The Promotable Woman

Advancing Through Leadership Skills

Second Edition

The Promotable Woman

Advancing Through Leadership Skills

Second Edition

Norma Carr-Ruffino

San Francisco State University

Wadsworth Publishing Company

Belmont, California
A Division of Wadsworth, Inc.

Editor: *Al Hansen*
Production: *Del Mar Associates*
Print Buyer: *Diana Spence*
Designer: *Michael Rogondino*
Copy Editor: *Robin Witkin*
Cover: *Susan Breitbard*
Compositor: *Thompson Type, Inc.*
Printer: *Malloy Lithographing*

This book is printed on acid-free paper that meets Environmental Protection Agency standards for recycled paper.

8 9 10 — 97 96 95

Library of Congress Cataloging-in-Publication Data

Carr-Ruffino, Norma.
   The promotable woman : advancing through leadership skills/Norma Carr-Ruffino.
       p.   cm.
   Includes bibliographical references and index.
   ISBN 0-534-18984-9 (alk. paper)
   1. Women executives.   2. Executive ability.   3. Management.
   I. Title.
   HD6054.3.C37   1993
   658.4'09'082 — dc20   92-8350
                                                                                    CIP

To Fredo
And to the women in my family:
Andrea, Bobbie, Elisha, Lauren, Meghan, Natalie,
and Vickie Smith, Erica and Frances Carr,
and Linda Ruffino Benvenuto

Contents

How This Book
Can Change Your Life

You are on your way to becoming a promotable woman, and this book can increase your level of promotability by making you a more confident, competent leader. The fact that you're reading this book indicates that you have either moved into a leadership position or that you are thinking very seriously about making a commitment to a career. That means you're able to picture yourself in an assertive, decision-making position of responsibility.

But can you picture yourself solving the problems unique to women leaders? And, how do you plan to overcome cultural barriers to acquiring the skills necessary to any successful leader? For example, you may have to overcome cultural conditioning that can create internal conflict between your personal-life roles (woman, wife, mother, other) and your role as an upwardly-mobile leader. And you will probably have to deal with the stereotypes others have of women, their acceptable roles, their place in business, their leadership traits.

Most of the specific problems unique to women leaders are rooted in two general elements: (1) the woman's own image of what her role and behavior should be and (2) the stereotypes others have about women. Finding the appropriate level of femininity, firmness, friendliness, and assertiveness is directly related to understanding these two elements and how they affect the woman leader.

This book can change your life dramatically if you take advantage of the opportunities it offers you to (1) understand how your self-concept affects your leadership style, (2) make constructive behavioral changes that help you function more effectively as a person, (3) understand how the stereotypes of others affect your leadership style, and (4) develop specific skills that establish your competence and deal effectively with stereotypes. In this way, the book can help you take advantage of the *opportunities* unique to career women and at the same time deal effectively with their unique *problems*.

What's Different About Career Women?

Both men and women must recognize opportunities and overcome obstacles to reach their career goals. Because the opportunities and obstacles are different for women, however, the process of reaching their goals is also different.

Different Obstacles Before the 1960s career women were relatively rare. Women were expected to devote their lives to homemaking and child-rearing. Some women had jobs; some worked for pin money or because they were poor. Women were not expected to be educated or groomed for careers, or to fill leadership roles in government, business, politics, or the professions. Women earned on average about half of what men earned. Although civil rights laws have opened new career doors for women, many traditional attitudes and practices still constitute barriers to women's careers, and a backlash to women's advancement became evident during the 1980s. Now, thirty years after the Civil Rights Act changed the rules of the workplace, women still average only 70 percent of men's wages, and many have hit a glass ceiling to top-level positions.

Women must learn how to hurdle internal and external barriers to achieve their career goals. External obstacles include others' stereotypes and prejudices about women's suitability for careers, their level of career commitment, their emotional stability, their ability to gain acceptance in leadership roles, and their decision-making capacity. Corporate career paths and policies that ignore women's family needs and obligations are examples of other external obstacles. Internal obstacles, on the other hand, include self-limiting beliefs women may have about their own leadership potential, ability to exercise power, and freedom to speak up about goals, ambitions, and strengths. Internal obstacles also include role conflict between the achieving woman role and the desirable date, mate, or mother role, and subconscious self-sabotage as a way of dealing with this role conflict.

Different Opportunities   Opportunities for career women have never been more abundant and enticing. Futurists such as John Naisbett predict that the United States will lead the world in the highly competitive 1990s, and that women leaders will make the difference. Women have been socialized to forgo ego and status concerns in favor of building close personal relationships, accepting and valuing all types of people, remaining flexible in dealing with people, intuitively tuning in to people and events, and bringing people together in synergistic, collaborative team efforts. These are just the leadership skills organizations need to galvanize work teams in the Global Nineties.

Career women must understand what the opportunities and challenges of the 1990s mean for them—and how typically feminine values and approaches can contribute to meeting those challenges. Women can take the lead in honoring their humanistic values and in encouraging men to activate the feminine side of their nature. Women have a special advantage in developing a leadership style that balances feminine connectedness and nurturing support with masculine competitiveness and assertiveness. Women tend to adopt a leadership style that respects and values individual differences and encourages shared goals and experiences. All this adds up to a style and substance that will enable the United States to take the lead in global cooperation, productivity, and abundance. Although women's *goals*— the leadership functions they must master— are the same as the *goals* of male leaders, the *process* of reaching those goals, of mastering those functions, is significantly different for most women.

The Women Who Will Profit from This Book

This book is for women who are moving into relatively lonely, but very exciting, leadership positions. Such women come from a variety of backgrounds:

Women who are currently in the work force as workers and who have been (or anticipate being) promoted

College students enrolled in courses to prepare them for careers

Women returning to the work force who want to prepare for leadership positions

This book is designed to be used

In college courses

In seminar groups

In training sessions within organizations

By women studying on their own

If you are in one of these categories, this book should help you prepare for the move into a leadership role, make a smooth transition, and become an increasingly effective leader. If you keep the book at your desk after you have completed it, it should serve as a handy reference guide for

Handling difficult situations

Regaining perspective after crises

Reviewing certain principles and techniques

Reinforcing new awareness, attitudes, or perspectives you have gained in the process of completing the book

How Your Learning Will be Enhanced

Every effort has been made in this book to provide opportunities for you to actually experience situations, actions, and viewpoints — either vicariously through reading and analyzing cases or directly through participating in simulations or role-plays of situations. Each chapter includes a statement of learning objectives so you can know what you should achieve by completing it. You can also evaluate how well you have actually achieved those objectives after completing a chapter by going back and reviewing them and making a self-analysis.

You can vicariously experience situations typically encountered by the woman manager through following Erika Kerr and her colleagues as they successfully and unsuccessfully cope. You will get to know Erika as she is promoted through the ranks of the Sales Department of a large clothing manufacturer.

These case incidents provide role models of successful actions and approaches. They can also help you become aware of some pitfalls to avoid. The problems and opportunities are analyzed and discussed within the chapter. Then the principles and techniques involved in these cases are pinpointed and listed.

Each chapter has a number of experiential learning devices to help you apply the principles and techniques so that they are reinforced. These experiences can help you have strategies readily available in your memory and feel confident in applying them to actual business situations in the future. These learning devices include self-analysis through completing checklists, answering questions, and making evaluations; analysis of cases; role-playing; games; and other exercises. Many of the exercises and games are ideal for working with a partner or a small group. Most of them can also be done by a person alone.

What You Will Work on in This Book

In Part 1, "Surveying the Leadership Scene," you will see the big picture of women's opportunities and challenges in the Global Nineties. You will survey the megatrends of this century, especially those of the 1960s and beyond, as they involve and impact women's careers. You will understand how traditions have erected barriers to women's career success; these barriers include both external barriers within the organizational culture and internal barriers within women's minds. You will connect current megatrends with women's leadership opportunities of the 1990s and beyond.

In Part 2, "Developing Personal Skills for Leadership Effectiveness," you will focus on self-development — on increasing the kind of awareness, attitudes, skills, and approaches that will make you the *kind* of leader most likely to succeed. Women's particular problems in developing or maintaining an appropriate self-concept and healthy self-esteem are addressed. The image you convey to others is stressed. In Part 2, then, your goal is success first as a person and second as a leader.

In Part 3, "Developing Leadership Skills," you will focus on developing the viewpoints, strategies, and skills that are most essential to such leadership functions as visioning, role-modeling, motivating, initiating, planning, organizing, coaching, empowering, and facilitating team synergy. As in Part 1, problems women often encounter, and strengths they typically bring to work situations, are highlighted along with basic leadership concepts. Part 2 culminates with a chapter on career strategies for moving up the ladder.

What You Will Achieve by Completing This Book

If you apply yourself to reading this book and completing the applicable exercises, then you will

Understand women's roles and status in organizations — how traditions still affect us, the major opportunities and problems now facing career women, and predicted changes

Know more about your talents and interests, the types of jobs and careers that fit your profile, your major life purposes, and the contributions you want to make in the Global Nineties

Build your personal skills and power for leadership effectiveness in such areas as goal-setting, time management, assertiveness, stress management, and communication

Increase your level of self-esteem and self-confidence and know how to project the image you want — that of a competent, savvy professional woman

Develop the types of viewpoints, strategies, actions, and personal traits you'll need in leading workers of the Global Nineties — by building on your current strengths and expanding into new areas

Use some personal strategies for career development, such as making the transition to a leadership position and moving up the ladder

Gain some basic leadership skills to build on, including motivating, problem-solving, decision-making, planning, organizing, and team development

This book is intended to help you grow personally and professionally. As you build your reputation as a successful person and effective leader, you also build the reputation of career women in general. I urge you to share with other women the knowledge and awareness you gain through this exciting process of growth and development. As we support one another, we not only help ourselves, we also increase the level of acceptance for women in leadership roles. We help open up new career paths for women everywhere.

Such mutual support and self-effort can also help us build a stronger democratic society, create a better world for both sexes. Shirley MacLaine shares a message from a very special being called Mayan:

> All women need to believe in themselves as women; they need to be secure in that belief. . . . Women have the right — even with the independence already achieved in the United States — to be even more independent and free. No society can function democratically until women are considered equal on every basis — particularly to

themselves. And women will never attain such a thing except through their own self-effort. In fact, nothing is worth having, except that which is won through self-effort.*

The People Who Contributed to This Book

I am especially grateful to Wadsworth's President Dick Greenberg for asking Al Hansen to oversee this book. As my editor, Al has picked up where former editors Carol Butterfield and Nancy Taylor left off. These three colleagues have made invaluable contributions to *The Promotable Woman*, as have former marketing specialist Karen Richardson, production coor-

dinator Nancy Sjoberg, and copy editor Robin Witkin. Suggestions from reviewers at National Seminars have been most helpful. And a special thanks goes to the many women who have attended my seminars throughout the United States and my courses at San Francisco State University in Women in Management and Leadership Skills for Women. Their feedback was essential in refining these materials, especially the exercises. Several graduate assistants also made contributions: Frances Gusman worked on the key terms, Sonia Media on the model of the job-getting process, Mary Ann Koliopolis on the women's networks list, and Nini Wang on the references.

Many of the women mentioned here have shared with me the ways in which the materials in this book have changed their lives. Our goal is to create a book that will help you change your life.

Norma Carr-Ruffino, Ph.D.

Out on a Limb by Shirley MacLaine. New York: Bantam Books, 1983.

The Promotable Woman

Advancing Through Leadership Skills

Second Edition

Surveying the Leadership Scene

Before the 1970s, women were almost never considered promotable. Whenever organizations needed new managers or leaders, the general rule was men only. Business and government have traditionally been a man's world, however, since the 1970s, women have increasingly been included in the pool of potential leaders. The women who have risen to the challenge of these opportunities tend to be especially bright, willing, and assertive. But they have also been strangers in a foreign land, dealing with the culture shock of moving from a woman's world to a man's world. For example, virtually all women internalize self-limiting messages about woman's place, messages that society communicates in many forms.

Women have also had to deal with the problem of being the foreigner in a well-established territory. For example, some people have not welcomed them nor the changes that opened the doors. Most people harbor stereotypes about how women are and what they are generally capable of doing.

The first chapter of Part 1 describes some traditional beliefs about woman's place and the changes that are challenging those beliefs. Chapter 2 is an overview of the male-dominated business arena, most of which is also applicable to the government arena, and leadership challenges that now beckon women.

Chapter One

A Woman's Place

"A woman's place is in the House . . . and the
Senate, the executive suite, the boardroom."

Eleanor Smeal

Women have come a long way in the workplace during this century, but they still have a long way to go before they achieve equality in opportunity, treatment, pay, and promotions. More women have moved into leadership roles in business than at any other time in U.S. history and than in any other country in the world. Yet less than 5 percent of top business, governmental, and political leaders are women. And U.S. women trail behind women in other industrialized countries in gaining political power and legislation to help them cope with the pressures of combining a career and motherhood.

This book is about helping women gain the skills they need to advance to leadership positions—not only to the first levels, such as working supervisors, first-line managers, city council members, or school board members, but all the way up the ladder to top management, higher administration, governor, U.S. congressional representatives, president—and into their own enterprises as entrepreneurs. People who become leaders are people who are willing and able to take responsibility for visioning where an organization, or a part of an organization, can go or should go. And they can communicate that vision, gain commit-

ment from others to work toward that vision, and empower themselves and others to work together to make the vision a reality. So whatever arena you plan to enter—big business, a sole proprietorship, a nonprofit organization, government, politics, or a professional career—you will find helpful ideas and suggestions in this book.

In this chapter you will have an opportunity to

1. See how women's roles evolved and how they are changing

2. Understand how our recent developments and trends have affected women's opportunities and problems in the workplace

3. Compare the progress of U.S. women with women in other countries, and see how the trends and predictions for the 1990s affect women's leadership opportunities

4. Gain insight into how women can become leaders in the "Global Nineties" by understanding new organizational demands, refining and expanding their skills to fit these demands, and overcoming critical external and internal barriers

HOW WOMAN'S PLACE HAS EVOLVED

Before we go too deeply into leadership opportunities, we will step back and survey the evolution of women's roles and their impact on the business and government scene in the United States today.

Changing ideas about what constitutes "a woman's place" are having far-reaching effects on nearly every person and every aspect of our society. Male/female relationships, family life, work life, educational programs — all are in the process of change as women move into new roles. But the rate of change is not consistent; it varies from community to community and from organization to organization.

In a few communities and organizations, general agreement about woman's place has changed very little in the past fifty years. In many others it may depart drastically from the traditional ideal, even to the extent that woman's place is little different from man's place. It depends on the woman, what she wants to do, and what she's able to do.

Women like you who are moving into leadership roles will encounter a variety of changing attitudes and practices, depending on where you live and the company you work for. These attitudes and practices, and your responses to them, will have a large impact on the opportunities and the barriers you meet throughout your career.

To put all this in perspective, we'll briefly look backward to see how this state of affairs came about. Then we'll survey the most important ways in which it is changing and how these trends may affect your future. This perspective can help you identify and overcome traditional barriers that you may face as a woman manager. It can also help you recognize new opportunities, which we will explore as well.

In the Beginning

"Woman's place is in the home." This predominant idea about a woman's role is the foundation of division of labor by sex. Some people say it's always been that way because it's natural and essential to the survival of the species — this is known as the nature theory. Others say that we can never know for sure how it all began. What we do know is that throughout history both sexes, and the community as a whole, have trained children to conform to the roles implied by the division of labor by sex — this is known as the nurture theory.

The Nature Theory Based on the premise that the average male apparently has always been larger and stronger than the average female, this theory holds that the male was the logical one to hunt for the family food and to defend the mother and babies. The female was the bearer and nurser of children and therefore stayed near the home to carry out her nurturing and caretaking functions.

The Nurture Theory Advocates of this theory say that regardless of how division of labor by sex originally came about, its existence is reinforced when a community believes that that is what works best. Here is how the nurturing, or socialization, process works: When women act in nurturing, dependent, serving ways, they are rewarded through such payoffs as approval, support, recognition, help, and protection. These rewards are given in the interest of keeping women in the home to care for their men and children. Men receive the same types of rewards when they show the strength, aggression, and independence considered desirable for defending and providing for their women and children.

At the same time, both women and men are punished for acting in ways that conflict with these basic roles. Community members may show disapproval, shun or ostracize violators, withdraw support, or carry out similar reprisals. For example, people might openly criticize a woman who acts in ways normally associated with the male role, such as venturing alone into the forest or going hunting. The criticism intensifies if she also neglects some of the housework. Likewise, the man who prefers household activities to hunting will be criticized.

The general belief that women are not good at performing masculine activities, and vice versa, reinforces this socialization process. For example, people in the community might expect women to fail or do poorly if they attempt to hunt or to tame a wild horse and men to be ineffective at cooking, child care, and sewing.

This type of socialization is still practiced in some communities today and its vestiges are felt in virtually every community and organization in our society. But it's been changing, especially in the last twenty-five years.

Before the Industrial Revolution

Before the 1800s most pioneer women in the United States were married to farmers or small-business owners. It was a family economy jointly occupied by men and women. The men tended to be responsible for producing commodities or providing services for the community, while the women's major responsibilities revolved around providing for family needs. Some of a wife's specific duties depended on her husband's occupation; she was expected to help him and respond to his specific needs. If he was a farmer, she might help with the milking and gardening. If he was a storekeeper, she might help out as a store clerk or record keeper. However, the average wife was not expected to work outside the home or family business. Black slave women were the only major exception to this arrangement; they were expected to care for their own family's

needs while also working outside their homes for their master. Black or white, rich or poor, women were generally thought to be inferior to men; their roles, therefore, were "properly" subservient to male roles.

The Development of Industrialism

During the 1800s family activities and economic activities began to emerge as distinct spheres. More and more husbands provided for their families by working in corporate factories and offices. The successful man won the struggle for wealth through competition with others and ultimately through power over others. His wife won approval through supporting his advancement and that of the children and ultimately through subordinating her personal desires and needs to theirs.

The ideal wife's sphere of "social homemaking" gained value. In fact, the privileged woman probably went to school or college to train for this role. She was held responsible for establishing the emotional bond of love within the family and for molding the personalities of the children. In her social homemaking sphere, individual personalities and the willingness to cooperate and to share were appreciated. This realm contrasted with her husband's economic sphere of impersonal, competitive, "you scratch my back, I'll scratch yours" relationships.

The contrasting sets of life principles that emerged were distinct and complementary: for men, an impersonal, public, competitive set; for women, a personal, private, charitable one. This difference in life principles and spheres was asserted to be natural and God-given by many nineteenth-century writers.

If a married woman worked outside the home, it was almost always assumed that her husband was unsuccessful in the struggle to provide for his family. In 1890 only 19 percent of all women worked outside the home, with less than 5 percent of all married women in this labor force. The female labor force was made up predominantly of young, not-yet-married women.

Most of these women worked in jobs considered compatible with "woman's function" and some in menial factory, office, or sales jobs. Over 95 percent of the servants in private homes were women [21].* Even when women found a position of authority and power outside the home, it was within a primarily female space, such as the public schools, hospitals, libraries, and welfare agencies. To this day, the only professional roles dominated by women are public school teacher, nurse, librarian, and social worker.

Developments During the Twentieth Century

Several recent developments that have further undermined the sexual division of labor are (1) the streamlining of housework, (2) the temporary need for women to fill men's jobs during World War II, (3) more reliable birth control methods, and (4) increased life expectancy rates.

The Streamlining of Housework Housework has come a long way since 1910, when it was tedious, often backbreaking drudgery, all done by hand. Today virtually every American home is equipped with an array of labor-saving devices, and supermarkets offer numerous prepared foods at reasonable prices. Such developments have allowed women to reduce drastically the hours they must spend doing essential household chores.

---

*See item 21 in "References" at the end of the chapter; books and articles cited within each chapter and other books of general interest are listed there. The number in brackets in the text corresponds to the item number in the reference listing.

World War II As this streamlining process was occurring, World War II created a dire shortage of workers in the United States. Women — even married ones — were urged to take over jobs vacated by men who were now serving in the military. Not only did women prove to be quite capable in filling these jobs, but they enjoyed doing needed work and bringing home an extra paycheck. Their families found they could function quite satisfactorily with a working mom; in fact many families were happier because Mom was happier. But when Johnny came marching home again, he wanted his job back. And women were urged to have babies and devote themselves full-time to the homemaking role. Family togetherness was the order of the day. It translated into husbands in the workplace and wives at home. Many women reluctantly complied, but the entire experience was not lost on their daughters. Some noticed, for example, that home life was more pleasant when Mom was purposefully occupied with her paid job. Most sensed the general acceptance (even approval) of working moms. And they noted that some moms continued working.

More Reliable Birth Control Methods Along with a greater acceptance of tubal ligations and vasectomies to limit the childbearing years, the development of the birth control pill during the 1960s meant that for the first time women could control the timing and number of their pregnancies. This made them less dependent on a husband's ability to provide and more in control of the pattern of their work lives.

Life Expectancy Rates Throughout this century life expectancy rates have been increasing. At about the time that the career doors were opening legally for them, women began to realize that they had many productive years to fill, even after their childbearing years were over. Many women who had thought of themselves as part-time or temporary workers now had all their children in school and could confidently choose to have no more children; yet they were only in their 30s. Now what? Suddenly they realized they would probably be working another thirty years, and many decided they might as well make the most of it. They wanted careers that were satisfying, challenging, exciting, and well-paying.

Many of today's women managers, therefore, were late bloomers. During their 20s and early 30s — when their male counterparts were busy "paying their dues" in the organization by putting in long hours, learning the ropes, getting promotions, and gaining invaluable expertise — these women were mainly concerned with raising children. Perhaps you're one of these women.

Or perhaps you're one of their children, one of the new breed of women who are moving into their own careers. A major concern for many of these women is how they will integrate the wife and mother role with the career role. These new career women are *not* late bloomers; they know they want managerial or professional careers, and many of them plan to make it to the top.

MEGATRENDS THAT OPENED DOORS

Beginning in the 1960s a series of megatrends combined to accelerate the pace at which women moved into managerial, professional, technical, and leadership roles that had been almost exclusively the territory of white males.

Women and Megatrends of the 1960s and 1970s: The Civil Rights Movement

The 1960s brought major social upheavals. Those upheavals that most affected women's careers included greater acceptance of divorce, greater sexual freedom, and greater acceptance of equality of opportunity for women and minorities. The Civil Rights movement led by blacks spawned the women's movement. These social changes allowed women more freedom of choice, while economic changes that accelerated in the 1980s created financial pressure for them to earn more.

The Civil Rights Movement The 1964 Civil Rights Act was mainly targeted to help blacks. Some Southern congressmen who opposed the pending bill tacked on a sexual discrimination clause, thinking that clause would surely cause its defeat. Much to their dismay, the bill passed. During the 1960s and 1970s, all three branches of the federal government established and enforced equal opportunity and **Affirmative Action programs*** for women and minorities. (See Exhibit 1-1.) Title VII of the act established the Equal Employment Opportunity Commission (EEOC) to define specific organizational practices that enhanced or blocked equal opportunity and to handle employee claims of discrimination. EEOC decisions and definitions could provide the basis for individual and class-action lawsuits.

*Terms in bold type are defined in Appendix Four, Key Terms.

EXHIBIT 1-1: Legal Aspects of Women's Advancement

Government Branch	Legislative	Administrative	Judicial
Source	Civil Rights Act of 1964	Executive orders	EEOC lawsuits Individual Class action
Type of law	Equal opportunity	Affirmative action	
Enforced by	Equal Employment Opportunity Commission	Office of Contract Compliance Programs	Courts

Aileen Hernandez, the only woman appointed to the commission, became so frustrated with the EEOC's failure to address women's issues that she appealed to Betty Friedan and others, creating the spark needed to ignite the women's movement throughout the United States [15]. These women appealed to President Lyndon Johnson to include women in his 1967 Executive Order that required Affirmative Action (AA) plans from companies doing business with the government. The resulting executive order is probably the first and only law in the world that provides adequate penalties for companies that do not take action to open up jobs and promotions to women. These penalties are significant enough to persuade companies to comply—the ultimate penalty being exclusion from doing business with the government. The Office of Contract Compliance Programs (OFCCP) actually enforced the order, reviewing AA plans and eventually imposing penalties if necessary. That possibility, combined with the possibility of being hit with an EEOC-related class-action lawsuit, convinced medium- to big-business to open more doors to women and minorities.

As a result, during the 1970s the percentage of women managers in the United States leaped far ahead of those in other countries (see Exhibit 1-2). A report prepared in the early 1980s by the Labor Department [33] but never released by the administration shows that

EXHIBIT 1-2: Percentage of Managers Who Are Female, Selected Countries, 1980s

	All Management	Top Management
United States[a]	40	5
Canada	32	5
Norway	31	9
Singapore	18	—
France	17	—
West Germany	17	1.5
Great Britain	15	6
Australia	15	—
USSR	15	—
Sweden	14	—
South Africa (nearly all white)	14	—
Portugal	13	—
Israel	12	—
Italy	n/a	1
Indonesia	12	—
China	10	—
Switzerland (primary sector)	9	—
Japan	7	—
Middle East Countries	—[b]	—

[a]All management, 1989; Top management, estimated; see discussion.

[b]Almost none.

Adapted from Nancy J. Adler and Dafna N. Izraeli, *Women in Management Worldwide* (New York: M. E. Sharpe, 1988); State Statistical Bureau of People's Republic of China, *China: A Statistics Survey in 1985* (China: New World Press, 1985); Cary Cooper and Marilyn Davidson, "Female Managers in Britain," *Human Resource Management* (Vol. 26, No. 2, Summer 1987), pp. 217–42; Larry S. Carney and Charlott G. O'Kelly, "Barriers and Constraints to the Japanese Labor Force," *Human Resource Management* (Summer 1987), p. 193. Less than 1 percent of managers in large corporations are women; U.S. Department of Labor, Bureau of Labor Statistics, Employment and Earnings, 1990; Francine Du Plessix Gray, *Soviet Women: Walking the Tightrope* (New York: Doubleday, 1990).

firms with AA plans hired seven times more women than firms without AA plans. In firms with plans, women in management grew at 2.5 times the rate of firms without plans. Firms whose plans were reviewed moved women into management at twice the rate of those whose plans were not reviewed. Black women moved en masse from janitorial/maid jobs to clerical jobs. (In 1960 about 50 percent were cleaning women, in 1980 only 10 percent. In 1960 only 8 percent of black women had office jobs, in 1980 about 40 percent.)

Women and Megatrends of the 1980s

The 1980s saw a conservative backlash to Affirmative Action led by people who never wanted such changes in the first place and the further evolution and impact of social changes that had erupted in the 1960s. In addition, trend expert John Naisbett described ten megatrends that offered exciting opportunities for career-oriented women [22].

The 1980s Backlash   Pulitzer prize winner Susan Faludi documents the reaction to women's progress in her best seller, *Backlash*. Beginning in 1981 and continuing into the 1990s, conservative members of government made headway in addressing what they call *reverse discrimination* against white males and *quotas* that force companies to hire and promote poorly qualified minorities and women. This, according to the critics, tends to lower the organization's standards and productivity. Conservatives argue that Affirmative Action is not the best way to provide opportunities for women and minorities because it *stigmatizes* them. They say that people doubt the competence of women and minorities promoted under such circumstances. Women would have more respect and self-esteem if they "made it" on their own merits. On the other hand, civil rights advocates, including the U.S. Civil Rights Commission, in a formal 1981 statement [32], make the following arguments:

- *Reverse discrimination* Preferential treatment of women and minorities must be viewed in the context of past socialization and discrimination throughout the culture and in terms of past and present tradition, hierarchy, and power alliances. A 1969 United Nations treaty, ratified by 107 nations by 1984, but not by the United States, declares that such special measures shall not be deemed reverse discrimination, provided that such measures "do not lead to the maintenance of separate rights for different racial groups and that they shall not be continued after the objectives for which they were taken have been achieved" [18].

- *Quotas* Neither the EEOC nor the agency that monitors affirmative action (the OFCCP) has the power to require quotas. Companies can set voluntary hiring and promotion goals, and the OFCCP can review them and may recommend higher goals. Only judges can require quotas in the resolution of lawsuits and have done so only in the most extreme cases.

- *Qualifications* Goals, and even quotas, have never meant that companies must use underqualified people; plans may call for training programs that will help women and minorities become qualified.

- *Standards* Nothing in the laws calls for lowering valid standards, although companies may have to show that standards have a significant relationship to successful performance.

- *Productivity* An extensive, rigorous study of the productivity of women in all manufacturing firms indicates that by 1977 women, on average, were 1 percent more productive than white men, while being paid an average of 54 percent of male wages [19].

- *Stigmatization* Before Affirmative Action, many doors were closed to women, so they were not given a chance to prove themselves or to "make it on their own." The possibility that some people may attach a stigma to those who come through the doors AA opens is not sufficient reason to eliminate the program. Once women are given opportunities, they can gain self-esteem by performing well and making a valuable contribution to the organization, thus disproving stereotyped stigmas.

The 1980s brought an interplay of the checks and balances of the three branches of government on the fate of AA (see Exhibit 1-1). The administration gave up its plans to rewrite the AA executive order, due to a predominantly liberal Congress's stated intention to pass new, more rigorous laws in response to such an action. However, the administration was able to greatly reduce enforcement of EEOC and AA laws in the executive branch. Although the proportion of women managers continues to increase, the growth rate has slowed considerably, is uneven at best, and is usually not accompanied by comparable growth in income. (The glass ceiling at the top levels and pay issues are discussed later in this chapter.) Next, by appointing conservative Supreme Court justices, President Ronald Reagan set in motion a judicial trend that led to the "Summer of '89," when six rulings were virtually all against AA [30]. The same Court began chipping away at abortion rights for women. President Bush appointed two more conservative justices during the early 1990s and the chipping away continued.

In response, Congress began drafting the 1990 Civil Rights Act to restore what the Court was taking away. When President Bush vetoed the act, he gave an "aversion to quotas" as the major reason. When Congress tried again with the 1991 act, the president referred to the "quotalike effect" of such laws. Civil rights advocates hailed his recognition that no laws — past, present, or anticipated — have called for quotas, but they regretted his use of the quota ar-

gument, seeing it as a distorted symbol tied to emotional reactions. Then, a few days after the Senate confirmed his minority candidate to the Supreme Court, Clarence Thomas, who was opposed by most civil rights leaders, the president signed the act. He apparently floated a trial balloon statement that the executive orders on Affirmative Action would no longer be implemented. He later withdrew the statement amid a chorus of outraged responses [30].

During the 1980s and early 1990s, Presidents Reagan and Bush also vetoed maternity leave and child-care bills submitted by Congress, stating that the bills placed a hardship on business. As we have seen, the top U.S. administrations of the 1980s and 1990s attempted to accommodate the conservative, traditional forces behind the backlash and appointed conservatives to the Supreme Court. This left only the Congress to protect the laws that had opened so many doors to women and minorities.

Socioeconomic Changes   Single parenting and divorce became much more prevalent after the social upheavals of the 1960s. By 1990 children were twice as likely to have divorced parents, compared to children of the mid-1960s. In most instances the mothers became head of the household and provided all or most of the income. This trend boosts the number of mothers who must work.

Naisbett's 1980s megatrend predictions that would most affect women turned out to be on target. They included (1) the movement of women into new, more powerful roles outside the home; (2) the transition from an industrial to an information society; (3) the resulting increased need for the human touch; (4) the decentralization of many centralized institutions, which eliminates much red tape and allows more autonomy at local levels; (5) the related focus on improving sagging productivity in American businesses through encouraging more cooperation, participation, and individual decision-making at all levels; (6) a tendency to depend more on self-help and less on institutional help; (7) more reliance on informal networks and less on formal communication through the organizational hierarchy; and (8) multiple lifestyle options as opposed to either/or choices [9]. These trends are favorable for women who want careers in management.

New Roles, New Technology The new roles of women and the transition from an industrial society to an information society are by far the most profound changes of this century. In an organization that relies on securing, processing, and disseminating information, physical size and strength are obviously not bona fide job requirements. In addition, the increased use of the computer and other high-technology applications tends to create a greater need for personal involvement, the human touch—empathy, warmth, understanding, supportive conversation, cooperation—skills most women have been encouraged to develop from childhood. We urge women to expand on these skills and to become knowledgeable and comfortable with computer functions. Since the computer is an essential tool that affects virtually all important jobs in the information society, women must overcome any reticence they may have about gaining computer skills.

New Organizational Cultures Other important trends of the 1980s—toward decentralization of organizations, participation in decision-making, networking within organizations and among business and professional people, self-help, and multiple lifestyle options—all represent a movement away from traditional, hierarchical, authoritarian organizations. This translates into less elitism, fewer directives from on high, and more participation and cooperation from all levels of the organization. Such a movement helps remove many traditional barriers to full participation in organizations that women have typically encountered, and many women are ready to accept the challenges and demands of the new responsibilities.

Women and Megatrends of the 1990s

The 1990s promise to be a time of expansion and growth in the following ways:

- People of the world growing in unity and common purpose

- People, companies, and whole societies growing in technical and psychological knowledge

- Employees advancing from using a few limited skills in doing the same old grind—and doing it as they're told—to exerting creativity and power as members of self-managing work teams

- Leaders growing from attempting to control their followers to empowering people

We looked back on the 1890s and called them the Gay Nineties. Perhaps we'll look back on the 1990s and call them the Global Nineties.

In *Megatrends 2000* John Naisbett follows up on his predictions of the trends of the 1980s and tracks key trends of the 1990s [23]. Naisbett's megatrend predictions that affect women's careers include a global economy, free-market socialism, a global culture and cultural nationalism, ethics in the workplace and in biotechnology, improvement of the individual, diversity in the work force, and women in leadership roles.

A global economy All large businesses will compete and cooperate with businesses in other countries and will be multinational to some extent. Companies must become increasingly adept at identifying market niches, adopting innovative approaches, and offering top-quality products and services. Leaders must think in global terms. The European Community as of 1992 is the largest consumer market in the world. The Pacific Rim is expected to be the most rapidly growing consumer market. India and China are edging toward consumer societies, and the formerly Communist countries of Europe are pounding at the door.

Free-market socialism and privatization of the welfare state Communist and socialist countries are undergoing a profound shift from economies run by governments to economies run by markets. They are shifting away from centralized government planning that tells industry what goods and services to produce and distribute toward decentralized production driven by market demand. They are moving away from a welfare state and state-owned assets toward individual ownership of homes, businesses, and retirement plans.

A global culture and lifestyle counterbalanced by cultural nationalism A global culture will become more pervasive, as symbolized by such icons as McDonald's, Levi's, Benetton clothing boutiques, the English language, and rock-and-roll. Naisbett predicts a simultaneous reaction to this global uniformity: Some people will begin to place a higher value on the native music, cuisine, language, and customs that make their culture unique.

Biotechnology and ethical values Biotechnology is poised to solve many of our health and poverty problems, but there is a corresponding need to define ethical values to regulate the industry. The excesses of the 1980s — from the spending of Donald Trump to the grand larceny of Wall Street dealers and savings and loan officers — will also bring a new respect for ethical principles. Several recent surveys indicate that people believe women can bring special talents to dealing with and cleaning up such issues, and that people tend to trust women's ethical standards and level of honesty [4]. This applies to both business and politics; that is, women represent a "fresh face" without the backroom connections and long years of deal making.

From management for control to leadership to empower individuals The underlying theme of these megatrends is the individual. Although people will work together in more dynamic ways than ever before, group power will come from the power of individuals within the groups. Most women are socialized to win commitment from people rather than to autocratically give orders and apply controls. Women tend to adapt more naturally to the role of teacher/facilitator/coach than to the role of director/overseer. Most women have historically been trained to subordinate their own success and focus on helping others, such as husbands and children, achieve success.

Diversity in the work force As baby boomers (born in high-birth-rate years 1950–65) become middle-aged, the baby bust generation (born during the low-birth-rate years after 1965) will begin to enter the work force. The shrinking labor pool means business recruiters must rely increasingly on all potential sources of qualified employees: women, ethnic minorities, older people, the handicapped, those with a nontraditional lifestyle, new immigrants, younger teenagers working part time. The largest potential source of qualified workers will be the estimated 14 million nonworking mothers. The only way companies will attract these women is to provide flexible arrangements, such as flexitime, part time, job-sharing, contract work, home offices, and flexible benefits, such as day care and family medical leave. In 1990 only 10 percent of organizations with ten or more employees provided such direct benefits as day care or financial assistance [28]. Most companies would have to make significant changes to provide the type of flexibility that career mothers need.

Women managers are in an ideal position to take leadership roles in bringing about such change. They have a special advantage in understanding the needs of working mothers and minorities: (1) They have direct experience in dealing with stereotypes and self-limiting beliefs rooted in the socialization process, and (2) they have traditionally assumed most of the responsibility for children, elderly parents, and the environment.

Women in leadership roles The needs and opportunities posed by the new global economy, free-market socialism, privatization of the welfare state, and high-tech industries (further fueled by the biotech industry) mean that savvy corporations will be scrambling to find people who can produce and perform in rapidly changing, highly competitive markets. In the 1980s talented women advanced faster in rapidly growing high-tech companies than in traditional ones. So women in the savvy corporations of the 1990s will find doors at the top swinging open.

Naisbett predicts that the United States will take the lead in the global economy and that women's leadership will make the critical difference. His rationale: Women's numbers in business have reached a critical mass. And, as they've bumped against the glass ceiling in large corporations, many women have started their own businesses — at twice the rate of men — and these businesses are looking for new markets. Nancy Adler points to the successful track records of American women doing business in Asia. Although a culture may frown on its own women going into business, foreign women are viewed differently. "If you have the best price, they'll buy," says an American woman based in Hong Kong [2].

Economists predict that **economic pressures** for women to work will intensify and that married women's incomes will continue to be a family necessity. Working mothers, once a sign of liberation, became an economic necessity during the 1980s. In 1975 there were 13 million working mothers; by 1989 that number had almost tripled to 33 million. Even so, family income growth slowed dramatically. Between 1950 and 1970 family income grew 97 percent, but between 1970 and 1990 it grew only 15 percent [34]. In 1990 first-time home buyers faced mortgages that were 50 percent larger than in 1965, when they accounted for only 20 percent of the buyer's income. By 1990 that figure had risen to 33 percent. Fewer renters could scrape together the down payment or qualify for a loan. The purchasing power of the average

worker's weekly take-home pay fell 11 percent between 1970 and 1990. Most economists expect these trends to continue until the United States adapts to the new rules of the global marketplace and business improves its productivity. This could take fifteen to twenty years, unless business and government leaders find innovative ways to meet global challenges.

OVERCOMING EXTERNAL BARRIERS

Many women must overcome both external and internal barriers in order to achieve their career goals. Three major external barriers of the 1980s are still with us: (1) a glass ceiling blocking women from top jobs, (2) pay disparity, and (3) lack of flexible arrangements for working mothers.

The Glass Ceiling

Although the United States leads the world in percentage of women managers (see Exhibit 1-2), the 40 percent figure may be somewhat deceptive for the following reasons:

1. Women managers tend to be clustered in the lower-paying, entry levels of management, such as working supervisor and first-line supervisor.

2. Women managers' pay lags behind men's at every level.

3. When women move into an occupation in significant numbers, the occupation loses status and decreases in pay, and men tend to move out of it. Conversely, if an occupation loses status and pay for other reasons, women are more likely to be hired into it.

4. Women are likely to hit a **glass ceiling** to top-level, and even middle-level, positions, according to a 1991 Labor Department study, "The Glass Ceiling Initiative" [34]. This bar-

rier to further advancement is invisible but solid, like glass. Few women see it before they hit it because the organization's leaders don't admit it's there. Therefore, few women are making it beyond lower-level management and may have little hope of doing so in the near future. The 5 percent estimate of female top-level managers shown in Exhibit 1-3 includes women who started their own firms and carried them beyond the small-business stage.

Labor Secretary Lynn Martin says the Labor Department is seeking voluntary compliance from business to move women up the ladder and will publicly recognize and reward firms that independently remove their glass ceilings. However, the department will conduct few AA reviews of top-level management.

A 1987 survey of women managers revealed that 90 percent think the glass ceiling is the most important issue facing women managers of the 1990s [5]. Virtually all women who did not head their companies (80 percent) said women were underrepresented at the top in their firms. The major reason given was the reluctance of the men at the top to include women. The following barriers, in the order

EXHIBIT 1-3: Women's Progress in the United States, Share of Management Positions and Pay Ratios

	1900	1950	1960	1970	1980	1983	1986	1988	1990
Percentage of All Management Positions Held by Women[a]	4	12	15.6	16	26	33	37	—	40
In firms with 100 + workers[b]	—	—	—	—	—	—	—	—	28
In Fortune 1000-sized companies[c]	—	—	—	—	—	—	—	—	17
Percentage of Senior Management Positions Held by Women[d]	—	—	—	—	3	4	5	—	5
Women's Pay as Percentage of Men's[e] (full-time workers only)	—	64	59	59	60	62	64	68	70
Vice-presidents	—	—	—	—	—	—	—	68	—
Managers	—	—	—	—	—	—	—	62	—
With college degrees	—	—	—	—	—	—	—	59	—
Black women/white men	—	—	—	—	—	—	—	59	—
Older women[f]	—	—	—	—	—	—	—	58	—
Engineers[g]	—	—	—	—	—	—	—	86	—
Computer programmers	—	—	—	—	—	—	—	83	—
Medicine, law	—	—	—	—	—	—	—	70	—
Government workers	—	—	—	—	—	—	—	80	—
Human resources, personnel	—	—	—	—	—	—	—	57	—

[a]U.S. Department of Labor, *Employment and Earnings*, 1990.

[b]U.S. Equal Employment Opportunity Commission, 1990.

[c]U.S. Department of Labor, *A Report on the Glass Ceiling Initiative*, 1991.

[d]Estimates based on surveys by Heidrick-Struggles, Korn-Ferry, *Fortune*, and *Business Week*. In 1990 fewer than .005 (.05%) of senior officers listed on proxy statements of the Fortune 1000 companies were women [Jaclyn Fierman, "Why Women Still Don't Hit the Top," *Fortune* (July 30, 1990), p. 40].

[e]U.S. Bureau of Census, "Current Population Reports, Consumer Income Series," P-60, No. 157, 1987; No. 166, 1988. "Average Earnings of Year-Round Fulltime Workers by Sex and Educational Attainment," Table 35, February 1989.

[f]James P. Smith and Michael Ward, "Women in the Labor Market and in the Family," *Journal of Economic Perspective*, Vol. 3, No. 1 (Winter 1989), p. 10.

[g]Anne M. Russell, "Women Vs. Men: Where We Stand Today," *Working Woman* (January 1991), p. 66.

listed, were considered the most important to overcome:

- Top management harbors stereotypes about women, especially regarding their ability to gain acceptance in a top role, their level of career commitment, and their decision-making ability.

- Women are often excluded from key informal gatherings where information and opinions are exchanged and deals are made.

- Women's contributions and abilities are not taken as seriously as men's.

- Women have more difficulty finding mentors.

- Women don't get equal opportunities to serve on important committees and project teams.

Pay Disparity

Although the United States leads the world in proportion of women managers, we are not as advanced in providing pay equity (see Exhibit 1-4). Full-time female workers earned only 68 percent of male workers' wages in 1988, as Exhibit 1-3 indicates. (In Exhibit 1-3 note that relative pay increased to 70 percent in 1990.) Some argue that women generally have less training, experience, and job commitment than men, and that this accounts for the pay gap. However, Exhibit 1-3 shows that women vice-presidents also earned only 68 percent of male vice-presidents' wages. It's highly unlikely that women who have made it to the vice-presidential level have less training, experience, and job commitment than their male peers. Some studies indicate that most women who make it this far must have higher qualifications than their male peers.

The Equal Pay Act of 1963 has not been as effective as hoped because it is easy to vary job duties so that male and female workers are not technically engaged in "equal work." **Pay equity** (or comparable worth) carries the equal

EXHIBIT 1-4: Average Women's Pay Relative to Men's, Selected Countries, 1980s[a]

Country	Women's Pay as a Percentage of Men's
Sweden	90
Norway	88
Denmark	80
Australia	79
Great Britain	75
United States	68[b]
USSR	66
Canada	60
Singapore (managers)	54
Japan	53
China (factory workers)	50
Brazil	33

[a]Although the year for which a figure is given may vary from country to country, all are during the 1980s.

[b]U.S. figures are for 1988. Pay for full-time women workers in 1990 was 70% of men's.

Adapted from Nancy J. Adler and Dafna N. Izraeli, *Women in Management Worldwide* (New York: M. E. Sharpe, 1988); *Canada, Survey of Consumer Finances*, 1983; *China*, Jennie Farley, ed., *Women Workers in Fifteen Countries* (New York: ILR Press, 1985); Dorothy McBride Stetson, *Women's Rights in France* (New York: Greenwood Press, 1987); Cary Cooper and Marilyn Davidson, "Female Managers in Britain," *Human Resource Management*, Vol. 26, No. 2 (Summer 1987), pp. 217–42.

pay for equal work idea a step further. Equal pay laws require, for example, that a female senior accounting clerk receive the same base pay as a male senior accounting clerk within the same company. Comparable pay rulings, where enforced, might require that a junior secretary receive the same base pay as a journeyman electrician working in the same community. Pay scales would be based on a system of analyzing and evaluating jobs based on such factors as level of education and experience required, level of responsibility and difficulty, and hardships involved.

Advocates of comparable pay laws believe their passage may be the only way to eliminate the "female ghetto" of low-paying jobs found in most organizations. They point to statistics showing that when an occupation formerly dominated by male incumbents — such as high school instructor or sales clerk — becomes dominated by women incumbents, the pay and status decline. At the same time, jobs held mainly by men — such as the building trades or maintenance jobs — may increase in pay, if not in status. As a result, female high school instructors with college degrees may receive less than half the pay of plumbers or city street sweepers without high school diplomas. A system of comparable pay would be designed to eliminate such inequities. A major barrier is the cost to organizations. Since lowering the pay of male workers would be impractical, they must raise the pay of female workers. One solution involves gradual increases for underpaid female workers and decreases in the starting pay of **new hires** in overpaid male positions.

Canada's Pay Equity Act took effect in 1988. It covers both government and private workers, but neither the structure nor the penalties are rigorous enough to have much impact on business. In the United States about half the states have implemented pay equity for their government employees, and the remaining states are examining the issue. Numerous city and county governments, many on the West Coast, have adopted pay equity for their employees. However, few corporate executives have admitted that pay equity is an issue being explored in their companies, probably because they are afraid of being sued. Courts have generally been unwilling to require pay equity of employers, although it has not been tested in the Supreme Court.

Inflexible Working Arrangements

If women are to have uninterrupted careers, rather than just jobs, they need (1) adequate paid maternity leave; (2) help in obtaining affordable, quality child care and eldercare; and (3) flexible job structure such as flextime, job-sharing, part-time arrangements at certain stages, and work in home offices. Rather than lose competent women who want more time for their small children for a while, some companies are giving these employees whatever they need to do their work — fax machines, computers, car phones — and letting them do most of their work at home, sometimes packing it into three days instead of five. While they often still need child care at home, these working mothers are near their children and don't spend energy fighting traffic from home to day care to office, and back.

The Search for Solutions

The trends discussed earlier may have more power to resolve these issues than any political or legal actions. If organizations need women badly enough, they will become flexible enough to meet their needs. If the choice becomes letting women exercise their talents in top leadership positions or letting the company fall victim to global competition, the doors will open. If women flock to those organizations that offer pay equity and flexible working arrangements and that have women in top jobs, other firms must follow suit if the labor market becomes as competitive as predicted. Women can also make a difference

- By speaking up and letting firms know what they want and selecting firms willing to give it to them

- By exercising their joint political power to elect legislators who are responsive to women's needs

- By staying informed concerning the issues and learning which companies and politicians have good track records at meeting those needs. It is now common policy to claim support for women's issues. Women must look beyond such claims and determine what the past performance has actually been.

The proportion of female national legislators is shown in Exhibit 1-5 for countries where this data has recently been published. Electing women to office has made a difference to women in Norway and Sweden, where paid maternity leave is required (see Exhibit 1-6), pay equity is greater, and child-care support is provided. Although U.S. women have made little progress toward equal representation in Congress (see Exhibit 1-7), their proportion has increased in state legislatures, from 5 percent in 1971 to 18 percent in 1990, and in the number of mayors, from 7 to 151 (cities over 30,000). Many of these women will soon be ready to win congressional seats. Pollster Mervyn Field predicts that the 1990s will be the decade of women in U.S. politics [4].

EXHIBIT 1-5: Women in National Legislative Bodies, Selected Countries, 1990s

Country	Percentage of Positions Held by Women
Norway	36
Cuba	33
Denmark, Finland, Sweden	25 to 30
China	21
West Germany	20
East Germany	13
USSR	15
Iraq	10
France	5
United States	5
Korea	3

From "Year of the Woman," *Time* (Fall 1990), special issue.

OVERCOMING INTERNAL BARRIERS

Traditions from the past affect today's career woman in two basic ways: (1) how she pictures herself and therefore the roles and behaviors with which she is comfortable, and (2) what others expect of her—their preconceived notions of her abilities, traits, strengths, and weaknesses, and their resulting beliefs about proper roles and behaviors.

Self-Limiting Beliefs

The beliefs held by many women create gaps in their preparation for a managerial role. Such beliefs lead to typical behavior, or traits, that may be quite appropriate in some situations but is frequently self-defeating in business situations. Which of these typical traits might create a career barrier for you?

- A tendency to suppress or hide ambitions and goals, to wait to be asked, to expect those in command to notice and acknowledge your potential and achievements and to direct your career progress

- A reticence to talk about your abilities and achievements, even in a business setting with people who need to know about them

- Avoidance of being the focus of attention, of taking action that will result in increased visibility within the organization

- A lack of confidence in your ability to handle financial matters, projects requiring math or technical skill, situations requiring astute problem-solving and decision-making abilities

- Avoidance of office politics, the gaining and effective use of power

- A lack of curiosity about the inner workings of organizations: the hierarchy, the chain of command, sources of power, career paths

- A tendency to capitulate quickly to the wishes of others, especially men, when they attempt to dominate

EXHIBIT 1-6: Maternity Leave Provisions, National Laws in Selected Countries, 1980s

Country	Minimum Leave (in weeks)	Leave Pay as Percentage of Full Pay
Great Britain	40	90
Sweden	38	90
Finland	35	100
West Germany	28	100
East Germany	26	100
Norway	24	100
Italy	22	80
France	16	90
Canada	16	90
Japan	12	60
United States	—	—

Adapted from *Woman* magazine, July 1989; Harry G. Shaffer, *Women in the Two Germanies* (New York: Pergamon Press, 1981); The Baroness Lockwood and Wilf Knowles, "Women at Work in Great Britain," *Working Women: An International Survey* (New York: Wiley, 1984).

EXHIBIT 1-7: U.S. Women as Political Leaders, 1970–1990

	1971	1981	1991
Percentage in the House of Representatives	2.0	3.0	6.0
Percentage in the Senate	2.0		2.0
Percentage of governors	0.5		1.5
Percentage in state legislature	4.8	10.0	18.2
Number of mayors (in cities over 30,000)	7	58	138

From National Women's Political Caucus survey, 1991; National Organization for Women brochure, 1991.

- A tendency to personalize events, criticism, and messages of others, to react emotionally, and to act out such reactions

- A tendency to react to risky situations by focusing on the possible loss or danger involved rather than by balancing the probabilities and magnitude of possible gain versus loss

- More focus on developing oneself than on working as part of a team to meet organizational goals (and in the process some personal goals) and on developing an organizational power base

- A tendency (conscious or subconscious) to fear success in the business world

Conflicting Beliefs

Role conflict is a common problem for career women. Both men and women are sometimes afflicted with fear of failure—fear that if they let people know they're trying to achieve a particular goal and actually go for it, they will be humiliated and perhaps rejected if they don't succeed. The fear of success is generally a woman's problem and is based mainly on the belief that if she becomes a successful career woman, she will not be viewed as a desirable mate. Dr. Matina Horner found that 65 percent of the women she studied indicated a fear of success, compared with only 10 percent of the men.

The fearful reactions range in intensity from disturbing to terrifying. Horner concluded that women's desire for a close relationship is more primary than men's and takes precedence over everything else. The results, mostly subconscious, take several forms, including (1) mild to severe paralysis — the woman allows her career to lie stagnant between the two conflicting needs; (2) self-sabotage — she manages somehow to take actions and make moves or decisions that undermine her career goals; (3) energy drain — she uses so much emotional energy trying to repress those parts of her personality she subconsciously believes are unacceptable, threatening, or otherwise frightening that she has little energy left to devote to achieving goals.

Author Colette Dowling [8] labeled one version of this fear of success the "Cinderella complex." She described the tendency of some women to sabotage their careers because they fear they'll become so independent, and perhaps aggressive, that they won't appeal to a potential "Prince Charming." The major problem is that their expectations, fears, and resulting self-sabotage are all going on at a subconscious level and therefore are difficult to pinpoint. Deep down, such a woman fervently hopes that someone will come along to make her happy, which implies that she lacks confidence in her ability to assume control and responsibility for her own life.

Do you have just a touch of the Cinderella syndrome lurking in the back of your mind? Deep down, are you really waiting for Prince Charming to come along and make you happy ever after? There are other versions of Prince Charming, such as Santa Claus or Sugar Daddy. It's important to identify such fantasies and decide if you need to replace them with more re-

alistic goals that allow you more autonomy. After all, Cinderella was a victim who needed rescuing — hardly a role compatible with that of a leader. The fantasy usually implies that the male rescuer would be resentful and probably threatened by an independent, competent woman. Do you really need such a man?

Doesn't it make more sense to build a satisfying life of your own and hold out for a partner who has a deep inner confidence in his own competence and manhood, one who prefers to relate to a woman on an equal basis? Such a man is unlikely to resent your accomplishments or to try to dominate you. This approach to close relationships can free you to grow and develop and to advance unfettered toward all your goals. It allows you to be open and direct about your abilities and achievements in your dealings with men. In turn, you can gladly let those men who are threatened by your competence move on, rather than cluttering up your life with problem relationships.

Many women reach adulthood with a number of these self-limiting beliefs and resulting fears that they picked up from their families and the people in their communities. These beliefs are also absorbed from the culture at large via books, newspapers, and television. Such beliefs are usually based on what we perceive as the expectations of others about how we probably are and how we should behave. Later we'll explore some alternate behaviors you may want to consider adopting — approaches that will enhance your leadership image. The fact that others' expectations of appropriate behavior for leaders often conflict with their ideas of appropriate feminine behavior creates problems for many women.

Others' Beliefs and Stereotypes

The expectations of others about appropriate roles and behaviors for women (or any other category of persons), as well as the rewards and punishments women experience as a result of these expectations, help mold women's behavior. When nearly all women conform to the expected behavior patterns generation after generation, it becomes impossible to determine whether such behavior is innate or learned. Many people have acted as if such behavior is innate, however, and have treated women in a stereotyped manner.

A **stereotype** is a belief about a certain group of people and their predictable characteristics. We use stereotypes as shortcuts — to categorize people and free us from having to judge each person independently. In the process, however, we usually ignore important information about individuals within that group. More important, stereotyped expectations frequently lead individuals to behave in the expected ways and therefore fail to act naturally or to develop alternate behaviors and skills. We see a cycle in operation here: Community expectations of desired behavior from a subgroup within the community can lead to fairly rigid behavior patterns, which in turn lead to stereotyped expectations about the subgroup, which further reinforces the limited behavior patterns.

These stereotyped expectations of others exert a powerful influence in our lives, especially when we are young. This socialization process, discussed earlier, molded much of our behavior as children because we got payoffs — admiration, approval, and other good things — for acting in expected ways. By the time we're adults, we've forgotten how the process occurred, and we've internalized many of the expectations as our own beliefs about proper behavior.

Even if your community, family, or personal beliefs about appropriate behavior for women differ from that of the culture at large, operating on your own terms can be most difficult in the face of cultural expectations.

A 1990 Gallup Poll [11] indicates that differences between traits valued in men and women have not changed much since the 1972 study done by Rosalind Loring and Theodora Wells [20]. The Gallup Poll asked what characteristics

are generally true of men more than of women. The response included these traits: aggressive, strong, proud, confident, independent, courageous, disorganized, ambitious. Loring and Wells had asked what traits are most admired in men. The response was aggressive, independent, unemotional, objective team player, dominant, likes math and science, not excitable in a minor crisis, active, competitive, logical, worldly, skilled in business. Notice that these traits (except disorganized) are also the traits typically expected of successful leaders.

The characteristics more generally true of women than men include emotional, talkative, sensitive, affectionate, moody, patient, romantic, cautious, thrifty. Men also said manipulative, and women said creative. The traits most admired in women were as follows: does not use harsh language, talkative in appropriate situations, tactful, gentle, aware of feelings of others, religious, interested in her appearance, neat, quiet, strong need for security, appreciates art and literature, expresses tender feelings. Women who find themselves in communities and organizations still adhering to these expectations of feminine behavior must convey a professional image that is usually identified with masculine traits and still retain the best aspects of their femininity. It takes skill, but numerous women have managed it and have won over the people they need as a support base to succeed. They've done it by building on their present strengths, adapting them to business settings, and developing other traits typical of effective male managers.

Do you need to develop strengths you've neglected because they weren't typically expected of women in your community? Alice Sargent has identified *some typical male strengths* that you can develop further and *some typical female strengths* that you may want to enhance [29]. See Exhibit 1-8.

Sargent [29] found that most men and women managers describe themselves as having an equal mix of traits that are considered

EXHIBIT 1-8: Masculine and Feminine Strengths

Typical Masculine Strengths Women Can Develop	Typical Feminine Strengths Women Can Expand
■ Learn how to be powerful and forthright.	■ The ability to recognize, accept, and express feelings.
■ Become **entrepreneurial.**	
■ Have a direct, visible impact on others, rather than just functioning behind the scenes.	■ Respect for feelings as a basic and essential part of life, as guides to authenticity and effectiveness, rather than as barriers to achievement.
■ State your own needs and refuse to back down, even if the immediate response is not acceptance.	■ Acceptance of the vulnerability and imperfections of others.
■ Focus on a task and regard it as at least as important as the relationships with the people doing the task.	■ A belief in the right to work for self-fullfillment as well as for money.
■ Build support systems with other women and share competence with them, rather than competing with them.	■ A belief in the value of nonwork roles as well as work identity.
■ Build a sense of community among women instead of saying, "I pulled myself up by my bootstraps, so why can't you?"	■ The ability to fail at a task without feeling failure as a person.
■ Intellectualize and generalize from experience.	■ The ability to accept and express the need to be nurtured at times.
■ Behave "impersonally," rather than personalizing experience and denying another's reality because it is different.	■ The ability to touch and be close to both men and women without necessarily experiencing or suggesting sexual connotations.
■ Stop turning anger, blame, and pain inward.	■ Skill at listening empathetically and actively without feeling responsible for solving others' problems.
■ Stop accepting feelings of suffering and victimization.	■ The ability to share feelings as the most meaningful part of one's contact with others, accepting the risk and vulnerability such sharing implies.
■ Take the option of being invulnerable to destructive feedback.	
■ Stop being irritable, a "nag," and/or passive-resistant about resentments and anger.	■ Skill at building support systems with other women, sharing competencies without competition, and feelings and needs with sincerity.
■ Respond directly with "I" statements, rather than with blaming "you" ones ("*I'm* not comfortable with that" rather than "*you* shouldn't do that").	■ The ability to relate to experiences and people on a personal level rather than assuming that the only valid approach to life and interpersonal contact is an abstract, rational, or strictly objective one.
■ Become an effective problem-solver by being analytical, systematic, and directive.	
■ Change self-limiting behaviors, such as allowing interruptions or laughing after making a serious statement.	■ Acceptance of the emotional, spontaneous, and irrational parts of the self.
■ Become a risk-taker (calculating probabilities and making appropriate trade-offs).	

Adapted from *The Androgynous Manager* by Alice G. Sargent (New York: Amacom, 1983).

feminine (being excitable, gentle, emotional, submissive, sentimental, understanding, compassionate, sensitive, dependent), masculine (dominant, aggressive, tough, assertive, autocratic, analytical, competitive, independent), and gender-neutral (adaptive, tactful, sincere, conscientious, conventional, reliable, predictable, systematic, efficient). Women who describe themselves as predominantly feminine or gender-neutral report a higher level of followership among their female workers than women who describe themselves as masculine.

Which of these traits and skills are part of your repertoire? Like most traits and skills, they can be either a strength or a liability, depending on the situation and how you use them. How can you build on these special skills in your leadership role? How can you adapt them to the rules of the business game so they create opportunities rather than barriers? We'll discuss various aspects of this issue in later chapters.

MOVING INTO LEADERSHIP OPPORTUNITIES

If companies are to meet the challenges of a competitive global economy in a high-tech information age, they must rely on work teams made up of new types of employees. To develop effective leadership styles, Global Nineties leaders must understand the Global Nineties workers. Let's look at some characteristics of these new workers and their leaders and see how women can use their particular strengths to move into leadership opportunities.

How Workers of the 1990s Are Different

Global Nineties workers have the following traits and expectations that leaders can draw on to create dynamic, innovative, self-directed work teams:

- They can think critically, plan strategically, and adapt to change. They are better educated, more highly skilled, and more creative than yesterday's workers.

- They understand that neither the government nor the corporation can be depended on to take care of them and that their security lies in the skills and attributes they can take to their next job.

- They are mobile. They will probably change careers three times, according to the Labor Department; five times, according to most career consultants. And within each career, a person may change companies several times.

- More Global Nineties workers insist on balancing the top priorities of career, family, and personal interests. In the 1980s it was mainly women who operated from these values. In the 1990s both men and women of the new generation insist on balanced priorities.

- In the industrial society, most workers performed assembly-line tasks; in the information society, they perform mental tasks. They are paid for their knowledge more than for manual labor. More and more, work is what goes on inside workers' heads. It's how they communicate, what they write, and what they say in meetings. It cannot be supervised in the same way manual tasks are supervised.

- Most Global Nineties workers do not function optimally under traditional control-oriented, top-down management and will not stay in such situations.

How 1990s Leaders Differ From Yesterday's Managers

What kind of people do organizations need to lead the Global Nineties workers? Most management experts agree that the demands of the

Nineties call for innovative leaders, not traditional managers. When we discuss more fully the topics of developing leadership style (Chapter 9) and developing a work team (Chapter 13), we will explore some *specific* approaches, attitudes, and activities that distinguish leaders from managers. To start your wheels turning, however, here are some *general* differences:

- Global Nineties leaders have a broader perspective than yesterday's managers. They are committed to creativity and action on the global level in response to the new global economy with its free markets, global scope, and technological diversity.

- At all levels they develop powerful visions of what the organization can be and do. Yesterday's managers tend to keep doing whatever worked. It's no longer enough to say "If it ain't broke, don't fix it." The focus now is on continual improvement, scanning for new opportunities, and anticipating how changes in the environment call for new or modified products or services.

- They know how to gain certain essential knowledge about the external environment of their business. Technological change, compressed product cycles, and global competition demand that leaders scan the global environment and organize the company's strategies and tasks accordingly, while remaining sensitive to market demands and opportunities.

- They are active in preserving and healing the environment. Yesterday's managers were often oblivious, uncaring, or grudgingly responsive to public demands.

- They place more importance on sharing power with all members of the organization, thus empowering others to achieve the visions.

- They make a full commitment to the visions, take full responsibility for achieving them, and encourage others to do the same.

- Leaders of the 1990s must be democratic but demanding facilitators of change rather than parent figures. They must respect people and encourage self-management, self-directed teams, and entrepreneurial units.

- These new leaders place less importance on the traditional hierarchy and more on informal processes to achieve rapidly changing goals.

- They create followers by operating consistently from fair, honest principles and by creating an environment where the unique potential of each person can be actualized.

- They see their greatest role as helping people reach their potential. A main strategy is to constantly challenge people to learn new skills.

- Their main goal is to encourage today's better-educated workers to be more entrepreneurial, self-managing, and oriented toward lifelong learning.

- Global Nineties leaders place less emphasis on formal job titles and descriptions and more emphasis on learning a variety of tasks (cross-training) and on ever-changing performance goals geared to individual strengths and interests as well as organizational needs.

How Women Can Emerge as Leaders in the 1990s

Women can be ready for new leadership opportunities by strengthening key feminine traits they already possess, by using their experiences as women to inspire loyalty and understand workers' needs, and by understanding that the world will open its doors to anyone who can get the results that organizations so desperately need.

Using Socialized Traits In the past, men's socialization gave them an advantage in managing within the military model, with its authoritarian values and rigid hierarchy. As more and more organizations move away from this model to a more open, informal, democratic model, women can be equally capable of inspiring commitment and bringing out the best in people. In fact, being socialized as a male may no longer be an advantage. Women who do not need to unlearn old authoritarian behavior may have a slight edge. Women now in middle-management jobs tend to have people skills to build on.

Inspiring Loyalty It takes better leadership than most managers have shown in the past to encourage worker loyalty to a particular firm, especially when that firm may change hands tomorrow and when workers change jobs and even careers more frequently than ever. Great leaders not only expect loyalty, they earn it by acting in ways that inspire loyalty. Women who have had to earn respect and loyalty every step of the way in their careers understand this unwritten rule and are primed to apply it.

Modeling Ethical Values and Principles
Naisbett found that most Americans are fed up with greedy, dishonest leaders and tend to trust women leaders more than men. Women can validate this trust by consistently rising to the occasion. Demonstrate that you are a good role model for employees by identifying your values and principles — where you draw the line on various issues — and making decisions accordingly.

Everyone faces tough ethical decisions at work. The real problem stems from (1) not seeing an ethical dilemma coming, (2) not recognizing that there *is* a dilemma, and (3) not realizing the choices available — the range of responsible options. The solution lies in thinking ahead and practicing your responses. Start observing the ethical issues that others face — in your office, in news stories, in books. Get in the habit of applying these questions to situations [26]:

- Is it legal?
- Will any policies, regulations, or rules be violated?
- Is the proposed action consistent with past practice?
- Does the situation require that I lie about the process or the results?
- Do I consider this an unusual situation that demands an unusual response?
- Am I acting fairly? Would I want to be treated in this way?
- Will I have to hide or keep my actions secret? Has someone warned me not to disclose my actions to anyone?
- Would I be able to discuss the proposed situation or action with my immediate supervisor? The president of the company? My family? The company's clients?
- How would I feel if the details of this situation appeared in the media?
- If a close friend took this action, how would I feel?
- How do I feel about this? Am I feeling unusually anxious? Fearful?
- Does my conscience bother me?

Understanding Needs Women have been through the fire of experience to reach an understanding of the Global Nineties worker's need to balance career, family, and personal interests. They have a personal knowledge of the ways in which the workplace must be made flexible enough to attract and retain highly qualified women and minorities.

Forming a Critical Mass For the past twenty years, U.S. women have filled two-thirds of new jobs and will continue to do so well into the next century. According to Naisbett, women dominate the information society as workers, professionals, and entrepreneurs.

Women over 30 set their career goals in the days when women were a minority. Many probably set them too low and may be holding themselves back because they don't visualize themselves in leadership roles and because they hold self-limiting beliefs about their role. Women who were 25 in 1975, when larger numbers of women started getting MBAs, will be 50 in the year 2000. The average age of senior executives is 51 [17]. In such fields as finance, computer, and advertising, women are well represented and many have the experience and savvy to break through the glass ceiling. Also, while consensus reality has always accepted "rare, exotic birds" as leaders, such as Margaret Thatcher or Golda Meir, we are finally moving toward general acceptance of women in leadership roles.

Being Career Oriented Top-level decision-makers in most organizations are still men who may assume you are not career oriented unless you fit the profile of the typical *Promotable Woman:*

- An achieving person

- A high level of motivation and achievement need

- An identification with a field or profession

- A high degree of individuality, but relates well with people

- A strong sense of self-esteem, and respect for others' individuality

The Promotable Woman acts out of her own convictions rather than merely reacting to people and situations. She focuses on living up to her own expectations, not other people's expectations for her. She doesn't need to acquiesce passively to others' demands nor to automatically rebel against them. She is her own person.

Gaining Key Team Skills Leaders of self-directed teams must be highly skilled at performing key management functions that all members must use. See Chapter 9 on Leadership Style and Chapter 13 on Team Development for more comprehensive discussions of skills. To summarize, the team leadership skills are:

- Planning strategically in longer time frames

- Thinking in terms of renewal

- Understanding and using the politics of getting along and getting things done

- Causing change

- Affirming values

- Achieving unity

- Inspiring commitment and empowering people by sharing authority

SUMMARY

Although the proportion of women managers has more than doubled since the 1970s, about 95 percent of top-level managers are still men. Women who made it up the ladder realized they were operating in a male culture where the rules are made and enforced by men. So they learned the rules of the game.

Traditionally, the woman's place was thought to be in the home. The Industrial Revolution separated male and female spheres even more; men ran the businesses and women ran the homes. During World War II, women were called on to do "men's work" and discovered they were good at it. Several developments since then—such as longer lifespans, better birth control, and the Civil Rights movement—have caused a large increase in the number of career-oriented women. Affirmative Action laws probably opened more doors for women than any other factor, causing the United States to lead the world in proportion of women managers. But this period of relative openness was followed by a backlash in the 1980s that has slowed the growth rate for women achieving leadership roles.

Also in the 1980s we made the transition from an industrial society to an information society. This transition and related organizational developments—such as decentralized structures, broad participation in decision-making, and networking—helped remove many traditional barriers.

The 1990s promise to be a time of expansion and growth into a global economy and culture that includes the new Soviet commonwealth and Eastern Europe, a simultaneous emergence of cultural nationalism, the growth of biotechnology, and a renewed appreciation of ethical and spiritual values and the arts. Organizations will see increased employee diversity at all levels and a movement away from management for control to leadership for empowering individuals and work teams. All these emerging trends should continue to erode the traditional barriers to women. And because women have reached a critical mass and have the skills needed for the Global Nineties, they are poised to move into top leadership roles, in turn sparking U.S. business's role as a leader in the global marketplace.

To fulfill that destiny, women must still overcome external barriers to equality, such as pay disparity, inflexible working arrangements, and the glass ceiling to the top. They must also overcome internal barriers that derive from socialization: their self-limiting beliefs, conflicting beliefs, and the beliefs and stereotypes of others. They must become well-rounded, identifying and expanding on typical feminine strengths that they possess and developing key masculine strengths. Women must understand how the workers of the 1990s differ from those of the 1970s and 1980s, how 1990s leaders differ from yesterday's managers, and which of their traits and skills fit the new leadership profile.

REFERENCES

1. Adler, Leonore L. *Women in Cross Cultural Perspective*. Westport, Conn.: Praeger, 1990.

2. Adler, Nancy J., and Dafna N. Izraeli, eds. *Women in Management Worldwide*. Armonk, N.Y.: M. E. Sharpe, 1988.

3. Anderson, Gregory, ed. *The White Blouse Revolution. Female Office Workers Since 1870*. New York: St. Martin's Press, 1989.

4. Carlson, Margaret. "It's Our Turn." *Time* (Fall 1990), p. 16.

5. Carr-Ruffino, Norma. "U.S. Women: Breaking Through the Glass Ceiling." *Women in Management Review & Abstracts,* Vol. 6, No. 5 (1991).

6. Center for Creative Leadership Staff. *Breaking the Glass Ceiling: Can Women Reach the Top of America's Largest Corporations?* Palo Alto, Calif.: Addison-Wesley, 1987.

7. Clausen, Jeanette, and Helen Cafferty, eds. *Women in Germany Yearbook.* Lanham, Md.: University Press of America, 1989.

8. Dowling, Colette. *The Cinderella Complex.* New York: Simon and Schuster, 1981. The author examines the tendency of many women unconsciously to sabotage real career success for fear it will prevent their rescue by "Prince Charming" from the workaday world. The tendency to back away from career success once marriage takes place is also examined.

9. Eagly, Alice H. *Sex Differences in Social Behavior: A Social-Role Interpretation.* Hillsdale, N.J.: Lawrence Erlbaum Associates, 1987. This author examines research theory and method as it affects sex differences in helping behavior, aggressive behavior, and other social behaviors. She also delves into possible meanings of such differences.

10. Epstein, Cynthia Fuchs. *Deceptive Distinctions: Sex, Gender, and the Social Order.* New Haven, Mass.: Yale University Press, 1988. Epstein cites research that challenges the position that inherent differences between the sexes result in greater achievement by men. Such research implies that the most apparent distinctions are the social product of a sexist society.

11. Fierman, Jaclyn. "Why Women Still Don't Hit the Top." *Fortune* (July 30, 1990), p. 40.

12. Freeman, Sue J. *Managing Lives: Corporate Women and Social Change.* Amherst, Mass.: University of Massachusetts Press, 1990.

13. Garland, Susan. "Throwing Stones at the 'Glass Ceiling.'" *Business Week* (August 19, 1991), p. 29.

14. Greene, Kathanne W. *Affirmative Action and Principles of Justice.* Westport, Conn.: Greenwood Press, 1989. A thorough presentation of AA issues and philosophy, Title VII history and case law, and landmark AA cases.

15. Hernandez, Aileen. "EEOC and the Women's Movement 1965–1975," Symposium paper, Rutgers University Law School, November 28, 1975.

16. Joekes, Susan. *Women in the World Economy: An INSTRAW Study.* New York: Oxford University Press, 1987. A study of the International Research & Training Institute for the Advance of Women (INSTRAW) of the United Nations. It gives a broad overview and focuses on policy and trends rather than on specific statistics or countries.

17. Korn/Ferry International and UCLA Survey. *Working Women* (October 1986), p. 107.

18. Krauthammer, Charles A. "A Defense of Quotas." *The New Republic* (September 16 & 23, 1985), pp. 9–11.

19. Leonard, Jonathan A. *Antidiscrimination or Reverse Discrimination: The Impact of Changing Demographics, Title VII, and Affirmative Action on Productivity.* Berkeley, Calif.: Institute of Industrial Relations, 1984.

20. Loring, Rosalind, and Theodora Wells. *Breakthrough: Women into Management.* New York: Van Nostrand Reinhold, 1972. This book reports a landmark study of attitudes and cultural factors that facilitate or hinder the movement of women into leadership roles.

21. Matthaei, Julie A. *An Economic History of Women in America.* New York: Schocken Books, 1982. A history of women's work in America since colonial times, this book focuses on how the sexual division of labor developed and changed with the advent of industrialism.

22. Naisbett, John. *Megatrends: Ten New Directions Transforming Our Lives.* New York: Warner Books, 1982. A well-known trend expert, Naisbett's identification of trends and predictions for their consequences during the coming decade were uncannily accurate.

23. Naisbett, John, and Patricia Aburdene. *Megatrends 2000: Ten New Directions for the 1990's.* New York: William Morrow and Company, 1990. Naisbett predicted women's rise in organizations in the first *Megatrends.* In this one he says many women will move into top leadership roles by the year 2000.

24. National Women's Political Caucus. *Study of Women in Politics.* Washington, D.C.: National Women's Political Caucus, 1990.

25. Nuss, Shirley, et al. *Women in the World of Work: Statistical Analysis & Projections to the Year 2000.* London: International Labour Office, 1989.

26. Orlov, Darlene. In "Career Insight." *Managing Your Career* (Fall 1991).

27. Rogers, Shirley. *The Invisible Woman: Target of the Religious New Right.* New York: Dell, 1983. The author discusses the political impact and specific strategies of religious fundamentalism. Includes attacks on working (career) mothers, sexual freedom, feminism, and abortion rights.

28. Rossman, Marlene L. *The International Businesswoman of the 1990s: A Guide to Success in the Global Marketplace.* Westport, Conn.: Greenwood Press, 1990.

29. Sargent, Alice G. *The Androgynous Manager.* New York: Amacom, 1983. This author discusses how to blend male and female management styles for today's organizations.

30. Sekaran, Uma, and Fred Leong, eds. *Womanpower.* Newbury Park, Calif.: Sage, 1991. N. Carr-Ruffino, "Legal Aspects of Women's Advancement."

31. "Survey of Employer-Provided Child Care Benefits," *Monthly Labor Review* (September 1988), p. 42.

32. U.S. Commission on Civil Rights. *Affirmative Action in the 1980s: Dismantling the Process of Discrimination.* Clearinghouse Publication 70, 1981.

33. U.S. Department of Labor, Employment Standards Administration. "Employment of Minorities and Women in Federal Contractor and Noncontractor Establishments, 1974–1980." Unpublished final draft known internally as the Crump Report.

34. U.S. Department of Labor, *A Report on the Glass Ceiling Initiative,* 1991.

35. U.S. Department of Labor, *Workforce 2000,* 1987.

Chapter Two

A Man's World: Paths to Power

*"If you're going to play the game properly,
you'd better know every rule."*

Barbara Jordan

It's important that you know how your viewpoints, attitudes, and habits compare with those of men (and other women) who are functioning successfully in leadership positions. It's also helpful to know something about others' expectations of you as a woman and as a leader. Being able to identify the **fast track** to advancement and to distinguish between **dead-end jobs** and those that lead to further advancement is crucial to your career. Just as crucial is understanding something about how power is gained and used within the typical organization and the resulting "politics" that inevitably accompany power bids and power struggles. And, when you start recognizing how upward mobility, visibility, and power interact and go hand in hand in achieving career success, you'll know you're developing the kind of savvy necessary for the promotable woman.

In this chapter you will have the opportunity to

1. Compare the traditional organizational hierarchy with the more fluid models that are emerging, especially as they impact women

2. Ascertain whether a job is primarily supervisory, middle management, or top management by looking at key job factors

3. Know how line and staff jobs differ and how they may impact women's promotability

4. Distinguish between potentially dead-end and fast-track jobs and know how to break out of dead ends

5. Understand how lack of opportunities for advancement and resulting powerlessness lead to "typical female behavior" in organizations

6. Identify key types and sources of organizational power

7. Know some ways of gaining organizational power and how to evaluate the power potential of a position

---

 Career Decisions

To help you achieve these objectives, we'll follow the career path and the skill development of Erika Kerr throughout this book. Erika will be finishing the MBA program at State University in three months. For the past three years, she

has been working for Lighthouse Designs, Inc., and attending evening classes. Her first year Erika worked as a sales representative, and for the past two years she's worked as assistant to Jan Arguello, Vice-President of Sales. Lighthouse Designs is a large company that manufactures women's clothing. Its headquarters are in Dallas, and it has a number of regional branch offices throughout the United States.

Today Erika has career plans on her mind. Sipping a cup of coffee in the employees' lounge, she confides to her co-worker Gail Blocker, "Gail, some of the big corporations will be interviewing on campus in a couple of weeks. I started working on my résumé last night, and I just realized that I'm not sure exactly what type of job I'm looking for, much less what kind of company."

"I thought you wanted to be a manager, Erika. Isn't that all you need to know right now?"

"Evidently not. The Placement Center sent out a list of questions interviewers often ask about your career plans, job objectives, and so forth—and I'm not really prepared to answer any of them!"

"I thought you were going to stay with Lighthouse, Erika, and try to work into a management position here."

"I think I would like that, Gail. But why should I put all my eggs in one basket? I mean, it seems to me that I'll be in a much stronger position to negotiate for a promotion if I can generate some other good job offers."

"Well, I don't envy you having to go through the ordeal of being interviewed. I *hate* looking for a job. It just makes me a nervous wreck. And I feel so rejected when I don't get the job I applied for."

"I guess that's one way of looking at it, Gail. On the other hand, I think it may be an exciting experience. The seminar instructor for the Placement Center suggested that we view any jobs we *don't* get as lessons in job campaigning." She smiled at Gail's puzzled look. "You know—we ask ourselves what lessons we can learn from that experience and use it to increase our effectiveness in the next interview."

"Well, I'm still more comfortable just staying here with a company I'm familiar with, even if it doesn't carry much status or pay. I know Mr. Barker appreciates my work as his assistant, and one of these days he's bound to recommend me for promotion to a management job."

"Hey, Gail, I can understand that. I may end up here myself. In the meantime, I'm planning to wage as effective a job campaign as I can. To me it's like a game—it will be a kick if I can play it really well, but it's not the end of the world if I blow it. Say, haven't you been waiting around for a promotion for three or four years now?"

"Yes, I have. In fact, I've watched several men come through this department who learned most of what they know from me. They've moved on to better-paying positions, and here I sit."

"Gail, have you ever talked to Mr. Barker about this?"

Looking upset, Gail pushes back her chair and begins gathering up her things. "Well, I don't want to complain. Mr. Barker knows all this, and he knows the kind of work I do. I've always felt that when the time was ripe, he would see that I got a good promotion."

As Gail walks away, Erika smiles and shakes her head.

These two situations, Gail's and Erika's, provide food for thought. Both women are in the process of making and implementing career decisions, but in different ways. Can you identify some of the differences?

1. List specific actions and attitudes mentioned in this case that tend to enhance a person's promotability.

2. List specific actions and attitudes mentioned in the case that tend to sabotage career goals.

3. What words do you associate with the word "risk"? (Be spontaneous.)

4. How do you think most successful business people view risk?

Throughout the next few chapters, we'll be generalizing, indirectly, from both Gail's and Erika's experiences as we look at approaches women can take to their careers.

Because about 95 percent of the top decision-makers in American organizations are men, you're going to be operating in a male culture where the rules are made by men. To be successful, you must learn the rules of the game, which are quite different from the rules governing a woman's traditional place in the home. To further complicate matters, some of the rules are beginning to change.

The term "business game" does not necessarily imply game-playing in the sense of ulterior motives, dirty tactics, and negative results for the losers. Like the game of life, the business game can be played in many ways and does not require losers or negative results. Some rules vary from one organization to another, while others tend to be common to most organizations. If you don't like the way the game is played in one firm, perhaps you can find another organization more to your liking. In this chapter you'll get an overview of the business game, which should help you put specific situations and problems you encounter into perspective.

Do you have a "promotable" viewpoint? Exercise 2-1 can give you some clues.

EXERCISE 2-1: ASSESSING VIEWPOINTS THAT AFFECT PROMOTABILITY

Place a checkmark beside the response that best reflects your viewpoint at first glance. Don't try to analyze your answer or figure out which response is "right." For some specific comments and interpretations of answers, see the answer key at the back of the book.

1. Several important people in your life seem to believe that highly successful career women are not good wives or mothers, are not "truly feminine," and by implication are not successful as women. Your response is
   (a) Maybe you're right.   (b) I'll live my life the way I see fit!
   (c) Women, as well as men, can be successful in both their personal and their professional lives, if they learn how to set priorities that reflect balanced life goals.
2. How long do you expect to be working?
   (a) Until I have children   (c) Until I get married
   (b) Most of my life   (d) Other (list)
3. What do you expect in return for these years of work?
   (a) Money for the "extras" in life   (c) Money for the essentials of life
   (b) A high income plus a chance   (d) Other (list)
       to make a contribution and
       develop my talents

4. What position do you expect to hold within the next ten years?
   - (a) Vice-President
   - (b) Department head
   - (c) Chief Executive Officer
   - (d) I don't know
   - (e) Other (list)

5. Which type of job is most likely to lead to advancement?
   - (a) Personnel specialist
   - (b) Salesperson
   - (c) Administrative Assistant to the President

6. A fast track is
   - (a) An express method for getting services or products to customers
   - (b) The most direct career path to middle or top management
   - (c) A computer-aided procedure for executive decision-making

7. You're most likely to gain favorable visibility in an organization by
   - (a) Taking calculated risks and succeeding
   - (b) Dressing for success
   - (c) Attending all social functions and talking to the top decision-makers

8. A calculated risk is mainly
   - (a) A chance to make a gain
   - (b) Dangerous but can pay off
   - (c) To be taken only if necessary

9. Teamwork in organizations mainly involves
   - (a) Joining forces with people you work well with
   - (b) Working toward specific goals with people you like, despise, or feel neutral about
   - (c) Helping those who need your help

10. Your boss tells you he's thinking about expanding your unit or department to include a new area of responsibility. Your group is already overloaded with work. What would you do?
    - (a) Wait for him to come up with the detailed plans and instruction for implementing them
    - (b) Work out your own ideas for the best way to plan and implement the expanded areas of authority and responsibility, then discuss them with him
    - (c) Tell him your group simply can't take on more work

THE TRADITIONAL ORGANIZATIONAL HIERARCHY

In planning your career, you need to be aware of the various levels of management positions, as well as the differences between **line** and **staff jobs.** You need to be able to identify the career path most likely to lead directly to the ultimate position you set your sights on. You'll want to avoid getting side-tracked into what the organization views as a dead-end position. And you'll want to know which job moves represent the fast track to the top, why women have traditionally been excluded, how barriers to advancement usually affect people's behavior, and some ways of identifying companies that actively promote women. In this section we'll discuss the organizational hierarchy as it applies to your career decisions. In Chapter 12 we'll examine in detail various types of organizational structure and their implications.

Levels of Management

At least three levels of management are found in most traditional organizations: supervisor, middle manager, and top manager. Very large organizations may have a dozen or more levels, but they can usually be further categorized into one of the three basic levels. Figure 2-1 shows the corporate hierarchy in a large organization.

The First-Line Supervisor   The person in this position directly supervises a group of workers who are usually doing similar kinds of work. They therefore perform a single function within a department, such as the Pattern Makers Unit in a **Production Department.** Sometimes the first-line supervisor is called a foreman, sometimes an office manager. The key to identifying her level is to determine the function she fulfills. She is usually technically competent at the work itself and spends most of her time directly involved with the workers and the work; that is, she is usually considered a specialist in the work being done.

The Managerial Supervisor   The person in this position has a broader scope of authority within the department and usually has two or more first-line supervisors in separate functions reporting to her. For example, the supervisors of the Pattern Makers Unit and the Fabric Cutters Unit might report to her. She may be responsible for scheduling and coordinating the tasks of different work sections, or she may simply be responsible for a larger variety of functions or work than the first-line supervisor.

At the managerial level a supervisor is no longer a specialist. She does not *do* the work her subordinates do, and she needn't know *how* to do it. Her job involves getting work done through other people. She judges results and

ensures the performance of others. She spends more time planning, coordinating, motivating workers, handling personnel problems, and dealing with aspects of company finances, such as budgets or profit figures.

Middle Managers   These people are responsible for all aspects of an entire division, department, region, plant, branch office, product line, or service area. They not only coordinate the activities of the supervisors who report to them, they spend a great deal of time with other middle managers and top managers to see that companywide objectives and policies are integrated and coordinated. They are normally much more involved than supervisors in making decisions about long-term company objectives and in setting policies.

Top Managers   The top managers are responsible for determining the long-term direction the company will take, its major purpose for being, and its broad, overall strategies for dealing with competition, change, and the external environment. Top managers are also responsible for establishing companywide objectives and policies and for providing leadership and guidance to the firm as a whole. They coordinate the activities of the middle managers who report to them, and they work with other top managers to integrate activities to achieve companywide objectives. They also interact with managers of staff departments, who provide them with information, expertise, and advice. Top managers often spend much of their time interacting with other business, government, and community leaders, as well as the company's owners (board of directors) or other governing body.

Line Versus Staff Positions

Staff departments are made up of people who specialize in various fields. Their function is to assist the line executives. They *may* include such departments as personnel or human re-

FIGURE 2-1: The Hierarchy in Traditional Organizations

Note that line jobs lead to movement up the chain of command into the ranks of top management. Staff positions lack authority outside the immediate staff departments and may be career dead ends.

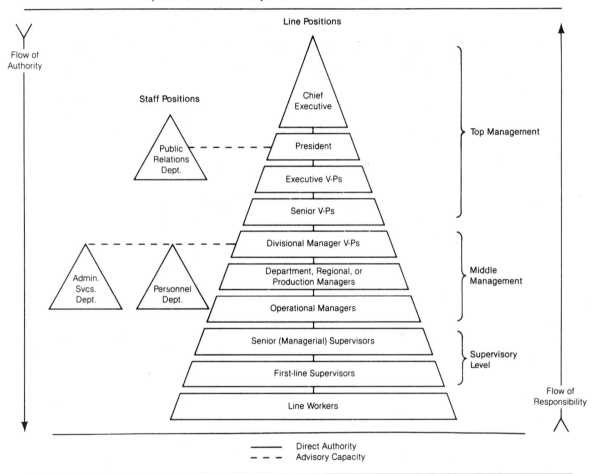

sources, accounting, data processing, advertising, public relations, research, traffic, billing, medical, legal, and such technical specialties as engineering, sciences, and architecture, *if they are not the main service provided by the organization.*

Staff jobs are *not* in the direct chain of command. Staff specialists and managers make recommendations and give advice to the line manager to whom they report. Although staff departments may have internal authority levels and chains of command, the top job is head of the department. Staff department heads make decisions that affect their own departments, but they do not normally make decisions that affect other departments, simply because they have no other departments under them. In contrast, the top job in the line structure is Chief Executive, as shown in Figure 2-1. Line managers make decisions that can affect everyone below them in the organization. More important, when top managers are looking within the company for promotable candidates, they usually select line managers. We'll discuss some exceptions to this practice later in this section.

Line jobs in private enterprise may be viewed as **profit centers,** responsible for generating a portion of the company's profits, or **entrepreneurial units.** Managers in these jobs find it relatively easy to pinpoint their contributions to company profits. In any firm that handles a product, sales jobs are line jobs. If the company makes products, jobs in the production department are line jobs. If it's a wholesale or retail firm, buyers as well as salespersons are in line jobs. If the company provides a service, jobs directly connected to selling or providing that service are line jobs. In banks, it's getting and investing money; in insurance companies, it's getting and investing the money from premiums and handling claims; in a repair company, it's making the repairs; in a computer services firm, it's providing the actual service. Top management views these departments as absolutely essential to the survival of the organization; therefore, the budgets required to operate these departments are accepted as a necessary cost of doing business.

Staff departments, on the other hand, are sometimes considered by top managers to consist largely of "extras, frills, or nice-to-haves." It follows that their budgets may be viewed largely as expenses — that is, as profit drains. While staff services may be valuable, even vital, to optimal company operation, staff budgets and jobs are usually the first to be cut when business falls off.

The Trend Toward More Fluid, Open Organizations

The organizational design symbolized in Figure 2-1 tends to be extremely rigid and hierarchical. Firms of the 1990s are beginning to move toward more fluid, organic, open structures. A simplified model of an extremely fluid and open organization is shown in Figure 2-2. In this model, top management is shown as an Executive Team (or Executive Committee), with a number of Operational Teams reporting directly to them.

The Operational Teams represent various departments and functional areas, both line and staff; and the difference between line and staff becomes blurred due to the teams' fluid tasks and responsibilities. The dotted lines to and from the Example Operational Team represent the free-flowing interaction and communication that each team has with other teams within the organization. If these lines were drawn in for all the teams, you would see a mass of dotted lines to and from all parts of the organization, indicating rich, informal communication patterns. In such a fluid structure, the teams' tasks, functions, lines of authority, and responsibilities may change rapidly, and people may move frequently from one team to another.

Most companies have a design that falls somewhere between the two extremes shown in Figures 2-1 and 2-2. Most businesses still look more like the traditional model, but many firms are becoming more fluid in order to meet the demands of the rapidly changing global marketplace. Women tend to have a greater chance to learn about many phases of company operations and to expand their support networks in fluid organizations. They can also become more visible to peers, through interaction of teams, and to top management because there are fewer layers of management between the workers and the top. Organizational structure is discussed further in Chapter 12.

Potentially Dead-End Jobs

Companies vary widely in their commitment to opening up management opportunities for women. Therefore, you should be aware of the

FIGURE 2-2: Model of a Fluid, Open Organization

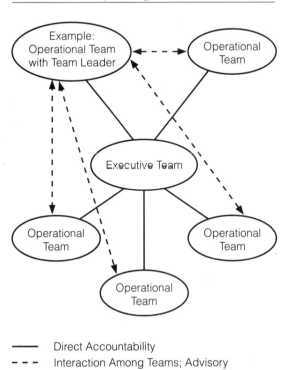

——— Direct Accountability

- - - Interaction Among Teams; Advisory

types of dead-end "management" positions you may get stuck in. (We'll discuss breaking out of dead-end positions later in this chapter.) Here are some examples of dead-end jobs.

The Working Supervisor This job may be labeled a management position for Affirmative Action purposes, but the label is misleading. Actually the woman still has responsibility for producing her own work while receiving a relatively small increase in pay and authority in return for a large increase in responsibility and time demands. She probably lacks adequate time for proper planning, organizing, directing, and controlling because she is too busy doing her own work.

First-Line Supervisors in Highly Routinized Functions Women in these positions are

often functionally powerless. They are frequently caught between the conflicting demands of a management hierarchy they are not likely to have an opportunity to enter and the resistance of workers who resent their own highly routine and repetitive work. Women are especially likely to be given such jobs overseeing other women clerical or secretarial workers. Even when they are relieved of their own work duties and given adequate time to supervise or manage, these women are likely to be powerless and stuck in dead-end positions.

Certain Staff Jobs Women in staff positions, such as human resources (personnel) or public relations, may be organizationally powerless because they have no line authority and must depend on line managers to carry out their recommendations and implement their decisions. Staff managers usually lack the authority given line managers to make operational decisions and see that they're carried out. The staff person must be an expert in a particular area, such as research, word processing, or personnel relations. Association with operational employees is indirect. In staff positions the most important requirement is *expertise* in a specialized area of an operation. Women are especially likely to find themselves in a "stuck" position in the human resources department, which is thought of as a "woman's area" in many companies.

Jobs Likely to Lead to Advancement

Line jobs are more likely to lead to advancement than staff jobs, especially line jobs that directly affect company profits. However, staff jobs that are directly connected to solving a major company problem can also be a steppingstone to promotion.

Line Jobs That Contribute Directly to Profit These are potentially the most powerful positions in most companies. If you can, find out how the people in top management in your company made it to the top. Chances are they came up through the ranks of the Production and/or Sales Departments. At times, some top executives emerge from Financial Operations, since managing money once it has been made becomes a high priority for many companies when interest rates are high.

In simple terms, the jobs connected with the dual functions of producing and selling are potentially the most powerful. The dual functions involve (1) buying something, making something, or bringing in something and (2) selling something or servicing something for a profit.

Key Line Jobs in Nonprofit Organizations The jobs most likely to lead to the top in government and other nonprofit agencies are those most directly connected with providing the major service of the organization. In health care organizations, the key jobs are the administrative positions involving direct patient services; in educational institutions, these jobs are providing programs of study; in the postal service, they are collecting, processing, and delivering mail; in the Salvation Army, they are collecting contributions and distributing meals and other help to the needy.

In these examples the positions that include responsibility for attracting users of the services or for securing the necessary funds to provide the services vary in importance, depending on the purpose and nature of the organization. For example, attracting students to private universities has become a key responsibility in recent years. Securing funds has always been a key responsibility in charitable organizations like the Salvation Army.

Jobs on the Fast Track Top management in many organizations tags the most promising management trainees for promotion along an accelerated career path often called the fast track. These candidates usually spend shorter periods in fewer jobs before being promoted to key middle-management positions. They may

then become the prime candidates for top-management positions.

Jobs in Areas Crucial to Solving Current Company Problems When a company needs to computerize its operations, the staff position of systems analyst can become quite visible and important. When a company is threatened with a ruinous lawsuit, the legal staff gains status. Although such jobs may have relatively temporary value for advancement purposes, you may be able to gain visibility and be "in the right place at the right time" by accepting such a position. If the job is a staff function, however, think twice.

Why Women Have Been Excluded

Prior to the 1970s, women were traditionally excluded from management, especially middle and top management. Their opportunities for advancement were practically nonexistent for three major reasons: the conformity pressures on managers to look and act alike, management's need for certainty about the attitudes and actions they can expect from people they bring into their inner circle, and the fact that the secretarial positions in which many women begin are completely outside the corporate hierarchy.

The Secretarial Ghetto

In this century women's roles have centered around secretarial and clerical functions; this has powerfully affected women's self-concepts and aspirations. In nearly all companies the secretarial ladder is short, and rank is usually determined by the boss's status. In other words, secretaries derive their formal rank and level of reward not from the skills they use and the tasks they perform but from the formal rank of their bosses. Rosabeth Kanter discovered other potential traps for women following the secretarial route; some of them could be traps for any woman worker [3].*

Narrow specialization and orientation to one boss and one job Ambitious secretaries who try to get ahead through the initiative/efficiency route run the risk of becoming a threat to their bosses. Most secretaries find it safer to learn the *boss* rather than the company. In this way he comes to depend on her ability to anticipate his needs and to respond to requests without detailed orders.

Timidity and self-effacement Because of their lack of independence and autonomy in the job and because of their dependence on one man, older women especially tend to display timid, self-effacing, nonassertive behavior.

Praise-addiction Many secretaries tend to become addicted to praise because the boss gives them regular doses of thanks and praise in return for compliance with a continual flow of orders. Most secretaries are protected from responsibility or criticism because their boss serves as a buffer between them and "problem" managers. This condition tends to intensify their dependence on the boss.

Emotionality and gossip Many secretaries resort to assumed helplessness and emotional manipulation to get what they want. They take advantage of the discomfort of many men with displays of emotion, such as anxiety or tears. These secretaries, of course, pay the price of becoming more and more accustomed to emotional displays that are considered inappropriate for managers.

Some secretaries also use their privileged access to information to gain status with others through gossip. Men in most status and power positions also earn status with others through gossip. However, it is usually referred to as "rumor" or "the grapevine." When secretaries use these power and control tactics, they tend to reinforce stereotypes of women as gossipy and emotional.

*Since Kanter found that nearly all bosses in the corporation she studied were male and nearly all secretaries were female, this discussion refers to the boss as "he" and the secretary as "she."

How Opportunities for Advancement Affect Attitudes and Behavior

In most companies the incentives are all for upward mobility. Therefore, the people who believe they're in line for advancement are "turned on" by the prospects of reaping rich rewards. On the other hand, those who believe they're stuck in dead-end positions must adjust to the prospect of limited rewards. The resulting attitudes and behavior of the two groups are quite different.

The Movers A typical career path to the best managerial positions is a track providing opportunities for a person to hold a variety of jobs across functions for two or three years each, including time in the company's central headquarters. The promotability that results from such diverse experience is essential not only to success but to other human values as well — to autonomy, independence, growth, a sense of challenge, and a chance to learn. In most companies the message is clear: Be promoted or be stuck. Upward mobility enhances a person's self-esteem dramatically and also affects the way people involve themselves in their work.

For those who are upwardly mobile, opportunity is seductive. Those on the fast track to middle or top management invest themselves heavily in work and concern themselves with learning the things that will be useful to them on their journey upward. They learn how to be political and how to watch what they say and to whom. As they move, they are usually willing to take on any extra tasks that will advance their careers. Once the excitement of opportunity takes hold, people's aspirations tend to soar. People can be turned around and turned on by realizing they have a wide-open opportunity to move up.

The Stuck It's a different story with the "stuck." These people have low ceilings in their jobs; they are at dead ends. Blocked from movement, lacking opportunity in a system where mobility means success, the stuck make a variety of adjustments to their situation. They relate to work, to the organization, and to its people in a very different way from high-opportunity movers.

The largest category of stuck people never had much opportunity to begin with. Low promotion rates, or short ladders and low ceilings in their job category, mean that they developed little or no expectations of upward mobility. Rosabeth Kanter found that most women clerical workers, supervisors of office workers, and some staff managers, especially in personnel, were in this situation [3, pp. 30–163]. Since their expectations were low from the start, these people were not necessarily alienated from the organization. Instead, they became more involved with their peers. Staff people might invest more time in their "professional" organization.

Another stuck group either (1) competed for promotions and were turned down or (2) were promoted along dead-end career paths. These people are more likely to be frustrated because their expectations of opportunities have been encouraged and then blocked.

Male and Female Responses to Being Stuck
Women and men tend to respond in similar ways to the realization that their jobs offer them little hope of advancement.

1. *Low commitment to the company and to their work.* They become marginal employees, doing just enough to hold onto their jobs.

2. *Lack of initiative and withdrawal from responsibility.* Even if they continue doing an excellent job, they make no effort to expand it or to look for opportunities for the company to excel or prosper. They play it safe, shying away from new assignments outside their job description.

3. *Loyalty to their stuck peer group.* Cliques of the stuck may find their solidarity in open rejection and criticism of managers farther up

the ladder. Such criticism tends to take the form of passive resistance such as gossip, jokes, and ridicule.

Members of any closed peer groups are under pressure to remain loyal to the group. Leaving the group, even for a promotion, may be seen as disloyalty. This tends to be especially true for women in clerical and secretarial jobs. To compound the problem, as a woman moves up, social contacts usually become fewer and more difficult, while men usually find a male peer group at every level. Concern about "leaving friends" and the social discomforts that go along with a promotion are often expressed by women in the secretarial or clerical ranks.

4. *Preoccupation with social recognition.* The stuck seek status through social, rather than technical or professional, skills—perhaps by having the juiciest gossip, the latest inside information, or the best jokes. Some gain status by being the most compatible on the golf course, at the convention, and at other semisocial functions, especially where they're in frequent contact with outsiders who don't know their true position within the company. Others focus on getting recognition from younger or newer employees within the company.

5. *Resistance to innovation.* The stuck may get their kicks by resisting the ideas and projects of those people who did make it to higher positions. These chronic complainers and criticizers tend to offer no new ideas, only barriers to the implementation of others' ideas. Barriers often take the form of foot-dragging or delaying projects through bureaucratic red tape.

Several studies have shown that men in low-opportunity situations take on the characteristics usually attributed to women in their orientation to work. Kanter found that such men "limit their aspirations, seek satisfaction in activities outside of work, dream of escape, interrupt their careers, emphasize leisure and consumption, and create sociable peer groups in which interpersonal relationships take precedence over other aspects of work" [3, p. 161].

If most women seemed to be less motivated or committed to business careers, then, it is probably because their jobs carried less opportunity. When they perceive they have the same opportunities as men, women tend to behave in ways usually attributed to men on the job: They become more ambitious, task oriented, and involved with work.

Breaking Out of a Dead-End Position

Your best strategy, of course, is to avoid getting stuck in a dead-end position by exchanging the right information with your potential boss when you interview for a job or a transfer. Make your career goals known, and find out about alternate career paths and the likelihood of their leading to your goal. Understand the difference between low-mobility and high-mobility positions, and ask questions that will help you determine which type of job you're being offered. (See Exhibit 2-1.) Also refer to Exhibit 2-2 for clues on evaluating the power

EXHIBIT 2-1: The Promotability Factor of Jobs

High-Mobility Positions	Low-Mobility Positions
A high probability of advancement	Low promotion rates
A short time-span between advances	Long time-span between moves
The chance for increasing challenges	Unchanging tasks
Eventual access to the most rewarding jobs	Static level of skill and mastery
	No pathway into rewarded positions

EXHIBIT 2-2: Evaluating the Power Potential of a Job

Job Factors	Potential for Power (+)	Potential for Powerlessness (−)
Number of rules that must be followed	Few	Many
Number of predecessors in the job	Few	Many
Number of routines already established	Few	Many
Variety of tasks involved	Many	Few
Quantity and quality of rewards for unusual performance	High	Low
Degree of flexibility about how to use people	High	Low
Amount of approval needed for nonroutine decisions	Little	Much
Proximity of physical location to company headquarters	Central	Distant
Extent of publicity about job activities	Great	Small
Relevance of tasks to current organizational problem areas	Central	Peripheral
Focus of tasks	Outside department	Inside department
Extent of contact with top management	Great	Small
Number of opportunities to participate in programs, conferences, meetings, problem-solving task forces, committees	Many	Few
Advancement prospects of subordinates	Great	Small

potential of a job, which is related to job mobility and promotability. Suggestions for specific interview questions are provided in Chapter 3.

After you accept a position, keep your eyes and ears open and keep evaluating whether you are still in line for a promotion that will be a good step toward your goal. Once you've been in a position for two years, start making inquiries about when you're scheduled to move up. If you're still in the same job after three years, it's likely that you're stuck.

Here are a few strategies for breaking out of a dead-end job; they should give you some ideas for developing your own strategy (see also Chapter 3 on setting career goals and selecting a job and Chapter 14 on moving up the ladder):

- Make your goals known to appropriate decision-makers; gain their support. (See the section on mentors in Chapter 8.)

- If a better position is unavailable, try to expand your job responsibilities and get the title changed; later ask for a pay raise commensurate with your increased responsibilities.

- Ask for a lateral transfer if it would provide necessary experience and put you in a better position for promotion later.

- Look for ways to become more visible to decision-makers and to impress them favorably with your abilities and potential. See the discussion of gaining power later in this chapter, as well as relevant discussions in Chapter 14.

- Ask if there are some seminars, courses, or training programs that will prepare you for promotion; see if the company will provide funds.

- If you cannot get a commitment from your boss for a promotion by a certain date, start planning your move to a company that offers better opportunities for advancement.

ORGANIZATIONAL POWER

How do you feel about gaining and using power? Exercise 2-2 at the end of this chapter is designed to help you identify your attitude toward power. Many women associate negative feelings and thoughts with the word "power" and are somewhat uncomfortable with the idea of assuming and using power. This attitude contrasts vividly with the typical male attitude. Most men assume that they will be expected to wield power in many capacities throughout their lives and tend to be comfortable with the idea. The first definition of power in the *American Heritage Dictionary* is "the ability or capacity to act or perform effectively." In other words,

> Power is the ability to make things happen, to influence people and events.

Implied in this definition is the ability to influence yourself — that is, to direct your own life and to command your inner resources.

Because the ability to gain and use power effectively and to be comfortable with a powerful role is essential to managerial success, we'll discuss power from several angles throughout this book. In this chapter we'll take a broad view of power as used in an organizational setting. In Chapter 5, we'll discuss personal power (the ability to command your inner resources), in Chapter 8 interpersonal power (your power as perceived by others), and in Chapter 10 the need for power (a drive that motivates some people).

All these discussions are based on the premise that power itself is neither good nor bad; it's the ways in which power is used — and the effect of those methods on others — that may be judged either positive or negative. If you are uncomfortable with the idea of wielding power, this thought may help: Wherever you find groups of people, you find leaders — people who exercise power. Someone therefore is going to exercise power in any group; if you have leadership qualities, the leader might as well be you. In fact, the way you exercise power might have a more positive effect on the group than the way your competitors might go about it.

Organizational power represents different things to different people. For some, organizational power meets a real need. Most people, however, are interested primarily in gaining enough organizational power to survive within the system. They merely want enough power to carry out their responsibilities — to conduct their business with relative autonomy and to get the resources they need to meet their objectives. The formal, hierarchic power that comes automatically with a manager's job is rarely adequate. To function effectively, managers must also gain informal power through organizational politics. In any organization the powerful are the ones who have access to tools for action; so as a manager you must figure out what tools you need and how to go about getting them.

Types and Sources of Informal Organizational Power

Kanter found general agreement among managers about what constitutes credibility — competence plus power, the known ability to get results [3, p. 169]. People will do almost anything for a boss when they believe he or she has their interests at heart and will fight for them. However, they must see that the boss has the power to produce for them; they must believe the fight will pay off for them. This means that the boss must have some power within the system.

To be an effective manager, therefore, you must tap into informal organizational power and project the image of a powerful boss. And to maximize your power and promotability, you must seek a powerful boss any time you interview for a new job. Some sources of organizational power are (1) upward influence in the decision-making process, (2) the ability to

get needed resources and information, (3) the ability to reduce people's sense of dependency and uncertainty, and (4) upward mobility. Although these categories are closely related and sometimes overlap, they are helpful in identifying power sources.

Upward Influence Work groups with high morale invariably believe that their leaders have upward influence — that is, they are able to influence their own bosses and have a say in decisions affecting the department as a whole. When a boss has both good human relations skills *and* power, the workers tend to have high morale. Both men and women attach more importance to having a boss who can get things done than to working for someone who is "nice." Praises and promises mean little if the leader can't deliver.

Resources/Information People invariably sense who is powerful and are most likely to accept direct attempts to influence them from people they perceive as powerful. The most effective and best-liked leaders can command more of the organization's resources, can bring something that is valued from outside into the group, and have access to the information that directly affects those in the work group.

Dependency/Uncertainty The larger and the more complex an organization is and the more rigid the hierarchy within the organization, the more people depend on others to get the things they need to carry out their tasks. People are generally willing to work quite hard to reduce this sense of dependency. One way is to become allied with powerful people who can make them more independent by bringing more certainty to their lives.

People who want to gain power, then, must be able to solve others' dependency problems and have some control over the major sources of uncertainty. People who have some control over the situations currently creating problems for the company tend to have access to this type of power. Finance and accounting people have more power when business is bad or when money is tight. Production experts have power when materials are scarce and demand is high. And so forth.

Upward Mobility Workers want to ally themselves with managers they perceive as powerful for several reasons: (1) powerful managers can get more for their workers; (2) they can back up both their promises and their threats; (3) they can more easily make changes in the workers' situation; (4) they can take the workers along with them when they move so that a worker's upward mobility is affected; and (5) they are more likely to adopt a participatory management style in which they share information, delegate authority, train the worker for more responsibility, and give the worker more responsibility and autonomy.

Powerful bosses are promotable bosses, and they want to show that they are not indispensable in their current jobs. They train people to take their place when they advance. They delegate authority as a means of training replacements. This is in vivid contrast to powerless and unpromotable bosses. They tend to try to retain control and to restrict opportunities for workers to learn new skills and attain a higher level of responsibility. They're insecure and want to make it clear that no one else can take their place. A capable subordinate represents a serious replacement threat to the unpromotable boss, and the subordinate's growth and advancement are seriously blocked.

Being upwardly mobile in an organization confers a degree of power upon a person. Conversely, individuals who know how to gain power are likely to *become* upwardly mobile within the organization.

Ways of Gaining Organizational Power

People within large organizations gain power through growth activities and alliances. Activities that result in an increase in power must be (1) out of the ordinary, (2) visible to key people within the organization, and (3) seen as part of a solution to a crucial organizational problem. Ways of achieving something considered extraordinary include

1. Making organizational changes

2. Taking major risks and succeeding

3. Being the first in a new position

Reorganizing New managers must handle changes or crises to demonstrate their abilities. If their department has been running smoothly and continues to run smoothly, no visibility is gained. By reorganizing, a manager can ensure that his or her own team is well placed and that opposition is eliminated. Reorganizing provides the manager with rewards to bestow on followers in the form of new opportunities and job changes. Such managers create new uncertainties that can make people more dependent on them; in this way they can increase their power. In addition, the reorganization can be presented as a problem-solving innovation, which by design is highly visible.

Risk-Taking This approach requires a willingness to take calculated risks. Since many women have a negative view of risk — focusing on what may be lost in case of failure instead of what may be gained in case of success — it's a good idea to analyze your approach to risk-taking. Most men view calculated risk-taking (awareness of the probabilities and the implications of both failure and success) as a welcome challenge. (See Chapter 11 for a discussion of risk-taking in connection with problem-solving and decision-making.) Fewer managers are able to pull off extraordinary risks. When they do, the payoffs can be very high. Successful risk-takers show the company they can perform in the most difficult of circumstances, and they develop charisma in the eyes of others.

Visibility Jobs in which people are heavily involved in more than one department or with other organizations tend to have the most visible activities. Serving on task forces and committees can also gain visibility for the participants. Some managers gain visibility for their activities by making sure they appear relevant to solving company needs. This strategy may involve finding an acceptable label for an activity, then finding an organizational need to hang the label on, and finally selling the project to the appropriate persons.

Power Base In a large company it's also necessary to make social connections with people outside the immediate work group; these relationships need to be long term and stable. Gaining power, in fact, requires developing a support network, or **power base,** throughout the company that includes (1) workers, (2) colleagues, (3) mentors, and (4) other decision-makers. The value of a **mentor** (a decision-maker who befriends a younger manager and serves as teacher and supporter) will be discussed in Chapter 8, along with a general discussion of support networks.

How can you size up a potential job in terms of the power you may be able to generate within that position? One way is to get as much information as possible about the job factors, as listed in Exhibit 2-2. You can add other relevant factors for the position you're considering. Then analyze the factors for their power potential; for example, if the job functions are governed by few rules, that's a plus. If you're following a long line of predecessors in the job, that's a minus. Compare and evaluate the pluses and minuses for all the relevant factors to determine the job's potential for power.

The Powerless

Although it is no longer unusual for women to be given jobs of heavy responsibility where they are accountable for the results of workers, it's still relatively unusual for women to have much power within the organization. This lack of power affects management style.

Sources of Powerlessness Frequently women supervisors or managers find themselves without the informal power that their formal roles demand—for some or all of these reasons:

They lack informal political influence as well as powerful mentors or sponsors; they are not on an upwardly mobile career path.

They are unable to get adequate **resources,** such as budget money, staff services, supplies, and additional workers.

They have little input to or influence in the planning and decision-making that directly affect them and their subordinates, and their area of independent decision-making is too limited.

Their situations don't permit them to take risks. Their bosses solve their problems for them rather than serving as **resource persons.**

Their authority is sometimes undercut by their bosses.

They convey a sense of insecurity as a leader and appear to anticipate resistance from their subordinates rather than cooperation.

Being aware of the sources and symptoms of powerlessness can help you avoid job "traps" that appear to be desirable promotions but are actually dead ends. Look carefully at the positions of working supervisor, supervisor of clerks or secretaries, and staff jobs. They may be steppingstones to powerful jobs, or they may be dead ends.

How Powerless Managers React Powerless managers—whether male or female—tend to concentrate their power needs on their subordinates, over whom they have at least some degree of authority. The following behavior patterns are typical:

1. *Controlling Behavior and Close Supervision*

   Powerless managers tend to "lord it over" their subordinates. They find talented subordinates threatening and rarely help such people get ahead. They usually select their immediate assistants from the mediocre rather than from the outstanding members of the group. Powerless managers also tend to resort to discipline or threats to gain cooperation from workers more frequently than their powerful counterparts do.

They tend to make most or all of the decisions.

They frequently do an excessive amount of the routine work.

They rarely or never let a subordinate represent them at meetings.

They attempt to control communications coming in and out of their department, so that all communications pass through them.

They may attempt to take all the credit themselves for what is accomplished in the department. Because technical mastery of job content is one of the few areas where they do feel powerful, they are likely to take over tasks of subordinates or supervise them too closely.

They may exert excessive control over their subordinates.

They tend to jump in too quickly to solve problems for subordinates.

They nitpick over small things subordinates do differently.

They may overdo demands of strict conformity to their procedures, thus blocking subordinates from learning or developing their own styles.

Rather than devoting themselves to more general leadership activities, they spend too much time taking over the work of the next level down.

2. *Overconcern with Rules and Procedures*

Powerless managers give subordinates no room for freedom or experimentation with procedures.

Since their superiors may not back them up, powerless managers depend on the rules as their only safe and sure legitimate authority.

Getting everything "right" according to the rules is one of the few ways they have to impress superiors or to secure their positions.

Control of the rules gives them some added power. They bend the rules for subordinates who are compliant and reward favored subordinates with a lighter application of the rules.

3. *Excessive Focus on Territorial Rights*

Powerless managers tend to narrow their interests to their particular small territory or piece of the system.

They try to insulate and protect it.

They attempt to prevent anyone else from engaging in similar activities without their approval or participation as "the expert."

They focus on meeting their own goals. They show little interest in company goals.

Staff managers indulge in territoriality more frequently than line managers. Staff managers usually have fewer subordinates to supervise closely and fewer rules and procedures to resort to.

These findings have three important implications for women. First, powerless managers tend to display the types of behavior often attributed exclusively to women managers. Such behavior results from organizational powerlessness, *not* from any sex-related characteristics. Second, upwardly mobile women should seek to work for powerful bosses. They are more likely to encourage growth and development and to help talented women move up the ladder. Third, women can avoid behaving as if they were powerless by avoiding the behaviors listed here and by adopting behaviors typical of the powerful. (See Chapters 3, 6, and 8.) Acting as if you have power is frequently half the battle! Many of the powerful got that way by surrounding themselves with the "aura" of power.

Now you know some basic rules of the business game, including how it came to be a male domain and how it's changing. If you don't like the business game or its rules, you have two choices: (1) Find something else to devote your energies to. (2) Play the game until you have enough power to change some of the goals or rules in your organization. Women can play a vital leadership role in transforming their organizations in ways that promote a balanced life and a sense of community and connection for employees.

If you're wavering, read on and find out more about the game. Start asking successful executives how they view the game. Most say it helps them to think of their work world as a game. Then they're not likely to tie their sense of self-esteem and value as a person to winning a mere game. They can put skirmishes — and even major battles — into perspective. The setbacks and defeats that inevitably occur in even the most successful careers can then be viewed philosophically. The executive can ask, "What

lesson can I learn from that one?" — "What new opportunity does this open up?" — and move on to the next round. This approach can be especially helpful for women who tend to take things too personally, overreact to criticism, let their emotions get the best of them, or carry a chip on their shoulder. It is conducive to "rolling with the punches." We'll discuss these particular problems in further detail in Chapter 5.

Keep in mind too that any organization — including government agencies, schools, churches, and other charitable or volunteer organizations — has its hierarchy, politics, and questionable practices. Whatever career path you choose, it's important to learn the rules of the game. Then you're in a position to decide how they fit in with your values, which of your viewpoints you're willing to change, and just how far you're willing to go toward compromise. Above all, it's important to deal with reality. This book is designed to help you do that. The next step is to identify the specific niche you want to aim for — to set your goals and priorities and to develop an action plan for reaching them.

SUMMARY

Although businesses are moving away from rigid, authoritarian structures, women still need to understand how they work. Upward mobility, visibility, and power go hand in hand for career success. The following jobs *may* be upwardly mobile but are frequently dead ends: working supervisor, first-line supervisors in highly routinized functions, and certain staff jobs, such as personnel. Jobs most likely to lead to advancement are (1) line jobs that directly contribute to profit and (2) jobs in areas considered crucial to solving current company problems.

Most women classified as "managers" are actually supervisors. It's important to recognize the difference between supervision and middle management. Middle managers are more closely involved in making decisions about objectives and developing policies for entire functional areas in order to integrate and coordinate companywide operations. Supervisors make fewer decisions, and their influence is usually limited to matters that directly affect their unit.

People who believe they have a high opportunity for advancement tend to become highly motivated. Conversely, people who believe they have little opportunity to advance tend to show (1) low commitment to the company and to their work, (2) lack of initiative and withdrawal from responsibility, (3) loyalty to their "stuck" peer group, (4) preoccupation with social recognition, and (5) resistance to innovation. Both men and women respond the same way to high-opportunity and low-opportunity situations.

Access to power is important for success as a manager. Work groups with high morale invariably perceive that their leaders have upward influence. Ways to gain power include (1) doing something out of the ordinary, (2) being visible to key people within the organization, and (3) being seen as part of a solution to a crucial organizational problem. Some actions that people might consider extraordinary are making organizational changes, taking major risks and succeeding, and being the first in a new position.

Male and female managers tend to react in similar ways to powerlessness: (1) exhibiting controlling behavior and closely supervising workers, (2) being overly concerned with rules and procedures, and (3) focusing excessively on territorial rights.

Additional Exercises

EXERCISE 2-2: YOUR POWER PROFILE

Write the first things you think of in response to the following five statements. Don't try to analyze what you "should" respond. The first thoughts that pop into your mind will be the most valuable for this exercise.

Statement 1. *Power.* When I think of power, I think of . . .

Statement 2. *Powerless.* Some situations in which I have felt powerless are . . .

Statement 3. *Powerful.* Some situations in which I have felt powerful are . . .

Statement 4. *Power Drains.* Some typical behaviors that drain away a woman's professional power image (that make her appear less powerful) are . . .

Statement 5. *Power Boosts.* Some typical behaviors that boost a woman's professional power image (that make her appear more powerful) are . . .

Recap. Now, go back and categorize your responses to Statement 1 by identifying each response as (1) a positive aspect of power, (2) a negative aspect of power, or (3) a neutral aspect of power. Which category is predominant in your responses? What do you think this reveals about your attitude toward power?

Compare your responses to Statements 2 and 3. How can you eliminate or minimize situations in which you feel powerless? How can you expand or increase the situations in which you feel powerful?

Compare your responses to Statements 4 and 5. How can you eliminate or minimize your power drains? How can you expand or increase your power boosts?

EXERCISE 2-3: PINPOINTING YOUR ATTITUDE

Step 1. Finish the following story. Be as spontaneous as possible; don't try to analyze or figure out the best response. This exercise will have the most value to you if it reflects your first reactions. Write anything that occurs to you, whether it makes sense or not.

Step 2. If you are meeting with a group, your instructor may want you to print your initials on the back of your story and turn it in for analysis or redistribution to another group member.

Step 3. See the answer key for instructions on analyzing your paper and, if appropriate, another group member's paper.

The Story: When Erika Kerr entered graduate school to work on her Master of Business Administration degree, about one-fourth of the graduate students were women. Only one of her instructors was female. When grades came out at the end of the first semester, Erika learned she had the highest grade point average in the Business Department. (Continue the story to its conclusion.)

EXERCISE 2-4: OVERCOMING FEAR OF SUCCESS

Is it possible that you have hidden reservations about achieving a successful career? Could it be that you actually fear some aspects of success? Such fears can result in self-sabotage of career goals. The analysis of your response to Exercise 2-3 may indicate that you do harbor some of these fears. The best way to overcome them is to uncover them and then to establish new beliefs about success. Steps 1 and 2 of this exercise are designed to help you further identify success fears and their sources. Steps 3 and 4 are designed to help you establish new beliefs about success (more about this in Chapter 3).

Instructions for Steps 1 through 3: Read the statement; then close your eyes, breathe deeply, and relax. Focus on the statement; don't analyze it or try to figure out what the "best response" should be. Notice what comes up, what spontaneously occurs to you. Then open your eyes and finish the statement by writing your responses in approximately the sequence in which they occurred to you.

Step 1: (a) I want to reach my career goals, but . . .

   (b) To achieve my career goals, I might have to give up . . .

   (c) Maybe I don't really deserve to succeed because . . .

Step 2: Some "don't deserve" or warning messages my parents or others gave me are . . .

Step 3: (a) I can handle abundant success because . . .

   (b) My top three priorities are . . .

   (c) I deserve abundant success because . . .

Step 4: Put each item you wrote in Step 3 on a separate card. Each week select a different card and place it where you'll see it several times a day. Become your own best supporter. Repeat one of these affirmations at least once a day.

EXERCISE 2-5: YOUR SELF-CONCEPT

Draw a picture of yourself

1. When you feel down

2. When you feel your very best

3. As you are in your wildest fantasies

4. The way people see you who think you're "just great"

5. The way people see you who think you're "for the birds"

6. As your ideal self—who you would really like to be and think maybe you could be

REFERENCES

1. Belasco, James A. *Teaching the Elephant to Dance: Empowering Change in Your Organization*. New York: Crown Publishers, 1990. Belasco says that most American companies, like powerful elephants, are shackled by the chains of conditioning and inertia. Those businesses that survive will be fleet of foot, not slow to change.

2. Kanter, Rosabeth Moss. *The Change Masters: Innovation for Productivity in the American Corporation*. New York: Simon and Schuster, 1983. Kanter tells why the key to the revival of U.S. world leadership is the development of participation management skills and environments. This development will make possible the full use of new ideas that arise from within the organization.

3. Kanter, Rosabeth Moss. *Men and Women of the Corporation*. New York: Basic Books, 1979. A classic in the field of women in management, this book is especially valuable for its insights into the ways organizational power and mobility affect women in the corporate world, the status of women, and some barriers women must overcome to succeed as managers.

4. Peters, Thomas J., and Nancy Austin. *A Passion for Excellence: The Leadership Difference*. New York: Random House, 1985. The authors give practical methods and actions to implement the conclusions set out in Peters' earlier book *In Search of Excellence*.

5. Peters, Thomas J., and Robert H. Waterman, Jr. *In Search of Excellence*. New York: Harper & Row, 1982. This ground-breaking analysis of the strengths and weaknesses of U.S. business identifies the need for change in organizational design, culture, and leadership.

6. Porter, Michael E. *The Competitive Advantage of Nations*. New York: The Free Press, 1990. Porter identifies what makes a nation's firms and industries competitive in global markets and thus what propels a whole nation's economy. He provides a blueprint for government policy to enhance national competitive advantage.

7. Sheehy, Gail. *Passages*. New York: Bantam, 1984. This is an excellent book for helping you understand the predictable crises of adult life. It helps to know you are not alone!

Developing Personal Skills for Leadership Effectiveness

Effective leaders blend a wide variety of skills. Some of those skills are related to basic management functions; others are more general, the skills that make you an effective human being. These personal, social skills are becoming even more important to leadership success than technical or management skills.

In Part 2 we'll discuss the personal beliefs, attitudes, thoughts, feelings, choices, and decisions that will lead to personal growth, help you develop personal power, and overcome barriers to acceptance in your organization. One barrier — men's discomfort in working with a woman leader — centers around seven complaints: She's not confident, she doesn't have clout, she doesn't know how to play the game, she comes on too strong, I don't know how to treat her, working for a woman makes me look bad, and I'm paying the consequences because she's only a token.

The major goal of Part 2 is to help you overcome these preconceived notions by becoming a more balanced, grounded, assertive, and sensitive woman. As such, you will be a more effective leader and a more productive, valuable resource to your organization. To help you overcome these seven complaints (and others), we'll focus on ten keys to leadership success:

- Review your strengths and achievements daily.

- Choose a career doing something you love.

- Clarify and balance your goals and priorities.

- Manage your activities to achieve your goals.

- Relax and visualize yourself achieving your goals.

- Take calculated risks every day.
- Use your emotions and intuition constructively.
- Get rid of any victim mentality you may have.
- Communicate in an assertive, results-oriented manner.
- Learn the political ropes in your organization.

Chapter Three

Creating Your Own Success: Life Plans and Career Plans

"To each one is given a marble to carve for the wall
A stone that is needed to heighten the beauty of all
And only your soul has the magic to give it grace
And only your hands have the cunning to put it in place
Yes, the task that is given to each one, no other can do
So the errand is waiting; it has waited through ages for you
And now you appear, and the hushed ones are turning their gaze
To see what you do with your chance in the chamber of days."

Edith Highman

You can create your own success. In fact, deciding what *you* really want, clarifying those goals, setting your priorities, and making life plans and career plans, is probably the most important work you'll ever do. Goal-setting can range from deciding what you want to accomplish in a ten-minute meeting to getting in touch with your life purpose and destiny. Goal-setting skills are the basis for many leadership skills, from personal time management to organizational strategic planning. Gaining such skills marks you as a promotable woman.

The people in power in business organizations are looking for promotable men and women. They want people who know what they want and where they're going, people who can develop goals as well as action plans to implement their goals. They also want people who are able to balance conflicts between work demands, family responsibilities, and personal needs. In this chapter you will focus first on identifying your key skills and interests. Then you can use that self-awareness to develop personal goals and action plans for your career, your family or private life, and your personal growth and development, so you will be able to balance or resolve conflicts that occur. Later, in Chapter 12, you'll apply goal-setting skills to developing organizational, departmental, and other job-related goals.

In this chapter you will have the opportunity to

1. Analyze and package your unique set of skills and interests

2. Distinguish between goals and activities

3. Formulate effective goals that lead to achievement

4. Develop skills in balancing your career, your private life, and your personal development

5. Develop action plans that lead to the attainment of your most important goals, and use your plan to improve your career and your life

6. Develop a plan for getting the job you want

7. Design a résumé that helps you sell yourself

8. Write an application letter that captures favorable attention

9. Learn how to handle job interviews so that you get the job that's best for you

---

 Life Directions

"Come in, Erika, have a seat." Jean Simon, University Placement Counselor, points toward the chair beside her desk. "I looked over the résumé you left with the secretary yesterday, but I'm afraid I wasn't able to do much with it."

"Is it that bad?"

"No, no. It's just that your job objective is so broad — 'a management position.' You see, your résumé should focus on those aspects of your background that qualify you for the particular job you're after. And when you don't identify a particular kind of job with a specific type of company, then it's impossible for me to evaluate effectively how well your résumé highlights your qualifications."

"I knew I should have been more specific. Believe me, I've wrestled around with this problem for over a week. But I hate to just pick a type of job and a kind of company out of the air. The truth is, I can't decide exactly what I want to do. I feel that I don't know enough about what's out there."

"Okay, Erika. I can see you have lots of work to do before you begin any serious interviewing. Job objectives are based on career goals and on life goals — and a week is hardly an un-

due length of time to consider these matters. You need to hammer out your goals, decide which ones have top priority, and set up some action plans for the major ones. And all this should be done in writing, so you'll have something concrete to refer to when you're conducting your job campaign and later when you're making on-the-job decisions about how to manage your time."

Erika sighs. "I suppose so, but it's such a drag. I mean I'm so busy already — with school, and my job, and now these interviews. Besides, I'm not really comfortable with the idea of planning every aspect of my life for the next ten or twenty years."

"Whoa! I can see you've thrown up some real barriers to the whole planning process. First of all, goals should be stated in concrete terms, but they should never be set in concrete. The best plans are always flexible, and the best planners are alert to times when their goals should be changed." She smiles at the spark of interest in Erika's eyes. "You see, goals should serve you — you should never become a slave to your goals."

"I like that idea."

"Sure. Your goals and plans simply provide you with a mental map to help you direct your energy. They help you create the life you want for yourself. Instead of wasting a lot of energy in hoping and wishing, you use that energy to achieve what you want in life. Even if you make some false starts, you'll probably be moving in the general direction of your heart's desires. It's fine to dream, but people with just dreams — no specific goals — tend to drift along through life, never really getting anywhere."

Erika nods. "Waiting for their ship to come in."

"Yes, and later wondering why it floundered. That's why I'm convinced that your chances of creating the life you want in minimal time are far greater when you're armed with some goals that are based on honest soul-searching."

"You're beginning to convince me," Erika replies.

"Let me share with you a story I came across the other day. It says it so much better than I can." Jean pulls a little booklet from her desk drawer and begins reading:

The coast was shrouded in fog that fourth of July morning in 1952. Twenty-one miles to the west on Catalina Island, a 34-year-old woman waded into the water and began swimming toward the mainland, determined to be the first woman to do so. Her name was Florence Chadwick, and she had already been the first woman to swim the English Channel in both directions.

The water was numbing cold that July morning, and the fog was so thick she could hardly see the boats in her own party. Several times sharks had to be driven away with rifles. As the hours ticked off, she swam on. Fatigue had never been her big problem — it was the bone-chilling cold of the water.

Fifteen and one-half hours later, numbed with the cold, she asked to be taken out. She couldn't go on. Her mother and her trainer alongside in a boat told her they were near land. They urged her not to quit. But when she looked toward Long Beach, on the mainland, all she could see was the dense fog. After another twenty-five minutes — when she had been in the water almost sixteen hours — she quit and was lifted into the boat.

It was not until hours later, when her body began to thaw, that she felt the shock of failure. To a reporter she explained, "Look, I'm not excusing myself. But if I could have *seen* land, I might have made it."

After swimming over twenty miles of the twenty-one-mile channel, she had been pulled out only a half-mile from her goal! Later she was to reflect that she had been licked not by fatigue or even by the cold — but by the foggy coastline and the fuzzy images in her mind. She had no clear picture of her goal — nor of the path leading to that goal. The external and internal fog had blinded her reason, her eyes, and her heart.

It was the only time Florence Chadwick ever quit. Two months later she swam the same channel, and again the fog obscured her view, but this time she swam with a clear vision of her goal in her head — a mental map of where she was going. Not only was she the first woman to swim the Catalina Channel, but she beat the men's record by some two hours!*

Erika blinks. "Sold! When is your next goal-setting seminar?"

---

1. Do you think Erika's initial attitude toward goal-setting is a typical one? How would you describe that attitude? What new insights do you think Erika gained from Jean Simon's suggestions and the story she read about Florence Chadwick's experience?

2. Have you made a practice of setting specific goals for yourself and developing plans to achieve them?

3. How would you describe your attitude toward goal-setting up to this point in your life?

4. Did the Florence Chadwick incident bring to mind any related experiences from your own life? If so, explain.

5. How can you use insights similar to the ones Florence Chadwick experienced to achieve what you want in your life?

IDENTIFYING PLANNING BARRIERS AND PAYOFFS

If your answers to these goal-setting questions reveal some internal resistance to setting goals and developing a career plan, you are not unusual. The first step toward success for many people is getting over the planning barriers they erect for themselves. Exercise 3-1, Identifying Planning Barriers and Payoffs, is

---

*Adapted from *Bits & Pieces,* ed. by Marvin G. Gregory (Fairfield, N.J.: The Economics Press, 1979).

EXERCISE 3-1: IDENTIFYING PLANNING BARRIERS AND PAYOFFS

1. "Set your goals and plan your life." Do you have any resistance to that suggestion? If so, list your negative or doubting responses.

2. "If only I had . . ." Does that phrase bring to mind any regrets you've experienced? If so, list the first few that come to mind.

3. Look over the situations you listed in No. 2. Note how the results might have differed if you had clearly identified your top goals and thought about some key activities for reaching them.

4. "I did it!" "I made it!" "I got it!" Do these words bring to mind some high points in your life? List the first few that come to mind.

5. Look at the situations you listed in No. 4. Compare them to the situations listed in No. 2. Were you more committed to achieving the results you got in the No. 4 situations? Did you put more thought and planning into them? How many of them were "lucky breaks"? How much of your desire or commitment was subconscious? Conscious? Do you think your subconscious desires and intentions may have helped create any of the lucky breaks? Explain.

6. Are you willing to depend on lucky breaks or subconscious desires to determine the kind of life you have? Or do you want to exercise a higher degree of conscious control in creating the life you want? Comment.

7. What payoffs can you identify for setting goals and planning your life direction? Refer to the resistant responses you listed in No. 1; list any rebuttals that come to mind.

---

designed to help you identify your own barriers and move on to a greater awareness of the payoffs for planning.

Perhaps you can identify other barriers to success from your responses to the exercises at the end of Chapter 2. Do you feel uncomfortable about exercising power? Are you afraid to set goals because you may fail? Do you fear success even more than failure? How about your self-concept? Who are you? Can you picture yourself in a role that symbolizes success ɔ you? What is success to you? Three troubleme types of fears that form barriers to success are (1) fear of success itself, (2) fear of failure, and (3) fear of risk-taking.

Success means different things to different people. Here's a definition that could apply to everyone:

> Success is the ability to visualize what you want to do next with your life — what you want to be, do, and have in life — and to enjoy the process of moving toward that vision, achieving it, and creating new visions.

To visualize the life you want, you must be able to see yourself functioning comfortably in it.

You must have a sense of who you are. Did the drawings you made of yourself in Exercise 2-5 (p. 48) help you identify who you are in your own mind? How would you answer the question, Who are you?

Many people respond to that question in terms of the roles they play or what they do. But you are something more all-encompassing than that. Ruth Ross, author of *The Prospering Woman* [26, p. 18], goes even further and says you are not your feelings, your body, or your mind. She says:

> You are a center of consciousness — designed to be self-aware.

Many of the exercises in this book are designed to help you reach new levels of self-awareness. For example, becoming aware of your fears is often a first step to overcoming the three barriers to success discussed next.

Fear of Success

Did Exercise 2-4 (p. 47) uncover some fear of success you may have subconsciously been harboring? If so, you'll need to work out any role conflict that underlies the fear. The best way to root out fear is to get down to specifics and examine it in detail by asking yourself questions similar to the following ones:

Do you fear that success will have some scary consequences? Dig them out and face them. Here are some common ones: I won't be as attractive to men. I won't be able to catch (or hold) a husband. It will involve too much responsibility. I'll be in the spotlight too much. I'll be blamed when things go wrong. I won't have enough free time for a personal life. People won't like me if I'm the boss . . . a strong, aggressive woman . . . more successful than they are.

Do you fear that success doesn't fit your self-image? Maybe you need to work on changing it. Deep down, do you picture yourself as an underprivileged type? Slightly inferior in some way? A follower, not a leader? A victim? A sweet young thing?

Are you afraid of your parents' reaction to your success? Are you afraid your mom won't like you if you're more successful than she was? Do your parents generally resent successful people?

Conversely, are you afraid you *will* fulfill your parents' wishes? Perhaps you still resent their pushing you. Or maybe there's another reason you decided as a child that you would "show them" by not giving them what their hearts desired.

Do you merely fear the unknown aspects of success? Moving into new roles, especially leadership roles, is risky. So much of the territory is uncharted.

Or, maybe you fear that you don't really deserve success. This ties in with self-image again. If as a child you received messages from important people in your life that you interpreted as, "You don't deserve success," then you may have decided you aren't deserving. Or perhaps your behavior didn't meet the standards you had internalized, so you decided you were undeserving. Chances are you don't remember making that decision, but it can exert a strong subconscious influence on your actions. In fact, psychological research indicates that we'll do almost anything to prove we are right in these basic life decisions. We'll focus on proving we don't really deserve success instead of focusing on opportunities for achieving it. After all, achieving success would make us wrong, a situation our subconscious selves will fight valiantly to avoid!

You can reverse such negative cycles through self-awareness and through changing your subconscious beliefs and goals. We'll focus on the latter in Chapter 5. It also helps to take a realistic look at the alternatives to success — in the long run you are much more vulnerable and have far fewer options in life without success!

Fear of Failure

The other side of the coin is fear of failure, which involves the fear of revealing yourself as inadequate or wrong. It involves focusing on wrong versus right instead of moving toward the life you want. When you experience fear of failure, focus on this thought:

All is to my benefit.

The idea is based on the concept of life as a game in which we are constantly learning, growing, and improving. Situations in which we don't get what we aim for can serve as valuable lessons and signals for future guidance if we choose to use them that way. Ask, "What can I learn from this experience?" Then move on.

Fear of Risk-Taking

Both the fear of failure and the fear of success are often based on a fear of taking risks. Throughout this book we'll be discussing various aspects of risk-taking, including calculating the probabilities of success. It's easy to forget, also, that avoiding a risk can be a risk itself — a risk that we won't grow or be all that we can be.

Our fears can exert power over us only so long as they are vague or nebulous. When we keep them in a mental closet and refuse to bring them into the bright light of awareness to examine them and their possible consequences, they retain the scary power of ghosts or goblins. Exercise 3-2, Handling Fear, is designed to help you face your fears. If you can become comfortable with handling the worst that can happen, the consequences cease to have the power to bring fear and tension into your life. Only then can you truly let go of your fears and focus on setting and achieving your goals. Letting go of the desperate need to avoid fearful consequences is one of the keys to self-mastery. In Chapter 5 we'll discuss letting go

of the intense need — versus the relaxed intention — to achieve your goals, which is another self-mastery key.

Handling your fears can help you deal effectively with risk and estimate more objectively the actual probabilities of various outcomes. Taking calculated risks is essential for success in life and is certainly a key to success in business. Nothing ventured, nothing gained is one of the rules. What types of risks have you been unwilling to take? How does this unwillingness affect the goals you set for yourself? Often people miss opportunities because they won't risk rejection. As one wit has said, "If you haven't experienced rejection at least once this week, you're simply not out there trying." In other words, playing it safe may make you feel better temporarily, but to experience that heady excitement that comes from a high level of achievement, you must go after challenging goals, goals that involve the risk of rejection or failure.

Identifying with Successful People

How do you relate to other people's successes? With envy? Resentment? Awe? Appreciation? Enjoyment? Sincere applause? Your responses are clues to your self-concept and to your fears. If your feelings are negative or involve a sense of awe, you are separating yourself from success. Chances are you don't want to be reminded that you are not risking and achieving. On the other hand, when you identify with success and see yourself moving toward your vision of success, your feelings about others' success tend to be positive.

It's important to identify your own barriers to successful goal-setting and planning and to overcome them so they don't dominate your thoughts. Your dominant thoughts are what you will get next in your life. Learn to focus on what you want, not on your supposed inadequacies. Then you'll be open to the opportuni-

EXERCISE 3-2: HANDLING FEAR

Step 1. List all the fears that come to your mind.

Step 2. Rank the fears you listed according to the power you think they have over your willingness to set goals and achieve them.

Step 3. For your most crippling fear ask, "Why do I experience fear in this type of situation? What am I really afraid will happen?" Write your answer next to the fear statement. Then ask why again and write your answer. Keep asking why until you feel you've discovered the root of the fear, the ultimate consequence you're really afraid of.

Step 4. Visualize the ultimate consequences you uncovered in Step 3. (See Exercises 5-4, 5-5, and 5-6 on pp. 150, 152, and 153 if you need help with this step.) Ask yourself, "What are the worst things that can happen in this situation?" Imagine all the consequences. List them here. Next, relax and let go of the desperate need to avoid those consequences. See yourself handling them comfortably. (You may have to spend days or even weeks getting to the point where you can honestly say, "I can handle those consequences; it wouldn't be the end of the world. I could move up and out from there.")

Step 5. Ask yourself, "What goals was this fear blocking my wholehearted commitment to?" List them here. Next, picture yourself moving toward each goal with the relaxed intention of achieving it. Whenever you think about this goal, relax and focus on achieving it, free of fear. (See the exercises in Chapter 5 for tips on achieving a deeply relaxed state of concentration.)

Step 6. Repeat Steps 3 through 5 for your other major fears, one fear at a time.

---

ties that come along—you're more likely to see them and grab them. You'll focus on what you *can do*, not on what you can't.

IDENTIFYING AND PACKAGING YOUR SKILLS AND INTERESTS

One of the keys to success is to choose a career doing something you really care about. What you care about, what you enjoy, is closely related to what you're good at doing. But many people are not clear about the kinds of things they're good at and really enjoy. They feel there may be many things they could do or would like if they only knew more about them or had a chance to try them—especially in the career area.

The only way to identify your skills and interests is to start with what you know now. Then as you learn more about various jobs and careers, you have a basis for evaluating how well they fit your set. Exercise 3-3, Analyzing Your Key Interest/Skill Areas, is designed to help you identify your skills and interests and to go a few steps farther.

EXERCISE 3-3: ANALYZING YOUR KEY INTEREST/SKILL AREAS

Part A. Interests — Activities You Most Enjoy

Step 1. In the first column randomly list, as they come to mind, twenty things you most enjoy doing. Do not attempt to respond to the other columns until you have completed the first column. This should take no more than twenty minutes.

Step 2. Analyze each activity listed in the first column by responding to the other columns.

In column 2, opposite the first activity, place a dash (–) if you most enjoy doing this alone; a plus sign (+) if you enjoy this activity with another; or a slash (/) if either (or no preference).

In column 3, place an *I* for activities in which you experience intimacy, perhaps *I+* for deeper levels of intimacy.

In column 4 note activities that carry a risk factor with an *R*.

In column 5 write the approximate date and year you last engaged in the activity.

In column 6 identify the primary need filled by engaging in this activity; that is, what motivates you to get involved? A need to achieve (*A*), to exercise power (*P*), or to interact socially (*S*)?

In column 7 identify the types of skills or knowledge that you use when you engage in the activity.

See Exhibits 3-1, 3-3, 3-4, and 3-5 for ideas. Write one word that symbolizes each skill or knowledge area used in this activity.

Step 3. Rank the activities in order of the degree of enjoyment you derive from each.

1. Twenty things I most enjoy doing	2. Alone (−) With another (+) Either (/)	3. Intimacy factor (*I*)	4. Risk factor (*R*)	5. Date I last did it (mo/yr)	6. Motivator *A* = achskill *P* = power *S* = social	7. Type of knowledge

Part B. Skills and Knowledge — Activities You Do Well

Step 1. If possible, complete this part a day or so after you complete Part A. Complete column 1 by listing, in random order, ten things you honestly do well; take no more than twenty minutes.

Step 2. Complete columns 2 through 7 as instructed in Part A.

Step 3. Rank the activities in order of their importance to you, also considering your level of expertise in each activity.

1. Ten things I honestly do well	2. Alone (−) With another (+) Either (/)	3. Intimacy factor (I)	4. Risk factor (R)	5. Date I last did it (mo/yr)	6. Motivator A = achskill P = power S = social	7. Type of knowledge

Part C. Patterns and Insights

Step 1. What interrelationships do you see among the different factors, such as alone/with another, intimacy, risk, need fulfillment/motivation, and types of skill and knowledge? What patterns seem to emerge concerning what you enjoy (interests) and what you do well (skills/knowledge)? Notice the dates column. Are you developing your most likely talents or neglecting them? Are these truly the interests and skills you most enjoy and that seem most important to you? Or do you wish they were, or believe they should be? If so, where do these wishes and beliefs originate? From family? Friends? Teachers? Describe the interrelationships and patterns in writing. From this deep inner source comes your passion for your work and for life.

Step 2. What insights emerged from this exercise? State in writing how these insights affect your image of yourself, what you want in life, and what talents and contributions you have to offer.

Part D. Career Building Blocks

Look over your interests, skills, patterns, and insights. Identify some common building blocks of skills and interests that could form the foundation for a career. Refer to Exhibits 3-1 and 3-3, and to your own knowledge of career fields and jobs. Take several sheets of paper; consider each page a block. Give each block a label, and within it list the types of interests, skills, and knowledge that apply. Play with your blocks, moving them around in different combinations and configurations to fit various types of jobs and careers.

You may need to learn more about what people in various careers and positions actually *do*, rather than rely on what most outsiders assume they do. Examine John Wright's *The American Almanac of Jobs and Salaries*, which includes job descriptions [31]. Each year, usually in July, *Working Woman* magazine describes the twenty-five hottest careers for women. Ask your librarian for other resources.

Your most valuable resource can be women who are working in the field, industry, company, or position you are considering. Use your networking skills to locate these women and to arrange some informational interviews. See the interview questions on women's issues given later in this chapter. In addition, ask such questions as:

- Where do you see the industry going in the next few years?

- What is the average salary for this type of position?

- What is your career path?

- How did you get your job?

- What is the single most impressionable thing I can tell you about myself that would help me get a job?

- Is there anyone else I could speak to? In a particular job or department? In another company?

DEVELOPING CLEARLY STATED GOALS

Now that you have dealt with potential barriers to effective goal-setting and have analyzed your unique package of skills and interests, you should be ready to move into the goal-setting process. The process of developing clearly stated goals involves first getting in touch with some sense of a life purpose as a large framework within which to develop your goals. The next step is understanding the difference between goals and activities and learning to state goals in specific terms. Then, after brainstorming a comprehensive set of goals, you can refine and rank them. To clarify your priorities, categorize your goals according to career, personal development, or family orientation. Finally, recognize the relative importance of these categories for you at this phase of your life.

Getting in Touch with Your Life Purpose: Your Mission Statement

If you can get some sense of a life purpose, it can serve as a framework for all your short-term and long-term goals for each major area of your life. When you operate from such a framework, the achievement of your goals is likely to be most rewarding for you. In this mode the line between work and play becomes fuzzy, because those activities that you see as part of your life work you also see as important, satisfying, and even the source of fun and joy in your life. In other words, work that you love to do, you learn to do well, and the work that you do well is the most likely to bring in the money you want. Isn't it elegant that the work that brings you joy is most likely to bring you abundance?

Find regular quiet times when you can relax and tune in to your inner self. See if you can get a sense of a deep, quiet core self within. Refer to Chapter 5 for suggestions on relaxing, visualizing, and letting go. Clues to your life purpose may come through from that deep core self as loud, clear messages. They may come through as a series of quiet, subtle whispers. The key is to keep focusing and listening until you have some sense of the general direction your life should take. The clues will become the basis for your mission statement, which you will write as one or two clear, brief sentences. This statement can be the underlying rationale for all the goals, activities, and priorities you develop in the remaining exercises in this chapter.

EXHIBIT 3-1: Repackaging Your Skills

Your Current Key Skills	Related Business Needs/ Applications	Transfer to Business/ Employment Areas of
Creative/Artistic Writing, editing, graphic arts, announcing, performing arts, modeling	Communication skills, public relations/media skills, establishing/building client relationships, technical supervision	Managers/administrators, marketing/sales, communications, clerical/ administrative support, services
Business Detail Clerical, bookkeeping, accounting, administrative, computer operations, interviewing, claims handling, statistical analysis, records processing	Organizing, coordinating, processing, follow-up and control, evaluation, information management, administrative procedures	Managers/administrators, marketing/sales, computer-related jobs, finance/real estate/ insurance, professionals, communications
Humanitarian Child care, counseling, religious or social work, nursing, therapy, rehabilitation services	Consensus-style management, service orientation, direct client/ customer contact, skills in communicating, motivating, training, supervising	Managers/administrators, marketing/sales, finance/real estate/insurance, professionals, communications
Accommodating Services Social/recreational services, food services, beauty/barber services, customer services, attendant services, passenger services	Customer/client orientation, building and maintaining business relationships, skills in communications/public relations	Managers/administrators, marketing/sales, finance/real estate/insurance, services
Selling Retail, real estate, and technical sales, advertising and promotion, clerical work related to sales	Persuasive communication, human relations skills, establishing business relationships, customer/client orientation, results/profit focus	Managers/administrators, marketing/sales, finance/real estate/insurance, services, communications
Physical Performing Coaching and instruction of sports, officiating	Decision-making, problem-solving, training, coaching, directing workers, setting motivational work climate, setting goals, managing achievement, productivity	Managers/administrators, marketing/sales, services, communications
Plants/Animals Farming, forestry, animal services, nursery/ groundskeeping, specialty breeding	Planning, organizing, coordinating, technical applications/supervision, achievement/productivity orientation, problem-solving, decision-making, follow-up and control	Managers/administrators, professionals, services, technicians

(continued)

EXHIBIT 3-1: Continued

Your Current Key Skills	Related Business Needs/ Applications	Transfer to Business/ Employment Areas of
Leading/Influencing Educational/library services, social research, law, politics, public relations, health and safety services, finance communications	Managing information, handling authority/accountability, being responsible for results and productivity, dealing with the public/media	Managers/administrators, marketing/sales, computer-related jobs, finance/real estate/ insurance, communications
Industrial All production work, manual work, equipment operation, quality control supervision	Technical applications/ supervision, union relationships, productivity orientation	Technicians, services, computer maintenance, contract construction
Scientific/Technical Physical/life sciences, laboratory technicians, medical practitioners	Math skills, technical applications/supervision, design and use of rational procedures, problem-solving, decision-making	Managers/administrators, professionals, technicians, computer-related jobs, marketing/sales, services, mining, finance/real estate/ insurance

Developing your mission statement will probably take many hours of introspection, writing, and rewriting, but it's the most important work you may ever do. Once you feel a sense of clarity. of organization and commitment, of exhilaration and freedom, then you probably have a mission statement that is right for you. Remember to review it every so often and rewrite it when it's time for your life to take a new direction. With your mission statement or life purpose in hand, you will not be thrown off course by ill winds or stormy seas. You're likely to stay the course toward your goals and to go about your activities with a sense of purpose, passion, and enthusiasm that energizes your efforts.

Defining a Goal

The term "goal" as used here is synonymous with "objective." Let's define it further: (1) A goal is a specific end result you want by some stated point in time. (2) Activities are things you *do* in order to achieve your goal. (3) You may *enjoy* an activity, but that doesn't make it a goal. (4) There may be a variety of feasible and acceptable activities that can help you reach your goal.

The activities are a means to an end. The end is your goal. That's why it's so important to separate goals from activities — so you'll be clear about what you're really after and feel free to consider alternatives for getting there.

It's also important to have a clear picture of your goals. Write them down. Exercise 3-4 asks you to list your five most important goals. You're much more likely to achieve written goals than mental ones. They're more specific, as you will see in the pages that follow. You'll also see that written goals are easier to remember, to update, to revise, and to mark off once they're achieved. And the marking-off increases your sense of satisfaction and your motivation to keep achieving.

EXERCISE 3-4: INITIAL STATEMENT OF GOALS

Step 1. Write your personal mission statement (life purpose) in one sentence.

Step 2. Keeping in mind that a goal is a specific end result, list your five most important goals. Include goals related to family, career, and personal development.

Distinguishing Between Specific and Vague Goals

Most of us tend to carry around a mixed bag of "wants." Many of them are vague; some we picture as activities instead of what we hope to gain *from* those activities. We usually wish we had these wants now, and we dreamily hope to have them someday. We must transform such dreamy wants into clear, specific goals in order to achieve them.

Most of us need to clarify what we really want to *be,* what we want to *have* in our lives, and what we can *do* to achieve our goals. We need to be specific about exactly what we plan to achieve. How specific? Preferably specific enough so that on the target date we've set for attainment of the goal, we *know* for sure whether we've achieved it or how close we've come to it, and anyone knowledgeable on the subject could also tell. To illustrate, let's compare the stories Erika recently heard from two friends, Pat and Ann.

Pat's story: Last summer my sister came to visit for a couple of weeks. We've always been able to wear the same clothes. One day I tried on one of her skirts and couldn't close the zipper. Sis teased me about "putting away a few too many groceries." After she left, I looked in the mirror and said to myself, "Pat, ole girl, you've got to do something about this flab." I'm going to join an exercise class and cut down on desserts. I'm determined to lose this excess weight.

The next time Sis visits me, I want her to see that I'm my old, trim self.

Ann's story: The other day I got out my fall and winter clothes. When I tried on my after-five things, I couldn't get the zipper closed on some of them. Later, I weighed myself. That's when I realized for the first time I had gained fifteen pounds since last Christmas. I have a clear picture of how I want to *be* physically and that includes *being* slender. My goal is to lose fifteen pounds—about two pounds a week over the next eight weeks. By December 1, when the holiday parties begin, I will be down to my previous weight and able to look great in all those party clothes hanging in my closet. I figure that in order to achieve this, I'll have to cut my food intake to twelve hundred calories a day. I'll use the balanced diet my health club recommends. I'll also exercise an extra thirty minutes each day in order to use up a few more calories and improve my muscle tone.

Which person do you think is most likely to achieve her goal? Why? We can see several factors operating in these two cases.

1. *Ann* is clear about what she wants to *be:* slender, slender enough to fit into her party clothes. *Pat* is focusing on what she is going to *do:* get rid of the flab.

2. *Ann* is clear about the end result she wants. Her goal is specific, and she has a time

target: lose fifteen pounds, about two pounds a week, by December 1. She will know for sure how well she has achieved her goal by December 1, or just how close she came to achieving it. And anyone else could tell if they watched her as she stepped on the scales on the beginning date of her project, October 1, and again on the target date, December 1.

Pat will have no way of knowing for sure how well she has met her goal. It is too vague. She has specified neither how much weight she plans to lose nor a specific target date for losing it. Since her goal is vague in her own mind, it will be easy for her to mentally change her ideas about how much she needs to exercise, what and how much she should eat, and so forth.

3. *Ann* is separating her goal from what she will *do* to achieve it. He activities include cutting her food intake to twelve hundred calories a day and exercising thirty minutes more each day. She could choose many alternative activities to achieve her goal. Notice that her activities, like her goal, include specific and measurable standards. She has also included a standard of quality for her activities—a balanced diet and exercises that are designed to improve muscle tone.

Pat is focusing on activities and not separating them from her goals: "to do something about this flab," "to join an exercise class and cut down on desserts," "to lose this excess weight." Her activities are as vague as her goal, and she hasn't thought about what standards she wants to maintain in the course of this project.

Additional examples of vague and specific goals are listed in Exhibit 3-2.

Distinguishing Between Goals and Activities

In many cases, only you can decide whether a "want" is a goal or just an activity. Ask yourself, "*Why* do I want to do this?" If the act or process of doing something is what you desire, then it's probably a goal for you. If the activity is mainly a *means* to having something you desire, then it's not a goal for you. For example: *Why* do you want more free time? Is it to have more time to pursue a hobby, develop a skill, travel? If so, then those activities are your goals and having more free time is a *means* to that end. On the other hand, you may want freedom to do things on the spur of the moment, to pursue whatever tickles your fancy from time to time. If so, then having more free time is indeed your goal.

Here is another example: *Why* do you want to have a college degree? Is it to get a better job, make more money, or feel the personal satisfaction of having the degree, regardless of its other advantages?

Analyzing your "wants" in this way will help you determine what you really desire. If an item is more an activity than a goal, you may be able to find an alternate activity that is much

EXHIBIT 3-2: Vague Versus Specific Goals

Vague Goals	Specific Goals
To make more money	To earn $30,000 next year
To move up in the company	To be General Manager of a regional branch by 19xx
To get ahead in life	To have a net worth of $500,000 by 19xx
To go back to school	To have an MBA degree by 19xx
To have more free time	To have at least one month of free time per year by 19xx
To travel more	To travel to the Far East in 19xx for three weeks

easier to engage in and will lead to comparable or even superior results. For example, suppose you find that the major reason you want a degree is to increase your earnings. You might find a number of alternate career paths or ways of becoming qualified for a particular career path that would take less money, time, and energy than getting a degree.

When you find it difficult to make that kind of decision, try this: Get comfortable; relax as fully as possible. Close your eyes and try to visualize yourself once you have achieved your goal. How do you feel? Are you satisfied with that particular end result? Are you satisfied with the *way* you got it? Is anything missing? What would you have done differently if you could?

Sometimes visualizing the end results and how you feel about them can help you decide what you really want. For example, if you visualize yourself holding a particularly desirable job *without* having gotten the degree, you may determine whether having a degree is your true goal. (See also Richard Bolles's paperback *What Color Is Your Parachute?* [4], or order his brochure *The Quick Job-Hunting Map* [6].)

Refining and Ranking Your Goals

Exercise 3-5, Refined List of Goals, is designed to help you state your goals specifically and reflect on their relative importance. Some of the items are probably variations of the goals you listed in Exercise 3-4. If you have trouble deciding what your goals really are, complete Exercise 3-6, Self-Starters to Help Clarify Goals. Be sure to complete Exercise 3-7, Self-Starters to Add Power to Your Goals.

Prioritizing Three Areas of Your Life

Your goals probably include several kinds of "wants"; few people lead a one-track life where *only* their careers or *only* their personal growth

or *only* their family is important. Women frequently have more difficult choices to make than men when it comes to conflicts between career and private life. In the past, highly trained women have usually given up their career aspirations when they married. Today, some women attempt to be Superwoman. They set unrealistically high goals and standards for all areas of their lives, which may lead to frustration, exhaustion, and even depression (currently referred to as "burn-out"). Other women are unaware of the implications of the choices they're making until problems begin cropping up.

To have a clear picture of your career goals, you'll need to analyze their importance in relation to the other goals in your life. Exercise 3-8, Deciding Your Most Important Life Areas, presents an opportunity to do this. It asks questions concerning the choices you will make among three areas of your life—career, private life, and personal development. Base your responses on your *current* life circumstances, not on possible later phases. In attempting to answer the first question, about private life versus career goals, picture yourself in a situation where you must make a choice. For example, you might have the opportunity to obtain a high-level position in a foreign country in which you've always wanted to live for a while, but your husband can't go with you. Even if you live alone, you probably have some family or private life considerations and goals. If not, you can concentrate on the other two categories.

In answering the second question, concerning conflicts between your career and personal development, you might visualize a situation in which you must regularly give up your personal reading time or your favorite sport to attend job-related meetings or seminars. In resolving conflicts between personal development and private-life goals (question 3), a sample scene might be giving up Saturdays with your family for four months to attend a creative-writing class.

EXERCISE 3-5: REFINED LIST OF GOALS

Step 1. *Distinguish between goals and activities.* Look at the list of goals you made in Exercise 3-4. How many are actually activities? Eliminate them.

Step 2. *Redefine your goals to make them more specific.* Select the following items that reflect your goals and fill in the blanks to make your goals specific. At this point, don't rank or evaluate their practicality or relative importance.

Rank

_____   To have $_____ in assets by _____ (date)

_____   To be _____ by _____
            (job position)   (date)

_____   To earn $_____ next year

_____   To have a relationship with _____ in which we
                                        (description of person)

            _____ by _____
            (feel, believe, do . . .)   (date)

_____   To weigh _____ by _____
                     (pounds)   (date)

_____   To have a _____ by _____
                      (degree or certificate)   (date)

_____   To retire with $_____ a month income (or equivalent) by _____
                                                                        (date)

_____   To have _____ days of free time per year by _____
                                                            (date)

_____   To learn _____ by _____
                     (specific skills or knowledge)   (date)

_____   To travel to _____ in _____ for _____
                                              (date)   (no. of days, weeks, or months)

_____   To spend _____ hours a _____ in mutually satisfying activities
                                       (day, week, month)

            with _____
                 (name)

Step 3. *Brainstorm.* List other goals that don't fit into the preceding categories. Be as outrageous as you like. Use the enthusiastic, creative-child part of your personality to brainstorm. Send that critical, practical part of you "down the hall" till later. Make your goals as fantastic or as simple as you like. Anything goes! (Remember to try Exercise 3-6 if you're blocked.)

Step 4. *Evaluate and rank.* After you've freely and wildly listed any goals you can think of, start asking which one of all your goals is the most important (include all goals in steps 2 and 3). Put the number "1" in the space to the left of that goal. Continue the process for the second most important goal, the third, and so forth until all are ranked. Do you want to delete any goals? Can any outlandish ones be modified or combined to make them more realistic? Are they all specific?

EXERCISE 3-6: SELF-STARTERS TO HELP CLARIFY GOALS

Prognosis: Six months: Pretend that you have been given six months to live. Close your eyes and visualize the situation in as much vivid detail as possible. Assume that you'll be in perfect health up to the day you die and that all the necessary arrangements for your death have been taken care of. List the first five things you think of that you would want to achieve in your last six months.

Sudden wealth: Pretend someone just gave you $5 million tax-free. Close your eyes and visualize the situation in vivid detail. List the first five things you think of that you would want to achieve in the next six months (remember, these are your last six months).

Analysis: Which items on these lists are not connected with pressures of time or money? Which can you achieve now, even without a gift of money? Which can you have in the next six months, even without the pressure of time? Can those items be phrased as goals? How many of them can become obtainable goals with some simple modification to your current situation?

Now go back to Exercise 3-5 and continue refining your goals.

EXERCISE 3-7: SELF-STARTERS TO ADD POWER TO YOUR GOALS

Step 1. *Visualize end results:* During a quiet time, relax deeply and visualize yourself living the end result of each goal. (Refer to Chapter 5 for suggestions.) Focus on what you are doing, having, and most of all *being;* that is, how you feel, how others feel, how relationships are affected. Note any conflicting feelings or thoughts that come up — thoughts about barriers to achieving the goal or about payoffs for not achieving it.

Step 2. *Check the source of each goal.* Are you sure this is *your* goal? It is very important to establish this. If you are trying to achieve a goal because someone else thinks you should, you can never give it the full level of commitment, passion, and enthusiasm you give to goals that come from deep within you. The achievement of others' goals can never bring you the joy and fulfillment you deserve, and you will never reach the same level or quality of success as you will with your own goals. So analyze each important goal in this light. Have you chosen this goal because it's what you think someone else would admire? For example, a parent figure, spouse, influential friend, teacher? Or is it truly what *you* want in your life?

Step 3. *Apply the energy/emotional level test.* If you have difficulty ranking a goal — or if at any point in the goal-setting or goal-implementing process, you are pulled between two alternatives — try the following analysis: First, be sure you have developed an adequate foundation for making the decision, through self-analysis of your life purpose and deepest desires and gathering the information you need. Then ask yourself the following questions:

- Do I feel energized when I think of a particular choice?
- Do I sense a drop in my energy level when I think of the choice?
- Which option has a special glow around it when I picture it? An emotional attraction?

Then ask yourself, if the decision were based solely on emotion, which alternative would I choose? You will probably experience the greatest success when you go for the alternative that energizes you and brings up positive feelings, such as a sense of freedom, well-being, growth/expansion, or enthusiasm.

Step 4. *Turn old blocks into new cornerstones.* For each major goal, examine your current and past beliefs and attitudes, thoughts and feelings, decisions and choices. Are any of them likely to block your success in achieving the goal? What new beliefs and attitudes could you adopt that would support this goal? How can you change your thoughts, letting go of nonproductive ones and focusing on positive ones that enhance your chances of success? What old decisions — about yourself and others or your place and your roles — might be inappropriate now for what you want to achieve? What types of choices (based on your beliefs, attitudes, thoughts, feelings, and decisions about you and life) have you made in the past regarding goal achievement? What new types might be better?

a. List Goal No. 1.

b. List current beliefs, attitudes, and so on, that conflict with achieving your goal. Identify new ones that would support it.

Current:	*New:*
Beliefs	
Attitudes	
Thoughts	
Feelings	
Decisions	
Choices	

c. Repeat the process for each major goal.

EXERCISE 3-8: DECIDING YOUR MOST IMPORTANT LIFE AREAS

1. If you had to choose between career goals and private life goals during this phase of your life, what would you choose? (If you have no private life goals, skip this question.)

2. If you had to choose between pursuing career goals and personal development goals, which would you choose? (It may be helpful to refer to your list of goals in Exercise 3-5.)

3. If you had to choose between private life goals and personal development goals, which would you choose?

4. If you had to choose one life area to work on this month, what would it be?

5. List the three life areas in order of importance to you.

Don't worry about the complexity or inter-relatedness of the questions. It's obvious that you may be a better daughter, wife, or mother when you're a better person generally. For now, just try to choose among the categories so that you can set priorities and determine the most important area of your life.

After you have analyzed your life areas in Exercise 3-8, go back to the goals you refined in Exercise 3-5 and decide whether each is a career, private life, or personal goal (or some combination of the three). Which are so important that you would like to work on them in more than one area of your life — by taking a course with your husband, for instance? Which aren't leading to achievement or satisfaction for you in one area but might fit well in another area? For example, getting training in making presentations through company-sponsored seminars versus joining a toast-masters group on your own time.

You'll probably find that one broad goal applies more to a specific area rather than to all three areas of your life. For example, you may want increased freedom in your job but feel no need for it in the private life or personal development area.

Balancing Your Life Areas

People who make it to middle and top management almost invariably must pay their dues by putting their career first during some phase of their lives. This emphasis can have real payoffs: A 1980 study revealed that most millionaires gain their fortunes through their work or profession, not through inheritance [2]. However, if you keep putting your career first throughout your adult life, you may miss out on some of your most cherished goals. For example, most happy couples report that they both put each other first in the scheme of things. So there may be times when you'll place your career second, though let's hope not because of any Cinderella complex.

A 1978–1980 study to determine what contributes most to women's self-esteem and enjoyment of life led to the conclusion that married women with children and careers are the happiest [3]. Several studies during the

1980s yielded similar results [1, 10]. So the good news is that many women are managing to "have it all," and they seem to be the happiest women in our society.

The bad news is that no matter how hard they work, women still do most of the housework and child care. According to a 1990 Gallup poll of 1,234 men and women, working wives are responsible for between 70 and 80 percent of the child care, grocery shopping, meal preparation, house cleaning, and laundry [10]. This response confirmed a 1977 [3] study that indicated that while couples were struggling toward equality, many of the traditions that make careers difficult for married women still prevail [1]. These researchers also report that husbands with successful wives are happier in their marriages, but most of them don't want the wives to take over the provider role. And there seems to be a point at which most males feel threatened. The more successful wives had a higher breakup rate unless their husbands achieved a similar level of success.

All this is a further indication of the need for selectivity in close relationships. In addition, some frank discussions about areas of responsibility in the home may prevent later stress and undue burdens on you. Here are a few questions you might want to consider: Who should manage the money? Do the cooking? Clean the house? Take out the garbage? Mow the lawn? Be responsible for the children? Stay home when a child is sick? How are you going to handle career opportunities that require travel? Relocating? Will it depend on which career phase either of you is in, or will the decision be automatically in favor of his career? It's important to discuss priorities and joint decision-making techniques *before* becoming too committed to a relationship, rather than after.

Career women who marry career men must be alert to the potential problems that occur when two workaholics team up. Workaholics are addicted to work, so they have difficulty

enjoying family time, leisure time, and perhaps even personal development time. The children of such parents will have great difficulty getting some of the basic needs met, needs for parental guidance, support, and affection. Workaholic parents often find it difficult to turn the precious time they spend with their children into "quality time" because they are preoccupied with thoughts of work.

Balancing your life areas requires skills in assertiveness, delegation, and time management, topics that are discussed in later chapters. If you are to avoid the burn-out caused by playing a wonder-woman role for too long, you must identify your rights within your close relationships, especially where children are involved. Assertiveness on your part will probably be required to reach constructive agreements on how everyone in the household will contribute toward its maintenance. You will need delegation skills to assign tasks to your children and paid household helpers. And you'll need time management skills to be sure you're taking care of your own top priority items rather than unwittingly spending too much of your precious time on other people's priorities.

REACHING YOUR GOALS: PLANNING ACTIVITIES AND SETTING PRIORITIES

You probably have a sense now of what goals are most important in each area of your life. The next step is to consider what activities will provide the best avenues for reaching these goals by completing Exercise 3-9.

Exercise 3-9 lays out an activities list for all three areas of your life. (You'll probably wish to elaborate on it on your own worksheet.) To use it, you'll need to check back to Exercise 3-5; then list your three most important goals in each category in Exercise 3-9. Fill in the life area priorities you developed in Exercise 3-8, item

EXERCISE 3-9: ACTIVITIES FOR ACHIEVING CAREER, PERSONAL DEVELOPMENT, AND PRIVATE LIFE GOALS

Career (Life Area Priority No. _____)

Step 1. List Goal 1. Then list at least four activities that would lead to the achievement of Goal 1.

Step 2. List Goals 2 and 3 and their activities, as you did for Goal 1.

Step 3. Repeat the process for personal development and private life goals. After you have listed activities for *all* goals, rank the importance of the activities listed for each goal.

5. You'll then have a summary of what you want in life, right now.

Next, start writing down any and all activities you can think of that might help you achieve your goals, taking one goal at a time. At this point, do not rank the activities. Again, fantasize, brainstorm, let the creative-child part of you take over. Send your judgmental counterpart out of the room; she can come back later and help you evaluate the activities. Be daring. Be outrageous. If you're stymied in the career category, see Exhibit 3-3, Finding the Best Field, turn to Exercise 3-10 as a self-starter, and then return to Exercise 3-9.

When you have listed activities for all life areas, summon your critical, practical, reasonable side to help you select the activity that is the most feasible and the most likely to contribute to your first goal. Rank that activity number 1 on the list in Exercise 3-9. Rank the second most likely activity number 2, and so forth down to the least likely activity. Repeat for each goal.

Does your list of activities boggle your mind? If so, start picking out the activities *you are willing to spend at least five minutes on during the next week.* Now remove from your list all activities

you are *not* willing to spend five minutes on. Such activities may be important, but obviously they're not important enough to occupy your time right now. Since *now* is all any of us has, remove them from your list.

Do some of your goals now have no activities listed for them? Then go back and list other activities, ranking them and deleting them. Keep going until you have for each goal a list of activities that are important to you and are things you are willing to begin acting on right away.

Once you've completed all the exercises to this point, you should be closer to knowing (1) what you want, (2) what you can do to get it, and (3) what you will do about it in the next week.

Developing Short-Term and Long-Term Action Plans

Here's the total process you'll be following to get what you want in life: (1) setting goals and priorities, (2) developing specific action plans with prioritized activities to help you reach those goals, and (3) periodically reevaluating your goals, action plans, and priorities.

EXHIBIT 3-3: Finding the Best Field

	Keys to Power	Need for a Mentor	Tolerance for Individuality	Style	Future
Accounting	Personal influence; building relationships with clients, partners	Great	Very low	All-American	Clients may start shopping for brilliance and originality, which will change internal power game
High technology	Original ideas in product development, marketing, productivity	The larger the organization, the greater the need	Much greater than in the past; innovators who can work within system in great demand	Consensus-style management pushing out former autocratic styles	Risk-taker's paradise; high stakes, huge payoffs
Banking/finance	Profitable ideas; technical analysis; building relationships	Helpful, not essential if self-motivated with money-making ideas	Growing	Low-key; facts/numbers focus; serious, fairly trendy, not overly ambitious	Much change, rethinking about mission, services, methods
Health care	Influence with M.D.'s, administrators	Not great if skilled politician; hard to find	Medium to high	Analytical; firm, sticking to point; respectful attitude toward doctors	Booming, but government and insurance companies are setting limits
Nonprofit	Often on edge of organization, managing special projects; fundraising skills, consensus management skills, public relations skills	May be only way to learn ropes	Fairly high	Project image of idealism; practice rules of political survival	Change; erratic spurts of growth and decline
Glamour/media	Ideas supreme; profitability all; risk-taking essential; boldness a must	Self-promotion more important in many cases; access to powerful people important	Highest	Outgoing; negotiating skills, political savvy	Always important; perhaps some altered forms

Adapted from "The Keys to the Kingdom" by Marilyn Moats Kennedy, *Savvy* (February 1984), pp. 48–55.

EXERCISE 3-10: SELF-STARTER TO HELP IDENTIFY THE MOST PRODUCTIVE CAREER ACTIVITIES

Part A. Ask Career Questions
By now you should have a specific type of job in mind as your key career goal. You should also be able to describe your ultimate career goal — the top position you're aiming for. To help you identify the activities most likely to help you reach that goal, look at these questions:

1. What type of company do you have in mind? Can you pinpoint a specific company?

2. What type of degree, courses, or other training will you need?

3. What specific skills and knowledge will be required? At what level of ability?

4. What kinds of people could tell you more about the job, help teach you what you need to know, help you get your foot in the door, help you gain favorable visibility within the company, introduce you to people who can help?

5. What jobs will you need to hold in order to prepare yourself for your *ultimate* career goal? What functions do you need to have experience with? How do these functions link up with each other? (For example, what are the links between production and sales, sales and marketing?) Can you get some actual job descriptions your target company has prepared for these jobs? Which staff positions would give you the best chance of moving into a line job? Which line jobs provide the basic experience you'll need? (See also John Wright's *The American Almanac of Jobs and Salaries* [31].)

6. Once you have a career plan, who can give you the most helpful evaluation of its effectiveness? Is the plan workable in view of the other top priorities in your life?

Use your answers to help complete Exercise 3-9.

Part B. Brainstorm with a Friend
Brainstorm with a partner about ways to achieve a particular goal. What types of activities might work? If your goal is to go to Paris, what do you need to get there? How can you get the time, the money, and any other resources you'll need? Next, work on your partner's goal.

Part C. Mutual Support with a Friend
Discuss a key goal with a friend. Tell her the specifics of the goal and the actions you plan to take. Verbalizing your commitment, as well as writing it down, tends to strengthen it. Your friend should also share one of her goals with you. Set regular dates to discuss what actions you actually took and how

they worked out. Two nationally known authors recently explained how this process worked for them when they were each writing their first books. They agreed to phone each other every Friday to discuss their progress. Each wanted to be able to tell the other that she had moved along in her project. If Thursday arrived, and she hadn't written all week, she was motivated to write something rather than admit on Friday that her project had been neglected.

Part D. Make Your Goals Visible
Find methods of keeping your goals up front, of staying focused, of making them real to you.

1. Pick three top goals: Write them on a business card, along with the target dates. Put the card where you will see it many times a day: tucked in your dresser or bathroom mirror, in the clear-plastic window of your wallet, on your desk calendar, or in another visible place.

2. Draw vivid symbols of your top goals, using colored pens or pencils if possible. Put them on a card and display them as discussed in number 1.

Exercise 3-11 provides a format for a one-month action plan. Exercises 3-12 and 3-13 provide for a one-year plan and a five-year plan. Think broadly as you complete the longer-range plans, focusing on goals rather than on activities. Do you need to plan even farther ahead? For ten years? If so, use a similar format.

To accomplish the most, make a one-month plan *every* month. Use it as the basis for your weekly and daily **"To Do" lists** (see Chapter 4). Compare months to see how you're progressing toward long-term goals. Finally, remember to reevaluate your decisions regularly to be sure that your goals reflect what you really want in life and that your activities are the best ones for getting you there.

Tips for Implementing Your Plan

Here are some general suggestions for using your plan:

1. *Visualize.* Use relaxed concentration and visualization as a technique to command your inner resources so that all your actions tend to move you toward your goals.

2. *Act.* Begin this week, even if you undertake only a five-minute activity for each goal.

3. *Communicate.* Let the important people in your life *know* about the goals they may be able to help you with. For example, let your boss or mentor know about appropriate career goals.

4. *Get support.* Make a list of the people who can help you and give you support as you work toward your goals. Decide the best way to enlist their aid. Include support systems in your plan.

5. *Enjoy.* Make the *process* of achieving your goal as enjoyable as possible. It's important to keep your eye on the end result you want, but it's also important to relax and enjoy yourself along the way. In fact, your enjoyment of an activity should be one of the criteria for selecting it.

EXERCISE 3-11: ONE-MONTH ACTION PLAN FOR _____ 19 __
(MONTH)

Step 1. List career goal 1. In order of importance, list the major activities, with their target dates, that you plan to complete this month. Put the most important activity on your To Do list for *today* and keep it on the list until you have accomplished it. If you haven't acted on this activity within seven days, go back and reevaluate your goal and activities.

Step 2. Repeat the process for career goals 2 and 3.

Step 3. Repeat the process for your top three personal development goals and top three private life goals.

EXERCISE 3-12: ONE-YEAR ACTION PLAN FOR 19 __

Last updated on:

Step 1. List the top three career goals, with target dates, you plan to accomplish in one year.

Step 2. Repeat the process for your personal development goals.

Step 3. Repeat the process for your private life goals.

EXERCISE 3-13: FIVE-YEAR ACTION PLAN FOR 19 __ TO 19 __

Last updated on:

Step 1. List the top three career goals, with target dates, that you plan to accomplish in five years.

Step 2. Repeat the process for your personal development goals.

Step 3. Repeat the process for your private life goals.

6. *Negotiate.* Use your goals to help you achieve specific results on the job that will serve as the basis for negotiating promotions and raises later.

7. *Stay focused on your goals.* Don't get so carried away with the *activities* that you lose sight of the *goal.* Use your action plan to chart activities; mark them off as they are completed and as the goal is achieved. As mentioned earlier, it helps if you keep a list of your top three or four goals handy and refer to it regularly. Some successful women keep their list (or symbolic pictures of their goals) posted where they'll see it daily in their home or office.

8. *Overcome barriers to achieving goals.* Don't let procrastination, interruptions, and distractions keep you from achieving your goals. See the discussion of time management in Chapter 4 for suggestions on overcoming these barriers.

9. *Reevaluate.* If you are having unusual difficulty in achieving a goal, ask yourself whether the goal is right for you. If it is, then reevaluate the activities you have selected and look for new ones. If it's not, spend some time formulating another goal that's more appropriate and focus on it.

10. *Keep goals flexible.* Your goals are not set in concrete. They're just part of a plan that can be changed as *situations* change.

11. *Congratulate yourself.* When you achieve a goal, remember to give yourself credit and reward yourself.

12. *Keep setting goals.* Once you have achieved a major goal, set another one to take its place. You say you've earned a rest? You don't want another major project for a while? Then your new goal might be to have a specific number of additional unstructured hours each week, month, or year to do as you please. The object is to be clear about what you want and what you are doing with your time and your life — so that you are making clear choices rather than drifting.

USING YOUR PLAN TO GET THE JOB YOU WANT

You can use the goal-setting process for developing on-the-job goals for yourself and for coaching members of your work team in setting their own job goals. We will discuss this type of goal-setting in Chapter 11. For now, let's focus on getting a job. Once you have a clear picture of your interests, likes, dislikes, skills, abilities, and resulting career goals, you're in a better position to develop an effective action plan for getting the specific job you want next. In this section we'll discuss the other steps to landing that position, as illustrated in Figure 3-1.

If you are a college student, you'll need a job-getting action plan before you graduate. If you're in a secretarial, clerical, or staff position, you may have to wage a job campaign and change companies in order to have the best chance of moving into management. Even if you plan to move up within your present company, many of the suggestions that follow can be helpful to you. If you're not sure exactly what you want to do next, you're not alone. That's why the "reevaluate" step is shown in Figure 3-1. Once you've done your best to analyze your situation, make a wholehearted commitment to the resulting action plan and give it your best shot. At least you'll be gaining valuable experience and learning more about yourself.

Designing a Winning Résumé

The right kind of résumé can open doors for you. Even if you already have the job you want, it's a good idea to periodically update your ré-

FIGURE 3-1: The Job-Getting Process

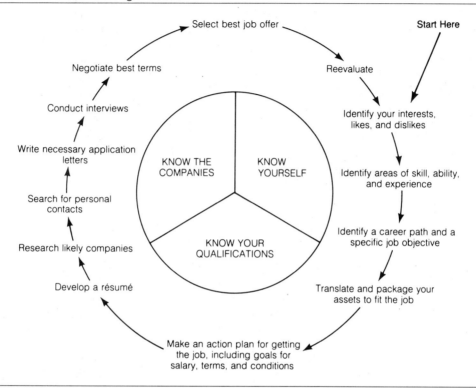

sumé. The process can sharpen your awareness of your strengths and achievements.

Keep your résumé in a file folder. From time to time add to the file any letters, reports, memos, honors, or awards that reflect your achievements, career growth, and personal development. At least once a year pull the file and update your résumé. Review it before you ask for a promotion or raise. If someone asks you for your biography or for background information for a news release or a group introduction, use your résumé as a basis for preparing it quickly. Your résumé is a handy reference document, and you will probably find other uses for it.

The most important use of résumés is in applying for a job. Interviewers review them to determine which applicants probably have the right "product" to sell.

Selling Yourself   Your résumé is a selling document. Its major purpose is to persuade the reader to grant you an interview. To do that, it must hook your reader's attention immediately. Interviewers frequently screen large numbers of résumés in order to select three or four candidates to interview. Therefore your résumé may have only about thirty seconds to make an impression, good or bad, on the reader.

Put only your name and phone number at the top of the page. Don't clutter it with personal data, because this is the place to state your job objective and a summary of your most attractive qualifications. Should you include a picture at the top? Normally, no. If you use a high-quality reproduction process in which the picture becomes an integral part of the résumé, interviewers might back away from the slickness of the presentation. On the other hand, if you merely glue a small photograph to your résumé, the effect tends to be a little corny and unprofessional. A major exception is when you're applying for a job in a distant city and you feel your appearance is a definite asset for the job. The interviewer naturally prefers maximum input before incurring the expenses involved in a personal interview in such cases.

You'll have a better chance of selling yourself to the right company if you aim for a specific type of position. It's standard practice to reproduce the résumé and send it to several companies. However, the most successful applicants avoid the "shotgun approach" — that is, hoping to get interviews for a wide range of jobs by stating a general job objective — for example, a management job or leadership position — and mailing the résumé to numerous companies. Remember, résumés that get results usually include (1) a specific job objective and a clue to the type of career path desired, (2) "bait" lines stating major qualifications for the job, and (3) a detailed but concise description of experience and education, all tailored to fit the job objective. (See the example in Exhibit 3-7.) If you wage a job campaign that zeroes in on your first-choice job objective, you're likely to get that type of job. At the same time, you avoid giving the impression you'll take almost anything or that you don't know your own mind.

Your résumé must answer some basic questions, such as what sort of position you want and perhaps your ultimate target position or career path. At the beginning, therefore, state clearly your own specialty and the area you're aiming for — for example, a systems analyst with a large bank, a management position in the production department of a textile manufacturing firm, a financial manager for an investment counseling firm.

Follow the statement of job objective with a brief summary of your *major* qualifications for the position. This is your selling pitch, your bait to hook the reader into reading further. The way you phrase your job objective and your summary of qualifications can mean the difference between success and failure in getting a chance to interview, so spend time perfecting this section of your résumé. (See the bait lines following the statement of job objectives in Exhibit 3-7; see also the Summary of Qualifications section in Exhibit 3-8.) Put yourself in the interviewer's place and ask which of your qualifications he or she will view as most important for success in the position you're seeking. Then select those items from the experience and education sections of your draft résumé and rephrase them concisely into three or four bait lines. Use the kinds of management terms we'll discuss next.

Describing Past Experience in Management Terms In the experience section of your résumé, back up what you claimed in your bait lines. Stress experience that relates to the job you want (no matter how insignificant or limited it was, if you're relatively inexperienced). List it first. You must learn to view these past experiences in terms of the management functions you performed. Think back over the functions you have fulfilled in previous jobs, at home, and in social, charitable, religious, or professional organizations. Then picture yourself doing something similar in a management position. Did you plan and organize a rummage sale? Then you can plan and organize business projects. Did you call club members and persuade them to take on responsibilities and work toward club goals? You can do the same with employees in meeting company goals.

Exhibit 3-4 lists some verbs that might be appropriate for describing what you actually did in the jobs you held. Choose the ones that express the highest level at which you performed ("implemented" instead of "assisted," "supervised" instead of "performed").

Even if the highest-level position you've held is sales clerk, secretary, or office clerk, you have performed many of the functions listed in Exhibit 3-4. For example, if you've been responsi-

EXHIBIT 3-4: Action Verbs That Describe Management Functions

Administered	Developed	Managed
Advised	Directed	Negotiated
Analyzed	Edited	Organized
Applied	Evaluated	Participated in
Approved	Executed	Performed
Arranged	Expedited	Planned
Clarified	Facilitated	Prepared
Communicated	Forecast	Promoted
Compared	Generated	Recommended
Compiled	Handled	Recruited
Computed	Have knowledge of	Reduced
Controlled	Implemented	Reported to
Cooperated with	Initiated	Researched
Coordinated	Improved	Reviewed
Counseled	Integrated	Solved
Created	Interviewed	Supervised
Decided	Investigated	Surveyed
Delegated	Made decisions	Trained
Demonstrated	Maintained contact	

ble for showing a new worker how to handle certain jobs, you've been involved in training and perhaps in delegating and supervising. If you've ever been responsible for even a part of a major project, you no doubt organized, handled, decided, and executed items in completing your assignment, and you were probably involved in other functions as well. Even if none of the action verbs apply to your involvement in a task, you can always use "was responsible for," "was accountable for," "am familiar with," or "reported to." By expressing your experience in this manner instead of merely listing job titles and duties, you show an executive orientation. Your résumé becomes more businesslike and impressive in tone.

If you have volunteered in charitable, academic, religious, or other nonprofit organizations, analyze your activities and responsibilities for their administrative or managerial components. If such experience helps fill in gaps in your qualifications for your target position, by all means include it in the experience section of your résumé. (Exercise 3-14, p. 88, can help you translate your experiences into management terms. If you will first read the dis-

cussion and examples that follow, however, the whole process will make more sense to you.)

Look over all your activities and recall specific achievements related to each. Were there instances in which you produced more than was expected? By how much? Estimate, if necessary. Use percentages, where appropriate. "I exceeded the target number of claims to be processed by 10 percent." Did you accomplish something with less money, time, or supplies than expected? Again, be as specific as possible and use numbers, dollars, or percentages. "I devised a way to save $1,500 a year on office supplies." Are you in the habit of meeting deadlines and target dates, even when the going gets tough? Say so. "My reports were regularly submitted on or before the deadline dates."

Now describe specific activities and achievements for each job you held. If one job is obviously more relevant to the position you're seeking than the others, consider listing it before other more recent jobs so it will attract more attention. Otherwise, list your most recent job first. While you're at it, relate each accomplishment to a given job unless you performed virtually the same functions in more than one job. Many résumés are so full of accomplishments—whole pages of them—that they neglect to tell what actual jobs the person has held and at what companies. To get an accurate picture of you, the interviewer needs a framework to hang your accomplishments on.

Once you have completed the experience section, analyze it to identify the broad functional business areas you've been involved in. Exhibit 3-5 lists a few of the functional areas of business to give you some ideas for categorizing your experience. Use these as headings in the left margin of your résumé so the interviewer sees your key skills areas.

Highlighting Appropriate Aspects of Your Education   If you have any work experience that can possibly relate to the job you want, present the experience section before the education section. This approach may set you apart from the numerous graduates who will probably be applying for similar positions. If not, then highlight your academic achievements. Mention your grade point average only if it's good ("B" or better). Call attention to any academic honors and special achievements. If you have a college degree, don't bother to list community college or high school information unless you received special honors or your

training there is more relevant to the job requirements than your university courses. Mention only those courses that are beyond the required courses in your field and that apply to your job objective. If your education was completed years ago, merely list the degrees or diploma and schools. If you've done any significant postgraduate work, including professional seminars, that fill in gaps in your qualifications, list it.

Selecting the Right Personal Data and Interests   Normally the interviewer will be calling you for an interview, so your address is not important and can go near the end of the résumé under personal data. In the past many applicants also listed here such items as sex, marital status, number of children, height, weight, and health condition. With the advent of Equal Employment Opportunity laws, this practice is changing. The purpose of these laws is to help you have a fair chance to be considered for jobs you want. Therefore, you need only include such information if you think it will favorably impress the interviewer. If you believe the interviewer is looking for women to meet Affirmative Action goals, by all means mention that you're female. (It's perfectly legitimate to put only your initials and last name at the top of the page if you don't want your sex revealed.) If you think the interviewer might

---

EXHIBIT 3-5: Functional Areas of Business

Accounting	Merchandising
Administration	Operations Research
Administrative Services	Personnel/Human Resources
Advertising	Production
Budget and Control	Purchasing
Communications	Real Estate
Data Processing	Research and Development
Finance	Retailing
Industrial Relations	Systems
International Trade	Traffic
Inventory Control	Training
Legal	Transportation
Marketing	Wage and Salary Administration

prefer a single woman with no children, and you're married with two children, don't mention marital status or children. (Various aspects of EEO laws are discussed in the interview sections of this chapter and Chapter 15.)

The personal data section is the place to put *brief* relevant information about yourself that doesn't fit in any of the other categories. For example, you can mention your willingness or unwillingness to move to another locale, to travel, or to use your own car for company business. A graduate might mention that she worked to provide partial or full self-support while in college. Information given here should overcome possible obstacles or further enhance your chances of getting an interview.

In the interests section mention any activities, skills, or special interests that might enhance your success on the job or give you something in common with the interviewer or your future coworkers. If you have been recognized for special achievement in these areas, refer to it but keep this section very brief. Avoid a childlike show-and-tell tone. Analyze this information to see whether any of it can be moved into your experience section to round out your qualifications for the job.

Using Personal References Discreetly Interviewers do not normally check out references until after they have selected, interviewed, and screened the applicants for a particular job. Only when they are seriously considering the top two or three candidates do they bother with this step, which is somewhat of an imposition on the people listed as references. If you include their names, addresses, and telephone numbers on your résumé, which everyone knows you had reproduced and probably sent to a number of companies, you are in effect "advertising" your connections. You certainly want to avoid the possibility that inexperienced or thoughtless interviewers may contact your references unnecessarily. Protect their privacy and exhibit your savvy and thoughtfulness by merely mentioning that references are available on request.

Do spend some time deciding whom you should give as references when the time comes. The interviewer may want the names of the people you reported to in your former jobs as well as other people who can give a fairly objective evaluation of your personal habits and characteristics.

If you didn't get along with a former boss and were fired or quit in a huff, are you going to list him or her? If those job experiences are an important part of your qualifications, see whether you can get another of your bosses there to give you a good recommendation. List him or her instead; you may even want to go ahead and put that name in the experience section in case the interviewer checks job references before calling you. If you think you won't get a good recommendation, be vague on your résumé about the exact department or unit you worked in and handle the reference problem at the interview. (More about that in the interview section.)

If you have little or no work experience, you can ask teachers and others familiar with your academic performance to serve as references. In addition you may want to ask a business or professional person — one who is respected in the community and who has known you for several years — to vouch for your personal integrity and dependability.

Regardless of the types of references you give, be sure they will be fully supportive of you. Always contact them first and ask whether you may give their names. Let them know the type of job you're seeking and remind them of your qualifications. You may want to send them a copy of your résumé. After you get a job, acknowledge their help by writing them a note of thanks and telling them about your new position.

Learning from Sample Résumés Although you may benefit from the advice of a professional résumé-writer, you should write your own résumé. The process of writing it is as important as the finished product in helping you get your job. The process of translating past experiences into management terms and organizing your qualifications into a selling package is invaluable to you in preparing for the interview. Since the résumé is totally and uniquely yours when you write it yourself, you'll be able to back it up and expand on it with confidence. This approach also implies that copying a sample résumé almost verbatim, merely plugging in your data, is self-defeating. On the other hand, you can learn something about applying the suggestions given here to your situation if you analyze how they're carried out in sample situations.

Suppose, for example, your job-to-be called for selling fashion merchandise, and helping retail clients with sales promotion, merchandising, and sales forecasting. The career path might include advancement into higher-level management positions. This was the case with Joan Rogers, a senior at State University. She had been a part-time sales clerk, an officer of the honorary marketing fraternity, and a Girl Scout leader. How could that qualify her for this top-level sales job? Joan's first-draft résumé, the draft shown in Exhibit 3-6, doesn't make the most of her experience.

Joan discussed her first draft with her communications instructor. They agreed it needed revising. Working together, they first broke down Joan's job and organizational responsibilities into separate activities or functions. They found that she had valuable experience in sales promotion, merchandising, planning, and forecasting. After all, Joan had been selling women's clothing for years, arranging and displaying some of the merchandise. She had talked with her supervisor about sales expectations for upcoming seasons (part of sales forecasting). She looked at these ordinary duties to see which parts of them were transferable to a manager's duties; then she rephrased the description of her experience to reflect those skills. It's important for managers to produce measurable results, so Joan did some figuring and noted that she had regularly exceeded her sales quotas by an average of 15 percent.

Joan's teacher pointed out to her that she has performed a number of administrative functions as an officer of a school organization. As a professional fraternity officer, she has also gained marketing experience and understanding, which could be used as part of her bait. In the final version of Joan's résumé, shown in Exhibit 3-7, the words "part-time sales clerk," "student-organization officer," and "Girl Scout leader" are buried or omitted. However, her transferable skills *do* relate to the seemingly different job she's aiming for now.

How about the woman who has been out of school for several years and has a great deal of valuable experience, but not in the area of business management? This was the case with Helen Jay, who taught high school math for ten years. Helen wanted to move into a career path leading to top management, but she realized she knew very little about profit-making organizations. She does know about helping people gain new skills. She decided the best way to get her foot in the door was through personnel training. She figured she would learn about all aspects of a personnel department while in a training position and eventually move into a head slot. As head of personnel she planned to learn about the functions and interactions of other departments and move into a line-manager slot. Helen is willing to change companies each time she makes a major job move, if necessary, and she will tailor her experience to fit her new job objective at each step. The résumé Helen sent to the Personnel Director at Lighthouse Designs, Inc., is shown in Exhibit 3-8.

Pulling It All Together Before you write the final draft of your résumé, be sure you're making the most of what you have. Exaggerating your accomplishments is expected and tolerated by most experienced interviewers. In fact,

EXHIBIT 3-6: Joan's Résumé: First Draft

Joan Rogers
831 Foothill Drive
Little Rock, AR 72205
(501) 555-3809

Job Objective

A management position with a clothing manufacturer.

Education

B.A. in Marketing
State University
January 19xx

G.P.A. State University 3.67
G.P.A. Marketing 3.77

Marketing courses: *Units*

Intro to Marketing	3
Intermediate Marketing	3
Advanced Marketing	3
Sales Techniques	3
Advertising	3
Merchandising	3

A.A. in Retailing
West Community College
January 19xx

Salutatorian, Westmoor High School, 19xx

School Activities

President of student organization, Beta Gamma Psi. Arranged luncheons, dinners, and banquets with guests from business firms, the AMA, and government agencies.

Work Experience

Part-time salesclerk for Gemex Department Stores for seven years.

Personal Data

Date of Birth: January 27, 19xx
Marital Status: Single
Height: 5'7"
Weight: 135 lbs.

Interests

Helping girls in the Girl Scouts. Physical Fitness. Sports (tennis, swimming, surfing, etc.). Sewing.

References

Mr. Bill Jensen, Vice-President	Ms. Violet James
Acme Company	Violet's Boutique
4509 Green Road	98 Beach Road
Little Rock, AR 72205	Little Rock, AR 72205
(501) 289-3605	(501) 382-4621

EXHIBIT 3-7: Joan's Résumé: Final Version

Joan Rogers
(501) 555-3809

Job Objective	Marketing graduate with top grades seeking position as sales representative with women's ready-to-wear manufacturer.
	Seven years' experience in sales and merchandising.
	Experience with activities of marketing department; clothing manufacturers, wholesalers, and retailers; and American Marketing Association.
Experience *Sales and Merchandising*	Gemex Dept. Store—19xx to present Promoted sales of women's ready-to-wear. Participated in planning of merchandising strategies. Was responsible for implementing merchandising plans. Regularly exceeded sales quotas by an average of 15 percent. Exposure to sales forecasting.
Training	Trained new workers in the department.
Administration	President, Beta Gamma Psi, 19xx. Planned and supervised correspondence with members, national offices, firms, and agencies. Planned and directed meetings and banquets with guests from the marketing division of business firms and the AMA. Organized and administered a tutorial program for marketing students.
Education	B.A. in Business Administration, State University
	Degree to be granted in 19xx
	Overall G.P.A. 3.67, Marketing G.P.A. 3.77
	Concentration in Marketing, including advanced elective courses in Sales Techniques, Advertising, Merchandising.
	A. A. in Retailing, West Community College, January 19xx Westmoor High School, 19xx, Salutatorian
Personal Data	Address: 831 Foothill Drive, Little Rock, Arkansas 72205 Willing to travel and to transfer, although prefer Dallas area.
Interests	Civic activities, sports (tennis, swimming)

References available on request.

EXHIBIT 3-8: Helen's Résumé: Career Change

Helen Jay
(405) 362-8519

Job Objective	Assistant Director/Manager, Personnel-Training
Summary of Qualifications	A results-oriented organizer, able to establish and lead productive, creative group-learning processes. A background in education and administration that illustrates competency in managing, training, evaluating, coordinating, communicating, researching, and reporting complex situations.
Professional Experience	Planned, organized, and administered the High-Intensity Learning Center for basic math skills, which provided an innovative tool for creative teacher-student interaction. Bennington High School, 19xx–19xx.
Management	Responsible for the planning and organizing of the Demonstration Summer School. University of Okalahoma, Norman. Supervised the summer school office staff. Publicized the summer school by editing and distributing brochures. Completed summer school annual report.
	Responsible for adding new equipment in the Science-Math Lab as a result of the funding of a proposal I prepared.
Training	Conducted workshops to train teachers to use the High-Intensity Learning Center at Bennington High School.
	Managed full-time teaching load while involved in numerous professional activities, 19xx–19xx.
	Responsible for the Teaching Assistant Program.
Coordination	Coordinated new curriculum for a Biology-Math course and a Consumer Math course.
Education	B.A. Mathematics, University of Oklahoma, Norman
Personal Data	Address—4021 Maple Avenue, Bennington, Oklahoma 73110 Willing to travel and to relocate.
Interests	Toastmasters Club, honored as Outstanding Speaker in Region V. Skiing, tennis.

References available on request.

most instinctively discount claims by a certain percentage; therefore, you're at a disadvantage if you *don't* embellish your record. Take full credit for every project you've shared in and every management function you've performed. You can explain your claims when you come in for an interview. What you clearly should *not* do is take credit for projects or functions you were scarcely involved in at all. If you're still unsure about how to apply all this to your situation, complete Exercise 3-14.

Edit your final draft for conciseness. Most recent graduates should be able to include their essential information on one page. The absolute maximum for older, more experienced applicants is two pages. Never crowd the information on the page.

Be sure your finished résumé is neat and simple. A sloppy, smudged document that's hard to read won't impress anyone favorably. To be effective at all, the résumé has to look good. At the other extreme, one that's too glossy or artistic worries experienced interviewers. They wonder if the applicant is all glitter and razzle-dazzle. Your next step is to decide who gets copies.

EXERCISE 3-14: SELF-STARTER TO TRANSLATE EXPERIENCE INTO MANAGERIAL LANGUAGE

Objective: To help you identify and organize your past experience in ways that focus on your managerial skills, even if you've never held any sort of "management position."

1. List every job you've ever held, including officer and committee positions in any type of organization and any volunteer work.

2. Break down each job in terms of what you learned — new skills, upgraded skills, new knowledge. Include the level of ability you achieved.

3. List specific projects, achievements, deadlines met, as well as any incidents, crises, or tests you handled successfully.

4. How did you do it? What technical and behavioral skills were necessary?

5. Now describe in managerial terms the skills, knowledge, and achievements mentioned in items 2, 3, and 4 (see the list in Exhibit 3-4).

6. Now regroup. What broad functional areas have you had experience with (see the list in Exhibit 3-5). Which jobs, along with your skills and achievements in each, fall under this function? These functional areas become your marginal headings under "experience" in your résumé.

7. Keep rewriting and editing until you've refined your experiences into those that best represent your ability to succeed in the job you're seeking.

Finding the Right Organizations

You need as much information as possible about the types of companies that might use your services. You're looking for the best fit between your package and the company's needs and objectives. What are the advantages and disadvantages of large, medium, and small organizations, for example? In a large firm you might have the most opportunities for advancement and access to the most sophisticated operations, but you might also find yourself stuck in a highly specialized job. Talk to anyone and everyone who has knowledge or experience with the types of organizations you're considering. Ask your librarian for reading sources. Narrow the field to your first-choice geographical area and company size.

Geography and Opportunity In selecting a geographic area, it's wise to investigate prevailing attitudes toward new roles for women. When attitudes are generally supportive of career women, doors tend to open more readily, and support is more abundant and easier to find. According to Dun's Marketing Services, the best regional area is the West, based on the percentage of women who are managers. By state, California has the most women executives, followed by New York, Texas, Florida, Illinois, and Pennsylvania.

But opportunities can vary greatly by city within a state. Furthermore, in any large city, you're likely to find some companies that open doors for women managers and others that resist such trends. However, some cities do have more of one type of company than the other, according to surveys conducted by *Savvy*. Based on percentages of women who are managers and are active in management and professional clubs, local chambers of commerce, city government, and women's support groups, *Savvy* designated the following cities the best in 1988, in order of livability: Seattle, Boston, Pittsburgh and Washington, D.C. (tied), San Francisco, Chicago, Houston, Los Angeles, New York, and Atlanta.

Clues to an Organization's Openness Even though it's a real asset to live in a city where women tend to be welcome in management circles, it's even more important to find organizations with good track records in supporting women. The following list contains some policies, programs, and structures to look for in organizations you're investigating. When you're preparing for your job interviews, use this list to help you formulate questions you'll want to ask. Add them to your total list of questions. (See the section on preparing your questions, later in this chapter.)

1. *Antidiscrimination guidelines.* Progressive organizations publish a statement of organizational policy regarding equal opportunity and sexual harassment. They provide specific guidelines for behavior in situations involving women so that discrimination and harassment can be avoided.

2. *Decentralization.* More and smaller units are created within the organizational structure to increase the number of managerial positions available. Increased autonomy in work units gives supervisors and managers more opportunity for making decisions and taking risks. "Flattened" managerial hierarchies with short chains of command bring workers in closer contact with top management, increasing the influence of leaders and building worker morale.

3. *Project management.* Temporary teams are created to carry out particular tasks. Workers from different departments and hierarchical levels work on new tasks and share learning experiences, even though their routine jobs remain the same.

4. *Open communication channels.* System knowledge (information about budgets, salaries, minutes of some meetings, and so forth) is routinely available to all employees, eliminating a "closed club" effect.

5. *Management by objectives.* This formal system of objective-setting, problem-solving, positive reinforcement, and upward mobility can pinpoint performance requirements for promotions.

6. *Job opportunities within the organization.* Openings are posted and employees are free to apply for any job. Position descriptions list actual tasks to be performed, identify abilities needed, and identify special opportunities to move beyond the limits of the formal job title.

7. *Personnel assessment centers.* Such centers provide objective evaluative data about employees' performance. A male executive takes less risk in promoting a woman if he can back up his decision with impartial data from the center. (More information about assessment centers can be found by looking in the classified telephone directory under "Career Services" or "Vocational Consultants.")

8. *Opening up dead-end jobs.* Achievement at all levels — including secretarial and clerical — is rewarded by promotion. Job enrichment rewards skill development with new challenges and increased pay. Apprenticeship systems are developed. Managers are rewarded for helping low-mobility employees, like secretaries, develop skills, further their education, and move up the career ladder. New jobs are developed in a sequence of skill levels to bridge the gap between high- and low-status work. Project teams and committees include secretaries and clerical workers.

9. *Formal mentor-type programs.* A formalized mentor/protégé system can reward men-

tors for producing successful protégés, especially women. Similar programs can help ensure that someone will help women manage their career paths, including access to a progression of sympathetic and supportive managers they report to. (See discussion in Chapter 8.)

10. *Formal career review procedures.* Workers discuss their career goals and the means of achieving them with the appropriate person in the company on a regular basis. Workers receive constructive feedback about their performance.

11. *Management development programs.* Formal management training helps new managers eliminate inappropriate behaviors and develop skills and understanding necessary for working with groups. Formal training programs for new managers have an added bonus of bringing people together within the organization. They help lay the groundwork for powerful peer alliances.

12. *Aids for dual-career women/families.* Some company practices that may be especially helpful for career women with families are provision of maternity/paternity leaves, on-site day-care centers, **job-sharing, flextime,** and flexible job transfer and travel policies. For example, a few organizations provide for a choice or combination of paternity and maternity leaves, which signals that management considers child care a family issue, not a woman's issue. Job-sharing (two professionals or managers each working half-time to cover one job position) and flextime (choice of beginning and ending work hours) are company practices that help career women through the child-raising years.

After you collect information about specific companies that might fit with your package, select a few to focus on and learn all you can about them. Many reference sources at university and public libraries contain such information. Such directories as Moody's and Standard & Poor's can help you learn about company operations, financial performance, and key personnel.

Each June *Savvy* publishes a report on the sixteen large corporations they believe offer the best opportunities for women. They report that all have a rich tradition of change, aggressive recruitment, objective systems of promotion, management training programs, company-wide job postings, Affirmative Action programs, and an open management style. All show good prospects for growth and have a growing percentage of women in management. Each October *Working Mother* publishes a report on the "seventy-five best companies for working mothers." See also *The Best Companies for Women* [32].

Try to determine the salary range for the type of job you want. Also, find out about usual benefits and perquisites (these "perks" include such things as a company car, an expense account, and so on). The *American Almanac of Jobs and Salaries* [31] is a good place to start. Once you have some general salary information, see if you can identify what your target companies offer. This may be hard to come by; personal contacts can be invaluable sources of such information.

It's Who You Know   About 80 percent of all new jobs are found through networking [30]. Once you have a few likely companies firmly in mind, begin an all-out campaign to find personal contacts within them. Find out whether any of your friends, relatives, or acquaintances knows anyone connected with the companies. Don't forget people from your past: teachers, fellow students, business acquaintances. Personal contacts can not only provide valuable information, they can do wonders in helping you get your foot in the door, so effort spent developing them can really pay off. Both *what* you know and *who* you know determine your success in landing the right job.

If you're a student, doing a research project that requires interviewing someone in a business organization can help you get your foot in the door. Of course you won't mention at this point that you're interested in a job. Simply establish one or more contacts in the company and get as much information as you can about company operations. If you simply can't establish any kind of personal contact, you may have to send your résumé in "cold" and depend on an attention-getting, persuasive cover letter as the contact point.

Writing an Application Letter That Gets Attention

Each résumé you send out should be accompanied by an original cover letter or application letter. *Never* send a photocopy of your cover letter. Even the best résumés tend to have a mass-produced look. You can make your own individual mark most effectively in your cover letter.

Get the name and title of the particular person within each company who is most concerned with the skills and services you have to offer and address your letter to that person. Show how your particular experience, skills, interests, and traits fit the specific job you want in this particular company. Refer only to the high points of your résumé. Don't repeat large segments of it in your letter. Stress what you can contribute to the company's operations and goals. Where appropriate, show that you know something about what's going on in the field that affects this company as well as company achievements, objectives, and problems. The person who receives your letter should always feel that your pitch is directed solely to this one company.

Start off with a statement that's likely to grab the reader's attention; include your bait early. Remember, the recipient of the letter is mainly interested in the needs and problems of the company. She or he is interested in you only to the extent that you can help solve a problem or meet a need. So state briefly how you can do that.

You might need another paragraph or two to describe how your knowledge, skills, interests, and personal traits fit the needs of the company. Try to show how and why you are just the person the company is looking for. Remember to keep your letter brief, however; from three to five short paragraphs are plenty.

In the last paragraph ask for an interview. Make it as easy as possible for the reader to set up an interview with you. Give some specific dates for follow-up purposes so you'll have a good reason to call later and won't be left wondering and waiting. Before you sign the letter, proofread it carefully. Make it as letter-perfect as your résumé. Be sure to keep a copy so you'll know exactly what you said.

Exhibit 3-9 shows the letter Joan Rogers wrote to Jan Arguello to apply for a job on the sales staff. See how it illustrates the points we've just covered. Such a letter helps land you an interview. But how should you handle this important meeting?

Getting and Managing the Job Interview

The next step is getting interviews and generating job offers. Remember it's who you know when it comes to getting a job. Keep in mind also that the mind-set of really wanting a job and going for it is frequently what separates the winning candidates from the losers. This means taking an extra step beyond simply showing up for the interview and sending a thank-you note later. It means showing as much enthusiasm and excitement as possible during the interview process. It may mean making some bold move or statement that makes a point at some time during the process. Don't forget, though, that the steady drip-drip-drip of persistence is just as important. You may need to keep calling or finding innovative ways of reminding them that you're there. This is an art, for there's a fine line between being

persistent and being a pain in the neck. To identify that line, know your audience. Do not carry an innovative approach to the point of preparing a "gimmicky" résumé. Any innovation should be in the words, not in the paper, the container it's in, or the color. Substance with a fresh approach gets favorable attention, but gimmicks and stunts usually backfire.

The purpose of the interview is to give the company an opportunity to see whether you have the right "product" to sell them and to give you a chance to see whether the company has the right "product" to sell you. *Your* basic approach should be: I have a product that is good and that I want to sell to the right buyer. You will be in a better bargaining position if you can set up several interviews within two or three weeks of each other and generate at least two job offers.

Most interviewers are looking first for confidence and second for competence—not overconfidence or underconfidence, simply confidence. If necessary, they'll trade competence for confidence because they can't teach confidence or unteach overconfidence. The key to a successful interview is a combination of reasonable humility (not expecting to be president right away), enthusiasm, and strong self-respect.

The main part of the interview consists of explanations as well as questions and answers about job requirements and your qualifications. After the routine matters have been handled, it's your turn to show whether you have the mentality of an executive or a worker (see Exhibit 3-10).

Bring a folder with relevant information to the interview. As the interviewer talks, take a few brief notes about important information on the company and the job. Have a list of reminders on questions you want answered and points you want to cover.

Use the executive approach in your job application letter and résumé as well as in the interview. Every contact you have with a prospective employer is an opportunity to show

EXHIBIT 3-9: Job Application Letter

April 22, 19xx

Ms. Jan Arguello
Lighthouse Designs, Inc.
206 Market St.
Dallas, TX 75201

Dear Ms. Arguello:

The enthusiastic response to your new lines reported recently in the Dallas *Star* indicates your company will continue to grow and expand. You will no doubt be looking for additional top-notch sales representatives to handle your lines. I have over seven years of sales experience in fashion merchandising that includes sales promotion, merchandising strategies, and sales forecasting. It also includes the successful handling of various responsibilities that called for executive planning, organizing, administering, training, and supervising.

I think this experience, along with my college degree in marketing and my life-long interest in the fashion industry, can help me contribute to your goals of meeting the increased demands of your market.

I am sure you are looking for someone who also has the intelligence and ambition to advance to more responsible positions within the firm. The enclosed résumé shows that I have maintained a high grade point average in my college work, while taking a leadership role in professional and civic organizations. At the same time, I was also successful in assuming increased responsibility on the job.

I am graduating with a BA in marketing from State University and will be ready to move into a full-time position by June 1. My résumé lists some of my past achievements that show I am accustomed to getting results. I am eager to bring the same high level of drive, intelligence, know-how, and willingness to learn to my future position on the sales staff of a firm such as Lighthouse Designs.

May I meet with you between now and Wednesday, May 25, to discuss the possibility of joining your firm? I will call your office on Wednesday, May 1, to discuss a meeting date that is convenient for you. If you wish to reach me in the meantime, my home phone number is (501) 555-3809.

Very truly yours,

Joan Rogers

Enclosure: Résumé

EXHIBIT 3-10: Executive and Worker Mentalities

Executive Mentality	Worker Mentality
You are a self-confident salesperson. You approach job-getting as a courting-for-marriage relationship. Each party must have something of value to bring.	You have a "beggar" attitude. You approach job-getting as a master/slave relationship.
A Focus on Primary Concerns	*A Focus on Secondary Concerns*
The firm and its future	Fringe benefits
The salary	Holidays
Opportunities for continued advancement *after* you prove yourself	Working conditions
Second Part of the Interview	*Second Part of the Interview*
You know about the company and the job.	You reveal that you know little or nothing about the company.
You are able to provide relevant information.	
You smoothly point out how your experience fits the job — what you have to sell.	You seem to want a job, any job.
	You imply that your main concern is "What's in it for me?"
You ask for information about what the company has to offer you. Show no fear about doing this.*	You focus too intently on secondary concerns — work hours, holidays, coffee breaks, fringe benefits, carpets, windows, desks.
You do not ask about secondary concerns.	
You discuss salary in terms of an *annual* amount and negotiate assertively.	You show little or no interest in primary concerns.

*Put the responsibility on the interviewer to volunteer information about primary concerns. If the interviewer doesn't and starts to discuss secondary concerns, you should politely put aside the secondaries and zero in on the primaries. In this way you will show the interviewer that you're aware of the difference between the two and are interested in the primaries.

you are executive material. Here are some pointers.

Dress the Part   The way you dress communicates a great deal about your self-concept and about the type of person you are. Your image is especially crucial during job interviews and the first few weeks or months on the job. The people selected for higher-level positions tend to look and act as if they fit the new role even *before* they're given the nod.

Many articles and books have been written on the subject of appropriate dress for the business woman. Here is a very simple formula: When in doubt, select

A conservative approach

Simple lines, classic styles

Neutral colors (gray, navy, black, brown, beige, tan)

Clothes and accessories that are as expensive as you can afford (It's better to have a few expensive items than several cheaper ones.)

Natural fibers (wool, silk, cotton) or at least fibers that look natural

Real leather pumps, bag, briefcase

Minimal, simple, "real" jewelry (gold, pearls, classic styles, appropriate heirlooms)

Simple, neat, natural hairstyles

When dressing for a job interview, you frequently know very little about the people you'll be meeting, their viewpoints and values. However, as a potential manager for a company, it's better to be considered slightly plain or dowdy than to be considered the least bit far-out, cheap, or flashy. Once you are on the job and get to know the organization and the people in it, you will find out how much leeway you have. But for the interview, be conservative.

Keep in mind that we form our initial impressions about people within thirty seconds of meeting them. The decisions we make at that time are difficult to change. You don't want your appearance to create unnecessary barriers in the decision-maker's mind. For more specific details and information, read John Malloy's *Woman's Dress for Success* [21]. Malloy's research included sending pictures and live models dressed in different outfits to business people. The follow-up interviews and questionnaires helped him determine what impact various types of clothing, colors, styles, and accessories have on business decisions.

Malloy recommends a business woman's "uniform" of conservative, skirted suits, and he describes in great detail how to apply this simple formula for business dress. You won't go far astray if you follow his advice. Remember, you can always add your own touches of individuality and color with blouses, scarves, and other accessories. The main point is to avoid "costumes" that distract from your main purpose: acceptance as a credible, professional business person. Save the "far-out," the "really in," and the latest fads for your nonbusiness social life and leisure time.

Stress Specific Achievements The job interview is *not* the time to be shy or modest, regardless of your childhood training. Toot your own horn, just as you did in the résumé, when you discuss your qualifications. You might say, for example, "I'm good at problem-solving." Then be ready to back it up by giving some examples—how you solved a problem, how you would do it again. Look for interdisciplinary experience and skills that make your product unique or at least special: "I've been especially successful in solving problems involving research design, product quality, and sales promotion. I think this experience will be especially helpful in promoting your new product line."

When you discuss your experience and educational background, describe projects you successfully initiated, participated in, or completed; company savings you effected; contributions to company profits and goals; activities that show you're in the habit of producing results. If you developed your own résumé, following the suggestions given earlier, you will probably be comfortable and confident in discussing your achievements and skills in a businesslike way.

Be Prepared to Handle Difficult Questions and Situations Some interviewers may, through ignorance or by design, set up uncomfortable situations. For example, you may be kept waiting in the reception room. If so, take the time to review your résumé and notes for the job. Breathe deeply and relax. Or when you are ushered into the interviewer's office and introduced, the interviewer may glance up briefly and keep on working. If that happens, ask whether you should come back another time when she or he is not so busy. Standing around nervously or fading into the woodwork does *not* signal self-confidence.

Here are some difficult questions you should be prepared to answer. You might want to role-play them with a friend. In general, avoid one-line answers. The interviewer's purpose is to find out as much as possible about your qualifications and your personality. Expand on appropriate questions in order to give the information *you* want the interviewer to have.

"Tell me about yourself." Be ready to focus on the aspects of your background that qualify you for the job.

"Where do you want to be in five years?" Your career goals are well planned. Review them just before the interview. Relate them to a specific career path within the company, if possible.

"What is your major strength?" Talk about strengths that are especially important for success on this particular job.

"What is your major weakness?" Don't fall for this one (and of course don't be the one to bring up weaknesses). It's up to you to present your *best* self at the interview. Turn this negatively phrased question into a positive by saying something like, "I tend to take my career too seriously," "I'm a perfectionist in my work." "I sometimes get carried away with exciting projects on the job and push myself too hard." "I sometimes put too much pressure on myself to achieve."

"What did you like best about your last job (or in school)?" Your answer should reflect your ability to succeed in this job. For example, if human relations is an important part of the job, you can say "the people" and then tell why.

"What did you like least about your last job (or in school)?" Again, turn a negative question into a positive one. A good answer might be, "the limits on my ability to use all my skills to the fullest," or "the limited opportunities for advancement." Studiously avoid saying anything negative about any person or organization you've been involved with. You want to come across as a person who has a positive outlook, who foresees and prevents problems, who handles any problems that do occur effectively, and who doesn't harbor resentments or grudges. Also, the interviewer may figure that if you bad-mouth your previous boss or company, you'll eventually bad-mouth your new boss or firm.

There is one exception to the advice about avoiding negative comments: when you are reasonably sure that the person the interviewer will contact will not give you a favorable recommendation but you must list that company on your résumé because your experience there represents an essential part of your job qualifications. In this unfortunate situation, it's best to inform the interviewer of the circumstances from your viewpoint. If you are reasonably sure that the interviewer will check out this job reference and will therefore probably get some negative feedback about you, give your side of the story at the initial interview. Be as objective and matter-of-fact as possible. Describe the unfair *situation* and avoid condemning the *people* involved. If personalities played a part, your attitude can convey "how unfortunate" it is that certain personality traits were involved. You can stress that you learned a great deal from the experience and know how to avoid such problems now.

"What salary are you earning now?" If you're after a job that pays more than you are now earning, you may weaken your bargaining position if you reveal your current salary. The interviewer probably has an idea of your general salary range but will be unable to verify it. You can answer, "Actually, quite a bit less than I think I am worth and will be able to get. That is one reason I'm looking for an opportunity elsewhere."

"Can you type?" If you have the experience or education to qualify for a managerial or management trainee position, don't let anyone steer you into a clerical or secretarial position except as a last resort. You can respond either "No," or "I'm not interested in a position in the clerical or secretarial area." The latter response implies, ". . . even if it has a glorified title."

If you do your homework in identifying and packaging your skills and interests, developing a career action plan, translating past experience into results-oriented management action terms, and investigating potential employers, you'll be ready for many of the questions that are difficult for less-prepared candidates. Questions such as, "Why do you want to work here?" "Why should I hire you?" "How have you helped sales/profits/cost reductions?" and "How many people have you supervised?" will merely serve as opportunities for you to highlight your key qualifications and your preparation for the interview.

You need to think about responses to such questions as, "Why do you want to change jobs?" if you're currently employed full time.

"How long will you stay with the company?" and "Are you willing to go where the company sends you?" are other questions that should not catch you by surprise. If your potential boss asks, "Would you like to have my job?" a good answer might be, "I would certainly like to follow in your footsteps when you move up — of course, a job at a similar level to yours might be quite appropriate, too."

View the following types of questions as opportunities for you to highlight your key qualifications and your preparation for the interview:

Why do you want to work here?

Why should I hire you?

How have you helped sales/profits/cost reductions?

How many people have you supervised?

Give a specific example of a time you had to reprimand an employee — the action you took and the results.

Give an example of a challenging job objective you achieved — how you developed an action plan and gained the cooperation of others.

Anticipate Sexist Questions Federal legislation and court decisions now make it unlawful to ask certain questions *before* hiring that might be used to discriminate against an applicant because of sex, race, age, religion, disability, or arrest record. Some questions are essential to establish whether you can meet a bona fide occupational qualification. Other inquiries — about your previous name(s), family status, age, health, race, birthplace, people you live with, home ownership, arrests, club memberships, credit rating, religion — may be unlawful, if the answers might eliminate you from consideration for a job you're actually qualified for. (See Chapter 14 for more details.) What will you do if an interviewer asks you a question

that you believe is discriminatory? That depends on how sexist the interviewer seems to be, how much you want the job, and how you feel about the particular situation in which the question occurs. Here are some possibilities:

1. *Sidestep the question* by not responding directly to it. Instead, mention a related bona fide job qualification you meet, or make a reference to your professionalism, commitment, or relevant trait. For example, a response to, "What arrangement have you made for the care of your children?" might be, "My personal responsibilities won't interfere with my job."

2. *Downplay the question* by answering as briefly as possible, and then move on to a related topic. For example, in response to, "Will your husband object to your traveling?" your answer might be, "We support each other's career objectives. What sort of travel does the job entail?"

3. *Challenge the relevance* of the question by asking if it refers to a requirement for the job and just how it is connected with your qualifications. For example, a response to whether you plan to have children might be, "Is motherhood a requirement for this job?"

4. *Return the question* to the interviewer by saying, "Yes, are you?" or some similar question that fits. This can make a pointed statement, especially with male interviewers.

5. *Tactfully confront the legality* of the question by asking, "Isn't that type of question now considered sexually discriminatory?" or a similar question.

Decide in advance which kinds of attitudes you're willing to tolerate and which you will not (as well as which attitudes will probably limit your advancement, if held by one of your bosses). If the interviewer's questions reflect an attitude that you find intolerable, you probably should think twice before accepting a position with the firm. In this case, do you want to confront the interviewer with the illegality of the question (or later report it to the EEOC, after you find a job with another firm)?

As a practical matter, let the interviewer know the facts that you think will put you in a favorable light. Sidestep or downplay possibly unlawful questions that might be unfavorable to you. If the interviewer persists, return the question or challenge its relevance and/or legality. You may have to make the choice of cooperating if you want the job or calling the interviewer's hand if you don't.

In developing your answers, keep in mind the ten basic qualities that typify the people most employers are looking for: (1) intelligence and analytical ability — people who, when presented with an analytical challenge, take the time to define the parameters, understand the goal, and work step by step toward a conclusion; (2) creativity and flexibility — people who are able to approach problems in new and unusual ways; (3) communication skills; (4) work experience and technical skills; (5) leadership and team-playing ability — people who can excel in either mode; (6) initiative and entrepreneurship; (7) energy and stamina; (8) maturity — people who plan ahead and make carefully thought-out decisions, who have realistic goals and a sense of what they can contribute to the firm; (9) interest in the job — people who love what they do and have taken the time and trouble to find out about the firm; (10) personal qualities and personality — people who know how to dress and behave in a business setting, who seem trustworthy and well balanced, who are likely to improve the work atmosphere.

Prepare the Questions You'll Ask   Remember, you're interviewing the company too, so prepare a list of questions. You certainly won't read from it during the interview, but you'll probably want to glance at it before the interview is over to be sure you've covered the important items. The items listed as clues to an organization's openness in this chapter should trigger some questions you'll want to ask. See Exhibit 2-2, Evaluating the Power Potential of a Job, page 39, for more ideas. Here are a few other questions to get you started:

- What percentage of your employees are women? What percentage of supervisors, middle managers, and top managers are women? Are there any women on the board of directors? Have percentages increased in recent years?

- Do you have an Affirmative Action program? What does it include?

- What sort of career paths were followed by your top managers?

- What job moves are actually possible from this position?

- Which moves would be vertical and which lateral?

- What capabilities and experience are needed to move from one job to another?

- Are jobs with similar requirements grouped as job families? If so, what moves within job families are available to broaden experience and gain exposure to different working situations?

- Is there any systematic way that career paths are managed in this company? Do you have a formal career development program?

- Do you have a special career track for top performers?

- Is it company policy to promote from within (as opposed to looking outside the company for top managers and staff people)?

- What percentage of trainees make it to middle management? Top management? (Or perhaps a specific staff position you have in mind)

- What departments or areas are expanding most rapidly?

- Do you have a career development program? If so, how does it work? What services does it offer employees? Do you have a career resource center or something similar?

- Does management support individual career planning? If so, in what ways? (For example, counseling, workshops, self-development assessment centers)

- Is information about career opportunities and career development resources made available to employees? How? (For example, by posting available job positions, through workshops, or through counselors)

- How many women managers report directly to the CEO?

- Can you explain the typical career pattern of someone in this position?

- What are the common satisfactions and frustrations with this job?

- Can you tell me what a typical day on this job would be like?

- What is the firm's policy on paying for educational tuition and fees?

- How flexible are company work arrangements? Does the company offer flexitime, job-sharing, telecommuting, extended leaves, part-time tracks, child care/elder care referral, or on-site child care?

Negotiate the Best Terms   If your research has been successful, you will know the salary range the company pays for the type of position you want. You should at least know the salary range most companies generally pay for that type of position. Your goal is to get the top of that range. If your information about what

the company pays is sketchy or nonexistent, try to ask about the salary *range* before the interviewer asks what salary you expect. Then you can set your asking price at the top of the range or a little above the annual salary the interviewer mentions.

Delay talking about money as long as possible. Wait until you feel the interviewer wants you for the job, if possible. You're more likely to get your price once the interviewer is convinced of your worth and is psychologically committed to trying to hire you.

If the interviewer tries to pin you down to a salary figure too soon, a tactful delaying maneuver might be: "I'm really intrigued with the areas of responsibility in this job. Tell me more about those first. I'm sure we can arrive at an agreeable salary figure if everything else fits." Be aware that most interviewers claim the salary scale is fixed and that in fact all organizations have ways to offer you more.

Once you get an offer that seems acceptable, thank the interviewer, say you're very interested, and ask when he or she wants your decision. If you avoid accepting right away, you can review your job offers at your leisure and try to find out what perks and benefits you may be able to negotiate (such as an expense account, stock options, or company car) as well as a higher salary. Your chances of getting these extras are small just after a salary discussion. You have a better chance to negotiate for them during the next meeting. If the interviewer balks, perhaps you can tie them to additional job responsibilities you're willing to accept. If you have a slightly better offer, you can say you really prefer the interviewer's company but Company X has made you an offer that's hard to refuse.

Logical and patient insistence on an annual salary that is within reason will win you respect that will probably be remembered in the future. It sets the stage for assertiveness in future negotiations for promotions and raises. Since raises are usually figured on a percentage of what you're already earning, negotiating the best starting salary provides a basis for larger raises as long as you're with the firm.

As part of your preparation for interviewing, prepare one or two possible parting comments that may enhance your prospects: "I've enjoyed learning more about Lighthouse Designs. You're doing some exciting things." Or: "I think this job is my cup of tea."

Within a few days after the interview, send a follow-up letter referring to key points that were covered and thanking the interviewer for the opportunity to discuss the position. Such a

follow-up (1) shows you are thoughtful and considerate, (2) keeps your name on the interviewer's mind, and (3) provides you with a record of the transaction via the carbon copy.

When you select the best job offer, keep in mind the intangibles as well as salary and extras. Weigh your feelings about chances for advancement, attitudes toward women managers, lifestyles and attitudes of management, and your emotional reaction and enthusiasm toward the job. Remember, your passion for the work and your joy in achieving job goals will be major factors in your success.

SUMMARY

Before you begin setting goals, you may need to identify barriers in your own mind to planning your life direction. Typical barriers are fears concerning regimentation, failure, success, and risk-taking. If you handle such fears, define your ideas of success and who you are, and focus on the payoffs for planning, you will be able to set your goals with more energy and direction. The next phase is identifying and packaging your skills and interests so you have a better idea of the type of career that will spell success for you.

A goal is a specific end result you want by some stated time. Activities are things you *do* to achieve your goal. You may enjoy an activity, but enjoyment doesn't make it a goal. There may be a variety of feasible and acceptable activities that can help you reach your goal.

Specific goals include amounts, places, exact items, and time targets. The more specifically you state your "wants" as goals, the more likely you are to get them. If you have difficulty determining if a "want" is a goal or an activity, ask yourself *why* you desire it.

To identify your major goals, follow these steps: (1) Brainstorm all the "wants" you can think of. (2) Separate goals from activities. (3) Rank your goals in order of importance. (4) Restate goals, if necessary, so they are specific and clear. (5) Decide the relative importance to you of the major areas of your life: career, private life, and personal development. (6) Categorize your list of goals according to the major areas of your life.

After you have identified your major goals, your next step is to find activities that will help you achieve them: (1) Start with the top-priority goal in your most important life area. Brainstorm activities that can help you reach this goal. (2) Rank the activities according to their likelihood of helping you achieve the goal. (3) Select the activities you're willing to spend at least five minutes on during the coming week. (4) Repeat this process for your other goals.

Next develop action plans, beginning with a one-month plan: (1) List the top three goals in each life area. (2) Under each goal (a total of nine goals), list the three top-ranking activities for achieving those goals, along with target dates (a total of twenty-seven activities). Adapt the number of goals and activities to reflect your situation and preferences. Use the most important activities as the basis for your daily "To Do" list. Make long-range action plans—one-year, five-year, ten-year—to suit your needs.

Use your action plan to move ahead by designing a résumé that reflects your goals. The process of preparing your résumé should sharpen your awareness of your strengths and achievements and help you sell yourself. The main purpose of the résumé is to persuade the reader to grant you a job interview. It should begin with a clear statement of your specific job objective, followed by a brief statement of your major qualifications for that position. This selling pitch or "bait" is designed to capture the reader's attention and interest immediately. Describe your past experiences in terms of the management functions you've performed even if you haven't actually held a management position. List specific activities and achievements, using administrative action verbs and quantifying where possible. Get all the information you can about the companies you may want to interview. Make every effort to establish personal contacts.

A cover letter is necessary any time you mail your résumé. Write it especially for the person who can grant you an interview. Show how your particular experience, skills, interests, and traits fit the job you're applying for and meet the needs of this firm. Stress what you can contribute.

The job interview is your opportunity to show that you are executive material. Focus on the primary concerns: the firm and its future, the salary, and the opportunities for advancement after you prove yourself. The way you dress for the interview also communicates a great deal about your self-concept and the type of person you are. When in doubt, select a conservative, simple, classic, well-tailored suit and accessories.

During the interview, stress your most relevant skills, specific achievements in past situations, and unique combinations of skills and experience. Be prepared to handle difficult questions and situations so that you (1) project self-confidence, (2) take advantage of every opportunity to communicate your strengths and achievements, (3) avoid bringing any shortcomings into the conversation, and (4) tactfully sidestep or confront unlawful, discriminatory questions. Know the going salary range for the position, and try to get the top of the range by postponing the salary discussion until you feel the interviewer is ready to offer you the job.

Try to set up several interviews and generate more than one job offer so you'll be in a better bargaining position. Respond to offers with a show of interest and an agreement to give a decision within a reasonable time. Then see which company will up its ante in salary or other benefits before accepting the best offer.

REFERENCES

1. Baruch, Grace, Rosalind Barnett, and Caryl Rivers. *Lifeprints: New Patterns of Love and Work for Today's Woman*. New York: McGraw-Hill, 1983. In a two-year study financed by the National Science Foundation, the authors concluded that married women with children are the happiest women.

2. Blotnick, Srully. *Getting Rich Your Own Way*. New York: Doubleday, 1980. This study uncovered facts about the wealthy and how they got that way (mainly by working productively in careers they loved).

3. Blumstein, Philip, and Pepper Schwartz. *American Couples: Money, Work, Sex*. Seattle: University of Washington Press, 1985. The authors surveyed 12,000 people to determine new trends in couple relationships.

4. Bolles, Richard N. *What Color Is Your Parachute?* Berkeley, Calif.: Ten Speed Press, 1991. This classic in career planning includes excellent exercises for determining what you really want to do and how to create an ideal job for yourself.

5. Bolles, Richard N. *The Three Boxes of Life*. Berkeley, Calif.: Ten Speed Press, 1984. This text contains excellent exercises for life planning.

6. Bolles, Richard N. *The Quick Job-Hunting Map*. Berkeley, Calif.: Ten Speed Press, 1985. This handy packet of key exercises from *What Color Is Your Parachute?* can be ordered from the publisher (Box 7123).

7. Butler, Diane. *Future Work: Where to Find Tomorrow's High-Tech Jobs Today*. New York: Holt, Rinehart and Winston, 1984. The author explains the various technologies and presents a method for finding openings.

8. Deal, Terrence E., and Allan A. Kennedy. *Corporate Cultures: The Rites and Rituals of Corporate Life*. Menlo Park, Calif.: Addison-Wesley, 1982. The chapter on how to analyze a company's culture is especially helpful for a job campaign, to determine how well company values fit with your own.

9. Ferguson, Trudi. *Answers to the Mommy Track: How Wives-Mothers in Business Reach the Top and Balance Their Lives*. Far Hills, N.J.: New Horizon, 1990. Learn more about how career wives and mothers can reach the top and balance their lives.

10. Gallup Organization. *Gallup Mirror of America Poll*, 1990. This report compares the results of a 1975 poll with a 1990 poll of 1,234 adults concerning the women's movement, women's changing roles, and comparisons of male and female experiences.

11. Good, Nancy. *Slay Your Own Dragons*. New York: St. Martin's Press, 1990. Moving into new, more independent roles is the theme of this book.

12. Grossman, Earl A., and Gerri L. Sweder. *The Working Parent Dilemma. How to Balance the Responsibilities of Children and Careers*. Boston: Beacon Press, 1986. Dis-

cussions include the impact on children of working parents and strategies for handling common problems and crises, as well as creating quality time.

13. Hancock, Emily. *The Girl Within.* New York: Fawcett Columbine, 1989. Hancock discusses how adolescent girls lose their sense of self and how they can regain it.

14. Highman, Edith. *The Organization Woman: Building a Career.* New York: Human Science Press, 1985. A sensitive and practical guide for business women.

15. Jackson, Carole. *Color Me Beautiful.* New York: Ballantine Books, 1987. All items in your wardrobe will work together for a well-coordinated look once you identify your best colors. The secret is discovering your underlying skin tone. Carry the removable color chart with you when you shop.

16. Kennedy, Marilyn Moats. "The Keys to the Kingdom." *Savvy* (February 1984), pp. 48–55.

17. Kolbenschlag, Madonna. *Kiss Sleeping Beauty Good-Bye.* San Francisco, Harper & Row, 1979. This ground-breaking classic is designed to awaken women from the spell that feminine myths and models hold over us. The author looks at the hidden meanings and impact of such fairy tales as Sleeping Beauty, Snow White, Cinderella, Goldilocks, and Beauty and the Beast — as well as the roles of the Frog Prince, Handsome Prince, and Knight in Shining Armor.

18. Lakein, Alan. *How to Get Control of Your Time and Your Life.* New York: P. H. Wyden, 1989. This is a basic text on using goals to manage time.

19. Lee, Valerie. *Pregnancy in the Executive Suite.* McAllen, Tex.: Success Publications, 1988.

20. Levering, Robert, and Milton Moskowitz. *The 100 Best Companies to Work for in America.* Reading, Mass.: Addison-Wesley. This book includes not only the best places for women but the best companies for ambience, pay, job security, and benefits. First published in 1984, it is updated about every three years.

21. Malloy, John. *Woman's Dress for Success.* New York: Follett, 1987. This is a basic resource for proper business dress. All suggestions are based on extensive research into actual reactions of business decision-makers.

22. Medley, Anthony H. *Sweaty Palms: The Neglected Art of Being Interviewed.* Berkeley, Calif.: Ten Speed Press, 1984. This book includes the many aspects of going through a job interview.

23. Moskowitz, Milton, Michael Katz, and Robert Levering, eds. *Everybody's Business: An Almanac.* New York: Doubleday, 1990. The authors call this book an irreverent guide to corporate America. It lays it on the line about all the large corporations with little nuggets of information and big patches of corporate history. This reference book is a must for researching companies during your job campaign. Updated about every three years.

24. *National Job Market.* This newspaper reprints help-wanted ads gleaned from nearly 3,000 newspapers each week. Buy at some newsstands or order the full edition that includes helpful articles and other data (P.O. Box 286, Kensington, Md. 20895).

25. Rogers, Henry C. *Rogers's Rules for Business Women.* New York: St. Martin's Press, 1988. The author discusses how to start a career and move up the ladder, from a man's perspective.

26. Ross, Ruth. *The Prospering Woman*. New York: New World Library, 1985. This book can change your life by helping you know yourself and what you truly want, showing you how to adopt a viewpoint of abundance versus scarcity, and explaining how to make room in your life for success.

27. Sher, Barbara. *Wishcraft: How to Get What You Really Want*. New York: Ballantine Books, 1986. This book presents a detailed, step-by-step plan to pinpoint your goals and make your dreams come true.

28. Sinetar, Marsha. *Do What You Love, The Money Will Follow*. New York: Dell Publishing, 1987. Discusses the psychology of right livelihood and the power of believing in your right to express yourself through your work.

29. Thompson, Jacqueline, ed. *Image Impact: The Complete Makeover Guide*. New York: Arrowood Press, 1990. A valuable addition to Malloy's work on business dress, this book also covers personality and public speaking.

30. "Working Smart." *Female Executive* (November/December, 1988), p. 8.

31. Wright, John W. *The American Almanac of Jobs and Salaries*. New York: Avon. Here's a wealth of previously unobtainable information about salaries for all types of positions. Covering both profit and nonprofit organizations, it includes job descriptions and salaries by region and metropolitan area. You must buy or borrow this reference before launching your job campaign. First published in 1982, it is updated about every three years.

32. Zeitz, Baila, and Lorraine Dusky. *The Best Companies for Women*. New York: Simon and Schuster, 1988.

Chapter Four

Managing Your Time Productively

> *"I discovered I always have choices and sometimes it is only a choice of attitude."*
>
> Judith M. Knowlton

The goals and action plans you developed in Chapter 3 will serve as the foundation for managing your time. If your new goals call for a new image, be sure to complete Exercises 8-2 and 8-3 on fine-tuning your image and integrating your new image, for your image affects your attitude toward time. The way you use your time and the way you expect others to use theirs will, in turn, affect all the leadership skills we discuss in Part 3 of this book.

In this chapter you will have the opportunity to learn more about

1. Developing a constructive attitude toward time, its value, and its use

2. Making the best use of time for your individual working style and energy-level patterns

3. Creating a personal environment for effective time management

4. Focusing on results instead of activities

5. Scheduling your day to accomplish *your* goals rather than other people's goals

6. Making and using "To Do" lists

7. Cooperating with your boss, work team, assistant, and peers to weed out time-wasters

8. Streamlining paperwork so that you normally handle each piece of paper only once

9. Minimizing interruptions so you can complete your top-priority tasks

10. Analyzing activities in order to improve the workflow in your department

11. Using your travel time productively

12. Planning, directing, and completing large, complex projects with minimal procrastination and a greater sense of satisfaction

Freewheeling or Frantic?

8:00 A.M.: Jan Arguello smiles as she sails by Erika's desk. "Another gorgeous day, Erika. And I'm ready to tackle that summer sportswear project." Jan enters her office. "Ah, nothing like a nice, clean desk to start a nice, clean day."

"Oh, come on," laughs Erika, poking her head in the door. "Sometimes your efficiency becomes absolutely Pollyannish. I assume you want me to keep the pack at bay for the next hour."

"You bet," responds Jan, picking up the file folder lying on her otherwise empty desk and patting it. "The good old sales campaign for summer sportswear gets my undivided attention till 9 A.M. or a dire emergency — whichever comes first."

9:00 A.M.: Jan checks with Erika to see who has called or asked to see her. Randy Perkins, a regional sales manager, wants to see Jan before he leaves the office to call on a customer this morning. Jan asks Erika to call Randy and ask him to drop by now. Meanwhile, she starts going through the high-priority mail that Erika has sorted and placed on her desk. She makes instructional notes to Erika on a few of them. (Erika writes many of the letters in response to requests for information and other routine transactions. She also delegates routine items to others in the department.)

9:15 A.M.: Randy enters Jan's office. "Hi, Jan. Thanks for taking the time to see me this morning. I know you're busy with the new sales campaign."

"Glad to see you, Randy. The sales campaign is coming right along. It's exciting to work with such a well-executed line of sportswear. I think your team will enjoy selling it, too. It should make a lot of money for us and for our cus-

tomers. Here, take a look at these preliminary sketches."

"Say, these *are* good looking! They'll practically sell themselves."

"I agree. Now, what can I do for you this morning, Randy?"

"Well, I'd like your opinion on the Wingate account . . . (Randy discusses a potential problem concerning one of Lighthouse Designs' oldest and largest customers. Jan listens, making appropriate, helpful comments from time to time.) I see now exactly what I've got to do. I think I mainly just needed to talk to someone who understands the situation. Just talking about it and getting a few pointers from you has clarified the whole situation for me."

"Good, I'm sure you can handle it well, Randy. If you want to discuss it further, though, be sure to drop by."

"Thanks, Jan. See you at the next staff meeting, if not before. By the way, when will our next meeting be?"

"I'm not sure yet, but I'll give you plenty of notice. Things are going pretty smoothly right now, and there are not enough discussion items to warrant a meeting at this time. As soon as we need a meeting, I'll let you know."

"Okay. See you later."

9:30 A.M.: Randy stops at Erika's desk on the way out. "You know, Erika, we're both lucky to have a boss like Jan. I don't know how she manages to get so much done and still have plenty of time to listen to everyone's problems and requests. Are you the one who keeps her organized?"

"Well, let's just say we work together to keep the office running smoothly. Jan *lets* me help her — more so than any boss I've ever had. And she helps me, too."

Kate Blakeley's assistant, Phil, is sitting by Erika's desk, going over some items Erika is sending to the Administrative Services Department.

"You really are lucky, Erika. Kate drives me buggy sometimes. I wish she'd get her act together the way your boss does."

"Oh, Phil. Surely it's not all that bad."

"Okay, yesterday was a typical day. Let me give you a rundown. Pretend we're hiding behind a candid camera."

8:00 A.M.: Kate Blakeley comes bustling in. She rushes toward her office, barely nodding to people as she dashes by. She has several meetings to attend today, including the weekly staff meeting. She simply must spend an hour or so with Phil, going over important correspondence and giving him instructions on handling some matters.

K: Good morning, Phil, would you come in right away and let's get on these requests.

P: Sure thing. Ah . . . Frank LeFavor just came by. He needs to see you to find out what you want him to do about the materials for Schroeder's Department Store.

K: Well, get him on the phone and tell him I'm here. I'll try to get this over with as soon as possible and then we'll work on those requests. Meantime, I'll start on these telephone calls. (She picks up several telephone message slips left over from yesterday afternoon.)

8:20 A.M.: When Frank gets to Kate's office, she's on the telephone and waves for him to come in and sit down. Frank waits patiently as Kate tries to finish the call. She occasionally glances at Frank, raises her eyebrows, and shrugs her shoulder as the long-winded person on the other end of the line keeps talking.

8:30 A.M.: Finally Kate is able to complete the call and turns to Frank.

K: Now, Frank, let's discuss the Schroeder problem . . .
Frank tries to explain to Kate what he has learned about the Schroeder problem. Dur-

ing the discussion, Kate excuses herself two different times to take important phone calls. She's aware that the morning is slipping by and she still hasn't finished preparations for her staff meeting. She glances at her watch several times. Finally at 9 A.M. she interrupts Frank.

K: Why don't you put this all in a memo to me and let me study it.

F: But I'm supposed to call Schroeder tomorrow . . . Well, all right. I hope you can give me an answer within the next few days.
Kate manages to complete most of the instructions to Phil. Then she takes a few minutes to prepare for her weekly staff meeting, which is scheduled for 10 A.M.

10:10 A.M.: Kate rushes into the meeting.

K: Good morning, people. Now we've a number of items to cover this morning, so I'll get right down to business . . .

11:05 A.M.: The meeting adjourns. Frank LeFavor and Bill Waldheim walk together toward their offices.

B: You know, I'm wondering what we really accomplished in that meeting.

F: I thought the same thing after several of the meetings lately. It seems to me that at least half of these meetings could be eliminated and everyone would be a lot better off.

B: Yeah. I need to finish the Viva job today. Now the day's nearly half gone.

F: Why does she think we have to meet every single week?

B: Oh, she thinks we need the regular contact so that we feel like one big happy family.

F: Some family! I went in this morning to try to get an answer from her on the Schroeder job, and I felt like I was talking to a brick wall.

Erika sighs. "Yeah, I see what you mean, Phil. Kate needs help. Well, maybe I can drop a hint to Jan. She's great at working with people on these problems — and she does it in a way that makes people feel good about themselves."

---

1. As you read this story, what effective time management attitudes and actions did you notice?

2. What impact or effect did these effective practices have on people? (For example, on motivation and productivity?)

3. What ineffective time management attitudes and actions did you observe?

4. What impact or effect did these ineffective practices have on people?

DEFINING ATTITUDES TOWARD TIME

Yesterday is a cancelled check.
Tomorrow is a promissory note.
Today is ready cash. Use it!

This statement by an anonymous philosopher vividly conveys the importance of making the most of the present moment. Think about it. The present moment is all you *really* have.

How can we make the most of time? First of all, even though we speak of managing *time,* what we can actually do about time is manage our *activities* so that they produce the most effective results. We conduct our activities within a frame of reference called "time." Time marches on, and there is nothing we can do to change that. What we *can* do is change our activities so that they give the best results.

It has been said that "Time is money." Most effective managers share that viewpoint. When employees' time is wasted, the dollars the company pays them in salary are being wasted. Not only that, but wasted time can mean lost opportunities to make money, costly delays that not only tie up other workers' time but perhaps lose customers and increase storage costs, transportation costs, insurance costs, and other costs.

Thinking of your time and your subordinates' time in terms of hourly pay will help you put wasted time in proper perspective. To figure approximate hourly pay, divide annual salary by 2,000 hours. For example, if you make $20,000 a year, your hourly rate is about $10 per hour ($20,000 ÷ 2,000). The hourly rate for $100,000 a year is $50. Remember, though, that this doesn't include "perks" or fringe benefits, which frequently amount to one-third of the salary. The estimated cost of some typical executive time-wasters is shown in Exhibit 4-1.

When you adopt the attitude that indulging in time-wasters is similar to taking a match to company money and burning it, you are likely to guard your precious time and make the most of it. This attitude can influence your subordinates too. You can go over the monetary value of their time by calculating with them the cost of a coffee break or bull session, interruptions, and other time-consumers.

Using your time productively is intertwined with other good management practices, such as setting objectives so that you focus on effectiveness rather than on efficiency; setting priorities and time targets so that the most important objectives are given top priority; planning activities ahead by identifying and ranking them on a "To Do" list so that you schedule your day for the activities most likely to achieve the objectives; concentrating on a single item at a time; delegating effectively and establishing a good follow-up system; and making timely, appropriate decisions. All these practices also tend to prevent harmful tension that leads to stress. Instead, they promote beneficial tension — that is, challenge and enthusiasm. Stress management and time man-

EXHIBIT 4-1: Estimating the Cost of Wasted Time

Someone comes into your office uninvited = $10

> That's the average value of the time you lose from the interruption of your work and the unproductive time you spend.

You accept a phone call outside your preset phone hours = $13

> If you're not a salesperson or a customer relations specialist, you can restrict unwanted calls and save this expenditure.

You pick up a piece of paper = $1

> If you put the paper down without working on it, you've thrown that money away.

You stop what you're doing to do something else = $3.50

> That's the approximate cost of switching from one task to another, especially when the first task isn't finished.

You dictate a letter = $10 to $30

> The exact cost depends on your salary and your assistant's salary. Is this letter really necessary?

---

agement are both enhanced by an awareness of personal energy-level patterns **(body time)** and a soothing external environment. To take advantage of the time-management techniques suggested here, however, you must analyze your attitude toward time and focus on payoffs for practicing time-saving techniques.

Delegating: The Key to Time Management

An important benefit of delegating effectively is the time it frees up for you to devote to higher-priority items such as planning and organizing or mastering higher-level leadership skills. (See Chapter 13.)

Focusing on One Task at a Time

Your attitude toward balancing projects is important too. Regardless of your individual working style, you must focus on one task at a time for maximum effectiveness.

Some people work best with several irons in the fire at once. They like to have several projects going — each at a different stage in its development. In that way they can be thinking about one when they have a breather in another. They can assign the solution of certain problems on one project to their subconscious while the conscious part of their mind focuses on another project. When they feel blocked, tired, or bored with one project, they can frequently make progress on a different one.

If this is your style, you can still focus on one task at a time, even while "keeping all your irons hot." Try these suggestions.

1. As soon as one project is underway, look for another that is ready for action.

2. Make a step-by-step plan for each project.

3. Delegate as much of the work as you can.

4. Set a schedule for following up on each one.

Other people prefer to focus on one project at a time. They become intensely involved with it, living with it almost day and night until it is completed.

If this is your style, try these techniques.

1. Choose the one project that promises to be most fruitful and is best suited for you.

2. Make a plan for completing it.

3. Delegate other projects that will need attention before your number-one project is completed.

4. Stick with your project until it is finished.

Regardless of which style best suits you, it's important to focus on one *task* at any one point in time. Other tasks and other projects may be simmering in your subconscious, or your workers may be working on them. But at any one moment you are totally focused on the task at hand—whether it is planning a step, discussing a task with a subordinate, carrying out a task yourself, or handling some other aspect of the multiple projects you may have going.

Using Awareness of Body Time

Your attitude toward your activities and the pace at which you accomplish them is strongly affected by your energy level at various times of the day. As a rule, workers between 18 and 30 years of age start the slowest, begin to peak after lunch, and are still going strong even when the office is closing up. Workers between 31 and 40 start to peak earlier in the day and slow down by 2 P.M. Workers between 41 and 55 peak at midmorning and taper off gently throughout the day. On average, the energy of all workers is highest at 10:30 A.M. By the end of the day, 20 percent are "exhausted."

Try to schedule projects and tasks that require the most concentration, creativity, analysis, synthesis, and decision-making for your higher-energy hours. If you find that your peak hours simply don't coincide with the needs of your job, it may be possible to change your peaks by changing your sleeping habits. People who are convinced they are "night people" are often surprised to find that they become more of a "morning type" after a few months of changed sleeping habits. When they are required to arise early every morning for a few

months and in turn to retire early, they soon find themselves waking earlier on their own and peaking at an earlier hour.

Locating Time-Wasters and Energy Drains

The first step in locating the major time-wasters and energy drains in your life is to keep a log of your activities for a week or two. Exercise 4-1 offers suggestions for setting up such a log and analyzing it to determine how well your activities support your top priority goals.

Developing a Constructive Attitude Toward Time Management

Your viewpoints about the value of time, the role of delegation, your individual working style, and the use of your body time patterns all work together to form a constructive (or not so constructive) attitude toward time management. Another vital factor is how you use rewards to motivate yourself to reach your time-management goals.

First, give yourself permission to have regularly scheduled rewards. You may find yourself torn between what you *should* do and what you *want* to do. It's natural to want immediate payoffs—to have fun and feel good *now*. Therefore, if you don't arrange some regular short-term payoffs, you may end up sabotaging your own efforts, usually without knowing why.

Find rewards that are satisfying but create minimal delay and expense in meeting your objectives. Only you can decide how simple or sophisticated, how large or small, how often and in what pattern they must be to keep you happy. Experiment with rewards such as these to find out what works for you:

A snack break, coffee break, special lunch or dinner, cocktail, weekend trip, or vacation

EXERCISE 4-1: LOGGING AND ANALYZING YOUR ACTIVITIES

Step 1. *Identify goals.* If you are working, first analyze your job description or determine what is expected of you; then identify your major areas of responsibility. In any case, identify your top-priority goals in all areas of your life.

Step 2. *Set up a time log.* A fairly large daily appointment calendar with space to record items for each hour of the day can be purchased at an office supply store, or you can easily set up your own log sheets.

Step 3. *Log activities and body time.* Pick two weeks that are fairly typical and log all your activities. Include weekends. Note times when your energy level is especially high or low, when you especially enjoy being with people or prefer to be alone (sociability level), or when you feel especially influential or ineffective (charisma level). Also note any variations in the work pace you prefer at various times.

Step 4. *Set up summary sheets.* Prepare a summary form for each week that will help you analyze the percentage of time you spent on various types of tasks. You can use the form shown in Exhibit 4-2 or design your own.

Step 5. *Fill in summary sheets.* Identify the main activities that occupy your time and make up your work load, as shown on your log sheets. Each major activity becomes a column heading on your summary form opposite "Task." The sample summary sheet shown in Exhibit 4-2 is abbreviated. Your own summary sheet will probably have a dozen or so major types of activities. Referring to your log sheet for each day, record the hours you spent on each type of task under the task column heading and in the appropriate horizontal row indicating the day the task was worked on.

Step 6. *Analyze summary sheets.* You should be able to see how much time you spent on each task and the daily and weekly pattern of effort toward each task by looking down each column. You can also see the daily and weekly pattern of time allocated to all major types of tasks by looking horizontally across the row for each day.

Step 7. *Identify time-wasters and energy drains.* Does the amount of time you're spending on each type of task adequately support your top-priority goals? If not, how can you reprioritize your activities? Are you making best use of peak body times? If not, how can you change the timing of your activities?

---

days off — once you complete a certain task or project

A shopping trip, the purchase of a little luxury item, or simply a stroll through an interesting shop or mall — upon completion of a task or project

An interesting new "toy" such as a car phone, laptop or palmtop computer, or other equipment that turns you on and helps get the work done

A favorite beverage or goodie to sip or munch as you concentrate on an especially

EXHIBIT 4-2: Example of Summary Sheet for Analyzing Logged Activities

Task: / No. of Hours:	Research for Marketing Report	Reading for Management Seminars	Team Meeting	Food Shopping Preparation, Cleaning	Total	BODY TIME SUMMARY:* Energy	Sociability	Charisma	Work Pace
Mon.	2 ½	2 –	3 ½	3 –	11	9-11 H / 5-6 L			9-11 = F / 2-3 = S
Tue.									
Wed.									
Th.									
Fri.									
Sat.									
Sun.									
Week's Total									
SUMMARY TOTAL (all weeks)									
PERCENTAGE OF TOTAL TIME									

*H = High
L = Low
F = Fast
S = Slow
M = Moderate

tedious project (watch out for calories, sugar, alcohol, too much caffeine, and other problems)

A thick piece of carpet under your desk to work your toes into after you've quietly slipped off your shoes

A red marker for drawing nice big lines through items on your "To Do" list as you complete them

A trip down the hall or to another floor to chat or enjoy a nice view for a few minutes

You may be carrying around old parent messages that interfere with your enjoyment of these rewards, such as: "You're just coddling yourself and wasting time." "Buckle down and get your work done." "Quit acting like a child." If so, simply remind yourself that you'll be more productive in the long run if you enjoy yourself along the way.

If you still have trouble motivating yourself to use constructive time-management techniques, find out what payoffs you're getting for *not* managing your time well. Use the same process discussed in Chapter 6 for analyzing payoffs for nonassertiveness.

Setting the Stage for Effective Time Management

Not only is your internal environment important for effective time management, your external environment has a strong impact also.

Eliminate or improve as many situations as possible that regularly irritate you. For example, if your daily route to work is unpleasant, the trip to the office may have a depressing effect on you. It may be worth a few extra minutes of commuting time to take a more pleasant route. If you find yourself in regular contact with people who are insulting, confront them assertively or find a way to avoid them. If you find yourself waiting in lines and hating it, use problem-solving techniques to figure out ways to avoid lines. In other words, clean up your life as much as possible by eliminating any negative junk that is surrounding you. These irritants and depressants are energy drains.

Remember, your physical working environment has a strong psychological effect on your attitude and your work habits. Determine what you need to make you feel comfortable with your office and enjoy being in it and modify your work space. Set the stage for effective time management by organizing your desk, setting limits on your weekly work hours, and learning to say "no" to some requests.

Keeping an Uncluttered Desk   Nearly everyone finds that a well-ordered desk improves mood and efficiency; it also signals an executive attitude. In most companies the higher up in the corporate hierarchy one goes, the cleaner are the managers' desks. So get papers off your desk and onto someone else's (or into the file cabinet or wastebasket) when possible. Avoid in- and out-baskets; keep them on your assistant's desk or use your desk drawers for this purpose.

Limiting Your Work   Except for short periods when you're learning the ropes of a new job or completing a special project, avoid working more than forty-five hours a week. If you must work overtime, consider doing it early in the morning rather than staying late; this signals that you're on top of things instead of floundering.

You will profit from directing most of your energy toward career-related objectives, espe-cially while you're trying to make your mark. Everyone who succeeds pays those kinds of dues. However, don't confuse long hours and hard work with achieving objectives. Don't bury yourself in piles of work and neglect opportunities to make important contacts, become professionally involved, and learn important new skills.

Try to get all your work done at the office so you won't need to carry it home. If this is your intention and your goal, you'll rarely need to take work home and you'll probably be a better manager. When you get in the habit of thinking, "If I don't finish it today, I can always do it at home tonight," your *intention* changes and your incentive for managing your time effectively takes a nosedive.

Learning to Say "No"   If you don't learn to say "no" to tasks, nominations, meetings, and other time-consuming activities people ask you to participate in, you will end up managing your time according to other people's objectives and priorities rather than your own (see Chapter 6 on assertiveness). Of course your priorities should be congruent with your boss's. If they are not, perhaps you should think seriously about changing jobs. At times, it may even be wise to say "no" tactfully to your boss. At least discuss how completion of the activities the boss is requesting fits in with the objectives the two of you agreed on for your job.

USING OBJECTIVES AND PRIORITIES FOR DIRECTING ENERGY

Before you can direct your energies into channels that are most productive for you, you must know what you are trying to achieve. Time management rests on management by objectives, which implies effective action rather than merely efficient action, getting results rather than merely making an effort. To lay the necessary foundation for using your time effectively, therefore, look at the list of activities you made for achieving your career objectives (Exercise 3-9, p. 73). Are you actively engaged in these activities now? Are they moving you toward your most important objectives? Do you need to add new activities and weed out unproductive ones? How about the time targets for completing them? Do you need to rethink the deadlines you've set?

Setting Deadlines

It's important to set deadlines for completing your activities and achieving your objectives — and to have your workers set deadlines. It's also important to observe them. According to **Parkinson's Law:** "Work expands to fill the time available for its completion."

People who don't have a deadline tend to put off getting started on a task and to dawdle once they do start. Some keep working toward perfection rather than being satisfied with reasonable effectiveness or excellence. Perfectionism is extremely costly. In fact, it's prohibitive over the long term. Successful business people adopt the principle of "sensible approximation." Ask yourself, "If my life depended on doing this task in half the time I have allocated, what shortcuts would I take? Is there really any reason *not* to take them?" Set intermediate deadlines for long-term projects so that you keep working at a steady pace rather than find yourself swamped near the deadline date.

Scheduling Your Day

If you don't plan your day, you'll end up doing whatever comes up. This means that other people's actions may determine your priorities instead of the goals you have set for yourself. It also means, as Edwin Bliss points out in *Getting Things Done,* that you will make "the fatal mistake of dealing primarily with problems rather than opportunities" [1, p. 81]. You're likely to be solving other people's problems instead of looking for new things to do and new ways of doing things. Remember, one of the most productive uses of your time is planning ahead. The better you plan a project in advance, the less time it takes to complete it successfully. Don't let busy-work crowd out your innovating and planning time.

Using a "To Do" List   The key to successful use of "To Do" lists is actually *using* them. That means referring to your list the first thing every morning and checking it regularly during the day to be sure you are making the best use of your time all through the day. Especially good times for checking your list are just after an interruption, when you're torn between two activities, or when you're running out of energy or interest in your current activity. Use whatever format and materials work best for you but avoid using small pieces of paper. They tend to get scattered all over the place, making you feel scattered rather than organized and integrated. Put everything on one sheet of paper or in one notebook.

Perhaps you need to get a clear picture of your major responsibilities and deadlines for each week, each month, or perhaps even for a year. Experiment by either trying out various "To Do" sheets and pads from office supply stores or by designing your own format. After a tryout period, stock up or have your own format reproduced. Keep an adequate supply of sheets at your desk. If you date your "To Do" sheets, they can do double duty as an appointment calendar and tickler file. Figure 4-1 shows a format that is helpful for many managers. Use the "follow-up" section for jotting down reminders by turning ahead to the appropriately dated "To Do" sheet. Later, on that day, your reminder will be waiting for you.

Preparing for Tomorrow   Not only is it important to check your "To Do" list first thing every morning and at intervals throughout the day, it's also important to take a few minutes in the afternoon before going home to work on your

FIGURE 4-1: Format for "To Do" Lists

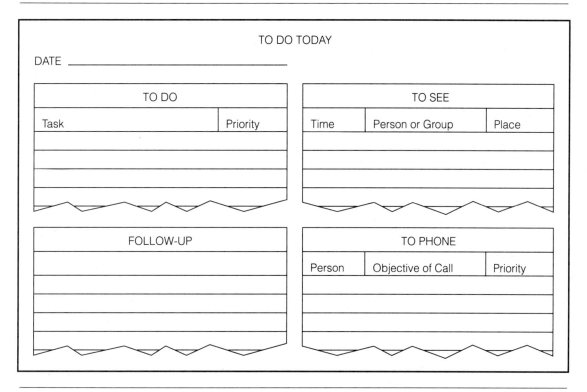

list for the following day. Why should you make it in the afternoon? For one thing, doing so gives you a feeling of closure and completion of the workday. Also, in the morning, you are pressured by other duties and are likely to prepare the "To Do" list haphazardly. The main reason, however, is to give your subconscious mind time to work on your list during the intervening time, even while you sleep.

After you have made your list for the next day, clear your desk before leaving the office. Try setting just one important project out on your desk and putting everything else in a file drawer or cabinet that's easy to reach. When you come in the next morning, work on that one project as long as you can.

Eliminating Activities   Remember that sometimes the activities that are most important for reaching your objectives are not urgent — for example, writing an article, working up a proposal, or working out the details of a new idea. If you find yourself transferring an item from your "To Do" list day after day, ask yourself: "Is this item really important?" "Am I procrastinating?" "Should this go in the tickler file?" There is no need to list routine items that you do regularly. List only the items that have high priority today and might not get done unless you give them special attention.

For each item, ask yourself, "What can I delegate?" Then, for each activity, beginning with the one ranked lowest, ask, "What would happen if I didn't do this?" If the answer is "maybe nothing" or "not much," give the activity an aging period. If there is no follow-up from anyone and no repercussions, you have saved that time to spend on high-priority items.

Custom Tailoring Your List As you schedule your time, keep in mind three major considerations.

Practical considerations: Match items that require concentration with times when you are reasonably certain of having an uninterrupted period of peace and quiet. If special equipment or facilities are necessary, are they available only at certain hours? Might there be a waiting time to consider? Do you need to see other people in order to complete the task? When will they be available?

Body time considerations: Wherever possible, schedule activities to take advantage of your prime times. Reserve routine tasks for times when you are fairly alert but not at your peak. Try to use peak hours for top-priority projects, tasks that require intense concentration or original thinking, or tasks that are stressful or unpleasant but important. Use your low-energy times for catching up on professional reading, proofreading and signing letters, planning the next day, and so forth.

If you must schedule a task that calls for high energy during a low-energy time, boost your energy by taking a brief rest period followed by a nutritious snack (and see the relaxation exercises at the end of Chapter 5).

Preferred pace considerations: Some people require pressure to work at top capacity. If that is your style, use it. However, be sure you plan ahead enough to get the information, approvals, documentation, and other items you need to complete the job so that pressure doesn't turn into panic or disaster. If you like to schedule your day very closely, from hour to hour, be sure you still build in at least an hour a day for unexpected events and for breathing space.

For most people, crash programs are far inferior to well-planned and well-timed programs. Knowing when to stop work on a project is as important as knowing when to start because overwork leads to diminishing returns, such as increased errors and slowed-

down responses. When your muscles are aching or you find yourself reading the same sentence two or three times, it's usually time to quit.

Whenever you possibly can, schedule your time in large blocks so you won't have to constantly switch back and forth from one type of activity to another. Leave some unscheduled time for visitors, phone calls, unforeseen emergencies, and other unexpected tasks. If it turns out you don't need all that unscheduled time, count your blessings and return to the next item on your "To Do" list.

Remember to schedule some quiet time for relaxation and meditation. At least find some time to back off from the rat race; stand back and gain some perspective on what is going on. This can help you be more objective about minutiae and pettiness when you go back to your tasks.

Setting Special Emphasis Goals Allan Lakein, in *How to Get Control of Your Time and Life*, suggests that to increase your level of motivation and enthusiasm, you should set a "special emphasis goal" that lasts from a week to a couple of months [4]. The goal might be to come up with one new idea for some special project each day, to go after one big customer each day, or to figure out a way to streamline one activity (yours or a team member's) each day. Then do something every day to squeeze in at least one top-priority activity for each special emphasis goal.

This technique is a great morale-booster because every day you see yourself come closer to your top-priority objectives by remembering what you want to do and doing it. Obviously, then, working with team members to set special emphasis goals can also pay off handsomely.

Using "Dead" Time We all have a certain amount of "dead" time when we are not doing anything that directly leads to the accomplishment of top-priority objectives—the time we spend waiting for someone or something, sleeping, engaging in early morning activities or inertia, commuting, taking lunch and coffee breaks, and so forth. It is up to you to decide how much of that time should remain "dead" and how much of it you want to liven up by making it do double duty.

There is no need to become an overworked time-management "nut" by frantically packing every moment full of activity. But you will no doubt experience times when dead-time activities are boring. You may feel a sense of frustration at such a low-level use of your time when you are itching to work on a top-priority activity. It can be fun to figure out your own preferred pace and see how creative you can be in making the best use of your dead time.

Try keeping a file folder of "quick tasks." During the day, drop into it items that can be done during dead time. Drop the folder in your briefcase when you leave the office. Then when you are faced with dead time and want to work on some high-priority activity, you will have some quick tasks with you. Also, be sure to take your file folder along to meetings and appointments when you may need to wait for someone.

Use your commute time to think about activities for the coming day. This time can be extremely valuable in mentally rehearsing the best ways to handle problems, situations, and tasks. Consider carrying a small tape recorder so you can dictate "To Do" list reminders for the future, items for your expense report, and dates you want to remember. If you are not doing the driving, you can even dictate detailed memos and letters. Your secretary can sort out the items and transcribe them later.

Evaluating Objectives, Activities, and the Daily "To Do" List   Frequent evaluation helps you stay flexible and ready to change plans and priorities as circumstances change. Once every month or so keep a detailed log of how you spend one day. Choose a fairly typical day; then ask yourself as you get ready to begin an activity, "If I weren't already doing this, would I start it now?" If the answer is "no," why not cut your losses and drop it? If the answer is "yes," calculate how much time that item deserves and limit your involvement to that much time and no more. This practice will keep you aware of good time management. It will help you focus on objectives that enhance your effectiveness and activities that get results rather than on merely keeping busy and working hard.

Documenting Your Achievements   Keeping track of what you've accomplished is easy if you keep your used-up "To Do" lists in special file folders. Be sure they include a notation indicating whether you completed each item. For special activities or projects, note (1) everything you did well, what made it successful, and how you went about it; (2) everything that went wrong, why, and how to prevent problems from happening again. File these sheets where you can easily find them when you begin planning a similar activity or project.

Some people make an "I Love Me" (ILM) folder for their achievement records. They add to it letters of appreciation, congratulation, and praise written to them by others. They also include special reports, articles, or letters they have written that reflect high-quality work or special achievement. Keep this file at home to maintain privacy and prevent loss.

Review your special files when it's time for a performance appraisal, a raise or promotion request, or an update of your résumé or biography, and on any other occasion involving your performance. In this way you can base your comments on specific achievements that you can back up with accurate facts and figures.

FINDING TIME-SAVERS AND WEEDING OUT TIME-WASTERS

In Chapter 3 you developed a list of clearly stated objectives, ranked in order of importance, and a list of activities that will lead to achieving those objectives, ranked in order of priority. In this chapter you have reviewed techniques for using a daily "To Do" list that includes those activities and other tasks, ranked in order of importance. You're well on your way to managing your time as effectively as possible. All that remains is for you to weed out time-wasters that may creep into your well-planned day and replace them with time-savers—whether the source of the waste is your boss, your team members, your peers, or the system.

We'll look at cooperating with others on time-savers first and then at effective ways to handle workflow, interruptions, the telephone, paperwork, and travel time. Finally, we'll cover procrastination, which is especially common, and deadly, to large, complex projects that tend to be rather overwhelming.

Cooperating with Others on Time Management

Your best efforts at managing your time effectively can be sabotaged by your boss, work team, and peers. It is up to you to use Murphy's Law (Chapter 11) in order to foresee and circumvent as many obstacles as possible.

Your Boss   If your boss pushes you to complete an item that is low on your priority list, tactfully discuss your conflict rather than meekly complying. Talk in terms of achieving objectives and doing what's best for the boss, the department, and the company. Make sure your boss knows what other items are pending on your "To Do" list and is aware of their impact on your objectives.

If your boss is difficult to find when you need an approval, decision, or information, plan ahead to avoid delays. If that doesn't work, discuss the problem with the boss.

Some bosses don't delegate effectively; others postpone decisions too long. No matter what time-management problem your boss is

creating for you, a tactful, open discussion about the impact of the boss's actions on your productivity is usually the key to improving the situation. Of course you never want to appear critical of your boss's behavior. To avoid the impression of evaluating your boss in a negative fashion, take a problem-solving approach. Stress the possibilities for improvement of your performance with the boss's help.

Your Work Team   Encourage your team to think about time management and to speak up when you ask them to do things they think are ineffective or time-wasters. Work with them on making the best use of your time and theirs.

You can waste team members' time by communicating instructions poorly or in other ways delegating ineffectively—for example, when you don't select the right job for the right person or don't train the person properly. When you keep them waiting, you are wasting their time and the company's money. Be prompt for appointments and meetings. If you see that you're going to be late, let them know so they can be using their time constructively until you *are* ready to see them.

Be sure that you don't interrupt people's work unnecessarily. Ask yourself: "Is this interruption really necessary, or could it wait?" "Could I ask this person to drop by when he reaches a stopping point?" "Could she call me?" "Could an assistant or receptionist give this person the message during a break?"

That Special Team Member: Your Assistant The most important team member, so far as helping you manage your time is concerned, is your assistant or secretary. The first step in using this asset is to select an intelligent, well-trained person who approaches the job as a professional. Pay him or her as much as you can. The next step is to *treat* your assistant as a professional who will be working with you as a teammate. Delegate as much of the paperwork and as many of the communications tasks as you can to your assistant. Keep your assistant fully informed so that he or she knows what you would do in most situations.

Upgrade your assistant's duties. Work with him or her to eliminate useless chores and to streamline paperwork. In this way you will free up some valuable administrative talent. Work together to make the best use of it. Set decision-making guidelines and define areas of authority for your assistant. Inform others of these developments and instruct them to co-operate with your assistant.

Keep your assistant's workflow in mind as you plan and execute yours. Some managers sit on their paperwork all day and then dump it on their assistant late in the afternoon. That practice can be harmless *unless* you expect to have it all handled before quitting time.

Remember that work variety is important, and that assistants can suffer from mental fatigue and boredom. Help your assistant have variety in the course of a day, week, and month. Be sure your assignments provide adequate challenge and opportunity for growth. Your assistant will probably respond by working more efficiently and effectively. It pays, therefore, to work out a pattern of assignments that meets both your needs and your assistant's needs.

Keep your assistant informed about your priorities. Assign priority numbers to tasks you give your assistant, or have him or her rank the items after checking your "To Do" list. Prioritizing avoids the overwhelming effect of dumping work in a heap on your assistant's desk. It lets your assistant know which tasks to tackle first even when you assign a large number of tasks at one time.

Work together. Work with your assistant to devise procedures for screening calls, visitors, and mail. For example, some managers enlist their assistant's help in bringing appointments to a close: When someone is scheduled to see you in your office, decide how much time you want to allot to the meeting, and tell your assistant to call you when the time is up. Respond in a way that clearly indicates to your visitor that the meeting will have to end.

Keeping your desk organized can also be a joint project. One way to work together on this is to have a couple of "Do Not Disturb" paperweights. Your assistant can then be authorized to straighten or clear anything that doesn't have one of the signs on it. He or she can keep you organized in other ways, too. For example, your assistant can suggest items for your "To Do" list, help you monitor the progress of projects, and handle the follow-up on actions delegated to other team members at staff meetings. Here are some additional time-saving practices that require working cooperatively.

Be prepared for work sessions to avoid delays, searches, and changes.

Every time you leave your office, let your assistant know where you're going and when you'll return.

Ask for suggestions on how you can help your assistant be more effective.

Give your assistant feedback, professional development, support, decision-making autonomy, and recognition.

Work together to follow up with information and decisions others have requested of you.

Your Peers   The heads of other units or departments in your company can create all sorts of bottlenecks and delays in your plans. It's up to you to foresee and prevent as many of these problems as possible. When you are discussing the need for action with a peer, stress how the completion of the task in question helps achieve a specific objective. Tie the objective in with an organizational objective that your peer is committed to. In other words, find a common goal in order to motivate your colleague to cooperate more fully.

Here are additional techniques for eliminating time-wasters in your dealings with peers (as well as with team members and others) in meetings and discussions.

Set a closing time for all meetings and keep them as short as possible.

Consider scheduling meetings just before noon so that everyone will leave for lunch at the appointed time.

When you want to end an informal discussion, simply push back your chair, stand up, and start walking slowly toward the door as you end the discussion.

When someone drops by your office unannounced and you don't have time for a visit, stand up and remain standing as you talk. This signals that the conversation will have to be brief and prevents a "settling in" for a long session.

If you don't have time for a discussion in your office, but you want to at least acknowledge someone, walk out of your office and talk with the person on his or her way down the hall.

Improving Workflow

Sometimes the source of time-wasters — and a fertile area for finding time-savers — lies in the workflow system rather than in the people you deal with. To improve the workflow to, within, and from your unit, the first step is to work out regular times for doing *your* routine or recurring tasks so others can adjust *their* workflow, timing of calls, and other contacts with you accordingly.

Next, analyze routine tasks to see which ones (yours and your team members) can be performed more effectively so that workflow is improved. Do this by breaking down the tasks into steps and then concentrating on all aspects of each step, searching for alternative ways of handling each one.

Obviously the tasks that occupy the most time offer the most opportunity for real breakthroughs in time savings. So look first for problem areas where you can get the highest possible return on the time you invest in analysis and improvement. Focus more on what can be improved than on what is being done wrong. See whether you can make even small changes that will have big results. If you can, your motivation — and your workers' — to continue working toward improvement will be boosted.

Here are suggestions for finding *breakthrough problem areas*.

1. Develop a specific objective for the improvement; state it in measurable terms.

2. Start with the bottom line and work backward. For example, start with profits, items produced, costs, savings, or some other measure of effectiveness. Then work backward until you find an activity that controls or significantly affects this measure of effectiveness in some way.

3. If you come up with several ideas for change, look for the one that requires the least change, effort, cost, or lead time. The easiest, smallest changes are often the best, especially to begin with, unless there is a basic flaw in the entire system or procedure.

4. Before focusing on special tasks, look at repeated routine tasks, which offer greater opportunity for savings. The most typical types of problems to look for include:

Bottlenecks: A person, task, or spot that creates delays in other people's work by backing up everything that precedes it, holding up everything that follows it, or both. Do a separate study of each delay to find out why it's happening and how it can be corrected.

Time-consumers: Tasks that take a long time to finish.

Run-abouts: Tasks that involve a great deal of dashing around or flurries of phone calls and paperwork.

Hidden time-wasters: These are the most difficult problems to identify because the scene *appears* productive and people *seem* extremely busy. Remember, however, that well-organized tasks create a minimum of fuss and bother. Therefore, be suspicious of too much hustle and bustle. Ask, "Are the *right* things being done?"

Exercise 4-2 gives you an opportunity to analyze a workflow problem in your organization.

As you make your analysis, be sure to include the people involved in each step. Ask them for their ideas and suggestions for improvement. It is a good idea to ask for input even on your own workflow problems—the ones that you create. Sometimes we are blind to solutions that an outsider can readily see; we are just too close to the problem. You may benefit by stepping aside and letting someone else take a look.

EXERCISE 4-2: ANALYZING WORKFLOW PROBLEMS

Identify a job or task in your organization (or any personal task); then analyze it step by step, listing each step in sequence. Ask yourself why each step is necessary. Begin with the performance steps because if you can eliminate any of them, you'll probably automatically eliminate some planning and follow-up steps. Next ask yourself what else could be done that might give you the same or even better results. To further analyze each step, see the suggestions that follow.

Job: _____

Job Step	*Why Is It Done?*	*What Else Could Be Done Instead?*
	Performance Steps	
1 _____	_____	_____
2 _____	_____	_____
	Planning Steps	
1 _____	_____	_____
2 _____	_____	_____
	Follow-Up Steps	
1 _____	_____	_____
2 _____	_____	_____

Were you able to eliminate or change any steps in the job you selected for Exercise 4-2? Now look at the performance steps that are left. Ask some "where, when, who, and how" questions for each one. Follow each question with a "why" question and a question that searches for alternatives.

The sequence in which you ask the questions is important. How the task is done should *not* be the first question. Changing the location, time, or person doing a task can be a great deal easier and simpler than coming up with an improved method for doing it. Therefore, the answer to the where, when, and who questions may eliminate the need for the how question. Here are specific questions about each step.

1. Where is this task being done? Why there? Where else can it be done as well?

2. When is it done? What is the timing and sequence of the actions taken? Why then? What other time could it be done as well?

3. Who does it? What individual, group, or classification of persons has responsibility? Why is it done by them? Who else could do it as well?

4. How is it done? Why that way? How else could it be done as well?

As you search for ways to overcome workflow problems, it's important to deal with facts; look for causes; look for reasons, not excuses; and make the activity a team effort. As you look for improved methods of completing jobs (the "how"), you might decide to

Eliminate steps. Ask, "What would happen if we didn't do this?"

Combine steps to consolidate time, space, or people.

Rearrange the sequence of steps. Identify steps that can be done at other times or at any time. This will show where your flexibility lies.

Simplify steps. Can an existing step be simplified? If you come up with a *new* method, ask yourself, "Is each step in the new procedure done as simply and easily as possible?"

When you are ready to try out your improved procedures, approach, or system, continue to involve those who will carry out the plan.

Minimizing Interruptions

A common complaint of new managers is that they can't find time to work on high-priority projects because of constant interruptions. Finding large blocks of uninterrupted concentration time can be a real time-saver. It takes ten minutes for most of us to get deeply focused on a task that requires our full attention and intense concentration, and we can sustain this concentration for twenty minutes or so. After that, most of us take a break of some kind. Therefore, when your top-priority activity requires concentration, you may find yourself actually spending about half of your time on getting into the task, resting, switching to lower-priority items, and so forth. If you can build up your concentration span from twenty minutes to forty minutes, you get a real bonus in prime productive time. So time yourself and see whether you can stick it out for a few more minutes each time.

As you learn to concentrate for longer periods, you may find that you can focus in much faster and feel less tired when you are done. As a matter of fact, for most people one hour of continuous concentration on a project usually yields better results than two hours spent in ten- to twenty-minute work sessions. Eventually you may be able to concentrate for as long as three hours, if necessary, with only a ten-minute break each hour.

To make the best use of your concentration time, then, you must have at least one-hour blocks when you are free from interruptions. Nothing is more tiring and frustrating than handling continual interruptions when you are attempting to concentrate on a task. It's especially important to have a quiet time when you are faced with a high-priority project that is rather large or complex. You can accomplish this by establishing a daily **quiet hour** and by using other techniques for minimizing interruptions, such as scheduling "open-door" times and screening telephone calls.

The Quiet Hour   The key to minimizing interruptions during times when you need to concentrate is to establish a quiet hour in your schedule. During this time, have your assistant hold all your calls and tell visitors that you are unavailable. If you don't have an assistant and you can't stand ringing telephones, devise some way to keep your phones from ringing and people from knocking on your door. Put a sign on your door saying "Quiet Time" and perhaps the time when you will be available again. Alternatively, you might install a schedule board outside your door showing times when you will meet with people and times when you will be unavailable.

If you are convinced that the quiet hour is valuable and indeed necessary, you will probably be able to convince your boss and team members to respect it. In fact, you may able to institute a quiet hour throughout the unit, department, or company that might follow these procedures: During this hour no phone calls are put through, no visitors are admitted, and there is no unnecessary talking or moving about. Management teams can meet and concentrate on tasks and people can focus on individual tasks. Encourage your people to plan, get organized, dream up new projects or new solutions to problems, or concentrate on their single most important task of the day. During the quiet hour the clerical and secretarial peo-

ple can put their work in order, catch up on paperwork, and intercept stray phone calls and visits to their bosses.

If the quiet hour is the first hour of the day, the effect on customers is no more drastic than if office hours were 9 to 5 instead of 8 to 5. If you *do* institute a quiet hour for everyone, remember to renew commitment to it periodically. Otherwise "exceptions to the quiet hour rule" tend to increase until the quiet hour eventually becomes like any other hour.

Other Techniques   In addition to the quiet hour, you can try a number of other techniques for keeping interruptions to a minimum. An **open-door policy,** for example, reflects a willingness to listen to team members' ideas and problems and an openness to accepting and trying out their suggestions. If you take it too literally, however, you're likely to sabotage your own efforts to improve your productivity by inviting constant interruptions. To forestall that problem you can (1) require your people to schedule the times they will meet with you, (2) have them hold less-urgent matters until you can visit them, or (3) have them hold most matters for regularly scheduled meetings.

Let people know what times you prefer to be available. This approach doesn't necessarily violate the concept of an open-door policy, and it allows you to set aside large blocks of time in the morning and afternoon to concentrate without interruption. An added bonus is that during the waiting period workers often figure out solutions to problems on their own.

Placing a barrier in front of your office door can help prevent constant interruptions. Some possible "protectors" are your assistant's desk, a screen, or a table. Closing your office door at least part of the way also helps discourage people's tendency to interrupt.

Avoid needless communication by analyzing your company's communication system. Are appropriate people informed in advance of changes, events, and other matters so they don't need to call you for the information? Is the company's telephone directory clear, accurate, and current so you needn't spend time redirecting calls? To further minimize telephone interruptions, either have your assistant screen your calls, or simply say, "I'm busy (or tied up) now. May I call you back at eleven?"

If all else fails, when you must concentrate on a project without interruption, trade offices with someone else, find a quiet spot in the company or public library, or even consider working at home.

Taming the Telephone

Your telephone can either be a time-saver or a time-waster, depending on how you use it. Analyze the purpose and pattern of your calls. When you need to communicate with someone, take a moment to reflect on the advantages and disadvantages of doing so by telephone, face-to-face meeting, or written message. Is your purpose to discuss (1) detailed items that you need to confirm in writing anyway, (2) complex items that the receiver will have to think about before giving you a firm reply, (3) important items that require approval at several levels? Will a phone call now really do any good? If it will, then have your points and all materials at hand *before* you dial.

Bunch your telephone calls by making several calls during one time period. This leaves blocks of time when you can be uninterrupted.

Decide on a policy about being put on hold. Either avoid it and call back, or keep your file of quick tasks handy so you can keep busy while you're waiting.

Consider using special telephone equipment and arrangements, such as a speaker phone or a shoulder rest that leaves your hands free to handle files and perform other tasks. A telephone headset with a long cord frees your hands and still maintains your privacy. An automatic dial system for frequently called num-

bers also saves time. A telephone charge card for calls made away from the office can be handy. You don't have to worry about finding change for calls, and you'll get a record of all calls made with your card.

When your business is over with, get off the phone. Practice the quick ending: "I'll let you get back to your business." "Well, thanks so much. I must dash to a meeting now." "Fine. If we've covered everything, I'll let you go and get back to you later."

Analyze the pattern of both incoming and outgoing calls for a while to see which types can be eliminated through delegation, rerouting of written notices, screening, or other methods. Streamline incoming calls by finding out what a caller wants as soon as possible. Ask probing questions tactfully or say, "What can I do for you?"

Streamlining Paperwork

Now you know how to sidestep the worst hazards of the telephone. It's time to face a similar danger—becoming swamped in paperwork. Many articles and books have been written about handling the "paper explosion" and avoiding paper-pushing all day. The less paperwork an organization produces, the more effective its planning system is likely to be. When people are preoccupied with documenting actions, they spend less thought and energy on actually doing the things that contribute most to achieving specific objectives. Here's where working closely with your assistant can really pay off. Ask for suggestions.

The first step in streamlining paperwork is to work out a plan for minimizing and organizing the flow of paper. Establish procedures for sorting and handling your mail effectively. Experiment until you find the best procedures for your situation. Then stick with your plan until and unless you come up with something better. Minimize both the time you spend writing letters, reports, and other documents, and the number of papers you file. Organize your files so that you can make the best use of them.

The second step is a part of your plan. As a daily practice, make this your goal: Once your incoming mail is sorted, *handle each piece of paper only once.* This is a goal, of course, not a rigid rule. But if you haven't tried it, you may be surprised at how seldom you really need to violate it.

Handling Your Mail Effectively   A workable system for sorting and handling mail is a prerequisite to handling each piece of paper only once. You or your assistant divide mail into categories that work best for you. Here are some categories to consider.

Immediate action — high priority

Pending action — high priority (needs research, consultation, or approval)

Can be done later — low priority

To read later, file, or distribute

Throw away

Of course you judge the priority of each piece of mail according to how it fits in with your objectives and the activities designed to achieve them. Remember to give low-priority items an aging period because the need for many of them may disappear.

One of the most common sources of poor time management is the practice of working on low-priority items just because they seem to be immediate, demanding, easy, or short. At times the only high-priority tasks you have are either difficult or time consuming. Nevertheless, it's generally more productive to keep chipping away at large, high-priority tasks than to sail through low-priority ones. (Later in this chapter we'll discuss ways of breaking down large projects into quick tasks or manageable tasks.)

Train your assistant to handle as much of the mail as possible without your needing to see it. For the things you do read yourself, try using a four-color pen so you can signal by color the type of action your assistant should take on an item. One executive uses this system: When she uses red ink to jot a note on a piece of mail or related item, her assistant knows he must complete the instructed action himself. A note in green signals him to type an item, blue to file it, and black to route it to the person noted. Such color coding lets you avoid the time-waster of writing the same instructions over and over.

Streamlining Your Correspondence Procedures   Writing letters and reports in minimal time is also an integral part of handling each piece of paper only once. Use dictation equipment for most letters and reports. Dictate from a *brief* outline of points you want to cover. To make retyping unnecessary, include information about format, stationery, and number of copies needed at the *beginning* of each dictated item, and learn to make corrections on the tape properly.

Consider using form letters, preprinted cards, and form paragraphs. You and your assistant can keep a file of well-worded, numbered paragraphs. Then simply dictate the paragraph numbers and any other necessary information. If you have access to a word-processor, you can have the paragraphs stored and reprinted electronically. For many messages, of course, you can simply dictate key ideas and let your assistant compose the letter or memo.

Look for other ways to simplify your correspondence. On the bottom portions of the letters you receive, write short replies or have longer ones typed. If you need a copy of the transaction, have one made on the copy machine. Try speed forms for the correspondence you initiate; they provide a place at the bottom for quick replies. Use simplified formats for letters, memos, reports, and forms. Post bulletins for general-interest messages rather than making copies and routing them. Make changes and corrections on the carbon copies of your letters so that only the original needs to be retyped. Make creative use of new pre-inked rubber stamps for reducing writing and typing time.

Streamline reports by developing standard procedures for authorizing and auditing new forms and periodic reports. The procedures should provide a double-check for duplication of effort, real need, and distribution lists. Can some reports be combined? Can routine reports be computerized?

Keeping Lean Files   The third aspect of handling each piece of paper once is minimizing and organizing the papers you file. Always ask, "What are the probabilities of our ever needing this piece of paper again? If we eventually need some information it contains, could we get it elsewhere? What would happen if we didn't have a written record of it?"

Many people ask, "Could we possibly need this ever again?" In other words, they retain records on the basis of *possibilities* — remote possibilities — rather than on the basis of *probabilities.* Even if it might be handy to have an item in the file at some future time, the item may be relatively unimportant and the consequences of producing or not producing it may be trivial. Meanwhile, the item is adding to the clutter in your files, and you must contend with this growing profusion of paper every day. So think in terms of high priorities and probabilities and dump papers that don't measure up.

Avoid dealing with needless paper by asking to have your name removed from mailing lists and routing slips for materials that have little or no value to you. Don't file (1) memos that are routine and are on file somewhere else in the company, (2) announcements of meetings, (3) directives that have since been revised, or (4) company newsletters, minutes, announce-

ments, and other material that's on file elsewhere. It's been estimated that about 75 percent of the items in most files should have been thrown away. Be ruthless in throwing out papers, and you will avoid crowded files, a messy desk, an overworked assistant, and a confused mind.

Finally, experiment to find the filing system that works best for you. Your system might include such categories as "tickler," "current projects," "to read," "creativity," and "travel," as well as a general file.

A *tickler file* is kept handy to remind you to initiate or follow up on transactions. It consists of day folders numbered 1 through 31, for each day of the month. In the appropriate day's folder for the current month, you place letters, memos, reminders, notes, reports, and other items that you want to handle on that day and that do not need to be placed in some other file. You might also need folders labeled for each month of the year, which you'll review on the first day of each month, and folders labeled for each of the next several years, which you'll review at the beginning of each year. On the first day of each month, file all the items from that month's folder into the day folders. Then each January the items in that year's file are placed in the appropriate monthly folders.

Your tickler file can supplement the "To Do" sheets you dated ahead and jotted reminders on. Each afternoon when you work on your "To Do" list for the next day, pull the tickler file folder for the following day. You can think of it now as your "Do Today" folder that keeps all those notes and papers organized and off your desk.

A *current projects file* should also be within easy reach. It consists of file folders that contain the working papers, correspondence, reports, ideas, and plans for all projects you and your team members are currently working on. If you set up your folders well, you can easily and quickly clear your desk of all paper and still have everything at your fingertips. In fact, you will find it easier to lay your hands on an item at any one time than if you have stacks and piles of papers all over the place.

Create as many new folders for each project as you need, but categorize and title them in ways that are meaningful to you and work for you. You can put notes about priorities, starting dates, and deadlines for the projects in your tickler file or on your "To Do" list, depending on their length and detail.

A *"to read" file* is a handy place to group and store all the journal articles, reports, book summaries, newspaper items, and other information you need currently or will need in the future. Categorize the file according to subjects that interest you. For example, an accountant who works for a computer company and is involved in professional accounting associations might be interested in such subjects as tax law, accounting associations, computer technology, and standard accounting practices.

To make the best use of your "to read" file, have your assistant scan the tables of contents of books and journals, checking articles or chapters you might be interested in. She or he might even read certain items, marking important passages so that you can scan them quickly later. Have your assistant prepare a "reading record," a sheet for recording all items as they are placed in the "to read" file. Figure 4-2 is an example of how a reading record can be set up.

FIGURE 4-2: Example of a Reading Record

	READING RECORD							
Item No.	Source	Tax Law	Acctg. Assn.	Standard Acctg. Practice	Computer Tech.	Reports	Other	
1	The Accountant, June 10, p. 22	✔		✔				
2	Computing Newsletter, June 17, p. 43				✔			
3	CPA Journal, July 5, p. 67		✔	✔				
4	Jones Audit Report					✔		
5	Fortune, July 12, p. 105						Motivation	

The subject columns of your reading record become the subjects of your "to read" file folders. Each article placed in a folder and each journal and book placed in a box or on a bookshelf is recorded on the reading record sheet and is numbered sequentially. This identifying number is also written on the book, journal, or article so that it's easy to spot. The subject(s) the item refers to are checked in the appropriate subject column(s) of the reading record. This record is a handy reference of sources for projects, speeches, reports, or other assignments. Refer to it also when you want to quickly pull items for your briefcase — to have on hand for dead-time reading or a business trip.

A *creativity file* is a handy place to store new ideas for projects and improvements, future plans and goals, and other ideas, hopes, and dreams. We've stressed the importance of keeping pad and pen handy for jotting down ideas wherever they occur. Record all ideas and drop them into your creativity file. You may want to categorize them by subject matter, by project, or by more general categories such as "ideas," "plans," and "projects." You may also want folders that indicate a stage of development, such as "rough ideas," "developing ideas," and "refined ideas."

A *travel file* can be a great help if you travel often in your job. You might have a file folder for each location you regularly visit or anticipate visiting. Put into these folders items concerning people to see; information to gather or check on; information about plane, train, rental car, limousine, and other transportation services; tips on good hotels, restaurants, and entertainment; and any other information that might be helpful. Also, for each business trip prepare a file folder, such as "Boston trip — June 10." Keep it handy and as you receive your plane tickets, hotel confirmations, phone numbers, contracts, and other working papers, put them in it. By the time you leave, everything you need will be accumulated in your trip folder. This habit helps prevent leaving important items behind.

The *general file* is where you store everything else. You may categorize by subject, alphabet, geographical locations, number, or any combination of these. You and your assistant can devise the system that works best for you.

Finally, just as important as a system for categorizing and arranging items in files is developing a workable system for periodically removing from the files items with a low probability of being needed again. If space is limited, you may need to have an active general file and an inactive general file. Items should be periodically removed from the active file and placed in a less accessible inactive file. These items are usually kept for legal or tax reasons and shouldn't clutter prime filing space.

Organizing Travel Time

Telephoning and paperwork are time-consuming activities that all managers must control. For those managers who frequently travel, conserving their time and energy on the road is also a major time-management consideration. We've already discussed some ways to save travel time — by using conference calls and by keeping trip files, for example. Look for additional ways you can handle business in other cities without spending your precious time and energy in airports and taxis. At times, of course, there's no substitute for an in-person appearance. The more frequently you must travel, the more important it is to make the most of your travel time.

Packing Let's begin with packing. Stay partially packed all the time. Keep extra toiletries, medication, first-aid items, business cards, and other trip items in a bag at home. Some people include a travel hair dryer, special high-steam iron, and heating rod for boiling water.

Travel Agent   Next, get a good travel agent if your company doesn't already have one. Air fares are so complicated these days that even professional travel agents have difficulty keeping track of them. Because of their daily contact with the airlines, agents can usually get you a better deal and can do it quickly and efficiently. It costs you nothing and saves your time as well as your assistant's time.

Airline Clubs   If you travel often, consider joining one or more airline clubs. Some of the benefits may be

Access to a members-only lounge at most airports, which includes telephones and free local calls, free coffee, peace and quiet, and sometimes meeting rooms, free drinks, free continental breakfast, color TV, and other amenities

The airline's special telephone numbers for preferred customers (You can get through on these unlisted numbers even when the airline's other lines are busy.)

Special check-in privileges with no waiting in line

Hotel and car rental discounts

Check-cashing privileges

Car Rental Agencies   Consider opening business accounts with a couple of car rental agencies. You can negotiate a significant business discount, so shop around. Rental agencies with offices some distance from airports are frequently less expensive. It's a good idea to reserve your car ahead, especially if you are arriving on a weekend in a popular resort area. Also, during the fall months there are usually fewer cars available as agencies reduce their inventories and get ready to buy new models.

Itinerary   Be sure to leave a detailed itinerary with appropriate people so important messages can reach you. If you subscribe to an itinerary service, you can call in for messages at any time of the day or night. You give a special toll-free number to people who might need to call you. Also, some hotels will rent you a beeper so that you can immediately get messages left at the hotel desk. You don't have to keep calling the hotel to check for messages or wait in your room for calls to come through.

Notebook   A pocket-sized loose-leaf notebook or computer for your appointments, brief "To Do" lists, and other notes is a great organizer.

When it's time to go, you'll need to spend minimal preparation time if you have kept a trip file, your other files are in order, your bag is partially packed, and your pocket notebook is current. Of course, you can use part of your flight time to work on tasks. Rank them in order of priority just as you do in the office.

Pace Yourself   Last but not least make plans to pace yourself and to manage the stress that travel creates. Plan for extra rest on the first evening you arrive, especially if you take a two-hour or longer flight. Many people become ill immediately after they return from business trips. The reason is frequently fatigue, even though the traveler may not feel tired. Take steps to prevent illness by getting extra rest, even though you're full of nervous energy.

Don't try to pack too much into one trip. Decide what's most important and allow enough time to accomplish it, including time to rest and relax. Usually three major meetings a day are the most you can expect to handle well. After that, you will probably lose your ability to concentrate and perform well. Also, allow plenty of time to get from one place to another. Ask local people about distances and traffic patterns, and then estimate travel time within an area.

AVOIDING PROCRASTINATION IN TACKLING LARGE PROJECTS

Now you have the tools for managing your time on a day-to-day basis. Before you assume that your time problems are licked, however, you must face the question of how effectively you complete the large projects that are essential to achieving some of your major objectives. One of the problems with working on big projects—and one of the reasons people procrastinate on them—is the feeling of leaving loose ends after a work session on the project. Yet the project is much too big to finish in one time block. Here are some ways to overcome that problem.

Organizing Projects into Manageable Segments

First, be clear about specific objectives to be achieved through completion of the project, and write them down. Next, break the project up into major segments. Do this as soon as you receive the assignment (or conceive of it), and do it in writing. Block the project into tasks you can complete in one work session. Making a written plan helps you tackle each segment with minimal time-loss from building up momentum again, retracing steps, reviewing what you've done, and getting your thoughts and materials in order.

When you start a task, finish it. Savor the moment by congratulating yourself and taking time to enjoy the satisfaction of having completed that part of the project. This helps reinforce a sense of closure each time you work on it. Also consider rewarding yourself in other appropriate ways.

If you must leave a task uncompleted, note the next step so you won't waste time when you come back to it. Once you start a major project, be sure to keep working on the segments until you finish the project. Avoid having too many large projects going at once. If you accumulate a backlog of partially finished projects, it becomes more and more difficult to finish any of them and to have a sense of satisfaction and closure.

Figure 4-3 presents a format for planning large, complex projects. After you break the project down into major segments and the manageable tasks involved in each segment from start to finish, determine which tasks can be delegated. Then estimate how long each task will take. (Consider doubling that estimate to give yourself plenty of lead time and to build in flexibility.) Which tasks can be overlapped or done simultaneously? List starting dates and target completion dates. Put these dates on your "To Do" list daily calendar sheets as reminders of when to begin, assign, follow up, or complete each task. Finally, note the date each task is actually completed on your planning sheet.

Identifying Quick Tasks

If you have trouble getting started on a major segment of the project, look for "quick tasks" that can be done in five minutes or so. Quick tasks are great for getting overwhelming projects underway. To set the wheels in motion, try tactics such as these:

Contact someone to get information that you need.

Spend a few minutes planning some procedures for the project.

Set up a simple filing system for the project.

Do some reading that will be helpful.

Locate some sources of information or material.

After you have completed a few quick tasks, you may find yourself being pulled into the

FIGURE 4-3: Planning Sheet for Large, Complex Projects

Major Segments	Tasks	Do Myself or Delegate	Estimated Time for Completion	Starting Date	Target Completion Date	Actual Completion Date

Project _____   Objectives _____

project. Completing the tasks tends to generate interest and involvement and to build momentum.

Using Other Techniques

If you find yourself still procrastinating, try some other techniques.

Do the most unpleasant task first, if possible. Get it out of the way so you don't waste energy "doing it in your head over and over." Congratulate yourself for getting it done. Notice the light, satisfied feeling you get from completing the task and take time to enjoy that feeling. If you give yourself this positive reinforcement, you'll soon get in the habit of getting necessary unpleasant tasks done fast.

Take advantage of your current mood. Keep returning to the project in your mind. Keep asking yourself, "What am I especially in the mood to do today that could move the project along?"

List the advantages and disadvantages of starting now. You'll usually see that the disadvantages are trivial and the advantages significant. This can quickly boost you into action.

Analyze your motives. If these direct techniques aren't working, maybe you need to delve deeper. Perhaps fear of failure or fear of success is blocking you. Are you afraid of succeeding at the project? Women frequently *do* fear the changes in their lives that accompany success in a career. Look deep within. If that's your problem, ask yourself, "What's the worst that can happen?" You will probably realize either that your fears of the worst are absurd or that you *can* face the worst and handle it comfortably.

Are you afraid of failing at the project if you start it? If so, remind yourself that if you give it a good try, you may succeed; but if you don't, you guarantee failure. If you do your best and it's not good enough, you can at least learn from your mistakes. Studies show that people who work toward success are happier and accomplish more than those who fear (and therefore expect) failure. Everyone who makes it to the top experiences some failure along the way. It's what they do with that failure—the lessons they learn from it—that makes them winners.

SUMMARY

Your attitude toward time is the most important aspect of time management. Time is money. When your time and your team members' time is being wasted, the dollars the company pays in salary are also being wasted. Wasted time can also mean costly delays or lost opportunities to make money. Major attitudinal keys to time management include constructive attitudes toward delegating, balancing tasks and projects (the ability to focus on one task at a time even though you may have many irons in the fire), and using body time productively (scheduling your day to make best use of your energy, sociability, and charisma levels as well as your preferred work pace).

Another key is the ability to overcome nonproductive parent messages about what you *should* do and to provide yourself with small rewards for completing tasks, meeting deadlines, weeding out time-wasters, and discovering time-savers. Your attitude toward time management is also affected by your internal and external environment—your ability to eliminate or rise above minor depressants and irritants in your life, to say "no," and to arrange a pleasant, practical physical work space.

Using your objectives and priorities to direct your energy is the key to actually making the most of your time. Your goal is to focus on doing the right things at the right time, rather than merely working hard and doing things correctly and efficiently. This means making a daily "To Do" list of tasks that lead to achievement of your top-priority objectives.

Cooperating with others on time management can help you eliminate time-wasters and discover time-savers that others create in your workday. It also includes helping your boss, team members, and peers make the best use of their time. Getting your boss to practice more effective time management calls for tact; however, if you stress the good of the company in your discussions, your suggestions will probably be accepted.

Your greatest opportunity to influence others' time management practices, of course, is in dealing with team members. The way you handle *your* time makes the greatest impact because it sets a noticeable example; it's also important to respect their time. The person who can help you the most in your time-management efforts is your assistant. Treat your assistant as a professional, keep him or her informed about your priorities, listen to his or her suggestions, and work with your assistant as a teammate in keeping your desk, your calls, your correspondence, your calendar, and *you* organized.

Your peers can create all sorts of bottlenecks and delays in your plans. Therefore, when you are discussing the need for action with a peer, stress how the completion of the task in question helps achieve a specific objective. Tie the objective in with an organizational objective that the peer is committed to helping achieve. Be businesslike in your dealings with peers to avoid wasting time in needless chatter.

Improving workflow, both yours and your teammates', can pay off in big time-saving benefits. Working out regular times for handling recurring tasks is a first step in improving workflow. Analyzing routine tasks to see which ones can be performed more effectively so that workflow is improved is next. Look for typical barriers — bottlenecks, time-consumers, run-abouts, and hidden time-wasters.

Minimizing interruptions is essential if you are to make the best use of your concentration time. You need at least a one-hour block of uninterrupted time when working on complex projects. The solution is to establish a "quiet hour" in your schedule. Other techniques include scheduling meetings with teammates and others for certain times of the day, informing others of your work patterns so that they'll know when to contact you without needless interruption, working with your assistant to screen calls and visitors, and maintaining a businesslike manner.

Telephoning can help you save time, or it can be one of your worst time-wasters. Analyze the best way to handle a communication. Prepare adequately for placing calls. Bunch calls to eliminate unnecessary interruptions. Have your calls screened when you need uninterrupted time. And be businesslike and to the point when making telephone calls.

Streamlining paperwork is essential to avoid becoming swamped in the "paper explosion." Start by sorting your mail by priority (or having your assistant sort it). Keep in mind that your goal is to handle each piece of paper only once. Learn to use dictation equipment for most of your letters and reports, and use it correctly in order to save your assistant's time. Do everything you can to cut down on paperwork and files and to keep them out of sight. One way to organize current paperwork is to keep special files, such as a tickler file, a current projects file, a "to read" file, a creativity file, and a travel file. Everything else goes into the general file, which should be categorized in the way that works best for you and your assistant. Finally, develop a workable system for periodically cleaning out the files.

You can plan your travel time to make the most of it. First, look for ways you can handle your business in another city *without* having to be there in person. Then keep a bag partially packed with essentials you use over and over on your trips. Use a good travel agent and appropriate credit and membership cards. Leave a detailed itinerary so your office can get in touch with you. Take a pocket-sized loose-leaf notebook or computer for your appointments, "To Do" lists, and other essential notes. Protect your health by getting plenty of rest and pacing yourself properly. Use the time en route to accomplish some of your tasks, but don't overdo.

You can overcome procrastination and complete large, complex projects by first breaking them down into manageable segments. Give yourself an appropriate reward each time you complete a segment, and build in as much pleasure and satisfaction as you can. Remember to identify quick tasks that can be done in five minutes or so to help you get started and to build momentum.

REFERENCES

1. Bliss, Edwin C. *Getting Things Done.* New York: Scribner's, 1980. An excellent resource for managing your time and producing results.

2. Davis, Shirley E. *The Confident Traveler.* Littleton, Col.: Shiro Publications, 1988. The author claims this is a complete travel guide for the business woman.

3. *EXECU*TIME,* a monthly newsletter published by MRH Associates, P.O. Box 11318, Newington, Conn. 06111. This is an excellent source of ideas for making the most of your time.

4. Lakein, Alan. *How to Get Control of Your Time and Life.* New York: McKay, 1989. This is perhaps the most widely used source for time-management techniques. Lakein, a former Harvard professor, has done extensive business consulting.

5. MacKenzie, Alec, and Kay Waldo. *About Time: A Woman's Guide to Managing Time.* New York: McGraw-Hill, 1981. This book addresses the special time demands and constraints that working women experience.

Chapter Five

Empowering Yourself: Managing Stress

"For fast-acting relief, try slowing down."
Lily Tomlin

The leader's job is a demanding one, especially when you are aiming for visibility and promotion. It requires a high level of health and well-being and an ability to command your inner resources. Some of the leaders who fall by the wayside simply don't have the stamina or resources to stay in the running. They can't cope with the stress. Others keep running at high speed until they literally drop dead. Women leaders are not immune to the stress-related illnesses that plague male leaders. In fact, recent research indicates that women managers report higher stress levels than male managers, but most are able to manage it better. In this chapter you will have the opportunity to learn more about

1. The nature and impact of stress

2. Strategies for preventing and minimizing stressful situations, including taking responsibility for your own health

3. Empowering yourself by tapping your inner resources through deep relaxation, visualization of desired states, and **letting go** of anxiety

4. Making the most of your sleeping hours to empower yourself and minimize stress

5. Turning negative criticism into a positive or neutral experience

6. Redirecting emotional energy into constructive channels

7. Experiencing feelings without acting them out

 Getting Stress Under Control

Jan pulls Erika's résumé from her briefcase. "Erika, I'm glad you brought your new résumé to me first. I went over it last night. You're doing a great job as my assistant, and I don't want the company to lose your talents. If you'll stick with us, I'm sure the right type of position will open up before long. When it does, I'll recommend you for promotion."

Erika smiles. "That's wonderful, Jan. I like Lighthouse, and I've learned so much from you. I would rather work here than any place I know—as long as the company has a place for me where I can keep learning and progressing."

Jan picks up a thick folder labeled *Harbor Point*. "Let's start a new phase of your learning process now — with some on-the-job training. Would you like to take over the Harbor Point sportswear line? That would mean responsibility for all aspects of it. Of course, I'll work with you at first, and I'll be here any time you really need me."

"That's my favorite line! I think Julio's preliminary drawings for next spring are smashing. I already have a couple of ideas . . ."

Six weeks later, at one of their regular coaching sessions, Erika talks to Jan about the stress that's been building up since she took on the Harbor Point line. "Jan, I think I'm successfully handling the various aspects of the job, and I generally feel good about my interactions with people."

"I sense a 'but' coming up," Jan responds.

"Yes. Well, it's not any one thing, but the accumulation of deadlines, problems caused by mistakes my team members make, and miscellaneous pressures. Some of them are beginning to knock me off balance. For example, you know Tom Jenson, the Production Manager? Well, the other day he barged into my office waving a handful of orders . . ."

T: Kerr! Don't you ever learn? I've told you we've got to have at least nine weeks' lead time on orders for new styles of sweaters. Your people are promising delivery in six to eight weeks in some cases.

E: But it's only been a couple of weeks since you told me that, and I haven't had a chance to meet with the salespeople since then.

T: Only a couple of weeks? That was plenty of time for you to contact your people before they started showing the fall line. Don't you know how to communicate? Haven't you ever heard of memos or the telephone?

E: Of course I have. It's just that I've been so swamped trying to get everything ready for the fall sales campaign . . .

T: Oh, I get it: Other things are more important than cooperating with my department. Well, I'm not going to take the rap for losing these accounts when the orders aren't delivered on time. I'm telling Arguello that if you can't do this job, I think she ought to get someone who can.

E: *(Near tears)* You've picked on everything I've done ever since I took over this line. You've just been waiting for me to slip up so you could pounce on me. Get out of here!

T: As if I didn't have enough problems, now I have to deal with an overly emotional female! Just forget it. I'll take it up with Arguello. *(Walks out)*

"I just fell apart," Erika continues. "I slammed the door shut after him and gave it a hard kick. When I sat down I was shaking with rage. Then I felt the tears coming — along with all these awful physical symptoms: heart pounding, stomach tied in knots, hands and knees trembling, pulse rapid. It was just terrible."

Wrinkling her brow, Jan asks, "Erika, do you have such symptoms often?"

"More and more frequently lately. I love being married, but it seems so difficult to do everything I'm supposed to do since Scott entered my life. I guess it's time I took a look at my priorities."

"Yes. Listen, will you do me a favor? Make a schedule of your typical working day — from the time you get up until you go to sleep again at night. Include all your habits — activities, food, drink, cigarettes, everything, and send it to me. Then I'll get back to you."

Here's the typical day Erika records:

6:30 A.M.: Wake up, often tired and bleary-eyed. Shower, dress, grab a cup of coffee, sweet roll, and a cigarette.

7:15: Start the commute to the office.

8:00: Arrive at the office. Have a second cup of coffee and cigarette. (Coffee and cigarettes throughout the day.)

8:00–12:00 NOON: Handle problems, attend meetings, dictate correspondence, do whatever needs doing — always with too many interruptions, too little time, and too much frantic activity.

12:00–2:00: Continue working if no business luncheon is planned, eating a sandwich at desk. Business luncheons usually include a cocktail or two, then rich food and wine.

2:00–? Continue working. Always find it difficult to find a "stopping place." Rarely leave the office before 6 or 7 P.M., and when I do, usually carry some work home that I just couldn't get around to. It's not unusual to stay until 9 or 10 P.M. to meet deadlines.

Evening: After the commute home, usually need a couple of drinks to unwind. Usually smoke a pack or two of cigarettes a day to help relieve tension. Sometimes have dinner at a restaurant; frequently pop a TV-dinner in the oven or open a few cans or packages for a quick meal. Conversations with Scott usually center around the work day. Scott often gives helpful suggestions, but just as often needs advice on his own work issues. After dinner frequently work on an office project until bedtime, which may be well after midnight.

This pattern of living has taken its toll, and Erika is just beginning to pay the price.

1. What do you see as the major problems here?

2. What connection do you see between Erika's lifestyle and her job problems?

UNDERSTANDING STRESS

To discuss stress, we must agree on a definition of what it is. To understand stress more fully, we must understand some common sources of managerial stress **(stressors)** and whether they are mainly external, inherent in the job structure, or internal, affected by our socialization and how we choose to view situations. We need to know why certain types of situations are stressful for some people and not for others (i.e., how individual differences impact stress, especially male/female differences). We also need to know more about how people respond to stress: the emotional and physical symptoms and the coping behavior, both reactive and solution-oriented.

Dr. Hans Selye of the University of Montreal, a leader in the study of stress, believes we respond to stress with some version of the fight-or-flight biologically based survival reaction [3]. When a person interprets a significant disruption as a threat, powerful hormones are released into the bloodstream, and the sympathetic division of the autonomic nervous system prepares the body for instant action — either to fight or to run for it. We almost never get so physical in an office. Instead we tend to squelch our emotional and physical reactions, which can eventually damage our mental and physical well-being. Later in this chapter we'll discuss alternatives to this squelching process.

Stress as used here refers to significant disruptions in an individual's environment, whether the disruptions come from within (from unresolved hurts and fears) or from without (from pressures in her working, family, or social world). Even seemingly pleasant or neutral change, such as a job promotion or a vacation, *may* be a significant disruption for a particular individual and therefore create stress.

Sources of Stress

What are some common sources of stress? Dr. Selye mentions (1) psychological upsets, (2) anxiety (from your reactions to life events), (3) overwork, (4) drugs (including medications), (5) chemicals (including additives and residues in food), and (6) excessive noise and air pollution.

The more predictable these disruptions are and the more control we believe we have over them, the less stressful they are for us. Disruptions are changes in the status quo. We all need *some* change in our lives, of course, to provide interest and challenge. Some people welcome and thrive on change; however, we all have limits to the degree of change we can tolerate within, say, a year, without ill effects.

Dr. Thomas Holmes and Dr. Richard Rahe have studied the life events that tend to create anxiety or psychological upset for people. (The resulting "Social Readjustment Rating Scale" is reproduced in Exercise 5-1.) They have ranked some typical events in order of severity (left-hand column) and given each an average mean value that reflects the degree of disruption it tends to create in the lives of the persons studied (right-hand column).

Thomas and Rahe found that the number and severity of stressful incidents that occur in a person's life during a year's time can serve as predictors of the probability that the person will become ill within the following year. The probabilities are shown at the bottom of the

exercise. Assess your own status by completing Exercise 5-1.

How can you use the results of Exercise 5-1 to prevent or cope with the stress that may occur in your life? A good beginning might be to put your scale where you can easily see it every day so that you become thoroughly familiar with the life events that are likely to create stress for you. Think about the meaning of events for you, and try to identify some of the feelings you experience. In this way you gain practice in recognizing stress buildup before it gets out of hand.

Identify constructive ways to express your feelings and different ways you might best adjust to the more important events (more on this later). Ask yourself if focusing on guilt, humiliation, or resentment over past actions or worry over possible future events has ever been helpful to you in the past. An honest evaluation usually reveals that the only positive things we gain from past disasters are lessons for future guidance. Otherwise, they're best forgotten. And the only positive approach to future events is to take action now to prevent them or cope with them. Mere worry only drags us down *now*; it causes us to ruin our enjoyment

---

EXERCISE 5-1: ASSESSING THE IMPACT OF TYPICAL DISRUPTIONS

Step 1. Read the list of forty-three life events listed below. Add other events that might disrupt *your* life in a stressful way.

Step 2. Rank all the life events (the forty-three listed plus any you added) in order of their potential disruptive impact on *your* life.

Step 3. Assign a mean value for the relative degree of disruption each life event would probably create (100 points for total disruption; 0 points for no disruption).

Step 4. Identify those events that have occurred in your life during the past year. Write them down along with the mean value you assigned each one. Add the mean values together. Compare your total mean value rating with the probability of illness findings shown at the end of the exercise. What is the probability of your becoming ill during the coming year based on this exercise? (Example: If your score is between 150 and 299, there's a 50/50 chance you'll become ill during the coming year.)

Your Ranking (Order of Severity)	Life Event	Your Value (Relative Degree of Stress)	Your Ranking (Order of Severity)	Life Event	Your Value (Relative Degree of Stress)
1	Death of spouse	100	27	Begin or end school	26
2	Divorce	73	28	Change in living conditions	25
3	Marital separation	65	29	Revision of personal habits	24
4	Jail term	63	30	Trouble with boss	23
5	Death of close family member	63	31	Change in work hours or conditions	20
6	Personal injury or illness	53	32	Change in residence	20
7	Marriage	50	33	Change in schools	20
8	Fired at work	47	34	Change in recreation	19
9	Marital reconciliation	45	35	Change in church activities	19
10	Retirement	45	36	Change in social activities	18
11	Change in health of family member	44	37	Mortgage or loan less than $10,000	17
12	Pregnancy	40	38	Change in sleeping habits	16
13	Sex difficulties	39	39	Change in number of family get-togethers	15
14	Gain of new family member	39	40	Change in eating habits	15
15	Business readjustment	39	41	Vacation	13
16	Change in financial state	38	42	Christmas	12
17	Death of close friend	37	43	Minor violations of the law	11
18	Change to different line of work	36		Other _____	
19	Change in number of arguments with spouse	35		_____	
20	Mortgage over $10,000	31			
21	Foreclosure of mortgage or loan	30			
22	Change in responsibilities at work	29			
23	Son or daughter leaving home	29			
24	Trouble with in-laws	29			
25	Outstanding personal achievement	28			
26	Spouse begins or stops work	26			

Total Mean Value Rating:	Probability of Illness Occurring Within One Year:
300 or more	80%
150 to 299	50%
149 or less	30%

Reprinted with permission from *Journal of Psychosomatic Research*, Vol. 11, pp. 213–18. Thomas H. Holmes and Richard H. Rahe, "The Social Readjustment Rating Scale." Copyright © 1967, Pergamon Press Ltd.

of the present because of a future event that may never occur.

Your goal is to anticipate life changes and plan for them well in advance. The more you learn about your psychological and physical reactions to stress, the more adept you can be at managing it. You'll be able to pace yourself when events start building up.

Women and Stress

Career women may experience more disruptions than men for many reasons. For one thing, they may have more responsibilities. For example, when they accept the primary responsibility for the children and housework, there are simply more things going on in their lives — things they perceive as crucial. For another, women who have not resolved inner conflicts concerning their career role and their wife or mother role are subject to added stress. In addition, women are likely to experience more stress than men in the process of establishing their credibility and advancing within an organization because of the sterotypes and other barriers discussed in previous chapters.

According to Margaret Hennig, there are now many women in their mid-30s to late 40s who have been deeply involved in their careers for fifteen to twenty years. "They have already worked harder in terms of hours and stress anxiety than the traditional 65-year-old man." Most are not willing to sacrifice family relationships in order to move up in their careers. Therefore, when they are faced with the additional stress of children and family in their mid-30s, many drop out [18]. They are the victims of job burn-out — too much stress for too long with too little psychological nurturing in return, resulting in a loss of enthusiasm and drive.

You have a head start on preventing such burn-out because you've gained skills in establishing goals, priorities, and action plans, and therefore in balancing your life. We'll discuss

other preventive strategies in this and later chapters.

Several studies indicate that male and female managers vary in their experiences of stress. The model shown in Figure 5-1 reflects recent theories about some ways in which people experience events differently. Let's see how the model might explain a real-life situation. Lynn, a young, female first-level manager at an engineering firm, experiences tension and sadness in response to not being accepted as one of the gang. So far, she's the only woman manager at her branch, and the male managers have kept her at arm's length. To her work team in this culture, she's the boss, not quite one of them. Lee, the older, male senior manager down the hall, doesn't find this type of isolation stressful; he is accustomed to the gulf between manager and worker and has long since developed a support network that includes senior managers in other companies. The situations listed under *stressors* in the model are part of the structure of the job situation and are therefore a *structural explanation* of stress.

Males and females are *socialized* differently (as are people from different ethnic backgrounds). As a result, they will interpret job situations through the filter of their past training and experiences. The model contains a few *cognitive appraisal* factors. For example, Lynn's *self-image*, formed as a little girl and carried through to womanhood, is that of a warm person who finds it easy to be very close to people, who makes good friends quickly; so professional distance feels lonely to her. Lee's self-image is one of a leader, first of boys, now of adults; professional distance feels right and comfortable to him. The differences in the way they respond to isolation are due mainly to their *socialization*.

Lynn and Lee respond to stressful situations in the ways their role models responded and in ways that brought them understanding and approval as they were growing up. *Stress responses* include both *strain symptoms* (physical and emotional) and *coping behavior.* Many of the dif-

FIGURE 5-1: A Model of Individual Differences in the Stress Process

| | INDIVIDUAL DIFFERENCES (Gender, Management Level, Age) | | |

Structural explanation

Socialization explanation

| STRESSORS (situations) | COGNITIVE APPRAISAL (interpretation = felt stress) | STRESS RESPONSES | | |

Emotional   Physical   Behavioral

| | | STRAIN SYMPTOMS | COPING BEHAVIOR (to moderate stress) |

Job satisfaction	Self-image, confidence			
Participation in decisions	Career achievement needs			
Job authority	Achievement needs	Anxiety/fear	Insomnia	Reactive	Solution-Oriented
Job demands	Social needs	Confusion	Headache	Nervous gestures	
Goal clarity	Power needs	Sadness	Back/neck pain	Smoking	Distracting pastimes
Access to resources	Personal growth needs	Depression	Nausea/diarrhea	Reckless driving	Positive action
Stereotyping	Family needs	Frustration	Asthma/colds	Alcohol	Meditation
Discrimination		Anger/rage	Hyperactivity	Caffeine	Humor
Coworker acceptance		Indecisiveness	Eating disorders	Sweets/junk food	Confiding in friends
Experience/training		Tension	Skin problems	Drugs	Exercising
Physical work environment			Errors/accidents	Withdrawing	Hobbies
Total workload (job/home)			High blood pressure	Sleeping	Medical help
Job tedium				Violence	Psychological help
Job fit with needs				Hostile actions	

Adapted from the work of Todd D. Jick and Linda F. Mitz, "Sex Differences in Work Stress," *Academy of Management Review*, 10(3), pp. 408–20.

ferences in Lynn's and Lee's responses may have a *socialization explanation*.

Lynn's *emotional symptom* of tension and sadness triggers the *reactive coping behavior* of withdrawing from her managerial responsibilities. She tries too hard to please in order to be well-liked and to feel closer to the workers. She ducks tough decisions and avoids controversy at all costs. From the time she was a little girl, Lynn received approval from her parents, teachers, and most of her friends for such behavior. Reactive behavior usually creates more problems than it solves. If the behavior does

not include adequate expression of the *emotional symptoms, strain symptoms* escalate into *physical symptoms*. The tension builds up as Lynn tries to be all things to all people, and she begins to have headaches.

Lee received approval from his parent figures and friends for taking the bull by the horns and solving problem situations. For example, he becomes very frustrated if his job workload is so heavy he doesn't have time to explore new business opportunities. His *solution-oriented coping behavior* is to find ways to delegate. On the other hand, if Lee has no one to delegate to and cannot find an adequate solution to his problem, his frustration builds because he suppresses his anxiety at falling behind in his career progress. His unexpressed emotion surfaces later as high blood pressure.

A recent study that controlled for differences in age and management level, found that female managers report significantly higher stress levels than male managers [4]. So far as structural stressors (job situations) are concerned, a significantly greater percentage of female managers report experiencing (1) discrimination and stereotyping, (2) job and role overload, and (3) role conflict. Other findings apply to both male and female managers: Middle managers report significantly higher stress levels than senior managers. Higher stress levels are correlated with, and can be predicted by (1) difficulty picturing oneself comfortably exercising power, (2) unclear, unrealistic, or conflicting job goals, (3) heavy job demands, (4) a poor fit between one's job and one's personal needs for growth and development, and (5) lack of participation in higher-level decisions affecting one's area of responsibility. In our model, being a middle manager is classified as an individual difference. Picturing yourself exercising power (self-image) is a cognitive appraisal factor explained by socialization; the remaining four predictors are stressor situations that are a structural part of the job.

Responses to Stress

Stress responses include emotional and physical strain symptoms as well as reactive and solution-oriented coping behavior, as shown in Figure 5-1. Each person has a unique pattern of responses. A recent comparison of male and female managers' self-reported responses to stress [4] found few significant differences. Women are more likely to experience the strain symptoms of sadness, nausea/diarrhea, back/neck pain, and skin problems. Men, on the other hand, are more likely to experience high blood pressure.

The study found no significant differences in male/female coping behavior. Managers who report higher stress levels also report more anxiety/fear, frustration, back/neck pain, and nausea/diarrhea. They also report a higher frequency of taking prescription drugs, eating sweets/junk food, engaging in hostile actions, and sleeping longer than normal — all categorized as reactive behaviors. Surprisingly, they also seek medical help more often and engage in distracting pastimes more frequently — both categorized as solution-oriented behaviors. Seeking medical help may indicate that other solution-oriented behaviors have not been fruitful. It may mean the manager prefers dealing with symptoms, turning responsibility over to a doctor, rather than dealing with the root cause and then using solution-oriented actions appropriate to that root cause. And engaging in distracting pastimes may also deter one from finding a solution.

Exercising, or working out, is the solution-oriented coping behavior that has the greatest correlation with low stress levels and is the best predictor of low stress.

Certain job situations, or stressors, are correlated with a significantly greater range of stress responses and a greater frequency of experiencing those responses. Those job situations are (1) lack of job control, (2) stereotyping and discrimination, and (3) poor job fit.

The first step in gaining control of stress is to identify those situations in which you are aware of pressure, anxiety, or some other symptom that you experience when you are stressed. Exercise 5-2 is designed to get you started.

MANAGING STRESS

In this section we'll discuss ways to avoid the negative means of coping with stress and ways to focus on the more positive strategies and tactics for preventing and avoiding undue

EXERCISE 5-2: SORTING OUT YOUR STRESSORS

Step 1. On a separate sheet of paper, draw yourself. Now symbolize in some way all the pressures and demands that you're aware of—use drawings, words, or other symbols. Then draw arrows, bridges, or other connections between the pressure and you that indicate (by their size, thickness, darkness, or other means) the intensity of each pressure, demand, or anxiety.

Step 2. Now list each item from Step 1 in one of two columns.

Column 1
External Sources (Other people, situations, cultural factors, physical environment, etc.)

Column 2
Internal Sources (Self-doubt, repressed anger, fears, anxieties, etc.)

Step 3. What personal actions or attitudes tend to feed into or maintain the stress sources you listed in Step 2?

Step 4. For each pressure or demand shown in Step 2, list at least one way you can prevent its occurrence or handle it more effectively to prevent stress. (You may want to return to this step after you finish this chapter.)

Step 5. Think of an illness you've had in the past. List the major stressful factors in your life during the year prior to the illness.

Step 6. List payoffs for being ill. (Examples: Getting a vacation from work or class; getting sympathy from a loved one)

Step 7. How can you take care of yourself and provide reasonable facsimiles of these payoffs without becoming ill? (Example: Allowing yourself to accept more love and attention from others and from yourself when you're well)

Step 8. Do you see any patterns in the ways you respond to stress that may be harmful to your health? (Example: Interpreting a change as a defeat or sign of failure, or as proof that life is unfair, or as a trap) List.

Do you see patterns that are constructive and may prevent illness? (Example: Interpreting a change as an opportunity to move into more appropriate activities, or as a sign that it's time to move on) List.

---

stress. Mastering techniques that work for you will give you high-level payoffs—such rewards as maintaining high energy on the job, living longer, and enjoying your life more fully.

Dr. Selye and many other scientists believe that we are born with a fixed amount of vitality or "vital energy" that we can draw on to respond to stressful happenings throughout our lives. (Some scientists call this vital-energy account the "immune response"; it can provide us with the necessary immunity to avoid or recover from illness.) We can conserve our vital energy, but there's no way to increase it. It's there for us to draw on and eventually use up. When we don't use it effectively (for example, when we fail to pace ourselves or otherwise neglect our health), we get sick. When our total vital-energy account gets low, we show signs of aging. When it's all gone, we die.

Many medical experts believe we can cope effectively with stress by drawing intelligently on our vital-energy account. The degree of stress we experience depends on how we perceive and react to situations and how our bodies absorb the effects of stress. Therefore, an intelligent approach must deal with both psychological perceptions and physical health. Here is a three-pronged strategy:

1. *Take an assertive approach.* You can anticipate problems (both physical and psychological) likely to create disruption and pressure and develop strategies for preventing, reducing, or postponing them so that you don't become "swamped." This process requires an assertive approach to taking responsibility for your physical well-being by adopting and maintaining a healthful lifestyle. It also requires an assertive approach to dealing with people that gives you more control over your life and helps you avoid becoming the victim of others' manipulations, games, and whims.

2. *Command your inner resources.* You can learn to turn off stressful thoughts so you can relax, and you can learn to handle your emotions constructively. When you're in a position of responsibility that calls for risk-taking and decision-making, you may occasionally be hit with an overload of disruption and the resulting pressure, no matter how well you anticipate and prevent problems. The key to managing this stress and the "churning hormones" of the fight-or-flight response is to become skilled at relaxation, visualization, and letting go. A quick technique for staying centered or in balance

on the job is sometimes essential to regaining your perspective of the situation in order to handle it effectively. Regular periods of relaxation are also essential for maintaining a level of calmness, serenity, and stability that eliminates the need to overdraw your vital-energy account.

3. *Handle emotions constructively.* Learn to view criticism objectively and to express feelings in ways that don't compromise your leadership role.

Let's look first at some assertive approaches to stress management.

Using Time Management, Support Networks, and Assertion

Three major ways of preventing stress are managing your time well, developing an appropriate support network, and asserting yourself effectively. Time management is based on periodically listing major objectives and ranking them in order of priority. It also involves keeping a daily "To Do" list that is categorized and numbered according to priorities, delegating, and arranging "quiet times" for uninterrupted work. These and other techniques were discussed in detail in Chapter 4.

Developing a support network at all levels *within* the company is not only essential to survival as a manager, it's a source of help and comfort in preventing and coping with stress. A support network *outside* the company is also helpful. In Chapter 8, we discuss the importance of support networks in preventing stressful problems. We'll also discuss their importance and use in the coping strategies section of this chapter.

Asserting yourself at the right times is essential for preventing problems that create stress. People who can comfortably stand up for their rights and express their preferences and desires are seldom victimized. They exercise a relatively high degree of control over their lives, and they are more secure and confident as persons. You'll learn more about this in Chapter 6.

Taking an Assertive Approach to Health

Donald Ardell, in his book *High Level Wellness* [1], takes a **holistic** approach to health and stress management that recognizes the impact on your health of every aspect of your lifestyle. According to Ardell's theories, many managers' lifestyles are more conducive to "low-level worseness" than to "high-level wellness." If you decide you're one of these and want to change, try making changes one step at a time. As soon as you're comfortable with one step, add another.

The basis for an assertive approach to health is the belief that "I am the cause of my health." Once we accept that fact, we don't surrender responsibility for our health to the medical system; we use this system when necessary on a client/customer basis. Only when we become accountable for our own health are we likely to avoid such high-risk behaviors as excessive eating, smoking, and drinking. Because these high-risk behaviors are forms of self-abuse, taking responsibility may involve a consciousness-raising program for building self-esteem and becoming more aware of and responsive to the body and its signals. After all, no one else can know your body and what it needs the way that you can, for each body is unique.

Taking an assertive approach to health also specifically involves (1) taking care of nutritional needs, (2) exercising regularly, and (3) controlling your environment.

Taking Care of Nutritional Needs   A U.S. Senate Select Committee, in noting that the major diet-related problem in the United States is the deadly combination of overconsumption and undernutrition, reported:

> We have reached the point where nutrition, or the lack or the excess or the quality of it, may be the nation's number-one public health problem. The threat is not beriberi, pellagra, or scurvy. Rather we face the more subtle, but also more deadly, reality of millions of Americans loading their stomachs with food which is likely to make them obese, to give them high blood pressure, to induce heart disease, diabetes, and cancer—in short, to kill them over the long term [quoted in 3, p. 5].

To meet your nutritional needs, Ardell has suggested the following practices:

1. Eat as many natural foods as possible, such as fresh fruits, raw vegetables, whole grains, low-fat cottage cheese and yogurt, onion, garlic (combined with or followed by fresh parsley, onion and garlic leave little or no mouth odor). Eat plenty of high-fiber roughage (especially bran) every day.

2. Eat a balanced diet—no crash diets.

3. Avoid foods containing artificial colors, additives, preservatives, stabilizers, and other processed chemicals; also, foods containing nitrites (found in bacon, sausage, luncheon meats, and frankfurters).

4. Avoid refined, processed foods, including "enriched" foods. They usually have little nutritional value and many calories.

5. Avoid foods containing white sugar or white flour. Many degenerative diseases have been correlated with overconsumption of these foods. Avoiding them can be difficult since some form of refined sugar is added to a high percentage of our packaged, canned, frozen, and bottled food (for more information on this subject, see *Sugar Blues* by William Dufty [8]). Labels, however, reveal the contents in order of their proportion.

6. Minimize intake of salt, coffee, tea, alcohol, colas, and chocolate.

7. Concentrate on high quality in proteins. Many authorities believe Americans eat far

too much beef and pork for their own good. The right combinations of eggs, milk, fish, cheese, beans, legumes, brown rice, whole grains, and seeds can provide higher-quality protein for less money. They can also provide variety in your diet and improve your elimination.

Exercising Regularly   This may be your most powerful preventative. Strangely enough, most people find they have *more* energy when they get some regular form of exercise. Most authorities recommend exercising at least an hour a day; a goal of twenty minutes should be your absolute minimum. Include bending and stretching exercises for flexibility, lifting and pulling exercises for muscle tone, and build up to some cardiovascular-stimulating exercises (aerobic exercise that will make you "huff and puff" but not get out of breath) for respiratory and circulatory health and increase your metabolic rate so that you burn off calories faster. Doing twenty minutes of aerobic exercise morning and evening keeps your metabolic rate higher around the clock.

Busy managers often find it difficult to take time for adequate exercise. Often the only way is to give it top priority — "If I don't get anything else done today, I'm going to get some exercise." It also may help to keep reminding yourself, "If I take care of my body, it will take care of me."

At least one expert claims you can maintain cardiovascular fitness and weight level with his specific aerobic exercise routine in as little as twenty minutes a day for three days a week [2]. If you spend twenty minutes on three other days doing exercises for flexibility and muscle tone, you'll get all-around results and even a day off!

Keep in mind, though, that each time you get a *thorough* workout, you reap many benefits; some of them are (1) using up calories at a faster rate for the next twelve hours; (2) slowing the aging process; (3) improving your figure;

(4) keeping bones and muscles healthy and strong; and (5) preventing stress buildup.

It's best to find some forms of exercise you really enjoy, and some that provide social interaction. Above all, don't think of your exercise regimen as a crash program. Move into it one step at a time and make it a permanent way of life. The older you get, the more you need it.

Controlling Your Environment   Your environment has three aspects: the physical, the social, and the personal. The air you breathe, the water you drink, and the land around you make up the physical environment. The quality of the social environment depends on how economic, governmental, and cultural conditions affect your health and well-being. Your personal environment reflects the way you organize your living and working spaces, the kinds of friendships you create and maintain, and the kind of feedback about yourself that you invite by your actions. Here are some suggestions for developing sensitivity to all three aspects of your environment.

1. *Analyzing your physical environment.* Think about what interrupts, distracts, upsets, or prevents you from doing something constructive during the day. Then make a list of things, events, sounds, scents, and opportunities that could be *added* to your daily routine. Evaluate the positive and negative impacts of these things. Set goals that will help you structure space in ways that enhance your efficiency, effectiveness, well-being, and your continued progress toward achieving your major objectives.

2. *Reevaluating.* Periodically pause to get in touch with basic questions and purposes in your life. Then examine or reexamine the extent to which your personal and social environments hinder or enhance your progress toward your top-priority goals.

3. *Enhancing your personal environment.* Learn to arrange your personal environment to enhance the positive and minimize the negative elements in your life. Some possibilities: bottled spring water; air ionizer; soothing music; a deck or patio with greenery and flowers; reorganized closets, kitchen cabinets, or desk; a more relaxing commute; strategies for avoiding daily irritations like waiting in line or running too many errands.

4. *Turning your internal needs into preferences.* When you think in terms of *wanting* something to happen instead of *needing* it to happen, you retain a healthier perspective, are more likely to gain respect, and therefore improve your personal environment. Upgrading needs to preferences is often called

"letting go." It's one of the most important coping strategies, as well as a good preventive strategy. See Exercise 5-6.

COMMANDING YOUR INNER RESOURCES: YOUR PERSONAL POWER

A process for commanding your inner resources is shown in Exhibit 5-1. Specific techniques include living in the present, learning to relax, visualizing results, letting go of desperate needs, adopting "abundance thinking," and using your sleep time constructively.

Commanding your inner resources is the key to dealing with stress, as well as to reaching your goals, becoming an effective leader, and

EXHIBIT 5-1: Inner Leadership: Creating Productive Thought Patterns

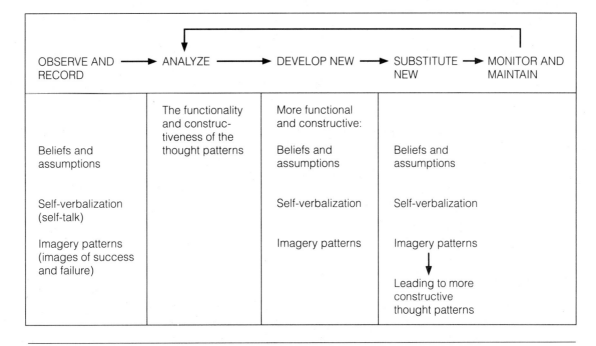

OBSERVE AND RECORD	→ ANALYZE →	DEVELOP NEW →	SUBSTITUTE NEW →	MONITOR AND MAINTAIN
	The functionality and constructiveness of the thought patterns	More functional and constructive:		
Beliefs and assumptions		Beliefs and assumptions	Beliefs and assumptions	
Self-verbalization (self-talk)		Self-verbalization	Self-verbalization	
Imagery patterns (images of success and failure)		Imagery patterns	Imagery patterns ↓ Leading to more constructive thought patterns	

From Charles C. Manz and Chris P. Neck, "Inner Leadership: Creating Productive Thought Patterns," *Academy of Management Executive*, Vol. 5, No. 3 (August 1991), pp. 87–95.

generally creating the life you want for yourself. It is your ultimate source of personal power. The three major steps are

1. *Deep relaxation* — focusing on the here and now, moving away from a focus on mind chatter, and moving into a state of deep relaxation

2. *Visualization* of the end results you want for virtually any situation that concerns you

3. *Letting go* of any tension-producing need to have the results you picture

Specific Techniques

Living in the Present This is the way to eliminate guilt, resentment, and worry from your life, as mentioned briefly in an earlier discussion. When you're feeling guilty or resentful, you're really living in the past. When you're worrying, you're living in the future. Acting in the here and now is the only way to influence events. The key is to focus on the present moment and determine what, if anything, you need to *do*. Exercise 5-3 is designed to bring you into the present moment by helping you focus on the sensations your body is experiencing now. Practice it frequently when you're *not* under stress, and you'll soon be able to use it quickly even in stressful situations.

Mastering Relaxation Techniques This is a more advanced approach to getting in the here and now, because the goal of these techniques is to cut through tension and mind chatter to reach a deeply relaxed state. As with all the techniques for commanding your inner resources, these may be relatively difficult and time-consuming to master in the beginning. With practice, however, you'll be able to use your skills even in the midst of a stressful situation, and you'll be able to go into deeper states of relaxation more quickly.

The ultimate goal is to be able to move into a state of relaxation so deep that you would be producing alpha brain waves if you were having an electroencephalogram taken. Although biofeedback mechanisms are available for helping you develop this ability quickly, you can learn well enough without them. Research indicates that when you are in such a relaxed state, you can communicate more effectively with your subconscious. You can give it new messages, even messages that override key decisions about life you made long ago — viewpoints that no longer serve you. You can enlist the aid of your subconscious in reaching your goals and solving problems — so that your verbal and nonverbal actions are well integrated and your entire being is moving toward achieving what you decide you want in life.

You get double payoffs, therefore, for learning to relax deeply. The relaxation alone is an immediate antidote to stress. It enhances your sense of well-being, your health, and potentially your longevity. In addition, when you combine it with visualization — that is, mental imagery — it helps you create the life you want. But more about that later.

Four conditions are necessary for mastering the relaxation techniques provided here: (1) a quiet, calm place as free from distraction as possible, (2) a comfortable body position, (3) a mental focusing device to help you shut off your mind chatter (internal dialogue) and go deep within yourself, and (4) a passive attitude that lets you merely observe distracting thoughts, let them go, and bring your mind back gently to your focusing device. Keep in mind that you can't *make* relaxation occur; you can only *let* it occur.

Once you've found a quiet place, experiment with comfortable positions. (A favorite of many is sitting in a comfortable but firm chair with back perfectly straight, legs and arms uncrossed, feet flat on the floor, and arms resting on the thighs.) Then experiment with the techniques included in Exercise 5-4, Deep Relaxa-

EXERCISE 5-3: GETTING IN THE HERE AND NOW

Variation 1 — Focusing on the Five Senses
Step 1. Take a few deep breaths.
Step 2. *Seeing.* Become intensely aware of what you see around you. Look at it in detail as if you've never seen it before. Pretend you just arrived from another planet. Notice colors, patterns, textures.
Step 3. *Hearing.* If the situation permits, close your eyes. What do you hear? Notice every little sound, identify it, describe it mentally.
Step 4. *Touching.* Now focus on your sense of touch — the feel of your clothes against your skin, the air on your skin, the floor under your feet, the chair under your seat if you're sitting. Describe the sensations to yourself.
Step 5. *Smelling and tasting.* If there are noticeable odors around you or tastes in your mouth, become aware of them; identify and describe them.

Did you notice that your focus moved away from your mind and its internal chatter about the past or future and into your body and what it was sensing in the present moment? Here's an alternate technique that may work better for you:

Variation 2 — Progressive Muscle Relaxation
In this process, you alternately tense and then relax all the muscle groups in your body beginning with the toes and moving upward. Tense up the toes of your right foot, hold it, then quickly release them all at once. Notice the resulting feeling of relaxation in those muscles. Continue up your right leg, tensing and relaxing the calf muscles and the thigh muscles. Then do the left leg; next, progress up through the various muscle groups in the trunk of your body, then the right and left arms, and finally the neck and head. Pay special attention to the muscles of the jawline and between the eyes; both are places where we tend to retain tension.

---

tion. Discover the ones that are most relaxing for you.

Visualizing the Results You Want   Once you're in a deeply relaxed state, you can talk to your subconscious and tell it what you want. Your subconscious is amazingly competent at moving you toward the results you request — if you'll only relax and let it do its work. It tunes in better to pictures and feelings, however, than to words. That's why visualizing results and getting in touch with the feelings you want

to experience along with those results is so powerful.

What if you have difficulty "making pictures" when you close your eyes? Never fear. Everyone differs to some extent in the way they visualize. If you see no pictures at all, think of what it might be like if you *could* see the pictures you're thinking about. That's good enough.

When should you practice your visualization skills? Shortly before going to sleep each night is a time preferred by many people because it's

EXERCISE 5-4: DEEP RELAXATION

Deep relaxation begins with deep breathing. The goal is to slow down your breathing pattern. So start with one of the breathing techniques. Then move into one of the focusing devices. If you have trouble moving out of a focus on mind chatter and into a passive attitude, do an exercise for getting in the here and now.

Deep breathing — Variation 1. Breathe in through your nostrils, counting slowly as you do so; hold the breath, starting your counting over again; breathe out through your mouth, lips slightly parted, again counting. The actual process: Breathe in 1-2-3-4-5; Hold it 1-2-3-4-5; Breathe out 1-2-3-4-5. Each time you repeat the process, extend the time you take to breathe in, hold it, and breathe out. See how much you can extend it.

Deep breathing — Variation 2. Visualize yourself stepping onto the top of an escalator. As you breathe slowly in and out, watch yourself descending on the escalator into a deeper and deeper state of relaxation and count: 10-9-8-7-6-5-4-3-2-1.

The backward counting described in Variation 2 serves as a focusing device. Variations 3 and 4 also incorporate focusing devices.

Deep breathing — Variation 3. Close your eyes, take a deep breath, and enjoy the pleasure of feeling yourself breathe. As you breathe in, say quietly to yourself, "I am." As you breathe out, say to yourself "relaxed." Or say, "I am . . . calm and serene" or "I am . . . one."

Deep breathing — Variation 4. Focus all your attention at the tip of your nostrils. Quietly "watch" in your mind's eye the breath flowing in and out past the tip of the nostril. Count from 1 through 10 each time you breathe in and each time you breathe out. Continue counting from 1 through 10 each time you breathe in and out until you're completely relaxed.

Focusing device 1 — Candle flame. Place a lighted candle about a foot in front of you and focus all your attention on the flame. As thoughts float by, notice them, let them go, and gently bring your attention back to the flame. This form of relaxed concentration can help you notice how your thoughts and senses keep grabbing at your awareness. The goal is to free your awareness from its identification with thoughts. We cling to our senses and thoughts because we're so attached to them. While focusing on the candle flame, you start becoming aware of that clinging and attachment and the process of letting go.

Focusing device 2 — Centering. Focus all your consciousness into the center of your head. Visualize a point of light about a foot in front of your eyes. Now focus all your attention on the point of light.

Focusing device 3 — Grounding. Visualize the center of the earth as a very dense place of rock or metal. Focus all your attention on the center of the earth, and picture a huge iron bar there. Next bring your attention to your spinal cord. Visualize a large cable or cord running from the base of your spine all the way to the center of the earth. Picture a big hook on the other end of the cord; now hook it into the center of the earth. Feel a slight pull toward the center of the earth and a slight heaviness of your body.

Focusing device 4 — Your peaceful place. Think of a place where you usually feel especially serene, relaxed, and happy, such as the beach, the forest, or the lake. Picture yourself there. Reexperience in your mind's eye all the sights, sounds, smells, and tastes you experience there. Focus on your sense of touch, too — the sun, water, and air on your skin, the sand or earth under your feet. Bring in as much vivid detail as you can. Get in touch with the positive feelings you experience there — your sense of well-being, confidence, serenity.

---

a quiet time when they're ready to relax fully. To make the most of your personal power, practice deep relaxation and visualization at some time every day so that it becomes a deeply ingrained habit — a way of life that you can put to use almost automatically. If you do this, you will soon discover that you can use these skills — quickly, with your eyes wide open, and with no one the wiser — any time you're dealing with potentially stressful situations. You'll be able to stay centered or to regain your composure quickly even if you're taken by surprise.

The processes described in Exercise 5-5, Visualizing Results, are designed to enlist the aid of your subconscious in handling specific types of situations. You can adapt them to any kind of situation; just remember that important final step, letting go.

Learning to Let Go   Have you ever observed someone sabotaging herself because she was trying too hard? You probably thought, "Why doesn't she relax a little?" Can you think of a time when you probably sabotaged yourself by trying too hard or caring too much? Why do people do this? Usually it happens because they are too strongly attached to having the situation turn out just the way they want. They

cling — perhaps desperately — to the idea or picture of certain end results. Therefore, they create a tension-producing need to achieve those results, often accompanied by fear that they won't.

Think of some situations in which you achieved the results you wanted — times when you moved relatively effortlessly toward your goal. Think of top athletes who have done that. Top achievement is usually a result of *relaxed concentration*. You fully intend to achieve certain results, and your mind and body are focused on the process of doing so. You *desire* those results, but you don't desperately *need* them, and you're not focused on fear connected with failure to achieve the results.

You prevent the self-sabotage caused by tension-producing needs when you add a letting-go step to the visualization process you use for goal-setting. Exercise 5-6, Letting Go of Results, offers several techniques for this final step of the personal power process. Remember, when you let go of your goal, you retain a clear picture of having it, but you release the needs and fears related to not having it. This process frees you to work toward your goal in a relaxed, confident way, which in turn makes it easier to gain the cooperation and support of others.

EXERCISE 5-5: VISUALIZING RESULTS

Step 1. Focus on the here and now and move into a deeply relaxed state by using any combination of techniques from Exercise 5-4.

Step 2. Select the visualization that applies to your situation from the ones listed here (or adapt one of them to fit your situation).

Step 3. Use one of the letting-go techniques from Exercise 5-6.

Visualization 1 — Problem resolution. Relax deeply. Get in touch with your problem situation. If thinking of it or picturing it causes you to feel anxious, focus again on a relaxation technique. Repeat until you're able to picture your problem situation without feeling anxious. What do you want the end results of this situation to be? How do you want it to be resolved? Picture that happening — in vivid detail, bringing all your senses into play: colors, patterns, textures you see; sounds you hear; and things you touch, smell, and taste. Picture your interactions with the other person(s) involved, focusing on your specific feelings and the feelings flowing between you and others; for example, understanding, acceptance, warmth, good will. Focus on the pictures and feelings until you feel quite comfortable and secure with them. Now use a letting-go technique to release them.

Visualization 2 — Goal achievement. Follow the process described in Visualization 1, but instead of focusing on a problem situation, focus on a goal you want to achieve. Picture yourself actually achieving the goal. Include all the people involved in helping you reach the goal; focus on the positive feelings flowing between you and them. Now let go.

Visualization 3 — Evaluating goals. You can carry the process used in Visualization 2 a step further to help you evaluate possible goals. (For example, if you're not sure whether getting a master's degree should be merely one alternate activity for achieving a career goal or a goal in itself, picture yourself having achieved the career goal without the master's degree.) Picture all the consequences of having achieved the goal. How do you feel about each? Is anything missing? What? Would a different goal have led to better results?

Visualization 4 — Handling stage fright. Use this process to overcome the "jitters" that accompany any type of presentation you must make before a group. For best results, practice the visualization several times before your presentation. Just before going to sleep the night before the presentation is an especially good time to visualize positive results. Follow the process described in Visualization 1, but instead of picturing a problem situation, picture yourself making a successful presentation. See yourself focusing on the major thrust of your message and getting it across in a clear, dynamic, persuasive way. See your audience understanding and accepting it. Get in touch with your positive feelings and theirs. Now let go.

EXERCISE 5-6: LETTING GO OF RESULTS

Step 1. Move into a state of deep relaxation (Exercise 5-4).

Step 2. Visualize the end results you want (Exercise 5-5).

Step 3. Let go of your pictures of end results by one of the following methods (or devise your own method for putting your goals out into the universe):

Variation 1 — Hot air balloon. Picture a beautifully colored hot air balloon with a lovely passenger basket. It's tied to the ground with velvet ropes. Put the pictures of your end results into the basket — all the pictures and the feelings related to them. Untie the ropes and watch the balloon float away, up into the sky and away toward the horizon. As it floats out of sight, repeat to yourself, "Let go, let go."

If you experience discomfort or negative feelings, such as sadness, regret, or unwillingness to let go, turn to Exercise 3-2 on page 59. Work on the fear of failure that is causing you to cling to the needed results until you are comfortable with letting them go.

Variation 2 — Space capsule. Follow the process described in Variation 1, substituting a sleek space capsule for the hot air balloon. Picture all the latest technology and equipment for controlling the capsule; put your end results inside; lock it; watch it blast off and disappear into space.

Variation 3 — Bottle at sea. Follow the process described in Variation 1, substituting a large glass bottle for the hot air balloon. Put your end results inside; place the cork in the bottle top; throw the bottle into the ocean. Watch the tide carry it out to sea; see it disappear toward the horizon.

However, you must truly become comfortable with the idea of *not* achieving your goal. If letting go is accompanied by sadness, regret, or unwillingness, you need to work on your fear of failure (see Exercise 3-2, p. 59).

You can also adopt a viewpoint that there is abundance in the world. When you let go of your goal pictures, you "put them out into the universe." The view that there is abundance in the universe implies that everything that happens eventually works toward your benefit. Therefore, if you give a goal situation your best shot, you are confident of achieving it. If it doesn't turn out the way you pictured, then your deep inner self had the wisdom to know that those results were not best for you in the long run. That's the time to ask, "What lesson can I learn from this situation? What's my next goal?"

Abundance Thinking Do you approach goal achievement from a viewpoint of scarcity? Do you think, "Since there are not enough resources for everyone to have all they need, then the more I get, the less there will be for someone else"? Think of all the things that are perceived as scarce. Jot them down.

Most people list food, fresh water, housing, education, health care, money, time, energy, love. Actually, all of these resources are in adequate — even abundant — supply if enough of us decide to manage them properly. According to a 1981 publication of the American Friends Service Committee, a supplement of $17 billion a year could have ensured adequate food, water, housing, health care, and education for every person in the world. In 1981 world governments spent this amount for arms—every two weeks [23]. If enough people decided it was essential, we could suspend the arms race for just two weeks a year and have adequacy; surely we could collectively choose to have abundance.

Abundance thinking reflects an individual or collective attitude. Take money—our creative energy becomes money; we can think of it as green energy. Or time—there are always twenty-four hours in a day; we have abundant time to achieve our top-priority goals once we clarify them and weed out the nonessentials. Or energy—all that exists in the universe is energy; the only problem is finding and using the best form of energy for each of our purposes. And love, which exists in our minds— the more love we give to ourselves and others, the more we tend to receive, and the more we have to give back again. The only limits are our fears that shield us from receiving love.

When you come from an attitude of abundance, you can move more freely toward your goals. Since there's plenty for everyone, your successes need not be built on someone else's failures; your having more need not mean that someone else has less. It's a win-win attitude: everybody can win.

Sleeping on It   You can even use your sleep time to move you toward your goals. For years we've heard managers say, before making an important or difficult decision, "Let me sleep on it and get back to you tomorrow"—and for very good reason. Research studies increasingly point to the importance of sleeping, and especially dreaming, to our mental health and ability to function well during waking hours. Your subconscious mind is very powerful, and you can draw on its resources almost effortlessly by using the dream state to help you solve problems, resolve conflicts, and come up with new ideas.

Suppose Erika Kerr decided to combine visualization and "sleeping on it" to help solve the problem of getting sales orders to Tom Jenson's people. Just before going to sleep, Erika uses deep relaxation and visualization to picture a positive solution to her problem. Next she expresses her wish in a concise statement: "I want a solution to the sales order problem." Another way of putting it might be "I'll discover a method for coordinating the sales orders." She tells herself that she will have a solution when she awakens. Finally she repeats her concise statement over and over as she drifts into sleep.

Here are the steps to take:

1. Just before going to sleep, use a deep relaxation and visualization process (see Exercises 5-4 and 5-5) to picture a positive solution to your problem.

2. Put your wish into a concise statement.

3. Visualize yourself waking up with the solution or ideas you want. Tell yourself you *will* have them in the morning.

4. Repeat your phrase as you drift into sleep.

5. On awakening, lie still and think about your subject. Write down any ideas that come to mind. The idea may come to you later in the day. Relax and be open to it.

This procedure can help you with any problem, including handling your emotions on the job.

Handling Emotions Constructively

Most women are blessed with the ability to express their emotions more freely than men. However, this blessing can become a curse to the woman manager who hasn't learned appropriate ways to express and channel her emotions in business situations. In fact, one of the most damaging and widespread stereotypes women in business have been stuck with through the years is that of the overly emotional female.

You've heard the comments: "Women are too emotional to be managers. They go to pieces in a crisis." (This overlooks the fact that nearly all mothers get their children through the numerous crises growing up entails without "going to pieces.") "You can't afford to hire a manager who might burst into tears in the crunch." "Women are just too flighty to handle a manager's job." "Women don't roll with the punches like men do." "A man can keep problems in perspective better than a woman."

Women do report being in positive moods and in negative moods about twice as often as men [5], which would indicate that women experience feelings more intensely. However, it does not follow that women are helpless victims of their feelings or must somehow act out all their feelings.

A key factor that has led to these stereotypes is the different payoffs our culture tends to give to little girls and boys when they express emotions. Girls usually get payoffs of sympathy or approval when they cry, show fear, express sadness or other tender feelings, show sympathy for others, and nurture others. Boys frequently get disapproval or even punishment for such behavior. ("Big boys don't cry." "Don't be a chicken.") On the other hand, boys often receive approval, admiration, or at least acceptance for expressing various forms of anger or aggression. Such "masculine" expressions of emotion by girls, however, are usually met by disapproval or rejection.

In the male-dominated business world, therefore, it is generally acceptable to express anger or aggression within certain limits. However, a display of tears or fear signals you can't handle the game; that is, you can't handle real responsibility on the line where key decisions are made and where the real power is wielded. It's especially important to manage fear because

some political game players can sniff out the nonverbal signs of fear like bloodhounds, and they'll quickly move in for the kill if it suits their purposes.

What should you do with your tears, fears, and anger? Squelch them? Pretend they aren't there? That approach just leads to more problems. We'll discuss several ways to prevent emotional buildup and to handle emotions you don't care to display on the job. You can control the viewpoint you take toward others' actions, including their criticism of your performance. When you choose to change viewpoints, your emotional reactions will also change. For example, if you see the threatened little boy thrashing behind your boss's angry outburst, you may feel empathy, not anxiety. When "problem" feelings do intrude, you can learn to express them in ways that are acceptable in the business world (see Chapter 6), to experience them without acting them out, or to release them through substitute acting-out or expressing them to a trusted friend.

Now let's look at some suggestions from people who have stopped being the victims of their feelings and have learned to use their feelings in ways that keep them in closer touch with themselves and others.

Avoiding the Tendency to Take Things Personally   The tendency to view other people's actions and criticisms as a personal put-down stems from the fear of some sort of personal failure. Why do women seem to take these things more personally than men? Perhaps because men have generally been more single-minded about their career objectives. They are more likely to keep focusing on such questions as "What do I have to *do*, what do I have to *learn* in order to advance?" That focus makes it easier to keep things in perspective. When the intention to *learn* from our mistakes overcomes our fear of failure, we're less likely to take people's criticisms and actions personally.

It may help to view business as a game. First, what's your major objective in this game?

Discovering the limits of your capability? Financial independence? Making a specific kind of contribution to the planet? Once you're clear about your major objective and let go of any tension-producing *need* to achieve it, you can relax and begin to enjoy the *process* of playing the game in order to achieve the objective. The actions of others become part of the challenge and complexity of the game, and you make your moves with your goals foremost in your mind. Your focus changes from avoiding the risk of failure and protecting yourself from failure to winning the game. Problem situations merely alert you to the need to take corrective action. You switch from agonizing over the fact that a problem was allowed to develop to getting on with the job of correcting the problem. Your ego is not on the line. After all, it's just a game.

In addition, when you learn to identify your rights (the rules of the game?) and to stand up for them, you're better able to view others' actions objectively. When you consistently assert your rights, you avoid the buildup of emotional resentment that leads to the "chip-on-the-shoulder" attitude that hampers some women. Assertion is discussed in Chapter 6.

Putting Criticism in Perspective   Ask yourself about your critic's qualifications on the subject at hand. Suppose you were to take a visitor on a tour of your department and explain major departmental goals, organization, procedures, and controls. He sees some potential problem with the way you're running things and suggests some ways you could improve the setup. The range of possibilities about his qualifications to criticize and advise you is shown on this scale:

1	2	3	4	5	6	7	8	9	10

Ignoramus   Expert

Let's look at the two extreme possibilities. Possibility number one is that your critic doesn't know a thing about running the business. In fact he's so ignorant that he doesn't know the difference between a work schedule and an organization chart. In that case, if you allow yourself to become upset because of the criticism of a business ignoramus, you are acting even more foolish than the person who criticized you.

At the other extreme, your critic may be a world-renowned expert on business organization. In that case, his observations are probably valid and his suggestions extremely valuable. In fact if you acted on those suggestions, you might become a top officer of the company in a very short time. To be upset by such criticism, then, would be inappropriate and self-defeating.

Most of your critics' qualifications will lie somewhere between complete ignorance and incomparable expertise. The point is that if you automatically respond negatively to feedback, you are showing that you lack self-esteem in that area of your life. Such negative reactions not only waste your energy, they tend to sidetrack you from your major objectives and goals. When you are criticized, ask yourself: What are the qualifications of my critic? What validity does this criticism have? Are ulterior motives involved? Can I use this feedback to help me reach my goals and objectives [10, p. 192]?

Stewart Emery tells a story that further illustrates this concept.* He describes the autopilot and the inertial navigation system on the plane he flew to Hawaii. The plane's crew refers to the autopilot as George and to the inertial navigation system as Fred. The relationship between these two pieces of equipment is called a "closed-feedback mechanism" in engineering terms. Emery explains that this is just a fancy way of saying that Fred and George never get out of communication. They always supply each other with feedback; they don't make each

---

*Adapted from *Actualizations: You Don't Have to Rehearse to Be Yourself* by Stewart Emery. Copyright © 1982, by Stewart Emery. Used by permission of Doubleday & Company, Inc.

other wrong; and they don't take anything personally. If Fred and George communicated with words rather than by mechanical means, their conversation on the trip to Hawaii would go something like this:

F: George, we're off course two degrees to starboard.
G: Okay, Fred, I'll fix it.
F: George, we're off course three degrees to port.
G: Okay, Fred, I'll fix it.
F: George, we're Dutch rolling.
G: Okay, Fred, I'll fix it.
F: George, we're forty knots below our airspeed.
G: Okay, Fred, I'll fix it.
F: George, we're three hundred feet below our corridor.
G: Okay, Fred, I'll fix it.

This type of communication would continue all the way to Hawaii. Now, if Fred and George also happened to be human beings, the conversation might go something like this:

F: George, we are off course two degrees to starboard.
G: Okay, Fred, I'll fix it.
F: George, we're off course three degrees to port.
G: (*Pause*) Okay, Fred, I'll fix it.
F: George, we're Dutch rolling.
G: All right, Fred, I will fix it.
F: George, we're forty knots below our airspeed.
G: Will you knock it off, Fred! Gripe, gripe, gripe! All you ever do is gripe.

As a person, it's difficult for George to avoid the tendency to take the feedback as a personal affront. Yet this feedback is the essence of the Fred/George relationship that allows the safe arrival of the plane in Hawaii.

Do you welcome feedback? Ask yourself: Is it better for me to know what's going on in my department — the problems, conflicts, others' reactions — or not? If having all pertinent information, negative or positive, about what's going on in your area of responsibility is important to you, then your logical response to feedback will be, "Thank you. I'm glad you brought that to my attention. I'll look into it."

Sometimes people will criticize you in such a negative, hostile way that it's difficult to remain emotionally detached. It may be appropriate to tell such a person that you appreciate the feedback but you *don't* appreciate the manner in which it was given. At the same time, it helps to keep in mind that the hostility is the other person's problem. She or he would react that way to *anyone* who represents to him or her what you do at the moment. It's a part of the individual's own conditioning and working out of his or her own life story and really has nothing to do with you personally. And, if you *still* feel strong emotions, you don't have to act them out. You can choose a substitute acting-out method.

Experiencing Feelings Without Acting Them Out   As you master the techniques we've been discussing, "problem" emotions will become less and less a problem. Here's a strategy for constructively handling those "problem" emotions that do occur. Many male managers have learned to control their feelings by suppressing them and pretending they don't exist. This practice creates a number of negative side-effects.

Suppressed feelings don't go away; they tend to build up inside until they reach the "explosive stage." We tend to forget the incident that triggered the feeling and the fact that we suppressed the feeling. Therefore, our outbursts of anger, self-pity, fear, and so forth come as a surprise to us and are out of our control.

Suppressed feelings that simmer and fester within us continue to create stress long after the stressful situation has passed. We then become vulnerable to stress-related illnesses, especially ulcers, high blood pressure, migraine headaches, allergies, asthma, and heart disease.

Denial of feelings as a way of coping with life takes us more and more out of touch with ourselves — the way we are, the true effects of people and events in our lives, all the facets of the ways we really respond to those people and events. Such denial will inhibit your personal growth and development as a creative, autonomous person. As a result, you'll find it more and more difficult to be clear about your values and therefore your goals and to evaluate situations and opportunities in the light of those goals.

It is important that we fully *experience* the feelings we have without judging those feelings to be good or bad. It may be inappropriate and self-defeating to *act-out* some of those feelings.

For example, in the second case described at the beginning of this chapter, Erika felt frustration, then self-pity, then rage. She expressed her frustration and self-pity in ways that upset Tom Jenson, intensified her problems, and were therefore inappropriate and self-defeating.

How can you fully experience feelings so that it's not necessary to act them out? Here are some suggestions.

1. *Accept your feelings.* Be glad that you're able to experience the whole range of human emotions and that you're aware of being able to do so.

2. *Don't judge your feelings.* Tell yourself that a feeling is not right or wrong, good or bad; it just is.

3. *Let yourself fully experience a feeling.* Be aware of it in the present moment. Don't begin focusing on guilt (about past experiences associated with a similar feeling) or worry (about what will happen in the future). Stay in the here and now by focusing on your senses: Focus on what you are seeing, hearing, touching, and so forth.

4. *Choose not to act-out.* Tell yourself that you are choosing not to act-out your feelings because to do so would be inappropriate and self-defeating.

5. *Decide whether and when to give feedback.* You may decide it is appropriate to *tell* the person who triggered the feeling what you are feeling. If this is done effectively, it is not acting-out, and the feedback can be constructive to that person. (See Chapter 6 for suggestions on giving feedback constructively.)

6. *If you can't give feedback calmly, postpone it.* As a general rule, you don't have to respond immediately to anything. When your feelings are too overpowering for you to "experience them out" quickly, it's more professional to delay responding. You can act-out your feelings in privacy. Later, when you're ready to deal with the problem situation, you can do so without having to deal with explosive feelings at the same time.

   To postpone gracefully, it helps to have some "exit lines" in mind. Your exit line is what you say before you change the subject or excuse yourself from the scene. For example: "I'd like to check on a few things before I give you my answer (or respond to that, discuss that). May I get back to you at/on . . . ?" "Let me think about that for a while. I'll get back to you at/on . . . ." "I'm glad you brought that up. I must leave for a meeting (or appointment) now, but I want to talk with you about this as soon as I return."

   Use Exercise 5-7 to help prepare your own exit lines.

7. *Use substitute acting-out.* Tell yourself that you'll enjoy acting-out your feelings in an appropriate way later. Sometimes just telling yourself this can defuse the situation enough for you to deal with it effectively at the time it occurs.

   You can visualize throwing darts at a picture of the person on a dart board. (Some people even have dart boards in their office for this purpose.) Other substitutes are

   Any game that requires hitting a ball: Pretend the ball is the person or thing you resent and really smash it.

EXERCISE 5-7: ARMING YOURSELF WITH BUSINESSLIKE EXIT LINES

Recall three situations in which you acted-out your feelings and got poor results. After noting each situation, make up an exit line that would have been appropriate. Keep these lines in mind for future use in similar situations. (Note: When you become skilled at relaxation and visualization, exit lines may become unnecessary.)

Tense Situation 1 _____

Exit Line _____

Tense Situation 2 _____

Exit Line _____

Tense Situation 3 _____

Exit Line _____

Jogging or walking: Pretend you're stepping on the person you resent (if you need to!).

Karate: Pretend your opponent is the person you resent (but don't get carried away!).

Any physical exercise: You can work off the bottled-up energy of unexpressed feelings by reminding yourself while you're exercising that you're working out those feelings. Be aware of the situation and the resulting feeling you're now working out. You'll probably be free to rest peacefully once the tension and energy drain of unresolved feelings is eliminated.

Hitting a large stuffed doll: Try to knock the stuffing out of a large doll, animal, or dummy, using either your fists or a baseball bat.

A quick mental acting-out: Instead of visualizing the dart-throwing incident, you can picture yourself telling off the other person, kicking him or her in the seat of the pants, and so on. You may be able to work out the feeling in a few seconds and go on to deal with the situation calmly.

Expressing Feelings to a Trusted Friend   Another way of handling your emotions is to talk them out with someone. The more stressful your job, the more essential it is to have at least one trusted friend that you can "let your hair down" with. It's best if such friends are not connected with your job. Although business friends may understand the problems better than someone outside the company, it's risky to be completely open with them. True friends are rare: Most people are lucky if they have five or six at any one time in their lives. Someone who might serve as confidant(e) could be your husband, someone you live with, some family member or relative, or simply a friend. For the relationship to be mutually supportive, it should include aspects such as these:

You can be yourselves with each other.

You are interested in each other's well-being.

You really listen to each other.

You don't make judgments about each other's character, feelings, or behavior. (To avoid making judgments, think in terms of behavior that works or doesn't work, that appears to be constructive or destructive, rather than what is right or wrong, good or bad. Deal more with what is rather than with what *should* be.)

You confide in each other about the joyous events in your life as well as the problem situations.

You both feel more lovable and capable as a result of the friendship.

You can trust each other's judgment about revealing shared confidences.

Frequently you can gain insights into problem situations and learn more about yourself by discussing things with a friend. Such discussions can also be very helpful in "experiencing out" any leftover, bottled-up feelings you may have. This type of friendship can help both parties keep a balanced perspective on life. When things get rough, it can have a healing, therapeutic effect.

SUMMARY

Empowering yourself involves tapping your inner resources and managing stress. "Stress" as used here refers to significant disruptions in an individual's environment, whether the disruptions come from within (from unresolved hurts and fears) or from without (from pressures in her working, family, or social world). Even pleasant or neutral change can be a significant disruption of a person's environment and therefore can create stress. The more predictable disruptions are and the more control we believe we have over them, the less stressful they are for us. We can manage stress effectively (1) by anticipating problem areas likely to create disruption and pressure and developing strategies for preventing, reducing, or postponing them; (2) by learning to command inner resources so we can relax; and (3) by handling emotions constructively. Keep in mind these strategies.

1. Use time-management techniques. Develop a support network of peers, bosses, workers, and people outside the company. Know when and how to assert yourself appropriately.

2. Take an assertive approach to health, based on the viewpoint: "I am the cause of my health." An assertive approach means not surrendering responsibility for your health to the medical system. Instead, use the system when necessary on a client/customer basis. Place a high value on your health and be aware of and responsive to your body and its signals. Avoid high-risk behaviors.

3. Take care of nutritional needs and exercise regularly.

4. Control your physical, social, work, and personal environments.

5. Learn how to command your inner resources by using specific techniques for (a) staying in the here and now, rather than dwelling on past guilt and grudges or future worries; (b) mastering techniques for reaching a state of deep relaxation; (c) visualizing the results you want; (d) learning to let go of tension-producing needs; and (e) using your sleep time to move you toward your goals.

6. Handle emotions constructively and avoid the stereotype of the overly emotional female by (a) avoiding the tendency to take criticisms or slights personally; (b) putting criticism in perspective by evaluating your critic's qualifications and motives, the validity of the criticism itself, and how the feedback can help you reach your goals; (c) experiencing your feelings without acting them out by accepting them rather than judging them as good or bad, consciously choosing whether to act them out, giving feedback about your feelings in a calm manner, postponing your response by using businesslike exit lines when you can't respond calmly, and using substitute acting-out to release strong feelings. Remember that expressing feelings to a trusted friend can help you handle them constructively by getting them out in the open and gaining insights about yourself and others.

REFERENCES

1. Ardell, Donald B. *High Level Wellness.* Emmaus, Pa.: Rodale Press, 1987. The author gives an effective presentation of the holistic approach to health with a number of self-checks and an excellent annotated bibliography.

2. Bailey, Covert. *The Fit or Fat Woman.* Boston: Houghton Mifflin, 1989. A detailed guide to developing an aerobic exercise plan that takes into account your age and physical condition, this book includes explanations of body processes and dietary suggestions.

3. Benson, Herbert. *The Relaxation Response.* New York: Avon, 1976. Dr. Benson discusses the various types of diseases and illnesses directly connected to stress and presents relaxation techniques to help decrease blood pressure, relieve stress, and prevent illness.

4. Carr-Ruffino, Norma, and David Lambert. "Managerial Stress: Gender, Age, and Management Level as Moderators of Stressors." Paper presented at the Association of Management 1990 Annual Conference, Orlando, Florida.

5. Diener, Ed. Urbana: University of Illinois, Department of Psychology, 1991. In a study of more than 5,000 days of people's moods, subjects reported being intensely happy on fewer than 3 days in 100. Women reported more intense joy than men.

6. Davidson, Marilyn, and Cary Cooper. *Stress and the Woman Manager.* Oxford: Martin Robertson & Co., Ltd., 1983.

7. Delaney, Gayle. *Living Your Dreams*. San Francisco: Harper & Row, 1988. This detailed guide describes how to use your sleep to solve problems and to help create the life you want.

8. Dufty, William. *Sugar Blues*. New York: Warner Books, 1986. Dufty presents scientific evidence for the connection between refined sugar and a host of diseases and chronic conditions. He also discusses the high sugar content of many processed foods we don't think of as "sweets" and gives suggestions for determining sugar content.

9. Dyer, Wayne W. *You'll See It When You Believe It*. New York: Avon Books, 1990. The author of many best-selling books on personal change and success, including *Your Erroneous Zones*, discusses self-limiting beliefs that lead to stress and block success. He explains how changing your beliefs can change your life.

10. Emery, Stewart. *Actualizations: You Don't Have to Rehearse to Be Yourself*. Garden City, N.Y.: Doubleday, 1982. This book offers some excellent insights into becoming more comfortable with yourself and your relationships, maintaining perspective, and handling criticism.

11. Gallwey, W. Timothy. *Inner Tennis: Playing the Game*. New York: Random House, 1983. This book might be titled "Inner Life." Gallwey discusses ways of rising above the "ego self," whose anxieties and fears cause us to suffer defeat in the game of life as well as in tennis. He suggests ways to relax and let the "inner self" take over.

12. Freudenberger, Herbert J., and Gail North. *Women's Burnout*. New York: Penguin, 1986. Sources of stress that career women experience are explored, including how unmanaged stress can lead to burnout.

13. Handley, Jane, and Robert Handley. *Why Women Worry*. New York: Prentice-Hall, 1990. The authors tell how to deal with the stress of worry stemming from women's multifaceted roles and unique job pressures.

14. Maltz, Maxwell. *Psycho-Cybernetics*. Englewood Cliffs, N.J.: Prentice-Hall Pocket Books, 1960. A classic on how to use internal experiencing, or visualizing, as a direct and controlled method of changing your self-image and developing skill mastery.

15. Maltz, Maxwell. *Psycho-Cybernetic Principles for Creative Living*. New York: Simon and Schuster, 1974. Maltz gives additional processes for applying his self-image theory to positive action in your life.

16. Mason, Marilyn. *Making Our Lives Our Own*. San Francisco: Harper Collins, 1991. This is a woman's guide to six types of major changes that create challenge and excitement or worry and stress: leaving home, facing shame, forging an identity, integrating sexuality, claiming personal power, and tapping into the creative spirit.

17. Morse, David, and Lawrence Furst. *Women Under Stress*. New York: Van Nostrand Reinhold, 1982.

18. Rivers, Caryl. "Reaching for the Top." *Working Woman* (September 1983), p. 138.

19. Ross, Ruth. *Prospering Woman*. New York: Bantam, 1985. This excellent guide to achieving a full, abundant life includes detailed suggestions for commanding your inner resources.

20. Shealy, C. Norman. *90 Days to Self-Health*. New York: Bantam Books, 1988. Dr. Shealy's book is full of many types of techniques for relaxing.

21. Simonton, O. Carl, Stephanie Matthews-Simonton, and James L. Creighton. *Getting Well Again*. New York: Bantam Books, 1988. The Simontons achieved amazing results with "hopeless" cancer patients at their clinic in Fort Worth, Texas, using relaxation/visualization techniques along with conventional medical therapy. See especially *A Mind/Body Model of the Development of Cancer* and *A Mind/Body Model of Recovery*.

22. Watkin-Lanoil, Georgia. *The Female Stress Syndrome*. New York: Newmarket Press, 1984.

23. "World Hunger Actionletter," Ed. by American Friends Service Committee. *Ms Magazine* (August 1981).

Chapter Six

Asserting Yourself

"You can control your destiny without leaning."

Ellen Burstyn

The more positive and constructive your dealings with the people you work with, the easier your job as manager will be—and the more effective you will be. Understanding your own and others' behavior is crucial in getting along with people. During childhood, many women learn to be "too nice" (overcompliant or nonassertive) because they believe it pleases others or prevents problems. Every once in a while they may get fed up with being "walked on," rebel in an aggressive manner, and then return to a basically passive, indirect way of dealing with people. At both extremes, they give up control of how they will express their feelings. The cycle also creates further problems.

An essential rule for getting along with people on the job requires **assertiveness** in your transactions. The rule:

Go directly to the person(s) involved.

If you have a problem, foresee a potential problem or opportunity, need or want something, or merely want to give constructive feedback, go first to the person(s) most directly involved. State your case candidly and tactfully. Asking someone else to broach the subject or merely complaining or dropping hints and "hoping" something will change or someone will pass along the word often creates problems

of its own. This is a passive, timid approach. However, going over the person's head to get results is usually even worse. It may rightfully be viewed as an act of aggression, violating another person's rights.

When you complete this chapter, you should have the assertiveness skills for handling problem situations. In this chapter you will have the opportunity to

1. Become aware of ways in which communicating assertively can help you prevent problems, manage stress, improve your self-confidence, and become a more respected, effective manager

2. Define some of your basic rights and become committed to standing up for those rights

3. Identify assertive, nonassertive, and aggressive behaviors

4. Become more assertive in a variety of situations by applying the most appropriate techniques or combination of techniques

5. Learn how to change nonproductive behavior by changing your internalized parent messages, irrational beliefs, and self-statements through focusing on the pay-

offs for assertiveness, and trying out new behaviors

6. Become comfortable with behaving asser- tively in appropriate situations with your workers, other managers, and your bosses

---

  Recognizing Assertiveness Gaps

"Jan, you were right, as usual. I just wasn't man- aging the stress in my life. That seminar you recommended was just the ticket. You should see the changes I've made! And they're working."

"That's wonderful, Erika. And you're looking wonderful, too, I might add." Jan smiles as she and Erika settle into the restaurant booth for lunch.

"Well, I'm off cigarettes, and I'm substituting spring water and herbal teas for some of the coffee and booze I used to drink. A healthy diet and making time for exercise has worked won- ders—along with picking up some good time- management techniques."

"Yes," says Jan, "they all seem to work to- gether, don't they?"

"That's right, and you know, the skill that's been most helpful so far has been the relaxed concentration—it not only works to calm me down, but I'm convinced it's helping me solve problems and achieve my goals."

"I'm sure you need all the skills you can get to handle Tom Jenson. Any run-ins lately?"

"I thought you'd never ask," laughs Erika. "Just the other day he came barging in with the same old complaint . . ."

T: Can't your people ever do anything right? They're driving my people crazy!

E: What's the problem, Tom?

T: You don't seem to be able to train them well enough to fill in a simple order form cor- rectly. If we don't get the information we need, how can you expect us to get the right orders to the customers on time?

E: Do you have copies of the incorrect orders so I can see who's leaving off what?

T: Well, no, not with me. I just know that nearly every day we have a problem with one of your orders, and today we have a whole stack of them.

E: Tom, I'm glad you brought this matter up. It's important that I stay on top of this so your department gets the proper information. First, if you'll send me the orders you're hav- ing difficulty with today, I'll have someone in my office locate the information for you at once. Second, if you'll send me copies of incomplete orders you've received in, say, the past month, I'll analyze them to see who needs further training and in what areas. Then I'll set up a training session. Finally, let's work out a system where your people divert any incomplete orders to my office in the future so we can handle the problems before sending the orders back to you.

T: Well, I don't know. Maybe it will work. But you'll have to do something about this in- competence in your department.

E: Tom, I want to cooperate with you in every way I can to get the right orders to the cus- tomers on time. Can you meet with me at ten in the morning to go over a plan for diverting incomplete orders to my desk?

T: Okay, we can give it a try.

Jan nods approvingly. "That's more like it. You played it cool—and you were assertive. By the way, I hope your seminar leader pointed out that being assertive can also prevent stress from building up."

"Yes, but I think I need some work on that. I'm doing pretty well with my work team and my peers, but I'm still intimidated by men who are old enough to be my father. I know I handled this one badly. I asked Perry Walker, head of the Credit Department, to bring a couple of his people to a staff meeting. I wanted to go over several billing matters and get their cooperation in giving more liberal credit terms to new Harbor Point customers. The first few items were pretty routine. But when it came to the new credit terms, Perry interrupted me before I really had a chance to explain."

P: That would be a mistake. You'll make our other customers angry.

E: But I think —

P: We tried that once before, about five years ago, and the results were disastrous.

E: Well, I believe we can justify it for new customers.

P: Our other customers will find out. They won't like it. You'll lose some of them — and all for new customers who are an unknown factor. Besides it's against company policy, and I for one will not go out on a limb for this.

"So, I just dropped the subject and ended the meeting without getting what I wanted, or even making my case. You see? I just knuckle under to older men like Perry."

Jan smiles. "Looks like your next training seminar will be on developing assertiveness skills."

---

1. What are the major differences in the way Erika handled the meeting with Tom Jenson and the one with Perry Walker?

2. What actions and attitudes do you think were especially effective or ineffective?

3. What should Erika do next about the credit-terms issue?

4. What risks are involved in behaving assertively with authority figures?

5. List some possible payoffs for assertiveness in such situations.

ASSESSING YOUR AWARENESS OF ASSERTIVENESS

It's obvious that Erika was assertive in the first example and not in the second. But how do *you* know when *you're* being assertive? How do you decide on appropriate behavior? What do you base your decisions on? We'll discuss these questions in detail later.

First, let's briefly define "assertion," "nonassertion," and "aggression" as we'll use them in this book. Assertion is confidently expressing what you think, feel, and believe — and standing up for your rights while respecting the rights of others. Nonassertion is a reluctance or inability to express confidently what you think, feel, and believe — allowing others to violate your rights without challenge. Aggression is expressing yourself in ways that intimidate, demean, or degrade another person — and going after what you want in ways that violate the rights of another.

Before we go into more detailed descriptions of behavior, let's establish a clear understanding of the foundation on which assertive actions are based: human rights.

If your assertive actions are to be effective, they must be convincing. You must believe in what you're doing. This means you must be clear about your rights and the rights of others in the situation. Later, we'll discuss what other authorities say about rights; first, get in touch with what you (as your own authority) believe by completing Exercise 6-1. After you've formulated your own ideas about basic human rights, see how they compare with lists compiled by others. See Exhibits 6-1 and 6-2.

Has this brief discussion of rights helped you clarify what assertiveness is based on? Hopefully, you're already feeling more committed to standing up for your rights (and respecting the rights of others). Now test your understanding of the differences between assertiveness and other kinds of behavior by completing Exercise 6-2.

EXERCISE 6-1: DETERMINING YOUR RIGHTS

Think about some basic rights you are entitled to. List them. (If you're meeting with a group, you may want to jot down your own ideas first; then discuss them with the others. Perhaps the group can formulate its own list of basic rights.)

EXERCISE 6-2: IDENTIFYING ASSERTIVE, AGGRESSIVE, AND NONASSERTIVE BEHAVIOR

Indicate whether you think the response to each of the following situations is assertive (As), aggressive (Ag), or nonassertive (N). After you've completed the exercise, turn to the answer key to see how you did.

Situation	*Response*
1. Husband expects dinner on table when he arrives home from work and gets angry when it is not there immediately. You say:	I know you are tired and hungry and would like to have dinner immediately, but I have been doing some sculpting which is important to me. I will have dinner ready soon.
2. You are having trouble writing a paper and don't know exactly what further information you need. You say:	I really must be dumb but I don't know where to begin on this paper.
3. You are at a meeting of seven men and one woman. At the beginning of the meeting, the chairman asks you to be the secretary. You respond:	No, I'm sick and tired of being the secretary just because I'm the only woman in the group.
4. A woman is being interviewed for a job, in the process of which the interviewer looks at her leeringly and says, "You certainly look as if you have all the qualifications for the job." She responds:	I'm sure I am quite capable of doing the work here.
5. You're walking to the copy machine when a fellow employee, who always asks you to do his copying, asks you where you're going. You respond:	I'm going to the Celtics ball game . . . Where does it look like I'm going?
6. You are asked to serve on a committee. You respond:	I'm sorry. I'm not available to serve on that committee.
7. Man asks you for a date. You've dated him once before and you're not interested in dating him again. You respond:	Oh, I'm really so busy this week that I don't think I will have time to see you this Saturday night.

Situation	*Response*
8. You are in a line at the store. Someone behind you has one item, and asks to get in front of you. You say:	I realize that you don't want to wait in line, but I was here first and I really would like to get out of here.
9. Employer sends a memorandum stating that there should be no more long-distance business calls made without getting prior permission. One employee responds:	You're taking away my professional judgment. It's insulting to me.
10. You'd like a raise and say:	Do you think that, ah, you could see your way clear to giving me a raise?
11. Student enjoyed the teacher's class and says:	You make the material interesting. I like the way you teach the class.
12. Your husband promised you that he would talk to your daughter about her behavior at school. The promise has not been carried out. You say:	I thought we agreed last Tuesday that you would have a talk with Barb about her behavior at school. So far there's been no action on your part. I still think you should talk to her soon. I'd prefer sometime tonight.
13. A committee meeting is being established. The time is convenient for other people but not for you. The times are set when it will be next to impossible for you to attend regularly. When asked about the time, you say:	Well I guess it's OK. I'm not going to be able to attend very much but it fits everyone else's schedule.
14. In a conversation, a man suddenly says, "What do you women libbers want anyway?" The woman responds:	Fairness and equality.
15. You've been talking for a while with a friend on the telephone. You would like to end the conversation and you say:	I'm terribly sorry but my supper's burning, and I have to get off the phone. I hope you don't mind.
16. A married man persists in asking you out for a date, saying, "Come on honey, what harm can it do to go to lunch with me just this once?" You respond:	I like our relationship the way it is. I wouldn't feel comfortable with any kind of dating relationship — and that includes lunch.
17. At a meeting one person often interrupts you when you're speaking. You say,	Excuse me. I would like to finish my statement.
18. You have been pestered several times by a caller who has repeatedly tried to sell you magazines. The caller contacts you again with the same magazine proposition. You say:	This is the third time I've been disturbed and each time I've told you that I'm not interested in subscribing to any magazine. If you call again, I'll simply have to report this to the authorities.

Situation	*Response*
19. Wife tells husband she'd like to return to school. He doesn't want her to do this and says:	Why would you want to do that? You know you're not capable enough to handle the extra work load.
20. An employee makes a lot of mistakes in his work. You say:	You're a lazy and sloppy worker.

Reprinted from Arthur Lange and Patricia Jakubowski, *Responsible Assertive Behavior,* copyright © 1983 (Champaign, Ill.: Research Press, 1983), pp. 41–52. Used by permission of Patricia Jakubowski.

EXHIBIT 6-1: A Bill of Assertive Rights

1. You have the right to judge your own behavior, thoughts, and emotions, and to take responsibility for their initiation and consequences upon yourself. (This is your prime assertive right. The other nine rights listed here are derived from this one and serve to elaborate on it more fully.)
2. You have the right to offer no reasons or excuses for justifying your behavior.
3. You have the right to judge if you are responsible for finding solutions to other people's problems.
4. You have the right to change your mind.
5. You have the right to make mistakes — and be responsible for them.
6. You have the right to say, "I don't know."
7. You have the right to be independent of the goodwill of others before coping with them.
8. You have the right to be illogical in making decisions.
9. You have the right to say, "I don't understand."
10. You have the right to say, "I don't care."

In other words, you have the right to say "no" without feeling guilty.

Excerpted from the book *When I Say No, I Feel Guilty* by Manuel J. Smith. Copyright © 1985 by Manuel J. Smith. Reprinted by permission of the Dial Press.

EXHIBIT 6-2: Everywoman's Bill of Rights

1. The right to be treated with respect
2. The right to have and express your own feelings and opinions
3. The right to be listened to and taken seriously
4. The right to set your own priorities
5. The right to ask for what you want
6. The right to get what you pay for
7. The right to ask for information from professionals (doctors, lawyers, counselors)
8. The right to choose not to assert yourself

Descriptions of Assertion, Nonassertion, and Aggression*

To clarify the differences between assertive, nonassertive, and aggressive behavior, assertion trainers Patricia Jakubowski and Arthur Lange have developed excellent definitions of the three categories.

Assertion   You assert yourself when you stand up for your personal rights and act in ways that express your thoughts, feelings, and beliefs in direct, honest, and appropriate ways that don't violate another person's rights. You assert yourself as much by your actions (if not more so) as by your words. By your actions and your words you convey to people: This is what I think. This is what I feel. This is how I see the situation. You convey this in a way that doesn't dominate, humiliate, or degrade the other person.

Assertion is based on respect for yourself and respect for the other person. You express your preferences and defend your rights in a way that also respects other people's needs and rights. The goal of assertion is to get and give respect, to ask for fairness, and to leave space for compromise when your needs and rights conflict with another person's. Such compromises respect the basic integrity of both people, and both get some of their wishes satisfied. This approach to assertion helps you avoid the temptation of using assertion to manipulate others in order to get what you want. It frequently leads to both people getting what they want because most people tend to become cooperative when they're approached in a way that respects both parties.

Nonassertion   When you let others victimize you by failing to act in ways that express your honest feelings, thoughts, and beliefs, or when you express them in such an apologetic, unsure, or self-effacing way that others can easily disregard them, then you're allowing your rights to be violated through **nonassertiveness.** By such actions you tell others: I don't count for much: You can take advantage of me. My feelings aren't very important: Yours are. My thoughts aren't important: Yours are the only ones really worth listening to. I'm nothing: You're superior.

Nonassertion reflects a lack of respect for your preferences. In an indirect way it reflects a lack of respect for the other person's ability to take disappointments, to assume some responsibility, or to handle problems. The goal of nonassertion is to please others and to avoid conflict at any cost.

Passive-aggressive behavior is a variation of nonassertion. Some experts theorize that nonassertion is always accompanied by some degree of resentment that is experienced at some level, whether conscious, subconscious, or unconscious. Passive-aggressive behavior always results in some type of hostile action. For example, you may secretly pout, stew, fret — all the while being "nice" and giving no clue to your real feelings. If you are unaware of the source of your resentment, you may suddenly explode, surprising even yourself. If you are aware of your resentment toward the "aggressor," then you may quietly sabotage that person's efforts or projects. You may resort to passive-aggressive behavior because you fear the consequences of speaking up. You may feel another is trying to dominate you, and this is your way of resisting. Such relationships frequently have a persecutor-victim aspect.

Aggression   When you stand up for your personal rights and express your thoughts, feelings, and beliefs in ways that violate the rights of another person, you're behaving with **aggressiveness.** Such actions and words are often dishonest and usually inappropriate. Such behavior carries this message: This is what I think: You're stupid for believing differently.

---

*Based on the work of Arthur Lange and Patricia Jakubowski, *Responsible Assertive Behavior,* copyright © 1983 (Champaign, Ill.: Research Press, 1983), by permission of Patricia Jakubowski.

This is what I want: What you want isn't important. This is what I feel: Your feelings don't count. The goal is domination and winning—which means the other person loses. Winning is achieved by humiliating, belittling, degrading, intimidating, or overpowering other people so that they become less able to express their preferences and defend their rights.

Examples of Assertive, Nonassertive, and Aggressive Responses

You ask for a long-overdue raise.

Aggressive: "You've been ignoring the fact that I'm underpaid for what I do. I think you're taking advantage of my good nature."

Assertive: "I've prepared this analysis showing that my job responsibilities and productivity have increased by more than fifteen percent since my last raise. I would like a fifteen percent raise based on these increases."

Nonassertive: "Uh . . . I know things are tight just now, but . . . uh . . . do you think you could see your way clear to give me a raise?"

Your subordinate is habitually late for work.

Aggressive: "Do you really think you can come dragging in late all the time and keep your job?"

Assertive: "Let's discuss this problem of getting to work on time."

Nonassertive: You send a memo to all subordinates regarding the need for punctuality, hoping the late worker will get the message.

A boss asks you to take on tasks that are not your responsibility and that you don't want to get saddled with.

Aggressive: "Get someone else to do your dirty work."

Assertive: "I realize you must find someone to do this, but I don't think it's part of my job responsibilities and I don't want to take on tasks that will prevent me from doing my best with my own responsibilities."

Nonassertive: "Well, okay, I guess I can handle it."

To Assert or Not to Assert?

By now you have an idea of appropriate assertive behavior, and you know that you have a right *not* to assert yourself. How are you going to decide when to assert? In making this decision, keep in mind that the choice may involve the rights of others. If so, are you willing to compromise?

How will others interpret your nonassertiveness? The men you work with may interpret your behavior in ways you never intended. For example, many women use silence as a way of ignoring a situation, avoiding an embarrassing confrontation, or "rising above" unpleasant circumstances. For men, silence may signal consent, or they may interpret it as weakness—a sign that you'll have trouble in the tough business world.

Will assertiveness improve your relationships and your self-respect? This is a key factor to consider when you're deciding whether to assert yourself. Nonassertive behavior creates problems for many women. Aggressive behavior is less frequently a problem because most women have accepted the **socialization messages** they received in childhood and the cultural stereotypes of ways they should act. However, some women believe they must behave aggressively "to make it in a man's world." They feel they will become vulnerable and lose control if they don't. This viewpoint overlooks the fact that most people "go underground" in their relations with aggressive people. They find indirect ways to undercut the aggressor's control. The most successful relationships are based on assertive behavior, and they help prevent and reduce the degree of stress you experience.

Will assertiveness prevent or reduce stress? This is another key factor to consider when you're deciding whether to assert yourself in your relationships (see Chapter 5). We teach people by our actions how we will and will not be treated and how we think, feel, and believe about certain matters. When someone violates our rights and we *don't* say anything, we teach them that it's okay to exploit, dominate, or manipulate us, and we therefore create stress in our lives.

What if you alienate another in the teaching process? If you've shown respect for that person while asserting yourself, then it's fairly safe to assume that a mutually beneficial relationship was impossible to begin with. In such cases it's best to lay your cards on the table early; otherwise, you are likely to get hooked into playing the other person's games. If you eventually decide to assert yourself and break up the games, your "friend" is likely to react much more negatively at this point than in an initial encounter. And you are more likely to have an emotional stake in the relationship the longer it continues, and therefore experience more upset when it runs into trouble.

In short, you prevent stress by asserting yourself in the beginning in any new situation or relationship. If you do, you are likely to find yourself surrounded by people who honestly accept, respect, and admire you — a true support network. Others pass on by, and you will probably find yourself with *fewer* enemies.

Strangely enough, people like most those people they respect, and you don't gain respect by letting yourself be dominated or manipulated. In fact people may pity you even while they take advantage of your nonassertion. This pity may eventually become irritation and even disgust. In the long run more people that you really want to be around will like you if you

behave assertively. People who appreciate you for who you are and who support your growth and autonomy will respect your assertiveness, and you'll respect yourself more. As you feel better about yourself, more self-confident, you'll start getting more of the things you want in life. You'll prevent many of the problems that create stress, including the frustrations and resulting pressures created by nonassertion.

As you are deciding when to assert yourself, ask the following questions: (1) How important is this situation to me? (2) How am I likely to feel afterward if I *don't* behave assertively (rather than aggressively or nonassertively) in this situation? (3) How much will it cost me to assert myself in this situation?

Once you decide to assert, follow the advice offered by psychologist Wayne Dyer in *Pulling Your Own Strings:*

> Try to make all your assertive encounters happy, fun, and challenging experiences, rather than battlegrounds in which you place your humanity on the line. *Have fun* seeing how effective you can be. If you succeed in this, but don't invest your entire self-worth in the process, you need never again be a victim. Avoid plowing through with deadpan seriousness or "trying hard." Relax and enjoy the challenge. [3, p. 89]

SELECTING THE BEST ASSERTIVE APPROACH

Situations calling for assertiveness can vary widely. Therefore, you need to become familiar with a number of different approaches to asserting yourself, so that you can select the most appropriate method or combination of methods for each type of situation.

We'll define ways of behaving assertively according to the following categories: (1) basic assertion, (2) assertion with empathy, (3) I-messages, (4) assertion with increasing firmness, (5) assertion that confronts broken agreements, (6) persuasive assertion in groups, and (7) feedback assertion.

These approaches should provide you with a broad range of practical, constructive actions to take in order to assert yourself in most of the situations you will encounter.

Basic Assertion

The direct, simple actions involved in standing up for personal likes, opinions, beliefs, or feelings are known as basic assertion [6, p. 14]. Basic assertion also involves expressing affection and appreciation toward another person. Here are some examples:

1. You're asked a question for which you have no ready answer. You reply: "I'd like a few minutes to think that over."

2. The person in the next room has a radio playing loudly. You say: "Your radio is disturbing me. Would you turn it down?"

3. Your boss keeps interrupting you while you're trying to make a point. You say: "Excuse me, I'd like to finish making my point."

4. A colleague makes a good presentation. You say: "I enjoyed your talk. Your descriptions were so clear."

Assertion with Empathy

Sometimes you want to express empathy along with your preferences or feelings. You want to show that you recognize the other person's viewpoint or feelings. The empathetic statement is followed by one that stands up for your rights [6, p. 14].

Assertion with empathy is often effective because people are more likely to accept your assertion when they feel you have some understanding and respect for their position. It's especially valuable in situations where you tend to overreact in an aggressive way. If you take a moment to try to understand the other person's viewpoint before you react, you're less likely to respond aggressively. On the other hand, your expression of empathy must be sincere to be effective. People can usually spot insincere expressions of empathy, and they resent such attempts to manipulate. Here are some examples of assertion with empathy.

1. The boss wants a time-consuming report submitted tomorrow. You say: "I know you need this report as soon as possible, but I have important plans for this evening and won't be able to work overtime."

2. A subordinate is trying to get you to serve as referee in his personality clash with a co-worker. You tell him: "I can understand why you want help with this problem, but the two of you will have to work this out together on your own."

I-Messages

You are most likely to retain the goodwill of the person you're standing up to if you stick with your own thoughts, feelings, and beliefs and avoid direct or implied criticism of his or her thoughts, feelings, or beliefs. One way to do that is to think in terms of **I-messages**. In *Effectiveness Training for Women*, Linda Adams has described an I-message as

> a statement that describes you; it is an expression of *your* feelings and experiences. It is authentic, honest, and congruent. And since I-messages express only your inner reality, they do not contain evaluations, judgments, or interpretations of others. Since you are saying what you really feel, your verbal and nonverbal expressions are in harmony. Your messages come through confidently and congruently. [1, pp. 31–32]

Think about your own reaction to the **you-message** "You talk too loudly" versus the I-message "I have sensitive hearing." Let's look now at some specific instances in which I-messages can be effective.

Preventive I-messages let people know ahead of time what you will need and want. They can prevent many conflicts and misunderstandings. To send preventive I-messages successfully, it's important to (1) know what you want, or need, in life and in specific situations, (2) decide to take personal responsibility for meeting your preferences, (3) express your preferences in an assertive way to the person whose cooperation you need, and (4) be willing to shift gears to listen if the other person becomes defensive. Here are some examples.

1. "I'd like to set up a time to meet with you to plan what we're going to do at the conference, so I'll feel prepared and less anxious when we get there." (Instead of a you-message: "You shouldn't wait until the last minute to plan what you're going to do at the conference.")

2. "I'd like us to figure out what needs to be done before the week is over, so we can make sure we have time to get it all done." (Instead of, "You need to manage your time better.")

3. "I'd like to know what we're going to discuss in our meeting tomorrow, so I can bring the necessary information with me." (Instead of, "You should send out an agenda.")

These I-messages all begin with "I'd like" to point out that they express your preferences. They may also be phrased as questions: "Could we set a time . . . ?"

Declarative I-messages help others know more about you. They are self-disclosures that tell people about your beliefs, ideas, likes, dislikes, feelings, reactions, interests, attitudes, and intentions. They let others know what you have experienced, what it feels like to be you. They describe your inner reality. Here are some examples.

1. "I'm excited about the project."

2. "I'm worried about completing the project on time."

3. "I'm looking forward to more business travel."

4. "I appreciate the time you've spent on this."

Responsive I-messages clearly communicate "no" when "no" expresses your authentic feelings. They can also clearly communicate "yes" when "yes" expresses your authentic feelings. In addition to saying "yes" or "no," you may also want to express how a request will affect you or the reason you are saying "yes" or "no." Here are some examples.

1. "I have decided not to."

2. "No, I can't have the report to you on Monday because I have another project that I want to complete first."

3. "Yes, I will be glad to tackle that project. It will give me a chance to learn more about . . ."

Assertion with Increasing Firmness

Frequently a simple statement of assertion made in a friendly manner will be effective. On the other hand, you'll sometimes have to deal with people who persist in violating your rights or ignoring your stated preferences. In such cases you can state your position with increasing firmness without becoming aggressive [6, pp. 16–20]. Here are some examples.

You have helped out a married male colleague, and he keeps insisting on taking you to dinner to "return the favor."

First response: "That's very nice of you, but I never go out socially with business friends. You can return the favor by helping me out sometime."

Second response: "No thanks. I really feel very strongly about not accepting dinner invitations from business friends, especially married men."

Third response: "The answer is 'no.' Please don't ask me again."

A worker is repeatedly late in submitting an important periodic report. When you speak with him about it, he argues about the necessity of giving it top priority.

First response: "I know it's time consuming to collect all the figures you need for this report, but it has top-priority status. I must receive it on time in order to prepare for the regular staff meetings."

Second response: "You'll have to manage your activities so that this report gets done on time. Make certain you're not late in submitting it again."

Third response: "If you can't manage your work so that the most important jobs are done on time, I'll have no choice but to reassign you to a position with less responsibility."

In these cases the third responses were appropriate because the earlier assertions were ignored. They would have been inappropriate if they had been the initial responses.

In the second situation a **contract option** was offered. The speaker said what her final assertion would be and gave the listener a chance to change his behavior before that occurred. Some people will believe you're serious about standing firm only when you reach the contract-option point. The option should be said not as a threat, but merely as a fact. Therefore, it's important to be calm and rational when delivering this type of assertion, speaking in a matter-of-fact tone of voice. You simply give information about the consequences if the problem is not satisfactorily resolved.

Assertion that Confronts Broken Agreements

When another person fails to keep his or her agreements with you, **confrontive assertion** is appropriate. This involves describing specifically and nonjudgmentally what the other person said he or she would do, what he or she actually did do, and what you want [6, pp. 16–20]. Again it's important to express yourself in a matter-of-fact tone of voice with nonevaluative language. Here are some examples.

1. "I thought we agreed that my department will receive two additional personnel assistants, and I confirmed that in my memo of June 2. Yet the new budget shows no provision for new assistants. I would like for you to revise it to provide for them."

2. "I agreed that you could use the services of my assistant occasionally as long as you check with me first. She said you asked her to do some work yesterday, but you didn't mention it to me. I'd like to find out why you did that."

The confrontive assertion normally involves more two-way interaction than is shown here. You'll usually want to learn more about the circumstances of the broken agreement in order to solve the problem it has created. It's important to avoid a critical, accusing attitude, which usually results in an aggressive confrontation that judges the other person and attempts to make him or her feel guilty. For example: "You broke your promise! Obviously I can't depend on your word and will have to get everything in writing from you from now on."

Persuasive Assertion in Groups

We've been discussing types of assertion that apply mainly to one-on-one transactions. Now let's look at ways to assert yourself in group situations. To have the greatest impact when expressing honest opinions in task-oriented groups such as staff meetings and committee meetings, you can learn to use timing and tact [6, pp. 16–20].

Timing involves not only choosing the right time to express an opinion but avoiding taking up too much group time by expressing your opinion too frequently. Therefore you need to decide which of the agenda items being discussed have top priority for you and are worth taking a stand on. Otherwise you may end up talking far too long about nearly every topic that's brought up. If the other group members decide that you just like to hear yourself talk and that you need to be the center of attention, they'll be likely to ignore your opinions on the issues that are really important to you.

Probably the best time to state your opinion on an issue is after a third or a half of the committee members have already expressed their positions. By then you have a sense of the group's position, and you can respond to the points that have been raised. It's unlikely that the group has made up its mind on the issue, so your position has a good chance of influencing the group's decision.

When you express your opinion on your top-priority item, state it as clearly and concisely as possible without belittling yourself.

Nonassertive: "Well, I've been known to be wrong before, but it seems as if maybe we should think of some other ways of doing this."

Assertive: "This approach to marketing the product involves some high-risk factors. I think it would be a good idea to consider some other approaches that could reduce our risks."

To have the greatest impact, assertive words must be accompanied by assertive body language: Look directly at the various members of the group. Speak with appropriate loudness and firmness. And use your hands in a relaxed

way to make reinforcing gestures. Of course, you must do your homework before the meeting so you know what you're talking about (see Chapter 7).

Tact is extremely important when your viewpoint differs from that of the majority of the group or from that of an influential member. Find something that you honestly think is good about the opposing viewpoint and acknowledge that before stating your viewpoint. For example:

1. "I agree that we need to expand our market in the southern region. However, if we expand too rapidly, we won't be able to deliver the goods on time, and eventually we may lose more customers than we gain."

2. "That's a good analysis of our internal budget problem. It's also important to examine the role that our competitors play in the problem."

Assertion That Gives Feedback

Assertive managers are able to give feedback that clarifies their thinking, feelings, opinions, and understanding of what others have said and done. We'll discuss constructive approaches to giving feedback, including suggestions for describing others' behavior specifically and nonjudgmentally and for expressing your feelings appropriately.

Giving Feedback That Clarifies   You can develop skill in giving feedback that clarifies situations and keeps communication lines open. When you use a constructive approach such as we discuss here, your feedback can help build and maintain good relationships rather than destroy them.

Give regular feedback so that the receiver gets at least as much positive as negative feedback. Give negative feedback early, before a situation builds to the point that strong emotional reactions may be involved. Approach situations in a spirit of helpfulness and willingness to solve any problems.

Let's take those most difficult situations in which you need to assert yourself by giving someone feedback about how their behavior is affecting you. Such **feedback assertion** should clarify your viewpoint and help resolve the problem situation. For best results include these four basic aspects:

1. *When you* . . . (You nonjudgmentally describe some specific behavior of the other person.)

2. *The effects are* . . . (You describe as specifically as possible how the other person's behavior *concretely* affects your life — the practical problems it creates.)

3. *I feel* . . . (You describe the feelings you experience as a result; avoid the expression "you make me.")

4. *I prefer* . . . (You describe what you want — preferably after giving the other person a chance to state what she or he thinks might be done.)

The first three parts of the message can be given in any sequence using any words that express the ideas shown. Here's an example of this type of feedback message: "When I don't get the information I need from you about the number of orders your department has processed each day, I'm unable to make appropriate work schedules for the next day. This has happened twice in the last two weeks, and I'm getting frustrated. What procedures can we work out to make sure I get the information I need each day?"

Now test your initial understanding of feedback messages by evaluating this example: "When you don't send me information about the number of orders your department has processed each day, you really frustrate me. I'd like you to be more reliable."

In that example, the speaker hasn't stated what effect the problem behavior has on her

life. By the way she expresses her feelings, she puts herself in the position of a helpless victim. Instead of asking for a preferred type of behavior that is specific and objective, she makes a vague request that implies a condemnation of the receiver's character.

Here are some general suggestions for giving feedback constructively in situations where tension has been building: First, focus on your viewpoint by analyzing what it is that's really bothering you and how you feel when it occurs. Form this into an I-message that incorporates the first three elements of feedback assertion just listed. Find an appropriate time, and state your I-message to the other person. Describe accurately and completely enough to give a clear observable picture, but don't talk too long (a response known as "overloading") or introduce a great deal of evidence (sometimes called the "courtroom technique").

Next, focus on the receiver's viewpoint. Ask the other person how she or he sees this situation and listen with an open mind, as nonjudgmentally as possible. Acknowledge what the receiver says (for example, "You feel that . . ." or "You think we should do . . ."). Avoid the tendency at this point to defend your position by reiterating your point and trying to prove it. Instead focus your energy on understanding the other person's viewpoint while not losing sight of your own.

Once you are sure you clearly understand the other person's viewpoint, you may want to come back to your position but almost as if you are approaching it from the other person's side. For example, "So the way you see this is that I am making it very difficult for you to cooperate by expecting too much too soon? Is that right?"

Finally, reach an agreement. When both viewpoints are adequately clarified, determine whether some action needs to be agreed on or whether communicating thoughts and feelings is all that's needed for now. For example, "How are we going to do this from now on?" or "I think it's enough for now if we just understand each other's viewpoints and feelings about this." Establish a feeling of closure by expressing how you feel *now* at the end of this discussion and asking the other person how she or he feels now. Accept these feelings without trying to change them. For example, "I feel relieved for having shared my thoughts and feelings, but I'm worried that you may resent my telling you this," or "I do feel a little defensive, but I think I'll get over it. I appreciate your letting me know about this."

Now that you've had an overview of giving feedback assertively, we'll look at the two most common barriers to doing so effectively and at ways to overcome them.

Giving Feedback Specifically and Nonjudgmentally   Most people give feedback about problem behavior in vague, accusatory language and therefore trigger a defensive reaction from the listener. Here are some suggestions for giving another person specific feedback about his or her behavior and the effects it has on your life.

1. *Be specific.* State exactly who did what, when, where, and to whom or what it was done. If appropriate, give a detailed but brief step-by-step replay of exactly what happened. Don't bog down in detail. Keep your purpose clearly in mind.

2. *Paint an observable picture.* Describe the situation so that the listener can see a picture of what you saw, as if he or she were a disinterested observer watching the situation.

3. *Clarify your statements.* Be exact and accurate. Avoid the tendency to exaggerate behavior that bothers you by using all-or-nothing expressions such as "never," "always," and "every time." To describe behavior accurately, it's important to be exact by using phrases such as "three times this month," "every day this week," "sometimes," "often," "occasionally."

4. *Use nonjudgmental words.* When people discuss behavior that offends them, they're prone to use judgmental words such as "sloppy," "lazy," "inconsiderate," and "stupid." These words not only judge a person's behavior, they are frequently used to overgeneralize about a person's character traits. Because they tend to put down a person and imply he or she is wrong, they are aggressive rather than assertive. They usually trigger defensive or guilty feelings. In addition they give little or no information that can help the listener identify specific behavior that will be acceptable to you, as these examples reveal:

Nonspecific, judgmental feedback: "I would appreciate it if you would at least be considerate and polite in your dealings with me."

Specific, descriptive feedback: "When you came over to my desk yesterday, you spoke in a very loud voice and demanded the Carter Company invoice. When we were unable to furnish it, you called us incompetent . . ."

Nonspecific, judgmental feedback: "We have a problem with your invoicing unit."

Specific, descriptive feedback: "During the last three weeks, your invoicing unit has not informed us of delays in their invoice-processing. We have received several telephone calls from angry customers because of these delays . . ."

Expressing Feelings Effectively   Most people have difficulty identifying and expressing their feelings appropriately, but this skill can also be mastered. Even in business situations it can be important to communicate your feelings about another's behavior. Doing so increases the impact of your feedback message. The listener is more likely to get it and to remember it. To be effective, however, your message must also make clear that you take responsibility for your own feelings.

When people first attempt to communicate their feelings, they are likely to make such statements as "You make me angry when you accuse me like that." This you-message implies that the other person is responsible for your angry feeling and that you're blaming the other person for your feeling and accusing him or her of causing it. This further implies that the other person can control the way you feel, which places you in a weak, helpless role.

"When you called me incompetent, I felt angry" may appear to be an almost identical statement to the one above. But in fact it is a quite different I-message in which you take responsibility for your feelings. You have the ultimate control over how you choose to view an accusation (or any other event) and therefore over how you will feel when it occurs. The way you phrase your messages about your feelings may seem unimportant. However, each time you phrase them in language that blames someone else for them, you are telling *yourself* — as well as others — that you are a victim controlled by others' actions.

Stating feelings directly and honestly is difficult for many people. They find it much easier to (1) state an evaluation of the other's behavior, (2) state the solution they want to the problem, or (3) imply their feelings indirectly. Many people expect a listener to be a mind-reader, or more specifically a feelings-reader. Here are some suggestions for avoiding those traps.

1. *State feelings, not evaluations.* Imply that your underlying attitude is "I'll tell you very directly what I'm feeling in response to your behavior, but I won't judge your behavior." This attitude carries a quite different message from one that implies "I'm going to tell you when you're good or bad, based on your behavior toward me."

2. *State feelings, not solutions.* When you state solutions to the problem instead of expressing your feelings about it, you imply that you're superior to the other person. You are able to figure out the problem and a solution without even discussing it with him or her. This approach also implies a lack of trust, that you don't expect the other person to be able to figure out an acceptable solution to his or her own problem behavior. Also, stating a solution before discussing the problem omits vital problem-solving steps. You haven't agreed on a definition of the problem, much less a solution that is acceptable to both of you. The problem may now become one of enforcing the solution! People may resist your high-handedness even if they agree with your solution.

3. *State feelings directly.* Simply say you are hurt, pleased, happy, annoyed, or frustrated. Don't imply your feelings by your voice tone, emphasis, sarcasm, or other indirect means; and don't expect people to infer them from your cutting remarks, questions, denials, or cloaked messages. For example, instead of saying directly; "I really become annoyed when you borrow my directory and don't return it," you say, "If people in this office would be more thoughtful, it sure would make it a nicer place to work." Such indirect messages usually communicate only a vague, underlying negative feeling. They are often interpreted by receivers as a generalized rejection of them as persons rather than as a specific reaction to a specific event. Instead of thinking, "She's upset because I didn't return her directory," the other person tends to think, "She doesn't like me; I wonder why."

Now you have the tools to give feedback assertively in problem situations. Even if the feedback doesn't lead to your preferred solution of a problem, it can help you become more open and direct with your thoughts and feelings. As a result, people are more likely to learn they can trust you. They know "where you're at," for better or worse. They tend to become more open in their dealings with you and with others in the work group.

You can enhance this openness and trust by using feedback assertion about constructive behavior, too. Here's an example: "Thank you for getting these reports to me on time every week. That makes it easy for me to be well prepared for staff meetings. I feel happy when I get that kind of cooperation. Keep up the good work." Feedback assertion helps you build an atmosphere for dealing with all kinds of behavior and at the same time minimizing defensiveness. Exercise 6-3 is designed to help you learn more about giving effective feedback, especially about describing behavior non-judgmentally.

Combinations for Maintaining Assertiveness

You'll probably be surprised at how readily others accept and respect your assertiveness. You must be prepared, however, for the occasional "tough cookie" who responds aggressively by coming back with verbal attacks, demands, or put-downs. Think about appropriate combinations of techniques you can use as shown in the following example of dealing with a person who won't take "no" for an answer.

Assertion with empathy to show that you have

EXERCISE 6-3: GIVING FEEDBACK MESSAGES

Read the following story:

You have a new apartment-mate, Lois. You have been sharing an apartment for about a month now, and things have been going fairly smoothly. However, two or three times you have come home from the office to the following scene: In the entry hall, Lois's coat is thrown over the chair; her shoes are lying in the middle of the floor; and her briefcase is on the floor, leaning against the wall. In the living room, the newspaper is spread all over—part of it on the floor and the rest of it on the tables and the sofa. Various articles of clothing are also scattered around the room. Lois, wearing an old robe, is sitting in the easy chair with her feet propped up on the arm of the sofa. She's drinking a can of beer and eating a package of peanuts. A few peanuts and an empty beer can are on the living room floor. The television is playing loudly.

Now it's Friday. This morning a man you've been interested in getting to know better called you at the office and asked you out to dinner. You agreed and suggested he come by your apartment about 7 P.M. for a before-dinner drink. You rush home from the office and reach your apartment at 5:30. As you enter, you see a repeat of the previously described scenario. You decide that the time has come to give Lois some feedback about her behavior.

You say; "Lois, I want to talk with you . . ."

Now you finish the statement. On a separate sheet of paper, write what you would say to Lois. (If you're doing this exercise as part of a class activity, your instructor may ask you to complete the message and then exchange papers. If so, don't sign your name to the front of the paper. Instead turn the paper over and print your initials in the upper right-hand corner.)

actually received the other person's message can be used initially: "I understand that your work is important to you and therefore you think it's unfair that I don't give your work top priority, but we can't complete it before Thursday."

Repeated assertion, in which you firmly repeat your original point while still responding to *legitimate* points made by the other person, can be used when the other person persists. The repetition helps you avoid becoming side-tracked by justifying your personal feelings, preferences, or opinions or arguing about irrelevant issues: "I must use my own judgment about the priorities I assign to the work that comes into my department." Or, "I understand the importance of this work to you, but we still must complete two other projects before we start yours."

Active listening questions (see Chapter 7 for more on this) about the other person's assumptions or positions can help clarify while you remain firm: "Are you saying that I should ignore everyone else's requests except yours?" Or, "Do you think that just because I don't grant this request that I don't want to cooperate with your department?" Or, "Are you angry because there's other work ahead of yours?"

Feedback assertion can be used if the discussion reaches an impasse: "I'm getting irritated. When I tell you we can have your project completed no earlier than Thursday and you keep insisting that we complete it by Tuesday, I begin to think you're trying to interfere with the way I run my department. I would prefer not to take up any more time discussing this."

NONVERBAL MESSAGES: ACTIONS SPEAK LOUDER THAN WORDS

Regardless of the assertive approach you select, you must learn to communicate your message nonverbally as well as verbally. One reason it's so important to be convinced of your rights is that your true convictions will come through in your nonverbal behavior. Many nonverbal aspects are virtually impossible to consciously control. They reveal how you really feel about a situation or person. They have far more impact than the verbal part of your message. Research indicates that our words, our vocal expression or tone, and our facial expression have the following impact on a listener's perception and decoding of a message [8, p. 44]:

Impact of words (verbal impact)   7%
Nonverbal impact   93%
   Vocal expression
     or voice tone   38%
   Facial expression   55%

If a speaker's facial expression or voice tone conflicts with what he or she is saying, the listener will normally accept, remember, and act on the nonverbal message. This makes sense when you consider that feelings have much more influence on actions than rational, logical thoughts do. People are more likely to act on their feelings. (So when you get conflicting messages, pay more attention to the nonverbal portion of the message.)

Types of Nonverbal Communication

Nonverbal communication takes many forms besides vocal and facial expression. The clothing people wear, the way they establish and observe territories and status symbols, whether and how they shake hands, and their body positions and postures can speak volumes.

Facial Expression High-status, assertive males tend to be more impassive than most women are. They are more "poker-faced" in business situations and thus express less emotion. They also smile less often and less broadly than women.

Voice Tone and Expression Most people equate a strong, deep male voice with power and authority. While most women neither want nor could have such a voice, you can almost certainly improve the assertiveness level of your voice. You can work to make your voice firm, strong, relaxed, self-confident and appropriately loud, forceful, low-pitched, and well-modulated.

Many women retain the voice pitch and tone of a little girl throughout their lives. Voice pitch can be lowered with practice. We all have a range, from high to low, that is comfortable for us. Record your voice on a tape cassette and play it back. Now record yourself as you practice speaking at a deeper pitch; as you practice, think of yourself as an extremely important, powerful leader. Can you detect the difference in your playback? When you listen to your playbacks, be alert for voice tones that are apologetic, tentative, meek, imploring, whining, prissy, nagging, or schoolmarmish. If you make a practice of taping your telephone conversations, you may pick up some voice patterns you'll want to change.

Some women speak so softly it's difficult to hear them from more than a few feet away. A stronger, louder voice is essential to an assertive image, so practice until you're comfortable speaking so a person twenty feet away can easily hear every word.

High-status male executives are usually somewhat less expressive in their voice modulation, as well as in their facial expression, than low-status women workers. This is one way they project a more self-possessed, rational image — one of cool moderation, carefully revealing only what they intend another to know. While an expressive, well-modulated voice can be a real asset, it can signal low status if it's overdone.

Clothing and Grooming   Your appearance tells people a great deal about your attitude toward yourself and others, your competence, and your role in the company. Your clothing and grooming signal how well you fit in with the company image and with others in the

company. (See Chapter 3 for a discussion of appropriate dress.)

Eye Contact   The eyes are considered by many to be the most important means of nonverbal communication. Often they are a clue to thoughts and feelings the sender may be trying to hide. In normal conversation you glance at a person for about a second and then glance away to show the speaker you're listening but not staring. If you avoid eye contact, it will probably be interpreted as a sign of low self-esteem, weakness, or guilty feelings. A longer meeting of the eyes is uncommon and therefore can have special importance, indicating anger, challenge, or sexual attraction, for example. Research also indicates that people tend to maintain a higher degree of eye contact with those they believe will be approving or supportive of them.

Use of Space and Territories   The way space is used is also a means of nonverbal communication. Humans, we well as other animals, tend to lay claim to and defend a particular territory. There is a psychological advantage to meeting with someone in your own territory. Lawyers like to hold important meetings with adversaries in their own offices just as athletic teams prefer to play on their "home" court or field.

In *Organizational Communication*, Gerald Goldhaver expands this concept and identifies three principles relating to territory and status in an organization [4, p. 150]. People with high status (1) control a larger territory (space, subordinates, decision-making authority, and other aspects of power) than people with lower status, (2) protect their territory better, and (3) invade the territory of lower-status employees more readily. Look at the people in your organization. In most firms, the higher the status, the larger the office and the more private. As executives move up, their territory is better protected by the number of stories in the building, the length of hallways, and the presence of walls, doors, receptionists, secretaries, and other barriers to immediate access.

Executives usually presume familiarity with subordinates by casually dropping by their desks or offices. And executives usually feel free to sit down without being asked, implying that they are relaxed and intend to stay awhile. Most subordinates, on the other hand, would hesitate to invade the territory of their boss in this way. The larger the gap in status between the executive and the subordinate, the freer the executive tends to feel to invade and the more hesitant the subordinate is to do so.

Male peers and subordinates may attempt to subtly dominate you through such territorial moves. Unless you're aware of the significance of such actions, you may unconsciously respond with submissive behavior. Your most effective defense is to mentally "hold your ground." You can also signal your own sense of status in any number of ways, including: (1) rising and moving casually around your office during the conversation, (2) excusing yourself on the pretext of keeping an appointment, (3) setting up a barrier to screen visitors to your office or desk, (4) assuming the same familiarity with peers by dropping by their offices.

Status Symbols   Nonverbal status symbols trigger strong feelings because they can satisfy or frustrate ego needs. People are usually quite sensitive to the messages implied by the ways managers handle status symbols such as their names on routing slips, lists, directories, organization charts, office doors, and stationery; the size and location of their offices; their furniture and equipment; their secretarial and clerical support; and their access to other company resources. The more visible these status symbols are to others, the stronger are the feelings likely to be attached to them, especially if they're taken away.

A Handshake   In our culture a handshake is almost universally obligatory for men when they are introduced, and frequently when they meet or say goodbye. Women have traditionally used the handshake selectively and at their own option. Psychologist Albert Mehrabian says that a person's general level of preference for handshakes reflects how positively he or she feels toward others [8, p. 7]. A firm handshake indicates a greater liking and warmer feelings, but a prolonged handshake is considered too intimate for most situations. A loosely clasped hand is usually interpreted as a sign of aloofness and unwillingness to become involved. A downright limp, cold handshake is repugnant to most people and is taken as a signal of an unaffectionate and unfriendly nature as well as an unwillingness to become involved in any way.

When a businesswoman volunteers a firm, friendly handshake in appropriate situations, it is usually interpreted as a sign of professionalism, assertiveness, and strength. Any time you're introduced to someone or encounter someone you haven't seen for awhile, initiate a handshake. Use it to congratulate and to seal agreements.

Body Position and Posture   Through your body language you signal either weakness or dominance and status. Dominant postures also convey a sense of personal power or fearlessness. According to Mehrabian, "In our culture relaxation-tension is a very important way in which status differences are subtly conveyed" [8, p. 115]. Mehrabian's research into the significance of relaxed, as opposed to tense, body positions indicates that males in our culture assume more relaxed postures than females do. This pattern predominates in a variety of circumstances, whether the men are in the presence of women or of other men. Dr. Diane Warshay has studied these power postures and ways women can respond to them (as shown in Exhibit 6-3). She stresses the importance of responding with a message of strength, since most men know the signs of weakness and look for them (though not necessarily at a conscious level).

Research by John Malloy [7] indicates that the most effective power stance for both men and women is almost military, spine and head erect and straight, feet slightly spread, arms at sides with fingers lightly cupped. He also discovered that standing with one or both hands on the hips is a power stance for a man but a nonpower stance for a woman.

Malloy also found that upper-middle-class males (most top executives fall into this category) have somewhat different body postures than lower-middle-class males. A key difference is the angle of head and shoulders — the upper-middle-class head is more aligned with the spine — neck back and head erect. "Lowers" stoop their shoulders more, which throws their heads forward and downward, as shown in Figure 6-1. These head angle differences are also found in females of both classes. The walk of the "uppers" is different, too — shoulders are straight, head aligned, eyes forward, arms in toward body, fingers lightly cupped, walk almost military with even strides of about twelve inches. The most powerful individuals walk with the relaxed power of a panther — unhurried, smooth movements, but ready to spring.

"Lowers" walk with the shoulders and body rolling more, hips swinging, arms swinging out, head thrown more forward and downward, and long or erratic strides.

Height The average woman (5 ft. 4½ in.) is 4½ inches shorter than the average man (5 ft. 9 in.). In the business world being taller usually means being more respected, more powerful, and more affluent. Several studies have established these relationships; in fact, a 1985 study showed that each additional inch was worth an extra $600 a year to male MBAs. A 4½-inch average difference would have been worth $2,700 that year.

In business tall women tend to have the same advantages as tall men. On the other hand, the short man may be even more threatened by a tall woman than by a tall man. He may see the short woman as less threatening than anyone in the office and therefore let down his guard and confide in her. Overall, however, the taller your *image,* the better for your career. A few suggestions for projecting a taller image are given in Exhibit 6-3. Some additional suggestions include:

FIGURE 6-1: Head Positions Signal Status

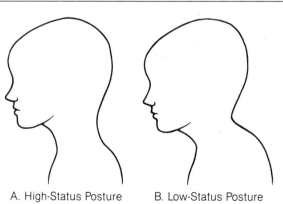

A. High-Status Posture B. Low-Status Posture

Based on research by John Malloy, *Live for Success* (New York: Perigord Press, 1981).

- *Think of yourself as tall.* Your self-image can have greater impact than your physical size.

- *Walk tall.* Pull yourself up to your full height; practice this as often as you can think of it. Picture a cord anchored to the base of your spine, running through the crown of your head, and attached to a crane above you. Let the cord gently tighten, stretching your spine upward, helping you walk, stand, and sit tall.

- *Dress tall.* Find some good books on how to dress for the illusion of greater height, which are often the same principles as dressing for an illusion of slenderness. Typical techniques include a one-color effect from head to toe, solid colors or small-scale patterns, softer fabrics that follow body lines, simple lines, vertical or diagonal lines, and uncluttered necklines.

- *Project an assertive professional image.* If you begin to feel intimidated or overpowered when someone is towering over you or is stereotyping you as childlike or weak because of your size, focus on your career goals and picture yourself as a confident, assertive professional.

Developing New Nonverbal Messages

Managers who are most effective tend to engage in nonverbal behavior that conveys self-confidence, liking, involvement, and interest in others. People who are relatively outgoing,

EXHIBIT 6-3: Nonverbal Power Postures

Male Power Postures	Female Weakness Postures	Alternative Female Responses
The Power Position: A woman walks into a man's office. He leans back in his chair, puts his hands behind his head, spreads his elbows wide, and straightens his knees. The message is that the woman is inferior.	The woman clasps her hands, leans forward. If seated, she crosses her legs and looks slightly downward.	Assume a relaxed posture. Put your fingertips together with your hands pointed upward, a gesture called "steepling." Stand over his desk. Sit on his desk.
The Power Stance: A man approaches a woman's desk where she is seated, and he talks to her from above.	The woman remains seated, straining to look up at the man during the conversation.	Move casually back and then stand up.
Or, a man who is much taller than a woman moves close to her during a conversation.	The woman throws her head back in order to look up at the man.	Step back. Find an excuse to casually move far enough away that your gaze seems to be level with his. Get him to sit down.
The Power Touch: A man puts his arm around a woman to discuss an office procedure. (People can show their power by acting in an intimate way with someone who wouldn't act in an intimate way with them.)	The woman touches her hair, wets her lips, smiles.	If you're standing or walking, step back and turn toward him in a relaxed way as you continue to talk, listen, and/or walk along, forcing him to drop his arm. If you're seated, turn in your chair and/or get up. If he repeats the touch, fold your arms and move away. If he persists, tell him he's invading your personal space.

friendly, and approachable are more likely to take charge of situations. Managers tend to be dominant persons who have controlling and relaxed styles.

The nonverbal behavior of women tends to convey more liking than that of men, but also more tenseness and submissiveness. Women's nonverbal behavior also reflects a greater measure of empathic and affiliative tendencies [8, p. 67]. As a woman manager, you'll want to develop and project the tendencies and behaviors you already express that are typical of effective managers. It's also wise to become aware of necessary traits that you're *not* projecting.

Are you projecting an assertive, powerful image through your body language? Watch the high-status business executives you know. Then observe low-status workers. You may want to consciously practice some of the nonverbal behaviors that signal personal power and strength.

Exhibit 6-3 can help you identify new responses to male power postures, and Exhibit 6-4 can help you identify other nonverbal behaviors you may want to modify.

The good news is, you can change the way people perceive you by consciously changing your nonverbal messages. When you send high-status messages, people peg you at that level whether you're actually there or not [9]. Any time you try out new assertive verbal messages, it's important to practice the nonverbal actions that must accompany your words. Although the new ways of behaving may seem difficult and awkward at first, they'll become a natural part of you with practice. So practice before a mirror and with friends at first, use videotaping and cassette recording where you can, and soon you'll have a new power image.

How can you be sure your nonverbal messages match your verbal ones? Perhaps most important is being very clear about what you *intend* to communicate. Before the anticipated confrontation, periodically relax and focus on your intended message (see Exercise 5-5, p. 152). Visualize coming across assertively, both verbally and nonverbally, behaving naturally and appropriately, and achieving your intended goals. When the time comes to be assertive, your subconscious mind will take over the nonverbal aspects if you'll let it. Relax, keep your ultimate goal in mind, and play it by ear. (See Exercises 6-4, 6-5, and 6-6.)

EXHIBIT 6-4: Nonverbal Behaviors Signaling Nonassertiveness, Assertiveness, or Aggressiveness

	Nonassertive Behavior	**Assertive Behavior**	**Aggressive Behavior**
Facial expression	Smiling often, broadly; relatively animated, expressive	Relatively impassive; less smiling	Tight with anger; jaw and brow tense; sneering or scornful; patronizing; come-on smile, manipulative
Voice tone	Relatively expressive, sometimes apologetic, tentative, meek, imploring, whining, or prissy	Relatively impassive; objective, self-confident, firm, decisive	Angry, sarcastic, sneering, flippant, nagging, scolding, scornful; extremely loud; menacingly low
Voice pitch	High, little-girl quality	Relatively low, forceful	Manacingly low; yelling

EXHIBIT 6-4: Continued

	Nonassertive Behavior	**Assertive Behavior**	**Aggressive Behavior**
Hands	Playing with hair or earrings; nervous movements, mannerisms; primly folded in lap	Still or purposeful, smooth movements; hands at sides, fingers lightly cupped	On one or both hips; pointing or shaking finger
Eyes	Cast downward; little contact while speaking; watching speaker intently; avoiding direct contact	Frequent eye contact while talking; steady, firm, decisive gaze; casual, relaxed observation while another is talking	Staring—angry, challenging; or cold, expressionless
Head	Tilted, nodding, moving from side to side, up and down; ducked	Still, straight	Stiff, erect
Posture	Slumped, stooped, but tense; or ramrod tense, at attention, nervous	Almost military but relaxed; head and spine straight, erect, feet slightly apart, well-grounded, arms at sides	Tense—knees locked, feet spread widely apart, firmly planted; fists clenched
Positions	Hesitantly standing; sitting forward tensely; knees and feet together; arms folded tightly in lap; other balanced, tense positions; vigilant	Asymmetrical, expansive positions— arms on sides of chair, sometimes leaning to one side in relaxed way; leaning back, clasping hands behind neck; males: turning chair around and straddling it or putting feet on desk; casually turning one's back on another to get something	Tensely, forcefully leaning forward; pointing fingers; pounding desk
Movements	Small, controlled, tense; covering face with hand; fiddling with an object; rhythmic shaking of leg or foot	Expansive, relaxed, free; pressing fingertips together in a steeple; staring through them; free of nervous mannerisms	Waving arms angrily; closely towering over another; invading another's personal territory without asking
Other patterns	Allowing others to interrupt; won't turn back on another	Not allowing others to interrupt; "competitive turn-taking" at interrupting	Interrupting others frequently; passing an acquaintance, making eye contact without speaking or smiling; failing to step aside when on a collision course with someone

EXERCISE 6-4: NONVERBAL POWER POSTURES AND RESPONSES

If you can, do this exercise with a partner. If not, practice the postures in front of a mirror until you become comfortable with them. (See Exhibit 6-7 for suggestions on giving feedback to a partner.)

1. Practice the male status or dominance postures (described in Exhibit 6-3) that you would like to work on.

   a. As you talk with your partner, deliberately use expansive gestures. Then try small, controlled movements. Compare how you feel when using each type of movement. Get feedback from your partner (or your mirror) on the impression you make in each mode.

   b. Practice walking and sitting taller. Think of yourself as actually being the height you would like to be in business situations. Then draw yourself up, beginning at the base of your spine and continuing to the top of your head, to your full height. Now go back to your regular height. Next try slumping or bending. Compare the different ways you feel in each posture. Get feedback from your partner on the impression you make.

   c. As you talk with your partner, consciously relax. Move around in a relaxed manner, occasionally turn your back on your partner, and then face her or him again. Next, practice tense movements in a vigilant manner as you talk. Compare the differences in the way you feel in each mode and get feedback from your partner on the impression you make.

   d. As you talk with your partner, sit in a relaxed manner with legs crossed, leaning back slightly, and slanting sideways a little, with arms asymmetrically placed (for example, one arm on the table and the other in your lap or on the chair arm). Now change your posture so that you are leaning forward in your chair and carry on a discussion while in this posture. Compare how you feel in each posture and get feedback from your partner on the impression you make.

2. Practice the *female* postures (described in Exhibit 6-3) with your partner.

   a. Have your partner play the male role and you play first the female weak role and then the alternative female role.

   b. Compare the way you feel in the female weak postures with the way you feel in the alternative female postures.

   c. Get feedback from your partner on the impression you give in each posture. If some of the improved postures seem awkward, practice them some more until they become more natural.

   d. Switch roles with your partner. You now play the male role while your partner plays the female role.

EXERCISE 6-5: NONVERBAL AWARENESS

This activity will help you get a feeling for the differences between assertive, nonassertive, and aggressive postures and gestures and the impact of these movements on the way you feel about yourself and others [2, pp. 154–56]. Do it with a partner, if possible (see Exhibits 6-4 and 6-7).

Nonassertive behavior. Think of a situation in which you have trouble asserting yourself. Close your eyes for a few seconds and picture yourself being nonassertive. Now stand up and *without words* act-out the way you behave in that situation. Move around doing the things you would normally do and thinking the things you would normally think and say. Fully experience the situation and your actions. Then sit down. Close your eyes again and recall how you felt acting nonassertively. Now erase the memory from your mind.

Aggressive behavior. Think of a situation in which you would probably over-react, perhaps something you have been feeling angry or frustrated about for a long time. Close your eyes for a few seconds and picture yourself behaving aggressively. Now stand up and *without words* act-out the way you would behave in that situation. Fully experience the situation and your feelings as you move around. Then sit down. Again close your eyes and recall how you felt when you were behaving aggressively. Now erase that memory from your mind.

Assertive behavior. Think of a situation in which you are comfortable asserting yourself (or a situation in which you think you could become comfortable behaving assertively). Close your eyes for a few seconds and picture yourself behaving assertively. Now stand up and *without words* act-out the situation in an assertive manner. Fully experience the situation and your feelings as you move around. Then sit down. Again close your eyes and recall how you felt when you were behaving assertively.

Comparison and feedback: Discuss the exercise with your partner.

1. How did you feel in each role?

2. How did each type of behavior make you feel about yourself? About others?

3. Which role were you most comfortable with? Least comfortable with?

4. Which role was the easiest to get into? The most difficult?

5. How did your partner perceive each of the roles?

6. What suggestions does your partner have for a more effective expression of assertiveness?

Replay: Take the assertive role again. Incorporate your insights and your partner's suggestions as you act-out without words.

EXERCISE 6-6: NONVERBAL AND VERBAL AWARENESS

With a partner or by yourself, say each of the following statements in three ways: assertively, nonassertively, and aggressively. Be aware of how your nonverbal behavior changes the message. If you are doing this exercise with a partner, ask her or him to identify the kind of behavior you are acting out. Ask for feedback about the effectiveness of your assertive behavior [2, p. 156]. Add your own list of statements to practice. (See Exhibit 6-7 for guidance in giving feedback to a partner.)

1. "That's all right."

2. "I'd rather do it myself."

3. "I didn't say that."

4. "I don't care to go."

5. "Please don't do that."

6. "Can you take my place?"

USING YOUR ASSERTIVE SKILLS ON THE JOB

By now you should be clear about your level of assertiveness and how it's affecting your life. Later we'll discuss some specific steps you can take to change nonproductive behavior into effective behavior that gets the results you want. First, let's survey some ways you can use assertive skills to become a more effective manager.

To Lead Workers

To be firm, women managers generally must develop a little toughness. This ability to dish it out and take it without complaining is expected of good managers. Only you can decide the best place on the scale for you in dealing with your particular group of workers:

1	2	3	4	5	6	7	8	9	10
Soft					Firm				Hard

Here are some steps you might take to develop the appropriate degree of firmness.

1. Get to know your subordinates.

2. Think through the personalities and the requirements for full productivity.

3. Anticipate the various types of situations you will encounter and the decisions you'll have to make.

4. Decide where you will draw the line in each type of situation. Stick to it, unless you discover valid reasons for changing your mind. If this occurs, ask yourself if you are rationalizing the switch in positions as valid when it is actually based on insecurity or fear.

Being Firm and Fair   Your workers want you to be assertive. They admire a sense of fairness that includes equal rights for all. Most of them will resent seeing a coworker getting away with something. Some will see if they can get away with it too. Therefore, it's important to assert your rights and the company's rights. Your workers expect that and will generally approve it. Even when they are the ones being "called on the carpet," they will usually agree with the idea that "It's not fair to your coworkers for you to behave this way," or "It's not fair to the others for me to condone this."

Giving Criticism or Feedback on Performance
When it's necessary to confront workers with poor results or unacceptable actions, use a problem-solving approach assertively. Focus on what can be done next, how to solve the problem, and how similar problems can be avoided in the future. Where possible, tie desirable behavior to achieving objectives a worker has helped set for his or her job, or tie the behavior to departmental or company objectives.

Avoid the trap of comparing or implying comparison of one subordinate with another. Focus on the worker's own performance according to the standards and objectives the two of you have previously agreed on.

Focus on *behavior*, not attitudes or personality traits that produced the behavior. Give **feedback** as soon after the behavior occurs as possible. If performance needs improvement, give the feedback in private. Be prepared to make suggestions or give instructions on how performance can be improved.

Dealing with Tardiness   If a worker's tardiness is a potential problem, it's best to nip it in the bud. Try a variation of feedback assertion. Confront the worker and describe in nonjudgmental terms the specific behavior that is creating the problem: "I noticed that you arrived at 8:40 on Monday, 8:50 on Tuesday, and 8:45 today." Ask whether there is some problem. If there is a legitimate problem, let the worker know you will appreciate being informed of such problems at the time so you will be able to plan accordingly. If there is no legitimate reason, mention the effect tardiness has on your work and on the others in the department and the kinds of feelings it triggers. You might want to point out that it's unfair to permit some people to violate agreed-on work hours while their coworkers are careful about keeping this agreement. Make it clear that you expect the worker to honor this agreement in the future.

Dismissing Workers   Sometimes, after you have taken all the usual steps of discussing performance problems, coaching, giving deadlines for improvement, and searching for alternatives (see Chapter 13), you must dismiss a worker. Every situation is different, and you will have to decide how to handle each according to its own peculiarities. Here are some suggestions to consider.

1. Be cordial but get straight to the point.

2. Give specific reasons. Discuss performance and behavior, not personalities, attitudes, or personal characteristics.

3. Give a specific termination date and tell the worker how much termination pay she or he will receive.

4. Answer questions.

5. If asked for suggestions about what the worker might do next, be prepared to respond helpfully. Think of the dismissal as an opportunity to support a worker in

finding a more appropriate niche. Help the worker see the dismissal as a learning experience and a growth opportunity.

To Deal with Peers

It is essential to be able to assertively ask for favors from peers and colleagues. Trading favors is an important factor among male colleagues in getting things done, taking advantage of opportunities, and moving up the ladder. Grant as many favors as you can. But be assertive about refusing to grant those that are inappropriate.

Also be ready to handle some common problems assertively.

Someone takes credit for your ideas. Confront the person in private. Tell him or her you don't want it to happen again.

You are hesitant to speak up at meetings. Be prepared for the meeting. Review your facts, then be positive about expressing yourself ("I think . . . I believe . . ."). If you find yourself thinking negative thoughts ("They'll think this is silly," "I'm no good at expressing myself at meetings"), stop that train of thought by saying "stop," then "calm," and deliberately relaxing your muscles for a few seconds. If you are alone, say the words aloud.

You are by-passed at meetings. The meetings consist of a dialogue between a few people speaking mainly to each other. Even though you speak up, your opinions are generally ignored. Try feedback assertiveness. Describe the behavior nonjudgmentally. For example, "I have been listening to this discussion for the past twenty minutes and three people have spoken, mainly to each other. Prior to that I contributed my opinion a couple of times and it received little or no comment. I've had the same experience at other meetings. I would like to contribute to this committee, but I feel frustrated in my efforts to do so." Then be prepared

to make specific suggestions for increasing your level of participation. If you are stumped for suggestions, at least ask the group what can be worked out to increase participation by all members. Here are some possible suggestions.

1. "Perhaps each speaker could remember to speak to everyone by looking at each of us."

2. "If each speaker would pause after making a point, we can ask questions or get clarification without interrupting."

3. "Perhaps the chairman can stop the discussion before going on to a new item and ask for contributions from others."

4. "If members would listen carefully to all input and formulate appropriate questions about statements that need clarifying, perhaps more of us could make a real contribution."

A peer is keeping you from doing your job. First, go to your colleague and confront him or her with the problem. Be as tactful and as candid as possible. If this doesn't get results, let the boss know what's going on.

To Hold Your Own with Your Boss

Your boss may be the person you have the most difficulty with in asserting yourself. However, you must learn to be assertive with your boss in order to gain his or her respect and to communicate your wants, goals, and requirements. You must be able to assert yourself in every area, from requesting office space and equipment comparable to that of your male peers to requesting a promotion and raise. No one person has the power that your boss does to implement or block your immediate career goals. Dealing assertively with this important person can be a real bonus to your career. Here are examples of typical problem situations that can be handled in an assertive way.

Your boss takes credit for your ideas. Start putting your ideas in writing. Send your boss a memo with a copy to his or her boss.

You have difficulty saying "no" to your boss. If you feel you want to say "no" and should say "no," be prepared to give your boss a reason, preferably without going into a lengthy explanation. Practice your refusal mentally when you are calm. Picture yourself being calm when you say it.

You have difficulty asking for a promotion or a raise. Read Chapter 14 for information about preparing your facts and picking the right approach. If you are nervous, rehearse with a friend. Have your friend offer all the objections and responses you fear. Practice handling them until you're comfortable.

Your boss makes a decision affecting you that you disagree with. Not only that, you are convinced that if you carry out the decision, the results will be disastrous. Counter with another suggestion or slant your boss's suggestion differently: "That ties in with something I had in mind." "What would you think if we did it this way?" "Perhaps the most *professional* way to handle it would be . . ."

You are excluded from a meeting or a trip you think you should attend. Write a memo saying you understand there will be a meeting (or trip) concerning (topic) on (date). Tell your boss that you have some ideas on this subject or that you think the experience will help your job performance, and ask whether it is all right for you to attend.

You're uncomfortable calling your boss by his or her first name. If your boss and your peers use first names, you should too. It's important for your assertive stance that you think of yourself as basically equal to your boss as well as to your peers. Being on a first-name basis can help you feel equal and reduce the possibility of being intimidated or dominated.

Your boss tries to compare you (or your behavior) with others. Confront the issue. Wayne Dyer [3, pp. 85–89] suggests some assertive strategies for dealing with this.

Remember that the boss's comparison has nothing to do with you as a person. He or she would do the same to any subordinate willing to take it.

Say, "You are using other people's examples as reasons why I should be a certain way, but I am not any of those other people."

Use sentences that begin with "you" to indicate that you are not internalizing the boss's efforts to compare you: "You think I should be more like Bob?" "You think I should do things the same way as Jim?" Be sure to sound incredulous and bewildered.

Give an honest evaluation of what you see going on: "You are comparing me with someone else so that I will stop trying to do what I believe in."

Ask yourself "What do I want from this encounter?" rather than "Who does he think he is, telling me I should be like someone else?" In this way you can avoid becoming angry. You start focusing on getting what you want rather than on the boss's behavior.

Ask yourself "Does he need to feel powerful, understood, important, effective?" If you can see what the boss needs out of this encounter, you are more likely to see an appropriate way to let him (or her) "save face" while you still assert your rights.

If your boss later makes comparisons in spite of what you have done, confront the issue again — and again, if necessary. It's important to be persistent and consistent.

Your boss overloads you. If your boss asks you to take on an unreasonable amount of work, it's important for you to assert your rights and communicate your situation. "I know there's a lot to be done, but I'm overloaded right now. Let's discuss what your top priorities are and I'll work on those first."

You're afraid you aren't pleasing the boss. Many women are caught in the "trying to please trap." They depend on others, especially authority figures, for approval of their behavior, decisions, or ideas. Your boss will respect you if you are clear about what you want in your life and in your career. If you please yourself, you're likely to gain the respect of your boss. Keep cooperation and achievement on an objective level: company goals, department goals, your personal job goals. Find a boss you can honestly admire and respect enough to support and be reasonably loyal to. Then focus on achieving your professional goals, not on pleasing the boss.

You get a new boss. When a new administration takes over a company, they frequently bring in some of their own staff. You may suddenly find your job in jeopardy. Consider meeting with your new boss. Before the meeting, review your achievements and update your objectives. Tell your new boss you have heard about possible layoffs and you would like to discuss why you think it would be a mistake to let you go. Tell him or her what you have accomplished in specific, measurable terms and provide documentation. Then lay out future plans for you and your department. Avoid becoming defensive or belittling anyone in the company.

You feel your boss is behaving incompetently or unfairly. If you believe your boss is not handling matters competently or is dealing unfairly with you, discuss the situation with him or her. Present the problem as you see it and be ready to give possible solutions. Try to work it out. If you get nowhere, seriously consider talking to the appropriate superior on up the ladder. Decide whether or not it's best to inform your boss in advance of your intention. Either way, try to

time your moves so that your boss doesn't have a chance to influence *his* or *her* boss's attitude before you give your side of the story.

When you talk with your boss's boss, be clear about why you are asking for the meeting and what you want as a result of it (that is, the action that you want). Give a brief overview of the situation, the major problem, and your major concern. Don't get bogged down in details. Let them come out as needed in response to the executive's questions. Remain objective and stick with facts. Avoid bad-mouthing your boss, but be frank about the facts. Stress what's "for the good of the company."

Your boss dismisses you. Ask the boss to give you adequate reasons for the dismissal. If he or she cannot, get your files in order. Be prepared to document your case and go to your boss's boss. Bring along a complete file of ideas you have given your boss as well as letters and memos recording your achievements.

If the boss *does* give you adequate reasons for your dismissal, make your departure as gracious and positive as possible. Tell your boss how much you have learned from this experience. Ask for a letter of recommendation. View your dismissal and its causes as a learning experience and possibly an opportunity for a new direction in your life. Analyze your behavior to determine if you want to make any constructive changes.

CHANGING YOUR THINKING AND BEHAVIOR

You've had a chance to become aware of your current attitudes and actions in the area of assertiveness and to see some ways in which assertiveness enhances a manager's effectiveness. What aspects of your behavior do you want to change in order to enhance your *own* effectiveness? The rest of this chapter is devoted to guiding you through the change process.*

If you're dissatisfied with your level of assertiveness, it's best to work on changing your thinking and behavior in one area of your life at a time. Begin with situations where little is at stake: interactions with strangers and acquaintances who have little impact or significance in your life. (If you blow it, it doesn't really matter.)

Don't *condemn* your ineffective behavior or actively try to squelch it. This kind of attention tends to reinforce it so that it becomes more deeply entrenched than ever! Simply notice it and start *substituting* assertive behavior. Build on the strengths you already have: You're behaving assertively in some types of situations already. Spend more time acting in this manner. Gradually expand that assertive behavior to similar kinds of situations.

Take it one step at a time, and you'll find that a small success in one area of your life will provide incentive to make changes in other areas. You'll gain confidence in asserting yourself in more and more significant situations where the stakes are higher.

Many psychologists believe that behavior is learned through (1) modeling, (2) association, and (3) payoffs. *Modeling* is copying the behavior of your parents and other role models. *Association* refers to the external and internal messages and experiences that you associate with your behavior. Messages from parent figures have a significant impact. These messages, along with your interpretations of them and the feelings you experience, lead to both rational and irrational beliefs, which determine

what you say to yourself in stressful situations. *Payoffs* are the rewards you got from parents and others who reinforced the behavior, the "something pleasant" you got or the "something unpleasant" you avoided as a result of the behavior.

You can learn new, more productive behavior in exactly the same way you learned the old, now nonproductive behavior. The basic change process is described in Exhibit 6-5. We'll discuss each step generally and its specific effect on your life. Then you'll put it all together to deal with a situation you want to change.

Role Models

Copying the behavior of role models is easy for most of us. Although you may have trouble finding numerous female managers for role models, you can surely find plenty of male managers to learn from. Of course you'll retain your own personality and autonomy. You'll simply be picking and choosing certain actions and approaches others use that you think will work well for you too.

Parent Messages

All of us operate at times on **parent messages** that we internalized in childhood. But we're frequently unaware of these messages and their impact on our behavior. When you become aware of the parent messages underlying your nonproductive behavior, the behavior changes you make are likely to be more profound and long lasting than when you remain unaware.

Take shyness, for example. Its root cause is an excessive concern that you'll be evaluated, plus an assumption that the evaluation will be negative and that you'll be rejected in some way. Dreading or fearing rejection, the shy person hangs back, "freezes," becomes self-

---

*An understanding of transactional analysis can help you in every area of the change process. **Transactional analysis** (TA) is a comprehensive approach to becoming aware of the subtleties and meanings that underlie people's behavior, interactions, motivations, and games. It offers a model or framework for understanding yourself and others and for changing nonproductive behavior.

EXHIBIT 6-5: The Change Process: From Nonproductive to Assertive Behavior

1. Identify the problem situation clearly and specifically and decide exactly what your goal is. State your current behavior and your desired behavior. Determine how much control you have over these outcomes. (Does the outcome depend mostly on your behavior or on another person's?)

2. Look for, or think of, *role models*, both male and female, who handle similar situations well. Pick up verbal and nonverbal cues from them, and absorb their attitude and style as they go about dealing with these situations.

3. Identify any *parent messages, irrational beliefs,* and consequent *self-statements, feelings,* and *anxiety* about what would happen if you acted assertively.

4. Dispute and challenge nonproductive parent messages, irrational beliefs, and self-statements about your rights and behavior in this situation. Eliminate them by substituting more rational, productive ones.

5. Identify the *payoffs* you get from the old and the new behavior.

6. Identify your *personal rights* in the situation and act on these convictions.

conscious, and won't risk taking assertive action. Simply developing and practicing relevant verbal and nonverbal skills can do much to remedy shyness—for example, practicing assertiveness, public speaking, and social skills.

Such behavior change will be longer lasting, however, if you look at underlying causes and make changes at a deeper level. That means becoming aware of parent messages you internalized, such as "You must achieve, you must compete, you must win to be okay." The implied message is, "If you fail, it's because you're a loser, not okay, didn't try hard enough." The cure for nonproductive parent messages is to refute them in your own mind now and make new messages to yourself. Then focus on your strengths, keep substituting your new messages, and spend more time being involved with activities and people who enhance your feeling of self-worth. Exhibit 6-6 and Exercise 6-7 list common messages parent figures stress to children through verbal and nonverbal communication. The messages in Exhibit 6-6 are followed by explanations of how children frequently interpret them, the effects such interpretations can have on their rights and their assertive behavior, and alternate messages that are more realistic and workable. Exercise 6-7 lists only the parent messages, not the effects or alternates. See whether any of these messages, or similar ones, are affecting your viewpoints and actions.

Irrational Ideas

Irrational ideas are often the basis for nonproductive behavior; they frequently give rise to emotional reactions to situations. If we irrationally believe that it would be "awful" and "catastrophic" to fail to accomplish a major goal or to be rejected by a significant person in our lives, then we will feel anxious, depressed, or guilty. Another irrational idea is that it's terrible if others treat us unfairly and those who do so should be blamed and severely punished. This idea leads to intense anger when others behave unfairly toward us.

The key difference between irrational and rational ideas is that irrational ideas are based on the belief that "I need" or "I must," while rational ideas are based on the viewpoint that "I want" or "I prefer."

Here are some irrational beliefs and alternative messages that are especially significant for women [2].

If I stand up for my rights, others will get mad at me.

Alternate belief: If I stand up for my rights, people may get mad, they may not care

EXHIBIT 6-6: Parent Messages That Affect Assertion

Parent Message	Effect on Rights	Effect on Assertive Behavior	Alternate Message to Enhance Enlightened Self-Interest and Assertiveness
Think of others first; give to others even if you're hurting. Don't be selfish.	I have no right to place my needs above those of other people.	When I have conflict with someone else, I will give in and satisfy the other person's needs and forget about my own.	To be selfish is to place your desires before everyone else's, ignoring others' rights and needs. However, you must take responsibility for meeting your own needs and goals. Your needs are as important as other people's. Try a compromise when needs conflict.
Be modest and humble. Don't act superior to other people.	I have no right to do anything that would imply that I am better than other people.	I will discontinue my accomplishments and turn aside any compliments I receive. When I'm in a meeting, I will encourage other people's contributions and keep silent about my own. When I have an opinion that is different from someone else's, I won't express it.	It is undesirable to build yourself up at the expense of another person. However, you have as much right as other people to show your abilities and take pride in yourself. It is healthy to enjoy your accomplishments.
Be understanding and overlook trivial irritations. Don't be a nag or shrew and complain.	I have no right to feel angry or to express my anger.	When I'm in a line and someone cuts in front of me, I will say nothing. I will not tell my girlfriend that I don't like her constantly interrupting me when I speak.	It is undesirable to deliberately nitpick. However, life is made up of trivial incidents, which are sometimes irritating. You have a right to your angry feelings; if you express them somehow as they occur, they won't build to an explosion.

Based on the work of Patricia A. Jakubowski, "Assertive Behavior and the Clinical Problems of Women," in *Psychology for Women,* ed. D. Carter and E. Rawlings, copyright © 1982 (Springfield, Ill.: Charles C Thomas, 1982). Used by permission of Charles C Thomas.

much one way or the other, or they may like and respect me more. When I assert a legitimate right, chances are the results will be at least partially favorable.

If people do get mad at me, it will be terrible. I will be shattered.

Alternate belief 1: I can handle other people's anger without feeling devastated.

Alternate belief 2: When I stand up for a legitimate right, I don't have to feel responsible for another person's emotional reaction.

EXERCISE 6-7: EXAMINING PARENT MESSAGES

1. Examine the parent messages that follow. Did you receive any of these messages as a child? Think about what effect they had on your sense of your own rights.

   Be perfect.

   Hurry up. (And grow up. And get out of my hair.)

   Please me. (Act in ways that are important to me at the expense of your own growth or desires.)

   Try hard. (And make me proud. And never notice that you've made it.)

   Be strong. (Don't be afraid. Don't be sad. Don't cry.)

2. List these and any other parent messages you can think of, especially messages that affected your right to be yourself, to do the things you wanted in your own way. List each message you received on a separate sheet of paper.

3. Identify the effect of each parent message on your rights and write about it, in the space under that message.

4. What effect on your assertive behavior do you think each parent message may have had? Write about it.

5. What alternate messages can you now give yourself? For each parent message that may have had a negative impact on your beliefs and attitudes about your right to assert yourself, write a new message that supports your right to assert.

6. Give the new messages to the child who is still within you. The child part of you still has a powerful effect on your current life. Try a deep relaxation technique. Go back in memory to your childhood and find the child who received these messages. Ask her what she needs and wants. Give her the support, love, and comfort that she needs, along with new messages that give her the confidence and security to communicate assertively.

If I am honest and direct with people and say "no," I will hurt them.

   Alternate belief 1: People may or may not feel hurt if I say "no" directly.

   Alternate belief 2: Most people are not so easily shattered that they can't handle another's honest, straightforward message.

If the other person does feel hurt when I say "no," then I am responsible.

   Alternate belief 1: Although they may be surprised and perhaps a little embarrassed when I say "no," most people are not so vulnerable that they will be devastated by it.

   Alternate belief 2: I can let people know I care

EXERCISE 6-8: SELF-STATEMENTS: CHANGING FROM NEGATIVE TO POSITIVE

Step 1. *Nonassertive incidents.* Think of three or four incidents in which you behaved nonassertively with poor results. List them. What did you say to yourself about these situations at the time? Write these self-statements in a separate list.

Step 2. *Assertive incidents.* Now list three or four incidents in which you behaved assertively with good results. Write down what you said to yourself about those situations. List these assertive self-statements.

Step 3. Now go back and change the nonassertive self-statements in Step 1 to assertive ones.

---

for them at the same time that I am saying "no."

Alternate belief 3: The other person's hurt or angry feelings may be his or her own problem.

It's selfish and bad for me to turn down others' valid requests. They will think I am mean and won't like me.

Alternate belief 1: Even valid requests don't necessarily warrant my time and energy.

Alternate belief 2: I can find myself continually carrying out other people's priorities rather than my own.

Alternate belief 3: It's okay to take care of my own needs before the needs of others.

Alternate belief 4: The more decision-making power and visibility I have, the more critics I will have. This is true for all managers, executives, administrators, and other leaders.

I must be extremely cautious about making statements or asking questions that might appear "dumb."

Alternate belief: No one is perfect and no one knows everything — even about his or her area of expertise. Asking apparently "dumb" questions at times reflects confi-

dence and competence. ("I figure if I don't understand it, something must be wrong.")

People label women who stand up, speak out, and fight back. They will call me a nag or a shrew. They will say I am grouchy or difficult.

Alternate belief: When I am direct, honest, and stand up for my rights appropriately, others are likely to respect me. Those who don't would probably not respect my nonassertiveness either; rather, they would probably use my timidity, fear, or anxiety to manipulate me and take advantage of me.

Nonproductive Self-Statements

What you say to yourself just before, during, and after an incident is based on your parent messages and beliefs. It has a very important influence on your behavior. Exercise 6-8 gives you an opportunity to become aware of these "self-statements" [6, pp. 141–44]. Examples of nonassertive self-statements are "They'll think I'm dumb"; "I'll probably blow it." Examples of assertive self-statements are "I'll relax and let my best self handle this"; "I can do it."

Compare the two sets of self-statements that you listed in Exercise 6-8 for differences in negative/positive, destructive/constructive, and distorted/realistic content. Most statements that lead to nonassertive or aggressive behavior have one or more of these characteristics [6, pp. 141–44]:

1. Draws conclusion when evidence is lacking or even contradictory: "He said there was no need to discuss next year's vacation now. I'll bet he's planning to let me go before the first of the year."

2. Exaggerates the meaning of the event: "I never thought I would get the news that I was a failure in front of the copy machine on a Monday morning."

3. Disregards some important aspect of the situation: You overlook the fact that the boss has a hangover and is running behind on current projects.

4. Oversimplifies events as good or bad, right or wrong: "He's had it in for me ever since we lost the Acme account. He probably thinks it's all my fault."

5. Overgeneralizes from a single incident: "It's terrible to be a failure at thirty-five. I'll bet no one will want to hire such a failure."

Negative self-statements can cause you to cycle down into a state of anxiety. One way to break the cycle is to stay in the present moment and deal with current reality by asking yourself questions such as these: What is my anxiety level (on a scale of 1 to 10)? . . . What am I doing (verbally and nonverbally)? . . . What am I feeling? . . . What am I thinking? . . . What do I *want* to be thinking, feeling, and doing? . . . What thoughts, opinions, desires, or feelings do I want to express in this situation? . . . What do I want the other person to know? . . . What thoughts are keeping me from doing what I want? . . . What do I think is appropriate to express? . . . How can I go ahead and express what I want?

Addressing these questions can help you change your pattern of irrational or self-defeating thinking, become aware of your thoughts, and stop them in midstream. Then you can make your thoughts more rational and workable by using *constructive* self-statements:

Before the event: "I know how to deal with this even though it's upsetting." "Easy does it! Remember to keep your sense of humor." "I'm not going to let him get to me." "I'll look for the positives and not assume the worst."

During the event: "Getting upset won't help." "My anger (or anxiety) is a signal of what I need to do; it's time to instruct myself." "Keep your cool."

After the event: "Don't take it personally." "Can I laugh about it? Is it really so serious?" "Don't let the bullies get you down." "I can win this game if I play my cards right." "I handled that one pretty well!"

Now, to assert yourself appropriately, practice making new, more constructive self-statements. Also, when your anxiety level is high, remember to use an effective relaxation technique or self-mastery visualization (see Chapter 5). Excuse yourself as soon as possible and find a private place to relax and get things in perspective.

Payoffs

Many women are comfortable with the "security" payoffs that nonassertiveness helps them hold onto. They're either unaware of the higher-level payoffs assertiveness brings, or they're afraid to risk losing what they're sure of.

In other words, although they are not satisfied with what their current behavior is getting them, at least they know more or less what to expect. They fear they may lose more than they gain if they begin asserting themselves. When women begin realistically to weigh what they gain against what they lose, however, the risks of assertiveness become more attractive. Here are some typical comments.

"My boss will protect me, but I never develop the confidence of standing on my own two feet."

"I avoid rejection, but I give up lots of opportunities to learn and grow."

"I was driving down the street listening to the car radio. Someone said, 'If you are not being rejected at least once a week, you are simply not trying.' What a revelation! Most men risk rejection all the time. That's when I started coming out of my protective shell."

"At first it was scary coming out of my cocoon. But at least my achievements are my own now. There's no way I would go back again."

"I *like* myself better when I speak out and stand up for my rights. It may be more trouble at the time, but it feels so good afterward. I no longer have to deal with conflict over what I should have said and done."

"Sure, some people don't like having their hands called, but I've been surprised at how many of them show increased respect and eventually like me more than before."

Let's focus for a moment on those situations in which you have behaved nonassertively, with poor results. Understanding *why* you acted that way—what payoffs you get from such behavior—can help you decide to assert. We only repeat behavior that brings us some reward or payoff. (Sometimes we even perceive negative attention as a payoff, though usually at a subconscious level.) Exercise 6-9 can help you identify the payoffs you get from nonassertion.

Here are some payoffs other women report; see how they compare with yours: avoiding risk, getting approval (avoiding losing another person's approval), playing it safe, not rocking the boat, avoiding a scene or hassle, being able to blame someone else if things don't work out, being polite, being helpful, avoiding rude or aggressive behavior. These payoffs obscure the greater rewards assertiveness can bring. If you focus on "safety payoffs," you forget that standing up for your rights can pay off in increased respect *and* goodwill from others.

Whenever you find yourself *not* taking assertive action because of fear, ask yourself, "What am I getting out of this?" You know the typical payoffs to look for.

Now for the other side of the coin: situations in which you *are* assertive and the payoffs you get. Identify them by completing Exercise 6-10.

Women who've just finished an assertiveness training course have made the following comments: "I haven't been being nice . . . I've been chicken." "I see now that dependency just invites people to encroach on my rights and my space." "Now I want to find out who I am and give up letting everyone else define me." "I've decided it's better to be a lion for a day than a sheep for life." "When I set a low value on myself, in a way I make life hard for all

EXERCISE 6-9: PAYOFFS FOR NONASSERTIVENESS

Describe recent situations in which you found yourself not taking assertive action because you feared the consequences. Ask yourself, "What did I get out of that behavior?" Then describe the payoffs. (Example: "I avoided alienating him/her.") If your first answer is "nothing," recall your feelings afterward, both positive and negative, and any thoughts they led to.

women." When you examine the feelings you've had after behaving assertively, do they include feeling stronger as a person? You have many strengths and many assertive experiences in your background. When you operate from those strengths, you're most effective.

Now you have the tools and the framework for deciding when and how to assert yourself effectively. Exercise 6-11 gives you a chance to apply the step-by-step change process as we've discussed it. You can also select appropriate exercises from those presented at the end of the chapter for practicing new behaviors and rehearsing anticipated situations. Build on your successes. Take time to notice your growing sense of strength and self-confidence. And above all *enjoy* being the creator of your own life.

EXERCISE 6-10: PAYOFFS FOR ASSERTIVENESS

Describe recent situations in which you took assertive action. Ask yourself, "What did I get out of that behavior?" Then describe the payoffs. Record the feelings you had about yourself afterward and the feelings you think other people had toward you and the situation.

EXERCISE 6-11: APPLYING THE CHANGE PROCESS TO YOUR LIFE

Briefly describe an activity or situation that you want to handle assertively. Then respond to each of the instructions listed below.

1. Identify your goal, your current and desired behavior, how much control you have.

2. Identify role models, their verbal and nonverbal actions, attitudes, and style.

3. Identify parent messages, irrational beliefs, self-statements, feelings, and anxiety level.

4. Dispute and challenge the nonproductive responses you listed in number 3. List new responses that you will substitute for the old ones.

5. Identify payoffs from old behavior and from new behavior.

6. Identify your personal rights.

7. With a partner, practice new verbal and nonverbal behaviors you'll use.

8. Visualize yourself behaving assertively in this situation, using the process described in Exercise 5-5. (p. 152).

SUMMARY

The concept of assertiveness as discussed here is based on standing up for your rights while respecting the rights of others. To assert yourself convincingly, you must be aware of and committed to those rights. When you let others victimize you because you don't express your honest feelings, thoughts, and beliefs in a confident way, you're behaving nonassertively. When you violate the rights of others by overreacting, or by overpowering or belittling them, you're behaving aggressively.

Appropriate assertiveness actually improves your relationships with others, gains you respect, and increases your self-respect. Because it's based on honest communication, assertion prevents some of the human relations problems that create stress. It also reduces stress that does occur because it enables you to handle problem situations productively, which leads to self-confidence and tranquility.

When you acquire skill in basic assertion and in a variety of assertive approaches — assertion with empathy and with increasing firmness, assertion that confronts broken agreements and is persuasive in groups — as well as I-messages, active listening, and giving feedback, you'll be in a better position to handle any type of situation. To back up and reinforce your verbal assertiveness, you'll find it helpful to practice nonverbal behaviors that signal assertiveness.

Here are some suggestions for becoming more assertive. Find role models to selectively emulate. Become aware of nonproductive parent messages and irrational beliefs and replace them with more productive, rational ones. Examine self-statements that trigger uncontrollable emotions and raise your anxiety level or otherwise inhibit assertive action and change them to positive statements. Identify the payoffs you get for nonproductive versus productive behavior. Confirm your personal rights in each situation.

Finally, you must practice your skills, taking one situation at a time and beginning with low-risk, simple transactions. Eventually you'll find it easy to assert yourself with your workers, your peers, and even your boss. The result will be a more effective management style. The ultimate payoff: You increasingly become the active creator of what you have in your life.

Additional Exercises

WITH A PARTNER

NOTE: These exercises may be used for videotaping; see also Exercises 6-4, 6-5, and 6-11.

Before doing exercises with a partner, study Exhibit 6-7, which is designed to help you give feedback in ways that will be most helpful to your partner.

EXHIBIT 6-7: Guidelines for Giving Feedback During Exercises with a Partner

1. Start off with the strengths of the performance. Specify exactly which behaviors were positive.

Verbal Behaviors

Was the statement direct and to the point?
Was the statement firm but not hostile?
Did the statement show some consideration, respect, or recognition of the other person?
Did the statement accurately reflect the speaker's goals?
Did the statement leave room for escalation?
If the statement included an explanation, was it short rather than a series of excuses?
Did the statement include sarcasm, pleading, or whining?
Did the statement blame the other person for the speaker's feelings?

Nonverbal Behaviors

Was eye contact present?
Was the speaker's voice level appropriately loud?
Was the statement filled with pauses?
Did the speaker look confident or were nervous gestures or inappropriate laughter present?
Was the statement flat or expressive?

2. After all positive feedback has been given, offer feedback suggestions.

Describe the behavior, rather than give a label. Be objective rather than judgmental.

Offer a possible way of improvement. This should be expressed in a tentative rather than absolute manner. Do not impose a suggestion.

Ask the group member for a reaction to the suggestions, allowing the member to accept, refuse, or modify the suggestion.

Note: Stick to the basic assertive problem and do not get involved with long and complex descriptions of the history of the problem or the anticipated negative reactions of the other person.

Reprinted from Arthur Lange and Patricia Jakubowski, *Responsible Assertive Behavior*, copyright © 1983 (Champaign, Ill.: Research Press, 1983), p. 195. Used by permission of Patricia Jakubowski.

EXERCISE 6-12: VOICE LOUDNESS

The purpose of this activity is to make you aware of the full range of loudness available to you and to contrast it with the range of loudness you are accustomed to [6, pp. 76–77].

Say the word "yes" and ask your partner to respond at the same loudness level. Repeat back and forth for a minute or two. Then vary the loudness of the word "yes" from very quiet to as loud as possible. Your partner should match your loudness level with "no" each time. Switch roles.

Is your present range of loudness wide enough? How much loudness control do you use? (How well are you able to match the loudness level of your partner when you are answering "no"?)

EXERCISE 6-13: MAKING AND REFUSING REQUESTS

This activity will give you an opportunity to practice discriminating between effective and ineffective refusals and requests. Here's your chance to practice standing up for some of those personal rights you identified earlier [6, pp. 102–03].

1. Create a role-playing situation in which a fellow worker, friend, or roommate makes a reasonable request of you that you want to refuse.

2. With your partner playing the role of the other person, you respond to the request with a simple "no"; then switch roles so that you play the person making the request.

3. Is saying "no" all you wish to communicate? What else do you wish the requester to know? Is the additional message an excuse that avoids the real issue?

4. With your partner, again act-out the scene, this time intentionally offering excuses that avoid the real issues. The "requester" should persist and confront the "I can't" responses either with solutions or with alternatives that still include a request.

    a. Are the "I can't" responses easier to give? Are they satisfactory?

    b. How does the fear or wish to avoid being selfish or hurtful to others affect your responses?

5. Identify your thoughts and beliefs that led you to avoid *making* requests and refusing requests. Write them down. Which beliefs are rational or faulty? What are some alternatives to those beliefs?

6. If you are not comfortable making and refusing requests and you wish to work on that, identify specific situations and work on them when you do behavior rehearsal with a partner.

7. With your partner practice making and refusing requests in an honest and direct way. Emphasize "I don't want to" or "I won't" messages rather than "I can't."

Explanations and expressions of concern for the requester are appropriate if they are said in a direct, honest way that doesn't put down the other person. Practice making requests without apology or low expectation of getting what you ask for.

EXERCISE 6-14: MAKING STATEMENTS WITH AND WITHOUT EXPLANATIONS

In this activity you will have a chance to discriminate between *wanting* to explain your behavior and *having* to explain it, and to practice making statements with or without explanation [6, pp. 104–06].

1. Think of a situation in which you have avoided taking action because you were afraid you didn't have a good explanation for your behavior.

2. Think of a situation in which you *have* taken action but you felt obligated to give a lengthy explanation (perhaps untrue) to justify your behavior. The following are examples that might help you think of your own:

   a. Leaving a shop without buying anything after a salesperson has spent a great deal of time and energy trying to make a sale.

   b. Canceling or changing plans.

   c. Returning merchandise.

3. Think of a situation in which you normally feel a need (as opposed to a preference) to give a lengthy explanation. Act-out the scene with your partner; then switch roles and respond while your partner gives a lengthy explanation from her own scene.

4. Reenact the scene *without* the lengthy explanation. Compare the effect on both you and your partner.

EXERCISE 6-15: DEFINING YOUR OWN BEHAVIOR — OR THE OPPOSITE OF TRYING TO PLEASE

This activity will help you recognize when your behavior is misperceived or misinterpreted and when incorrect motives or meanings are attributed to your behavior, and it will enable you to practice direct and nondefensive ways of responding to such redefinitions [6, pp. 111–112].

1. Think of a situation in which someone has redefined the meaning of your behavior and you did not respond assertively. Here are some examples to help you get started:
   a. You refused a friend a favor and he or she defined the refusal as a personal insult or rejection.
   b. You spent time with a friend and another friend reacts jealously and takes it as a personal put-down.
   c. You arrived late and someone assumes the meeting is not important to you.

2. With your partner create a role-play situation in which your partner will redefine your behavior.

3. Act-out the scene several times, trying various responses to the other person's redefinition. Compare your feelings and the effectiveness of the various ways of responding to the situation. Switch roles.

4. Optional additions:
   a. Express irritation or concern toward a partner who has redefined your behavior.
   b. Have your partner persist in redefining your behavior in the situation. Try out various ways of dealing with that.

REFERENCES

1. Adams, Linda. *Effectiveness Training for Women*. New York: Wyden Books, 1979. A good book for women, with a special focus on making decisions about what is and what is not your problem and on eliminating worry and guilt over other people's problems.

2. Bloom, Lynn Z., Karen Coburn, and Joan Pearlman. *The New Assertive Woman*. New York: Dell, 1975. One of the most valuable assertiveness-training books written especially for women.

3. Dyer, Wayne W. *Pulling Your Own Strings*. New York: Thomas Y. Crowell, 1983. Although not advertised as an assertiveness-training text, this book is the best one in the field.

4. Goldhaver, Gerald. *Organizational Communication*. Dubuque, Iowa: Wm. C. Brown, 1984. A comprehensive guide to organizational communication. The chapter on use of space and territory is especially valuable.

5. Lange, Arthur, and Patricia Jakubowski. *The Assertive Option*. Champaign, Ill.: Research Press, 1984. An excellent book for anyone who wants to become more assertive. Written for participants in assertiveness-training groups.

6. Lange, Arthur, and Patricia Jakubowski. *Responsible Assertive Behavior.* Champaign, Ill.: Research Press, 1983. An excellent manual for trainers. It includes all aspects of assertiveness, as well as numerous exercises.

7. Malloy, John. *Live for Success.* New York: Perigord Press, 1981.

8. Mehrabian, Albert. See Ronald B. Adler and Neil Towne. *Looking Out/Looking In.* New York: Holt, 1984. Includes Albert Mehrabian's research findings regarding the impact of the verbal and nonverbal aspects of messages and his work on nonverbal messages conveyed by relative tenseness and relaxation.

9. Parlee, Mary. "Women Smile Less for Success." *Psychology Today* (March 1979), p. 16.

10. Smith, Manuel J. *When I Say No, I Feel Guilty.* New York: Bantam Books, 1983. A helpful discussion of defining your rights.

Chapter Seven

He Said . . . She Said: Communicating Effectively

"If you can't be direct, why be?"
Lily Tomlin

Most work problems can be traced back to a failure in communicating. Every skill you gain will be either enhanced or undermined by your ability to communicate effectively. You use all your personal and managerial skills to get work done by leading your team, gaining the cooperation of your peers, and inspiring the support of your bosses. This leadership process relies on your skill at communicating effectively, which links everything together. Your communication skill is the key to personal and managerial success — it's a basic linking tool.

As a woman, you probably have an advantage over your male peers when it comes to listening and speaking effectively. From the time we were little girls, most of us were encouraged to tune in to other people's feelings and messages and to interact empathetically with them. Most of us were constantly reinforced in our verbal attempts and in our efforts to develop interpersonal skills — probably to a much greater extent than our male counterparts were. Here is a strength, then, that you can capitalize on.

The only *new* communication skills you may need to develop involve *adapting* your messages to the special requirements of your new leadership role, where your male peers may speak a "different language." We've already discussed communicating assertively, perhaps the most important adaptation the typical woman leader must make. Now we'll turn our attention to sharpening the listening and speaking skills that are especially appropriate to you as a leader.

In this chapter you will have the opportunity to learn more about

1. Viewing communication as an ongoing process

2. Sending messages that get the results you want and closing the male-female communication gap

3. Listening for the total message and overcoming some listening barriers

4. Developing active listening skills that support your leadership role

5. Arranging business meetings that achieve specific objectives

6. Conducting meetings that are group centered instead of leadership centered

7. Using the jitters constructively when making presentations and talks

209

8. Preparing and giving talks that get the results you want

9. Determining when to send oral or written messages

10. Writing effective proposals

 A Focus on the Message

"Erika, have you marked June 1 on your calendar?"

"You bet. I wouldn't miss that national sales meeting in Atlanta for anything. I hope you're lining up some good Southern cooking for us."

Jan smiled. "I have a better goodie than that for you. I want you to report on the Fall Fashion Preview you put on last month. The buyers are saying it's the best one we've had. I'd like you to tell the Regional Sales Managers about it. They can use the tips, and the visibility won't hurt you. Our top executives and most of the board of directors will be there too."

"Say, I'm impressed! What an honor. Sure, Jan, I'd love to do it. I'll start working on it right away." Pulling a scratch pad toward her, Erika starts to write. "Now, how long should the presentation run? . . ."

A few weeks later, Brian, Erika's assistant, enters her office carrying several large charts and a few five-by-eight note cards. "Here's the stuff for your speech." He holds up the note cards. "Brief outline of main points plus opening sentence and first sentence of conclusion." Then he holds up the charts, one by one. "I think Graphics did a pretty good job, don't you? A few simple items on each chart, large and bold — even those old codgers on the Board who are half-blind should be able to see these."

"Good job, Brian. Now, listen while I go over my part of the presentation. Tell me if there's anything you don't understand or any parts that drag."

A few days later in Atlanta, shortly after her presentation, Erika relaxes in the hotel coffee shop with Jan.

"Congratulations, Erika. You did a good job of explaining how you made your Fall Fashion Preview so successful. Your talk was well organized, and the visuals were great."

"Thanks, Jan. Some day I hope to make presentations that are as smooth and professional as yours. I'm not too happy about my talk today. Actually, I left out some fairly important details."

"Oh, I do that too, Erika. But I don't worry about it. I nearly always have time to ask for questions afterward, so someone asks something that triggers my memory — if it's really an important point. Talks can be more spontaneous and interesting to the group when some of the facts come out that way. People like to get involved in the talk."

"My main problem is nervousness. It doesn't go away once I start talking, either. It either gets worse or it comes and goes. I always seem to end up cutting my talk short and practically running for a seat. I just can't take being in the spotlight one more minute!"

Jan smiled gently. "I guess we all tend to get the jitters when we make these more formal types of talks."

"You sure don't! How do you stay so cool and calm, Jan?"

"Oh, I get my share of the jitters. But I make sure I'm well prepared, without memorizing my talk. Then I just keep focusing on getting my message across. Part of my preparation is getting clear about the main points I want to get across — what it is I want the people to come away with. Then any time I start feeling nervous — before *or* during the presentation — I just focus on my message. I picture the message going across from my head to their heads. In fact, if I get anxious in the days before the talk, I focus on that picture during my deep relaxation times."

Erika thought for a few moments. "I like that idea. But sooner or later I always start worrying about how I'm coming across. That's when I lose my cool."

"I know. But I think you'll find it's impossible to concentrate totally on two things at once. So if you concentrate totally on the *message*, you can't focus much on *yourself* or what people think of you."

"Well, Jan, so far every one of your suggestions has worked for me. I can hardly wait for a chance to try this one."

---

1. What were probably the strong and weak points of Erika's presentation at the national sales meeting?

2. Can she apply Jan's suggestions to situations other than formal talks? Explain.

FEMALE/MALE TALK PATTERNS

While the basic communication process is the same for everyone, women and men handle each step of the process quite differently. Women tend to be more tentative in sending a message. The message focuses more on connection versus status, on establishing rapport versus reporting information, on cooperating versus competing, and on playing down expertise versus displaying it.

The Communication Process

You can improve your verbal and nonverbal communications if you think of communicating as a process rather than as a series of isolated events. Consider your receiver's personality, experience, and feelings, and your previous transactions. Watch and listen for feedback that indicates the reaction to your message; otherwise you won't know how it was perceived, understood, and accepted. Feedback from the receiver constitutes a new message to you and closes one cycle in the communication process.

Models of the **communication process** can help us better understand what happens when we communicate (see Figure 7-1). The essential elements of the process include a sender, a message, a receiver, and feedback from the receiver to the sender. This feedback may be present even if it consists merely of silence [3, pp. 1–4].

The communication process starts with thinking—the formation and framing of an idea in the sender's mind. This idea is then **encoded**—that is, the thought is put into some form for possible communication. We think in terms of language and express our thoughts in verbal forms—speaking and writing. We also experience feelings that we express (or encode) in both nonverbal and verbal forms. Nonverbal forms of expression include physical touch, visible movement of some part of the body, crying, and the creation of symbols such as music, pictures, and sculpture.

Next, we **transmit** our message to the receiver—by the spoken word, the written word, nonverbal language, or by some combination of the three. The message is transmitted to the receiver through some **medium**—for example, it may be transmitted through the telephone, telegraph, radio, television, a letter, a report, or a face-to-face encounter.

The receiver actively enters the process when she or he perceives the message by means of the senses (seeing, hearing, smelling, tasting, touching). The receiver then **decodes** the message by translating it, interpreting it, or organizing it to fit into her or his background of experience.

The next step is for the receiver to understand the message, then accept it, and finally have it lead to some sort of action or behavior. This feedback gives clues to the sender about the impact of the message on the receiver.

FIGURE 7-1: A Model of the Communication Process

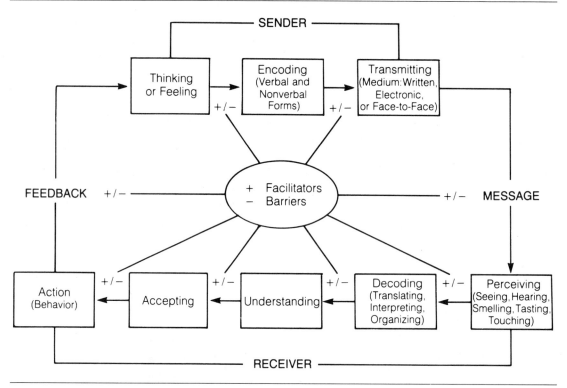

As Figure 7-1 indicates, various factors either facilitate the communicative process or form barriers to it at each step. The major purpose of this chapter is to help you identify ways to overcome barriers and facilitate the process.

Some of the key barriers created by typical female speech patterns (or stereotypes of those patterns) in business situations are shown in Exhibit 7-1. Identify those patterns that may be holding you back. Recall your past conversations; ask trusted friends for feedback; tape-record some of your conversations.

Then decide on alternate speech patterns that will facilitate understanding and acceptance of the meaning and image you want to convey to your business associates. (The sec-

ond column in Exhibit 7-1 offers suggestions.) After all, the male-dominated business culture does have its own patterns of speaking and listening. On the other hand, some men carry the cultural pattern to the extreme—and women attempting to adapt may do this too. So watch out for the types of overcorrection shown in the third column of this exhibit.

A major factor in facilitating communication—a factor not shown in Figure 7-1—is the timing and quality of the feedback. Feedback may be verbal or nonverbal, immediate or delayed. The most effective feedback is usually immediate and both verbal and nonverbal—in a face-to-face conversation, for example, where you can both see and hear the receiver's total

EXHIBIT 7-1: Key Communication Barriers and Facilitators for Women Managers

	Typical Barriers for Women: Speech Patterns/Stereotypes	**Facilitators in Male Business Culture: Alternate Patterns**	**Barriers Created by Overcorrection of Female Speech Patterns**
Gossip	Always ready to participate; indulges in idle, even malicious, gossip	Well-informed, alert; listens but rarely participates	Ignores all gossip
Content	Focus on trivia, chit-chat	Focus on relevant topics (business, politics, etc.)	Business talk only
Quantity	Babbles on too much; *or* keeps silent rather than "create conflict"	Usually speaks with a purpose or keeps her counsel; takes a stand on relevant issues	Every word carefully monitored; lacks spontaneity
Quality	Emotion-charged words ("just love it, so sweet, too gross")	Objective, operational words ("appreciate, thoughtful, inappropriate, effective")	Never expresses feelings
Reactions	Chip-on-shoulder, "women's lib," angry reactions; *or* gives in easily; backs off from conflict	Assertive, problem-solving responses	Swings from rebellion to submission or vice versa
Clarity	Ms. Vague ("the nicest meeting, a super group")	Clear, specific descriptions ("well-organized meeting, top-performing team")	Overdoes details and explanations; tedious, boring
Logic	Illogical; disconnected conclusions, idea-hopping	Coherent, connected, provides closure	Computerlike logic
Credibility	Tentative, overpolite, uncertain, indecisive ("We'll be able to do this?" "This is a sales problem — isn't it?" "Could I please see that for a second when you're through with it?" "I sort of think we should wait a little while?")	Confident, assertive, decisive ("We can do it!" "This appears to be a sales problem." "I'd like to take a look at that too." "I suggest we wait till the progress report comes in.")	Arrogant; overbearing
Interrupting	Avoids; thinks it's impolite; men may assume she has nothing to say	"Competitive turn-taking"; holds ground if peer overdoes it	Constantly interrupts; never gives ground

Continued

EXHIBIT 7-1: Continued

	Typical Barriers for Women: Speech Patterns/Stereotypes	Facilitators in Male Business Culture: Alternate Patterns	Barriers Created by Overcorrection of Female Speech Patterns
Profanity	Responds with disapproval, shock, embarrassment, giving males a "reason" to feel uncomfortable when women enter "their domain."	Communicates without profanity.	Starts swearing too
Jargon (military, sports, business)	Unclear of meanings of many words; rarely uses	Selectively uses jargon to create a sort of fraternity	Relies on jargon to impress and intimidate "outsiders" who don't understand it

reaction as soon as you send the message. When you telephone your receiver, you sacrifice the advantage of observing facial expressions and other body language. And when you send the receiver a written message, you further sacrifice the immediacy of the feedback as well as all its nonverbal aspects, including voice tone and inflection.

Obviously both verbal and nonverbal forms of communication are necessary to effective communication. Verbal forms are most helpful when you want to send logical, **analytical messages.** Let's look at what you do when you analyze: You break down messages, such as reports, into parts. Then you examine each part to see how it relates to a particular situation or problem.

On the other hand, how do you "analyze" the boss's mood or a worker's frown in response to your suggestion? These nonverbal forms of communication are most helpful in **synthesizing** a variety of messages. If you're smart, you'll use these nonverbal messages — along with the verbal ones — to make sense of company politics, the sphere the company operates in, and the "big picture." You'll put it all together (synthesize it) to understand the relationships between the parts and to build

mental models of the world. Whenever you're deciding on an action, use your model to anticipate outcomes. Let's look at verbal forms of communication in more detail.

Assertive or Tentative?

Many studies indicate that men and women literally live in different worlds; this creates numerous gaps in the communication process. Because the business world is accustomed to an assertive male approach to communication, women's credibility is undermined by a tentative, overly polite, uncertain, or indecisive approach, as indicated in Exhibit 7-1. Several studies indicate that women perpetuate the lower-credibility stereotype with the following types of behavior:

- *Women ask more questions,* about three times as many on average.

- *Women make more statements in a questioning tone,* with a rising inflection at the end of a statement.

- *Women use more tag questions;* that is, adding a brief question at the end of a sentence:

". . . don't you think?" ". . . okay?" ". . . you know?"

- *Women lead off with a question* more frequently. "You know what?" "Would you believe this?" Researchers note this and other striking similarities between the conversations of men/women and the conversations of adults/children.

- *Women use more qualifiers and intensifiers.* Qualifiers or "hedges" include "kind of, sort of, a little bit, maybe, could be, if." They soften an assertive statement, but also undermine its assertiveness. Intensifiers include "really, very, incredible, fantastic, amazing," especially when these words are emphasized. The metamessage tends to be: "Because what I say, by itself, is not likely to convince you, I must use double force to make sure you see what I mean."

This indicates that women tend to express their thoughts more tentatively and work harder to get someone's attention, which may in turn reflect basic power differences, or at least perceptions of power differences. Your most effective conversational style as a leader usually conveys your sensitivity *and* your commitment to your beliefs and statements.

Connection or Status?

Deborah Tannen's studies reinforce the idea that men and women live in different worlds; women live in the world of intimacy and men in the world of status concerns. In their world, women focus on connecting with others via networks of supportive friends [7]. Much of their communication is aimed at minimizing differences and building on commonalities and agreements. The ultimate goal is to attain maximum consensus and to function in relationships where people are interdependent. Men certainly have their old-boy networks, but their

world of status places higher priority on independence, where the focus of much communication is on giving or taking orders. The ultimate goal is to attain more personal freedom.

People begin taking these divergent paths as toddlers. Girls are encouraged to play in small groups or pairs, often indoors. They jump rope and play house, hopscotch, jacks, or other activities in which there is much sharing, and everyone gets a turn. Many activities involve no winners and losers, no rules and regulations, and are flexible, flowing from suggestions the girls make to each other: "Why don't we pretend that . . ." Boys are more likely to play outdoors and in large groups, especially when they enter school. Their team sports are more hierarchical, with group leaders dominating and giving orders. There is more focus on gaining center stage and thus gaining status, on winning and losing. The rules are more elaborate and arguments about rules abound. There is more boasting about personal skills and more focus on who's best.

As boys grow into men, their time and activities gain respect and tend to be viewed as important, whereas girls' time and activities are seen as less important. This tendency is tied to the fact that beginning with the Industrial Revolution, men went off to work they got paid for, while women stayed home and did not get paid. In our society income is seen as an indicator of a person's importance and value. Women are expected to be respectful of men's more important responsibilities. As little boys become adults, they take on the parent role with women, serving as their protectors. Men are thus seen as competent and tend to indulge women. On the other hand, as little girls become women, they retain much of the child role, needing to be protected and indulged, and thus less competent than men. Some social scientists are speculating that the recent increase in violent acts against women and girls (rape, child or wife abuse, assault and battery) may be an acting-out of men's confusion, resentment, and fear of women's increasing independence and power.

Many studies have shown that males are considered more competent than females, at least outside the home. For example, in 1988 people were asked to evaluate an article, some copies with a woman's byline and identical copies with a man's byline [4]. The article with the male byline was rated as better by 98 percent of the evaluators. In another study of mixed-group conversations, 97 percent of interruptions were made by men. There were few interruptions when women were speaking with women or when men were speaking with men. In mixed-group studies of who does most of the talking, men talk from 58 percent to 92 percent of the time. Most women are unaware of this type of domination, perceiving that they did a fair share of the talking in 75 percent of the situations.

Men are allowed to take the lead and dominate in many subtle ways. For example, both men and women tend to regard topics introduced by women as tentative, whereas topics introduced by men are treated as material to be pursued. Men use humor to take the lead. They tend to remember and repeat jokes, using the opportunity to take center stage and gain control. Most women tend to forget jokes, rarely attempt to repeat them, and serve as a supportive audience, laughing at the jokes men tell.

Rapport Talk or Report Talk?

Most communication by the typical woman could be called "rapport talk" because its major purpose is to establish or maintain rapport with others [7]. The focus is on feelings and includes personal thoughts, reactions to the day's events, and the details of her life. Typical male talk could be called "report talk," focusing on factual information that the listener needs to know and what's going on in the world. Women tell people things mainly to increase interpersonal involvement, while men do it because others need to know. Women's major aim in listening is to communicate interest and caring; men's major interest is to get information. Women will frequently reveal their weaknesses, especially when the other person is feeling discouraged. The rationale: Sharing such personal information will make the other person feel equal, and thus closer. Men nearly always feel that revealing a weakness would merely lower their status in the other person's eyes.

Cooperative or Competitive?

Women's communication often revolves around giving understanding, while men's is more likely to revolve around giving advice [7]. These tendencies are probably based on the different ways men and women measure power. Women view helping, nurturing, and supporting as measures of their power. The activities they engage in include giving praise, speaking one-on-one, and private conversations. The main arenas for these activities are the telephone, social situations, and the home. Men perceive different measures of their power, such as having information, expertise, and skills. The activities they engage in include giving information, speaking more and longer, and speaking to groups. The main arenas for these activities are the workplace and public places.

In the work arena women tend to approach decision-making in a participative way: I cannot and should not act alone when it comes to important decisions. Men tend to feel they must act alone and must find their way without help [7]. Women focus on mastering their jobs and increasing their skills, consulting and involving others in the process, and developing positive relationships with their peers. Men tend to focus on competition and power, hierarchy, and status. Women may not stand up for their rights because they want to avoid conflict. Men are less likely to be afraid of conflict and more willing to confront issues in order to clear the air. Men are also more likely to be intimidating, while women are more often perceived as approachable.

Women are more likely to be uncomfortable taking the initiative. Because they tend to be more accommodating and self-sacrificing, they are also more likely to allow frustration to build. To overcome problems arising from these tendencies, women can develop assertiveness skills and habits. Men need clear facts in the communication process. They experience more difficulty in coping with unclear situations and expressing mixed feelings. To overcome this, they can get in touch with their emotions and intuitive side.

Expertise: Play It Up or Down?

A major source of power for managers, professionals, and other leaders is expertise. Tannen's studies indicate that women tend to downplay their expertise, act as if they know less than they really do, and operate as one of the group or audience [7]. Men are more likely to display their expertise and act as if they know more about their area than others in the group know: they are comfortable taking center stage. The male expert's main goal is to persuade, and he often firmly states his opinions as facts. Moreover, when female experts speak with males, their approach tends to be assenting, supporting, agreeing, listening, and going along. They want to emphasize similarities between themselves and listeners and to avoid showing off. Their concerns: Have I been helpful? Do you like me? The male experts' approach tends to be dominating, talking more, interrupting, and controlling the topic, whether they are speaking with males or females. They want to emphasize their superiority and display their expertise. Their concerns: Have I won? Do you respect me?

The typical female response to male experts' communication is to either agree or disagree. On the other hand, male listeners usually don't understand that the female expert's main concern is to not offend, so the males often conclude that she is either indecisive, incompetent, insecure, or all of the above. They respond by offering their own opinions and information and by setting the agenda themselves; that is, they incorrectly perceive a power vacuum and try to take over.

Agreeing or Disagreeing?

Feedback, or listening responses, tend to be different for males and females. Women's feedback tends to be more positive and copious [7]. They keep a running feedback loop going with such responses as "mmmm, uh huh, yes, yeah." They ask questions, take turns, and give and want full attention. They usually agree, and they laugh at humorous comments. They focus on the metamessage even more than the literal message. Men, however, give fewer listener responses. They are more silent and listen less. They are more likely to challenge statements and to focus on the literal message.

Because women listen so attentively, they may think a man's silence implies concentration on their metamessage, when in fact he may not be listening. Later she says, "But I told you all about that yesterday!" Most men challenge any statement they disagree with, thus a man tends to interpret a woman's silence as consent or agreement. Later, when her actions are incompatible with her "agreement," he concludes that she is insincere or changeable: "Women!" As we begin to understand the different worlds that men and women live in, we can begin to bridge such communication gaps.

WAYS OF LISTENING AND SPEAKING

Even the most fluent women must adapt their talents to the language of business, both spoken and written. Let's concentrate first on the spoken word: developing some basic skills, listening, conducting meetings, and making presentations.

Sharpening Your Basic Skills

The spoken word can be a powerful tool for gaining and using personal power. Therefore, it will pay to continually sharpen your skills in persuading people and in getting through to them with clear instructions, questions, and responses. Keep developing skills in tuning in to the other person's viewpoint and gearing your messages accordingly. And remain aware of your responsibility as boss for taking the initiative to establish lines of communication with your people and to keep the lines open. Let's review some suggestions for sharpening these basic communication skills.

Practice Empathy   To be aware of what your listener will value as a payoff, try to put yourself in his or her shoes. How is your listener likely to feel about your message? What pressures is he or she under? How calm and confident is he or she feeling? What kind of relationship do you have? If the topic is controversial, is there anything the two of you *can* agree on to begin with?

Develop the Art of Persuasion   Remember that people usually base actions more on feelings, opinions, and beliefs than on logic and reason. A rational approach is one that considers all the variables, and in most situations there are many variables we cannot be sure of. True rationality also considers people's emotions and other "illogical" factors. Here is a five-step sequence for persuasive communication.

1. Establish rapport. Communicate to the listener, in both words and actions, that you see the problem or situation from his or her viewpoint, too.

2. Introduce your proposal or idea and suggest how it can help generally.

3. Try to determine what your listener's problems are and what payoffs are important to him or her by using good questioning techniques (see the discussion that follows).

4. Follow up with details to convince. Provide the listener with evidence that your proposal can help.

5. Maintain your credibility by avoiding too many strong adjectives, adverbs, superlatives, euphemisms, or worn-out phrases; words that imply a certain knowledge of future events; and inappropriate surprise or amazement.

Watch Word Choice   Be yourself and use language you are comfortable with, but modify it to fit the situation and your listener. Choose familiar nontechnical words when talking with people who might not understand technical terms or business jargon. Make this your goal: words and statements that are as short, simple, direct, familiar, and concise as is appropriate for the listener and the situation.

Use Specific Language   Another barrier to complete communication is the use of vague, abstract, general language. The more specific your message is, the more likely the listener is to interpret it correctly. You have a picture in your mind of what you're trying to get across. The more specific the language you use to describe that picture, the more likely the listener will be to get the same picture in his or her mind. Let's look at some comparisons:

General: We have got to get on the ball.

Specific: Everyone in the Field Audit unit must increase his or her production by at least 5 percent.

General: You can bring me the stuff now.

Specific: I'm ready to go over the Western Region account files now.

General: Some people are taking advantage of my good nature.

Specific: Both Jim and Bob have been leaving twenty or thirty minutes early several times a week for the past month.

General: It's time I got what I deserve for all the hard work I do.

Specific: Since I achieved all the objectives we agreed on — and even exceeded two of them — I think I deserve a $4,000 a year raise.

Notice that in order to be specific, it's important to use the names of things ("the Western Region account files"), names of people, and numbers where possible. Watch how you use indefinite words such as "there, that, this, it, thing, whatchamacallit, dilly." Even when you use "he," "she," or "they," be sure you are clear about exactly whom you're referring to.

Use the Active Verb Form   Active verbs generally signal a willingness to assume responsibility, a sense of being in control, and an assertive, positive approach. Active verbs are also more specific. They give more information and help the listener form a picture in his or her mind of someone doing something, of action taking place. Compare the active and passive forms:

Active: I will achieve the objectives by May 1.

Passive: The objectives will be achieved by May 1.

Active: On the basis of my investigation, I believe that the CRP is the best buy.

Passive: The investigation has led to the conclusion that the CRP is the best buy.

Don't Focus on Rules   The typical bureaucrat uses a variation of the logical approach when he or she keeps falling back on company rules or company policies as the reasons for decisions and instructions. Although some people will seem to go along, you'll get more cooperation if you communicate the *reason* for a policy or rule and the *payoffs* for following it. This approach conveys consideration of people as human beings rather than as cogs in the machinery. At times it's more productive to put people's feelings ahead of following the rules or even to allow them the freedom to make their own decisions.

Use Key One-Liners or Soundbites   Condense your thoughts and opinions on key issues, new proposals, and other company matters and be ready to express them at appropriate times. This is one way to stay prepared, avoid being caught with "egg on your face," and come across as an intelligent, well-informed, decisive, and assertive manager. Keep on top of issues that may come up in meetings or in chance encounters where you may have only a few minutes to communicate. Formulate your position and phrase it in one clear sentence. Write down these key one-liners and keep them up front in your mind.

If you are at the entry level, such one-liners can boost your image with decision-makers. Mastering the use of the one-liner is good practice for using soundbites when you become a team leader. Soundbites help you crystallize your vision, communicate it to coworkers, and inspire them to promote it. Some examples are

Ask not what you can do for your country

Make my day

Where's the beef?

The customer is king

The team's the thing

We're going to rocket-fuel this project

Our future's so bright, we need shades

Our three top goals are service, service, service

The most effective soundbites are short and catchy, have emotional impact, are often grammatically unusual, and are delivered with verve, a pause before and after, or a raised or lowered voice. How do you develop a good soundbite? Pay attention to the phrases that keep popping up in your mind. Jot down the ones that might become good soundbites. Use them on a trial basis to gauge their effectiveness. Once you adopt a soundbite, use it in key presentations, repeating it three times at various points for impact. Later, be alert to opportunities to interject it in conversations.

Avoid False Assumptions One of the most common barriers to communication is false assumptions about yourself or your listener. People frequently assume that the listener knows more about the content of the message than is actually the case. We can become so involved in a situation that it's easy to forget how unfamiliar a listener may be with important details. We therefore leave gaps in our messages, causing the listener in turn to act on incomplete information.

Allow for Face-Saving The listener may or may not be aware of gaps in a message. Someone who is aware may be unwilling to ask for more information for fear of appearing ignorant or stupid. As the speaker, then, it is often crucial that you make sure your message is clear and complete. For example, you can say, "Let's review. Will you give me your interpretation of what I just said so I can be sure I have covered everything?"

On the other hand, when you are the listener, don't resort to face-saving tactics when you are unclear about a message. Feeling free to say you don't understand can be a sign of confidence. Certainly no one signals a lack of confidence more clearly than the person who is pretending to understand.

Provide Closure Have you ever talked with someone who jumped from one topic to another, perhaps switching back and forth among topics? Some people even interrupt themselves in midsentence to digress to other topics, confusing and frustrating their listeners.

Listen to yourself. Do you usually stick with the topic until discussion of it is complete before moving on to another matter? If you find it difficult to stay aware of your conversational patterns, tape-record yourself. Telephone conversations are good ones to record because the listener doesn't have to be aware of what you are doing. When you play back the conversation, make notes on speaking habits and patterns that need improvement. Do this periodically until you have cleared up any poor speaking habits.

Maintain Relationships Keep communication lines open and let your people know you're interested in them as people through the appropriate use of small talk. You don't need to slip into "typical woman talk," but you can be warm and friendly while maintaining an air of professionalism. Consider using brief references to interesting current events or to the listener's interests, hobbies, family, home, pet, or vacation or holiday activities. By giving people this type of personal attention in the hallway, on the elevator, during breaks in meetings, and in other routine encounters, you can maintain relationships with little or no extra time cost. The manager who discusses *only* business can get the reputation of being more a machine than a person.

Take Initiative In addition to taking the initiative to maintain personal relationships with members of your staff, you must also let them know what's going on in the company and what you're thinking — if you expect them to let you know what *they're* thinking. Although some details may have to be kept confidential, you should communicate as much as possible about every phase of the group's operations to as many people within the group as possible. Take stock. Are you expecting your people to read your mind? Maybe they *should* know you need that report by Friday, but chances are they don't.

Get the Feedback You Need The key to getting feedback is letting people know you're open to it. Your people will give you the feedback they think you want, not what you need, unless you can accept criticism from them, help them bring facts and ideas into proper focus, and ask them for data properly.

When you ask for data, let people know why you need it and what you plan to do with it. In that way you're more likely to get exactly what you want in the best form for your purposes.

Helping your people bring their ideas into focus is the key to getting good feedback when you meet to discuss problems, plans, or the progress of projects. Draw out all the ideas and approaches your people have been thinking of. Don't just have a vague discussion. Get people to focus on specific questions: What are we going to do? What other information do we need to get? Who is going to do what and when? At the end of the discussion, ask for a summary. Once you get it, ask for a one-page memo itemizing what has been covered and agreed on.

Accepting criticism from your people without resentment is necessary if you want honest feedback that helps you lead your team to top performance. If you ignore or punish critical feedback, you'll probably become isolated from the effects of your decisions and therefore make increasingly poor decisions. The team member who is willing to tell you that you're going in the wrong direction may be far more loyal than the one who keeps telling you how wonderful your decision is. Such honesty may also indicate strength and self-confidence.

A major obstacle to getting constructive criticism from people is a lack of clearly stated, specific objectives. This lack prevents a subordinate from intelligently discussing how your decision affects departmental performance. Another major obstacle is fear that you will react badly. You can help your people overcome this obstacle by training them through example.

Listening for the Total Message

Saying the right things to the right people at the right time requires good listening skills. For example, the ability to determine when it's best to just listen and when it's best to become actively involved in a situation is important to the effective manager. Most managers can profit from spending some time on improving their listening habits and skills. Speaking and listening skills can work together to increase your personal power.

The ability to communicate empathy, encouragement, and acceptance of the speaker depends mainly on what you *don't* say. The ability to phrase questions effectively as well as to identify and follow up on the speaker's key points depends on your level of verbal skill. So does the ability to help the listener identify, analyze, and express her or his thoughts, beliefs, ideas, and behavior patterns. Finally, you must depend on your own judgment about the degree of personal involvement that is appropriate to your role as listener and as manager.

Exercise 7-1 provides you with an opportunity to review some of your listening habits. After you have completed it, take a look at your overall pattern of listening behavior. What areas most need improvement? How do you plan to change your habits in that area? Make changes one step at a time.

Developing the Art of "Being with" Another Person Perhaps the first step in improving listening skills is becoming aware of the importance of simply "being with" another person. This is an art that can be especially important in listening to team members.

When you meet with your teammates on a one-to-one basis, it's important to give them your full attention. First, put everything else aside and concentrate on merely being with that person—without adding anything to or taking anything away from the experience of just being there together. Take in everything the person has to communicate, both verbally

EXERCISE 7-1: REVIEWING YOUR LISTENING HABITS

After each statement, write the number that best reflects your habits:
Always = 5, Usually = 4, Often = 3, Seldom = 2, Never = 1. Add the
numbers. Maximum = 80, Minimum = 16.

1. If I cannot pay attention to the person speaking to me, I end the conversation or postpone it to a time when I can pay attention. _____

2. I look at the person who is talking to me. _____

3. I maintain almost constant eye contact when someone is talking to me (instead of reading or looking at other things on my desk or at other people who are passing by). _____

4. If I remain in a conversation, I concentrate on what the speaker is saying even though it may not be of great interest to me at the moment. _____

5. I listen to a person's ideas and facts, but at the same time I listen for the person's feelings and emotions. _____

6. I notice the speaker's body language and integrate it with the verbal message. _____

7. I allow the speaker to finish a complete thought without interruption. _____

8. I concentrate on what a speaker is saying even in noisy, distracting surroundings. _____

9. I listen for facts and information that other people can offer and that I do not possess. _____

10. I am not distracted by the way a person delivers a message. _____

11. If a speaker uses words that bring certain prejudices to mind, I try to be aware of prejudiced feelings and suspend them until I've got the full message. _____

12. If the speaker seems inappropriately dressed or speaks with an accent different from mine, I still listen intently. _____

13. If a speaker makes a statement that is not clear to me, I ask questions. _____

14. If the speaker answers my questions and I still do not understand an important point, I ask the person to explain the point again. _____

15. After I have learned what I want from a speaker, I still give him or her my undivided attention until the conversation is over. _____

16. I keep my mind focused on what the speaker is saying (instead of thinking about what I am going to say next or letting my mind wander to other topics). _____

and nonverbally. It may help if you think of yourself as an empty sponge being filled with that person's message. Take it all in and absorb it as fully as possible. Don't try to evaluate it as good or bad, right or wrong. It just *is*. Let the person know you are taking in the message. If parts of it are unclear, ask questions or feed it back in your own words to check for understanding. Once you are sure of the message, you can evaluate its validity and appropriateness, its effects on achieving objectives and co-operating as a group, and other factors. Absorb first; evaluate later.

Encouraging People to Talk   Drawing people out of themselves requires the use of some specific skills in addition to the ability to provide a supportive atmosphere. The first step is to put people at ease by acting relaxed yourself and giving sincere compliments. Remember to smile when it's natural and comfortable to do so. Once the speaker is relaxed, encourage talk by drawing him or her out. For example, make an opening statement that stimulates conversation: "That was the most complex set of specifications we've ever attempted!" Or ask an effective lead-off question: "How did you ever unravel that set of specifications?" Once the person starts talking, make encouraging listening responses ("Um-hum." "Yes?" "Right!" "Tell me more."), make supportive remarks, and ask questions at appropriate intervals. Maintain regular eye contact (no glazed-over or blank stares).

Avoid the habit of assuming you know what the other person is going to say after the first few words of a statement and finishing the sentence for him or her. If the speaker is too unassertive to give the correct ending, you may never know what he or she really intended to say. And don't tune out because you think you know what the speaker is going to say. While you're daydreaming, you may miss something important.

Getting others to talk can bring rich benefits to you. It helps keep the other person at ease as he or she becomes engrossed in verbalizing thoughts and experiences. It can start the person to thinking about a topic you want emphasized. You give the person an opportunity to show what he or she knows and understands. You bring out facts you might not otherwise find out about, and you get the opportunity to communicate that you understand his or her situation.

Phrasing Questions Appropriately   Another key to drawing people out and to pinpointing information you need is skill in phrasing questions. Open questions are phrased so that they cannot be answered "yes" or "no": "What do you think about this decision?" "Why are you late so often?" Use open questions when you want to encourage talk. Open questions usually begin with some variation of the "Five W's" of journalism fame (who, what, where, when, and why). Closed questions, on the other hand, frequently begin with some variation of the "be," "do," or "have" types of verbs. They are phrased so that they *can* be answered "yes" or "no" or with a specific bit of data: "Do you feel this is fair?" "How many units did you sell that year?" Use them when you want to zero in on a specific response. More examples of open and closed questions are given in Exhibit 7-2. See Exercise 13-9 (pp. 470–471), Interviewing Techniques, for applying open questions to job interviews.

Focusing on Important Aspects   You can guide a conversation so the most important facts come out and the key issues are explored. Listen for key thoughts and follow up by further questioning and discussion. A key thought is an idea, opinion, or experience that is expressed by the person talking and that appears to the listener to have an important bearing on the matter being discussed, even though it may be hidden in casual comments or very brief references. Become alert to the underlying meanings of the speaker's words, so you can note key thoughts and return to them.

EXHIBIT 7-2: Open and Closed Questions

Open	Closed
Who is in favor of the reorganization?	*Are* most of the accounting people in favor of the reorganization?
What information did you get?	*Have* you got the information?
Where is the best place for the new machine?	*Is* this the best place for the new machine?
When did you first notice the communication problem?	*Has* the communication problem been bothering you for long?
Why do you dislike the new schedule?	*Will* the new schedule interfere with your Baker project?

Learn to distinguish between the content and relationship levels in conversations. **Content level** refers to the topic being discussed, the verbal content of the message. **Relationship level** refers to predominantly nonverbal messages about the way one person values or accepts the other person; it is based mainly on feelings. We *feel* comfortable, free, anxious, or guilty in a relationship, for example, and the other person's messages of acceptance or non-acceptance can trigger these feelings. Messages at the relationship level usually contain the best clues to key thoughts and important aspects of a situation.

Communicating Acceptance Let people know that you accept not only the facts they present but the feelings and opinions they convey. If you accept only facts, you limit your acceptance, placing conditions on it. Since people's feelings and viewpoints help make them unique, you seem to be rejecting their individuality when you accept only the messages that *don't* include opinions and feelings. When you communicate acceptance at a relationship level, people feel trusted and respected.

On the other hand, when people feel rejected, they often respond by pushing harder, trying to prove that their feelings and opinions are justified. Messages at the relationship level tend to become pressured, accusatory, and defensive. The speaker may withdraw and withhold information. Therefore, it's worth sharpening your skills at communicating acceptance so your people can relax and give acceptance in return. When they feel free to listen to your messages, accept them, and act on them, they may allow other, perhaps deeper, feelings to surface.

Avoid the trap of thinking that acceptance of another person's opinions and feelings is the same as *agreement* with them. It's not, necessarily. Agreement is an alliance with the other person in his or her position that implies you feel basically the same way. Acceptance is merely an understanding that a person feels a certain way about a topic without condemning or denying the person's right to feel that way. To be a supportive listener, you must be able to accept people's feelings and opinions, whether you agree or not. When you and your people *share* feelings, opinions, and experiences rather than try to prove they're good or right, you have a chance to begin understanding one another.

Until people feel they can trust you, they tend to express themselves indirectly, perhaps by sending out trial-balloon problems. They present you with small, relatively innocuous problems. If you accept the total message and express acceptance of the total person, then she or he will probably feel safe enough to discuss more basic, meaningful problems with you. Effective listening, therefore, is essential

EXHIBIT 7-3: Responses That Can Communicate Nonacceptance

When You Make This Response:	Are You Implying This Message?
Ordering, demanding: "You must try . . ." "You have to stop . . ."	Don't feel, act, think that way; do it my way.
Warning, threatening: "You'd better . . ." "If you don't, then . . ."	You'd better not have that feeling, act, or think that way.
Admonishing, moralizing: "You should . . ." "It's not proper to . . ."	You are bad if you have that feeling, act, or think that way.
Criticizing, blaming, disagreeing: "You aren't thinking about this properly . . ."	You are wrong if you have that feeling, act, or think that way.
Advising, giving answers: "Why don't you . . ." "Let me suggest . . ."	Here's a solution so you won't have that feeling, act, or think that way.
Praising, agreeing: "But you've done such a good job . . ." "I approve of . . ."	Your feelings, actions, and opinions are subject to my approval.
Reassuring, sympathizing: "Don't worry . . ." "You'll feel better . . ."	You don't need to have that feeling, act, or think that way.
Persuading, arguing: "Do you realize that . . ." "The facts are . . ."	Here are some facts so you won't have that feeling, act, or think that way.
Interpreting, diagnosing: "What you need is . . ." "Your problem is . . ."	Here's the reason you have that feeling, act, or think that way.
Probing, questioning: "Why . . .?" "Who . . .?" "When . . .?" "What . . .?"	Are you really justified in having that feeling, acting, or thinking that way?
Diverting, avoiding: "We can discuss it later . . ." "That reminds me of . . ."	Your feelings, actions, and opinions aren't worthy of discussion.
Kidding, using sarcasm: "That will be the day!" "Bring out the violins . . ."	You're silly if you persist in having that feeling, acting, or thinking that way.

to communicating at progressively deeper levels.

Some typical responses that can communicate nonacceptance of a person's feelings, thoughts, and actions are shown in Exhibit 7-3, which is based on the work of psychologist Dr. Thomas Gordon. The responses illustrate the difficulty of merely listening, being with a person, and showing acceptance. Some of them may be appropriate and even constructive messages at certain times, but not when your major goal is to communicate acceptance at a relationship level. The receiver of one of these messages may become defensive and never allow you to hear anything deeper than the trial-balloon problem.

Developing Active Listening Skills This prepares you for a deeper level of involvement with the speaker once she or he feels accepted and trusts you. In *Effectiveness Training for Women*, Linda Adams has described active listening in this way:

Active Listening is a special way of reflecting back what the other person has said, to let her or him know that you're listening, and to check your understanding of what she or he means. It's a restatement of the other person's *total* communication: the *words* of the message plus the accompanying *feelings*. To shift gears to Active Listening, you must temporarily put yourself in the other's position, try to get a sense of the other's thoughts and feelings, and then share your understanding with the other to check its accuracy. [1, pp. 36–37]

This active listening sequence consists of these steps:

1. You receive the other's message, verbal and nonverbal.

2. You translate the message and get your sense of what the other is trying to communicate.

3. You feed back your understanding of the other's message, saying in effect: "Here's my understanding of what you're feeling or experiencing. Am I right?"

4. The other person then reacts to your active listening response, confirming or clarifying your understanding of her or his message.

Here's an example of active listening in a business situation:

You (*I-message*): I think you did a good job with that presentation, but I disagree that we should expand our product line just now. It would overextend our production facilities.

Peer (*resistance to message*): That's a pretty pessimistic point of view. I'm really surprised to hear you say that.

You (*shifting gears to active listening*): I see you are upset about what I said. I'm interested in knowing more about why you feel the way you do.

Peer: I believe we could put on a night crew and make better use of our production facility.

You (*active listening*): It's important to you to expand as rapidly as possible, right?

Peer: Yes, and one reason it's important is because the market is ready for our product now. It may not be so favorable a couple of years from now.

You (*another I-message*): I see your point; however, we've built our reputation on providing

top-quality products and excellent service. I'm concerned about the effect rapid expansion would have on that.

By shifting gears to active listening after an assertion, you can constructively explore *value* differences. Avoid assuming what the other's *motives* are, however. Frequently you can cool down a potentially volatile argument without either party backing away from her or his own feeling. You encourage rational discussion of controversial issues.

Determining the Right Degree of Personal Involvement How "actively" you listen will depend on the degree of personal involvement you think is desirable or necessary in the situation. One trait of a good listener is the ability to distinguish those times when the speaker doesn't want you to do anything except understand from times when the speaker is seeking guidance or action on your part. Let's explore three progressively deeper levels of listening.

Level 1: Listening to interpret and give feedback: To make sure you understand what the message is and to let the speaker know you understand, you can restate what you think you have heard, as in this exchange between a manager and a worker:

W: This problem has occurred several times, and I think I should change the way I handle these transactions.

M: You're considering rewriting the procedures?

W: Well, I think I should. I just don't like having people jump all over me.

M: You are really tired of being pressured to have the information in the form the Accounting Department wants it?

W: Yes, I want them to stop bugging me, and I'm going to tell them that, too. I'm tired of people thinking I'm a patsy and that they can take out their resentment on me.

M: You think people are in the habit of hassling you, but this time you're going to see that they stop it.

W: That's right . . .

This type of active listening can encourage the speaker to come to his or her own conclusions. You can restate the *content* of the message back to the speaker; you can also notice feelings and check them out.

Level 2: Listening for behavior patterns: A pattern of behavior indicates a readiness to respond in a typical way to certain types of situations. Our behavior patterns are determined by the basic underlying feelings we have about ourselves — for example, "People are always jumping on me," "I always get what I really want in the end," "People are always becoming envious of me," "No one really cares about my feelings." These decisions people make about themselves, often in early childhood, largely determine how they are going to react in certain situations. If you can listen and give feedback at this level, your interaction with the other person can become more meaningful. If people can reevaluate these childhood decisions in light of current reality, they often redecide and consequently change their behavior.

Level 3: Listening for deeper insights and guidance: At a deeper level of listening and involvement you look for deeper insights the speaker touches on, such as a desire for change, intentions, causes, and solutions.

W: This seems to happen to me frequently.

M: And you would like to change that?

When you assume a guidance role as a listener, you will sometimes need to decide which avenue toward a deeper insight to pursue. For example, if a team member tells you about what other people do to him, you can focus on the others or you can focus on the part he plays in the situation.

W: People are always pressuring me.

M: People expect too much from you?

In that response, the manager focused on "them," not on the worker. Contrast it with this:

M: You have difficulty handling other people's demands?

Here the manager focuses on the speaker.

It's usually more productive to focus on the speaker's role so that she can pursue ways of gaining control over herself and her life, regardless of other people's behavior. This focuses on what she can control rather than on her helplessness. If you want to be less directive, you can feed back both aspects and let the speaker pursue what is most relevant to her at this point. For example:

M: People expect too much from you and you have difficulty handling the demands?

Although some guidance can be helpful, it's important to avoid directing the flow of communication. When the speaker takes the lead and arrives at her own insights, the resulting conclusions and decisions will have the most meaning for her and she will most likely act on them. Your role as an active listener can be more productive if you facilitate this process rather than direct it.

Aim for an underlying attitude that asks ("Is this the way you feel?") rather than tells. If you have difficulty interpreting the speaker's total message, ask, "Is that right?" or "Does that seem to fit?" If your feedback is not accepted by the speaker, ask what he or she *does* mean. Focus on getting the total message, never on proving you're right in your interpretation or explaining why you interpreted in a certain way.

Being an active listener gives you a chance to communicate understanding and acceptance of a person's ideas and feelings, and it gives the speaker an opportunity to correct you if you have misunderstood. When you use this skill, your people will feel more comfortable about bringing ideas and problems to you and sharing deeper thoughts and problems. They'll be able to talk through their feelings and subsequently to solve many of their own problems. Test your listening skills by completing Exercise 7-3 at the end of this chapter.

Arranging and Facilitating Meetings

In many organizations attendance at meetings where little or nothing is accomplished is the biggest time-waster for managers. When you are in charge of conducting meetings, you have an opportunity to turn them into time-savers. You also have a chance to build group morale and team spirit through meetings that are well planned and group centered.

Exhibit 7-4 summarizes some of the differences between traditional leadership of meetings and group-centered leadership. In conducting meetings, as in other aspects of managing, your goal as the leader is to reach the optimal balance between accomplishing the tasks at hand and meeting the needs of individual members and of the group as a whole. A major barrier to adopting group-centered leadership is the leader's fears of appearing weak and inadequate to the group members. Many leaders fear the risks of sharing planning and decision-making with the group. Dealing openly with group conflict and emotional behavior is also viewed as risky. Doing so does indeed require courage and commitment. The payoffs include a high level of worker motivation and participation, plus strong support and commitment to team plans and projects.

To turn your meetings into time-savers that accomplish specific goals, you must take the lead in getting the team to decide when a meeting should be called, how long it should last, and who should attend. You must also prepare people to participate by briefing them and by distributing an effective agenda. You must be able to lead the meeting so people participate and necessary actions are taken. It's wise also to develop skills in contributing as a group member when someone else is leading the meeting.

Deciding When to Meet A universal complaint in large organizations is that too much time is wasted in meetings. We have all been to countless meetings where little or nothing was really accomplished, where business that took an hour or so to complete could have been handled in ten minutes with good planning and execution, where people didn't participate or go away committed to the plans made, and so forth.

How can you avoid the traps that seem to lure so many managers into arranging and conducting such poor meetings? Certainly the first step in avoiding wasted time in meetings is deciding when and when not to call a meeting. Let's look at the most common reasons for meetings.

To report or share information—for quick, direct presentation of reports or information, instructions, or assignments by individuals

To solve a problem or make decisions—to draw on the thinking of the various people or units of an organization, to clarify an issue or problem, and to form this thinking into a solution or decision

To develop or create—to create new ideas or to develop and expand as yet undefined concepts, strategies, theories, and so forth (This type of meeting works best when the leader serves as the facilitator of creativity and asserts minimum control.)

Calling a meeting is usually *not* a good idea when

You have inadequate information or preparation to deal with the issue

EXHIBIT 7-4: Meetings — Gaining Support and Commitment (A Comparison of Old and New Approaches)

Traditional Group Leader	Group-Centered Leader
Leader is in control of her group; her authority and responsibility are acknowledged by the group. She directs, polices, leads them to the best decision.	Group takes responsibility for the meeting; it is *their* meeting. Leader assists all members to contribute to group activities.
Leader focuses her attention on the purpose of the meeting and keeps the group focused on the task at hand. Leader performs all the functions necessary to arrive at the best decision.	Responsibility for reaching a decision lies with the group. All participate and the decision belongs to all. Leader serves the group and helps it achieve the purpose of the meeting.
Leader sets limits, uses rules of order to keep the discussion within strict topic and time limits set by the agenda.	Members are brought into the planning by setting goals and methods of achieving them, developing an agenda, and assigning tasks.
Leader encourages objective, logical thinking and discourages the expression of emotions. Leader explains the disruptive effect of emotions.	Feelings, emotions, and conflicts are accepted as realities that may be as important to address as the task agenda.
If a member's behavior becomes disruptive, it is the leader's responsibility to take the member aside to discuss the behavior and its effects.	Disruptive behavior is a group problem and must be solved within the group. As the group moves closer to the goal of mutual trust, members start monitoring their own potentially disruptive behavior.
The needs of individual members are less important to the leader than the need to arrive at a task decision.	Leader helps members realize that the needs, feelings, and purposes of each are important; that they are a unique group, and that they can continue to grow as such.

Adapted from Leland P. Bradford, *Making Meetings Work* (La Jolla, Calif.: University Associates, 1987).

You need to decide on personnel matters — hiring, firing, salaries, and so on

You could communicate better by one-to-one discussion, telephone, or memo

The topic is confidential

The issue is low priority, and therefore you can handle it yourself or delegate it

You have already decided what you're asking the group to help decide

Some people in the group are angry and hostile but will cool down with time (Don't run scared, but be aware of feelings and of good timing.)

When you are deciding whether to call a meeting and how to go about it, ask yourself such questions as these: Is a meeting actually the best way to accomplish the business at hand? Do I need group participation? Do I need to brief people on action plans that require cooperation among them?

What outcomes do I want from this meeting? What's the major purpose for calling it? What are my goals for it? What are the group's goals for it?

Who needs to participate? What is the best way to involve them in planning and in preparing for the meeting? A recurring theme in this book is the importance of involving people in planning and decision-making. Since there are so many payoffs for doing so — such as a higher level of interest, enthusiasm, and motivation; improved communication and cooperation; access to a larger pool of ideas and information; increased commitment to the achievement of goals — involve people in planning your meetings and in determining what outcomes you want. If it is not feasible to get this input beforehand, at least get it at the beginning of the meeting.

What agenda items, activities, people, and materials will best help us achieve the results we want from the meeting?

How can I get maximum feedback from the participants about their thoughts, ideas, beliefs, opinions, feelings, and suggestions? If you assume that a meeting you have held went well because no one complained, you are missing the boat. Take the initiative to get feedback from all participants on their reactions to the meeting so you can make appropriate changes and so people can see that they have a real influence on the meeting process.

What is the best procedure for assuring follow-up of the agreements, decisions, and action commitments made at the meeting? When the meeting is over, everyone should be clear about who will do what and when it will be done. You should be clear about your procedures for checking to see that commitments are carried out on schedule.

Developing an Agenda   Once you decide that a meeting actually needs to be held and determine the major purpose of the meeting, you are ready to develop an agenda. It's surprising how many meetings are called without an agenda and how many people show up at meetings without really understanding why they are there, much less being well prepared to contribute. Therefore it's important to prepare an agenda and to see that everyone who will be attending gets a copy of it ahead of time.

Consider keeping a folder of agenda items; then instead of calling regularly scheduled meetings, wait until you have enough agenda items to justify a meeting (or one item that is important enough).

The first item on any agenda should be a brief review of the purpose for the meeting. The group should rank the agenda items in order of importance. By *setting priorities*, the group can decide the amount of time that can

be devoted to each item. They may then want to set tentative time limits for each item. Also, when members suggest or submit agenda items, have them include time estimates.

It is much more effective to state the agenda in terms of what you (or the group) want to achieve or what you plan to decide, rather than merely listing the subjects to be covered. One way of doing this is to state agenda items as *questions to be resolved.* This format has the added advantage of encouraging people to think ahead about the goals of the meeting and to prepare more effectively for achieving those goals.

For example, instead of stating an agenda item as "XYZ product," state it as "Should we add XYZ product to our line?" Instead of listing "Profit goals," ask, "How can we increase profits by 10 percent next quarter?" Your agenda items should be clearly worded, brief, specific, and if possible listed in the order in which they will be covered. Exhibit 7-5 presents two versions of an agenda for a meeting of a committee formed to select a consultant. Assume you are a member of the committee and compare the way you respond to each version.

Perhaps the major advantage of phrasing agenda items as decision questions is that discussion at the meeting is more likely to be results oriented. It is therefore easier to keep the discussion focused on achieving the meeting objectives. Practice writing results-oriented agenda items by completing Exercise 7-2.

A common problem is trying to squeeze too much into one meeting. If your agenda is too long, prioritize and eliminate some of the items. In some instances you can divide the items or activities among small groups, which then can report results to the entire group for action.

Gaining Support for an Agenda Item   There will probably be times when you need to convince, persuade, or sell your group on goals, policies, or procedures that need to be implemented — either because top decision-makers

EXHIBIT 7-5: Sample Agendas for a Meeting to Select a Consultant

Meeting Objectives	Results-Oriented Questions
1. Establish criteria for selection.	1. What should be the criteria for selection?
2. Screen proposals and résumés of all candidates.	2. Which three candidates have the personal qualifications that best meet our criteria?
3. Choose three possible candidates.	3. Which three candidates submitted proposals that best meet our criteria?
4. Compose a letter of invitation for on-site visit by prospective candidates.	4. Are the top three candidates in terms of personal qualifications the same as the top three candidates in terms of the quality of their proposals? If not, would any of the personally qualified candidates be able to submit and implement a revised proposal?
5. Formulate questions for on-site visit.	5. What shall we include in the letter of invitation for on-site visits by prospective candidates?
	6. What questions shall we ask the candidates when they arrive?

EXERCISE 7-2: PREPARING ACTION AGENDA ITEMS

Change these agenda items to (1) meeting objectives and (2) results-oriented questions. Check your responses with the answer key.

1. Sales targets

2. New XYZ product

3. Layoff policy

4. Next meeting date

want them implemented or because environmental pressures call for it. In such instances you must consider the politics of planning and leading a meeting. Here are some key questions to ask yourself *before the meeting*.

- Who are the key people I must sell, persuade, or influence?

- How can I gain an adequate consensus of key people for my proposal?

- How can my support group help me achieve my goals?

- Who is the best person to propose this agenda item?

Briefing Speakers, Resource Persons, and Members   Decide who should participate in the meeting and brief them on what parts of the meeting they will be participating in and what they will be expected to contribute. Try to brief participants at least several days before the meeting. Then agree on what they will do, when and for how long, who will be attending the meeting, and what results you are after. If possible, brief people in person and follow up with a memo or letter, incorporating these suggestions.

1. Keep introductions short. Long introductions tend to put distance between the person being introduced and the group. Aim for a short, warm welcome and, if appropriate, provide a handout that gives the speaker's background and qualifications.

2. Make sure speakers and resource people are clear about time limits. Consider putting a large clock or watch where the speaker can easily see it. If appropriate, mention during the introduction that this will be a "fifteen-minute presentation."

3. Be clear about your purpose for having a speaker. Is it to stimulate the thinking of the group and get their inputs? If so, consider having at least two resource persons as speakers so that alternatives can be more openly and fully identified.

Deciding on Appropriate Time Limits and Group Size Generally, effective meetings last no longer than an hour and a half. With good planning, short, relatively simple problems can usually be solved in less than one hour. Aim for this goal. Ask yourself, "Can the purpose of the meeting be accomplished with a 'crisp conference' of the twenty-minute variety?" Often everyone concerned is extremely grateful for leadership toward this type of conference.

It's important to provide variety in regularly scheduled meetings. To keep people stimulated, alert, and thinking, consider changing the meeting time, place, or plans from time to time. Get feedback and suggestions from participants. If the meeting must last for several hours, consider some procedures for having people change seats so they won't get stuck in a rut.

Groups of more than fifteen people have difficulty achieving goals effectively. It becomes difficult for all members to relate to one another

and for the leader to interact with every person. Group action becomes unwieldy and awkward, especially for a decision-making meeting. If you must have twenty-five or more participants, consider dividing them into small groups.

You might also consider having a representative from each subgroup or unit attend the meeting instead of the entire group or unit. Keep the group small and tight, but urge unit representatives to determine the point of view of most of the people in their unit and to vote accordingly. Also, consider asking people to attend only the part of the meeting that they can contribute to or that they need to receive information from.

Providing Optimal Room Arrangements Try to hold meetings in rooms that are well designed for them. Provide for adequate space but not a space so large that the group rattles around in it. The room should have adequate air and light. Crowded, narrow, smoky, dim, or overheated rooms tend to promote tension, irritability, or drowsiness.

Arrange seating to facilitate optimal eye contact among and between all group members. The best setup is a single row of chairs in a semicircular or U-shaped arrangement.

Conducting Effective Meetings Once you have prepared adequately for a meeting, it becomes much easier to conduct it in an effective way. Let's look first at the importance of timing.

Make good use of meeting time. Begin meetings on time even if some people are late. This is especially important for regular periodic meetings. If you wait for latecomers, people who are on time soon realize they will waste *their* time in the future if they are prompt. So they start arriving late, the chronically late ones arrive even later, and starting times lose their meaning. If some people arrive early, try to arrange some constructive reading, activity, or discussion for them, so that they don't feel they are wasting their time while waiting for others to arrive.

Throughout the meeting, be aware of the time factor. Stick to the agenda unless the group votes to digress from it. Try to get a satisfactory answer to each question on the agenda and provide for necessary follow-up.

Consider making a short meeting double as a coffee break to save time. For longer meetings have coffee available throughout the meeting to avoid coffee breaks, especially if activities are planned that include some moving around.

If you have planned properly, started the meeting on time, and remained aware of the time factor throughout the meeting, you should be able to end the meeting on time. It's important to make every effort to do so. If you regularly have problems with overly talkative people getting off the subject and dragging the meeting on, consider setting your meeting time for just before lunch or closing time.

Keep the group focused. Just as important as proper timing is the way in which the group achieves the meeting goals. After you clearly state the purpose of the meeting, express your ideas about it as positively as possible. Indicate that the meeting can lead to successful results. If a solution or decision is needed, focus on the importance of the problem and the challenge, as well as the benefits, of resolving it. For maximum impact, include others in this initial discussion (more about energizing the meeting later). Move along crisply in your explanation. Don't dawdle or ramble. Try to make the pace of the meeting relaxed but lively.

Make frequent summaries during the meeting. A brief one- or two-line summary after each step helps everyone remember what has taken place. At each step of the way — including the written follow-up — stress the positive aspects of the meeting. This doesn't mean you should ignore differences or sweep problems under the rug, of course. If the group confronts and handles them, focus on the resulting benefits rather than on the differences.

Be sure to make adequate arrangements for recording what happens at the meeting. Using a flip chart and felt marking pen to record ideas and then posting them can be effective for some meetings. Participants get to see their inputs recorded and have access to them throughout the meeting so they can fully experience the feeling of participating and influencing results.

Steer problem-solving meetings through a solution-oriented process. The following steps can be posted and referred to from time to time:

1. What is the problem?

2. How did we get here? What are the effects of the problem?

3. What results do we want (goal)?

4. Is the problem too complex to arrive at a solution today?
   a. If the answer is "yes": What process or procedure for gathering information and developing solutions shall we use? The remainder of the meeting may be devoted to developing a process and deciding who will do what within the process. At a future meeting, items 5, 6, and 7 will be addressed.
   b. If the answer is "no," go on to item 5.

5. What solutions can we think of?

6. Which solution is best for us?

7. Who will do what by when? Where? How?

Using this format, or a similar one adapted to your particular problem, helps (1) keep the group focused on the question under discussion, (2) avoid needless digressions and confusion, and (3) keep all members informed about what has been accomplished and what still needs to be done.

Keep the meeting energized. The way a discussion is initiated at the beginning of a meeting is most important to the liveliness of the meeting. Plan in advance how you will get things started and keep them moving. Include others in the planning so they can be prepared to take responsibility and to help. It's up to you to promote contributions by all members; otherwise the group can quickly become passive and uninvolved. Be sensitive to the appropriate time for initiating further exploration of a new direction, and ask how the group feels about moving on.

The main energizing force in a meeting is the initiation of new topics and ideas by members and their general participation. Sometimes the group needs to move on but finds it is stuck. Techniques for energizing and moving the group are (1) introducing a novel idea, (2) expressing a feeling, (3) saying something in a humorous way, (4) devising an activity that involves all members and restores the momentum of the group, or (5) taking a short break. Exhibit 7-6 contrasts behavior that energizes a group and behavior that tends to have the opposite effect.

Deal with hidden agendas. The goals of a meeting can be sabotaged by persons or cliques who are attempting to carry out their own **hidden agendas.** A hidden agenda consists of personal goals that individuals do not reveal to the group spontaneously for fear of rejection. When these hidden individual goals are in opposition to the group's common goals, the meeting can be sabotaged. It's up to you as the leader to deal with this problem. Hidden goals might include playing power politics, impressing the boss, getting revenge, making another member look bad, or playing the comedian. Some commonly used techniques include monopolizing the discussion, asking for clarification on all points, and agreeing with everything the boss says.

Someone with a hidden agenda may come to the meeting committed to one particular solution to the problem and determined to persuade the group to that solution — regardless of the facts, others' opinions, and alternative solutions that are presented.

Frequently the members with a hidden agenda use strategy to manipulate the group. For example, they will listen attentively to the discussion, waiting for the best time to try to achieve their own purposes. Then, at the opportune moment, they pretend their input is

---

EXHIBIT 7-6: Energizing Versus Deadening Behaviors

Behavior That Helps the Group Achieve Task Goals	Behavior That Tends to Deaden Meetings
Identifying objectives	Avoiding eye contact
Speaking appropriately loudly and assertively	Using closed body language
Offering ideas	Speaking softly and hesitantly
Asking key or clarifying questions	Making unnecessary apologies
Keeping a clear focus on the task	Unnecessarily qualifying all statements
Summarizing the discussion	Asking nonessential questions
Behavior That Encourages People to Participate	Generalizing, rambling, getting off the track
	Moving the group away from the heart of the matter
Engaging in active listening	Monopolizing the discussion
Maintaining direct eye contact	
Encouraging participation	
Supporting others	
Soliciting ideas and responses from others	

spontaneous, something "I just thought of." If other members become aware that some strategy is being used on them, they may become defensive, and open communication and trust may be blocked. This defensiveness is intensified when the manipulative member is also powerful.

When you are dealing with a hidden agenda, the main thing to keep in mind is that individual members' goals do not represent the group's goals. Keep returning to group goals and group input. Try to see that less assertive members are not intimidated by the member with the hidden agenda. Encourage quiet members to state their opinions and offer their suggestions.

To encourage participation by all, and block hidden agendas, you must differentiate between criticizing and evaluating a person and that person's ideas or specific actions. Business meetings, as well as business situations in general, are no place to indulge in personal criticism. Feelings and attitudes may need to be aired, but they also need to be respected. It is up to you to be alert to personal attacks and to insist, if necessary, that the discussion be confined to an evaluation and exploration of effective versus ineffective ideas and actions.

You might even consider structuring seating arrangements to help foil persons with hidden agendas. If you anticipate cliques getting together to obstruct progress, consider physically breaking them up by seeing that they are seated apart from each other. Likewise, you can see that people who are personally hostile toward each other sit apart.

Finally, provide closure to the meeting so that members leave feeling that something has been accomplished. Some ways of providing closure are to (1) summarize what has been done, integrating the viewpoints that have been expressed into a unified whole as nearly as you can, (2) review what steps will be taken next, and (3) review action commitments — who is to do what by when. After the meeting, send a confirming memo of decisions made, assignments, responsibilities, and deadline dates for action. See the section on team meetings in Chapter 13.

Contributing to Meetings as a Member
When someone else is arranging and conducting a meeting, your input, preparation, and attitude are also important. If you approach meetings with the attitude that they are all a waste of time, they probably will be. If you approach them with the idea of making the most of them and contributing to the group's goals, meetings are more likely to be productive for you.

There is sometimes a fine line between cooperation and conformity in groups. When members don't feel free to openly express opinions, the group is in danger of overconforming and of indulging in groupthink. **Groupthink** occurs when members of a group appear to think as one and any deviation by one member results in severe negative sanctions by the others. In such an atmosphere, creativity and innovation are squelched. Both as a leader and as a member, you have a responsibility to point out situations in which you believe groupthink is operating.

As a group member, you are also responsible for

Being sure you understand the specific purpose of the meeting

Preparing adequately to contribute to the meeting

Expressing views that reflect some thought and preparation

Making and asking for suggestions

Clarifying and asking for clarification

Asking others' opinions

Even when you are not the leader of the meeting, it is still your responsibility to see that time is not wasted. Don't sit by and watch everyone's time being frittered away. Speak up.

If you don't get an agenda, call the group leader and ask what needs to be accomplished at the meeting. Try to get specific questions that need answering. Suggest that sending agendas to all concerned might help everyone prepare and stay on track.

Once the meeting has started, if you see the leader letting the group jump to a new topic before resolving the question under discussion, ask, "What have we decided to do about the item we have been talking about?" You don't want to give the impression that you're trying to usurp the leader's position, but you can still put your knowledge of effective ways of arranging and conducting meetings to good use. Simply ask appropriate, probing questions at the right times.

Making Effective Presentations and Talks

Your participation and leadership in meetings frequently involves informal talking and interaction. Occasionally, you will have opportunities to make formal presentations and talks. The ability to make effective formal presentations is one of the most important assets a manager can develop. Since so many people shy away from formal speeches, the person who is comfortable with them obviously has an advantage over competitors for promotion to higher-level positions.

Using the Jitters Constructively   The largest barrier to effective formal presentations is stage fright or fear of speaking. Therefore, controlling the jitters is really the key to becoming an effective platform speaker.

Your mind is incapable of totally concentrating on two concerns at once. Therefore, if you can focus all your conscious thoughts on getting your main message across, you *cannot* focus on worries about what people think of you personally. Try thinking of yourself as merely the medium or vehicle for sending the message. In the story at the beginning of this chapter, Jan focused on getting her message across. By doing so, she freed her inner self, allowing it to help her.

Your inner self is amazingly competent; but if you're like most people, you don't believe it is. You think you must put forth great effort to be "good enough." These great, intense efforts actually sabotage your movement toward achieving your goals. This doesn't imply that you should stop learning, growing, and preparing for new kinds of activities and roles. It *does* mean that when it is time to actually perform, you forget yourself, keep your attention focused on the end result you're after, and at the same time let go of any burning, intense need (as opposed to relaxed intention) to achieve that result. See Exercise 5-5, Visualizing Results — Visualization 4, Handling Stage Fright (p. 152).

An essential step in overcoming stage fright is to recognize it, face it squarely, and examine it. What do you fear will happen as a result of giving a talk?

A loss of esteem because of giving a poor performance?

The repetition of a traumatic experience? (If you've ever given a speech that you consider a disaster, you may have programmed yourself to connect speeches with disaster.)

Poor response from the audience leading to embarrassment? For example, not coming across the way you want to? People not laughing at your jokes? People leaving or nodding off? People asking embarrassing questions? People not asking questions when they should?

Amateurish performance because of your inexperience or because you're too introverted? (Do you believe only true extroverts make good speakers?)

Mediocre performance because you're not a podium star, dynamic and charismatic?

If you're a victim of any of these fears, it's up to you to develop a new set of attitudes that are more productive. First, keep in mind that the symptoms of stage fright are normal. Even the "podium stars" experience them. Anxiety can be a positive motivating force: It indicates you're concerned about doing a good job. The key is to control it so it doesn't become debilitating.

Next, focus on the fact that good speakers are made, not born. Public speaking is a skill you can master reasonably well with a little knowledge and a lot of practice. Granted, you'll probably never be a star or a silver-tongued orator. But, there are very few of these people in the entire world, so don't compare your performance with theirs.

Approach public speaking as a challenge rather than as an insurmountable barrier. Think of it as an exciting experience with many potential payoffs and many opportunities to learn. Then analyze your effectiveness and the results of your talks with the goal of constantly learning and improving. Ineffective behaviors then become learning experiences rather than disasters or defeats or embarrassments. And you're miles ahead of your shy peers, still cowering in the corner.

In addition to developing a new set of attitudes, there are specific steps you can take that will help you overcome stage fright during your talk.

1. Be well prepared.

2. Just before your talk, do some relaxation exercises. Meditate, ground yourself, visualize, do deep breathing.

3. *Before* the talk, try looking at a friendly face in the audience and focusing on it. *During* the talk, make eye contact with people in all parts of the audience, occasionally returning to the friendly face. A high level of eye contact can help you speak conversationally and spontaneously as well as give you feedback about how your message is getting across. According to research findings, it also increases the likelihood that people will perceive you as credible, well qualified, and honest.

4. For some people it is most effective to visualize the audience as basically open and friendly. They tell themselves how warm and supportive they feel toward people in the group and that people in the group return that feeling and support them.

5. You can combine such messages to yourself with ones concerning the importance of the *content* of your speech. Focus on the importance of conveying the "meat" of your message to the group. Be clear about the major points you want to get across and the results you want.

6. Know your opening sentence and the first sentence of your concluding remarks like the back of your hand so you can easily get into your speech and later move into your conclusion.

7. Keep in mind that mixing up words, skipping over points, forgetting the next point, and pausing to remember are all normal behaviors in everyday conversation. They can actually enhance your speech, making it come across as natural, conversational, and spontaneous. You can always mention the forgotten point later. Chances are, it will come up in the question-and-answer period and you can convey it in an even more interesting way then. If you have done a reasonably thorough job of preparing, you can relax and let your inner self take over. Your biggest enemy is *not* forgetting or stumbling; it's your expectations of perfection and the resulting tension and rigidity.

Preparing and Giving Talks That Get Results
Talks that hold people's attention and get results are designed to appeal to both the logical

and the psychological requirements of listeners. To make sense of a talk and to accept the speaker's credibility, most people need to grasp a logical progression of ideas, beginning with an overview of what the talk is about, moving on to major points that are rational and backed up by facts, and ending with a summary or wrap-up of what was covered.

You can deliver a talk that's accepted as credible yet still fail to persuade your listeners or to inspire them to action unless you also meet certain psychological requirements. You must determine what personal needs your listeners can satisfy by adopting your ideas and suggestions, show them the payoffs they will get, and touch their emotions. Only when people experience an emotional response to a talk are they likely to remember it and act on it. Exhibit 7-7 shows how talks can be structured to appeal to both logical and psychological requirements.

Now let's look at specific techniques for making the most of each aspect of the effective talk, beginning with determining the *purpose* of your talk. Decide exactly what end results you want from the talk. When the talk is completed, what do you want the effects or the outcome to be? What are you trying to accomplish? The answer to such questions as these will determine the title of your talk. Your purpose should be made clear or, where appropriate, intriguing, in both your opening and your closing remarks.

Don't try to achieve too many purposes or cover too many topics in one talk. The biggest mistake amateur speakers make is trying to cover too much ground and talking too long. Audiences generally cannot absorb more than three or four major points at one sitting, and they cannot pay attention to a speaker for more than about twenty minutes. If you must fill a longer time slot, plan some type of active audience involvement — an exercise, a game, a small group role-playing situation, a self-check or other type of quiz, for example.

A basic rule is to talk on topics and cover points that you know enough about and enjoy enough to be comfortable with. Audiences immediately detect the degree of authority and the amount of enthusiasm and enjoyment you have about your topic. It is therefore wise *never* to accept a speaking assignment on a topic that bores you.

On the other hand, it sometimes works well to accept a speaking assignment on a topic in which you are quite interested but lack adequate knowledge. The key to success here is doing your homework and gaining adequate background knowledge to speak with authority. The advantage is that you learn a great deal

---

EXHIBIT 7-7: Structuring Talks to Meet Logical and Psychological Needs

Logical Aspects	Psychological Aspects
1. Introduction	1. *Attention:* Catch the interest or attention of your audience.
	2. *Need:* Show how listeners can meet certain needs or gain rewards by focusing on the information you will give them.
2. Body	3. *Satisfaction:* Make a few clear major points, tying in to satisfaction of needs or desires mentioned earlier.
	4. *Visualization:* Illustrate your points. Show how listeners can apply your ideas. Help them picture themselves in specific actions or situations and enjoying the resulting benefits.
3. Conclusion	5. *Action:* Summarize and wrap up your points. Touch listeners' emotions. Where appropriate, make a specific and concrete recommendation — a call for action that will fulfill the need mentioned earlier in your talk.

about a topic in a short time. In addition, you tend to be more enthusiastic about a topic you've just learned about, and your enthusiasm comes through to your listeners. Also, you tend to speak at a level the lay audience can identify with since you have not yet gained a high level of sophistication.

One more word of warning: Never accept a topic or include points in your talk that conflict with your convictions or that you don't thoroughly understand, unless your purpose is to share conflicts or explore unknown territory as a group.

Plan an *attention-getting opening*. Your opening is the most important part of your talk. If you don't arouse the interest of your audience in the beginning, they may tune you out, and you may never have another chance to get them with you. The opening should catch immediate

attention and arouse interest. It may even be startling or surprising, but it should lead into or suggest the theme of your speech and not be totally "off the wall." Exhibit 7-8 shows some examples of attention-getters that can give you ideas for your own openings.

Once you get your listeners' attention, give them an overview of what you're going to cover in the talk. If it involves mystery and surprise, set the stage. Either way, your introduction should prepare listeners to understand and accept the main points that come next.

Now decide on *a few clear points and how to illustrate them*. Generally limit your main points to three or four and provide adequate illustrations, both verbal and nonverbal—examples, supporting facts, explanations, pictures, charts, models, demonstrations, or applications of each main point. The only way to make a lasting

---

EXHIBIT 7-8: Attention-Getters for Opening a Talk

1. A startling question or a challenging statement

   "Have you ever killed a man?"

   "Within two years you could be spending your winters in your own sunny villa by the sea."

2. An appropriate quotation, illustration, or story

   "All the world loves a lover."

   "Nuclear power plants are awe-inspiring monuments to man's manipulation of nature. As I was driving through the peaceful rural countryside recently, the sight of a huge monolithic white tower belching white steam startled me. It seemed so at odds with the quiet green pastures and grazing cattle."

   "When I was a little girl growing up in the rough, tough, he-man state of Texas, it never occurred to me that I might someday be a business executive. I remember walking to the local movie theater every Saturday and watching my heroines play sophisticated secretaries."

3. An exhibit: some appropriate object to use or to display, such as a picture or a sample

   Here's an example of using an object that created such a startling, exciting effect that the audience was spellbound throughout the talk: The speaker walked briskly over to a nail projecting from the wall. He was carrying several one-dollar bills in his hand. As he reached the nail, he impaled three or four dollar bills on it, saying "Bucks, bucks, bucks. Do you realize how many dollars are wasted every day simply because people do not communicate effectively with one another? Why, just last week a whole boatload of bananas rotted in the hold of a ship in the harbor of Managua, Nicaragua, just because no one got the message through to unload them." The speaker moved from this specific incident of waste caused by lack of communication to the generalized effects of noncommunication among computer programmers.

4. A generalization that is attention getting and ties in with what follows

   "People love to hear their own names spoken."

impact on listeners is to *develop* a few major ideas. When you merely touch on major idea after major idea, none of them is likely to stick in your listeners' minds.

Remember to provide for your listeners' logical needs by giving supporting facts, citing reference sources, and so forth. Also remember that feelings trigger action, so express your feelings, convey others' feelings, and appeal to listeners' feelings, where appropriate. If your talk is a persuasive one, show how your proposal will satisfy a need. Help listeners visualize themselves enjoying specific benefits and payoffs from doing what you ask.

A common mistake in preparing the body of the speech is failure to develop a good organizational plan and to communicate it to listeners. Communicate your organization of major points by stating a point clearly, then developing it fully, and finally summarizing it. Be especially aware of letting listeners know when you are leaving one point and moving on to the next: "That gives you an idea of what the XYZ model can do for your customers. Now let's take a look at how it can increase your sales volume next quarter."

Effectively illustrating or reinforcing your points through *visual aids* is a skill worth developing because it can contribute so much to the success of your talk. Keep visual aids simple — only a few words, figures, or items on each one. Use your visuals to reinforce points, not to tell whole stories. Make them large enough for everyone to easily see: Determine the maximum distance a viewer will be from the visual, pace it off, and check it out. Use heavy lines with plenty of contrast, and use color to advantage. (If you use handouts, distribute them *after* the talk as a rule; otherwise your listeners will focus on reading instead of listening to you.) Pointing to the items on your visuals as you discuss them can help you move and gesture naturally, relaxing and directing your tension.

The most helpful type of visual aid in most business situations is an appropriate graph or chart; they're especially effective for presenting quantitative information. Charts display information for quick comprehension. Graphs can show trends, fluctuations, relationships, and proportions more vividly than words alone could ever do.

Be sure your chart or graph is aptly labeled and the contents of any lines and columns are clearly identified with headings. Play around with the form it will take by making rough pencil sketches of key parts of it, using two or more different setups. Then choose the one that will best meet your recipients' needs and your purpose. Most computers have the capability to produce graphs, and most large organizations have graphics technicians.

Your discussion should expand on the data in the chart or graph by (1) explaining what it means, (2) pointing out implications for situations, problems, or decisions being considered, (3) analyzing it in some other way (for example, showing how it supports conclusions or compares with something else), and (4) making clear how it ties in with other information.

Deciding on the type of graph to use is easy when you understand the purpose of three basic types of graphs: (1) broken line, (2) bar, and (3) pie (see Figure 7-2). **Broken-line graphs** are best for showing progress over time. They're excellent tools for showing trends or fluctuations. For example, you might show how sales have gone up and down (fluctuated) during the months of the past year, or you might show how your company's overall sales trend has been upward during the past five years.

Bar graphs are the most effective means of grouping data when your main purpose is to help the reader make comparisons of figures that represent something that occurred at the same time or during the same period. They're appropriate for comparing the total sales of each of four sales representatives in a region or the total production of each of a company's five manufacturing plants, for example.

Pie graphs are best for showing the proportion of each of the items in a group to the whole amount. They're an excellent means of show-

FIGURE 7-2: Basic Types of Graphs

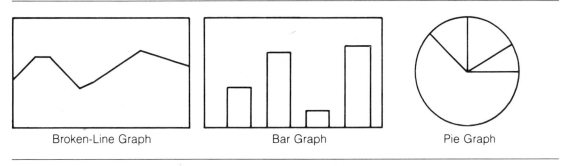

Broken-Line Graph   Bar Graph   Pie Graph

ing how each of the major items of a budget, for example, compares with the others and with the total budget. Pie graphs can also be used to show how each type of tax a company pays fits into its total tax picture.

For practice at choosing the best graph and constructing and interpreting graphs, see Exercises 7-4 and 7-5 at the end of this chapter.

Finally, plan to climax your talk with a *clear conclusion* that will reinforce the results you want. One of the most common mistakes beginning speakers make is failing to clearly conclude their talks — to wrap them up. Sometimes they merely stop talking and sit down, as if they can hardly wait to get the ordeal over with. At other times they give rather vague, "inconclusive" conclusions. Listeners aren't sure whether the speaker is trying to wrap up the talk, and they have difficulty pulling all the parts of the talk together in their own minds. If you're going to devote time and energy to preparing and giving a talk, don't drop the ball at the conclusion! Use it to leave a good last impression and to ensure a strong listener response by touching their emotions. Make your conclusion agree with your opening. Summarize your main points, tying them in to what your talk means for the listeners — the bottom line. Exhibit 7-9 shows examples of effective conclusions.

Now you're ready to rehearse, keeping in mind the goals of *comfort* and *spontaneity*. You need to rehearse your talk several times in order to feel comfortable with it. Your goal should be to prepare and rehearse just enough to feel adequately prepared and to come across as adequately prepared, but not so much that your talk seems to be "canned," mechanical, or lacking in spontaneity.

To achieve spontaneity, it is essential that you observe two rules: (1) Never memorize your talk, and (2) never read your talk. When you memorize or read a talk, you form an insurmountable barrier between the real you and your listeners. Your words tend to simply travel mechanically through your brain and out your mouth. They don't come in contact with your inner self. Audiences immediately sense this and tend to tune out. It would be better to send them a written report ahead of time and then chat informally about certain aspects of it when you meet. Reading or giving a memorized speech are both poor ways to communicate. When you have a group of people together, take advantage of the opportunity to interact with them and to get a message across from your inner self that has a chance of engaging the inner selves of your listeners.

To retain this spontaneity, make a brief outline of your talk. (The first sentence of your opening and of your closing are the only ones you write in full.) Write only a few words for each main point and supporting points and put them on a five-by-eight index card. Your

EXHIBIT 7-9: Ways to Conclude a Talk

1. A summary of points made and how they lead to a general conclusion

   "Now we have seen how the XYZ model gives your customers 20 percent more storage capacity and will process information twice as fast as any current model. We have also seen that by focusing first on the 30 percent of your customers whose present equipment is depreciated out, you can increase your sales volume by $200,000 to $500,000 during the next quarter. The resulting $2,000 to $5,000 boost in your income will buy lots of goodies! Therefore, I know you'll want to focus most of your energy during the coming quarter on sales of XYZ."

2. An appeal for definite action

   "Let's show the Board of Directors that we're tired of the situation and we're not going to stand for it any longer! Fill out your proxies now if you can't attend the annual stockholders' meeting, and vote against proposition B."

3. A pointed story, quotation, or illustration that fits and packages the subject

   "I was watching a little robin building her nest the other day, and I was taken by her persistence and determination . . . and so we can eventually build the best sales organization in the fashion industry, step by step, with persistence and determination."

goals are to (1) see your notes easily from the lecturn or podium, (2) find your place easily as you move from point to point, and (3) use the notes unobtrusively. Lay them down in one spot and leave them there. Glance at them only briefly and occasionally as you move from one point to the next.

Here are some further suggestions for rehearsing your talk.

1. Be sure you are familiar with your illustrations, anecdotes, and facts.

2. Know the basic sequence of thought.

3. Talk about the subject to others so that you become accustomed to spontaneously verbalizing your ideas about it.

4. Make a tape recording of your talk using your note cards. Play it back and note areas where improvement is needed. Incorporate improvements in the second rehearsal. Don't over-rehearse.

5. Before and during rehearsal, keep in mind the sources of your enthusiasm and conviction in order to maintain them.

6. During rehearsal, pretend you are actually talking to your audience and concentrate on your message and the importance of getting it across to your audience rather than concentrating on yourself.

Some people find the following procedure to be effective for rehearsing: In the first rehearsal, cover the first major point. In the second rehearsal, cover the first and second major points. In the third rehearsal, cover the first, second, and third major points.

During the rehearsal period, remember to follow the suggestions we discussed earlier for handling the jitters. Practice them, especially when you feel yourself getting nervous as you rehearse. Use a relaxation exercise, visualizing success, several times before you actually give your talk. At the very least use the visualization technique once before the talk, preferably the night before.

As you go through the preparation, delivery, and evaluation phases of giving a talk, keep in mind the value of this skill you're developing. It will help you gain visibility as a promotable woman, especially since so many of your peers avoid speaking opportunities. And remember to pat yourself on the back each time you conquer one more little fear.

WHEN AND HOW TO WRITE

Most of your managerial communications will be oral rather than written. However, the ability to write clear, action-oriented letters and reports is almost as rare as the ability to deliver effective speeches. Therefore, sharpening your writing skills and adapting them to business situations will certainly enhance your promotability. Your written messages can create visibility for you among the higher-level decision-makers and showcase your ability to think, reason, analyze, and make decisions as well as your level of sophistication and political savvy. Knowing when to document actions and agreements, for example, and when and how to use such documentation can be crucial to your survival and your advancement within the corporate environment.

Determining When to Write

Determining when to talk to someone face to face, when to make a telephone call, and when to write is every bit as important as developing a well-written, well-organized message. It pays to keep your eyes and ears open and to develop your awareness of the most effective ways to communicate in your organization. Since every organizational environment has its own peculiarities, you must use your own experience and judgment in determining how to communicate best.

A mentor can be invaluable in developing this ability, for there is often no substitute for years of experience in dealing with the communication requirements of the unique personalities and circumstances of an organization. There are, however, some general principles for determining when and how to communicate.

Sometimes it's best to communicate orally, in a face-to-face situation, especially when your message involves some break with custom, tradition, or usual procedures. People tend to become very touchy about such changes and often misinterpret the reasons for them. They frequently fail to understand such messages because they are not expecting a change; they may glance at the message and assume they know what it says without grasping the change. So whenever your message involves something basically different from the routine, it's usually best to communicate it first in a face-to-face conversation where you can fully explain and get feedback about how well it is understood. Then you may want to follow up with a written version of your message.

When deciding whether to write, ask yourself, "Is this the most effective way of communicating this message to this person?" "What are the advantages and disadvantages of writing, of talking face to face, of telephoning?" Most important, ask yourself if you are writing because it is easier for you to approach or respond to a difficult situation by writing than by eyeballing the person and asserting yourself. Face-to-face assertion requires more courage than a telephone call or a letter. An assertive telephone call requires more courage than an assertive memo.

If you decide to take the easy way out, at least be aware of what you are doing. Keep in mind that you may be merely postponing the necessity for face-to-face assertion. You may even be worsening the situation; initiating an assertive stance in writing may be interpreted by the receiver as more threatening than initiating it in person. The receiver may wonder if the reason for writing is that you are "building a case" against him or her with written documentation. You also run a greater risk that the receiver will misinterpret your statements because you have no opportunity to give nonverbal messages or to further explain.

Since you can't get and give nonverbal messages or immediate feedback through written communication, you'll probably use oral messages most of the time. *Do* use written messages, however, to protect yourself, to confirm and document agreements and actions, to save time and money, and to build goodwill.

Protecting Your Interests   There is a great deal of truth in Dean Acheson's rule of the bureaucracy: "A memo is written not to inform the reader but to protect the writer." Organizational politics are an inescapable fact of life. Determine those times, situations, and people who pose possible future problems for you. Then determine the appropriate ways of documenting your actions and theirs. Again, a mentor can be invaluable in suggesting appropriate ways and times for protecting yourself through documentation.

Confirming Oral Agreements and Transactions   Whether you are the sender or the receiver, consider documenting all assignments, projects, agreements, and other transactions. Be sure the concepts involved in the project or transaction are explained fully enough that you both have an understanding of what is entailed. Then put it in writing. Since it's easy for one or the other of you to forget exactly what you originally agreed to, documentation will tie it down. Any significant changes should also be communicated orally and in writing. Important insights and new ideas about a project should be discussed and documented before they're incorporated into a team member's work or a boss's expectations.

Documenting Your Ideas and Proposals   Use memos to document *any* new idea you have. If your boss or peers tend to take credit for your ideas, don't breathe a word of a new idea to anyone, including your boss, until you have it in memo form directed to your boss with a copy to his boss and any other appropriate people you can think of. Since good new ideas are

in short supply and are held in high esteem in most companies, they tend to be stolen. You might as well get all the credit you can for any new idea you may have. (The information about writing proposals that follows can help you implement your ideas.)

Saving Money   Sometimes long-distance transactions are just too lengthy, complex, or low priority to justify the travel necessary for face-to-face communication or the expense of lengthy long-distance telephone calls. Written messages will fill the bill here.

Conducting Routine Business Transactions   When you're sending routine letters, memos, and reports that all parties are familiar with and understand, you can probably do so without an oral preface or follow-up.

Building Goodwill   In addition to the more obvious routine business that can be handled by written communications, don't overlook the opportunity to send written notes of congratulations to business associates who earn promotions or win recognition. Thank you notes for special favors and notes remembering birthdays and company anniversary dates are also cordial and thoughtful.

Whatever you do, don't send a letter or memo that is written while you are angry. Write it if doing so makes you feel better, but sleep on it at least one night. Then ask yourself whether it really achieves your goals most effectively.

A final word to the wise that applies to all types of written communications: Limit them. Don't swamp people with paper. If you must send a written message that is especially important, make it stand out. Consider developing special signals for urgent or special messages, such as different paper, a special color, a special mark or heading, or a similar signal. If you reserve these special signals for really important messages, you have a good chance of regularly getting quick results from them.

Writing Convincing Proposals

If you can effectively formulate and present your ideas, suggestions, solutions, analyses, and recommendations in the form of a proposal for action to your boss (and perhaps to his or her bosses), you can gain favorable visibility. A proposal is a special type of report proposing that certain actions be taken, such as purchasing new equipment, contracting for services, implementing new procedures, reorganizing a department, or making a new product.

Writing a proposal, as opposed to merely discussing it orally, can help you shape your thoughts and think through the ramifications of a request or idea. By putting it in writing, you show you have covered all points, and you provide documentation for your boss and others to refer to when considering the action they'll take on your proposal. If you write it well, you show people you have good reasoning, planning, and communication skills, including that tough one, writing ability.

Writing an effective proposal requires careful preparation, as illustrated in the four-step PREP plan shown here.* "PREP" not only stands for preparation, but it's an acronym for the four steps:

P = Person who will receive the report

R = Results you want the report to have

E = Essential information that must be included

P = Presentation of the information for best results

By adequately covering these four aspects of report preparation and by applying the best business-writing skills, you can produce a proposal that gets the results you want. Here are specific suggestions to help you cover all bases when writing proposals and other reports.

Person: What persons will receive the report? If the situation is complex, important, or touchy, jot down key points so you can clarify them, grasp interrelations, and keep them in mind as you write. Ask yourself questions such as these:

1. Will several different categories of persons receive this report? If so, do they have different needs and uses for the report? Do I need to prepare more than one version of this report?

2. What sort of personal relationship, if any, do I have with the receiver? What past transactions have we had?

3. What do I know about his or her field of experience, approach to life, psychological needs, "games" he or she plays?

4. How is the receiver likely to misinterpret messages? What mistakes is the receiver likely to make in carrying out instructions, suggestions, or requests?

5. What is the receiver's position in relation to mine — up, down, or lateral?

6. Did the receiver request this report, or am I initiating it?

7. What is the receiver's general attitude about the subject?

8. Am I making a request or recommendation? If so, how will the receiver benefit from taking this action?

Results: What results do I want this report to have? Jot down the key results and keep them in front of you as you write. These questions

---

*Adapted from Norma Carr-Ruffino, *Writing Short Business Reports* (New York: McGraw-Hill, 1980).

can help you identify the results you need to aim for:

1. What effect, outcomes, or reactions do I want?

2. What are my purposes or goals? To help the receiver do the job? To help the receiver get necessary facts or understand the situation? To help the receiver make a decision? To save the receiver time and effort?

3. Am I writing this report to persuade the receiver to do something, change the receiver's viewpoint, establish or maintain a positive working relationship?

Essential Information: What information and ideas must I include to get the results I want? Brainstorm. Jot down key words for everything that pops into your head. Don't write complete thoughts. Don't evaluate or edit yet. Don't organize the items yet. Be sure you cover all bases by asking yourself these questions:

1. Do I need to cross-check the information to be sure it is correct?

2. What information does the receiver have on the subject already? Will the receiver remember it, need it, have problems looking it up?

3. Does the receiver need some background information to understand the basic material?

4. What basic information must I include?

5. What information can be omitted?

6. What questions might the receiver have as he or she reads this report? Can I include the answers? If not, have I recognized and discussed the questions in the report?

7. Do I need to review this report with the receiver at a later date? Follow up to see if instructions, requests, or suggestions were acted on? If so, have I provided for this in the report?

Presentation: How can I best present the essential information for the persons receiving the report to get the results I want? What is the best order of presentation for the report as a whole? Is this report analytical or informational? If it is analytical, will the receiver probably react negatively to the recommendations? If so, present the recommendations *after* the discussion. If the receiver will probably react favorably or routinely to the recommendations, put them at the beginning, in this sequence:

1. Subject line, title, or paragraph establishing purpose of report

2. For analytical reports: recommendations and summary of conclusions
   or
   For informational reports: summary of most important points

3. Background information, if essential to understanding of discussion

4. Findings or further discussion of points (Use subheads for easy reading.)

5. Additional details, if any

Next ask yourself some key questions to determine the best way to present your findings, basic information, or main discussion.

1. What is the best logical or psychological order for presenting the findings or discussion of facts? By order of importance? Size? Geographical location? Alphabetical sequence? Time sequence? Other?

2. Does the reader need to compare one set of facts with another (or others)? Have I organized them for easiest comparison? (By decision-making factors or criteria rather than alternative by alternative?)

3. Is it important for the reader to follow my thinking process? If so, how can I best present the facts and ideas to achieve this goal?

4. Can some of the information be understood more quickly and easily if it's presented in the form of a table, chart, or graph?

5. What information can I block in (itemize) and number?

Now go back and organize the items you jotted down earlier under "Essential Information." Gather any additional information you need. Evaluate and edit. Verify and cross-check information, where appropriate. Number all items of essential information in the order you want to present them. Now prepare a rough draft of the report from these brief notes. When you proofread, ask yourself whether you need to:

1. Be more specific, concrete?

2. Use more action verbs?

3. Use shorter words, sentences, paragraphs?

4. Add transitional words and phrases for coherence?

5. Add subheads that help tell the story?

Finally, decide the best way to transmit and sell your proposal. Is the receiver likely to respond more favorably to an oral presentation followed by the written report or vice versa? If you plan an oral presentation, who should be included? If you present the written proposal first, should you deliver it in person or route it through regular mail channels? Once you've developed a good proposal, follow through to give it the best chance for success.

SUMMARY

You can improve your communication skills if you think of communication as a process rather than as a set of isolated events. You can build on your talent for communicating well by adapting your skills to the business world. Monitor your tendency to communicate in a tentative rather than assertive manner. Understand the ways in which men and women differ in their communication patterns: Women focus on connection and men on status, women focus on developing rapport and men on reporting information, women concentrate on furthering cooperation and men on competing effectively, women are concerned with playing down their expertise and men on displaying theirs, women focus on listening responses that show agreement and men on ones that express disagreement.

By practicing empathy and developing the art of persuasion, you can gain the trust of others. By watching your word choice, using specific language, and selecting active verb forms, you can get clear messages across. When explaining rules, focus on payoffs for the person affected. Prepare key one-liners to express your viewpoint quickly on key issues. Keep communication lines open by avoiding false assumptions and allowing for face-saving by others. Increase your credibility by providing closure to your conversations instead of jumping and rambling. Take the initiative in using good communication techniques to maintain relationships. Structure those relationships so that you get needed feedback concerning your actions and messages and those of your people.

The ability to determine when it's best to just listen and when it's best to become actively involved in a situation is important for leaders. So are listening skills. The art of "being with" another person involves concentrating on that person and his or her message without adding to or taking away from it. It's important to distinguish between evaluating the content of the message and evaluating the person's feelings or beliefs. While being with another person requires accepting the speaker's message and feelings, it doesn't necessarily require agreeing with the speaker. Developing active listening skills involves restating the content of the speaker's message, noticing feelings and checking them out, listening for behavior patterns, and looking for deeper insights.

Meetings are notorious time-wasters in many organizations. Effective leaders turn them into time-savers that build group morale and team spirit. One way of accomplishing this is to make them as group centered as possible. The goal is to reach an optimal balance between accomplishing the tasks at hand and meeting the needs of individual members and the group as a whole.

Call meetings only when they'll be the best way of accomplishing specific purposes. Develop a results-oriented agenda that phrases items in question form, and set priorities for handling the agenda items.

Prepare well for each meeting by briefing any speakers, resource persons, and members that will participate, deciding on appropriate group size and time limits, and selecting the room arrangement so that members have maximum eye contact.

Conduct your meetings for maximum effectiveness by beginning and ending on time and keeping the group on target so the meeting goals are met. Make frequent summaries during the meeting and stress the positive aspects of what is occurring. In problem-solving meetings post the steps of the solution-oriented process and keep the group focused on each step. Keep the meeting energized by behaviors that help achieve task goals and that encourage people to participate. Look for hidden agendas and intervene where necessary. Provide for closure by summarizing what has been done, reviewing steps that will be taken, integrating viewpoints, reviewing action commitments, and providing for a record of the meeting along with written follow-up.

The ability to make effective formal presentations can be one of your most important assets in winning promotions because so many of your competitors will shy away from such activities. You can overcome the greatest barrier to effective speaking—stage fright—by focusing on the main message you want to get across and using relaxation and visualization techniques.

Prepare your talk by paying attention to both the psychological and the logical needs of your listeners. Plan an attention-getting introduction that hooks into your listeners' needs or desires; a body that gives necessary details and clarifies the major points, including how listeners' needs can be met; and a clear conclusion that wraps up the talk and focuses on the results you want to achieve. Use visual aids to reinforce the main points of your talk. Graphs and charts are especially helpful for presenting statistical information.

If a message is really important or involves a deviation from the routine, try to deliver it orally, even though you may want to follow it up later with a memo or report. Consider sending written messages for (1) confirming oral agreements and transactions, (2) protecting your interests by providing written evidence for your files, (3) conducting routine transactions and sending routine reports that all parties are familiar with and understand, and (4) conducting long-distance transactions that are too lengthy, complex, or low priority to justify travel or long-distance telephone calls. Avoid writing when you should really assert yourself in a face-to-face meeting.

Good written communications are one way to gain favorable visibility and win promotions. The higher you go, the more important they become. Skill in preparing effective proposals is especially important. Use a PREP checklist to help organize and present your data effectively by considering the persons who will receive the proposal, the results you want, the essential information to include, and the best sequence and format for presenting it.

Additional Exercises

EXERCISE 7-3: SPEAKING/LISTENING EXERCISE

From the following list of topics (or any other topics your instructor may add), select the three you feel most strongly about, regardless of whether you agree or disagree with the statement. List them on a piece of paper, putting the topic you feel most strongly about first with the word "agree" or "disagree" after it, and so forth. Your instructor will assign you a discussion partner.

You and your partner should decide which one of you will be Speaker first. The other partner will be Listener during the first round. For the second round, you will switch roles.

When you are Speaker, you will talk to your partner for from three to five minutes about the topic you have chosen. Discuss the reasons you agree or disagree with the topic statement. Concentrate on getting your message across. Notice any barriers you experience to communicating effectively.

When you are Listener, concentrate on just "being with" your partner and taking in everything she or he has to say, both verbally and nonverbally. Notice any barriers you experience to listening. Do not talk. You can, however, use nonverbal responses such as head nods and facial expressions.

Controversial Topics for Discussion

1. Abortion should be banned.
2. Interracial dating and marriage should be avoided.
3. Pornographic movies should be banned.
4. Gambling should be legalized in all states.
5. Prostitution should be legalized in all states.
6. Capital punishment should be abolished in all states.
7. Homosexuals should have equal rights.
8. The federal government should rescue large corporations that are floundering.
9. Blondes have more fun.
10. Every adult should have a guaranteed income.
11. An "open" marriage is a happier marriage.
12. Oil companies need tax advantages, such as depletion allowances.
13. "Oil sheiks" have the right to acquire American land, banks, and other assets.
14. We need more nuclear power plants.
15. All pesticides and herbicides should be banned.
16. Both men and women should be drafted for the armed services.
17. Advertising helps the average American consumer.
18. Your doctor knows best.
19. Gasoline should be rationed.
20. The average American diet is mostly junk food.

EXERCISE 7-4: CHOOSING THE BEST GRAPH*

Decide whether you would use a broken-line, bar, or pie graph to illustrate the following data. Check your responses with the answer key.

1. The number of women employed in business organizations from 1900 to the present

2. Total sales from each of the five district offices of Acme Company

---

*Adapted from Norma Carr-Ruffino, *Writing Short Business Reports* (New York: McGraw-Hill, 1980).

3. Money spent by your department last year for overhead, salaries, supplies, and miscellaneous expenses

4. The percentage of women in management during the past twenty-five years and in the next five years

5. A comparison of a company's net profits with expenses and cost of sales over the last five years

6. A breakdown by neighborhood of homeowners in Central City

7. Figures showing how sales have gone up and down during the past ten years

8. The portion of a company's taxes that went for federal income tax, state taxes, and local taxes

EXERCISE 7-5: CONSTRUCTING AND INTERPRETING A GRAPH*

As Marketing Manager for Lighthouse Designs, you want to include in a report to the president the total sales of ski wear for this year and last year. To help the president grasp this information at a glance, prepare a preliminary draft of a graph that illustrates the data shown in the table.

	Total Sales of Ski Wear	
	This Year	Last Year
January	$125,000	$140,000
February	90,000	105,000
March	60,000	70,000
April	12,000	16,000
May	7,000	5,000
June	8,000	4,000
July	13,000	12,000
August	160,000	80,000
September	210,000	190,000
October	190,000	225,000
November	175,000	215,000
December	140,000	175,000

*Adapted from Norma Carr-Ruffino, *Writing Short Business Reports* (New York: McGraw-Hill, 1980).

Then, suppose you were the reader of the report containing the graph you made from the data. Would you agree with the following statements about the information shown in the graph? Why or why not? Check your responses with the answer key.

1. The company sold more ski wear last year than this year.

2. The company will sell less ski wear next year.

3. Summer vacations cause a reduction in sales of ski wear.

4. The company is losing money on ski wear.

5. For the past two years the Marketing Manager has loved the fall months, at least for business reasons.

6. Sales of ski wear were generally unchanged in June, July, and October.

REFERENCES

1. Adams, Linda. *Effectiveness Training for Women.* New York: Putnam Publishing Group, 1987.

2. Bradford, Leland P. *Making Meetings Work.* La Jolla, Calif.: University Associates, 1987. A detailed discussion of the group-centered approach to conducting meetings.

3. Carr-Ruffino, Norma. *Writing Short Business Reports.* New York: McGraw-Hill, 1980. A step-by-step guide to effective business writing, with a special emphasis on writing proposals, memo reports, and letter reports.

4. Eisen, Jerry. *Powertalk!* New York: Simon and Schuster, 1984.

5. Kohn, Alfie. "She's Supportive, He Interrupts," *This World*, March 13, 1988.

6. Leeds, Dorothy. *Powerspeak.* New York: Berkley Books, 1991. This book is about the powerful use of persuasive communication. It covers ways to overcome speaking barriers, use fear to your advantage, command attention and never be boring, handle questions, and use visual aids.

7. Tannen, Deborah. *You Just Don't Understand: Women and Men in Conversation.* New York: William Morrow, 1990. Dr. Tannen, professor of linguistics at Georgetown University, reports the results of many years of study. Many critics have stated that her work will change our thinking about male-female communication.

8. Westheimer, Patricia. *Power Writing for Executive Women.* Glenview, Ill.: Scott, Foresman, 1988. This book focuses on the writing aspect of the communication process.

Developing Leadership Skills

In Part 2 you laid the foundation for success as a promotable woman by developing personal skills that are required of effective leaders. We've already discussed many business applications for those skills. Now you're ready to expand your knowledge to the more technical, traditional management functions.

The skill and knowledge areas we'll discuss in Part 3 are important for *all* leaders. As we cover these basics, we'll focus on the aspects that most often create problems for women leaders. You'll have a chance to (1) develop your own leadership style and make an effective transition to a leadership role, (2) enhance the motivation of your people, (3) solve problems and make decisions with confidence, (4) develop performance plans and organize for productivity, (5) build an effective working team, and (6) use your highly developed skills to get that next promotion!

That's a challenging list, but you'll have plenty of support in the form of explanations, examples, and exercises in every chapter.

Chapter Eight

Managing the Transition to a Leadership Role

"I don't ride to beat the boys, just to win."
Denise M. Boudrot (jockey)

You've already made your most important career decision: to move into a leadership role. Once that is done, the next step is actually landing a position. At that point you face perhaps the biggest test — and hurdle — of them all: surviving the transition from team member to leader. This chapter is about coming through that crucial period with flying colors.

In this chapter you will have the opportunity to learn how to

1. Identify the common pitfalls in making the transition from team member to leader and apply some techniques for avoiding them

2. Identify the top priorities of the leader's job and change your focus to getting the work done through your team.

3. Apply the politics of getting along by developing interpersonal power and a support network

4. Handle office politics and games

5. Avoid becoming identified by others with stereotyped female roles

6. Prevent or deal effectively with sexual overtures and harassment on the job

In this chapter we'll focus on some of the common pitfalls to be avoided as you make the transition from team member to leader. Most of them result from the lack of awareness of the politics and power structure within an organization that we discussed in Chapter 1. We'll expand on that topic in this chapter and discuss establishing your own power base of supporters. You will learn about the importance of including a mentor in that power base, along with suggestions for establishing, maintaining, and eventually outgrowing that important relationship.

We'll also discuss changes you may need to make in your approach, attitude, and goals in performing your job functions. You'll have a chance to review stereotypes, myths, and sexual games that you'll probably encounter as a woman manager, along with ways of sidestepping or coping with them.

Of course, you'll want to review your strengths and fine-tune them for your new leadership role. In Chapter 9 we'll discuss these aspects of developing your leadership style. You'll see more suggestions for establishing your leadership style and building your work team in Chapter 13. And in Chapter 14 we'll apply your strengths and skills to moving farther up the ladder.

First, though, examine your current attitude toward handling some of the situations new women managers often face by completing Exercise 8-1. When you have finished reading Chapter 8, take another look at your responses to this self-assessment to see whether you would change any of them.

EXERCISE 8-1: SELF-ASSESSMENT: MAKING THE TRANSITION TO LEADER

Select the response (*a, b,* or *c*) that best describes your opinion or the way you would handle the situation (3 = Strongly agree, 2 = Agree, 1 = It depends). Then determine how strongly you feel about that response and circle it. For example, if your response is "a" and you feel strongly about it, circle number 3. See the answer key for scoring and interpretation.

1. The most important task of the new woman leader is to
   a. Do her job the way her boss wants it done.   3 2 1
   b. Get the work done by her subordinates.   3 2 1
   c. Perform her job duties efficiently.   3 2 1

2. The first few weeks of the job, it is best to
   a. Pay attention to office cliques, gossip, and personalities. 3 2 1
   b. Ignore office gossip.   3 2 1
   c. Concentrate on learning the paperwork necessary to the job. 3 2 1

3. Your boss has been your sponsor or mentor within the organization. He constantly gives you advice and warns you about mistakes. Your best response is to
   a. Confront him with his overprotective attitude and tell him he must stop undermining your confidence. 3 2 1
   b. Encourage his nurturing tendencies in order to get all the information and help you can.   3 2 1
   c. Start changing the relationship from one of mentor/pupil toward one of two colleagues.   3 2 1

4. The best approach to molding your department into a more productive unit is to
   a. Make minor changes and improvements first.   3 2 1

b. Ignore minor inefficiencies in the beginning and concentrate on developing support for a major reorganization later.   3 2 1

c. Launch a comprehensive reorganization as soon as possible.   3 2 1

5. When you report for your new job as a leader, you find a typewriter by your desk. None of the other managers (all male) has a typewriter in his office. Your best response is to

    a. Say nothing. This is your chance to show how much more efficient you are than managers who can't (or won't) type. You can compose some of your own rough drafts of reports at the typewriter, type short business messages yourself, and so forth.   3 2 1

    b. Tell your boss that you are shocked at the blatant display of male chauvinism and that you will report the company to the EEOC if the typewriter isn't removed immediately.   3 2 1

    c. Arrange to have the typewriter removed to an area where clerical personnel can use it.   3 2 1

6. In your previous jobs, you developed a fairly high degree of skill in typing, taking shorthand notes, and filing. Your most effective use of these skills now is to

    a. Capitalize on your experience to supervise the clerical tasks of team members but don't use these skills yourself.   3 2 1

    b. Capitalize on them to improve your efficiency as a manager.   3 2 1

    c. Forget you ever knew them.   3 2 1

7. At the first weekly staff meeting you attend on your new job, your boss insists that you take notes and have them typed and distributed to the other leaders present. Your best response is to

    a. Do the job as quietly, efficiently, and professionally as possible.   3 2 1

    b. Tell him you'll be glad to take turns with the other leaders in performing this task and let him know you prefer to take your turn at a later meeting.   3 2 1

    c. Tell him it's too bad he has put you in such a spot but you'll have to refuse since this task is not appropriate to your new job assignments.   3 2 1

8. You are required to attend many company meetings as part of your new job. A good way to alleviate your restlessness during these meetings is to

   a. Take copious notes: This keeps you occupied and the notes may serve as a valuable source of information later.   3 2 1

   b. Keep some therapeutic project handy in your desk — such as knitting, crocheting, or needlework — that can help occupy your hands and mind during these meetings.   3 2 1

   c. Concentrate on observing the people in these meetings by noticing their nonverbal behavior as well as what they say.   3 2 1

9. You have been active in a charitable organization for the past several years. The people in your office have been supportive of the various projects of this charity by buying raffle tickets, Christmas cards, and so forth. Now that you are a manager, it is best to

   a. Dissociate yourself from volunteer projects completely.   3 2 1

   b. As far as the company is concerned, no longer associate yourself with volunteer projects unless they are also the pet project of a top corporate officer.   3 2 1

   c. Capitalize on the fact that you are involved in the community and continue to ask for support for your volunteer activities.   3 2 1

10. Your new boss starts confiding in you about his marital problems and asks you about your personal life. Your best response is to

   a. Keep steering the conversation back to professional and business interests.   3 2 1

   b. Tell him he is getting too personal and you won't put up with sexual overtures on the job.   3 2 1

   c. Capitalize on the opportunity to develop a close relationship.   3 2 1

Preparing for the Big Move

Jan, a big smile on her face, pokes her head in Erika's office door. "Are you ready for some news? Really big news?"

"Always. What's up?"

"Come on into my office. I'll go over all the details with you."

Intrigued, Erika follows Jan.

J: I *told* you that you did a great job with your presentation last November. Several people from the Executive Committee and the Board mentioned that we should make good use of your talents and give you all the responsibility you can handle. Sooo, when I learned that the Sales Manager at the Tulsa branch is taking early retirement, I naturally suggested you.

E: Fantastic. And?

J: And the Executive Committee agreed we should offer you the job — with a 30 percent raise, an expense account, an annual bonus based on sales volume, and your moving expenses. The CEO was concerned because you're married, but I told him that Scott has been spending about half his time in the area around Tulsa, so the move will probably work out well for him too. Right?

E: Exactly. Oh, Jan, this is like a dream come true.

J: Well, I believe our dreams tend to come true — if we hold onto them, and focus our energy on bringing them about. And you've been *very* focused lately.

E: Thanks to your guidance. Oh, I'm going to miss you, Jan. You know, I've never been totally on my own in such a responsible job before. What should I focus on *now*?

Jan, looking thoughtful, stares out the window for a while. Turning back to Erika finally, she says, "I'd say focus on the people you'll be dealing with. You already know a great deal about the actual work to be done — and you'll easily learn what you need to know about that. But your main job from now on is to get the work done through the people you'll be leading — instead of doing it yourself as you've been doing."

"Okay, but I'm not clear just how I go about focusing on the people."

"A good start is to become a listener, an observer, a sponge. Take in every detail about the people — their habits, likes, dislikes, working patterns, cliques, enemies, histories. Find out who the game-players are and what their games are. Office politics will make or break you, Erika. You can play it as honorably as pos-sible, but you can't avoid it or ignore it if you expect to survive in a large organization."

Erika smiles. "I think I have a lot to learn in that department."

"Yes, and you won't learn it overnight, but I'm as near as the telephone, and I'll support you any way I can. Which reminds me, another aspect of focusing on the people is to begin right away to build a support network."

"Well, I already have one supporter."

"That's for sure," laughs Jan. "And you'll need all you can get — among your people, the other managers like you, the higher-level managers, the customers — and don't forget to cultivate some support people outside the company circle."

"I guess I'd always thought of supporters as being my bosses."

"Many people make that mistake and pass up some important sources of power. Before you leave, you've got to hear one more of my little stories. I'm not sure where this one origi-nated, but it's been making the rounds, and it also makes a point about peers supporting each other."

Not long ago, there were two junior officers in the Dutch Navy who made a pact. They decided that when they were at various Navy social functions, they would always go out of their way to tell people what a great guy the other was. They would appear at cocktail parties or dances and say, "What an unbelievable person Charlie is. He's the best man in the Navy." Or, "Did you hear about the brilliant idea Dave had?"

They revealed that pact to the public the day they were both made admirals — the two youngest admirals ever appointed in the Dutch Navy. Their pact had influenced the perceptions of their su-periors and their peers in the organization. The point: Believing is seeing. It's much more effective than the old idea that seeing is believing.

"That's a powerful idea." Erika smiles. "When people believe you are exceptional, they're more likely to notice the good things you do — and to perceive your performance as exceptional. Can you imagine what would have happened if those guys had developed a whole support network?"

"I don't think the Dutch Navy could have handled that!" laughs Jan. "But getting back to our key points for making a smooth transition, let's talk about a couple of special points the woman manager must consider. First, you have to learn to sidestep stereotyped ideas about what women can and can't do."

"How?" asks Erika.

"By becoming aware. And by regularly and continuously picturing yourself as a competent professional person when you're at work. When you focus on this self-concept, it helps you project your chosen self-image to others, including guys at all levels who make sexual overtures."

"You mean I still have to cope with that — even when I'm a manager?"

Jan laughs. "The rarer and the bigger the catch, the more status it gives the man who does the catching. No, you'll probably find that the sexual game-playing just becomes more subtle and sophisticated. And you have much more to lose. Not only that, you'll almost certainly stand to lose more than he will — unfortunately, the double standard is still alive and well in most organizations." Jan glances at her watch. "Hey, it's almost time for that staff meeting."

Erika stands up. "Well, to be forewarned is to be forearmed. I can see there are many traps I could fall into, but you've shown me there are also ways to avoid them."

"Or cope with them — or redeem yourself. It would be nice if you could set some kind of record and avoid all the problems, but don't count on it. And remember, every problem offers an opportunity to learn and grow, and even win new supporters."

---

1. What do you think is the most important aspect of making a successful transition to a leadership position?

2. Of the potential problems or traps mentioned, which is most likely to trip you up? Why?

3. What can you do to prevent or cope with this potential problem?

4. What special strengths do you already possess that will help you make an effective transition?

REDEFINING YOUR TOP PRIORITIES

If you move from a trainee or team member position to team leader, your top priorities will shift from learning to leading. Of course, you were demonstrating your leadership potential before — and you'll continue to learn in your new role. But now your top priority is functioning effectively as a leader, and you'll spend most of your time in that capacity. Your top priorities will shift from technical effectiveness in doing the actual work to leading and directing others in the performance of the work. You'll shift from focusing on pleasing your boss in every detail to leading your team in achieving objectives you and your boss have agreed on.

To be an effective leader, you must be adept at organizational politics, for there will be times when you must outwit the politicians before they outwit you (and do you in). You must establish your credibility as a competent leader. If your working style has had a strong element of dependence and deference, you must develop autonomy and assertiveness. You must replace any out-of-balance need to please or to win popularity contests with the ability to establish appropriate distances in your work relationships. The effective woman manager has the self-confidence to "be her own person."

First, let's review some key elements you'll want to consider in redefining your priorities to suit your new managerial role. Later in this chapter, we'll expand on some of these elements in discussions of how to establish a support network and how to handle game-players.

Fine-Tuning Your Focus

Your new priorities call for fine-tuning your focus in two major ways. First, you'll need to shift from a focus on doing all the work necessary for meeting your personal job goals to a focus on leading others in doing the work necessary to meet department goals. Second, if you've relied on a dependency relationship in which your boss dealt with the unwritten mysteries of organizational power, rules, customs, and habits, you must now concentrate on gaining that kind of political savvy yourself.

Focusing on Leadership and Empowerment
As the leader of your work team, you must shift your focus from developing your own technical expertise and productivity to leading others in planning, organizing, implementing, and evaluating the work of the team or group. Your boss has delegated some of his or her objectives and authority to you, thereby empowering you. In turn, you will delegate to your work team and then coach them to successful achievement of each objective. Part of your work now is to clear out barriers — organizational, political, or financial — that your team may encounter in completing its tasks and objectives.

The process of empowering your work team includes

1. Getting to know each member

2. Listening to each of their needs and desires

3. Making agreements you can keep regarding their needs and desires

4. Telling them about key organizational needs and visions

5. Getting their agreement to cooperate

6. Coaching them in new ways to contribute

7. Meeting regularly as a group and finding ways to merge everyone's needs and contributions into a productive, dynamic team.

You must learn what you can expect from people — as individuals, as work teams, and as a total group. See the discussions of delegation and empowerment in Chapter 13.

Identifying the True Power   You'll check out the organization chart, of course, to identify formal power sources and relationships in your company. But keep in mind that informal power sources and relationships may be even more important to your success. Of course, you won't be so naïve as to ask directly about who the most powerful people are, but get all the information you can from old-timers, your boss, and others. Questions about how decisions are made, whether committee recommendations are acted on, and what jobs the top people previously held can be fruitful.

Do your career goals include reaching a top-management position? If you haven't been able to learn a great deal about the power elite in your company before joining it, now's the time to learn so you can weigh your chances of moving up. The most important step may be to determine if you have a disqualifying characteristic. For example, in some technically oriented companies, lack of a technical degree and background is a disqualifier. Your inquiries should also turn up clues about other organizational values — or dos and don'ts.

Learning the Unwritten Rules   Every organization has its own variation of the typical dos and don'ts we discuss throughout this book. Your indirect questions — and your careful listening and observation — will help you learn these. Here are some typical taboos you should investigate:

Talking too much about favors you've received from higher-ups, matters told you in confidence, others' shortcomings, and so forth

Being brutally frank about what's wrong with the company, someone in it, a client, or other aspect

Being a pest by making an issue of trivia or by constantly complaining

Throwing temper tantrums or displaying lack of emotional control

Cheating on the expense account—is it worth jeopardizing your career?

Complaining about a former boss needlessly

Deviating too far from custom in such matters as dress, speech, courtesy, habits

Violating the chain of command by going over your boss's head to complain about her or him or to get a decision revoked

Making a big issue of new male/female roles so that others feel put down or awkward in your presence or consider you touchy or difficult

Failing to cooperate with top management. For example, suppose you receive a request that would create an unreasonable burden. Instead of automatically refusing, consider some alternatives. If you can get the okay for additional staff to help you, you can cooperate *and* expand your area of authority.

Knowing the unwritten rules in your company will ease your transition to manager. Of even more immediate importance is learning about the department you inherit.

Learning About Customs and Habits in Your Department   These are the sorts of things you need to know: Who's called by his or her first name, last name, nickname? Is the order of names on distribution lists of great importance to people? Are memos sent to everyone or just to people who need the information? Does everyone get to work on time? How flexible are lunch hours and coffee breaks? What other habits and quirks may be important?

Learn the informal system but don't disrupt it at first; introduce small changes gradually. Every department has its own little idiosyncrasies. They may seem unimportant or silly to you, but they can have tremendous influence on your effectiveness in leading your group. If you get people upset over the little things, you'll have a difficult time winning their cooperation on major changes. You'll also reinforce one of the many stereotypes of women leaders—that they nitpick about trivial details and are overly concerned with efficiency.

Establishing Your Credibility

Convincing others that you are indeed an effective leader can be easy if you avoid the common pitfalls awaiting the woman manager. One pitfall is remaining dependent on an overprotective boss or mentor and not projecting the image that you are your own person. Other pitfalls revolve around the tendency of some women to reveal their thoughts and feelings too freely and indiscriminately in work relationships.

Being "Your Own Person"   Beware of the overprotective boss who is constantly giving you advice and warning you about mistakes. This is a subtle way of undermining your authority and confidence. Before taking a management position, get clear with your boss what your areas of responsibility and authority are. Make it clear that you're ready to use your authority and to accept responsibility for the consequences of your decisions and actions.

This can be especially difficult for you if your boss has been your mentor—the person who has promoted your interests, put in a good word for you with superiors, coached you in assuming more responsibility, and so forth. Once you become a leader, you must wean yourself from dependence on this person, while still retaining his or her support. One way to do this is to communicate your concern about dependence.

If your mentor or boss sometimes fights your battles for you, you can request that he or she not go to bat for you in problem situations unless you request it. You can say you prefer asking for his or her opinions and information and then making your own decisions. You can stress that you think you're at a point in your professional growth and development where you need to try your wings more, even if this means making some mistakes. Of course, it's wise to also stress how much you appreciate the advice and support — that you still welcome it at the same time that you're developing more autonomy. The idea is to maintain your boss's support, your subordinates' respect for your autonomy, and your growing self-confidence.

Distancing in Work Relationships   While you want to be known as a human, people-oriented manager, your leadership role requires that you earn and maintain respect. You are responsible for the productivity of your unit, and you must sometimes make decisions that will not please everyone. Developing intimate friendships and striving for popularity are therefore incompatible with your leadership role.

The tendency to become too personal in work relationships is a success barrier that affects women more often than men. If this is a potential problem for you, try thinking in terms of appropriate levels of intimacy, as depicted in Figure 8-1.

It is appropriate to reveal your inner thoughts, personal problems, deepest feelings, controversial beliefs, and other deeply personal aspects of yourself to your intimates — your most trusted family members and friends and, to a lesser extent, those you think of as close friends. Most people consider themselves lucky to have even six or seven such people in their lives at one time. These mutually supportive relationships are the sign of a well-balanced person and provide a safe place for expressing and sorting out your feelings and beliefs. Such

FIGURE 8-1: Emotional Distances: Putting Relationships in Perspective

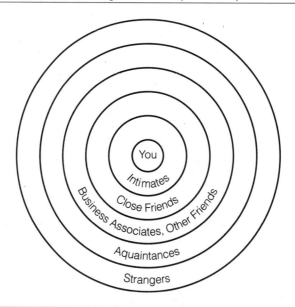

relationships are probably essential to managing stress effectively.

The third level of relationships, at a further distance from the innermost you, includes work relationships and other friends and acquaintances. With these people you discuss current events and activities of mutual interest. The focus is on events and activities — not necessarily on your personal feelings about them, your evaluations of the people involved, personal problems they create for you, how they affect your intimate relationships at home, and other private matters. Nor is it wise to delve into your deep personal beliefs about the religious or political aspects of situations.

Why the distance in work relationships? For one thing, you avoid needlessly stepping on toes and alienating people. For another, you avoid providing possible ammunition for future battles to people who haven't yet proved their trustworthiness. While you don't want to become paranoid, it is realistic to recognize that organizations are fertile ground for frequent power skirmishes, occasional battles, and even a rare all-out war. So why blab unnecessarily — about your past or current problems? Finally, if you keep your distance at work from the very beginning, you avoid the problems inherent in becoming the boss of former buddies. As you can see, by filling your need for close, intimate relationships with people outside the workplace, those in the first two levels of intimacy, you'll avoid a number of typical traps waiting for the unwary woman leader.

The fourth level of intimacy includes acquaintances, people you recognize, speak to, and perhaps conduct brief exchanges with, but whom you know little or nothing about. The fifth level is comprised of strangers. If you have a burning desire to blab and can't get to an intimate, it's usually better to tell all to a stranger you'll probably never see again than to let it all hang out with a business associate. Bartenders and passengers on public conveyances can attest to this phenomenon.

If you establish appropriate distances in your relationships, you will not alienate people. You will merely provide a framework for establishing the support network you need to be effective in your job and to advance in your career. Your support network is your power base, and as Figure 8-1 symbolizes, its inner core is you. This means you must be your own best supporter by continually giving yourself credit, acknowledging your own value, and taking care of your needs. The foundation of your support network, then, is made up of you, the keystone, along with your intimate and close friends. Let's explore ways of building on this foundation with your work relationships.

ESTABLISHING YOUR LEADERSHIP IN A NEW JOB

Let's assume you just got that promotion into a leadership role. What's your first concern? Normally, it's how to start off on the right foot with your work team.

Each time you take a new leadership position, you will be replacing someone who has had a distinct impact on the group — for better or worse. The approach you use to establish your own impact will depend somewhat on whether the previous boss led the group to good performance or to poor performance.

Replacing a Successful Leader

Following the act of a good leader can be tricky because the group may be highly critical of *any* replacement and feel no real need for new leadership. It's usually best to keep a low profile for a while in these situations. Get to know the abilities, resources, personalities, and quirks of your people and give them a chance to know yours. You will probably need at least a month to learn the game and the players in each new situation.

Use your creativity and sense of innovation. Sit down and go over the job and how your predecessor handled it. Ask yourself what there is about the current situation, team responsibilities, and team goals that suggest ways to do the job better. How can it be carried out more effectively? Which people can do what functions the best? Is the best combination of people being used? Are they overpaid or underpaid? Write down the things you think the team can and should achieve.

Next establish yourself as leader and consolidate your position. Consider holding a weekend planning meeting at a resort. If your operating budget is tight, at least try for an extended lunch or dinner meeting—anything you can manage that will break the usual routine. This helps you set the stage and the agenda so that *you* become the lead person. Assign topics ahead of time for study and reports. Let the team know you think they've been doing a great job. Look for and applaud every positive aspect of the team and its performance. Then suggest how the team can do even better. Invite them to search for ways of achieving better results—for their own sakes. Encourage discussion of team performance, including mention of the group's strengths and weaknesses, its possibilities for improvement, and possible opportunities and goals. Try to get some agreement on areas for further study or action. Before the meeting is over, make assignments accordingly.

This sort of meeting should be a turning point. People have been operating more or less in their old ways. Now they will take a new direction.

Replacing an Ineffective Leader

Following a loser can pay off handsomely for you if you succeed, but it's a tough assignment. You are, after all, inheriting a failure situation. The greatest barrier to success may be your own attitude. Since you are so aware of the liabilities, you may overlook the assets. Remember that the real problem is the failure of the unit or department to give other groups whatever goods, services, and support they expect and need. Your first step therefore is to question key people at every level in the groups that depend on yours for any goods or services. Get the answers to two key questions: (1) What do you expect from my group? (2) How have we failed you up to now? During this step, just listen. Be respectful of any ideas and suggestions submitted, but don't commit yourself yet.

The next step is asking your own people the same questions. See what discrepancies exist between their expectations and those of other groups. Which expectations are realistic or unrealistic? Look first for the simplest solutions, such as physical or mechanical rearrangement. Then lead the team to decide on the most appropriate problem-solving approach.

Once you are reasonably sure just what changes need to be made, don't delay. Move! The team will never again be so open to change as they are in the beginning. Everyone knows the previous situation was unsatisfactory, so get the changes over with now. And make them as sweeping as necessary. Personnel changes are of course the touchiest. See if people's talents are being misused. Change within the unit where possible. Next, look within the company for people you might recruit for your department. Then look for appropriate slots to transfer the people who are not working out well in your department. When no slots can be found, you will have to bite the bullet and do the necessary firing.

It is almost certain that at least one worker will defy you, no matter how well you carry out your changes. Don't back down, or your leadership may never be accepted. Handle challenges to your leadership assertively now, or you will find yourself continually having to deal with them. Pick an issue where you know you are right; then make it a matter of "you or me." *Don't* suggest going to a higher authority. But if the team member suggests it or does it, make it clear that only one of you is going to come away with a job.

LEARNING THE POLITICS OF GETTING ALONG

There are two sides of the coin of office politics: one side is coping with the office games people play, which we discuss later, and the other side is making positive use of office politics. Two keys to the politics of getting along are developing interpersonal power and establishing a support network.

Developing Interpersonal Power

People tend to be attracted to powerful people, especially when they sense that the power is used constructively and may be used to empower them. And powerful people are almost universally respected. For these and other reasons, you must gain some minimal level of power to be an effective team leader. Interpersonal power refers to the power you possess as others perceive it, the one-on-one power you exert in dealings with others. If you were to list all the types and sources of interpersonal power you could think of, they would probably all fit into one of the following five categories of interpersonal power.

Reward/Punishment — Your ability to provide meaningful rewards to people or to punish them in some way. The rewards you offer may be either concrete, such as a choice assignment, or personal, such as recognition, acceptance, even a smile. Rewards can increase motivation and build long-term goodwill when used intelligently. Punishments may likewise be either concrete, such as withholding a salary increase, or personal, such as ignoring the person. They are the least effective sources of power. Although recipients may try to please you in order to avoid the punishment, they tend to harbor resentment, passive resistance, and a desire for revenge.

Position/Role — The power inherent in your position in the organization or your role in relation to another person. You may expand your role and the power of your position by using other types of power. Over the long term, you must bring other types of power to your management position to succeed. The blatant use of your position power to achieve goals carries the same disadvantages as the use of punishment.

Skill/Expertise — Can refer to professional skills (such as those of an accountant, a lawyer, or a doctor), technical skills (such as computer or financial skills), managerial skills, social skills, or any type of skill that's useful or respected by the other person.

Information/Data — Your access to facts, figures, gossip, any information that another considers necessary, helpful, or interesting and that is not readily available elsewhere. Your power may come from providing the information, from doling it out to a selected few, or from withholding it at times.

Charisma/Identification — The extent to which another is personally attracted to you or is able to identify with you as a fellow human being. (See Chapter 10 for a further discussion of the elements of charisma.) This area is one of the few power sources that has not been gender stereotyped. To make the best use of your charisma/identification power within the organization, stress your organizational role over your gender. Stress the similarities you share with others rather than the differences.

The power you're able to gain in the position/role, reward/punishment, and information/data areas depends largely on your position within the organization. Your power in the skill/expertise and charisma/identification areas depends mainly on your own resources.

How do you normally use the power you have? Do you use it in a direct or an indirect way? Women have traditionally relied on indirect uses of power: first influencing their parents to get what they want, then marrying well and influencing their husband's career and achievements, and finally getting what they want through their husbands.

Such women tend to live vicariously through their husbands and later through their children, basking in the reflected glory of their achievements. In so doing they neglect developing their own sources of direct power and achievement. This syndrome often leads to the "empty-nest syndrome" when the children leave home. The problem can become a tragedy if the husband solves his midlife identity crisis by finding another (usually younger) mate, leaving the wife who sacrificed her own personal and career growth with little in the way of personal resources — that is, direct power.

Direct power is based on your own power sources rather than on those of a go-between. Instead of influencing a go-between to use his or her power in ways you think are desirable, you develop and use your own power to achieve your goals — or mutually agreed-on goals in business or personal relationships. Today more and more women are learning to use direct power more frequently.

You must become comfortable with the use of direct power to succeed in a leadership role. So identify your major sources of direct power, using the five categories to stimulate your thinking. Which areas do you need to develop further? How can you go about increasing your power in those areas?

Establishing a Support Network

Here's an example of how *men's* ("old boys'") networks operate. When a job opens, a contract goes out for bids, a stock splits, a story breaks, or a rumor spreads, the old boys meet and business gets done. They'll have cut through all the resistance and red tape with ease, simply because they knew each other well enough to get in touch informally.

Your support network consists of the relationships you've established — both inside and outside the company — that are based on mutual goodwill, trust, and willingness to help. They are business friendships that are mutually supportive.

Women are inclined to concentrate on proving themselves to their bosses when they first become managers. The *best* way to prove yourself to your boss is to develop your own interpersonal power and to build effective working relationships, starting with the people in your department. You must use your personal power and your ability to handle organizational game-players in order to build a support network of team members, peers, and higher management — including your immediate manager, top management, and a few mentors.

Your support network functions as your power base, which means it is an essential source of power for you. You'll probably be more effective in developing a power base if you understand the types of power people are attracted to. We've already discussed some ways power works within the organizational setup. Now let's take a closer look at one-on-one power — your power as other individuals perceive it. (See Chapter 5 for a discussion of personal [inner] power and Chapter 10 for a discussion of power needs as inner motivators.)

Getting the Team on Your Side   To build a supportive work team, start getting answers to some key questions as soon as possible: Did one of my people want this job? Who are the slightly mean or vicious people in this group? What combinations of people usually share confidences, trade gossip, and influence the group's thinking? Who is allied with whom? Which people are most likely to become my supporters? Whom can I probably trust?

Select friends or supporters from the people you can probably trust. You can identify these people by careful observation during the first few weeks you are on the job. As a general rule, select individuals who seem to be basically positive and constructive in their approach to life. People who feel threatened much of the time and are frequently defensive are usually unreliable supporters. You'll never know when they'll feel threatened by *you* and suddenly switch loyalties. Try to provide a supportive climate for these people (see the discussion of defensive versus supportive climates in Chapter 9), but don't depend on them as reliable supporters. Bide your time when making decisions about whom to cultivate as supporters. Then focus special energy on developing good rapport with those people.

In the process be sure to give everyone a fair chance as well as a fair share of your attention. Just as you have avoided becoming buddies with coworkers, you must avoid playing favorites; try to give everyone a chance to shine. Confine most of your conversation to business-related topics. Although you want to get to know your people and show concern for them as people, you can do this without close, emotional involvements. Keep it friendly but professional.

Establishing professional relationships requires special tact when some of your coworkers suddenly become your team members. You can avoid the worst aspects of this situation by not becoming close buddies with them as coworkers. Even so, it can be touchy. One way to prevent potential problems is to discuss your changed role with them in a friendly, sincere way. You can tell them how much you value their friendship. Although you haven't changed as a person, your role has changed. Therefore, your relationships will need to change somewhat. Point out that the other members of the department can make life difficult for them as well as for you if they sense you are playing favorites. Stress the need for teamwork, fairness, and good working relationships.

Keep your ears open, but evaluate what your workers tell you. Whether Jane is complaining about Jim's nasty attitude or singing the praises of Carol, ask probing questions of both Jane and others before making verbal or action commitments. Always ask yourself, "Why is he or she telling me this?" and follow up by getting other opinions or information—tactfully and discreetly, of course.

When your people aren't getting the results they should, look behind their reasons, especially if they're passing the buck. Ask yourself, "Is politics being used to cover up?" A related question is, "What methods are being used to impress me?" Sort out puffery from true achievement. See the discussion of handling political game-players later in this chapter.

On the other hand, do your share in the relationship by being a fair, supportive leader. Be sensitive to human relationships and to the need for productivity by considering some of these suggestions: Show respect for team members by promptly responding to their telephone calls, memos, and requests. Don't keep them waiting outside your office or in meetings. Accompany unusual requests with an explanation.

Let your workers know, subtly and without bragging, that you have powerful connections by mentioning their names in work contexts. ("J. B. and I were discussing this problem the other day.") Then go to bat for your people when they deserve it, and always follow through on your commitments to them. Workers like having a powerful leader they can respect.

Help your workers achieve their goals, then give them credit. Handle their errors and shortcomings in private and avoid pinpointing the blame when discussing errors to others. Back your workers up whenever you can. Above all, aim for fairness and equity within your department; your actions should reassure people that they'll always get a fair shake.

Cooperating with Peers   In most organizations you must be generally accepted by your peers or colleagues to develop an effective power base and to climb the ladder. As you move to higher positions, you will find it increasingly important to get peer cooperation in order to achieve the objectives you set for your job. Leaders who form strong peer alliances by sharing successes and helping peers are likely to be thought of as having leadership quality.

In the world of male leaders, one way to operate, survive, and get ahead is to trade favors with peers: "You scratch my back and I'll scratch yours." In this system, managers keep mental track of the IOUs they hold for favors granted as well as those they owe to other managers. They try to cash them in wisely to achieve their highest-priority goals.

Here's an example of turning a negative into a positive by establishing peer solidarity: Bob Pirosky, Advertising Manager, refused to cooperate with Erika in providing ads for one of her important customers. As a result, Lighthouse was in danger of losing the customer's business. If Erika had gone to Jan Arguello, Vice-President of Sales, to complain, she probably could have forced Bob to cooperate in the future, but she would have made an enemy. Bob would have "owed her one" in the negative sense and would have waited for her to stumble so he could cause trouble for her. Instead, Erika went to Bob and worked the problem out with him, promising him that once they worked it out, the matter would go no further. Erika would keep her mouth shut. In this way, she made an ally of Bob instead of an enemy. Now Bob owes her one in the positive rather than the negative sense — and he'll probably be more cooperative with Erika in the future than he would have been if his boss, Jan, had instructed him to cooperate.

Trading favors signals that you're a team player. Here are some other positive signals: You share the credit for your achievements with others who have helped. You look for opportunities to offer information and constructive opinions and to touch base with your peers. You also look for opportunities to compliment them, focusing on concrete accomplishments, passing on others' praise of them, and individualizing your compliments. You ask for their advice in their areas of expertise. You

avoid devious political tactics and, in general, appear more interested in the welfare of the firm than in feathering your own nest.

If you carry the team player idea a step further, you can show leadership. Take the initiative and find out what your colleagues' most pressing needs and wants are and what problems they're having in achieving their goals. You can learn a great deal *if:* (1) you're friendly and regularly available to chat; (2) you gain your peers' trust through showing supportiveness, solving problems, and keeping confidences; and (3) you listen well and ask probing but tactful questions. (See Chapter 7 for a discussion of listening and questioning skills.) Then do what you can to help your peers meet their most important needs.

Is Peer A having trouble relating well with his boss? Perhaps you can put in a good word for him at an opportune moment. If Peer A is present when you do this, so much the better. If not, let him know what you did, but tell him in a casual, tactful way. Does Peer B really want to find a job with a different type of firm? Help her make the right connections, and she will become part of your external support network.

Although virtually all successful women managers gain the cooperation of their male colleagues, women cannot really be a part of the "old boy network" that is a tradition in the male world. Therefore, women need to develop their own equivalent of it — women's networks, both within the company and externally within a particular field or area of interest.

Since women managers are still relatively rare in most organizations, it may be necessary to have some sort of formal network to get things started. This might be a task-related group with a meaningful function to perform for the organization. One possibility is a women's task force to aid in the recruitment and selection of other women. New women who are hired can then be brought into the network. Another example is an ongoing series of meetings where women help each other gain insight into any problems in their current job situations. The group could encourage its members to support each other instead of siding with men against other women. Regardless of the form the women's network takes, its main goal would be to give its members support and to offer feedback and valuable information.

Virtually every major city now has a number of women's organizations that serve the function of providing a support network outside the company. In addition, there are many national women's organizations and networks. For more details, check your telephone directory, watch for newspaper articles that give information about such organizations, and check issues of magazines directed toward business and professional women that frequently include information on networks. See Appendix 2, Magazines for Career Women, at the back of this book. Also see Appendix 1, Women's Networks: National Headquarters, for a list of the national offices of women's groups that may appeal to you. Call or write for information about groups in your area.

Supporting Your Leader   Your boss needs to know that he or she can depend on you. Show in every way possible that you will prevent and solve all but the hairiest problems in your bailiwick and that you recognize when to get the boss's input before blasting ahead on your own. Be alert to opportunities to make your boss look good, especially to his or her bosses. Develop trust by reporting only to your boss, honoring the chain of command in all but the rarest, most extreme cases. Going over your boss's head to complain or get a decision reversed is usually political suicide.

Help your boss reach her or his objectives. You may have to probe tactfully to get a clear picture of what the boss is trying to accomplish. All too frequently bosses don't have clear, specific objectives. It's worth your while though, because supporting your boss in achieving objectives is one of the best ways of winning his or her support in return.

If you think you can improve your boss's policies, procedures, or methods of operating, first gain his or her trust by focusing on what's good about departmental operations. Communicate your admiration and approval. Gain the boss's trust by showing you're a loyal team player. Then you can start suggesting ways to make "a good operation even better," one step at a time. If your changes are successful, give the boss credit, but be sure to file away memos documenting your role for use in promotion or raise negotiations. By giving your boss credit for successes, you lay the groundwork for acceptance of your future recommendations for change.

Consider documenting your boss's accomplishments as well as your own, passing on copies or accumulating information to produce at an opportune time. Look for opportunities to sincerely compliment, support, and touch bases with your boss in positive ways, as suggested in dealing with peers. Many of these same approaches are constructive in gaining the support of top management as well.

Becoming Visible to Top Management   Are you so in awe of the top people in a large organization, especially those who have some power over your life, that you avoid them or become tongue-tied in their presence? If so, refer to the relaxation and visualization exercises at the end of Chapter 5. Use them to become comfortable with powerful people, first through visualization and then in actual practice. Becoming visible to top management can put you on the fast track and may attract a mentor to your cause.

The most effective approach to impressing top management involves sensitivity, judgment, and balance. The impression you'll convey is that you're committed, deeply involved, and competent at your job, as well as friendly and good-natured in your dealings with bosses.

Getting to know the top people requires taking initiative and being assertive in a positive way. Look for opportunities to express sincere approval, admiration, and support of their programs and policies. If you can't sincerely support something, then stay quiet about it. If you have unique knowledge or information about why the program is headed for problems, relay it through proper channels in a manner that focuses on the benefit to management and the organization. But avoid appearing pushy, being an automatic yes-person, or using manipulative flattery. Most executives aren't dense.

Avoid trivia in conversations with bosses. A little small talk may be necessary to get started, but quickly shift to larger issues that involve or affect the company. Your opportunities to initiate conversations may be brief—in the elevator or hallway. Stay prepared. Formulate your ideas on current issues as they come up, practice verbalizing them to friends, and be ready when you have an opportunity to respond to an inquiry or to initiate a conversation. See the discussion of one-liners in Chapter 7.

Take advantage of opportunities to become visible to top management. Join business and social clubs that provide contacts. Send copies of articles mentioning the executive's achievements or items of interest to him or her. Send notes of congratulation. Keep appropriate people informed of your activities and progress by sending copies of memos or articles.

Show that you would fit into top management through your dress, manners, and habits. Display the right reading material and other items in your office, using top managers as role models but not overstepping your bounds by displaying items reserved only for them.

Become associated with special projects and task forces, especially those that will include meetings with top managers. Then make the most of those meetings by being thoroughly prepared, asking intelligent questions (but not questions that will put a top manager on the spot), volunteering crucial information at opportune moments, and sharing credit with others. Be objective, keep your emotions under control, and stay cool under pressure to show you're executive material (see Chapter 5).

Working with a Mentor In most organizations, entrance to middle- and top-management positions is not determined by mere competence. It depends on acceptance by those who are most powerful and influential. This is one reason virtually all people who make it to the top have at least one mentor or sponsor from this powerful, influential group. This fact is consistently reported by researchers who have investigated how men and women make it to the top. Here are some typical questions that arise.

What Is a Mentor? A mentor is a more experienced person at a higher level in your organization who takes a promising younger person under his or her wing as a protégé. The mentor takes a *personal,* somewhat parental interest in the protégé, to some degree above and beyond the usual professional relationship. Male mentors are referred to in some organizations as godfathers or rabbis.

What Does a Mentor Do? Most mentors are especially helpful in the areas of self-presentation, positioning, and connecting—the essential aspects of promotability that are above and beyond technical competence. In helping you, a mentor can

Teach, advise, counsel, coach, guide, and sponsor

Give insights into the business

Serve as a sounding board for decision-making

Be a constructive critic

Provide necessary information for career advancement

Show how to move effectively through the system

Help cut through red tape at times

Teach the "political ropes" and introduce you to the right people

Stand up for you in meetings or discussions with his or her peers; in case of controversy, fight for you

Suggest you as a likely candidate when appropriate opportunities come along

Increase your visibility; single you out from the crowd of competitors surrounding you and argue your virtues against theirs

Provide an important signal to other people that you have his or her backing, helping provide you with an aura of power and upward mobility

Regardless of the appraisal system an organization uses and its formal attempts at objectively rewarding and promoting people, mentors still make a difference.

How Do You Get a Mentor? If you can get a mentor to do for you even some of the things just listed, your chances of advancement are drastically improved. If mentors are necessary to the success of men in a large organization (as most authorities tell us they are), then they are probably indispensable to the success of women. After all, women have more barriers to overcome, less access to inside information, less training from childhood in areas essential for business success.

If you have the opportunity to relate to more than one, by all means do — as long as none is a political enemy of the others. Becoming the protégé of an appropriate mentor can be more difficult for a woman, however, than for a man. Mentors tend to identify with their protégés and see something of themselves in them. This means males tend to adopt males. Experienced women executives may feel the same way, but they are harder to find.

Like any friendship, the mentor-protégé relationship cannot be forced: Either the chemistry is right or it's not. However, you can certainly take some initiative in becoming a likely protégé, in such ways as these:

- Be sure you know where you want to go and are fully committed to getting there. Good mentors want to feel their efforts are not wasted.

- Do everything you can to become a promotable manager, including projecting that image.

- Become visible within the organization.

- Show that you are eager and able to learn.

You can also take steps toward locating potential mentors, getting to know them, and increasing the likelihood of their adopting you. The process goes something like this:

1. Identify the most powerful, secure, and upwardly mobile people in your organization. Which are the most likely candidates for mentor? Be sure they are respected and have influence.

2. Figure out ways to become acquainted with your candidates so you can see if a sense of rapport develops.

3. Seek their advice. Ask intelligent, thoughtful questions. Avoid acting helpless. Don't say, "I don't know what to do about this"; say, "I would appreciate your reactions to these two ideas I'm considering." Give the impression of a competent executive searching for input in order to make intelligent decisions. To avoid offending the person in case you don't follow the advice, use it as a takeoff for discussion of the problem and don't arrive at a clear-cut conclusion during the discussion.

4. Ask for further support if the relationship goes well. Use a direct approach at this point. Tell your potential mentor that you would like his or her help in learning the ropes, developing your potential, contributing to the organization, and/or reaching your goals.

5. Communicate that you are fully committed to achieving your goals. It's especially important for women to do this, because many men assume a woman is not really committed to her career.

If you are still in college, look for a professor who might serve as a mentor. The teacher/student relationship can naturally deepen into that of mentor/protégé. Your professor can throw many opportunities your way and even help you land a job.

As a student you can get an early start on both job-hunting and finding a mentor by enrolling in an internship program. Many business schools have them, especially those located near metropolitan business centers. Such programs involve part-time work in a business or government organization, and they give you an opportunity to apply the principles you learned in school and to gain firsthand experience of business operations. They frequently lead to full-time employment upon graduation.

What Are Some Dos and Don'ts? Here are some suggestions and precautions for dealing with potential and actual mentors:

1. Be sure your mentor gets her or his reward from the relationship. What does she or he want from it? The satisfaction of watching you grow? The knowledge that another key position is being filled by a competent person? A vocal supporter for his or her "team"? The mentor/protégé relationship should be a give-and-take one. Are you ready and able to give your mentor what he or she is looking for?

2. If your mentor's position is higher than your own manager's, you have to be careful how you use the reflected power. Avoid alienating your own boss or "cashing in your chips too soon."

3. Try to team up with a winner. If your mentor falls from power, you may fall also.

4. If your potential mentor is male, he may get the impression that sexual attraction is the basis for your interest in him. You can avoid misunderstanding by telling him directly that you are interested in being just friends and learning about the company and the job from him. (If you do become sexually involved with your mentor, you open the door to a whole set of potential problems, discussed later in this chapter.)

5. Some excellent potential mentors will be reluctant to adopt you as a protégé because *they* want to avoid the sexual innuendo that might result. This is another good reason for the woman manager to establish a reputation in the organization as an above-board professional who "keeps her skirt clean."

6. Be aware that some male managers will take on a high-performing woman protégé just to show they can handle a "tricky" management situation and solve a problem for the corporation. Where will you be once this mentor proves his point?

7. Finally, know when and how to change the mentor/protégé relationship. If your mentor is not helping you to grow and move along as you think you should, it's time to look for one who will. If you find you have chosen unwisely and your mentor is insecure in his or her job or is threatened by you, you must look for another one. Even if you have chosen wisely and find an ideal mentor, the day will come when you must outgrow your dependency and become more autonomous. It's up to you to be sure that the relationship moves from that of mentor/protégé to that of two professionally equal managers. If you don't outgrow the relationship, you'll almost surely get stuck in middle management. If you want to move on to top management, you must become more autonomous.

HANDLING POLITICAL GAMES

Battle-scarred veterans from all types of organizations have estimated that 75 percent of the managers who are forced out of their jobs fail because of organizational politics. Women are often more naïve and vulnerable to such treachery than men. When you move into a leadership job, you must assess your political savvy, for you will inevitably become the target of certain political game-players.

The extent to which you become embroiled in their games depends on your attitude toward people and your personal power in foiling game plans. As a general rule, if you respect people and are reasonably direct and honest with them, most of them are likely to respond in kind. On the other hand, if you initiate power games by using devious political tactics, most people will respond with their own games. Unfortunately, no matter how straight you play, you can suffer extreme agony, and even defeat, at the hands of the inveterate game-players found in every organization. To avoid such agony, you must study the various types of games you may encounter so you can recognize what's going on. Of course, you don't want to overreact and become unduly suspicious, but neither do you want to play Little Red Riding Hood, just waiting to be eaten alive.

Let's explore the games most likely to be played by bosses, rivals, and workers. Then we'll look at some general strategies you can adopt for foiling the game plans of even the master players, while keeping your dignity intact and perhaps emerging in an even stronger position.

Blocking Bosses' Games

Most bosses are fairly straightforward. In many organizations those who go the farthest are people who are fair and reasonable in their dealings with team members (even though they may be pretty foxy with their rivals).

Unfortunately, there are exceptions. Bosses' games are the deadliest, since they have the most power over your job security. In the early stages these games are designed merely to undermine you; later, in the "hardball" stage, the goal is to get rid of you. Let's consider first the "softball" games, those intended to undermine you.

Subtle exclusion is perhaps the most common game directed against women by men in power—both by bosses and rivals. For example, at meetings the men listen politely to your contributions, then continue the conversation as if you had said nothing. Later one of them may present a similar or identical idea phrased in a slightly different way, and it is accepted and perhaps adopted by the group. Of course you get no credit. Or they may fail to include you in planning and decision-making, meetings, business-related social functions, or business trips. The key to handling this game is to determine if the exclusion is an oversight, a test of your assertiveness, or the first step of an all-out war. Then develop your own game plan accordingly.

If it's an oversight or test of your assertiveness, you'll probably have to bring up the unpleasant fact that you're being excluded. You can easily fall into the role of shrew or nag unless you confront exclusion matter-of-factly without a trace of emotion. Keep your goal in mind (being included *and* accepted), stick to the facts, and assume that the exclusion is an "unintentional oversight." Project the image of a cool, rational, professional person; focus on the business reasons that make it important for you to be included. For example, at a meeting where your idea is adopted as the contribution of someone else, you might say, "Bob, I like the way we work together and bounce ideas off each other. You took my suggestion of . . . and gave it a slightly different twist, so we ended up with . . ."

If you decide the oversight means all-out war, consider setting up your own meetings, merely by-passing your boss or rival. Focus on strengthening your own support group.

Divide and conquer is an old game in which you and your peers are set up to be suspicious of each other or to fight among yourselves so you're less likely to form an alliance against the boss. Good managers encourage teamwork; so be on guard if your boss doesn't. Tactful questioning of peers can unearth this game, and peer solidarity can stymie it, even without forming an antiboss alliance.

Stealing ideas and credit is a particularly obnoxious game weak bosses play. You do the work or come up with the original idea, and the boss takes all the credit. To protect yourself, write memos to your boss that document your ideas and accomplishments — with one copy to his or her boss and one for the permanent file you keep on yourself.

Death on the vine refers to a game played with your plan or program. For some reason the boss doesn't want to oppose your plan, but she doesn't want it implemented. So she says she'll go ahead with it, then plays a stalling game until it eventually dies. Whether you call her hand or back off gracefully will depend on the circumstances.

Now let's go on to the hardball games, those intended to get rid of you. First we'll review the most common hardball games bosses play; then we'll discuss some tactics for coping with them.

The setup is probably the most common game male bosses have used against women they were forced to accept under Affirmative Action rulings. It involves setting you up in an assignment or project where you are likely to look bad or fail completely. Then they fail to give you the support and resources you need to succeed. If you blow it, the boss tells others, "Let's face it; a woman just can't hack this job."

Abolishing the position is an especially devious way of getting rid of opposition. Instead of firing a person, the boss gets the job position eliminated, then "regretfully" lets the person go since there's no longer a job for him or her to do.

Kicking up is a game to get an unfavored subordinate out of a meaningful job and into a meaningless one by giving her a promotion, a raise, and a fancy title, but little or no power or responsibility. Get full information about any job promotion offer, whether or not you suspect they may be trying to kick you up.

Threat of a bad reference is a game to force a subordinate to resign so the boss won't have to fire him or her. The person is promised a favorable reference if he or she resigns and threatened with a negative one if he or she does not.

Making life miserable may be played when the boss has inadequate grounds for firing someone he or she wants out. The tactics range from phrasing all communications in a negative tone to frequently transferring the employee from town to town, giving a family person a job requiring constant travel, transferring a city type to the "boonies," and other "legitimate" actions designed to make life miserable.

Preventing retaliation is a strategy of bosses for getting rid of people they have wounded in battle so they won't have to worry about past victims' getting revenge later. Your best protection from ruthless bosses — and rivals — who play power games to win is to stay out of their way and make sure they understand you are not a threat.

Defending Yourself in Hardball Games Before we move on to other types of games and ways of foiling them, let's discuss ways of handling this most difficult challenge: the boss who plays games designed to oust you. These games are difficult to counter without powerful contacts in higher management or a strong peer support group that can bring pressure to bear. Therefore, building a support network may be your most important defense. Another important preventive measure is to insist on specific, measurable goals and standards—for your job and for each major assignment (the boss's expectations for the end results). Make sure they're reasonable; then make sure you achieve them.

If all else fails, you will have to weigh several countermoves according to their chances for success: (1) confronting your boss with the situation and trying to work through the causes and possible solutions; (2) going over your boss's head to find a solution or to ask for a transfer; (3) making the best of the situation for a while if you think the boss may be moved soon; (4) finding another job; (5) fighting the boss through legal action. If you see you're losing the fight within the organization, however, the best career decision is usually to find another job. Resort to outside legal action only if you decide that proving a point about principles and fairness is more important than your career.

Redirecting Rivals' Games

Even though you signal that you are a team player, and even though you look for ways to cooperate with and help your peers, you'll run into an occasional game-player who considers you fair game.

Discrediting is the most common game rivals play to belittle their competition (you) through direct accusation or innuendo. Even more deadly is the back-stabbing game, in which the rival pretends to be nice and tries to befriend you. This tactic is intended to disarm you and encourage you to furnish information that the rival will later use as ammunition against you. A milder form of discrediting is to raise questions about your capabilities: Is she irreplaceable? Is she overloaded? Is she more of a specialist than a generalist?

Setup for a flareup is a strategy to provoke a rival into losing her temper, crying, or otherwise losing control. First the game-player discovers your most sensitive areas. Then in front of others the game-player innocently asks you a related, leading question designed to trigger your defenses. Your best protection is to keep quiet at work about sensitive areas, work on internally desensitizing those areas, and if you still feel your emotions going out of control, find a businesslike reason to exit—for example, "I must call New York in five minutes." See Chapter 5 for more suggestions on handling emotions.

Faint message is a technique used by peers who are obligated to pass on information to you but do so in an obscure way, hoping you won't grasp it and act on it. They might include it in a lengthy computer printout or long memo on other routine topics. Carried one step further, the rival actually double-crosses you by giving you incorrect information to lead you into mistakes.

Self-serving advice refers to the unfriendly tactic of giving advice that serves the adviser's own ends even when it has disastrous results for the advisee.

The case file is a devious tactic played by some rivals; some even keep files on everyone in the office. They jot down the dates and circumstances of any suspicious actions, for example, as well as reports, letters, and other documents containing errors or possible gaffes. Such file-builders hope to build a case against each rival and discredit him or her — or at least to protect themselves if attacked by another.

Weeding Out Workers' Games

Finally, there are games that tend to be played by workers — games that drain a manager's power unless she intercepts them.

Crisis creation may be played at several levels, but it becomes your problem when it's played by your team members. They create crises or exaggerate problems so they can be assigned the job of resolving them. Their payoffs may include getting to work on a project they like, gaining visibility and recognition for playing rescuer, or becoming known as an indispensable problem-solver. To break up this game, give workers greater rewards and more attention for anticipating and preventing problems than for solving them. See Chapter 11 on problem prevention.

Indispensable is a similar game that is usually based on keeping such poor records that no one else can step in and replace the worker when he or she is out. Review all record-keeping procedures, and require workers to prepare written procedures for all their recurring tasks.

Help the opposition right out the door is a strategy for removing rivals by finding a way to get them hired by other organizations. Since the more competent workers may be removed in this way, your department may be weakened as a result. Keep communication lines open with workers, and ask probing questions of any who mention leaving.

Highway robbery is a trick workers occasionally play to get a raise or other perks. Such workers know their services are critical for completing a key stage in a project, for ex-

ample, so they threaten to change companies unless their demands are met. You may have to give in, but you can start building a file on such workers' tactics and errors. If you can justify firing them as soon as the project is completed, the lesson won't be lost on their coworkers.

Let her hang is a game based on the notion that if some people are given enough rope they will hang themselves. The game-player would like to see you hang yourself, but instead of giving you something, he or she withholds things, such as information, feedback about your errors, or new developments.

Tell her what she wants to hear can have the same results as "let her hang," but it may have a different motive, such as a desire to avoid confrontation and unpleasantness. Feeling that the bearer of bad news will be unwelcome, this subordinate will turn it into good news, despite some reliable data to the contrary.

Steering Around Social Games

Socializing with people from any level of your organization may be tempting. Sometimes it's harmless; sometimes it's extremely helpful for gaining useful information, cementing relationships, and making transactions more effective on the job. In general, avoid the traps discussed so far: becoming too personal or intimate, getting involved unnecessarily in other people's battles, and engaging in negative gossip (it often finds its way back to its victim).

You'll avoid most of the potential problems if you view all work-connected social functions and contacts as primarily business occasions and contacts. The office party, therefore, is *not* the place to let your hair down, drink until you're feeling no pain, have a ball, or otherwise let it all hang out. Confine those activities to parties with your close friends or other groups.

While your work associates may enjoy your performance, you can be sure the decision-makers (and probably their spouses) are observing all your actions. So whether it's a casual drink after work, the company picnic, or the Christmas party, keep your professional image intact by carefully monitoring your behavior, as well as that of your escort (if unmarried), and your attire. This approach will pay off in the long run.

During these functions, how does the promotable woman handle such questions as who pays the restaurant or bar tab, opens doors, or helps with wraps? She simply follows the same commonsense rules of etiquette she uses when socializing with a woman friend: The person who did the inviting pays the tab, or they agree to go halves or take turns. The person who gets to the door first opens it for the other. If one of them is struggling to get into or out of a wrap (or a car), the other helps out.

Creating Positive Game Plans

We've covered briefly some of the political games businesspeople play and a few tactics for countering those games. One reason people are sometimes intrigued with political games, however, is that their variations are endless, and each situation with its particular players is unique. Therefore, you'll need to adapt the following general strategies for creating positive game plans to your unique situation.

Look for the Cause The first step in devising your own game plan is to look for the reasons behind the player's actions. What is he or she trying to accomplish or avoid? Is the game played at a conscious or unconscious level? Unconscious games are more difficult to counter because the player probably won't understand a direct confrontation. Is it really a game or just an oversight or misunderstanding? The latter may require only a tactful but direct confrontation. Is the game a test of your spunk or

savvy? Or is it the first skirmish in an all-out war to discredit or remove you? The longer game-players can keep you in the dark about their undermining activities, the better their chances of success. This means you must nip any war efforts in the bud without overreacting to mere tests, misunderstandings, or oversights. Figuring all this out is difficult for beginners and is a necessary part of gaining experience. Discuss problems with trusted mentors and more experienced friends.

Don't Take It Personally This is probably the most difficult—and the most important—key to foiling game plans. With experience and hindsight, you'll find it easier to realize that these people will inflict their games on anyone in your position—if they think they can get away with it. It has nothing to do with you as a person—in fact the game-players don't really know you. They don't bother to get to know people on an authentic, personal basis, but only on a manipulative basis. Their main motive for learning about you is to discover how to pull your strings. So don't assume there's something wrong with you, become defensive, or rise to their bait. Keep your counsel and decide on your own game plan. (See the discussion on taking things personally in Chapter 5.)

Stay Goal-Oriented Keeping your personal goals in mind can keep you from getting side-tracked with overemotional, ego-protecting responses. In each political situation, ask yourself, "How does this affect my personal goals? Company goals? What results do I want from this situation?" Then couch your responses in terms of company goals, if possible.

Develop a Support Network and Use It To succeed, political games must have the cooperation—whether knowing or unwitting—of people. Isolated victims are the most vulnerable. Therefore, a key to foiling game plans is the power base comprised of your network of supporters at all levels. To maintain balanced relationships, keep in mind the IOU system. Ask for supportive action selectively, where it will do the most good; then look for opportunities to repay the favor.

Be Knowledgeable   Begin by knowing the basics: everything in the company manual and employees' handbook; company policies, strategies, goals, procedures, and rules; legal aspects of employee relations and company activities. You can limit game-players' potential moves by knowing the score in these basic areas. Also learn as much as you can about the unwritten rules, and keep in touch with day-to-day events. Keep lines of communication open with as many people as possible, and keep your antennae up at all times. Never make the mistake of thinking you have it made so you needn't pay attention to political games. You're never immune.

Know Your Rights and Be Assertive   In addition to knowing your basic organizational and legal rights, identify your personal rights and learn how to assert them effectively. See Chapter 6 for a wider discussion on asserting yourself.

Read Nonverbal Messages   The most astute managers have learned to pick up and understand people's nonverbal messages. In fact, by merely taking a walk through the office, they can pick up reams of information. This skill is especially valuable in identifying and foiling game-players. Few of them are such accomplished actors that they can totally control their nonverbal behavior in order to hide their emotions and ulterior motives. Body language, facial expression, and voice tone will often give them away. See the discussion on this in Chapter 6.

Document Transactions   Follow up all important or questionable transactions with a written memo to the appropriate person, perhaps with copies to key people. Keep your copies on file where you can find them easily if you need them. They can be invaluable in backing up

your case when you need to confront a player's game. Document your achievements also.

Observe Behavior Patterns   People's behavior patterns tend to be consistent. If you observe one person stabbing another in the back, you can be pretty sure that person would stab you in the back sooner or later.

Focus on the Leader of a Group Game   Sometimes a game is played by several people, especially among your peers or team members. When they band together to work against you in some way, it's usually most effective to determine who is the leader of the attack. Then focus your counterattack on the leader only; ignore the others. You have a better chance of winning a battle with one person than with several. If you are successful, the others will quickly get the message and lay off.

Stay in Command of Your Inner Resources   This ability goes hand in hand with not taking attacks personally. Together they furnish the power you need to transcend games. The exercises in Chapter 5 for relaxing, visualizing, and letting go of needs will enable you to command your inner resources. They'll help you achieve a relaxed focus on your goals so your inner self, or subconscious, can pick up verbal and nonverbal clues to people's intentions. They'll enable you to put games in perspective and not take threats personally, as well as to respond in a relaxed but effective manner. Your key defense, therefore, is to maintain your self-confidence by commanding these inner resources.

STEERING CLEAR OF STEREOTYPED FEMALE ROLES

Changing your focus and mastering the politics of getting along will go a long way toward helping you make a successful transition to a leadership role. Success also requires that you steer around other people's stereotypes about the ways women behave, the roles women can fill, and the strengths and weaknesses characteristic of women.

Handling Sexual Stereotypes

Perhaps the largest single problem women managers face stems from sex-role stereotyping. Most men you'll encounter will probably try to place you in some category they are familiar with. Most variations on this theme can be placed in one of the following four categories.

Mother or maiden aunt. Men look to her for nurturing. If she accepts the role, she will probably at times be nurturing and at other times critical and demanding. She tends to be subjective and judgmental.

Daughter or kid sister. Men have a paternal attitude toward her. They tend to overprotect her but not take her seriously. She in turn may play the role of big sister to her female subordinates. Her friendliness may turn to jealousy if her subordinate becomes a rival for her job.

Sexpot. Men tend to look to her for a little excitement and flirtation, either covert or overt.

Hard-Hearted Hannah. Men learn that she refuses to fit into any of the first three categories. Her insistence on being her own competent self is interpreted as hardness. The men may leave her alone, especially when she most needs their assistance or cooperation.

Because of these stereotypes, women leaders find it difficult to be themselves, to act naturally. They may feel compelled to *react;* rather than just *act* naturally. They tend to respond in one of two ways: (1) They accept the stereotyped role rather than fight it. This means limiting their range of behavior, including some of the effective behavior appropriate to career advancement. Or (2) they try to avoid stereotyped roles by constantly monitoring their behavior and attempting to eliminate any action that might reinforce such stereotyping. This can also lead to unnatural or self-conscious behavior at times.

Men tend to protect women stereotyped in the first three categories. This protection, though sometimes essential to survival, prevents the woman from fighting her own battles. It limits and handicaps her. Men tend to feel threatened by Hard-Hearted Hannah and keep their distance. She may find herself without the help or cooperation essential to functioning, and perhaps surviving, when she needs it most.

Men often have problems establishing themselves in new jobs, but they don't encounter these problems with the frequency and intensity that women do. Women often have to deal with these problems in every new situation, with new associates, and so forth. They are probably even more affected than men by the need for self-repression and the need to refrain from certain kinds of expressiveness and self-disclosure. Women may find it difficult to comfortably participate in the customary ways of relaxing and easing tension, such as various forms of business socializing and joking.

Dealing with sexual stereotypes, then, tends to create unnaturalness and tension for women managers. Here are some general ways to handle this problem:

1. Separate conflicting role expectations— your own and other's. Realize that you can't exhibit opposite kinds of behavior at the same time. For example, you can't be both a "poor little me" helpless kid sister and a promotable woman. Keep the image you want in mind and act accordingly.

2. Don't automatically and unthinkingly fall into others' expectations about your role. Instead of fitting into a stereotyped role, rise

above it by firmly identifying your own professional image, goals, and priorities; identifying organizational and departmental work goals; and communicating with others in terms of goal achievement. (See Chapters 3, 4, and 7.)

3. Develop strong *outside* support groups that you can relax and be yourself with.

4. Use stress-reducing techniques to relax and to keep in touch with "who you are" (see the exercises in Chapter 5).

In addition to the stereotypical categories just discussed, you'll encounter the remnants of old stereotyped thinking about women's roles. So you'll want to steer clear of activities typical of clerks, secretaries, waitresses, hostesses, nurses, and volunteer charity workers. Here are some specific suggestions; keep in mind the purpose is to avoid being stereotyped. If all the men in your work group engage in one of these activities, then obviously it is not stereotyped in this situation. If both men and women rotate these chores, they aren't stereotyped.

1. Avoid letting anyone know you can type, take shorthand, or file.

2. Don't be responsible for the minutes of meetings or other note-taking tasks of the group.

3. Don't make the coffee, bring goodies to share, order the food, or perform other hostess duties.

4. Don't bring your knitting, crocheting, or other needlework to the workplace.

5. Handle any volunteer work for charitable organizations outside the office; don't encourage the idea that because you're "just a woman," you have plenty of spare time to donate.

Overcoming Perceptions of the Woman Leader

Attitudes toward women in leadership roles are changing, but women must still overcome some preconceived notions about their suitability for such roles. The *Harvard Business Review* surveyed the attitudes of nearly 800 executives in 1985 and compared them to attitudes expressed in their 1965 survey [17]. Responses to seven key questions, from a five-page survey, are shown in Exhibit 8-1. The Gallup Organization found similar attitudes when it asked about willingness to work for a female boss: 67 percent of the men said "yes" in 1987, compared to 36 percent in 1975; 58 percent of women said "yes" in 1987, compared to 37 percent in 1975.

A 1987 survey of women managers revealed that most believe male managers at top decision-making levels still hold stereotypes about women's shortcomings [4]. The most common and devastating stereotypes mentioned are (1) people won't accept them in top-management roles, (2) they are not committed enough to make it to the top, (3) their decision-making ability is inadequate, and (4) they are too emotional. Your best approach may be to analyze some general needs and concerns of your male team members, your male peers, and your male bosses. Then do the same for female team members, peers, and bosses.

Male Team Members A survey, conducted by Dr. Alma Baron [1], revealed a discrepancy between what men say about women executives and what they really feel. While nearly half the 8,000 men who responded agreed that in time women executives will become commonplace, over half believed that women are not generally as career oriented as men. Only half the men believed that women make good executives, and 40 percent had distinct misgivings about the woman boss. They offered seven reasons: (1) Women lack confidence in the role. (2) Women lack clout—real power.

EXHIBIT 8-1: *Harvard Business Review* Survey of Attitudes Toward Women Executives, 1965 and 1985

Question	Men (%)		Women (%)	
	1965	1985	1965	1985
1. The business community will never wholly accept women executives. Agree:	61	20	47	40
2. I would feel comfortable working for a woman. Agree:	27	47	75	82
3. Men feel comfortable working for women. Agree:	9	21	15	21
4. Women feel comfortable working for women. Agree:	40	31	63	54
5. Women rarely expect or want authority. Agree:	54	9	50	4
6. A woman has to be exceptional to succeed in business today. Agree:	90	59	88	83
7. Attitude toward women executives. Strongly favorable:	9	33	48	68

(3) Women don't know how to play the game. (4) Women come on too strong, try too hard. (5) Men are awkward with a woman boss, don't know how to treat her. (6) Men feel they lose face when they are subordinate to a woman. This holdover of the traditional belief that women are inferior, at least in business acumen, was most predominant in men over 35. (7) When they perceive that the woman is only a token for Affirmative Action purposes, men feel they must pay the price by having to function under an unqualified boss.

Men who report to a woman are sometimes almost impossible to please. If their female boss has an objective, businesslike approach, she may be labeled as a Hard-Hearted Hannah, a castrating female. On the other hand, if the boss shows some warmth and concern for them on a personal level, she may be labeled a pushover, and they are quick to take advantage of her. The line between being too hard and too soft may be a very fine one. The woman manager must find the proper balance for her particular situation.

Male Peers   Men on the same managerial level as the woman manager may feel threatened and resentful, especially if they are not par-

ticularly secure in their own jobs. As a result of their insecurity, the woman manager may get no information, help, or suggestions from them, and she may finally realize that her male peers are sitting back and waiting for her to fail.

Perhaps a more common problem is merely oversight on the part of male peers, stemming from the fact that women traditionally have not been included in *informal* communication channels. For example, the woman manager may be excluded from a great deal of useful information that is exchanged in the men's room, in the locker room, on the golf course, and at the corner bar. Women need to know what's going on in the company — which way the wind is blowing. Some information is available *only* through informal channels.

It's sometimes easy to overlook what amounts to an invitation from a male colleague. If he says, "I'm (we're) going to lunch," that's probably your cue to say, "Good idea. I'll be right with you." Sometimes your only workable solution may be taking the initiative yourself. For example, when you see the men going to lunch, join them, if possible, even without a formal invitation. Your attitude should be casual and confident.

When the men head for the corner bar, you can ask to join them. This may lead to certain pitfalls, obviously, but there are ways to avoid them. Depending on your capacity, drink non-alcoholic beverages or have only one or two drinks. Insist quietly on paying for your own drinks or on taking your turn in buying an occasional round. Leave with the group, at least the first few times. Then relax and have a good time. If you're fun to be with, the group is more likely to want to have you around in the future. Your goal is for your male peers to be comfortable with you and to think of you as just another colleague.

In assessing your position with your male peers, your primary concerns should be whether you are (1) treated fairly, with an equal share of the work, responsibilities, and rewards, and (2) allowed to participate in the events and decisions that affect your job.

Male Bosses   Bosses tend to fall into three broad types when it comes to stereotyped expectations of working women. The first is the *dinosaur* who has always believed that wives and mothers belong at home, that they simply aren't capable of coping as leaders in a "man's world." This type is easy to recognize.

The second type is the *two-headed monster* with one head professing sympathy for women's issues and supportiveness of women's career goals, and the other—whether consciously or subconsciously—thinking more like the dinosaur boss. He is probably the most typical and the most difficult type to recognize and deal with; it's like shoveling smoke.

The *enlightened man* who is truly free of the traditional, stereotyped expectations of working women is rare and of course delightful. With him you can move directly to dealing with the issues at hand.

Coping with the stereotyped ideas of bosses is especially difficult because they hold so much power over your career progression. We've already discussed some specific stereo-types and myths about women. The ones that may cause the most trouble when held by your boss are: Women are too emotional, they can't **"crunch the numbers"** (handle math, statistics, finance); they aren't good at decision-making—calculating risks, weighing rational alternatives, standing behind their choices; they aren't really dedicated to their careers—they'll probably quit when they start having babies; they can't take the hard knocks and roll with the punches—they take things too personally and can't handle criticism [1].

Female Team Members   Women tend to feel very strongly about the woman boss. They tend to think she is either one of the best or one of the worst. Here are some of their perceptions, both positive and negative:

Positive Traits of the Woman Boss

She understands what it's like to be a working woman. For example, she knows I must have some warning if I am going to work late.

She understands my problems. How can a man understand? Most of them have wives at home to worry about details.

She understands better than a man what motivates people.

She takes time to explain what she wants. She will tell me when I have done a good job, not just when I have made a mistake.

She makes it clear that she cares about people, not just machinelike performance. She has a way of bringing out the best in people.

Negative Traits of the Woman Boss

She's too moody and unprofessional.

She talks about me behind my back, when I can't defend myself. She doesn't level with me and tell me what she is thinking.

She doesn't help other women. You can't please her because in doing a good job you become a potential threat to her.

Female Bosses and Peers   Let's look at the two extremes you may encounter among female bosses and peers when it comes to stereotyped expectations of other working women. At one end of the spectrum the *queen bee* is usually a middle-aged or older manager who scratched and fought her way up in spite of the overwhelming odds against her advancement. She may have sacrificed much of her personal life and some of her femininity, leaving her pretty hard around the edges. She has enjoyed the attention of being a rare bird in the organization and does not welcome competition for the spotlight from bright, fresh-faced young women.

The best way to deal with her is to give her the respect she has earned; let her know you admire her achievements; ask for suggestions and information. Do *not* make the mistake of confiding in her. Don't tell her about your past or current problems, your personal life, or anything you would not want broadcast throughout the company. Remember, she is a fighter, and she will probably not hesitate to use such information against you when the time is ripe.

At the other end of the spectrum is the *liberated woman*, who is automatically biased in your favor. She believes career women should support each other and assumes you feel the same way. You would have to convince her that you were her enemy in order to alienate her. More and more career women are adopting this stance; most probably fall somewhere between the two ends of the spectrum.

Some Facts to Offset the Myths   The body of research concerning women's aptitudes and actual performance in new work roles is growing, providing a factual basis for repudiating some of the more damaging stereotyped ideas. For example, the Johnson O'Connor Research Foundation has been testing the aptitudes of

both men and women since 1922 [16]. The test battery includes measures of sixteen primary aptitudes plus English vocabulary knowledge. On ten of these abilities there is no sex difference. Females have consistently scored higher than males on five of the remaining six abilities and on English vocabulary knowledge.

The five primary abilities in which women excel are (1) speed and accuracy in comparing pairs of numbers, (2) short-term memory for meaningless verbal material, (3) short-term memory for strings of numbers, (4) ability to identify detailed changes in a picture, and (5) finger dexterity.

On the other hand, men excelled in structural visualization, an aptitude for picturing solid forms in space from various angles. This ability is needed for such occupations as engineer, architect, and physicist. People who score high in this aptitude tend to deal with problems by visualizing them, while others tend to use abstract reasoning. A 1982 foundation report states that an abstract reasoning approach indicates an aptitude for such occupations as manager, teacher, and lawyer. In other words, even in the one area where women scored lower than men, the lower score may indicate a higher aptitude for management.

Women not only have the aptitude for success as leaders, but significant numbers of women have shown they can excel in this role. They did it in the 1970s and early 1980s by developing their masculine strengths of assertiveness, rationality, and determination. In the changing business environment of the 1990s, women are more likely to rely on their feminine strengths of flexibility, openness, and empathy. This style is characterized more by consensus-building than order-giving, by listening than talking, by communicating more frankly with employees, by sharing information rather than withholding it, and by keeping the office door almost always open. The style focuses on a "problem-solving attitude that embraces coordination more than the masculine drive to have power," says Juanita Kreps, former Secretary of Commerce [10].

Your Balanced Image   In dealing with men and women throughout the organization, the woman leader will never please everyone. To gain the greatest acceptance and respect, however, you must learn to walk the narrow line down the middle between the extremes of behavior. When the Center for Creative Leadership studied how women reach the top in America's largest corporations, the researchers found that the women executives possessed this moderating or balancing ability [15]. The women who made it to the top invariably were able to tune into the corporate culture — values, expectations, and norms — and fine-tune their management style accordingly. This delicate balance is depicted in Figure 8-2. Other aspects that must be balanced include exercising authority and power versus being a team player and facilitator, making unilateral decisions versus collaborating to reach mutual decisions, focusing on specific goals and activities versus taking a broad perspective, and using charisma to inspire people to reach goals versus maintaining control in implementing goals.

AVOIDING SEXUAL PROBLEMS

Nowhere is sexual game-playing more rampant than in the corporate world. As you climb the ladder, you'll need to be more watchful and tactful than ever because you'll be an increasingly attractive "catch." Here are some suggestions from your predecessors.

The Woman Is Usually the Loser in the Office Sex Game

The major fact to keep in mind is that as a woman you'll probably be the loser if you get involved in office sex games. Remember that you're operating in a male culture and playing by male rules. Business woman Betty Harrigan has discussed sex games in great detail, along with some of the points that follow [8, pp. 287, 315].

Although nearly all organizations profess to be against office sex, unofficially it's usually condoned for the men as long as they stay in control of the situation and are properly discreet. Don't make the mistake of thinking this liberal view of sexual affairs applies to you. You represent the target of the conquest and eventually the victim if you give in.

Office affairs are almost never a secret. Since sexual conquests of female employees are male status symbols, they would have no value unless the male made sure he got credit. However, if the man shows any sign of emotion or if there's any indication that the woman began the affair or will decide when it's over, the man loses status among his colleagues. If you try to change the rules of the game, therefore, you can expect a real battle from him.

The higher the level of the woman who is conquered, the greater will be the value of the status symbol. As you climb the corporate ladder, you can expect more determined efforts to get you into bed.

Corporate wives are off-limits and are kept in the dark at all costs about the sexual conquests of any of the husbands. This also goes for wives of important clients and associates in the same industry.

Many married executives conduct their lives on two levels, which might be dubbed "top level" and "bottom level." The top-level life is designed to preserve the appearance of the good family man, responsible executive, pillar of the community. The bottom level is designed to enhance the male ego through sexual conquest, to impress other males with his apparent sexual prowess, and to add some fun, variety, and excitement to his life through sexual encounters.

Men cooperate with each other in the balancing act of keeping the two levels properly separated so that the appearances so necessary for

FIGURE 8-2: The Delicate Balance of the Female Leader

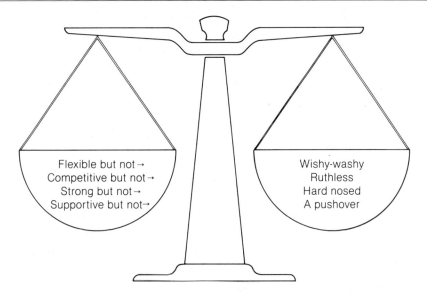

Flexible but not→
Competitive but not→
Strong but not→
Supportive but not→

Wishy-washy
Ruthless
Hard nosed
A pushover

Can you think of other areas where you as a woman manager must strike a balance?
If possible, discuss aspects of finding a good balance with a friend or with members of
your study group. Add your characteristics to those shown in the figure.

the top level remain untarnished. If you participate in the bottom level, you may be perceived as a threat to the top level once the affair is over. You will know too much about the bottom-level life of your former partner and perhaps about the lives of some of his colleagues as well. The safest way for men to handle this problem is to remove you from the scene; as a result, you may lose your job. Even if you get through this phase with your job intact, you may be automatically excluded from further promotions because you'll probably be branded "inferior."

Clients and suppliers are, generally speaking, included in the sex game along with people within the company. Your best bet may be to restrict your sex life to men in some completely different field.

To summarize: The objective of the office sex game is to increase the man's status with other men. This is one of the ways he becomes "one of the boys" who make decisions about promotions and salaries. You may therefore increase the status of every man you have sex with and at the same time decrease your own status.

Get the Wives on Your Side

Get to know the wives and cement your position in the top level. It helps if the wives view you as a competent professional. It's even better if most of them like you as a person, too. If you are happily married, be sure they know it and have opportunities to meet your husband. If you are not, it's even more helpful to get the wives on your side. Bring an appropriate man with you to any social occasion where wives are included, preferably a man who is *not* a business associate.

Your major focus and the message you want to convey is that you are not and will not be a candidate for an affair with any of their husbands; you are a competent professional with a busy, satisfying personal life of your own.

Say "No" Gracefully

Given the fact that sex in the office is a losing game for you, how can you keep from playing? Here are some suggestions.

Don't allow men to use endearing terms without challenging them. These terms indicate possessiveness and can imply a personal relationship beyond normal business dealings. You can privately inform men who use them that terms such as "Doll," "Dear," "Darling," "Honey," and "Babe" have negative connotations for you and you're sure they don't intend to continue making you uncomfortable by addressing you in that manner.

Ignore innuendos and subtle overtures. Pretend you don't get double meanings in this area. If the overtures become not so subtle, change the subject to a job-related topic. Become more businesslike than ever.

If he persists, say you're not interested and give him a legitimate reason why you're not. Above all, avoid hurting his ego. The person with a hurt ego tends to lash back sooner or later. Your goal is to win as much professional respect and support from him as possible and still say "no."

Here are some possible responses: *If he's married*, tell him you appreciate his interest but you never go out with married men. *If he's not married*, tell him you like him but you never accept social invitations from business friends. *If you're married*, tell him you'd like to join him but your husband would be hurt if he couldn't share the occasion. The underlying message you want to get across is that you like him but the answer to sexual involvement is "no" and will always be "no."

Have basically the same response for every man in the office, regardless of rank. The response is basically "no."

If a man in a higher position starts asking about your personal life, tell him about your career aspirations and plans. Give the impression that your career (or career plus husband) is your entire life. (See Chapter 6 for a further discussion and exercise on saying "no.")

Deal with Sexual Harassment

When does the office sex game become sexual harassment? When the behavior is unwanted, unsolicited, and nonreciprocal and when it asserts a woman's sex role over her function as a worker. In 1980 the EEOC identified two types of sexual harassment: (1) the overt "put out or get out" proposition and (2) behavior that creates a hostile work environment. During the 1980s and 1990s, courts expanded the definition of a hostile environment [13]. Sexual harassment can include (1) physical contact such as patting, stroking, hugging, kissing; (2) comments on your clothing, body, or appearance; (3) swearing, or "dirty" jokes, pinups, pictures, graffiti, and other visual depictions that are embarrassing or degrading to most women; (4) indirect harassment caused by being subjected to an environment where sexual harassment occurs even though you are not a target; and (5) favoritism that constitutes a hostile environment; for example, when one employee submits to sexual favors and is rewarded while others are denied promotions or benefits. In 1986 the Supreme Court ruled that:

- Sexual harassment can consist of nothing more than a hostile environment; no monetary loss is necessary for employees to establish a violation of Title VII of the Civil Rights Act.

- Sexual harassment can exist even if an employee voluntarily engages in sexual activity with a manager; the test is whether the manager's advances are "unwelcome."

- An employee's sexually provocative activity, dress, speech, manner, and so on can be used by an employer as evidence that sexual advances were not unwelcomed.

- For a violation of Title VII, harassment must be sufficiently severe or pervasive to alter an employee's condition of employment and to create an abusive work environment.

A U.S. Court of Appeals ruled in 1991 that the standards of a reasonable woman — not the traditional "reasonable man" standard — must be used to determine sexually offensive conduct in organizations. The Civil Rights Act of 1991 gives employees the right to jury trials and to limited punitive damages for sexual harassment — in addition to the reinstatement and back pay formerly provided.

Sexual harassment is pervasive in our society. A poll conducted by the National Association of Female Executives found that 53 percent of its 1,300 members have been victims. It is more about power, domination, and hostility than flirting or sexual attraction. When someone is attracted to you in a positive, respectful sense, he does not harass you. In about 99 percent of the reported cases, men harass women, not vice versa [13].

Men and Women View It Differently   In 1991 the Senate televised its hearings on a case involving sexual harassment, and the nation suddenly focused on the problem. Women became aware of the stereotypes many men attempt to place on women who complain of sexual harassment:

- *Seductress* — She asked for it. She led him on. This is the most common stereotype. In the 1980s a Southern judge ruled that a 5-year-old girl seduced an adult male to rape her.

- *She-Devil* — Watch that woman; she's trouble; she's trying to "demonize" him.

- *Bimbo* — She used him. She can't make it on her own merits; she has to get promotions, attention, money some other way.

- *Woman Scorned* — She had a crush on him and he wasn't interested, or lost interest.

- *Fantasizer* — She dreams of male attention and pretends it's there.

- *Frustrated Wallflower* — She can't get male attention and desperately wants it.

- *Martyr* — She loves playing the role of victim or martyr.

Before you file a formal complaint, be ready to deal with such accusations by keeping good records, as discussed later. Exhibit 8-2 presents some differences in how men and women tend to view a sexual incident.

Most women have some sense of the wide disparity between how men and women view sexual harassment and the stereotyped labels that may be pinned on them if they file a complaint. Understandably, most women have refused to file claims, believing that doing so would only make a bad situation worse.

What You Can Do   You cannot afford to allow any man to persist in actions that constitute sexual harassment. To do so would signal to other men that such behavior may be condoned by you and would set a poor example for the entire work team. Don't accept such a victim role. Here are some specific steps you can take.

1. *Document it.* Keep notes of what happened, when, and where. Note who, if anyone, witnessed it. Discuss the incident with any witnesses, to nail it down in their minds. Ask them to keep notes about it, with dates.

2. *Confide in someone.* If you wish to keep the matter officially confidential while you try to put a stop to his behavior, tell only trusted work associates. Ask them to keep

EXHIBIT 8-2: Male and Female Reactions to a Boss Flirting with a Female Employee

Male Observer	Female Observer
It's just a sexual dalliance.	It's a power issue.
It's okay to step out of the boss role to flirt a little.	A boss can't really step out of that role with an employee.
Harassment is rare; it's just when a guy goes over the line of acceptable flirting.	Harassment is pervasive and shows a difference in how men and women see power.
(Men often exercise power without noticing it.)	Power must be earned; women often don't get power.
What's the big deal?	I feel intimidated and threatened; this touches a nerve.

notes. These people can later serve as corroborating witnesses.

3. *Confront your harasser.* Tell him that this behavior must stop immediately. Follow up with a memo documenting what you said and hand it to him in the presence of a witness.

4. *Look for a pattern.* Chances are very good that he has harassed other women. Seek out women who have worked with him. Engage in discreet, probing conversations to learn if they have been harassed. If you can establish that he has a consistent pattern of harassment, your case is greatly strengthened.

5. *Report it.* If the harassment continues, report it to your Affirmative Action officer or Human Resources Department. If you need further emotional support or advice, look for a local women's organization that may provide such services.

6. *Weigh the consequences.* If you are not satisfied with the way your organization handles your complaint, you can carry it further — to the EEOC or to court. Consider consulting an attorney who specializes in such cases. Local women's organizations and bar associations may recommend someone. Carefully weigh the pros and cons.

7. *Be timely.* Determine the statute of limitation for reporting sexual harassment in your state. In most states you must file a claim within six months of the last occurrence.

What Your Organization Can Do You may have more influence than you realize within your organization to make sure it has policies designed to prevent and cope with sexual harassment. Preventive actions include

- Top management establishes and publicizes a strong policy that specifically describes the kinds of actions that constitute sexual harassment and sets out the consequences for offenders.

- Top management regularly signals that it is committed to fighting harassment.

- The firm provides training seminars designed to sensitize employees to the issue.

- The firm sets up grievance mechanisms that encourage private complaints of harassment and that bypass immediate supervisors, who are often the offenders.

Guidelines for resolving sexual harassment complaints include

FIGURE 8-3: The Executive Woman's Behavior: The Comfortable Mean

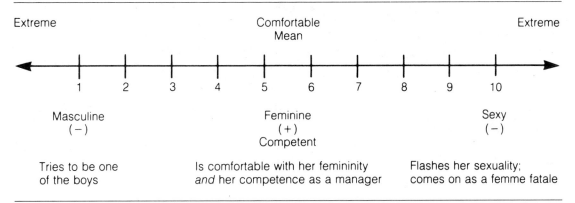

- Take sexual harassment complaints as seriously as other grievances; investigate them as thoroughly.

- Keep such matters entirely confidential.

- Find out what the complainant wants and try to accommodate her.

- Investigate it carefully. Appoint an investigative team: one man, one woman, preferably objective outsiders. Look for documentation, witnesses, confidants, observers.

- If the team cannot substantiate that sexual harassment has occurred (she says it did; he says it didn't), tell the complainant the firm cannot take definitive action and to report any further occurrences or any instances of retaliation. Tell the accused: The organization had a duty to investigate; he is cleared. But if another complaint is filed, it will have more serious implications.

- If the team substantiates that sexual harassment has occurred, use disciplinary procedures that are similar to those used in cases of nonperformance of job duties. Normally, the first offense calls for a warning and some sensitivity training. The second offense calls for some form of punishment: no bo-

nus, no promotion, a demotion, docked pay, temporary suspension. The third offense calls for dismissal.

- Ensure that no one retaliates against the complainant, no matter what the outcome.

Retain the Best Aspects of Your Femininity

Here's where that important matter of balance enters the picture again. It's important for you to accept yourself and express yourself as a woman *and* as a competent manager. That balance will be a little different for each woman and each job situation. The extremes are what you want to avoid. On the one hand, do not try to be "one of the boys" by adopting some of the men's coarser behaviors, such as using foul language, pounding on the desk, or overindulging in alcohol. On the other hand, be careful not to come across as a "sexpot" because of the way you dress and behave.

We might view the range of behavior on a scale from 1 to 10, as shown in Figure 8-3. What you want to aim for is the "comfortable mean" signified by number 5: You enjoy being a woman *and* you know you have what it takes to be a competent manager.

SUMMARY

When you become a leader, it's crucial to change your focus and your priorities in several ways: Concentrate on getting the work done through others rather than doing it yourself. Identify the true power structure within your organization. Learn about the customs and habits of the people you'll be working with. Project an image of being "your own person," and keep an appropriate emotional distance from work associates.

To be an effective leader, it's also crucial that you start at once to establish a support network among your workers, your bosses, and your peers. Get your *workers* on your side by gaining a reputation for fairness and objectivity and by keeping relationships on a friendly and professional level without close, emotional involvements. Collaborate effectively with your *peers* by sharing successes and helping them, by trading favors where appropriate, by attempting to work out differences directly before resorting to higher authority, and by becoming involved in women's networks, both within the company and externally. Support your boss by helping her or him reach objectives and offering constructive suggestions.

Make the most of opportunities to work with *mentors* who can guide and sponsor you in your upward climb. You're more likely to find mentors by taking some of the initiative to develop the relationship yourself, even though such a relationship cannot be forced. If you're fortunate enough to find a mentor, be sure he or she gets something from the relationship too.

Avoid becoming known as a game-player, but be aware of the typical office power games so you can recognize and intercept them. Games are played in the social arena as well, so maintain a friendly but professional image in all business-related social activities. These social contacts can be useful and even crucial to success. Your goal is to keep them constructive without getting too personal or emotionally involved.

To be your own person, you must avoid becoming identified with other people's stereotypes of female roles. Some typical categories to avoid are mother or maiden aunt, daughter or kid sister, sexpot, and Hard-Hearted Hannah. Focus on accomplishing results rather than fulfilling role expectations. Realize that most of the beliefs and stereotypes about women's ability to function effectively as managers are more myth than fact. According to some studies, women are better suited than men for top management.

Male peers who are insecure may feel especially threatened by competition with a woman manager. Others may exclude you simply from oversight. Be alert to opportunities to participate in their informal communication channels and even take some initiative at times to become one of the group. Both male and female team members may have stereotyped ideas about (and offer some resistance to) a woman as leader. The best way to cope is to be your best competent self, focus on results, and maintain a balanced image.

Being aware of sexual games and avoiding their particular traps will ease your transition to manager. Since the woman is almost invariably the loser in the office sex game, you need to be aware of the basic rules and be prepared to avoid problems. Your main protection is the ability to project a businesslike, professional image and to say "no" tactfully and consistently to all sexual overtures. Even if a powerful boss won't take "no" for an answer, you can take steps to successfully challenge him.

Additional Exercises

EXERCISE 8-2: FINE-TUNING YOUR SELF-IMAGE: To Fit a Leadership Role

This exercise is designed to help you change your mental self-image to fit the leadership role you want to fill; for example, your "change area" is "My Leadership Image." You will use a writing technique to raise your awareness of your current image and of the new image you want.

Step 1. *Pick a "change aspect."* Identify a specific leadership aspect in which your current image does not adequately support what you want to create (i.e., your image tends to block your goal). For example, if you want to be an outgoing leader who puts new team members at ease, but your current image is *not* "warm, outgoing, and easy to talk with," then "My Outgoing Image" will be your "change aspect." Other "change aspects" might be "My Visionary Image" or "My Empowering Image." You can use this exercise to fine-tune your image in any life area, such as physical image, personal relationships image, material wealth image, and so on.

Step 2. *Write freely and furiously.* Relax and let your intuitive, emotional side take over. Start thinking about your current image, especially as it relates to a leadership role. Write down what comes to mind. Write as freely and as quickly as you can. Do *not* evaluate or edit as you write. *Do* use free association, letting the writing go wherever it wants, but always coming back to the topic.

Whatever comes up is what you should write. Let it flow. This is the flow of your identity in this area of your life. When you've said all you have to say, stop. Put your writing away for at least an hour, or overnight if time permits. Then read it critically, making notes about contradictions, repetitions, emotions that are revealed, and any other insights that you receive from this process.

Step 3. *Write a paragraph.* This paragraph should describe your *identity* as it relates to a leadership role—a concise paragraph that captures the key thoughts and feelings expressed in Step 2.

Step 4. *Write a sentence.* The sentence should capture the essence of the paragraph in Step 3.

Step 5. *Write a current-image word.* The word should represent the essence of your current image as it relates to the leadership aspect you're working on.

Is it a word that ends in "ing"? If not, make it one; for example, your word might be "escaping, hiding, denying, depending, punishing, blaming," or "pitying."

Step 6. *Think of five new-image words.* These five words should represent the chosen aspect of your new leadership image. Make them "ing" words. Often they will represent the opposite of your current image word; for example, "accepting, shining, empowering, owning, achieving, asserting," or "supporting." Your words should feel right to you — perhaps make you tingle a little or hit you in the gut.

Step 7. *Pick one new-image word.* From the five words in Step 6, pick the word that captures the essence of your new image — a gem that represents the leadership image you will adopt.

Step 8. *Write a new sentence.* Base this sentence on your new essence word. Make it a sentence that describes your new image.

Step 9. *Write a new paragraph.* Expand on the description given in your new sentence by writing a concise paragraph defining your new image.

Step 10. *Make a reminder card.* Write the new-image word on one side of a three-by-five card. Beside it draw a symbol or simple picture that nonverbally captures the spirit or essence of your new image. If you need further information to remind you of your new image, write your new sentence or paragraph on the reverse side of the card. Put the card where you will see it often — in your billfold, on your desk, on your mirror — to remind you constantly of your new image. The card should readily trigger the new image for you, reminding you to feel and be that person (that aspect of yourself).

Follow-up: *Pick other "change aspects" or other "change areas."* Once you are comfortable with your new image in the "outgoing" part of leadership, work on other leadership aspects or other life areas, one at a time.

EXERCISE 8-3: INTEGRATING YOUR NEW IMAGE: Using Your Conscious and Subconscious Minds

Do this exercise after you have completed Exercise 8-2. You will be using a technique for communicating your new image to your subconscious mind, so that both your conscious and subconscious minds work together to project this new image to the world — nonverbally as well as verbally.

Step 1. *Relax and visualize.* Use the relaxation techniques presented in Chapter 5. Once you are deeply relaxed, use this seven-step reprogramming process:

Step 2. *Recognize and refuse the old image.* Just say "no" to it — reject it, refuse it, deny it, turn away from it. See yourself doing this; hear yourself doing it; feel the resentment, boredom, determination, or other emotions that impel you to do so. Bring into this mental experience as many of your senses as you can — seeing, hearing, touching, tasting, smelling.

Step 3. *Release the old image.* Just let it go, watch it float away. Notice the emotions that come up and encourage them; fully experience them. Continue using your five senses.

Step 4. *Forgive yourself and others.* Do not blame or punish yourself and others for the past. Forgive yourself for the fact that you formed the old image in the first place, held onto it, hurt yourself and others because of it. Picture others forgiving you. Let go of any guilt or blame you feel in connection with the old image. Watch this process, hear it, feel the emotions connected with it.

Step 5. *Create your new image.* See it vividly, hear it speaking, notice the fresh new smell and taste, experience how wonderful it feels. What do you feel? Freedom? Happiness? Joy? Anticipation of great things to come?

Step 6. *Announce and embrace your new image.* In your mind, watch and hear yourself announce loudly to the world that this is the new you. Do it with strong feeling. Let your emotions flow. Declare, decree, and demand that the new image is real. See yourself hugging the new image with great joy and love, making it a part of you. Hear yourself welcome it. Feel, taste, and smell the wonderful new image.

Step 7. *Accept your new image.* See yourself feeling totally comfortable with the new image, making it an integral part of your life, living it. See how your life is changing for the better. Picture yourself in specific scenes where you are in a leadership role. Become very comfortable functioning in this role. If problems come up in your scenes, focus on how to eliminate them; then refocus on a new positive scene. For example, if envious people try to sabotage you in your scene, create a scene where people are not envious, perhaps because you have nurtured and supported them or because you have surrounded yourself with confident people.

REFERENCES

1. Baron, Alma. "How We're Viewed by the Men We Boss," *Savvy* (July 1982), pp. 15–18.

2. Bernstein, Albert J., and Sydney Craft Rozen. *Dinosaur Brains.* New York: Ballantine Books, 1989. Coping with your own outmoded beliefs and behaviors and with those of others at work: the power-mad boss, the back-stabbing colleague, the surly subordinate, the office bully.

3. Briles, Judith. *Woman to Woman: From Sabotage to Support.* Far Hills, N.J.: New Horizon Press, 1987. The love/hate relationships of women in the workplace are explored. Strategies for mutual support are given.

4. Carr-Ruffino, Norma. "U.S. Women: Breaking Through the Glass Ceiling," *Journal of Women in Management Review & Abstracts*, Vol. 6, No. 5, 1991.

5. Collins, Nancy W. *Women and Their Mentors.* Englewood Cliffs, N.J.: Prentice-Hall, 1983.

6. Dubrin, Andrew J. *Winning at Office Politics.* New York: Ballantine Books, 1987. This is a hard-hitting on-the-job guide to understanding the political games you will encounter.

7. Gutek, Barbara A. *Sex and the Workplace.* San Francisco: Jossey-Bass, Inc., 1985. The impact of sexual behavior and harassment on women, men, and organizations is explored.

8. Harrigan, Betty. *Games Mother Never Taught You.* New York: Bantam Books, 1987. See also Harrigan's monthly column in *Savvy* magazine for discussions of playing the business game to achieve your goals.

9. Hearn, Jeff, et al., eds. *The Sexuality of Organizations.* Newbury Park, Calif.: Sage Publications, 1989. Many aspects of how sexuality affects the workplace are explored, including the domination of men's sexuality, lesbianism, sexual harassment, and the experiences of secretaries.

10. Helgesen, Sally. *The Female Advantage: Women's Ways of Leadership.* New York: Doubleday Currency, 1990.

11. Jones, Riki Robbins. *The Empowered Woman.* Hollywood, Fla.: Fell, 1990. This book covers strategies for surviving and thriving in our male-oriented society. It includes discussions of three "secrets" of empowerment: mutuality, autonomy, and authenticity.

12. Kennedy, Marilyn M. *Office Politics.* New York: Warner Books, 1987. Claiming that 75 percent of all office firings are political executions, the author discusses constructive use of office politics.

13. MacKinnon, Catharine. *Feminism Unmodified.* Cambridge, Mass.: Harvard University Press, 1989. See especially the chapter on sexual harassment, its first decade in court.

14. Madden, Tara R. *Women Vs. Women: The Uncivil Business War.* New York: AMACOM, 1987.

15. Morrison, Ann M., Randall P. White, Ellen Van Velsor, and The Center for Creative Leadership. *Breaking the Glass Ceiling.* Reading, Mass.: Addison-Wesley, 1987.

16. *Summary of Findings on Sex Differences.* A monograph. Fort Worth, Texas: Johnson O'Connor Research Foundation (650 South Henderson), 1989.

17. Sutton, Charlotte Decker, and Kris K. Moore, "Probing Opinions: Executive Women — 20 Years Later," *Harvard Business Review* (September–October 1985), pp. 42–66.

18. Tansill, George. *How to Succeed in a Man's World.* Los Altos, Calif.: Crisp Publications, 1988.

19. Tracy, Laura. *The Secret Between Us.* Boston: Little, Brown, 1991. Competition among women is the topic of this book — how it works against women; how to make it work for women.

Chapter Nine

Developing Your Leadership Style

"What you love to do, you do well.
What you do well will earn you money.
What brings you joy will bring you abundance."

Emmanuel

This entire book is about advancing through leadership skills. In earlier chapters we discussed the importance of identifying your strengths and weaknesses, what you want, and what you're good at. In this chapter we'll focus on the skills and styles that form the building blocks of success. We'll look at philosophies and theories of leadership, and you can see where your ideas fit in. We'll explore general and specific skills and which ones are perceived to be most common and most needed by male managers as compared to female managers. We'll look at the elements of leadership style needed for the Global Nineties, for leading work teams, and for **Total Quality Management (TQM)**—and you can analyze your current style tendencies. Then, we'll take a brief glimpse at the personality traits of high achievers and charismatic leaders. Finally, we'll see how leaders' attitudes and behaviors can work to create a supportive climate for their teams.

In this chapter you will have an opportunity to

1. Investigate some theories and philosophies of leadership

2. Determine your current philosophy about workers in organizations

3. Identify the leadership style needed by facilitators of self-directed teams

4. Recognize corporate cultures that support self-directed teams and the new leadership styles

5. Understand the difference between changemakers and implementers

6. Understand the necessity for leaders to scan the environment and envision the future

7. See how the ways women typically lead mesh with the needs of the Global Nineties

8. Assess your current leadership skills and compare them to the skills typical of other leaders

9. Understand the general clusters of skills that leaders build upon

10. Identify the specific skills needed for advancement, and examine typical assessments of female leaders' skills and needs for skill development

11. Understand which skills are needed for leading TQM

12. Identify personality traits of top achievers and charismatic leaders

13. Understand the behaviors that bring about a supportive environment or a defensive environment

---

 Different Strokes

When Erika was working as Jan Arguello's assistant, she did most of the planning and implementing of the Harbor Point line herself. She consulted with Jan on a regular basis, getting her approval on major decisions. Erika had to coordinate with production, sales, promotions, and other departments. She delegated most of the paperwork to a few clerks and secretaries. She found that working out some detailed procedures for each type of project helped her team produce the results she wanted. She always included deadline dates in her instructions and double-checked all her team members' work before releasing anything.

A few weeks after Erika assumed her duties as Sales Manager in Tulsa, she discusses her job with her husband, Scott:

"I just hope I can do as well with this assignment as I did with the last one. I've been analyzing the sales people's tasks and responsibilities, and I'm taking turns accompanying them as they call on customers. I've even tried my own hand at selling again just so I can keep in touch with what they're doing."

"Well, I hope they appreciate your dedication," responds Scott.

"That will take time, I guess," replies Erika. "Anyway, I'm working out some detailed job procedures I think will provide the sales reps with clear, precise ways of achieving the results I want. This should be really helpful, too, to our new people."

"How about the old hands?" Scott asks. "Will they accept these new procedures? What kind of group do you have, anyway?"

"Oh, the group. Well, I have twenty-one men and two women. Most of them have been with the company more than five years. In fact, a number of the salesmen have been with us fifteen or twenty years and have been quite successful. I'd guess that some years their commissions amount to more than the Sales Manager's salary. Anyway, these procedures are not that different from what the good reps are doing already. And there's always room for improvement, right?"

"Well, Erika," Scott smiles, "you know your people. I'm sure you're on your way to being a great Sales Manager."

That same evening two of the older salesmen, Frank Andreini and Ken Cypert, are chatting over a before-dinner drink.

"I don't know about Kerr," says Frank. "You know, Rodriguez wasn't that great a manager, but he stayed out of our hair and took care of the administrative work."

"She seems okay so far, but I'd feel more comfortable with someone like you as manager, Frank. Why didn't you take that job five years ago when they offered it to you?"

"You know better than that, Ken. An old drummer like me would never be happy behind a desk. I've got to be on the road and making sales. Besides, I make more money this way over the long haul."

Within the next few weeks, Erika completes the detailed job procedures and makes sure all the sales people have copies. She checks with them to be sure they understand what she wants them to do and how she wants them to do it. Then she makes regular checks to see that the sales people are actually following proper procedures. After three months on the job, her boss, John Brockfield, says one day:

"Erika, I know you're putting forth a great deal of effort in your new job."

"Yes, John, and it's quite a challenge, as you said it would be."

"How do you feel about the way things are going in your department?"

"Frankly, John, I had hoped to be making more progress. It seems as if I'm losing ground with my people instead of gaining."

"I agree, Erika. What do you think is the root of the problem?"

"I wish I knew! I'm doing the same kinds of things that were extremely successful when I was supervising the clerks and secretaries at headquarters. Somehow my approach just doesn't seem to be working with the sales reps. The office people seem to accept my leadership fairly well, but I'm having problems with the sales people—problems ranging from indifference to outright hostility."

1. How would you describe Erika's leadership style?

2. Why do you think it was effective in the past?

3. Why is it causing problems for her now?

4. How do you think she should change it?

Your leadership style is the way you function and relate to people at all levels within the company. It is also reflected in your dealings with people outside the company. Figure 9-1 shows how effective team leaders ideally relate to their subordinates, peers, and superiors in the organization and to customers and clients on the outside.

Now that you have an overview of the elements of leadership style and your current strengths and problem areas, we'll delve more deeply into the attitudes and viewpoints that make up your leadership philosophy.

FIGURE 9-1: Major Thrusts of Effective Team Leaders

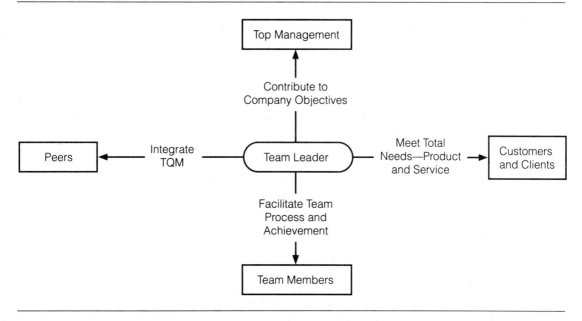

EXPLORING YOUR PHILOSOPHY OF LEADERSHIP

Whether you realize it or not, you have a philosophy of leadership. Your philosophy is revealed most clearly in the way you view workers in general. Exercise 9-1 can give you a rough idea about which of two typical, but opposing, leadership philosophies you are more oriented toward. In the next section of this chapter, we'll discuss these two extremes, known as Theory X and Theory Y, and other philosophies that incorporate aspects of both.

The elitist, autocratic leadership philosophy espoused by most bosses until nearly the middle of this century is now called Theory X. During the last fifty years, more and more managers have leaned toward a democratic, participative philosophy that is often referred to as Theory Y. Because this new approach is somewhat idealistic, managers who adopt it are sometimes disappointed in its results. In some cases productivity falls far below a satisfactory level. Recent philosophies that incorporate aspects of both Theory X and Y, depending on the situation, are Theory Z, and Fiedlar's contingency theory.

Theory X and Theory Y

In *The Human Side of Enterprise* [19], a management text that has been used for the past thirty years in business schools throughout the country, Douglas McGregor describes two predominant but opposing philosophies of management—Theory X and Theory Y. **Theory X** is based on three key assumptions about people.

1. The average person has an inherent dislike of work and will avoid it if possible.

2. Most people will not strive to achieve organizational objectives unless they are coerced, controlled, directed, and threatened with punishment.

3. The average person prefers to be directed, wishes to avoid responsibility, has relatively little ambition, and wants security above all else.

During the nineteenth century and the early part of the twentieth century, Theory X was the predominant management philosophy. It still exists in some companies, though usually in a modified form. Managers who believe the assumptions of Theory X rely on a "carrot-and-stick" approach to get workers to perform. They reward workers for exceptional performance and punish them for poor performance. Workers with a Theory X manager are motivated externally.

A Theory Y manager, in contrast, structures the job environment to enhance motivation from within. **Theory Y** is based on six assumptions about people.

1. The use of physical and mental energy in work is as natural as play or rest.

2. External control and threats are not the only ways to motivate workers to meet organizational objectives. A person who is committed to the objectives will exercise self-direction and self-control.

3. Commitment to objectives is a motivator and is a function of the rewards of achievement.

4. Under proper conditions, workers learn not only to accept but to seek responsibility.

5. The capacity to exercise a relatively high degree of ingenuity and creativity is widely distributed in the population.

6. The intellectual potentialities of most people are only partially utilized in modern organizations.

Assumptions 2, 3, and 4 of Theory Y depend mainly on the manager's ability to achieve company/worker **goal congruence.** The manager achieves goal congruence by showing workers that when they help the company achieve some

EXERCISE 9-1: HOW DO YOU VIEW WORKERS?

As you read each of the following statements, place a checkmark in the space that best reflects your thinking. Check the answer key and read the next section for an interpretation of your responses.

	Strongly Agree +2	Agree +1	Undecided 0	Disagree −1	Strongly Disagree −2
1. Workers tend to be more highly motivated when they help set the goals for their jobs and determine how to meet those goals than when the boss makes all the decisions.	___	___	___	___	___
2. Basically, people don't like to work. They'll try to get out of work whenever they can.	___	___	___	___	___
3. Most workers have the brain power to contribute a great deal more to their jobs than they are now permitted to do.	___	___	___	___	___
4. Most workers prefer a boss who gives them specific directions about exactly how and when to do various tasks.	___	___	___	___	___
5. Most workers would not only accept more responsibility, they would seek it, if they felt the payoff was high enough.	___	___	___	___	___
6. Most workers perform well when the boss is around but tend to let up when left on their own.	___	___	___	___	___
7. Most people would work, even if they didn't need the money, providing the work fulfilled their needs for a sense of purpose and achievement.	___	___	___	___	___
8. The main thing most people want out of their jobs is a regular paycheck along with some good fringe benefits.	___	___	___	___	___
9. Nearly all workers are capable of using imagination, ingenuity, and creativity when they recognize opportunities and payoffs for doing so.	___	___	___	___	___
10. Most people who think they want to be a manager actually just want the privilege and prestige of the job, not the responsibility and challenge.	___	___	___	___	___

of its specific goals they also achieve some of their specific personal goals. To motivate a worker to action, the reward for achieving company goals must meet some need that the worker feels—a need that he or she is willing to spend significant time and energy in order to satisfy. The worker's goals and the company's goals must be congruent in some way. (We'll discuss various types of needs and their motivating aspects in Chapter 10.)

Theory Y managers not only achieve goal congruence in motivating workers, they also encourage workers to participate in making plans, organizing workflow, solving problems, and making decisions that directly affect their job responsibilities. These managers encourage workers to suggest ways to improve any aspect of company operations. Workers have a relatively high degree of autonomy in performing their jobs and a high level of motivation to contribute to company goals.

In contrast, Theory X managers tend to tightly control all aspects of workers' jobs. These managers try to perform all the management functions themselves and instruct workers about how to carry out managerial plans and decisions. The motivation of workers to contribute to company goals tends to be low under these conditions.

McGregor's thesis is that Theory Y managers will experience greater success and their workers will be more productive and highly motivated than those of Theory X managers.

What if you are oriented toward Theory X? According to McGregor, you don't need to adopt all the assumptions of Theory Y to improve your management style. He urges managers to be open to assumptions about people that are more constructive than those of Theory X, which tend to limit a manager's approaches to dealing with subordinates [19, p. 245].

Theory Y appears to be the answer to the problem of getting from workers a high level of involvement, commitment, and performance

on the job—if companies and jobs are structured to implement its basic assumptions. In actual practice, however, attempts to implement Theory Y are often disappointing. From your experiences with people, what problems do you foresee in trusting people to exercise self-direction and self-control in situations where they have apparent reason to be highly motivated?

We've seen that Theory X reflects an authoritarian approach and Theory Y a participative approach. Both tend to be rather fixed and rigid. A more flexible approach has been called "Theory Z."

Theory Z

In studying both Japanese and American firms, management professor William G. Ouchi developed **Theory Z,** which defines an American adaptation of key aspects of the Japanese management style [23]. This style is characterized by mutual trust between employees and management, informal relationships, employee involvement in decision-making, nonspecialized careers, a slow evaluation process for employees, long-term employment, flexibility, and adaptability. In contrast, most Western firms, even those that are Theory Y in nature, have been characterized by mutual distrust between employees and management, formal relationships, decision-making confined to the executive level, specialized training for narrow career paths, quick employee evaluation, and short-term employment. Exhibit 9-1 gives further comparisons.

Very traditional corporate cultures have difficulty adopting Theory Z. Ouchi recommends taking the following preliminary steps to ease the transition:

- Have a reputable consulting firm make a corporate culture audit, analyzing the firm's

EXHIBIT 9-1: Traditional Management Versus Theory Z

Traditional U.S. Management	Theory Z
1. Impersonal	1. Personal
2. Direct employees	2. Work with employees
3. Suspicious	3. Trusting
4. Individual oriented	4. Group oriented
5. Mobile	5. Long-term employment
6. Inflexible	6. Flexible
7. Rapid evaluations	7. Slow evaluations
8. Specialized careers	8. Nonspecialized careers
9. Individual decision-making	9. Collective decision-making
10. Segmented concerns (firm's issues)	10. Collective concerns
11. Internally competitive	11. Internally noncompetitive
12. Formal relationships	12. Informal relationships
13. Resistant or slow to change	13. Adaptive

management philosophy and procedures and making recommendations.

- Develop new channels of two-way communication between workers and management.

- Do more "management by walking around"; that is, get to know workers and observe firsthand what's going on.

- Find ways to include groups of workers in Total Quality Management.

- Include workers in establishing objectives at all levels.

Fiedlar's Contingency Theory

In *A Theory of Leadership Effectiveness*, Fred Fiedlar suggests that leadership involves the exercise of influence over workers in the performance of a common task [4]. In fact, your effectiveness as a manager is determined by measuring how well your group performs. In Fiedlar's view, how far you as a manager can go

in implementing Theory Y will depend on (is contingent on) the amount of influence you have over your subordinates in three areas.

1. *Leader/follower relations* — The degree of mutual respect and friendliness between the manager and workers. The more positive such relationships are, the greater influence the manager will have.

2. *Position power* — The degree to which power is inherent in the position of leadership, regardless of leader/follower relations. The more actions (both positive and negative) the manager has the power to take, the more influence she will have over workers.

3. *Task structure* — The degree to which workers' tasks can be defined and provided with procedures and controls. The more structured a task is, the greater is the manager's influence over subordinates. A manager can more easily hold workers accountable for their performance when tasks are structured than when they are ill defined or vague.

Fiedlar states that a Theory X, or strong task orientation, works best in situations where managers have either very little influence or a great deal of influence. In other words, in situations where the manager (1) is extremely well liked by subordinates, (2) has a lot of power, and (3) is directing well-defined tasks, a Theory X or task orientation is most effective: The manager has everything going for her and nothing to lose by focusing on the task. Likewise, in situations where the manager (1) is disliked by her followers, (2) has little power in the company, and (3) is directing an unstructured, sketchily defined task, a Theory X or task orientation is also effective: The manager lacks the influence necessary to lead her workers to an acceptance of goal congruence and a high level of commitment and responsibility.

Theory Y, or a strong human relations orientation, works best when the manager has moderate influence. In other words, in situations that represent some middle ground between the extremes where Theory X is best applied, the most effective management approach will be some degree of Theory Y or human relations orientation.

Fiedlar's contingency theory is based on fifteen years of research that encompasses thirty-five different studies involving 1,600 groups of workers. He arrived at these conclusions about management style and leadership effectiveness:

How effectively a work group functions depends on how well the manager's style fits the particular group and work situation. A particular management style might be extremely effective in one situation and ineffective in a different situation.

How much influence a manager is able to assert varies from one group situation to another. It depends on the manager's relationship with the workers, power within the company, and the structure of the tasks to be performed. Therefore, which manage-

ment style will be most effective in a particular situation depends on the degree to which the group situation enables the manager to exert influence.

Since management effectiveness depends not only on the manager's style but also on the group situation, companies have two alternative ways to improve a managerial "fit": (1) They can design the selection and training of managers to fit specific group situations. This is usually the most workable approach. (2) They can design group situations to fit the managers' styles. Where a good fit exists, companies can select new workers who fit into the group situation. They can also continue the policies and procedures the manager is comfortable with.

LEADERSHIP STYLES FOR THE GLOBAL NINETIES

New types of leaders are emerging in the 1990s. These people are able to lead organizations through the challenges of global competition, deregulation, rapid technological change, and a demographically diverse workplace. Exercise 9-2 is designed to jump-start your thinking about your current style and how it may fit various organizational needs, situations, and specific types of job positions. Then we'll discuss the specific attitudes, traits, and skills that organizations of the 1990s need in their potential leaders.

Leaders as Facilitators of Self-Directed Teams

In *Megatrends 2000* John Naisbett states that during the 1980s many new businesses moved away from traditional approaches of *management through directing* to control people, toward a philosophy of *management through leadership* to bring out the best in people and respond quickly to change. Certain aspects of

EXERCISE 9-2: HOW DO YOU LEAD?

In each pair of statements, indicate which statement describes you. Some alternatives may seem equally characteristic, but please choose the alternative that is relatively more characteristic of you. For each item, divide 5 points between the *A* and *B* statements in one of the following six ways:

A B

5 0 **A** is completely characteristic of you and **B** is completely uncharacteristic.

0 5 **B** is completely characteristic of you and **A** is completely uncharacteristic.

4 1 **A** is very characteristic of you and **B** is somewhat characteristic.

1 4 **B** is very characteristic of you and **A** is somewhat characteristic.

3 2 **A** is only slightly more characteristic of you than **B**.

2 3 **B** is only slightly more characteristic of you than **A**.

As leader, I have the primary responsibility of

A	**B**
1. ___ setting goals for my work unit.	___ leading my people in setting our goals.
2. ___ giving workers feedback via formal performance appraisals.	___ talking about how we're doing every day or week.
3. ___ resolving conflict between workers; working toward compromise; making the final decision if necessary.	___ working with people to resolve conflict so that both sides are satisfied.
4. ___ enforcing work rules and procedures.	___ modeling expected behavior.
5. ___ staying within our budget.	___ getting the resources we need.
6. ___ solving problems.	___ getting workers to solve problems.
7. ___ making decisions for the work unit.	___ getting workers to make the decisions.
8. ___ explaining clearly what needs to be done.	___ asking workers what they think needs to be done and what they know about doing it.
9. ___ knowing the answers to workers' questions.	___ helping workers gain expertise; relying on workers' expertise.
10. ___ helping new workers learn how we do things.	___ learning how new workers are accustomed to doing things.
11. ___ helping workers develop goals that contribute to our work-unit goals.	___ getting everyone's commitment to some common work-unit goals.
12. ___ establishing processes for staff meetings.	___ asking workers to work out processes we'll use to manage the work.
13. ___ seeing that people get the work done.	___ finding ways to develop a sense of belonging, commitment, pride, and trust among the workers.

this shift were discussed in Chapter 1; for example, we discussed how workers of the 1990s are different, how leaders differ from managers, and how women can emerge as leaders in this decade. We will discuss how to develop and maintain self-managing work teams in Chapter 13. In this chapter we'll explore the leadership style that is essential for such teams.

Finally U.S. business is learning that people support what they help create, and that everyday operational decisions are best made at the levels where they will be carried out. However, top-down leadership and communication is still the rule in most U.S. organizations. Modern managers may encourage employees to ask questions, state opinions, and share information, but they seldom ask employees to make plans, solve problems, make decisions, create new procedures, or find out what went wrong. Companies are being forced by global competition to flatten their hierarchies, so middle management is thinning out and teams are taking on many of those responsibilities (see Figure 2-2, p. 35). When this occurs, top management comes closer to the ranks and is more directly involved with team leaders; there is no middle-management buffer.

The companies that are thriving and surviving in this global competition are those that Run Hot (as described in Chapter 13). They have work teams that improvise and innovate to fill the customers' total needs and deliver timely products or services at competitive prices. These new developments call for greater self-management by work teams and for leaders who know how to facilitate the problem-solving, decision-making, goal-setting, and development of work procedures that such teams do. Figure 9-2 shows how a controlling manager demotivates a team while a team facilitator empowers and motivates workers. Exhibit 9-2 compares the activities and traits of directive traditional managers (some are still around), consultative modern managers (the

most common type today), and the facilitative team leaders found in leading-edge organizations. Self-managing work teams and their facilitative leaders can thrive only in an organizational culture that nurtures and supports their existence. Exhibit 9-3 compares the attitudes and actions of these organizations with traditional organizations.

Leaders as Changemakers or Implementers

In traditional companies leaders (or managers) are viewed as people who carry out the five management functions of planning, organizing, staffing, directing, and controlling. When they plan, they set objectives, strategies, policies, procedures, and rules. When they organize, they decide on how work groups will be structured to do the work required to carry out objectives and strategies. When they staff, they hire, transfer, promote, and fire workers. When they direct, they command, instruct, and motivate people who do the work. When they control, they set up systems and procedures to be sure the work is done according to plan, and then they follow up and evaluate the work and the workers. All five functions require skill in problem-solving, decision-making, and communicating.

Recently, such management experts as John Naisbett [22], John Kotter [14], Abraham Zaleznik [29], and Warner Burke [15] identified differences in the leadership styles of those who thrive at the top and those who thrive at other levels. Exhibit 9-4 gives the profiles of each style. As you may guess, changemakers are best suited for top management, for starting and running their own competitive business, and for leading organizations during times of rapid change and stiff competition. Implementers are also essential. They provide the balance people need for some minimal sense of security, nurturing, and belonging.

FIGURE 9-2: Impact of Controlling Manager Versus Team Facilitator

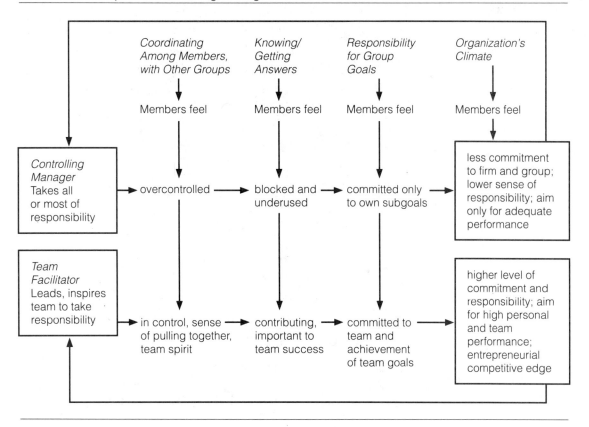

EXHIBIT 9-2: Evolution of Leadership Styles

Traditional Manager *Directive*	Modern Manager *Consultative*	Team Leader *Facilitative·*
Sets goals	Consults in goal-setting	Shares in goal-setting
Solves problems	Good problem-solver	Helps teams solve problems
Decides	Consults, then decides	Shares in decision-making
Tells	Sells	Asks questions, listens
Directs others	Delegates	Directs the team process
Uses authority to get things done	Motivates others to get things done	Empowers others to get things done
Cracks the whip; threatens		Coaches, teaches
Structured	More open, friendly	Flexible

continued

EXHIBIT 9-2: Continued

Traditional Manager *Directive*	Modern Manager *Consultative*	Team Leader *Facilitative*
Message to employees: don't think, keep quiet, cater to me	Receptive to others' ideas More participative environment	Develops teams: inspires, supports, sustains Models what is expected
Favoritism, "pets"		Gets people to focus
Little or no feedback	Performance evaluations	Frequent feedback
Unskilled at "the work"		Pitches in when needed
No counseling	More caring	Empathizes with team's struggles
One-way, top-down, poor communications	Two-way communication	Communication skills
Few people skills		Develops team to high performance, empowers
Knows all answers	Better people skills	
Sexist	Encourages people to share ideas	No longer the "expert"
Tight control		Can rely on others' expertise
Task oriented		
Little contact with other departments, functions	More contact with other departments, functions	Gets resources for team needs
Gets special privileges		Egalitarian
Gets ahead by knowing the right people		Understands change Computer savvy
Quantity above quality	More conscious of quality	TQM
Fulfills bosses' expectations	Dual focus: boss/workers	Focuses on team needs in context of firm's needs
Homogeneous groups	Others adapt to group	Richness in diversity
Takes credit for the work	Shares credit	Gives credit to team
Conflict: win/lose	Conflict: compromise	Conflict: win/win

EXHIBIT 9-3: Organizational Cultures — Old and New

	Traditional Organization	Leading-Edge Organization
Work Force	■ Expendable ■ Needs few skills ■ Narrow job definition	■ A resource to be developed ■ Needs many skills ■ Jobs with flexible scope; encouraged to develop more skills
	■ We-they relationship ■ Homogeneous	■ Partnership ■ Diverse
Focus	■ Specialization	■ Applying special knowledge to larger problems
	■ Driven by technology ■ Change is the exception	■ Driven by customers' needs ■ Change is the rule
Structure	■ Hierarchical ■ Teams formed when needed	■ Flatter organizational structure ■ Teams structured into organization; used to create synergy, to take over some of managers' work

EXHIBIT 9-4: Leadership Styles: Changemakers and Implementers

	Changemakers	Implementers
Key style elements	Creating	Conserving
	Arousing	Clarifying
	Active	Passive
	Visionary	Maintaining momentum
	Initiatory	Balancing interests of parties
	Charismatic	Empathetic
	Innovative	Stabilizing disruptive forces
	Developing strategy	Implementing tactical plans
Concerned with	Ideas/visions	Tasks/people
	Innovating	"Tinkering"
	Stirring up chaos	Stabilizing/order
Problems	Find/make them	Fix them
Decisions	Which to make	How to make them
Plans	Long range	Short range
	Strategic	Tactical
	What to do	How to do it
Personal image	Solitary	A "people person"
	Passionate	Measured/cool
	Emotional	Rational
Work vs. personal life	The same	Separate
Relationships	Intuitive/empathetic	Relates to role
Wants from people	Contrariness	Conformity
Gets from people	Intense feelings	Smooth relations
Communication	Hard, direct, clear	Implicit/"signals," ambiguous
Emotional involvement	With institution	With task and its people
Goals	Personal/active	Impersonal/reactive
	Very high	Realistic
	Risk-taker	Risk-averse
	End-oriented	Means-oriented
Self-esteem source	Context *independent*	Context *dependent*
	Personal mastery	Group identity

Implementers may even be ideal top-level managers and administrators in relatively stable organizations, such as large government institutions and agencies and some traditional industries, and during relatively stable economic periods.

What are your ultimate career goals? Do they include making it to the top levels of an organization or starting your own business? Or do you believe you are better suited to a position at another level—perhaps as a staff professional or department head? Compare your current leadership tendencies with those outlined in Exhibit 9-4. Are they likely to help or hinder you in achieving your goals? If you are strongly oriented toward one style, you may want to adjust your goals to your style; for it may be difficult to develop a style so different from your own. On the other hand, if your current approach incorporates elements from each style, you can probably rely mainly on your implementer skills for positions and situations that call for that style and hone your changemaker skills when it's time to switch styles.

A supposition sometimes used to explain the glass ceiling phenomenon is that few women have a changemaker leadership style and that most are implementers. Researchers at Russell Reynolds Associates refuted this supposition in 1990 by surveying men and women in positions just below top management of Fortune 500 companies [21]. The analysis indicates that the majority of the women were changemakers, whether they were in line or staff positions. On the other hand, most men in staff positions were implementers, whereas most men in line positions were changemakers. This does not mean necessarily that a majority of all women managers would be defined as changemaker-style leaders. It may imply, however, that if a woman wants to make it as far as "just under top management" in today's large corporations, she must develop a changemaker style.

Leaders Who Scan the Environment, Vision the Future

Leaders of the 1990s must think strategically and create visions of what the organization can be and do. They must involve others in creating a vision and then vividly communicate that vision. They must empower others to do their part in bringing the vision about. They must hook everyone into working individually and in teams to make the vision a reality.

Intuitive Visioning   Airline executive Frank Lorenzo equates vision with intuition. "I see chief executives in the airline business who just operate and never look ahead. A CEO's job is divided into two areas: looking into the future

and interpreting trends and steering the organization as strongly as possible on the basis of what's coming" [27].

Roy Rowan's research on intuition [27] indicates that managers who are creative changemakers and who have a participatory style rely heavily on their intuition. Here is the profile of an intuitive manager:

- *Farseeing* — Able to look beyond the obvious, while considering many alternatives simultaneously

- *Introspective* — A trial-and-error thinker with a mind that can turn in on itself and doesn't tune out internal stimuli

- *Impressionable* — Open, trusting, spontaneous, and often amazed

- *Independent* — Accepts the risk of going it alone and being ridiculed

- *Decisive* — Able to infer overall patterns from scraps of information, therefore capable of solving a problem, setting a course, or taking a leap of faith into the future with insufficient information

- *Practical* — Realizes that making new ideas work is more difficult than dreaming them up

- *Upbeat* — Confident that problems can be solved, and not just for the benefit of the firm but for society as well

- *Tuned in* — Wants to know what's going on at all levels and areas, so "keeps her ear to the ground"

- *Flexible* — Able to be cautiously bold by eliminating all unnecessary barriers while still taking chances; able to be ambiguously clear by defining a goal while allowing people a lot of leeway in how to achieve it

- *Enthusiastic* — Generates passionate heat for intuitive visions, winning the people and the money to put ideas across and bring visions into reality

The more effective intuitive leaders learn to avoid two of the most common traps: the illusion of mastery of all life's events and the illusion of immunity to bad luck. These leaders use their intuition to decide what to avoid. For example, they often sense when things are not right, when or where to check for something going wrong, who is being deceitful or playing games, and which situations should be avoided. See Chapter 11 for more information on how top-level leaders use intuition in making decisions, and how women compare with men in this area.

Environmental Scanning Changemakers must know how to scan the external environment for the information they need to vision the future. Changemakers and implementers alike must somehow build room for accelerating change and time for the renewal and innovation that change demands. They must deal with the competitive advantage of speed: getting products to customers faster, increasing market share while reducing inventory costs. Getting products to market before competitors is more important than ever, say consultants at McKinsey & Company. High-tech products that come to market six months late, but within budget, will earn 33 percent less profit (than if they had come out on time) over the next five years. On the other hand, products that come out on time, even if they're 50 percent over budget, will reduce expected profits by only 4 percent [22].

Vision-Creating One way that you empower yourself as a leader is to create a vision of excellence and start making it reality. You can empower your work team by helping them do the same as individuals and as a team; this is discussed further in Chapter 13. After you become clear about the vision, you bring it into reality by developing goals, action plans, structure, policies, and practices that support it. Here are some guidelines for vision-creating that highlight the key words: "inner self, contribution, guiding light, ideal, spiritual, heart."

- *Put your ego aside* and forget about being the boss. Look to your inner self, your higher self. Let your vision statement express the contribution you want to make to the organization, to society — not what the world is going to bestow on you. The organization is your vehicle for making a contribution.

- *Don't limit yourself.* Be imaginative, even "impractical." Let your vision express your idealistic, spiritual side. Let it come more from your heart than from your head. Think of it as a lighthouse, a guiding light to give you direction, rather than a specific end result. Don't worry about how to get there now.

- *Begin with your customers,* both outside the organization and within it. What do they need and want now? In the future? How do you want to serve them? Picture an ideal future.

- *Make your vision statement your own,* from the heart, challenging, and compelling. If it makes you feel a little vulnerable, that's a good sign. It probably means you're moving against the culture, or recreating the culture, in a positive political act.

- *Find the courage to make the vision a reality.* This may mean straying from the paths of "common sense," facts, imitation, and rules-following. It should mean forging new paths, making new maps of reality. Face the harsh reality of the difference, or gap, between your vision and current reality, what you now have. This helps you stop wasting energy on adapting, compromising, and positioning in ways that support your current reality. It strengthens you and gives you personal power, which you communicate to others. This in turn will help you get support for the projects that will bring your vision into reality.

- *Take responsibility for the current reality.* Forget guilt and blame. Focus on the choices you can make now, your commitment to the vision, and your beliefs that it can become reality.

- *Build support for your vision.* Identify people who can help you bring the vision into reality. Share the vision. Communicate with allies and negotiate with adversaries to get what you need. Build trust by communicating and acting honestly and authentically.

Being Authentic Leadership of constant change requires people who are comfortable with ambiguity and some degree of chaos. Don't depend on charm or on being a male impersonator. Become your own person, a person of substance — with values, principles, skills, and knowledge that form a unique pattern that is you. The great challenge for individual managers in the 1990s is to develop their own leadership style. Study the strategies of successful leaders in your organization, along with the events and environments that have brought out the best in its people.

Ways Women Lead

A 1989 study by Judy Rosener [26] indicates that women are less likely than men to use a traditional leadership approach, reward-and-punishment motivation, and the authority of position power. Women are more likely to use a participative approach, to rely more on the charisma of personal power, and to motivate by aligning employees' personal and work goals. Rosener summarized the women's leadership style as follows: encouraging participation, sharing power and information, enhancing the self-worth of others, and energizing others.

Encouraging Participation In nearly every aspect of their interactions with their people, the women in this study make people feel part of the organization. They established a group identity using the following techniques. They encourage people to have a say in almost every aspect of work, from determining strategy to setting performance goals. They use a conversational style that signals to people that they are invited to get involved. They create informal forums for people to interact. They draw people into conversations and solicit their opinions.

This type of inclusion has its disadvantages and risks: (1) It takes time; in fact, there may be emergencies that preclude taking time to involve people in the decision. (2) It often requires giving up some control. (3) It opens the door to criticism. (4) It exposes personal and turf conflicts. (5) Asking for ideas and information can be interpreted as not having answers. (6) Some people prefer being told what to do; they don't want to be asked.

The advantages of encouraging participation include (1) empowering people, (2) motivating those who want, or expect, to be included, and (3) enabling people to better cooperate, coordinate tasks, and even take over each others' jobs when necessary. Most women managers say they prefer participation but they are also comfortable using a variety of leadership styles to suit the situation.

Sharing Power and Information Part of making people feel included is establishing communication patterns that flow both ways. These women managers not only solicit input from workers, they willingly share power and information rather than guard it. They explain the reasoning behind their decisions. One manager describes a technique she uses: Instead of closeting a small group of key executives in her office to develop a strategy based on her own agenda, she holds a series of meetings over several days and allows a larger group to develop and help choose alternatives.

The advantages of sharing power and information include (1) creating loyalty by showing people they are trusted and their ideas are respected; (2) setting the tone for others to share information and power, helping to empower all and to expand communication flow; (3) helping bring problems to light before they explode onto the scene; (4) giving people the ability to solve their own problems, reach their own conclusions, and understand the reasons for decisions leaders make; and (5) responding to educated workers' expectations that leaders will be open and frank and will not act autocratically. These workers want to know the reasons for decisions and will buy in only if it makes sense to them.

The risks of sharing include: (1) People might criticize, reject, or otherwise challenge what you say, or even your authority. (2) People may feel resentment if you don't adopt their ideas after soliciting and listening to them. (3) Leaders who share power may be viewed as naive or seeking popularity.

Enhancing the Self-Worth of Others This aspect of women's style is in some ways a byproduct, or result, of the first two. People tend to feel important when their leaders encourage their participation and when they share power and information. Other ways women enhance workers' self-worth include: (1) frequently giving sincere praise and credit, looking for positive aspects of performance even when they must criticize; (2) sending many small signals of recognition, including personal notes, celebration rituals, and shared humor; and (3) treating workers as equals (for example, being averse to pulling rank, as well as to using separate dining facilities, reserved parking places, and other symbols that set them above and apart from others).

Energizing Others Women are more likely than men to rely on personal power and charisma to lead others. They speak of this as their enthusiasm for work and how they spread their enthusiasm around to make work a challenge that is fun and exciting. They use their own enthusiasm to get others excited. Some are almost evangelistic about their projects and want other people to be as excited as they are. They

"get up a head of steam" before they approach people about a project. They try to infuse others with energy and make them see that even boring jobs contribute to the fun of working in a dynamic business. They may focus on what it is about the business that turns them on: its glamour, mystery, challenge, fast growth, competitiveness, and so on.

Even this upbeat approach has its risks, however. It can be interpreted by staid onlookers as cheerleading and can undermine your credibility. The best way to offset this risk is to showcase the results you have gotten and are getting—measurable results, if possible. The other "risk" is that some of your people are like round pegs in square holes—they don't fit the job position and nothing can light their fire. Identifying these people and moving them on is discussed in Chapter 13.

SKILLS NEEDED TO ADVANCE AS A LEADER

As discussed in Chapter 1, the tasks of business have changed—from the tasks of an industrial economy to the tasks of an information economy. As the tasks changed, so did the work force and the workplace. From the predominantly male to the predominantly female, from workers with a high school education or less to college-educated workers, from assembly-line tasks to mental tasks, from workers paid for manual skills to workers paid for their knowledge. More and more, work is what goes on inside people's heads. It's how they communicate, what they write, and what they say in meetings. It cannot be supervised in the same way that manual tasks are supervised.

The new workers and the new tasks require a new leadership approach that focuses on:

- Planning strategically in longer time-frames
- Thinking in terms of renewal

- Understanding and using the politics of getting along and getting things done

- Causing change

- Affirming values

- Achieving unity

- Inspiring commitment and empowering people by sharing authority

In this section we will look at the *general* skill clusters that leaders build their success upon. Then we will examine some *specific* skills leaders need for advancement to the top and how male and female managers are perceived differently so far as the need for specific skills is concerned. Finally, we will discuss specific skills needed to lead Total Quality Management.

General Skills: Building on Skill Clusters

After extensive study, Richard Boyatzis arrived at an integrated model of skills clusters needed by leaders at all organizational levels, as shown in Figure 9-3 [2]. These skill clusters incorporate David McClelland's work on motivational theory (see Chapter 10). The four skill clusters are implementing skills, people skills, entrepreneurial skills, and visioning/inspiring skills. In addition to these major skill clusters, Boyatzis states that all leaders must possess a minimal level of the threshold skills of specialized knowledge and perceptual objectivity. You must have these threshold skills to get in the door but having more of them won't move you up the ladder.

The Implementing Skills Cluster The two most direct methods a leader can use in guiding or controlling the activities of team members are to provide performance feedback and to interpret the feedback and its consequences. The interpretation often results in a person feeling rewarded or punished. The three underlying skills that enable leaders to guide

team members toward improved performance are developing others, use of unilateral power, and spontaneity. Leaders with this set of skills express themselves to others to improve members' performance by giving directions, guidance, and feedback.

Developing others includes giving performance feedback with the intent of stimulating improved performance. Such leaders invite members to discuss performance problems. They make training and other resources available to help members improve their skills and get their jobs done. While helping others, they are careful to allow individuals to take personal responsibility for making changes and testing their effectiveness.

Use of unilateral power is a skill that leaders use to stimulate people to go along with their directions, wishes, policies, or procedures. These leaders see themselves as being in charge. They demonstrate influence skills that produce agreement or acquiescence in others. People who can use unilateral power give directions based on personal authority, positional authority, or the policies of the organization — with or without the input of others.

Spontaneity is a skill exhibited by people who can express themselves freely or easily. Leaders with this skill see themselves as being able to act freely in the present moment. In social and organizational settings they may take the role of provoker or jester. They demonstrate a variety of self-expression skills. They may express themselves with distinctly more emotion than others. They may act directly and without first thinking about the potential impact of their statements, and they may be surprised when someone responds adversely. They may make quick or snap decisions. But, basically, spontaneity is an individual's ability to feel secure or mature enough to recognize and express any thoughts, feelings, or opinions. (See Chapter 6 on assertiveness.)

The People Skills Cluster Leaders use people skills to coordinate groups of people. The

FIGURE 9-3: Model of Integration of General Skill Clusters

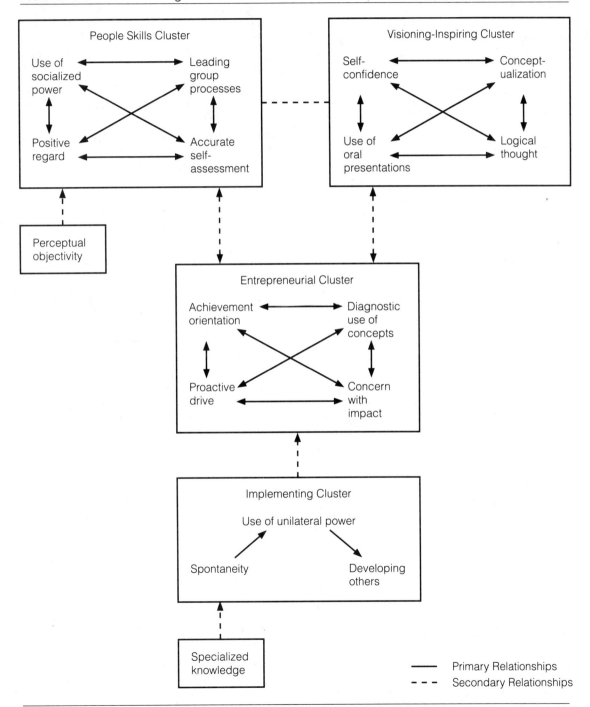

Adapted from *The Competent Manager,* by Richard E. Boyatzis. New York: Wiley, 1982.

coordination may involve promoting cooperative efforts, resolving conflicts, or exchanging information and goods among groups. The leader is responsible for stimulating a degree of pride in the team and the organization. This may take the form of loyalty, commitment to the team and organization, or team spirit. In whatever way this sense of pride is accomplished, it results in people working together toward the organization's goals. The four underlying skills in this cluster are use of socialized power, positive regard, leading group processes, and accurate self-assessment.

Leaders with this set of skills have positive expectations about others, realistic views of themselves, build networks or coalitions to accomplish tasks and solve problems, and stimulate cooperation and pride in their work teams.

Use of socialized power refers to forms of influence a leader uses to build alliances, networks, coalitions, or teams. Leaders with this skill see themselves as members of a team. They build commitment of various people to certain standards of behavior through modeling the desired behavior. Instead of describing the behavior and demanding compliance, they act in a manner consistent with the behavior and wait for others to appreciate its beneficial consequences. It's a matter of "do as I do." They bring conflicting members or groups to a resolution of the conflict through building coalitions or using existing coalitions.

Positive regard means the leader has a basic belief in others, a positive belief that people are good. These leaders see themselves as good people and adopt the role of optimist. They use verbal and nonverbal skills that cause others to feel valued. They often describe others as good or well-intentioned. They contend that, if given the chance, people will do "the right thing." This skill is based on a positive perspective on the people around the leader.

Leading group processes is a skill that leaders use to stimulate others to work together effectively as a team. Such leaders see themselves as able to make teams work well together. They adopt the role of collaborator or integrator. They understand the use and impact of various group processes and how to use individuals' motivation to affiliate with others as a basis for team collaboration and cooperation. They are able to get one work team to cooperate with another. They create symbols of team identity, pride, and trust that represent the team effort. They use personal contact and friendliness to build the team members' commitment to the team and their task effort. They involve all concerned parties in resolving conflict. They do not take on or perform tasks that should be a team effort.

Accurate self-assessment means leaders have a realistic or grounded view of themselves. They see their strengths and weaknesses and sense their potential and limitations. They test their perceptions and judgments about themselves against some other view. They are open to evaluation and criticism of their performance and use the feedback to improve. They are able to describe and evaluate the effectiveness of their performance in a particular situation. Results of their specific actions are attributed to personal strengths or weaknesses. They don't overestimate or aggrandize their strengths nor do they magnify or dramatize their weaknesses. They identify and seek help to remedy their shortcomings.

The Entrepreneurial Skills Cluster At the heart of every leader's job is the need to make things happen toward a goal, consistent with a plan. Leaders are required to oversee the process of establishing goals and action plans, determining how people and other resources will be used and solving problems to keep the organization functioning. To do this they must assume certain risks, have a clear image of the desired outcome, and understand when and how to take initiative. The leader must start with an idea, get things going, and breathe new life into the organization, or her part of it. The four underlying skills that enable a leader to respond to this entrepreneurial requirement are achievement orientation, proactive drive, diagnostic use of concepts, and concern with impact.

Leaders with these skills tend to see themselves as players in a game and see the organization as a player in a larger game. They see the present and future as a series of challenges and problems to be solved. They view life events as opportunities to test their ability, to take risks and succeed, and to accomplish something. Such leaders have a sense of where they and the organization are heading. They assume certain risks and look for signs of their progress. One focus is a concern for the bottom line.

Achievement orientation represents a concern with doing something better. Such leaders adopt the role of innovator. They tend to set goals or target dates that are challenging but realistic. They are usually able to describe clearly their personal standard of excellence for a particular activity or task. They have inner work standards and a need for advancement. They are able to identify specific actions to be taken, resources needed, and potential obstacles to be overcome. They organize resources to accomplish tasks or reach goals efficiently and effectively. They speak of relative returns on investments or relative results from allocation of resources.

Proactive drive represents a tendency to take action to accomplish something. Such leaders instigate activities for specific purposes. They see life events as opportunities for taking action and themselves as the agents who must be responsible for and initiate such action if they want events to unfold in a certain direction or manner. They believe they are in control of their life, not victims or pawns of others, of fate, or of luck. They use the skills of problem-solving and information-seeking to initiate such action.

They initiate various actions, communica-

tions, proposals, meetings, or directives to accomplish a task. They take the first step in a sequence of activities rather than wait for something to happen or for a situation to develop. They take multiple steps to circumvent anticipated or actual obstacles. They identify sources of information and find ways to gain access to them in order to investigate issues or solve problems. They accept and readily admit their personal responsibility for successes or failures in problem-solving or task accomplishment.

Diagnostic use of concepts is a way of thinking in which the person identifies patterns from an assortment of information, by bringing a concept to the situation and attempting to interpret events through that concept. For example, people are usually demonstrating this skill when they walk into a new setting and can quickly identify the leader, the major coalitions, and the informal influence network. They are applying a concept of interpersonal organizational influence and politics to a particular situation. This example is typical of one in which a leader recognizes patterns and interprets aspects of a situation by applying information from a specific event to an organizational model that they have in mind. Such leaders test the information they get by systematically applying it to their concept. They usually have a model, a theory, or a framework with which to interpret or explain the events and behaviors they observe in the organization or to anticipate how an event should unfold. They may adopt the role of analyst or scientist, analyzing situations and behaviors, looking for patterns that help them place an event within an overall concept or theory.

Concern with impact is a concern with the symbols of power that can be used to have impact on others. It reflects a power motive. Such leaders collect objects of prestige, become officers in organizations, and act assertively. They see themselves as important to the organization. They are interested in influencing and persuading others, and they are good at it.

They dress in a fashion and style considered desirable and attractive in their environment. They are concerned about reputation and status — their own, their team's, their organization's, its products, and its services.

The Visioning/Inspiring Skills Cluster
Leaders must have a clear vision of where the organization or team can go in the future, of how it can be. They must either develop or perceive a common vision, or shared vision, that will inspire people to have an interest in their work and the organization. To do this, they must be insightful. They must present ideas, concepts, beliefs, or goals that others find interesting, intriguing, or stimulating; that is, they must articulate the common vision they identify among the people. This common vision may be the workers' shared objectives, values, or concerns. It may also be a *new* direction, goal, or mission that others would like to follow. Often such leaders are skilled at identifying patterns of product performance and changes in the marketplace and communicate these observations internally. They are usually skilled at strategic thinking — at identifying the real business within which the organization is functioning, which may be different from the concept previously believed by management.

Four underlying skills that enable a manager to be inspirational and insightful are conceptualization, self-confidence, logical thought, and use of oral presentation. Leaders with this set of skills see themes and patterns in the common or shared objectives, values, problems, products, concerns, or performance of people and teams. They communicate them to others in a forceful and impressive manner.

Conceptualization refers to skills in finding and recognizing themes and patterns through concept formation. Leaders with this skill, when presented with a series of events, a variety of facts, or a phenomenon, can identify a theme that gives a pattern to the information. They can also label the pattern to communicate the meaning of the concept. They can examine

an issue or problem and provide meaning to it by breaking it down into its various parts, while using a new concept as the basis for the breakdown. Such leaders often use metaphors or analogies to help interpret or understand an event. When a group is exposed to a set of events that seem to be unrelated, such leaders come up with a concept to explain certain aspects of the events and how they are associated. Often the concept identified is different from any used previously by the group.

Self-confidence is often called decisiveness, presence, or positive self-esteem. Self-confident people feel that they know what they are doing and that they are doing it well. They tend to move into the role of natural leader and are often viewed as charismatic. They are surrounded by an aura. They are forceful, unhesitating, and impressive in verbal and nonverbal actions. They believe in the likelihood of their own success. Such leaders tend to express little doubt about the decisions they have made, but they are not arrogant or defensive about them. They might identify the pros and cons of a decision, but they are not reluctant to make a decision nor to live with it.

Logical thought refers to the ability to express ideas in ways that make logical sense to others. Such leaders demonstrate skills in organizing thoughts and activities and in sequential thinking. They can show how certain events precede or cause other events in a cause-and-effect series. They can bring a sense of order and coherence to the group. This skill is not associated with success at top-management levels and may interfere with the intuitive visioning so essential at that level.

Use of oral presentations refers to all presentations, from one-on-one meetings to speeches before hundreds of people. Leaders with this skill see themselves as able to communicate effectively. They adopt the role of communicator in groups, often summarizing or restating what others have said or are trying to say. They use symbolic, verbal, and nonverbal behavior to reinforce or interpret the content of the mes-

EXHIBIT 9-5: General Skills Critical to Success by Managerial Level in Order of Importance

Entry-Level	Middle-Level	Top-Level
Implementation skills	People skills	Vision/inspiring skills
Entrepreneurial skills	Entrepreneurial skills	Entrepreneurial skills
	Vision/inspiring skills	

sage and to ensure that the presentations are clear and convincing. When possible, they ask questions to ensure that people understand what they are saying. They often use visual aids and graphics to get their message across. They speak at a pace that allows the audience to understand and that maximizes audience interest, and they use language that the audience can understand.

In his research Boyatzis concluded that different skill clusters were crucial to entry-level, middle-level, and top-level managers. Exhibit 9-5 shows the general skills critical to success at each managerial level.

Specific Skills: Consensus and Stereotypes About Male/Female Leaders

We have been examining clusters of general skills that managers use as building blocks. Other studies reveal specific skills that organizations look for in performance evaluations of candidates for top-management positions. One study [3] examined how male and female managers view the skills of other managers, both male and female. The skills examined are shown in Exhibit 9-6.

Female/Male Skills — Consensus and Stereotypes A 1990 study of skills needed by women managers, as compared with managers in general, shows that men and women managers generally agree on the skills needed and that some stereotypes about women managers still prevail [3]. The top ten skills are in-

dicated by asterisks in Exhibit 9-6. Significant differences appeared in the need for female managers to work on the following skills:

- Respond professionally in tense or emotional situations

- Avoid impulsive reactions, act thoughtfully, considering the consequences of actions

- Make a commitment to reach the top; balance other commitments accordingly

These differences seem to reflect some typical stereotypes: (1) women managers cannot manage their emotions and tend to fall apart under pressure, responding impulsively, and (2) women managers lack the commitment and singleness of purpose it takes to make it to the top levels of business. Are these areas that you need to work on to overcome any problem tendencies? Regardless, you'll want to work on projecting an image that repudiates such stereotypes.

On the other hand, there were significant differences in the need for managers in general — as compared to women managers — to develop the following skills:

- Determine customer needs and wants that affect the business unit

- Understand and counter the effects of competition in meeting customer needs; be flexible in responding to rapidly changing needs ("Flexible" and "responding" may be the key words here.)

- Follow up to see that customer needs are met

EXHIBIT 9-6: Skills Leaders Need to Move to Top-Level Positions

1. Communicating a vision
   a. Clarify the organization's mission, specific objectives, and priorities
   **b. Make certain that employees understand the purpose of the work unit and how it ties in to the organizational mission
   c. Make certain that employees understand their specific job objectives and priorities
   d. Keep employees informed about progress toward goals
   e. Listen to and understand others' concerns

2. Taking initiative
   *a. Take action before being forced by the situation
   b. Take action to improve business results
   c. Plan ahead, check alternatives, make back-up plans
   d. Create, encourage, and use innovative approaches
   e. Devise new approaches that include others beyond the work unit
   **f. Show a basic willingness — to take charge, to take responsibility, to find out how to get results, to get the job done

3. Enhancing customer satisfaction
   *a. Determine customer needs and wants that affect the business unit
   b. Focus on TQM (Total Quality Management) in setting objectives, appraising performance, and rewarding employees
   *c. Develop new strategies for meeting customer needs
   *d. Gear procedures and methods to achieving customer satisfaction
   *e. Understand the effects of competition in meeting customer needs; be flexible in responding to rapidly changing needs
   **f. Follow up to see that customer needs are met

4. Leading the training and development of work-team members
   a. Develop short- and long-range plans for training and development of each employee
   b. Delegate tasks that will enhance employee's development
   *c. Delegate skillfully and effectively
   d. Provide or arrange for necessary training and coaching
   e. Provide opportunities for people to engage in challenging new tasks and projects

5. Maintaining self-confidence
   a. Apply judgment, skills, and abilities in a confident manner
   b. Express confidence in ability to achieve goals
   c. Approach problems as either opportunities or challenges
   *d. Take calculated business risks
   e. Appear comfortable in leadership role

6. Retaining poise under pressure
   a. Respond professionally in tense or emotional situations
   b. Select the management approach that is most effective for specific stressful situations
   c. Avoid impulsive reactions; act thoughtfully, considering consequences of actions
   d. Experience, express, and manage emotions in ways that prevent stress build-up

7. Getting results
   a. Measure employee progress toward goals
   b. Make employees responsible for results
   c. Appraise employee performance on basis of results, such as improving service or product, increasing revenues, cutting costs
   d. Give recognition and rewards on basis of performance

* Among the ten top-ranked skills
** Among the three top-ranked skills

8. Showing leadership
    a. Select from a variety of effective approaches to achieve results
    b. Guide and influence others in developing action plans to achieve objectives and carry out action plans
    c. Identify who has a stake in a given issue and how to involve them in its resolution
    d. Discover sources of individual and group resistance to implementing plans and develop strategies to overcome them
    e. Share relevant information in a timely fashion
    f. Cooperate and negotiate with others outside the work unit to secure resources and achieve goals

9. Increasing productivity
    a. Enhance the firm's competitiveness through increased productivity
    b. Base decisions on informed trade-offs between costs and benefits of alternate solutions
    c. Understand cost structure of product/service and effectively control costs
    d. Approve expenditures on basis of contribution to business objectives

10. Solving problems
    a. Analyze situations to get at underlying causes, implications, and significance
    b. Develop alternate solutions, including creative action plans
    c. Consult with people who are affected by problem and/or its solution
    d. Facilitate group effort toward problem solution
    e. Oversee appropriate computer technology or other technical skills to solve problems

11. Understanding the organization, its people, and its politics
    a. Be a team player to achieve goals
    b. Understand the difference between formal and informal organizational power and use both types to advantage
    c. Recognize political power games and successfully counter them

12. Taking a leadership role outside the organization
    a. Represent the organization to the media, business and professional associations, and community service groups
    b. Serve on the governing boards and important committees of such external groups
    c. Accept important fund-raising roles
    d. Make effective speeches to external groups

13. Managing own career to achieve realistic objectives
    a. Develop a realistic picture of your own potential, limitations, strengths, and weak areas
    b. Take responsibility for your own career development and advancement
    c. Make a commitment to reach the top; balance other commitments accordingly
    d. Work out any wife/mother role conflicts

This result indicates that women managers are perceived to be especially strong, or skilled, in dealing with customers. Some specific ideas about women that may underlie this perception include that women are particularly apt to show concern and care for others, listen to them, tune in to what they want, be flexible and responsive in meeting their needs, and nurture others. These may be strengths that give you an advantage and that you'll want to build upon.

Skills Needed for TQM Leadership Organizations whose cultures focus on TQM (see Chapter 11) are likely to survive and thrive in the 1990s. The type of person needed to lead the changeover to a TQM culture focuses on enhancing customer satisfaction via quality products and services. She engages in the following activities:

- Searching for challenging opportunities to change, grow, innovate, and improve

- Experimenting, take risks and learn from the mistakes that occur

- Envisioning an uplifting and ennobling future

- Enlisting others in a common vision by appealing to their values, interests, and dreams

- Fostering collaboration by promoting cooperative goals and building trust

- Strengthening others by sharing information and power and increasing their discretion and visibility

- Setting an example for others by behaving in ways that reflect your stated values

- Planning small wins that promote consistent progress and build commitment

- Recognizing individual contributions to the success of every project

- Celebrating team accomplishments regularly

PERSONALITY TRAITS OF EFFECTIVE LEADERS

To round out our exploration of skills and style, let's look briefly at typical characteristics of top achievers — those people who most would say are highly successful. The most successful of these people are said to have "charisma," so let's explore what makes such people tick and identify the elements of charisma.

Characteristics of Top Achievers

Sidney Lecker, a New York psychiatrist, did an extensive study of highly successful executives and entrepreneurs [17]. He found an interesting set of attitudes and traits that were common to these leaders. People with what Lecker calls "the money personality" exhibit certain characteristics. They

1. Are persistent and don't wilt with failure, rejection, or time

2. Are unafraid of bigness

3. Set simple objectives

4. Identify key data and actions for meeting objectives

5. Can carry complex, abstract ideas through to realization

6. Search for facts and weigh them

7. Take calculated risks

8. Take total responsibility

9. Have no guilt or fear about success

10. Love the *process* of success; seeking, achieving, savoring it

11. Are in command of inner resources: intelligence, creativity, and emotional strengths

Lecker notes that most people share many of these traits but don't use them as fully as the top achievers. Item 11, the ability to fully tap inner resources, is the key factor to success. Once people take command of their inner resources, Lecker says, "They experience more success and less stress than others who live less challenging lives" [17, p. 126]. In other words, the traits are not as important as the ability to use them.

The Elements of Charisma

Our actions reveal our philosophy and personality traits, but the *way* we do something is frequently more important than *what* we do. Top leaders of organizations usually have a type of charisma, a brilliance or personal magnetism, that attracts people. Max Gunther interviewed many prominent psychologists and psychiatrists and found that most of them believe the quality of charisma can be developed.

He has described six major components of charisma [7].

1. *Energy exchange.* A charismatic person gives off energy to other people. The major reason people are drawn to a person with charisma is that they go away with a sense of higher energy than they had before the encounter. This experience sharply contrasts with encounters with weak people who are always trying to get others to love them, cheer them up, or support them — who want to feed off others' mental or emotional energy. You can train yourself to become an energy giver, although doing so usually takes practice and enormous effort at first. The process can become painless and even enjoyable. The more you enjoy it, the bigger your energy reserves tend to become. Some people have developed their abilities to give energy through meditation and visualization.

2. *Physical appearance.* Although one need not be beautiful to be charismatic, it is essential to look interesting. Imaginative grooming, vibrant good health, and superb posture all contribute to the look.

3. *Independence.* Charismatic persons do not depend on others for their sense of well-being and self-esteem. People who are *anxious* to be liked are never charismatic.

4. *Verbal ability.* Magnetic people are highly articulate and skilled in the art of swaying people with words. Whether they use that ability constructively or manipulatively is a matter of values and ethics.

5. *Acceptance of admiration.* People with charisma are comfortable when others openly admire them, and they accept homage as a completely natural phenomenon — as simply part of the environment.

6. *The look of serenity.* Charismatic leaders have doubts like anyone else, but they tend to keep them to themselves. They discuss their worries only with close confidants. Once they make a decision, they go confidently ahead and implement it without hesitation even though they may have some serious doubts. They commit themselves to implementing the decision, and they maintain the look of perfect serenity during the entire process.

LEADERS WHO DEVELOP A SUPPORTIVE CLIMATE

R. M. Stogdill found that next to structure, consideration or support was the most important leadership trait [28]. As leader, you have more impact than anyone in your work group on the type of environment or climate that prevails. Your philosophy, your attitude, your approach to handling your responsibilities — that is, your management style — creates the work environment. It can be challenging or dull, supportive or defensive.

When people analyze the best work environment they've ever experienced, most discover it was challenging yet supportive — an environment in which they felt the need and desire to upgrade their skills and performance and at the same time felt free to take the risks involved in attempting new learning, new roles, and new assignments. They believed their manager was on their side and would back them up in their attempts to grow and learn.

As a result of an eight-year study, J. R. Gibb contrasted the characteristics of managers who tend to create either a defensive or a supportive work climate (see Exhibit 9-7). He found that in a defensive climate people are more likely to feel the need to defend their actions, beliefs, feelings, and motives than they are in a supportive climate. Such defensiveness creates a barrier to open, candid communication. In a supportive climate people don't feel threatened

EXHIBIT 9-7: Behavior Characteristics of Supportive and Defensive Climates

Defensive Climates	Supportive Climates
We tend to become defensive toward someone who seems to be	We tend to communicate openly with someone who seems to be
1. Evaluating our behavior	1. Describing our behavior
2. Trying to control us	2. Cooperating in solving a problem
3. Trying to manipulate us	3. Acting spontaneously
4. Indifferent to our welfare	4. Concerned with our welfare
5. Considering herself or himself superior to us	5. Considering herself or himself equal to us
6. All-knowing	6. Open to others' ideas

Adapted from J. R. Gibb, *Trust: A New View of Personal and Organizational Development* (Van Nuys, Calif.: Newcastle Publishing, 1991).

by the boss and are more likely to speak up and to take risks.

As you contrast the behaviors Gibb identified, think of your experiences and how you've reacted to such behavior.

Evaluating Versus Describing

When workers perceive that the boss is evaluating or judging them, they tend to become defensive. But if the manager is also supportive, this support will reduce or neutralize the defensiveness. For example, when your approach is one of seeking help to solve a problem, when you behave spontaneously, when you treat a worker as your equal or show that you understand the worker's viewpoint, then the worker is more likely to accept your apparent judgment of his or her behavior without becoming defensive. In other words, the six sets of behavior that Gibb identified work together and depend on one another for maximum effect on the work environment. How defensive the worker's response is depends on the overall work climate that currently exists and that existed in the past.

Evaluative messages that are especially likely to arouse defensiveness in workers are those that appear to place blame, fit people into categories of good or bad, make moral judgments about the worker or others, and question the value of others' ideas. In the terminology of transactional analysis, these evaluative messages frequently come from the Parent ego state and arouse the most defensiveness when the transaction is directed from the Parent ego state of the manager to the Child ego state of the worker.

Descriptive messages, in contrast, come from the Adult ego state, and the transaction usually involved is from Adult to Adult. The worker tends to perceive these messages either as genuine requests for information or as neutral messages (as opposed to messages conveying values that conflict with the values of the worker). Messages that do not ask the receiver to change his or her behavior or attitudes are most likely to be perceived as supportive.

Controlling Versus Problem-Solving

A manager may control a worker through a legalistic insistence on attending to detail, conforming to norms, and obeying restrictive rules, regulations, and laws. Control may also take the form of gestures and facial expressions as well as such simple acts as receiving a visitor from behind a large, imposing desk.

Workers will usually resist a message that they perceive is being used to control them in some way — to influence their behavior, restrict their activities, change their attitude. They may view attempts at control or change as signs of some sort of personal inadequacy — wrong or inadequate attitudes, inability to make effective decisions, ignorance, immaturity, lack of common sense. A worker who also perceives that an attempt to control is guided by hidden motives will increase his or her resistance.

The manager who communicates the wish to work with employees in defining a mutual problem and seeking its solution reflects a problem-solving orientation. When employees perceive that the boss is not going to impose a predetermined solution, attitude, or method on them, they are free to set their own goals, make their own decisions, and evaluate their own progress. At the very least, they will be able to share with the boss in doing these things. To communicate your willingness to take a problem-solving approach, you as a manager must do more than merely *say* that you have no wish to exercise control: Your nonverbal communications and ensuing actions must back up the verbal message.

Manipulating Versus Acting Spontaneously

A worker who believes the manager is playing a game with unclear and varied motivations will become defensive. He or she may perceive the hidden motivation to be larger than it really is and may resist being victimized by it.

Managers who are perceived to be playing a role, feigning emotion, toying with the worker, withholding information, or taking advantage of special sources of information are especially resented. And the resentment increases when the manager seems to be trying to make the game appear spontaneous.

In contrast, spontaneous messages — those that are interpreted as being free of deception, as having uncomplicated motivations, as being straightforward and honest, and as being authentic responses to a situation — are likely to arouse minimal defense in workers.

Being Indifferent Versus Being Concerned

Indifference usually indicates a lack of concern for the welfare of the worker. We all like to be received as persons of value having special worth and deserving of concern and affection. Messages that communicate little warmth or caring sometimes also communicate rejection.

Messages that communicate empathy and respect for the worker, however, are especially supportive and reduce defensive reactions. When you as a manager indicate that you are able to identify with the worker's problems, share his or her feelings, and accept his or her emotional reactions at face value, you provide reassurance to the worker.

Considering Yourself Superior Versus Considering Yourself Equal

If you communicate that you think you are superior in position, power, wealth, intellectual ability, physical characteristics, or some other way, you arouse defensiveness. Your subordinates are likely to feel inadequate and threatened. They may think you will try to reduce their power, status, or worth, and they may react by not hearing what you say, by hearing only part of your message, by distorting or forgetting it, or by competing with or becoming jealous of you.

Obviously, differences in talent, ability, worth, appearance, status, and power often do exist. But when you communicate that you attach little importance to these differences, you reduce the worker's defensiveness. If you communicate trust and respect and a willingness to enter into mutual planning and problem-solving, you can establish an atmosphere of equality.

Knowing It All Versus Being Open to Ideas

If you seem to know all the answers, to require no additional information, and to regard yourself mainly as a teacher rather than as a co-worker, you will tend to threaten your workers. If you act as if you need to be right, want to win an argument rather than solve a problem, or see your ideas as truths to be defended, you are unlikely to have your ideas or your approach fully accepted.

On the other hand, when you have a high degree of tolerance for workers who disagree with you and when you appear to be investigating issues rather than taking sides on them, problem-solving rather than debating, and willing to experiment and explore, you are more likely to communicate that the worker will have some control over the joint venture or the investigation of the ideas.

In TA terms, the person who seems to know it all is probably coming from the Parent ego state and is communicating from Parent to Child. When a manager comes from the Adult ego state and the transaction is an Adult-to-Adult one, she is then generally searching for information and ideas and does not resent the help or participation of her employees.

The business manager who arouses defensiveness makes it difficult, if not impossible, to communicate her ideas clearly and to solve managerial problems effectively. Effective business managers can listen without engaging in premature criticism or evaluation. They are open to their workers' ideas and information, even though they may make the final decisions.

This supportive approach results in a relaxed atmosphere where workers feel free to communicate openly. If the manager also expects top-quality performance from her workers and encourages them to achieve it, then the climate is also likely to be a highly motivating, productive one. See whether you can identify some of the behaviors that tend to produce a supportive climate by completing Exercise 9-3.

SUMMARY

Each of us has a management philosophy that contains elements of one or more well-known philosophies. Theory X is a traditional, authoritarian view of management based on the belief that people are inherently lazy, unambitious, and limited. Theory Y is a participative approach based on the belief that people will exercise self-direction and self-control on the job if they see that they are meeting their own personal needs and goals by meeting the company's needs and goals. A Theory Y manager believes people are capable of exercising a relatively high degree of ingenuity and creativity. Theory Z refers to an American adaptation of key aspects of Japanese management style. It is characterized by mutual manager/worker trust, informal work relationships, employee involvement in decisions, nonspecialized career paths, slow employee evaluation process, long-term employment, and flexibility/adaptability.

Fiedlar's contingency theory is another situational approach to implementing Theories X and Y, based on leader/follower relations, position power, and task structure. Fiedlar found that situations that represent either extreme

EXERCISE 9-3: IDENTIFYING BEHAVIOR CHARACTERISTICS OF DEFENSIVE AND SUPPORTIVE CLIMATES

Each pair of statements reflects behavior that is characteristic of one of the categories of defensive and supportive climates shown in Exhibit 9-6. Identify the appropriate category and write it down. See the answer key for an interpretation of your responses.

1. A. "Your petty cash account is short again. You'll have to get my approval for all petty cash expenditures in the future."
   B. "Let's go over your petty cash procedures and see what we can do about these shortages."
2. A. "My proposal is based on some sophisticated concepts you may not understand."
   B. "Please let me know if I'm communicating my proposal to you in an effective way."
3. A. "John, this report is well done. As soon as these minor errors are corrected, it will be ready to go."
   B. "I'm disappointed to see your poor proofreading habits are resulting in errors in your reports."
4. A. "This project must be finished by Friday, no matter what!"
   B. "Joe, how's your schedule this week? Our reputation with the Morton Company depends on finishing their project by Friday."
5. A. "These are my instructions, and I expect you to follow them precisely."
   B. "I've worked out some guidelines for this job. What do you think?"
6. A. "Well, Joan, I'll have to think about your request; I have a lot of other things to consider before I make my decision, you know."
   B. "Joan, as soon as I get the new production schedule, I can let you know about taking next Friday off."

Adapted from Norma Carr-Ruffino, *Writing Short Business Reports* (New York: McGraw-Hill, 1980), pp. 22–23. Copyright © 1980 by McGraw-Hill, Inc. All rights reserved. Reproduced with permission.

---

in these categories are best suited to a Theory X approach, and situations that represent some middle ground are best suited to a Theory Y approach.

You can adapt your leadership style to fit various organizational needs, situations, and job positions. A changemaker style is most often needed at the top of today's organizations, as well as in some lower-level positions in times of change or stiff competition. An implementer style provides the stability, security, nurturing, and belonging workers need to get the job done; that is, to implement the changemaker's vision. Most women just below the top levels of Fortune 500 companies use a changemaker style. Today's leaders must focus more on leading in order to respond quickly to change rather than on directing in order to control. They must constantly scan the external environment and respond appropriately.

Women are especially prone to lead by encouraging participation, sharing power and information, enhancing workers' self-worth, and energizing workers. They tend to rely more on personal power and charisma than on position power, and they motivate by aligning workers' personal and job goals rather than by traditional reward-and-punishment methods.

Leaders need special skills to deal with rapid technological change, as well as accelerated change in all areas. They need specific skills to lead a diverse, better-educated work force and to establish a corporate culture that focuses on TQM in a highly competitive global marketplace. General skill clusters that leaders build upon include implementing, people, entrepreneurial, and visioning/inspiring skills. Specific skills in all aspects of enhancing customer satisfaction are crucial, and women are perceived to be especially strong in such skills. Women must overcome stereotypes that they are unskilled in (1) managing their emotions and impulses and (2) focusing their career commitment and balancing it with other commitments.

The traits and attitudes of effective managers are quite diverse. However, certain characteristics have been found to be typical of successful executives and entrepreneurs. The key trait is the ability to fully tap inner resources in order to make full use of other traits. Also, top leaders usually have a type of charisma; they give off energy to other people. We know too that developing a supportive climate is extremely important to building a top-producing team. Such a climate enhances open communication, motivation, and a cooperative team spirit. Key behaviors are description versus evaluation, problem-solving versus control, spontaneity versus manipulation, concern versus indifference, equality versus superiority, and openness to ideas versus knowing it all.

Additional Exercise

EXERCISE 9-4: ANALYZING TRAITS OF YOUR WORST AND BEST BOSSES

1. *Worst boss:* Relax a few moments, close your eyes, then recall all the bosses you've ever had. Does one boss stand out as the worst? (If not, then concentrate on the worst aspects of all your bosses.) Think about specific actions, personality traits, characteristics, attitudes, and habits that made this boss so poor. Remember exactly how you felt about each of these items, the effects they had on you, and how you responded. Fully tune in to that time in your life and the specific items you remember. Then open your eyes and list all the traits, actions, and so forth that you can recall.

2. *Best boss:* Now repeat the process, but this time focus on the best boss you've ever had.

REFERENCES

1. Blake, Robert R., and Jane Srygley Mouton. *The Managerial Grid.* Houston: Gulf Publishing, 1984. See especially the overview in Chapter 1. The authors expand on the idea of a work-oriented versus a people-oriented management philosophy, along with the effects and impact of each.

2. Boyatzis, Richard E. *The Competent Manager: A Model for Effective Performance.* New York: John Wiley & Sons, 1982. The author bases his model on extensive research designed to determine which skills are most crucial to effective leadership.

3. Carr-Ruffino, Norma, Jane Baack, and Monique Pelletier. "Consensus and Stereotypes: Male and Female Managers' Perceptions of Key Skills Needed to Get to the Top," Association of Management Annual National Conference, Orlando, Florida, 1990.

4. Fiedlar, Fred E. *A Theory of Leadership Effectiveness.* New York: McGraw-Hill, 1982. Fiedlar gives a complete explanation of contingency theory, his research results, and practical applications.

5. Gibb, J. R. *Trust: A New View of Personal and Organizational Development.* Van Nuys, Calif.: Newcastle Publishing, 1991.

6. Griffin, Ricky W. *Management.* Boston: Houghton Mifflin, 1990. This is a good introduction to management textbook.

7. Gunther, Max. "Charismatic Leadership." *Journal of Business Communication,* Vol. 16, No. 5 (May 1982), pp. 82–85.

8. Helgasen, Sally. *Female Advantage: Woman's Ways of Leadership.* New York: Doubleday, 1990.

9. Hellriegel, Don, and John Slocum. *Management.* Reading, Mass.: Addison-Wesley, 1992. This is a good introduction to management textbook.

10. Hickman, Craig R., and Michael A. Silva. *Creative Excellence.* New York: Penguin, 1984.

11. Jelinek, Mariann, and Claudia Schoonhaven. *The Innovation Marathon: Lessons From High Tech Firms.* Cambridge, Mass.: Basil Blackwell, 1990.

12. King, Laurel. *Women of Power.* San Francisco: Celestial Arts, 1989.

13. Kinlaw, Dennis C. *Developing Superior Work Teams: Building Quality and the Competitive Edge.* Lexington, Mass.: Lexington Books, 1991. Kinlaw discusses the differences between work groups, work teams, and superior work teams and provides models.

14. Kotter, J. *A Force For Change.* New York: The Free Press, 1990.

15. Kouzes, James M., and Barry Z. Posner. *The Leadership Challenge.* San Diego: University Associates, 1988. How to accomplish extraordinary things in organizations through new ways of leading.

16. Kreitner, Robert. *Management.* Boston: Houghton Mifflin, 1992.

17. Lecker, Sidney. *The Money Personality.* New York: Simon and Schuster, 1983. The results of a psychiatrist's research on traits common to top executives and entrepreneurs.

18. Likert, Rensis. *The Human Organization.* New York: McGraw-Hill, 1981. Likert explains his application and adaptation of Theory X and Theory Y and describes other aspects of a workable management philosophy.

19. McGregor, Douglas. *The Human Side of Enterprise,* 25th anniversary edition. New York: Avon, 1982. This classic management text fully discusses the Theory X and Theory Y approaches to management, the implementation of Theory Y, and some case results.

20. Makoff, Barbara. *What Mona Lisa Knew: A Woman's Guide to Getting Ahead in Business by Lightening Up.* Los Angeles, Calif.: Lowell House, 1990.

21. *Men, Women, and Leadership,* a monograph. New York: Russell Reynolds Associates, November 1990.

22. Naisbett, John, and Patricia Aburdene. *Megatrends 2000: Ten New Directions for the 1990's.* New York: Morrow, 1990.

23. Ouchi, William G. *Theory Z.* New York: Addison-Wesley, 1981. Ouchi describes in detail the adaptation of Japanese management style by American companies, including case histories.

24. Peters, Tom. *Thriving on Chaos.* New York: Harper & Row, 1987.

25. Rees, Fran. *How to Lead Work Teams.* San Diego: Pfeiffer and Company, 1991.

26. Rosener, Judy B. "Ways Women Lead," *Harvard Business Review* (November–December 1990), pp. 119–25.

27. Rowan, Roy. *The Intuitive Manager.* New York: Berkley, 1987.

28. Stogdill, R. M., and Bernard M. Bass. *The Handbook of Leadership.* New York: The Free Press, 1981.

29. Zalesnik, A. *The Managerial Mystique.* New York: Harper & Row, 1988.

30. Jacobson, Aileen. *Women in Charge: Dilemmas of Women in Authority.* New York: Van Nostrand Reinhold, 1989.

Chapter Ten

Providing a Motivational Climate

"High performance is a <u>cause</u> of high satisfaction,
not a result of it."

Lyman Porter

When you have developed the skills needed to plan for results and adapt your management style so that it is appropriate and effective in the various situations you may choose to work in, you will have gone a long way toward providing a motivational climate for your people. In this chapter we'll discuss some additional specific actions and attitudes that affect the motivation of your team members.

In the final analysis, motivation comes from *within* a person. Therefore, you cannot truly motivate people: You cannot really control another person's inner drives and attitudes. What you *can* do is help team members channel their attitudes and inner drives by showing them how they can satisfy their needs and desires through working productively toward organizational objectives. You can take specific actions that encourage and enhance each person's inner motivation to perform well. Even though you cannot directly motivate another person over the long term, you can provide a climate in which motivation is encouraged, enhanced, and nurtured.

In this chapter you will have the opportunity to

1. Understand the needs, both innate and socially acquired, that drive people

2. Understand the role of expectations in worker motivation

3. Learn how a manager can help align worker and organizational needs and goals

4. See how motivating factors can be built into a job rather than tacked on

5. Recognize ways in which socially acquired motives both drive and inhibit women

 Firefighting Strategies

John Brockfield has been explaining the situational approach to management to Erika. Now he says, "What you were doing is perfectly logical and understandable, Erika—you were repeating behavior that had been successful in the past. The clerical staff you were dealing with were nearly all young and inexperienced, and the work they were doing could be structured. So a relatively directive, controlling leadership style worked well. The workers didn't mind the attention you gave them—in fact, it tended to motivate them to increase their productivity."

"Yes, that makes sense." Erika murmurs.

"But that bunch of salespeople you've got is a very different crew. Most of them are already highly motivated. They're skilled, experienced professionals, and their work is very unstructured. They generally have to figure out for themselves the best way to handle their various accounts. They have to establish the right relationship with the different buyers, and that frequently involves a delicate balance."

"Yes," Erika responds. "And they naturally resent a newcomer—especially a young female boss—like me coming in and trying to tell them how to do their jobs."

"Right. So what's your next step?"

Erika thinks that one over. Finally she says, "Well, John, it seems to me that I need to talk with all the staff at our next meeting. I'll ask them how the procedures are working out and encourage them to vent any feelings they have about that—and anything else connected with their jobs, for that matter. Then I'll let them know that I respect and appreciate their skills. My message will be that I'm here to assist and support them, but as long as they keep getting the results we're looking for, how they go about getting those results is basically up to them."

"Sounds like a good plan, Erika."

Erika feels good about moving toward a solution to her problem with the sales staff as she enters the restaurant down the street from the office. As she waits in a booth for her friend Audrey Frank to join her, Erika hears a familiar voice in the booth behind her. "Why, it's Lin Leslie, our new Customer Accounts Supervisor," she thinks.

"It's good to get away from that place, Pete, even if it's just a business lunch."

P: How's the new job going, Lin?

L: Fairly well. However, it was a lot easier being an Accounts Clerk than a Customer Accounts Supervisor. I had a lot fewer headaches in my old job. I like the feeling of doing something more important than being just a clerk, but trying to motivate these clerks to perform is a heavy responsibility.

P: Yeah. I guess that's the hardest part of a manager's job, isn't it?

L: It sure is! If I could just figure out how to get people to move! To take some responsibility! To take pride in their work!

P: True. You can try to light a fire under some people and they *still* don't do much.

L: It gets very discouraging sometimes. People nowadays just don't seem to care as much as I did when I was learning the business.

Erika decides it's best to keep quiet and moves to a table in the corner. After a quick lunch with Audrey, she returns to the office. Stopping by the employee's lounge, she overhears another conversation between two of Lin's clerks.

R: I guess we should get on back to work. We've been gone nearly an hour.

J: Why rush? The sooner we go back, the longer we'll have to sit there and work.

R: Yeah, but old Eagle-Eye Lin gets upset when we're late, you know.

J: Don't worry. She had one of her "business lunches" with a Maxi-Mart rep today. She won't be back before two. We can take it easy this afternoon. She'll have her mind on Maxi-Mart.

R: Good. I don't want her getting mad at me, though. I really need a raise. Maybe if I stay on her good side, I'll get one next month.

J: Don't count on it! I thought sure she would

recommend me for one last quarter and I got nothing. Zero.

R: I overheard Dawn telling someone on the telephone that she got a raise. I don't understand that. She doesn't do much.

J: It beats me. I don't know what Lin expects. I knocked myself out last quarter trying to impress her and do a good job. It sure didn't do me any good. I'm going to try to stay on her good side, but I'm sure not going to kill myself working around this place anymore.

R: I tried to find out what I need to do to get a raise, but she just said, "Do your job and do it right."

That night after dinner Erika snuggles against Scott's arm as they continue sharing the events of the day. "Sometimes, it's downright discouraging, Scott. I feel like a firefighter — about the time I see a way to get the fire under control in the Sales area, I stumble onto another one in the Customer Accounts area."

"Well, maybe that's what management is all about," he sighs. "The main thing is, you're hanging in there and you're handling it. I have a feeling that each time you learn to deal with one of these problems, you're also learning how to prevent it or cope with it in the future."

"Now that's a viewpoint I like!" laughs Erika.

---

1. Explain how you think Erika's original management style affected the motivation of the clerical workers she supervised.

2. Explain how you think it affected the motivation of the salespeople.

3. What do you think is the source of Lin Leslie's motivational problem with the clerks she supervises?

4. If you were Erika, would you bring up the problem to Lin? If so, why and how?

5. What advice would you give to Lin?

MOTIVATING THROUGH PERSONAL POWER INSTEAD OF POSITION POWER

Why aren't more employees really committed to their work and to the company's objectives? One reason is that too many managers still rely on the power of their positions rather than on their own ability to lead people. Although this use of power may be subtle and kept in the background, its effect is coercive. **Position power** stems from beliefs about the innate rights of the organization — beliefs that place the organization and its management on the side of the owners' interest and opposite to the employees' interests. As management expert Douglas Sherwin puts it, position power "is the root of the managing group's attitude as enforcer, driver, superior, privileged, and causative" [11, p. 672]. This somewhat arrogant attitude frequently triggers negative responses from employees.

Employees will generally *accept* (if somewhat grudgingly) the organization's concept of position power because they must accept it in order to earn a living. As a result, however, they think of work as a means to an end rather than a worthwhile end in itself. Since people commit themselves to ends, or goals, and not necessarily to ways of achieving the goals, employees often fail to commit themselves to the work itself. A key to exercising leadership is the ability to understand the psychological needs (and therefore personal goals) of individual workers and to help them satisfy their needs through their own actions.

An essential part of this process is identifying how the actions that help achieve the goals of the organization also achieve the personal goals of a particular worker. This type of leadership replaces position power and is made possible by disregarding it. This doesn't mean that as manager you must keep a low profile, that you must serve merely as a facilitator. Nor does it mean that your decisions should always be made by vote, caucus, or democratic process. You must be tough when necessary and perform your functions with firmness.

Since such leadership requires understanding people's needs, a study of motivational theories will be helpful, for people are motivated to act in ways that help them satisfy their needs.

RECOGNIZING INNATE MOTIVATORS

Before reading further, see what motivates *you* by completing Exercise 10-1. By understanding your own motivational priorities, you'll be in a better position to understand what motivates other people.

Different people will interpret job factors in somewhat different ways. For a few, salary may meet a purely physiological need to survive: "Will I have enough to eat in order to stay alive?" Most people would probably see salary as meeting a security need: "How can I ensure that I'll be able to survive safely in the future?"

EXERCISE 10-1: IDENTIFYING MOTIVATIONAL PRIORITIES

Determine whether each job factor in the following list belongs in Category A or Category B. Then rank the items you placed in Category A according to their relative importance. Do the same for Category B. After you've read this section of the chapter, compare your responses with those shown in the answer key.

Factor

Adequate salary	On-the-job achievement
Responsibilities assigned	Kind of supervision received
Relationship with fellow employees	Recognition
The work itself	Company policy
Opportunity for advancement	Opportunities for personal growth
Working conditions	

Category A: Factors That Produce Satisfaction or Dissatisfaction. You expect the job to provide an adequate quantity or quality of this factor. This factor does not cause you to work harder—either to obtain it or as a result of having it present. If it isn't present, however, you will look around for another job.

Category B: Factors That Motivate. You are willing to put forth additional effort and commitment as a result of having this factor present or in order to obtain it.

Other job factors often considered necessary for meeting safety and security needs are working conditions and company policy. These factors would fall into Category A for most American workers, but they're Category B factors for some, especially for workers in developing countries.

On the other hand, a certain percentage of Americans are motivated to high performance by rewards that fulfill the need for acceptance, to belong to a group. The factors of "relationship with fellow employees" and "kind of supervision received" are frequently interpreted as meeting these needs. Others have overriding needs for ego reinforcement in the form of recognition or status. "Recognition" and "opportunity for advancement" are often interpreted as meeting those needs.

According to psychologist Abraham Maslow [9], the need to discover and make the best use of one's talents is the highest-level need. The factors of "responsibilities assigned," "on-the-job achievement," "opportunities for personal growth," and sometimes "opportunity for advancement" are often interpreted as meeting this self-actualization need.

Maslow's Hierarchy of Needs

Probably the best-known motivational theory in the United States is the theory developed by Abraham Maslow. Believing that people act in order to satisfy certain needs, he developed a hierarchy containing five levels of needs (see Figure 10-1). According to Maslow, only when

FIGURE 10-1: Maslow's Hierarchy of Needs

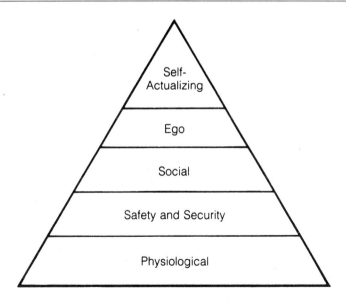

Adapted from Abraham H. Maslow, "A Theory of Human Motivation," *Psychological Review*, Vol. 50, No. 4 (July 1943), pp. 370–96.

needs at the lowest level of the hierarchy have been satisfied does a person feel an active need at the next level.

At the base of **Maslow's hierarchy** are *physiological needs* basic to physical survival—adequate food, water, and air as well as protection from the elements through adequate shelter and clothing. A person who is hungry and has no access to food will do almost anything to satisfy the need for food. Obviously, the way to get that person to do something is to offer food (or money for food) as a reward. Until the need for food, clothing, and shelter has been met, an individual will feel little or no motivation to satisfy the need for safety and security.

Security and safety needs drive people after their physiological needs have been satisfied. These are the needs to know that we can meet our physiological needs and do so in relative safety. Until we feel that our physical safety is adequately secure, we won't spend much time worrying about social needs, on the next level of the hierarchy.

Social needs include the needs to be liked, loved, and accepted. The need to belong to a group—whether to a family, peer, work, community, or some other kind of group—is also a social need. People who have not satisfied this need through family or social groups may be highly motivated to belong to a work group where they will be liked and accepted. Until social needs are met, they won't pay much attention to ego needs. In fact, if increased status makes them feel isolated, they may consider it more a punishment than a reward.

Ego needs are needs for respect, for recognition, for increased status, and for acknowledgment and appreciation of our work, our achievements, and our contributions. A person who feels that his or her physiological, safety and security, and social needs are being satisfied tends to focus on ego needs and is motivated by rewards that satisfy them. People operating at this level are more concerned with the favorable attention their actions, achievements, or contributions bring to them than they are with any personal satisfaction or growth that might be involved. Their rewards, then, are attention, applause, recognition, and fame.

Self-actualizing needs are needs for continuous personal growth and development, for the utmost achievement a person is capable of, for the full development of a person's potential capabilities. People operating at the highest level of Maslow's hierarchy are more concerned with personal satisfaction and growth than with popularity or recognition. They are even willing to pursue an unpopular course of action and perhaps alienate their peers if they feel such action plays an important enough role in their personal development. Self-actualization needs are never fully satisfied; the pursuit of **self-actualization** is a lifelong one.

Major Motivators of U.S. Workers

Most workers in the United States have come to expect that at least the first two and possibly the first three levels of needs in the hierarchy will be satisfied through their jobs (Category A in Exercise 10-1). Many of them also expect some satisfaction of ego needs for appreciation and respect. If physiological and safety and security needs are not met through their jobs, workers tend to be dissatisfied and will complain a great deal, look for other jobs, or find alternative ways to meet those needs (such as living on government subsidies). They will not be motivated to work harder to satisfy those needs because they can be readily satisfied by switching jobs or seeking government aid. Their focus is on the social, ego, or self-actualizing needs, and only rewards that satisfy the appropriate higher-level need will motivate them to greater commitment and productivity.

If you are to help people meet their needs through achieving company objectives, you must determine the level at which each individual is operating and gear the handling of rewards accordingly. We'll discuss suggestions for doing this in the last section of this chapter.

RECOGNIZING SOCIALLY ACQUIRED MOTIVATORS

Another approach to motivation has been developed by psychologist David McClelland [8] and others over the past thirty years. Maslow's hierarchy implies that all humans are born with the lower-level needs as well as the potential to develop the higher-level needs in a step-by-step progression. McClelland takes issue with this viewpoint by suggesting that many human needs are socially acquired, rather than innate, and therefore vary from culture to culture. The rewards a child gets for excelling at studies, winning a fistfight, or shooting birds, for example, depend on cultural values. Such values and the resulting rewards help shape the needs we develop in childhood. McClelland also questions the adequacy of the concept of self-actualization. He indicates that the kinds of rewards that actualize a person's potential vary more widely from society to society and from person to person within one society than Maslow's work recognizes.

According to McClelland, needs for affiliation, power, and achievement are prime motivators. We can see some similarity in his affiliation need and Maslow's social or belonging need. We can also better understand McClelland's power and achievement categories by relating them to Maslow's ego and self-actualization needs, keeping in mind that McClelland's needs reflect cultural values and an expectation–reward–learning process rather than an inherent progression of need levels. Before we discuss these **socially acquired needs** in detail, take time to complete Exercise 10-2.

Now let's look at the key actions that help you determine whether a person's primary needs are for affiliation, power, or achievement. Remember, many of the actions described under each category are exhibited by all of us at one time or another; therefore the behavior alone doesn't necessarily indicate a primary need. For example, most of us seek the company of others at times, and such behavior doesn't necessarily indicate a strong affiliation need. When a person places special emphasis on being with others along with other affiliative behavior, however, we can assume a high affiliation need.

Affiliation

The stories written by most people in response to an exercise like 10-2 reflect affiliation needs. They focus on thoughts about relations with other people. When people with high **affiliation needs** are relaxing or daydreaming, they tend to think about the quality of their personal relationships. They might recall with pleasure the experiences they have had with some people and worry about problems with their relations with others. Persons with high affiliation needs tend to place *special emphasis* on (1) seeking out others to gain confirmation for their own beliefs or to relieve the stress of their own uncertainties, (2) seeking the company of others and taking steps to be liked by them, (3) trying to project a favorable image in interpersonal relations, (4) smoothing out disagreeable tensions in meetings with others, and (5) helping and supporting others and wanting to be liked in return.

Here is a story that reflects needs that are predominantly affiliative:

This business woman is pausing in the midst of a busy day to think about her family. She's remembering the picnic at the beach they enjoyed so much last evening. She's concerned

EXERCISE 10-2: ANALYZING YOUR SOCIALLY ACQUIRED NEEDS

First, read the questions that follow. Then study Figure 10-2 for ten or fifteen seconds. Finally, close the book and — without looking at the picture again — spend no more than five minutes writing an imaginative story based on the picture. Relax and be creative instead of merely describing the picture. Your story may include anything that occurs to you, but here are some questions that you may want to answer in it.

1. What is happening? Who are the people?

2. What has happened in the past that led up to this situation?

3. What is being thought? What is wanted? Who is doing the thinking, the wanting?

4. What is going to occur next? What will be done?

After you've finished your story, read the discussion of socially acquired motives. Then analyze your story to determine the predominant motivational need it reflects.

---

about having enough time and energy to devote to her children, who still need a great deal of attention and guidance. She decides to plan more family outings like the beach picnic, even if it means delaying some of her professional ambitions for a while.

As you can see, this story reflects thoughts about people. It could just as easily reflect affiliative needs by focusing on relations with people at work, as long as positive, constructive relationships are seen as an end in themselves and not merely as a means to other ends that reflect an achievement or power orientation.

Power

People with high needs for power spend more time thinking about how to get and use power and authority than other people do. They tend to place *special emphasis* on (1) winning argu-

ments, (2) persuading others to accept and implement their viewpoints or action plans, and (3) prevailing or winning.

People with high **power needs** feel uncomfortable without some sense of power. Power may be used in two quite different ways.

1. *Power used to dominate.* People who want to gain power in order to dominate are sometimes said to be controlled by negative ego needs. We all have a positive and negative side to our ego. Your negative ego tells you that life is a win-lose game. It focuses on ways that you are better than or worse than others. Your negative ego is obsessed with surface appearances and how you impress others: getting cheers or boos, approving nods or raised eyebrows.

   People who use power to dominate are determined to have their own way. They control, intimidate, and manipulate others. As leaders, they may demand passive or

FIGURE 10-2: Basis for an Imaginative Story

submissive responses. Their followers often resort to passive-aggressive behavior; they may greatly resent the leader's style but are afraid to openly resist. If this type of leader is also charismatic, his or her followers tend to feel dependent, submissive, loyal, devoted, and obedient to the leader's will. Change in the status quo may threaten them. If you wonder what type of power a leader exercises, observe the followers.

2. *Power used to empower.* Global Nineties leaders use their power to empower themselves and others to achieve goals — to set meaningful personal goals, to connect them with organizational goals, and to attain these goals. These leaders tend to use inspiration, support, resources, and persuasion to lead people to higher levels of commitment, skill, innovation, and productivity. If the leaders are charismatic, their followers tend to grow in independence, personal power, confidence, competence, and creativity. The followers adapt well to change, usually welcoming those changes they understand.

Here is a story that reflects a high power need:

The woman is a top-level executive in a growing firm. Her family looks to her for guidance and inspiration just as people in her company do. She is preparing her presentation for the annual stockholders' meeting tomorrow. She must convince the Board of Directors that her proposal is essential to maintaining the company's present growth rate. If she is successful and her plan works as well as she expects, she will probably be promoted before the next annual meeting.

This story focuses on the rewards of power. Any mention of people or problem-solving is done in terms of power roles.

Achievement

People with high **achievement needs** tend to place *special emphasis* on (1) taking personal responsibility for finding solutions to problems, (2) setting moderate achievement goals and taking calculated risks, and (3) seeking concrete feedback on how well they're doing.

Here is a story that reflects a high achievement need:

The woman is a staff specialist and is quite good at what she does. She has been working on a project and is relaxing from her efforts for a moment. She is thinking how proud her family will be when she tells them about the difficult problems she solved and the extra effort she expended to complete this project on time. She will have special cause to celebrate the completion of the project this evening. It was her brainchild from start to finish, and test runs have already indicated its workability.

The Effects of Socially Acquired Motives on Women

These three motives — affiliation, power, and achievement — are acquired by people in response to the actions and attitudes of their parents and others. The effects of this socialization process have special significance for women. The process can help us understand some of the typical differences between men and women — differences that are not necessarily innate and that can affect managerial effectiveness. For example, if you're uncomfortable with assuming a power position, you may be able to overcome this barrier to upward mobility more readily if you understand the source of your discomfort. Such insights can also help you guide other women over barriers.

We start acquiring these needs in early childhood as an outcome of actively trying to cope with our environment. Because the process begins so early, by the time we reach adulthood it is operating mostly at an unconscious level. The process begins at birth when we start coping with the problems of satisfying our hunger and getting adequate attention. It continues as we cope with the problems that accompany learning and growing. An immediate outcome of this coping behavior is that it tends to be pleasantly rewarding or neutral or to have unpleasant effects, which in turn affect our long-term patterns of behavior and need.

Getting Rewards and Reducing Anxiety We frequently experience either reward or anxiety as a result of the way others respond to our behavior. These early experiments are powerful influences in shaping our long-term behavior patterns. When a reward follows an act, it reinforces the behavior and increases the probability that it will be repeated. When as a child your active, problem-solving behavior led to satisfying results, you learned more than just how to cope or solve a problem. You also learned to repeat the *type* of behavior that led to success. When some of these types of behavior were consistently rewarded over time, you learned to rely on them. As a result of this learning process, you developed your own pattern of affiliation, power, and achievement needs and motives.

The other force at work in the learning process is the reduction of anxiety. We tend to re-

peat the kinds of behavior that result in a reduction of negative states or unpleasant tension. If being warm and friendly paid off by relieving your pain and anxiety, for example, the warm, friendly behavior was reinforced and the foundation for a lifelong affiliation need was strengthened.

Effects of Socialization on Women's Leadership Effectiveness An analysis of socially acquired motives can perhaps shed some light on the assets and liabilities that women bring to the leadership role. It is safe to say that most women have received the greatest rewards and reduced more anxieties through affiliative behavior than through power and achievement-oriented behavior. In general, women therefore have an edge over men in sensitivity to people's feelings and in establishing warm, supportive relationships.

Some women also have received strong and consistent rewards for achievement-oriented behavior. The fact that until adolescence girls consistently get better grades than boys indicates at least some achievement orientation of girls at an early age. Even today, however, many girls respond to quite different messages during adolescence and early adulthood — such as "Boys don't go for bookworms," "Don't be too smart," "Start looking for a nice boy to settle down with." As a result, even girls who were previously oriented toward achievement found out that their greatest rewards came as a result of affiliative behavior, and they responded accordingly. Many channeled their achievement-oriented behavior into keeping the neatest house on the block, having the most successful husband in the group, raising the brightest, most attractive children, belonging to the most exclusive, desirable clubs and groups. They aimed at basking in the reflected light of their husband's and children's successes rather than in their own.

Very few women have found significant rewards or anxiety avoidance through power-oriented behavior. Quite the opposite, most women have experienced some degree of censure and anxiety-producing feedback when they have attempted to take charge, win arguments, prevail, and so forth — especially with men. Some studies indicate that the few women who make it to top management have usually enjoyed special relationships with their fathers. These women had relatively strong fathers who supported and encouraged them to excel and take charge. In most cases the father served as role model and mentor in a way that is common in father/son relationships but extremely rare with daughters.

Most women bring to the job a lifetime of experiences that have discouraged the very power-oriented behavior that is essential to becoming a top-level executive. Since this behavior is learned, however, there is no reason you cannot make new decisions about certain values and behaviors that will help you attain the job positions you desire. You might well keep in mind that *someone* must lead and must occupy these power positions. It is possible that women can more easily combine affiliative with power-oriented behavior to become more humane, effective leaders than men.

How have interactions with others affected your needs, your perceptions of rewarding and anxiety-producing situations, and therefore your own motivational patterns? Exercise 10-3 gives you a chance to examine these factors. The purposes of the exercise are to help you identify *patterns* of behavior and how they developed as you grew up and to give you some insights into the effects of your early experiences on your current motivators. How can you use your insights to motivate the people who work for you? We'll focus on that topic next.

RECOGNIZING THE MANAGER'S ROLE AS A MOTIVATOR

We've examined two major theories of motivation that are based on the assumption that certain needs impel people to behave in certain

ways. The theories of Maslow and McClelland deal with innate and learned needs that people bring to the job situation, and they can help you understand what you (and others) want as well as how you (and others) developed that pattern of wants. Now let's look at some theories that deal more directly with the job situation itself and the manager's role in enhancing worker motivation. These theories examine the roles of expectations and guidance.

Expectancy Theory

Since people's needs determine what is rewarding to them, they behave in ways they think will lead to those rewards. The actual behavior depends on a person's thinking, "If I act this way in this particular situation at this particular time, I will get a reward that I want."

According to **expectancy theory,** merely having a particular motive or needing a particular reward is not enough to turn a readiness to behave into behavior and performance. Where motivational theories such as Maslow's and McClelland's help us identify what people *want,* expectancy theory helps us understand how desire leads to *action.* Before people will act, they must generally expect two things.

1. If they try to perform, they will actually be able to perform. It *is* possible to do what they are trying to do in this particular situation, and they have the ability to do it.

2. If they perform, they will get the reward they want.

Another aspect of expectations (although not a part of formal expectancy theory) is the expectation of the manager concerning each worker's abilities and potential. Look at the situations where the worker respects the manager and is influenced by the manager's attitudes and actions. If the manager has reasonably high expectations for the worker's performance, the worker tends to rise to the

EXERCISE 10-3: IDENTIFYING SOURCES OF REWARD AND ANXIETY

As you read through each list of behaviors, respond only to the items that "ring a bell." Jot down the period of your life in which the behavior was significant—early childhood, elementary school, adolescence, or young adulthood. Finally, determine whether you experienced some type of reward or payoff for the behavior. If you did, put an *R* beside the behavior. If you experienced anxiety as a result of the behavior, write *A*. If the results were neutral, write *N*.

Don't overanalyze or try to respond to every type of behavior in every life period. First get the high points; then review your responses, looking for patterns and insights.

R = Reward
A = Anxiety
N = Neutral

Power-Oriented Behavior
1. Taking over in a situation
2. Arguing a point
3. Trying to persuade others to do what you want
4. Telling others what to do
5. Getting others to follow your lead
6. Breaking a rule when it interferes with a "valid goal"

List other power-oriented behaviors you have experienced.

_____

_____

_____

Achievement-Oriented Behavior
1. Initiating and completing projects
2. Figuring out what was wrong
3. Figuring out how to fix things
4. Making good grades
5. Taking "hard subjects" as electives
6. Doing well in or liking math or science courses
7. Doing well in or liking courses in shop, drafting, or other "male-oriented" vocations
8. Doing well in or liking football, baseball, or other "male-oriented" sports
9. Working or playing on your own
10. Asking how you are doing
11. Trying to find out how you are being evaluated

12. Competing with others
13. Trying to do better and better

List other achievement-oriented behaviors you have experienced.

_____

_____

_____

Affiliation-Oriented Behavior
1. Doing as you are told
2. Following the rules
3. Making lots of "nice" friends
4. Participating in the "right" group
5. Cooperating with others
6. Doing things to please others
7. Helping others
8. Putting others' wishes ahead of your own
9. Patching up quarrels or disagreements
10. Dating "nice" boys
11. Understanding others' feelings

List other affiliation-oriented behaviors you have experienced.

_____

_____

_____

occasion again and again. The manager's expectations reflect confidence in the worker's ability and therefore esteem for the worker. The worker's self-esteem and self-confidence are enhanced, and the manager's expectations create a self-fulfilling prophecy of worker achievement.

In effect, such managers help workers picture themselves functioning in certain roles, meeting certain goals, and receiving certain rewards. Three essential steps to maintaining a high level of motivation are (1) having the appropriate self-image, (2) setting appropriate

goals, and (3) applying the necessary self-discipline to overcome barriers and to reach goals. Managers can enhance workers' motivation by helping them through each of these steps.

The Path-Goal Approach

The manager who can understand and take effective action based on people's needs *and* their expectations is probably using some variation of a **path-goal approach** to motivation.

Effective managers are able to show their workers how meeting their job objectives will satisfy their needs and help them obtain some of the rewards they want most. (We described this in Chapter 9 as achieving goal congruence.) The manager's behavior will have a motivating effect on workers to the extent that such behavior (1) makes satisfaction of workers' needs dependent on effective performance (that is, challenges workers in appropriate ways) and (2) provides a supportive work environment by providing the coaching, guidance, support, and rewards necessary for effective performance.

More specifically, managers can increase (1) workers' motivation to perform, (2) their job satisfaction, and (3) their acceptance of the manager by taking the following kinds of action [3, p. 327]:

Recognize and arouse workers' needs for results over which they have some control.

Increase personal payoffs to workers for attaining job goals.

Make the path to such payoffs easier to travel by giving effective coaching and direction (see Chapter 13).

Help workers clarify their expectations.

Minimize frustrating barriers.

Increase opportunities for personal satisfaction dependent on job performance.

As you can see, the manager's skill in identifying appropriate rewards is a key to making the path-goal approach work. Here are some general principles of motivating through reward.

1. Identify the precise behaviors that you are rewarding.

2. Reward the desired behaviors as soon as possible. Be specific in communicating what you are rewarding and why.

3. When a new behavior is being developed, reward it in some way every time it occurs until it is firmly established.

4. When a new behavior is being developed, the learner must perceive that the reward will be worth the risk and effort.

The ideal management style for implementing the path-goal approach is the participative style described in Chapter 9, but other styles can be effective in certain situations. When the demands of the tasks are ambiguous or when organizational procedures, rules, or policies are not clear, *directive leadership* provides the necessary guidance and psychological structure for workers. When workers are performing stressful, frustrating, or dissatisfying tasks, *supportive leadership* can offset their dissatisfaction.

Achievement-oriented leadership strives for higher standards of performance to meet challenging goals. When workers are performing ambiguous, nonrepetitive tasks, the higher the achievement orientation of the leader, the more confident the followers will be that their efforts will pay off in effective performance.

Regardless of management style, the path-goal model is one in which the manager focuses on results, with a balanced emphasis on the objectives of the organization and the personal goals of the workers.

PRACTICAL APPLICATIONS OF MOTIVATIONAL THEORY

The path-goal approach is a good start toward bridging the gap between understanding pure motivational theory and making theory work on the job. In this section we'll focus on applying motivational theory to constructively select, train, and lead people and to organize work. To get the best results, the leader must try to find the best match between the requirements of the job, the needs of the persons who'll be doing the tasks, and the working climate (that is, the organizational structure, leadership styles, and related factors). Then the leader must choose among several alternative approaches in order to achieve two distinct goals:

1. To build a highly motivated team by such actions as hiring people who fit and counseling those who don't into other jobs or companies

2. To structure a motivational work environment by reorganizing job descriptions and tasks to take better advantage of the needs, interests, and drives of the people in the work groups and by modifying the working climate to achieve a better fit with the types of workers involved

Matching Jobs to Workers' Motivational Patterns

Of all the actions you can take, the one that will have the most dramatic effects on the motivational environment of your group is matching the right person to the right job. You can get the right match by hiring people who fit the job and the group, by transferring people within the group to achieve a better fit, and by reorganizing jobs for a better fit. (Removing employees who don't fit in or is discussed more fully in Chapter 13.) Let's look first at the kinds of jobs that are suited to people with high affiliation, power, or achievement needs.

Affiliation Motives = Coordinators, Integrators People with strong affiliation needs make the best coordinators and integrators. Place these people in jobs that require coordinating the work of others, such as specialists, or the work of departments. They are also ideal in jobs that require integrating the goals of various persons, units, or departments with organizational goals, as well as teaching and

coaching, and performing services that require directly helping others.

Power Motives = Upwardly Mobile Managers Anyone who is expected to move beyond the ranks of first-line or middle management must have a fairly high power need — at least in most organizational settings. The competition at higher levels is usually so stiff that people with less than a strong need to lead, influence, and prevail soon grow tired of the battle. The climb up the ladder usually requires skill and interest in organizational politics and skirmishes. Persons who enjoy the process are most likely to survive and come out on top.

Achievement Motives = Staff Specialists, Commission Salespersons, Professionals The salesperson on commission and the owner-manager of a small business are good examples of the person with a high achievement need. They are in a perfect position to see whether their performance is improving and to reap the rewards of that performance. Other job situations that require problem-solving skills are engineers, builders, and certain staff jobs requiring specialized expertise (such as computer specialists). Professionals such as accountants, lawyers, and doctors usually have high achievement needs.

Listening for Clues Pay special attention to people's thoughts and feelings and try to tune in to what motivates them [5, pp. 105–10]. How do workers talk about their experiences? What kinds of things seem to give them the most satisfaction? What do they think about when they are involved in their work? Detailed suggestions for analyzing the jobs or tasks to be accomplished and for identifying patterns of behavior of the people who might fill these jobs are shown in Exhibit 10-1.

Recognizing Multiple Orientations As you go about making the job/person fit, keep in mind that just because a person is strongly oriented toward one type of motive doesn't

EXHIBIT 10-1: Matching Workers' Needs to Job Requirements

When the job allows or requires workers to	Look for people who
Affiliation Orientation	

Interact with numerous people on a daily basis	Relate well to other workers and go out of their way to make friends with new workers
Have access to interaction with numerous people in his or her working area	Get involved in group projects
Have significant free time to interact with people on nontask matters	Are sensitive to other people's feelings
Gain the cooperation of coworkers to successfully accomplish the task	Make special efforts to get personally involved with bosses
Maintain long-term worker relationships	Don't like to work alone

Power Orientation

Personally direct coworkers	Especially like to be their own boss, even in situations where they need help or where cooperative effort is needed
Spend a significant amount of time dealing directly with the boss(es)	
Spend a significant amount of time in personal interactions	Enjoy a good argument
Have significant control over his or her work pace and methods	Seek positions of authority where they can give orders rather than take them
Be reasonably free to come and go as she or he pleases, as long as the work gets done	Like to take charge of situations
Have significant opportunities for advancement	View status symbols as especially important and use them to gain influence

Achievement Orientation

Have a great deal of freedom in setting his or her work pace and designing own work methods	Are eager to accept responsibility
Usually choose when and where to get help or direction	Like to set and meet measurable standards of high performance
Perform effectively and efficiently because company sales or profits are directly affected	Stick with tasks until they are satisfactorily completed
Always know how well she or he is doing	Enjoy difficult, challenging tasks
Be continually challenged to develop abilities and skills	Work better when the job is challenging or a deadline must be met
	Try to find out how they are doing, like to get as much information as possible to help meet goals and standards
	Enjoy a fairly high degree of freedom, responsibility, and competition

Adapted from George H. Litwin and Robert A. Stringer, Jr., *Motivation and Organizational Climate* (Cambridge, Mass.: Harvard University, Graduate School of Business, 1978), pp. 105–110.

necessarily mean that he or she will be "low" in another motive. For example, a person might be "high" in both affiliation and power needs — and possibly in achievement needs too. You'll need to consider the mix and the situation when making personnel decisions. In addition, people vary in their energy levels and in the degree of positive, constructive outlook. For example, it is quite possible that an energetic person with an approach to life that is usually very positive and constructive would be more highly motivated by needs for affiliation, power, *and* achievement than would a passive, lethargic person with a rather sour, pessimistic viewpoint. Test your matching ability by completing Exercise 10-4.

Structuring the Work Environment

We've been focusing on building a highly motivated work team by achieving the best fit of worker to job and situation. You can also plan and organize the work itself to enhance motivation. You can provide workers with relevant information, and you can encourage them to participate in planning and decision-making.

Structuring Jobs Five key characteristics of job tasks that significantly affect motivation have been researched by J. Richard Hackman and others, as shown in Exhibit 10-2. These five task characteristics determine the type and level of certain psychological states that are critical to high motivation and performance. The extent to which three of these task characteristics are present (skill variety, task or team/task identity, and task significance) directly affects how meaningful the work is to the worker. A fourth key task characteristic, the level of autonomy the worker has in performing job tasks, directly affects the extent to which he or she takes personal responsibility for work results. And the fifth characteristic, the kind of feedback the worker gets, directly affects his or her knowledge of the actual work results.

Three critical psychological states — (1) perceived meaningfulness of the work, (2) responsibility for work outcomes, and (3) knowledge of the end results of the work activities — in turn directly affect the workers' attitudes and behaviors. In other words, the level of your workers' internal motivation, work performance, job satisfaction, and attendance rate are all directly related to these psychological states. Your challenge, therefore, is to structure the tasks and the atmosphere in which they're done to provide the needed levels of skill variety, task identity, task significance, autonomy, and feedback.

Ideally, workers should be the first ones to get feedback on their performance so they can practice as much self-evaluation and self-control as is feasible, as discussed in the section on planning in Chapter 12. When you give feedback, take a problem-solving approach, as discussed in the section on delegating in Chapter 13. In addition to information on their performance, workers frequently need other kinds of information in order to take full responsibility for their jobs.

Providing Information If workers are to accomplish their job goals and make contributions to company goals, managers must see that they get all possible information that can be helpful. Workers should receive relevant information on a regular basis and as a matter of course. Therefore, managers must arrange for information to flow routinely to workers who need it. The information should be specific, readily identifiable, and readily digested by the worker. In other words, workers should not have to wade through pages of reports or stacks of computer printouts in order to sift out and interpret the information they need.

Providing for Planning and Decision-Making by Workers When the people who will actively undertake work assignments participate in making some decisions and have latitude to make others on their own, they gain stature

EXHIBIT 10-2: How Task Characteristics Affect Work Motivation

Task Characteristics	Critical Psychological States	Effects on Attitude and Behavior
Skill Variety — The number of different tasks, their level of challenge, and the variety of skills and talents needed to accomplish them *Task Identity* — How well a worker can identify with a distinct or tangible piece of work he or she can claim as the result of his or her effort *or* *Team/Task Identity* — How well workers can identify with a small team that can in turn claim a distinct piece of work as the result of its own joint effort *Task Significance* — How important the task is; how much it affects the work or the lives of others	→ *Meaningfulness of the Work* — as perceived by the worker	High internal motivation to work High quality of work performance → High satisfaction with work Low absenteeism, turnover rates
Autonomy — The level of freedom the worker has to plan tasks and to decide on procedures for carrying them out	→ *Responsibility for Outcomes of the Work* — as perceived by the worker	
Feedback — The extent, type, and immediacy of information about how well the worker is performing assigned tasks	→ *Knowledge of Actual Results of the work activities*	

Adapted from Richard Hackman and G. R. Oldham, *Work Redesign* (Reading, Mass.: Addison-Wesley, 1980).

within the company and in their own eyes. Their expertise and their capacity for rational action in making creative contributions is more fully utilized and developed. Their interest in their jobs and their sense of responsibility are enhanced.

If workers are not allowed to participate in planning and other decisions concerning their jobs, the company is in effect telling them that they have no prospect of becoming really in-

volved in the company's affairs. If they are not involved, how can we expect them to be motivated? (See Chapter 12.)

Putting It All Together

In the final analysis, you cannot motivate anyone but yourself. You certainly cannot successfully manipulate motivation in others for very long. Neither will occasional "rewards," such as company picnics, gold watches, or even a pat on the back have any real effect if the job itself and the work environment do not enhance the workers' self-motivation.

The key, then, is to determine: (1) What needs create a readiness in the worker to act and (2) what rewards the worker values and is willing to put forth extra efforts to obtain.

You can then structure job content and work environment to enhance the workers' self-motivation. You can help your people see how meeting the job goals and standards you have jointly set can help them satisfy personal needs and get the rewards they want. Finally, through the way you interact with your people and your communication with them — such as giving immediate feedback on the desired behavior — you can further enhance the workers' self-motivation.

Now, try your hand at applying your knowledge of motivational theories and approaches by analyzing the motivational problems involved in the Leslie case, Exercise 10-5.

SUMMARY

A major reason that most employees aren't committed to their work is that managers rely more on position power than on personal leadership. The key to exercising leadership is to understand the psychological needs of individual workers and to help them satisfy their needs through their own actions — actions that also contribute to organizational objectives.

Perhaps the most widely used motivational theory is Maslow's hierarchy of needs, which is based on various levels of innate needs. Only when a person has adequately satisfied a lower-level need, will he or she be motivated to satisfy needs at the next level of the hierarchy. Most American workers are motivated to higher performance through expectation of rewards connected with the higher-level needs.

David McClelland suggests that many human needs are learned rather than innate. He discusses three basic categories of socially acquired needs: affiliation, achievement, and power. These motivators have special significance for women. As children we acquire needs (and motives) in the process of solving problems and reducing anxiety. Most women have received the greatest rewards and reduced anxiety most effectively through affiliative behavior. Many women have also received significant rewards for achievement-oriented behavior, but usually only until they reach adolescence. On the other hand, most have experienced censure and anxiety as a result of power-oriented behavior. Since problem-solving behavior is learned, women can make new decisions about the values implied by the behavior and its rewards. They can adopt new behaviors that will enhance their career goals.

Maslow's and McClelland's theories focus on what people want. Expectancy theory focuses on how desire can become action. Before people will act, they must generally expect that they will actually be able to perform the act and that they will get the reward they want as a result.

You can increase your workers' motivation to perform, their job satisfaction, and their acceptance of you as manager by combining expectancy theory with a path-goal approach. Recognize and arouse workers' needs for results over which they have some control. Increase personal payoffs to workers for attaining job goals. Make the path to such payoffs easier to travel by giving effective coaching and direction. Help workers clarify their expectations. Minimize frustrating barriers. Increase opportunities for personal satisfaction dependent on job performance. Use directive leadership when the demands of tasks are ambiguous or when organizational procedures, rules, or policies are unclear. Use supportive leadership when tasks are stressful, frustrating, or dissatisfying. Use achievement-oriented leadership when ambiguous, nonrepetitive tasks are required.

Above all, focus on selecting the right people for the right jobs. In general, look for these matches: affiliation motive—coordinators, integrators, trainers, service people who help others; power motive—upwardly mobile managers; achievement motive—certain staff specialists, commission salespersons, professionals, entrepreneurial types.

Finally, structure the work environment to provide a motivational climate. Provide information needed to perform well. Design the flow of information so that people routinely get information they need in the form they need it. Structure jobs so that dead-end jobs are eliminated, workers' creativity and intelligence are used, and workers can set meaningful, attainable job goals. Provide for decision-making by workers.

Additional Exercises

EXERCISE 10-4: MATCHING NEEDS TO JOBS

Assuming you have a fair understanding of the predominant needs of the people you're placing in various jobs, what type of person would you place in each of the jobs listed below. (Use the categories *Aff* for affiliation, *Ach* for achievement, or *P* for Power.)

_____ 1. *EDP program librarian:* Responsible for maintaining the on-line and off-line libraries of production programs; keeps track of program revisions.
_____ 2. *EDP systems analyst:* Works with users to define data-processing projects or project segments, or to iron out details in specifications.
_____ 3. *Personnel interviewer:* Involved in all phases of screening prospective employees. Processes changes in employee status and conducts exit interviews.

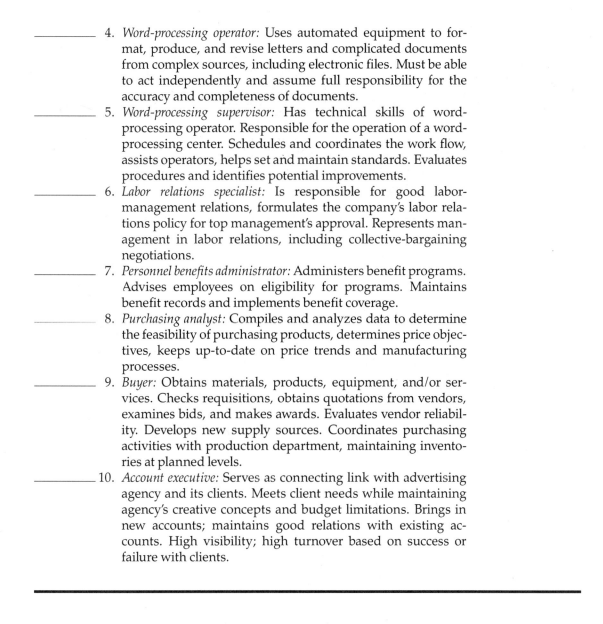

_____ 4. *Word-processing operator:* Uses automated equipment to format, produce, and revise letters and complicated documents from complex sources, including electronic files. Must be able to act independently and assume full responsibility for the accuracy and completeness of documents.

_____ 5. *Word-processing supervisor:* Has technical skills of word-processing operator. Responsible for the operation of a word-processing center. Schedules and coordinates the work flow, assists operators, helps set and maintain standards. Evaluates procedures and identifies potential improvements.

_____ 6. *Labor relations specialist:* Is responsible for good labor-management relations, formulates the company's labor relations policy for top management's approval. Represents management in labor relations, including collective-bargaining negotiations.

_____ 7. *Personnel benefits administrator:* Administers benefit programs. Advises employees on eligibility for programs. Maintains benefit records and implements benefit coverage.

_____ 8. *Purchasing analyst:* Compiles and analyzes data to determine the feasibility of purchasing products, determines price objectives, keeps up-to-date on price trends and manufacturing processes.

_____ 9. *Buyer:* Obtains materials, products, equipment, and/or services. Checks requisitions, obtains quotations from vendors, examines bids, and makes awards. Evaluates vendor reliability. Develops new supply sources. Coordinates purchasing activities with production department, maintaining inventories at planned levels.

_____ 10. *Account executive:* Serves as connecting link with advertising agency and its clients. Meets client needs while maintaining agency's creative concepts and budget limitations. Brings in new accounts; maintains good relations with existing accounts. High visibility; high turnover based on success or failure with clients.

EXERCISE 10-5: THE LESLIE CASE

Lin Leslie was enthusiastic when she first took over as Customer Accounts Supervisor for the SuAnne product line. She enjoyed her contacts with the customers and felt a sense of achievement in seeing that all the accounts were handled properly. Lately, however, her enthusiasm is waning because of a continuing problem with three of her clerical people.

The three clerks—Barbara, Vickie, and Alice—are fresh out of high school and seem to be interested mainly in boys, parties, girlfriends, and clothes. They are rarely absent or late for work, but they don't accomplish much once they are on the job. The three have become good friends in recent months. (They were hired at about the same time last June. Leslie became supervisor about six weeks ago, in August.) The girls usually take coffee and lunch breaks together and frequently stretch their breaks by anywhere from five to fifteen minutes. In addition, their legitimate discussions concerning accounts often get sidetracked onto personal matters, and prolonged personal conversations regularly take place in the hallway and restroom. All this results in a significant decrease of hours actually devoted to their work.

To compound the problem, all three frequently make errors in their work and fail to follow prescribed procedures. They just don't seem to care enough to thoroughly check their work and concentrate on doing it correctly.

1. If you were Lin, how would you handle this situation?

2. What motivational factors do you see in operation?

3. Can Lin do anything to enhance the motivation of the three clerks?

If your instructor has asked you to discuss this case with a group, jot down your own ideas first. If you're working on your own, write down your responses and then compare them with the main points mentioned in the answer key.

REFERENCES

1. Hackman, J. Richard. *Groups That Work (And Those That Don't)*. San Francisco: Jossey-Bass, 1990. This book focuses on creating conditions for effective teamwork.

2. Hackman, J. Richard, and Greg R. Oldham. *Work Redesign*. Reading, Mass.: Addison-Wesley, 1980.

3. House, Robert J. "Path-Goal Theory of Leader Effectiveness." *Administrative Science Quarterly* (September 1971), pp. 321–28.

4. Lawrence, P. R., and J. W. Lorsch. *Developing Organizations: Diagnosis and Action*. Reading, Mass.: Addison-Wesley, 1980. An excellent analysis of the origin of various needs and motives. Helpful for understanding the physiological aspects of motivation.

5. Litwin, George H., and Robert A. Stringer, Jr. *Motivation and Organizational Climate*. Cambridge, Mass.: Harvard University, Graduate School of Business, 1978.

6. Locke, Edwin A. *Goal Setting: A Motivational Technique That Works*. Englewood Cliffs, N.J.: Prentice-Hall, 1984.

7. McClelland, David C. *Motives, Personality, and Society: Selected Papers*. New York: Praeger, 1984.

8. McClelland, David C., and Abigail J. Stewart. *Motivation and Society*. San Francisco: Jossey-Bass, 1982.

9. Maslow, Abraham H. "A Theory of Human Motivation." *Psychological Review,* Vol. 50, No. 4 (July 1943), pp. 370–96.

10. Pallak, Michael S., Robert O. Perloff, and J. Richard Hackman. *Psychology and Work: Productivity, Change, and Employment*. Washington, D.C.: American Psychological Association, 1986.

11. Sherwin, Douglas S. "Strategy for Winning Employee Commitment." *Harvard Business Review on Management*. New York: Harper & Row, 1975.

Chapter Eleven

Problem-Solving and Decision-Making

"Don't agonize. Organize."

Florynce Kennedy

The major barrier to effective problem-solving and decision-making for most women is the myth that women are innately weak in these areas. The truth is that you are likely to have special strengths that will become ever more valuable as you move to higher levels of management that call for broader types of decisions. In this chapter we'll explore the value of such special strengths as practicality, intuition, and preventive or constructive attitudes toward problems.

Specifically, in this chapter you will have the opportunity to learn more about

1. Recognizing the special strengths and weaknesses of women as problem-solvers and decision-makers

2. Developing a decision-making style that enhances your management style

3. Developing executive ESP

4. Developing ways of preventing problems through the use of Murphy's Law

5. Focusing on prevention and rewarding preventive strategies

6. Stressing solutions instead of problems

7. Viewing problems as challenges to be met or as needs to be filled

8. Defining and analyzing problem situations and developing and evaluating alternate solutions to problems

9. Deciding on an action plan, committing to it, and then communicating, selling, implementing, evaluating, and modifying it

10. Deciding when and how to include groups in the problem-solving/decision-making process

---

 Breaking Murphy's Law

"Well, Erika, how goes your strategy for taming the savage sales staff?" asks John Brockfield as he sinks into the chair by her desk.

"Just great, John. I guess there's nothing like a little honesty. Without coming right out and saying it, I got the message across that I realized I had made a false start and wanted to get back on the right foot. They responded like troopers. Now not only are they producing well, but I sense a high level of enthusiasm and team spirit."

"That's the impression I'm getting, too. They respect your savvy and willingness to level with them. They know you want the department to excel, and they feel a lot of support from you in helping them do their part. Congratulations, Erika, I had a feeling you could carry it off."

A few minutes later Erika's assistant, Brian O'Hara, drops in. "Hi, Erika. I got your note about a new assignment. What's up?"

"Brian, you know Jan Arguello in headquarters has asked us to do something brand-new for the Resort/Holiday Fashion Preview this fall."

"Yes, I read a copy of the memo. It's going to be quite a job to play host to all the major buyers in the country."

"But it really gives us a chance to show what we can do, here in Tulsa. All the top headquarters executives will be here along with some of the top buyers in the country. Brian, how would you feel about handling most of the details for this show?"

"Well, I don't know. I would hate for things to go wrong when so much attention is being focused on us."

"You know, Brian, I had the same kind of fears about my first big assignment. Here was my chance to shine — or to blow it. Luckily I had a boss who showed me how to use Murphy's Law."

"Murphy's Law?"

"Yes. You know: 'If something *can* go wrong, it will.'"

"That's just what I'm afraid of, Erika!"

"Ah, but you can use it to *avoid* unpleasant surprises."

"How's that?"

"Well, for example, what are some of the things that *can* go wrong at the Resort/Holiday showing? Things that you fear happening?"

"You mean like some of the samples won't be ready on time? *(Erika nods.)* All the invitations

have the wrong date on them? Or they get lost in the mail? *(Brian warms to the subject.)* Or the hotel doesn't honor room reservations for some of the bigwigs . . . and they have to stay in some inferior, inconvenient place . . . and there's a howling rainstorm the day of the show . . . and taxis are practically impossible to find . . ."

"Enough, enough. You've got the idea. But that's just the first step in using Murphy's Law. The next step is figuring out ways to prevent those problems or to handle them most effectively if they can't be prevented."

"Like giving early deadline dates for completion of samples? *(Erika nods.)* And having alternate back-up samples? Like having two or three people check the master copy of the invitation list to be sure all details are correct . . . and having extra invitations run in case some get lost in the mail . . ."

"That's right. Now start organizing those points into a list. As your plans progress, stop periodically to visualize the entire process of putting on the show, all the necessary steps, and everything that could go wrong at each step. Keep adding to your list. Of course, some possibilities are so remote or the consequences so trivial that you won't need to bother with preventive action. The main idea is to have no unpleasant surprises."

"Say, I'm already learning things from this project."

Later that day, Lin Leslie, Customer Accounts Supervisor, bursts into Erika's office near tears.

"Why, Lin," says Erika, "what's the matter?"

"I'm at my wits' end. This job is just too much for me. People keep pestering me for decisions before I'm ready to make them. Besides that, there's just one crisis after another."

"Sit down, Lin. Now, first, who's pestering you for decisions?"

"Today it seems like everyone! But I guess it's mainly the clerks in my unit. I do my best to motivate them, but they just don't seem to be able to handle problems that come up. I'm not sure whether they're incapable or just don't care."

"So you end up solving most of the problems?"

"That's right, Erika."

"And making all the decisions?"

"It seems that way!"

---

1. As you read this story, what actions and attitudes did you think were especially effective? Why?

2. What impact are those effective actions and attitudes likely to have on others?

3. What actions and attitudes did you think were especially ineffective? Why?

4. What impact are those ineffective actions and attitudes likely to have on others?

VIEWING WOMEN AS LOGICAL PROBLEM-SOLVERS AND CONFIDENT DECISION-MAKERS

Many women have grown up with the assumption that girls are not as good as boys in math, science, sports, and finance — areas that call for logic, strategy, and good problem-solving and decision-making abilities. Therefore, many women feel inferior to men when it comes to logical problem-solving and confident decision-making. When we think of a competent executive who rationally, coolly, and calmly reviews the facts and reaches a decision, most of us picture a man. Lately, however, that picture has been expanded to include the female executive. As a matter of fact, some women have always been excellent problem-solvers and decision-makers. Others can acquire these skills with a little help and encouragement.

You may have to deal with others' stereotyped notions (and perhaps your own?) of the female decision-maker: She is perhaps charm-

ing but somewhat scatterbrained, vague, and emotional. She dithers and worries a great deal about problems and alternative solutions. "She just can't make up her mind." When she finally does reach a decision, she relies on intuition and emotions more than on the facts. She communicates her decisions in rather vague, emotional terms. She seems tentative about the entire matter.

Needless to say, this approach does *not* inspire confidence in those who must carry out the decisions. Finally, she confirms that age-old saying "It's a woman's prerogative to change her mind" by immediately reversing her decision when minor barriers to carrying out the plan arise.

Because of these stereotypes, you must communicate with people about your problem-solving and decision-making activities in as logical, rational, and businesslike a manner as possible. In this chapter we will discuss each step of the process. Some steps call for curiosity, creativity, intuition, the ability to tune in to people and their feelings — all traits that women have been blessed with and have developed to fairly high levels. Take advantage of your strengths in these areas, but watch how you refer to them in communicating with others. Stress the rational, logical, factual aspects of problem-solving and decision-making — as well as your know-how in preventing problems.

Just as important as being able to effectively solve problems and make decisions is knowing how to prevent problems (and the resulting need to make thorny decisions). Therefore, we'll look at some methods of prevention before going on to cures.

PREVENTING PROBLEMS

The best way to avoid problems is to plan and prepare thoroughly. The best way to teach your people to prevent problems is to reward them for doing it. In addition, give them training and information that will let them solve their own problems. Train them to have at least a tentative solution in mind if they must bring a problem to you, so that they won't get in the habit of dumping problems on you. Now for the details of these strategies.

Using Murphy's Law

According to **Murphy's Law:** "If anything *can* go wrong, it *will*." At first glance, this seems to reflect an extremely negative viewpoint. As Erika discovered, however, it can be useful in a very positive way. If you start by anticipating all the things that can go wrong instead of blithely expecting things to occur as planned, you can then make back-up plans to (1) prevent as many problems as possible and (2) handle problems that do occur with minimal disruption.

Let's look at some elaborations on Murphy's Law contributed by Arthur Bloch [3, p. 11]:

Murphy's Second Law: Nothing is as easy as it looks.

Murphy's Third Law: Everything takes longer than you think.

Murphy's Fourth Law: Left to themselves, things tend to go from bad to worse.

Murphy's Fifth Law: If there is a possibility of several things going wrong, the one that will cause the most damage will be the one.

We've all experienced such events, and the only reason for recalling them is to see what lessons we can learn. Ask yourself, "How can my experience of past disasters help me to prevent future problems?" The more important the project, the more thoroughly you'll need to apply Murphy's Law. An awareness of it can help you prevent problems, for example, when (1) you're tackling a certain type of project for the first time, (2) the results of the project will be highly visible and will affect your reputation, or (3) the assignment is a pet project of one of your bosses.

After you've planned the project, ask yourself some probing questions: Suppose Jones doesn't show up that day? What if Smith is late? What will we do if the equipment isn't available? Or breaks down? What if a key person didn't get my memo? Or forgets to look at her calendar? What if twice as many people show up as I expect? Half as many? Suppose the printer doesn't get the handouts done in time?

Your list of questions will depend on your particular project. Develop your own questions by mentally living through the implementation of your project step by step. Each step of the way visualize all the problems that could possibly arise. Develop a plan for either preventing or handling each one. Make this your motto: "No Surprises!"

Developing a Preventive Attitude

Constructively applying Murphy's Law is only one facet of avoiding problems. Another is making sure the right people are aware of the thought, expertise, and effort you put into managing your project so smoothly. To be really successful, one must overcome Zimmerman's Law of Complaints [3, p. 12]: "Nobody notices when things go right."

Who gets the most favorable attention in your company? The person who runs her operation quietly and smoothly? Or the person who is always having to cope with crises and somehow "pulls her people through them to go on to bigger and better things?" The manager who trains her people to prevent problems and make correct decisions? Or the manager who is "indispensable" and is always rushing in to rescue her people from messes? The person who works at a steady, unhurried pace? Or the person who is always getting "snowed under" (but who also has frequent slack periods)? Ask yourself, "What are the payoffs for managers and for workers in my company for preventing problems and crises?" It may be that managers and workers who *cope* with problems and crises are given more favorable attention than those who *prevent* them. People tend to behave in ways that get them favorable attention. You can help break such a cycle in your company.

To get the payoffs you deserve for preventing problems, you must be sure your bosses know about and understand what you are doing. By the same token, you need to be especially alert in order to give your team members more favorable attention when they prevent problems than when they merely cope with them. Let your people know what's important to you by training them to prevent problems and by giving them the information and guidelines they need for making decisions that are appropriate to their job responsibilities and their career potential.

Training Solutions-Oriented Workers

When problems *do* arise, you can minimize their burden to you or your boss by thinking in terms of solutions. Whenever possible, insist that your people bring you solutions along with the problems. If they keep dumping problems in your lap, don't automatically accept each problem and start trying to solve it.

If the decision can be postponed, ask the person to come back later with a list of all the possible solutions she or he can think of, along with the advantages and disadvantages of each. Ask for a ranking of the solutions according to their chances of success. If possible give the worker time to sleep on it and the next day or so go over the list and help her or him analyze the advantages and disadvantages of each solution.

If action is needed immediately, sit down with the worker and try to get her or him to come up with at least one possible solution. Ask the worker to identify the advantages and disadvantages of any proposed solutions and to recommend one over the others. Then give your opinion and jointly come to a decision. By

taking people step by step through the same process you use to make effective decisions, you help train them to make decisions on their own.

On the other hand, at times you will need further information, expertise, or authority from *your* boss to solve a problem. Even when you lack vital information, try to show your boss that you are thinking in terms of a solution rather than merely dumping a problem in her or his lap. Try to come up with some ideas or solutions, even if you feel they are not the greatest. Present your ideas or solutions along with your thoughts and feelings about them.

Preventing Problems Through Participative Decision-Making

There are many advantages to training your people to solve problems and to make appropriate decisions. Not only can you establish a preventive attitude, but you can also provide a more motivating work environment for most people. In Chapter 10 we briefly discussed some of the benefits of providing subordinates with the information and guidelines they need to make the decisions necessary to carry out their job responsibilities. In Chapter 9 we discussed participative versus authoritarian management. The more that managers tend toward Theory Y, concern for people, and therefore a participative approach, the greater is the area of freedom for their people to solve problems and make decisions, as indicated in Figure 11-1. The most extreme example of managerial control and authority is the leader who makes decisions unilaterally. At the opposite extreme is the leader who establishes regular decision-making limits for teammates so that they have maximum freedom to make their own decisions and to participate in higher-level decisions.

You must use your own judgment about the degree of freedom each worker should have in making decisions in various situations. Sometimes crises do arise even with the best of plan-

FIGURE 11-1: Extent of Participation in Decision-Making

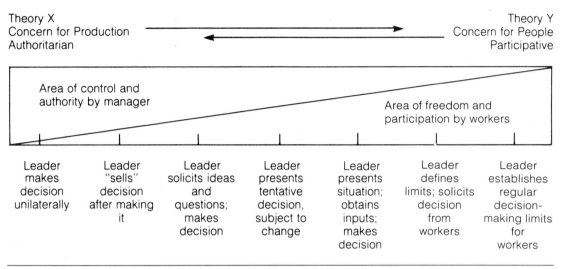

Adapted from the work of Robert Tannenbaum and Warren H. Schmidt.

ning, and it may be necessary for you to take charge and make timely, unilateral decisions. Moreover, some people need more training, experience, support, and encouragement than others before they are ready for increased decision-making freedom. If you keep these kinds of exceptions in mind, *as a general rule the more decision-making responsibilities you can train your people to handle, the more successful your group is likely to be.*

FROM WOMAN'S INTUITION TO EXECUTIVE ESP

The higher the executive level, the more likely the leader is to use intuition or extrasensory perception (ESP). After conducting experiments for ten years, two professors at the University of Pittsburgh's School of Engineering established this fact [5]. Then a *Harvard Business Review* survey of business managers and executives confirmed it [8]. Over 100 U.S. universities offer courses in parapsychology, including Princeton and Duke, and many professors who

teach these courses are studying executive ESP. Some of the reputable private research institutions doing research on leadership and ESP are SRI International in Menlo Park, California, The Mobius Society in Los Angeles, McDonnell Laboratory for Psychical Research in St. Louis, and the Institute of Noetic Sciences in Sausalito, California.

A nationwide survey of 2,000 business, government, and academic leaders was conducted in 1982 by Professor Weston Agor, University of Texas at El Paso [8]. He concluded that top-level leaders rely more on intuition than do lower-level managers. Moreover, women consistently scored higher than men in intuitive ability, and Asian managers scored higher than Westerners. The women were more reluctant to admit using intuition, however, fearing that it would be viewed as a sign of weakness. Agor did a follow-up study of the executives who scored in the top 10 percent in intuitive ability. Virtually all said they use intuition in making the most important decisions, though many said they do not reveal this fact to their colleagues.

Jo Durden-Smith, author of *Sex and the Brain*, says, "Scientists have found more connecting nerve fibers between the two hemispheres in women's brains than in men's" [6]. She says this could be why women are often better at skills that involve both hemispheres, such as reading, which requires the ability to translate visual symbols (right brain) into language (left brain). This may also explain why men have more difficulty talking (left brain) about their emotions (right brain), and why women have greater peripheral awareness and pay more attention to detail. Studies done in business settings reveal that men and women are equally efficient at recalling the verbal content of a conversation, but women are much better at remembering the person's physical appearance and the features of the room they were in. Women also recall more emotional information and personal impressions than men. Durden-Smith notes that men tend to say that emotional information is irrelevant, but this is not always so. "If a client seems unhappy, an astute businessperson ought to find out why" [6].

Here are a few suggestions for developing your executive ESP.

Set the Stage for ESP

- If it's a decision you're working on, determine how important a role intuition should play. Leaders typically rely most on intuition for decisions entailing a high degree of risk or uncertainty, and problems with little precedent but with several feasible solutions.

- Concentrate on what is unique about the problem.

- Be aware of the gaps in your knowledge and experience.

- Do your homework. Develop skills, get facts, build your experience bank.

- Avoid becoming overloaded with information. When the conscious mind receives too much data, it interferes with the subconscious mind. Then even if you get a flash of insight, the rational system is likely to destroy the intuitive component.

- Develop empathy. This opens up a path to other people's minds, enabling you to better read their thoughts, a key to intuitive data-gathering.

Let the Information Incubate in Your Mind

- Grab one corner of the problem and begin to unravel it.

- Use a process for relaxing, concentrating, visualizing, and letting go. While deeply relaxed, concentrate on your end goals in this situation, not on what you are doing to reach those goals. Then concentrate on *being* in the present moment, *allowing* your mind the freedom to let ideas float in and out. At this stage, direct assaults on the problem or new idea may smother the intuitive process. Visualize your end goals on a regular basis, allowing yourself to have them in the present moment, then letting go of any desperate need to achieve them.

- Be receptive. To open up a path to your intuition, be open, have faith, and believe that a flash of inspiration may come at any moment. Watch for a sense of being "light-bodied." Let it work rather than make it work.

- Be patient. New ideas are like flowers, so let the first tender shoots take shape before trying to consciously grasp what they are. Playing with the idea prematurely may prevent it from budding, but you must remain aware of its development so as not to neglect it.

- Avoid analysis paralysis. The analytic approach of breaking ideas down into components drives out intuition. It imposes order and structure, both enemies of creative thinking. Instead, use your imagination.

- Allow uncertainty. Get accustomed to proceeding with an incomplete picture.

- Be open and aware of *glimmers* of a new idea — often soft, subtle little whispers.

- Make loose connections between seemingly unrelated ideas, things, or problems. (Solving one problem often helps solve another.)

Be Open to the Light — Glimmers and Flashes

- Turn your attention to other matters, but keep listening until something clicks and you feel the right answer; keep watching till you sense a glimmer or flash.

- Free yourself from the way of thinking held by your associates and friends or the leaders in the field. Just because "we tried that before and it didn't work" doesn't mean it can't work now. Master the art of the fresh, clean look at old information. Give your mind a free rein and allow it to play. Most major new discoveries are made from people outside the field.

- Try imaginative lateral leaps and soaring flights of imagination instead of step-by-step thinking.

- Consider looking for poetry and analogies that lead to insight. Elizabeth Sewell wrote, "The mind knows in poems, a little more than it knows it knows. A poem will often tell the thinking mind where to think next." Analogies stir new ideas and concepts, especially those that use concrete images rather than abstractions. These images can trigger other concrete images and help ideas flow spontaneously.

- Tune in to a sense of timing. When is the right moment to go forward? One person

described timing in business this way: "You sort of ratchet yourself along by having a picture of the future that gradually changes as you learn more facts and add more pieces to it."

- Be willing to take a risk with a new idea or approach. Overcome fear of failure. Ask "What's the worst that could happen?" Can you become comfortable with that?

- Notice which ideas become stronger.

- Watch for a sense of "homing in" on an idea, solution, other.

- Look for the types of physical, emotional, and mental clues that persons identified as high in executive ESP report:
  * A growing harmony in the pit of the stomach
  * A feeling of total harmony
  * A total sense of commitment
  * A burst of enthusiasm and energy
  * A thought that is like a bolt of lightning or sudden flash that this is the solution

Verify Whether the Hunch Will Work

- Will your idea work? Check the facts. Does information exist that could eliminate some of the uncertainty?

- Discuss the idea with people you trust. Verbalizing it will help you develop it and test its merits.

- Daydream. Play over the new idea in your mind's eye, considering the many different ways to go forward and the barriers you might encounter along each path. Look for ways around them so you won't become locked in a death struggle with an unworkable solution.

- Conduct stray-bullet drills to identify all the unlikely bad news and obstacles that might shoot down implementation of a new idea.

- Listen to the rumblings from your team; sense the mood of your organization and tap into the collective wisdom of the rest of the employees.

- Test your idea. Figure out what you can and should try on an experimental basis, to minimize risk. Be open to feedback.

- Be prepared to back off if signs indicate that your initial hunch was flawed.

- Turn around adversity. Look to your intuition for protective clues about what can go wrong, so you can move around obstacles and avert disaster.

- Learn to recognize your intuitive clues. You can learn to distinguish between intuition and wishful thinking by reviewing your processes in light of outcomes. If your hunch turns out to be valid, you can usually chalk it up to intuition. After each outcome, review the mental, emotional, and physical clues you relied on. This will help you establish which ones are valid, for future reference.

AN OVERVIEW OF THE PROBLEM-SOLVING/DECISION-MAKING PROCESS

So far our discussion has focused more on attitudes toward problems and their prevention than on the actual process of solving problems and making decisions. Perhaps the clearest way to view the problem-solving/decision-making process is to divide it arbitrarily into three major phases: (1) problem-solving, (2) decision-making, and (3) implementing (see Exhibit 11-1). Include the team in as many phases and steps as possible.

Let's look at each phase in detail.

EXHIBIT 11-1: The Problem-Solving/Decision-Making Process

1. Becoming aware of the problem
2. Defining the root of the problem rather than its symptoms or results
3. Gathering information and consulting people who will be affected by the decision or have valuable information
4. Analyzing the information and formulating possible solutions

⎤ Problem-Solving

5. Weighing possible solutions (alternative courses of action)
6. Selecting what appears to be the best course of action
7. Making a commitment to the success of the action plan

⎤ Decision-Making

8. Communicating and selling the decision to those who will be involved in it
9. Directing the implementation of the plan
10. Evaluating the results of the action plan
11. Modifying the action plan in response to new situations and information

⎤ Implementing

Each step should be taken separately and in proper sequence. The extent of participation by subordinates in each step will vary. The maximum feasible participation will give the greatest payoffs in motivation and productivity.

THE PROBLEM-SOLVING PHASE

We've discussed the desirability of welcoming constructive criticism about work performance in your area of responsibility and of evaluating that criticism objectively and acting on it accordingly. One advantage of such openness is that it allows you to become aware of problems at an early stage of their development. Then you can analyze the problem to determine if it's merely a symptom of a deeper problem. Once you have defined the root problem, the best approach is to consult people who have valuable information about the problem and its possible solution and people who will be affected by the final solution you decide on. After you gather the information you need to formulate possible solutions; analyze it carefully. See how many workable solutions you can put together. This problem-solving approach is outlined in Exhibit 11-1 as the first four steps of the problem-solving/decision-making process. Let's examine each step in detail.

Becoming Aware of the Problem

Managers typically deal with two distinct types of problems: (1) problems in implementing currently accepted policies, procedures, and approaches to achieving company, unit, or individual job objectives, and (2) problems in developing new, improved approaches to achieving objectives — approaches that might result in the ability to set completely new and different kinds of objectives.

Managers deal most often with problems of the first type. This category includes small, everyday problems such as maintaining workers' productivity, as well as occasional major problems such as dealing with a sudden, unexplained decrease in company sales. You need to be alert to problems of both types, however. If you're aware of how well objectives are being accomplished and of new and better ways of doing things, you're likely to recognize quickly the problems that need attention.

Managers who do not dread dealing with problems are likely to be more open to recognizing and facing them. Therefore, it helps to view each problem as a need to be filled or as a challenge to be met. You can learn, grow, and profit from filling needs and meeting challenges. If you want to earn a reputation as a truly productive problem-solver — not just someone who puts out fires that should have been prevented in the first place — keep an open mind, be curious and inquisitive, and keep asking key, probing questions, both of yourself and of others.

Defining the Root of the Problem Rather Than Its Symptoms

Once you become aware of a problem, don't waste your time gathering information about it until you've satisfied yourself that it is not merely a symptom of a deeper problem. First ask, "Who is responsible and who has authority in this situation?" Is it really your baby? If so, be sure to include in the problem-solving process the people who have some responsibility and authority for solving the problem and reaching the decision. Then try to get at the root of the problem by asking certain questions in the sequence shown in Exhibit 11-2.

This process of problem definition is similar to the one described in Chapter 3 for setting objectives and separately listing activities that can help you achieve those objectives. By keeping activities or approaches separate from objectives or purposes, you may delve deeper into the reasons behind your objective and realize that there are many more ways to achieve what you want than you originally thought. You may even redefine your objective. (You may want to look at the personal objectives you set in Chapter 3. Use the process shown here to see

EXHIBIT 11-2: Finding the Root of the Problem

Problem: What is the problem?

Purpose: What do you want to achieve in this situation? What is the purpose of solving this problem?

Why: Why do you want to accomplish this purpose?

Possible approaches: What approaches could accomplish this purpose?

Best approach: All things being equal, which approach will let you accomplish your purpose in the most effective way?

Redefine purpose: Having worked through the preceding steps, do you think the purpose needs to be modified?

Redefine problem: Do you think the problem needs to be redefined?

Here is an example of the use of this method to define a problem.

Problem: Vince Dietz, head of the Accounting Department, has been by-passing Erika and negotiating with Jack Ames, one of the customer accounts specialists, to developing working agreements between the Sales and Accounting Departments.

Purpose: To prevent Jack Ames from taking over in areas where Erika should be taking the lead.

Why: To maintain Erika's authority and control over her department.

Possible approaches: (1) Talk with Dietz about procedures he should follow when he wants to negotiate agreements with the Sales Department. (2) Arrange a joint meeting with Dietz, Ames, and the General Manager to reach an understanding about procedures. (3) Instruct Ames to refer Dietz to Erika in the future. (4) Ask the General Manager to instruct both Dietz and Ames to make Erika a key player in any discussions that might lead to a new working agreement.

Best approach: Erika decides her best initial approach is number 2, arranging a joint meeting.

Redefine purpose: In reviewing the possible approaches, and in thinking about the outcomes, Erika decides she needs to redefine her original purpose, "preventing Ames from taking over in areas where she should be supervising . . . in order for her to maintain authority and control." Erika decides that this approach comes from a lack of self-confidence on her part. She believes that Dietz probably has difficulty accepting women in positions of authority and so is by-passing her to negotiate with a male member of her work team. She can choose to focus on (1) maintaining her position of authority or (2) arriving at what is best for both departments and the organization. She decides on the latter focus as a more powerful approach.

New purpose: To establish an understanding among all the parties about the process of negotiating and establishing new work agreements between departments.

New problem: Including the department heads (Erika) in establishing any important new working agreements that affect their departments.

---

whether any of them should be redefined. You can also apply it to planning objectives, which are discussed in Chapter 12.)

Gathering Information and Consulting People

Once you have clearly defined the problem, the next step is to gather information in order to identify, explore, and develop as many workable alternatives as possible.

Pinpointing Information Sources You need as many facts and knowledgeable opinions as you can afford to gather. *Decisions can be no better than the information they are based on. However, you must weigh the cost and time required to gather that information against its value in contributing toward a better decision.* How much potential profit and cost is involved in a decision? Obviously, you would want to spend more time and money gathering information to select a new computer system, for example, than to se-

EXHIBIT 11-3: Checklist of Information Sources

Publications of all types	Personnel records:
Company files, newsletters, magazines, brochures	Staff selection, retention, and promotion records
Knowledgeable people in your company and other companies	Job descriptions, standards, and performance records
Other experts in the field	Absentee and employee turnover figures
Interviews and conversations	Union agreements
Library reference files	Annual reports to stockholders
Computer files	Press clippings
Company policy or procedures manuals	Universities and other institutions — the appropriate department

lect a new brand of staplers. Set appropriate time limits, then make a list of the most likely sources of the information you'll need, using Exhibit 11-3 for ideas.

Being Objective Be sure you get the whole picture — not just the part you *want* to see. If you are in doubt about any important facts, double-check or cross-check. Look for another source, a person who has no personal involvement in the situation. For example, people in the Sales Department may exaggerate sales figures; people in the Production Department may inflate production figures and minimize errors and rejects. Double-check their reports by asking people outside their departments for the same information.

Keep asking questions until you're satisfied you have a fairly accurate picture of the situation. List appropriate questions, using those shown in Exhibit 11-4 for ideas.

Taking a Survey This is often one of the best ways to get information. Your survey may include people who have handled similar problems, experts in a particular field, or the people who will be affected by the decision you make in this situation. Get out and talk with these people; watch the people who will be affected as they go about their jobs. Experience for yourself the problems involved and people's

responses to them. Give these firsthand impressions time to knock around in the conscious and subconscious areas of your mind. They can lead to flashes of insight and later help you put the pieces of the puzzle together.

Try brainstorming (which we'll discuss later in this chapter). This technique can be effective in the fact-gathering phase. Ask a person or a group to brainstorm facts that might be relevant to solving the problem. You can also use brainstorming to get advice and opinions. Sometimes the seemingly least likely fact or bit of advice turns out to be a key to solving a problem.

It's sometimes a good idea to give people time to think about the questions you are asking and then follow up later. People will often come up with more and better ideas and comments after they have mulled a question over for a while. Treat these inputs with respect and give immediate positive reinforcement for all sincere suggestions, advice, and information. Be careful not to commit yourself to following a suggestion or idea too soon, however. Give yourself time to collect all the facts you must have and to analyze and weigh them.

It's also wise to test people's reactions to your ideas about the situation by asking them what they think. But avoid giving the impression that you've already made the decision and just want support for it.

EXHIBIT 11-4: Fact-Finding Questions

1. How is the problem situation similar to other situations? Different from others?
2. How long has this situation been in existence?
3. How did it get started?
4. What is its history?
5. What are the outstanding developments?
6. What are the major advantages of the current situation? The major disadvantages?
7. What are the major functions to be performed in this situation?
8. What functions are being neglected?
9. What is the situation related to, both in the past and currently?
10. What are the latest developments in the field that are relevant?
11. Are there opposing opinions?
12. What does the future appear to hold?
13. What further avenues should be investigated?

Consulting People This is perhaps the most important factor in the problem-solving/decision-making process. It gives you the best chance to get essential information and to get people involved. This suggestion is worth framing: *Before you make a decision, check out the facts you have gathered and ask for the viewpoints, advice, and information of the people who will be affected by the decision.*

You'll nearly always find there is something important you haven't grasped. Often you've missed important facts or gotten them wrong. By involving people, of course, you also make your job easier when you get to the later step of selling or communicating the plan. At the same time, you lay the groundwork for effectively implementing the plan. When people have been involved in making a decision, they're more likely to be cooperative, and even enthusiastic, about carrying it out than if it's handed down to them from "on high."

Analyzing Information for Possible Solutions

Once you have the necessary facts, your next step is to study them, analyze them, and use them to formulate creative alternate solutions.

Don't evaluate at this stage. Save that for the next step.

Get into a Creative Mood Creativity is not some mystical quality enjoyed by only a few special people. All of us are capable of creative thinking and problem-solving. The key is to keep an open mind and a flexible attitude. You can allow your natural creativity to come forth by encouraging certain tendencies that, to some degree, we all have:

An open mind: Willingness to change viewpoints and approaches and to try new things and experiences

Curiosity: A spirit of inquiry, a realization that there is much to learn, a keen enjoyment of learning

Ability to concentrate: An interest in delving below the surface of situations, willingness to apply energy and effort to solve problems, an enjoyment of working on complex problems, willingness to spend considerable time alone thinking

Persistence: Willingness to keep working on a problem until a satisfactory solution is found, patience in working out solutions

EXHIBIT 11-5: Special Analytical Techniques

Experiments and pilot projects	Program Evaluation and Review Technique (PERT)
Test runs	Critical Path Method (CPM)
Decision matrix	Force Field Analysis
Model making	Other types of flow charts and structured analytical procedures
Algorithms and decision trees	
Problem analysis and synthesis	Other quantitative and statistical techniques
	Other computer-based techniques

Confidence: Willingness to risk being ridiculed by others for unconventional ideas and approaches, optimism and enthusiasm about finding and implementing solutions to problems

Cooperation: An ability to work productively with others to define problems, formulate solutions, and implement action plans; flexibility in adapting to the realities of situations.

Review Your Purpose and All the Facts   Why do you want to solve this problem? What is the major goal you want to achieve? What facts are relevant? Organize them in a way that is meaningful to you so that you have them clearly in mind.

Analyze the Information   Ask yourself what ideas, facts, or things can be put together or combined; changed, modified, or rearranged; substituted for something else. What items can be magnified, increased, made larger (advantages or assets); minimized, reduced, made smaller (disadvantages or faults); reversed, handled in exactly the opposite way; broken down into smaller parts and then each segment dealt with? Can any ideas or items be applied to similar problems or products? Can any be simplified, removed, or added?

Questions like these can spur your creative thinking. Another technique is to list advantages and disadvantages of the present situation or system. This may help you form a better picture in your mind of what the ideal solution should include.

Consider role-playing at this stage, either in your head or with another person. This can be especially effective when the cooperation of two or more factions is required. Pretend you are a key member of one faction. Discuss the current situation and each alternate solution from that viewpoint. Then take the role of a key member of the other faction and do the same thing. Get a debate going. Play the Devil's advocate. This technique can help you identify needs and concerns that pertain to the problem. As you answer the needs with suggestions to fulfill them, you will stimulate new ideas for a solution.

Investigate other special analytical techniques that might throw light on alternate solutions. You'll have a chance to review three of them (Program Evaluation Review Technique, Critical Path Method, and Force Field Analysis) later in this chapter. Exhibit 11-5 lists these and some other types you might want to investigate on your own.

Formulate as Many Alternate Solutions as Possible   Don't stop when you have only one or two plausible solutions. Keep asking, "What else might work?" One of the most common barriers to effective problem-solving is putting unnecessary limitations on the number and variety of alternate action plans. Remember, at this stage *don't evaluate* the solutions that pop into your mind.

Write Down Alternate Solutions   Each time a solution occurs to you, no matter how wild or far-out, write it down. Schedule definite times to work on the problem, but be ready to record ideas any time they occur — even in the middle of the night. Try to have note pads on hand in strategic spots.

Verbalize Possible Solutions   After you've had time to analyze the facts and think about alternate solutions, discuss them with people. Strangely enough, you may find yourself describing an action plan you weren't even aware you had formulated until you started talking! Or you may find that you've selected one without being aware of it. The act of discussing the problem and its possible solutions in a relaxed atmosphere at this point may help all the pieces fall into place for you.

Following these steps should result in a top-notch list of alternate solutions. Next you're ready to make a decision.

THE DECISION-MAKING PHASE

Making decisions involves letting the alternate solutions "simmer" for a while, then weighing them, and finally selecting one. In this section we will examine specific techniques you can use for doing this, and pitfalls you'll want to avoid.

Weighing Possible Solutions

Some of the techniques for analyzing the information may be appropriate for evaluating the effectiveness of alternate solutions before you decide to adopt one of them.

Relax and Forget the Problem for a While   Once you have formulated as many alternate solutions or action plans as possible, shelve the whole project for a few hours, days, or weeks, depending on the magnitude of the problem and your time targets. If you choose a course of action too soon, you'll be overlooking one of your major assets — your wonderful brain and its ability to process information at a subconscious level. Some people call this waiting time the "incubation period." Others say it is a "simmering" process that leads to illumination, insight, regeneration, and the crystallization of ideas.

Turn your mind to other activities and forget the problem as completely as possible. If it's a major creative project, plan some activities or pastimes that are especially relaxing and pleasant to you. At least try to get a good night's sleep before you make your selection. If you have a tight time schedule, get it clearly in mind, tell yourself that you will come up with the best solution on time, then forget it. Most people find that the best solution will indeed pop into their minds unexpectedly and within the time target they specified.

The optimal simmering time needed for different types of projects varies for each person. Pay attention to your timing needs by noting the time-lag between when you shelve a problem and when you get a flash of insight or inspiration about how to handle it. The time-lag is *not* wasted time, especially if you are productively working on other matters. Once you get back to the problem after the proper simmering period, you'll come up with a far better action plan in a fraction of the time it would have taken if you had hurried into that phase too soon.

Weigh the Alternatives   There are several evaluative techniques that will let you weigh alternatives.

1. *List the goals and* **criteria** *for making the decision*. Criteria are specifications of the quality a good solution would have. They help distinguish between good and bad alternatives. They are the standards a solution must meet to be acceptable. How well does each alternative measure up? Exhibit 11-6 shows a **criteria matrix** for accomplishing this.

EXHIBIT 11-6: Criteria Matrix for Weighing Alternatives

Step 1. Determine the criteria for making the decision. List them across the top of the matrix, one criterion per column.

Step 2. Determine what alternatives are available. List them vertically below the "alternative" heading.

Step 3. Rate each alternative on how well it meets each criterion. Use either "yes" and "no" or a scale of 1 through 5 for rating.

Step 4. Find the total number of "yes" responses or the sum total for each alternative by adding across.

Step 5. Rank each alternative from highest to lowest.

Numerical System for Rating Each Alternative

5 = Highest Rating
4 = Good
3 = Fair to Middling
2 = Poor
1 = Lowest Rating

Alternative Word Processors	Criteria			Total for Each Alternative	Rank of Each Alternative
	1. Less Than $10,000	2. Will Work Well for at Least 5 Years	3. Good Editing and Storage Functions		
CBX Magtape	1	5	4	10	1
Vymax Display	2	2	3	9	2
Ramses Memory	2	2	1	5	4
Xerxes Model Z	4	1	1	6	3

The matrix is a table in which the alternative actions, solutions, or selections are listed vertically as line headings. The major criteria for measuring each alternative are listed horizontally as column headings. The criteria matrix allows you to organize and display all the alternatives and criteria related to a decision. Within the matrix, you record your evaluation of how well each alternative meets each of the criteria by assigning each evaluation a number. You then total the numerical ratings for each alternative and rank them accordingly. You should not decide automatically that the top-ranking alternative is the one to select because you'll need to weigh other factors too. But you can clarify complex situations and weigh alternatives with greater objectivity when you use the criteria matrix as a selection tool.

The criteria matrix shown in Exhibit 11-6 was developed by a group of workers who met with their manager to solve a written communications problem. They decided that the goal was to improve efficiency and timeliness of written communications through purchasing word processors. They established three criteria for selection of the equipment: The unit must (1) cost less than $10,000, (2) stay relatively free of repairs for at least five years, and (3) have storage and editing functions to meet their needs.

Four types of word processors appeared likely to meet the criteria—CBX Magtape, Vymax Display, Ramses Memory, and Xerxes Model Z. The workers rated each one according to how well it measured up to their criteria and ranked each accordingly. They found CBX and Vymax to be the superior

EXHIBIT 11-7: Factors to Consider When Weighing Alternatives and Risks

Costs, expenses, potential profits	Impact on company objectives and policies
Available resources	Attitudes and reactions of the people involved
Budgets	Long-range consequences
Trained staff or workers	New problems that the action plan may create
Tools and equipment	Union contracts and relationships
Facilities	Morality and legality
Efforts involved	

choices. Now they can concentrate on comparing these two alternatives.

In some cases, of course, one alternative emerges as the best choice and the decision can be made immediately. To simplify our example, we assumed that all criteria were of equal importance. In actual practice, however, the criteria can be weighted. In the example shown in Exhibit 11-6, if criterion 3, editing and storage functions, were considered twice as important as the other two criteria, you would place "× 2" above that column and multiply each number in the column by 2. The ratings for how well the four alternatives met criterion 3 would then be 8, 6, 2, and 2, respectively, instead of 4, 3, 1, and 1. The total for each alternative would be 14, 12, 6, and 7 instead of 10, 9, 5, and 6. Although the rank of each alternative wouldn't change in this instance, the degree of difference between the top two and bottom two alternatives is increased.

2. *List all events that are likely to occur in the future.* Include all events that might affect the action plan. Try to categorize events that have a cause-and-effect relationship or are related in some other meaningful way (see Exhibit 11-7). Which action plan would be best for each set of events?

This process can help you clarify how well each action plan fits with various types of future developments and circumstances. It can help you weigh the risks involved in adopting each action plan.

3. *List all possible consequences of each plan.* Project yourself into the future and visualize the plan in action. Try to foresee consequences and list them.

4. *Compare* **opportunity values** *of alternate action plans.* Keep in mind that when you select one plan you commit resources that would otherwise be available to take advantage of alternate or unforeseen opportunities. Try to estimate the potential value of the opportunities you'll be forced to pass up. Are the payoffs from your selected action plan worth it? Ask yourself and others some key questions: What would happen if we didn't do anything about this problem? What risks are involved in each plan? What payoffs are probable from each? What resources will we need for each? What limitations will be necessary for each? What tradeoffs are practical between the time and money invested and the possible payoffs for each plan? What specific conditions require specific actions?

Keep the timing factor in mind. Although you don't want to jump to the commitment phase too soon, you must be aware of the consequences of postponing the decision. Sometimes putting it off is disastrous. At other times postponing can be a blessing because it allows you to take advantage of new developments, new information, and—perhaps most important—new insights and ideas that occur to you or your people.

5. *List the advantages and disadvantages of each action plan.* Include the people who will be involved, if possible. Make your list as complete as you can.

6. *Clarify how each action plan will be carried out.* Answer these questions: Who will be responsible for each phase? How will they carry it out? What will they do? When will they do it? Where will they do it?

   Considering these questions can help you select an action plan that can be carried out. The people who will be responsible for carrying out the action plan must be capable of doing so. Assess the strengths and weaknesses of your people.

   The action plan must also be acceptable to the people who will carry it out. You must be sure you will have adequate resources to implement your plan. In addition, ask yourself how flexible each action plan is and how much it will cost in money, time, and effort to change the plan if new developments and conditions call for change.

7. *Review your purpose in solving this problem.* Remember what you wanted to achieve in this situation. Which action plan is most likely to lead to the achievement of those objectives?

Selecting the Best Course of Action

The next step is to choose the option that best meets the objectives and priorities of the situation. If you have followed the step-by-step process and suggestions given here, the best solution will probably become fairly obvious. Occasionally, one action plan stands out as far superior to any others. In most situations, however, you will have to think in terms of *degrees* of effectiveness rather than right versus wrong solutions. Since you will rarely find a perfect solution, you will have to be willing to take calculated risks.

Holding out for the perfect solution is only one of the decision-making traps to beware of. We'll review typical traps poor decision-makers get caught in, as well as suggestions for making especially difficult decisions.

Poor Decision-Makers   Many of the common decision-making traps managers fall into occur at the selection stage. Here are some common traps, adapted for the woman manager.

The *decisionless decider* keeps putting off decisions without proper regard to the optimal timing for making decisions. She overlooks the fact that making *no* decision is actually deciding to go along with the status quo, at least for the time being.

The *priority fumbler* is not clear about objectives and priorities, fails to put first things first, and overlooks the fact that a short-range decision may have a long-range impact.

The *detail person*, as she moves up, keeps making detailed decisions for her workers instead of focusing on higher-level decisions.

The *wheel-oiler* avoids making decisions whenever possible. She makes decisions only when people complain loudly and long enough. She "oils the squeaky wheel" by attempting to solve the problem they are complaining about. This means that the problems that most need solving may be neglected. Only problems considered important by the loudest, most aggressive people in the company may be addressed.

The *perfectionist* keeps waiting for the perfect solution. She thinks in terms of right and wrong solutions rather than degrees of effectiveness. She may become a facts junkie, going overboard in gathering more and more facts before making a decision. She overlooks the high cost, the time factor, and the possible loss of opportunity while she is looking for a riskless decision. She tries to substitute facts for her own good judgment.

The *know-it-all* mistakenly thinks she knows enough about the situation to make a decision without investigating or consulting people. She is "sensitive to the situation" or "has a feel for the problem" and doesn't want to be bothered with the facts.

The *mare with blinders* is so concerned with her bailiwick that she doesn't see the big picture. She therefore neglects to consider all the dimensions of the problem and its impact on others outside her department. She overlooks both positive and negative factors that should affect her decision.

The *yesteryear expert* doesn't take into consideration the constantly changing conditions that affect business decisions. She made some effective decisions in the past, and she keeps looking back to those successes rather than looking forward to current and future conditions.

The *face-saver* becomes ego-involved in her decisions and thinks in terms of right versus wrong decisions. If she makes a poor decision, she clings to it like a survivor clinging to a sinking ship. She may surround herself with "yes people" who keep telling her that she is right.

The *ball-dropper* makes a good decision and then drops the ball by not following through by effectively communicating and selling the decision to those who will be affected by it. She therefore fails to properly implement her plan.

Do you recognize any of these characters? We've all seen people who have fallen into one or more of these traps. Of course, *you* can avoid these decision traps by following the suggestions given in this chapter.

Now evaluate your own decision-making approach by completing Exercise 11-1. Then compare it with those of typical Chief Executive Officers and successful entrepreneurs by checking the decision-making profile shown in the answer key.

Difficult Decisions In some situations the best solution is so difficult to determine that you will have to rely heavily on your own judgment in reaching a decision. You probably have an edge over your male peers here since judgment involves intuition.

When you use your intuition effectively, you're in good company. Recent research indicates that the higher a manager goes in an organization, the more she or he relies on soft data and intuition in making decisions. Most top-level decisions involve broad policy matters rather than operational details, depend on future events, and have such general implications that managers cannot depend on hard facts and figures alone in reaching them. Although effective executives certainly won't ignore relevant facts and figures, they must also take into consideration the feelings and opinions of other people, information gleaned from the company grapevine, and their own feelings and intuition.

Some people are startled to discover that top executives depend on intuition so much. It's not surprising to others who believe that intuition is actually the result of a process of analyzing and synthesizing information and experiences that are stored in the brain's memory — and doing so at lightning-fast speeds — at a subconscious level. In other words, intuition may be a short cut to problem-solving and decision-making, not a completely different process. If this is true, top-level executives who rely on intuition are actually relying on the vast knowledge, information, and experience stored in their brains, as well as on a high level of intelligence and an ability to relax and tune in to what their subconscious is trying to tell them.

The time to use your judgment and intuition is when no one solution stands out as unquestionably better than the others. For example, the decision that is needed may not be the obvious one or the easiest one to choose. In some cases there may be no "good" decision; you may have to select the "least worst" option, which may even be sticking with the status quo. If many people have been geared up to anticipate a change, you may find this difficult to do. When you firmly believe that no change is best, however, it's a good idea to have the

EXERCISE 11-1: DISCOVERING YOUR APPROACH TO DECISION-MAKING

Each numbered pair presents two opposing attitudes or actions. Decide which attitude in each pair best reflects the way you respond to decision-making situations and the extent or frequency of that response. Then place an X in the appropriate space.

	Usually	Frequently	Frequently	Usually	
1. Solve problems.	___	___	___	___	1. Capitalize on opportunities.
2. Generally dissatisfied with things as they are.	___	___	___	___	2. Satisfied with things as they are.
3. Don't care what others think.	___	___	___	___	3. Want to know what others think.
4. Get things going.	___	___	___	___	4. Avoid making waves.
5. Want to continue doing what I'm doing.	___	___	___	___	5. Want to shift to more rewarding activities.
6. Keep learning within my area of expertise.	___	___	___	___	6. Still in the process of searching for my best area of expertise; quickly bored.
7. Tend to do things in well-tested ways.	___	___	___	___	7. Tend to develop new ways of doing things.
8. Get ready for tomorrow's job while doing today's job.	___	___	___	___	8. Concentrate on today's job.
9. Do it myself.	___	___	___	___	9. Seek available counsel and advice.
10. Do what I'm told to do.	___	___	___	___	10. Make continuing reappraisals of the value of what I'm doing.
11. Adhere to rules.	___	___	___	___	11. Will break rules; rules are only guidelines.
12. Avoid risk as a matter of principle.	___	___	___	___	12. Accept "calculated" risk when it may optimize achievement.

courage of your convictions and convince the people involved that you have made the best decision.

When it's impossible to tell which solution will turn out to be the best one, decide arbitrarily. If necessary, flip a coin. The essence of a good decision is timing. Once it is time to make a decision, don't falter, waiver, or dither. Decide! Then commit yourself wholeheartedly to making the decision work.

Making a Commitment to the Success of the Action Plan

Once you have sidestepped the pitfalls and have selected a solution, you must be committed to making it succeed — even if you flipped a coin to decide. This doesn't mean you should stubbornly refuse to see that the action plan is not working or that you cling to a sinking plan as the "face-saver" does. You must remain flexible to changing conditions and open to new information. At appropriate intervals you must reevaluate the plan and modify it when necessary.

Making a commitment to the success of the plan means giving it the best you've got, so it has the best chance to succeed. If *you* are not committed to making the plan work, you can't expect others to become committed. Your attitude comes through to the people who must implement the plans: Commitment and enthusiasm can be contagious. Your leadership may make the decision work out even if it was not the best one available.

THE IMPLEMENTING PHASE

If you'll always include the implementing phase when you think about the problem-solving/decision-making process, you'll avoid dropping the ball the way so many managers do. Often managers tend to think that, once they've solved a problem and made a decision, what remains is merely detail work for their team to carry out. However, even the most brilliant problem-solving and decision-making achievements can be worthless if the manager fails to guide the effective implementation of the action plan.

Communicating and Selling the Decision

Once you're firmly committed to a decision, you are in a good position to convince others that the team's plan is a good one. If you do so effectively, you help ensure that the plan will be carried out successfully. Plan to go over the plan with affected people as a group, then follow up as necessary with individual meetings and written instructions.

Briefing People in Groups   If you brief and instruct people together rather than separately, you'll save yourself innumerable communication problems. When everyone knows what everyone else is responsible for, it's easier for them to coordinate their work and to cooperate with each other to carry out the plan. Also, many heads are better than one; the questions of the various group members will help clear up vague or uncovered aspects of the plan. Overlooked points tend to surface and can be dealt with.

Another advantage of briefing people in groups is that you avoid the false rumors, the needless chitchat on the office grapevine, and the resulting possibility of misunderstandings and ruffled feelings that frequently occur when decisions are communicated piecemeal. For this reason it's a good idea to call a meeting as soon as possible after the decision has been made — before people hear about it from some other source.

In your briefing, you may want to cover these seven points: (1) the specific objectives to be achieved in this situation, (2) the action plan that's been decided on, (3) time targets for the plan, (4) changes that will take place — where and when, (5) how the plan will be carried out, (6) who will be affected, and (7) why this course of action was selected to solve the problem.

The "why" of the decision is often overlooked by managers. This is unfortunate because people rarely become committed to implementing a decision unless they understand how it was reached and why a particular action plan was selected. At this point it's up to you to sell the "why" of the decision. Point out all the benefits and advantages of the action plan.

As you prepare for the briefing meeting, put yourself in the place of those who will be attending. Be sure your briefing adequately informs each of them about (1) what is going to happen to them and why, (2) what they are responsible for and when, (3) any worries and misunderstandings they may have. You might want to try your briefing out on your assistant or another trusted confidant to see whether there are any noticeable gaps in the information you intend to convey. Since you have been immersed in the problem, it's easy for you to overlook points that may be vague or unclear to others.

Be sure to cover the major effects of the action plan as well as the side effects. If you are unclear about all the side effects that may occur, at least deal with this point in the meeting and give a tentative date as to when resulting side effects will be known and handled. If you fail to address these issues, people may go away feeling very insecure about what's going to happen to them as a result of the decision.

Following Up If the plan is complex, you'll need follow up meetings with individual team members to develop specific objectives for each individual. Everyone responsible for implementing the plan must be clear about the results they're aiming for and how these results contribute to the achievement of the specific objectives for the action plan as a whole.

Follow up with a written confirmation of the action plan. Include key points, who is responsible for what, and time targets. However, do not rely on a memo to communicate the action plan without first holding a briefing. It's important to communicate face to face when you first present a plan so you can sell the decision, answer questions, and clear up any misunderstandings.

Directing, Evaluating, and Modifying the Plan

Once you have communicated and sold an action plan, you must follow through by leading the people who will carry out the plan. Be sure that action commitments are clear to everyone involved. Spell out (1) who is responsible for what specific results, (2) exactly what each person will do, (3) when they will do it (give target dates), and (4) where they will do it.

If your action plan involves many changes, they may have to be phased in one step at a time. If the plan will be implemented over time, people must fix target dates for the completion of each stage. Mark your calendar or follow-up file and check to see what progress has been made at each stage. Where appropriate, make the rounds and observe what is happening and how people are carrying out the plan. Be prepared to work out problems that arise. Use the appropriate leadership techniques covered in other chapters of this book.

Even then your job is not finished, because there's only one sure thing about the business world: It is constantly changing. Therefore, your action plan should be subject to continuing review and update as required by changing conditions. Once you decide on a plan, don't close the door to revising it later. A good plan is flexible enough to be changed as times and conditions demand. Here are some suggestions for evaluating the results of a decision.

1. Keep the purpose firmly in mind.

2. Look at the specific objectives you developed for the action plan. How well are they being achieved?

3. Are target dates being met?

4. How well are the people responsible for carrying out the plan doing? Is each person achieving his or her individual objectives on target? If not, why?

5. What new or unforeseen factors are affecting the plan?

6. Do the objectives need to be modified or changed?

7. Does the plan need to be modified or changed? In what way?

8. How will any proposed changes affect other aspects of the plan?

Treat any major modifications just as you would a new problem and resulting decision. In other words, go through the entire process again, remembering to involve people as well as to communicate and sell the modification to the people who will be affected by it.

FACILITATING GROUP PROBLEM-SOLVING

So far we have discussed problem situations in which the manager takes the major responsibility for solving the problem. In most situations there's a high payoff for involving your people in the problem-solving process. Although you may have to make the *final* decision in some matters involving two or more team members, it's best to include them in as many phases of the process as possible.

Assessing the Desirability of Group Input

You as manager must decide the optimal level of group input in each problem-solving/decision-making situation. In each situation ask yourself, "Which phases of the process might benefit from group effort — defining the problem, gathering information, analyzing the information, weighing possible solutions?" In the process of setting unit or department objectives, you might include your teammates in all these steps.

At times you will undoubtedly be involved in group problem-solving and decision-making with your peers and colleagues. You can take a leadership role in these sessions if you are aware of effective approaches and techniques for group work. Whether you are leading team members or working with peers in one or more steps of the process, however, it is critically important to keep the steps separate and in sequence. Separate information from opinion or evaluation. If the group is evaluating a solution, be sure they know about *all* solutions and discuss them before evaluating *any* of them. Display all alternate solutions on a flip chart, chalkboard, or overhead projector so everyone can be clear about them.

Identifying the Type of Decision Needed

As a leader you must also be alert and aware of the best approach to each problem-solving/decision-making situation. You must define that approach to the subordinates involved in the process leading to a decision. Here are five distinct types of situations, each calling for an approach that is quite different from the others.

Debatable Decisions (Finding a Better Way) These are decisions to be reached when there is general agreement about the goal and methods for dealing with a problem. For example, everyone agrees that the goal is to increase sales by 10 percent and that the major method is through developing new accounts. The group needs to decide on a better way to build these new accounts.

Encourage the group to specify productivity objectives. In joint meetings with the leader of the group, each member makes quality and quantity commitments with time targets. After that there may be occasional joint meetings, but people generally coordinate their efforts by communicating and cooperating directly with one another. It's up to the leader to encourage professionalism, commitment to shared group objectives, concern for the quantity and quality of actions, as well as efficiency and effectiveness.

Exploratory Decisions These are decisions to be reached when no agreed-on method of dealing with the problem exists. For example, everyone agrees on the goal of finding a new product to develop and market, but people are unclear and undecided about the best way to go about it. Use brainstorming techniques to explore as many alternatives as possible.

Negotiated Decisions These are decisions to be reached when people are strongly divided and in conflict about methods or goals. Each side is committed to a different course of action even though the values or logic of both are generally acceptable to all.

For example, one group wants to adopt a new group insurance plan that provides increased benefits but will require larger monthly contributions from both the company and the employees. The members of the other group agree that increased coverage is valuable and

understand that it will cost more. However, they strongly believe that their monthly insurance costs should not be increased and that the current insurance coverage is adequate for most employees.

Negotiated decision-making calls for an impartial leader or chair who follows parliamentary procedures. If the number of people in the two factions is unequal, each group should have the right to veto any vote that they don't agree with. The goal is to reach a compromise acceptable to both sides. The leader should encourage participants to express their viewpoints frankly and to be open to opposing viewpoints and compromise solutions.

Also, participants should be encouraged to see conflict as a healthy and natural process for free-thinking individuals rather than as a disaster. You can point out that conflict can lead to better decisions because the ramifications of various alternatives are more thoroughly explored.

Routine Decisions These are everyday decisions for which there are adequate guidelines, rules, procedures, or policies to provide a framework for making a choice. For example, hiring new workers, preparing production schedules, or making ordinary purchases. When there are no new significant factors to consider or any major changes involved, the decision falls into the routine category. These decisions rarely require a great deal of time or energy, although they may require going through each of the steps.

Emergency Decisions These are decisions to be reached in problem situations that call for clear, quick, and precise action to prevent or handle a crisis such as an injury, accident, or breakdown. Your goal is to have *no surprises*. Apply Murphy's Law and try to anticipate every type of crisis that could occur. With each plan of action, visualize you and your people carrying it out and all the problems that could arise. Decide in advance how you'll handle crises that could occur even though every precaution has been taken. For example: What will you do if the computer is down when the payroll is due? What if there's a fire? What will you try to save if there's time? How will your people get out? What procedures will they follow? By thinking ahead in this way, you avoid making poor snap decisions. See the discussion of crisis management in Chapter 12.

Selecting Appropriate Tools for Group Action

Once you've identified the best approach to reach the type of decision needed, you're in a position to review specific techniques that can facilitate group problem-solving and decision-making. Your job as a manager or team leader is to select or suggest techniques that are most appropriate to each type of decision situation, the people who are participating, and the problems involved. Here is a summary of some group techniques that may be valuable to you. (Consult the business or educational section of your library for more details about these techniques.)

Procedure-Setting   The group should decide on procedures at the time it is formed and before beginning the problem-solving or decision-making process. A major question the group should consider when setting procedures is: Who will make the decision? *One person* who has the authority and responsibility for seeing that it is carried out? If so, who is this person? Is the authority and responsibility clear? *The majority?* If so, will a vote be taken? *The entire group?* Is consensus essential or possible? *The minority?* Can the objections of a minority cause one of the alternate solutions to be dropped? If an alternate solution is mentioned and there is no response or comments, does that mean it will be dropped?

Problem Determination   The chair gives everyone an opportunity to state what problems or matters pertaining to a problem should be discussed. Group members can state what aspects of the problem should be included and what alternative problems, solutions, or issues should be considered. The chair has a recorder list and post each suggestion so everyone can see all suggestions. These items may be used to guide discussion at the current meeting or to set a future agenda. This technique gets people involved and participating.

Force Field Analysis   The group is asked to think of any driving forces in the problem situation that tend to push toward improvement. These items are listed on a flip chart. Then the group identifies restraining forces in the situation — forces that resist improvement and change and keep the problem a problem (see Figure 11-2). These items are listed. Then the lists of driving and restraining forces are posted in a conspicuous place and kept in mind during the brainstorming phase.

Brainstorming   This technique is especially helpful when creative ideas are needed. If force field analysis is being used, the group will be looking for actions likely to strengthen the driving forces for improvement and to reduce the restraining forces that are resisting improvement. The goal is to come up with as many ideas as possible within a specified time period. A recorder is designated to list *all* ideas on a flip chart. The ideas are then posted where everyone can see them. The group suspends all judgment and criticism of ideas and encourages the flow of ideas.

After the brainstorming phase, members may participate in an evaluation phase. Then they give each idea a critical look and evaluate it for feasibility, practicality, and probable effectiveness. Sometimes ideas are combined, modified, or ranked in order of preference.

Buzz Groups   If you are working with a large group, there might be times when it would be effective to divide into small subgroups to discuss a specific aspect of a problem or solution. This technique tends to increase involvement

FIGURE 11-2: Force Field Analysis

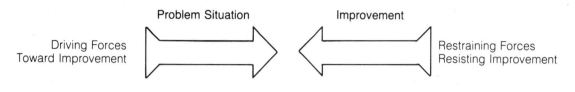

After the discussion, one member of each
and participation and to reduce the inhibiting
and cumbersome factors present in working
with large groups. The purpose of the discussion may be to brainstorm new ideas or to evaluate and discuss each item in more detail than
the larger group might be able to spend time
on. Such buzz groups may discuss the same
item, or each may be assigned a different item
to discuss.

After the discussion, one member of each
buzz group reports back to the group as a
whole. These reports may mention which issues members agreed on and which issues
need further discussion.

Listening Teams This is another technique
that involves forming small groups. When
you begin the meeting with a guest lecturer,
panel discussion, or other informational presentation, the participants may have difficulty
grasping and remembering all the information
presented to them. To eliminate this problem,
listening teams can be assigned to pay special
attention to particular aspects of the presentation. Members can later serve as resource persons when the discussion moves to the aspects
they were assigned to pay attention to.

Before the presentation, form teams and assign each team a different listening task. One
group may listen for causes of the problem, for
example, another for possible solutions, and a
third for the possible results of each solution.
After the presentation, each group takes a few
minutes to prepare a master list of their recol-
lections. When discussion begins, all members

of the team serve as resource persons on the
team's assigned topic.

Individual Polling This technique can be effective in conflict situations and situations
where a negotiated decision may be necessary.
It is used to get the viewpoints of *all* members,
regardless of their shyness or their intimidation
by the more powerful group members.

The chair asks each person to list the advantages and disadvantages of each solution being
considered. After twenty minutes, the lists are
turned in. A reporter posts a master list of all
advantages and disadvantages.

Next, members have ten minutes to rank all
advantages and disadvantages from highest
priority to lowest priority. These lists are
turned in, and an "average" master list is made
while members take their break or address
other issues. The rank-ordered lists are posted
and used as the basis for discussing alternative
solutions. The discussion now reflects the
viewpoints of all members, regardless of their
status or degree of assertiveness.

The Two-Column Method This method may
also be used in conflict situations where two
distinct viewpoints have developed. It can help
all members see that each position has merits
as well as weaknesses. The chair asks each
person to express favorable and unfavorable
points about each position. A recorder places
two columns on the chalkboard or flip chart,
one column for each position. Each point mentioned is placed in the appropriate column. The

goal is to list as many points as possible in the shortest time. The list forms the basis for discussion of the merits of each viewpoint, how to resolve differences, and comparison of the advantages and disadvantages of each position.

This procedure gets all the items on the table before members get bogged down in arguing over one point or another. It tends to reduce the tendency to become firmly attached to one viewpoint, and it facilitates compromise and negotiation.

Action Plan Risk   To facilitate the implementation of the decision, you may wish to learn what each member sees as the major "risk" involved with adopting and carrying out the action plan decided on. These concerns can then be discussed by the group one by one. This technique can help you nip in the bud any unfounded fears and perhaps uncover serious reservations of members that can't be easily overcome. If these kinds of barriers to implementing the plan exist, you need to know about them and deal with them *before* you adopt the plan.

PERT and CPM   PERT (Program Evaluation and Review Technique) is a good technique for reviewing all the steps necessary to carrying out a complex plan. It deals with the sequence in which steps should be performed, how long each step will take, and what resources and materials are needed. The steps are outlined in a flow chart.

CPM (Critical Path Method) is used to set time targets. Sometimes two or more of the steps or tasks necessary to implement the plan can be performed at the same time. The "critical path" is the cumulative time path for the most time-consuming task in each group of tasks that will be performed simultaneously. By following the critical path on the flow chart, the manager can determine the total number of workdays the project will require.

PERT and CPM involve setting a target date and working backward from that date to see when each task must be initiated. Here are the major steps.

1. Determine the final step—in other words, how the solution should appear when it is fully operational.

2. List any events that must occur before the final goal is realized.

3. Arrange these events in chronological order.

4. Develop a flow chart of the process and all the steps in it.

5. List all the activities, resources, and materials needed to accomplish each step.

6. Estimate the time needed to complete each step.

7. Determine which steps can be accomplished at the same time. Add all the estimates to get a total time for the implementation of the plan.

8. Compare the total time estimate with deadlines or expectations and correct as necessary (for example, by assigning more workers to a task or by allowing less time for a given step).

9. Determine which members of the group will be responsible for each step.

Decision-Making by Work Teams

Your most potent tool for problem-solving and decision-making is your work team. Since they are usually the key players in carrying out action plans, they can provide crucial insights. They tend to become committed to plans they helped formulate. See Chapter 13 for clues to the tricky business of building self-directed teams.

SUMMARY

Many women believe the myth that they are not good at rational, logical, cool-headed problem-solving and decision-making. This misconception, however, can easily be overcome. The techniques and procedures for reaching effective decisions are easily learned. Not only that, the higher an executive goes, the more the decisions to be made are based on soft rather than hard facts. Since women have usually received a great deal of reinforcement for sensitivity to people's feelings and the use of their intuition, they have a special advantage in making these kinds of decisions. The main thing for the woman manager to keep in mind is the importance of communicating with people about her problem-solving and decision-making activities in a logical, rational, and businesslike manner.

According to Murphy's Law: "If anything *can* go wrong, it *will*." If you use Murphy's Law to anticipate everything that can go wrong, it can help you (1) prevent many problems and (2) handle problems that do occur with minimal disruption. When you're tackling new projects, highly visible projects, or the boss's pet projects, it's especially important to apply Murphy's Law.

Your attitude toward preventing problems, rather than allowing crises to occur and then galloping to the rescue, affects all your team members. Be sure to give more favorable attention and rewards to individuals who prevent problems than to those who merely cope with them. Your boss may be delinquent in this area. Nevertheless, be sure to let him or her know when *you* are preventing instead of coping.

Train your people to think in terms of solutions rather than in terms of problems. Require them to formulate at least one solution for each problem they bring you. Do the same when discussing problems with *your* boss.

The sequence in which you tackle a problem and arrive at a decision is one key to success. For best results, use this sequence: (1) Be alert to problems. (2) Define the problem, not its symptoms or results. (3) Gather information and consult people who will be affected by the decision or have valuable information. (4) Analyze the information for possible solutions. (5) Weigh possible solutions or alternative courses of action. (6) Select what appears to be the best course of action. (7) Make a commitment to the success of the action plan. (8) Sell or communicate the plan to those who will be involved. Brief in groups first; if necessary follow up individually and in writing. (9) Direct the implementation of the plan by making assignments, setting target dates, and checking to make sure proper progress is being made. (10) Periodically evaluate the results of the action plan. (11) If necessary, modify the plan to respond to new situations and information.

It's impossible to have a really participative style of management without involving your people in the problem-solving/decision-making process. Doing so will increase the motivation of your people — and their productivity. In each situation ask yourself, "Which phases of the process might benefit from group effort?" Identify the type of decision needed so that you can determine the best approach to take. Ask whether the decision is debatable, exploratory, negotiable, routine, or emergency. Then review the techniques or tools commonly used in group problem-solving and select those that will be most helpful. Self-directed work teams are your most potent tool for solving problems and making decisions.

Additional Exercises

EXERCISE 11-2: THE MANNING CASE

Mary Manning has her work cut out for her. Her proposal for a campaign to publicize the Laura Lee line of resort wear was accepted by the Executive Committee, thanks to the support of Jan Arguello. This is Mary's first chance to gain some real visibility at Lighthouse Designs. Some members of the Executive Committee were skeptical about her ideas, but they went along at Arguello's insistence.

Manning works days, nights, and weekends for the next two weeks mapping out complete plans, procedures, and strategies for the campaign. When her plans are complete, she calls the people who will be working with her, one by one, and tells them about their duties and responsibilities in carrying out the campaign. She sends memos to the Regional Sales Managers explaining the campaign and giving instructions for cooperating.

The Laura Lee campaign is scheduled to begin on November 1 with simultaneous fashion shows, news releases, and department store advertisements. Suddenly Manning starts experiencing problems. For example, some of the Regional Sales Managers haven't coordinated the department store ads in their localities with the New York fashion shows and press releases. Some of the styles pictured in the ads and planned for the fashion shows are not ready in time, so customers become confused about what styles are available. Worst of all, Mary doesn't learn about any of these problems until it's too late to remedy them.

1. What do you see as some of the sources of Manning's problems?

2. How could she have handled the situation more effectively?

3. What effect do you think this project will have on her status at Lighthouse?

4. Can she recoup her losses or redeem herself? If so, how?

Compare your responses with the answer key in Appendix 3.

EXERCISE 11-3: MAKING DECISIONS UNDER PRESSURE

You left Monday morning for a one-week company-sponsored training program in supervisory leadership. Your department was turned over to Rose, but she became ill and went home. It was then turned over to Ken, but his mother became critically ill, and he flew home. You were called two hours ago to return on an emergency basis. You arrived five minutes ago. The time is 1:00 p.m. The day is Friday. As you walk into your office, you face ten immediate problems.

These problems are listed below. First read, evaluate, and decide on the relative importance of each problem. Then decide on the sequence in which you would handle the problems. Take only five minutes to read the problems, rank them in order of importance, and set up a sequence for handling them. Put (1) the rank order of importance and (2) the sequence of handling to the left of each problem.

Compare your responses with the answer key in Appendix 3.

Problem

A. You have received a report from Peggy in Personnel that Scott is looking for another job outside the company. She wants you to talk to him. You figure this would take you about fifteen minutes.
B. Your boss left word that he wants to see you in his office immediately on your return. Anticipated time: sixty minutes.
C. You have some very important-looking un-opened mail (both company and personal) on your desk. Time: ten minutes.
D. Your telephone is ringing.
E. A piece of equipment has broken down, halting all production in your department. You are the only one present who can fix it. Anticipated time: thirty minutes.
F. A most attractive young man is seated outside your office waiting to see you. Time: ten minutes.
G. You have an urgent written notice in front of you to call a Los Angeles operator. Both your mother and the company headquarters are located in Los Angeles. Time: ten minutes.
H. Jim, head of Production, has sent word he wants to see you, and has asked that you return his call as soon as possible. Time: ten minutes.
I. Ann, one of your workers, is in the women's lounge and claims to be sick. She wants your permission to go home. It would take at least fifteen minutes to get down there and get the facts.
J. In order to get to your office by 1:00 p.m., you had to miss lunch. You're very hungry, but figure it will take at least thirty minutes to get some substantial food.

REFERENCES

1. Adams, James L. *Conceptual Blockbusting.* Reading, Mass.: Addison-Wesley, 1990. Adams, a Stanford professor, discusses various types of blocks to creative problem-solving. He then provides individual and group "blockbusters" that provide breakthroughs to better ideas.

2. Albert, Kenneth J., ed. *Handbook of Business Problem Solving.* New York: McGraw-Hill, 1983. In this book, ninety top managers describe how to solve complex business problems in every major business function.

3. Bloch, Arthur. *Murphy's Law, Book Three.* Los Angeles: Price/Stern/Sloan, 1982. A humorous look at the trials and tribulations of managers. Reading this book can help you feel that you are not alone; it can give you a few laughs; and it might even trigger some insights.

4. Collins, Eliza G. C. *Executive Success.* New York: Wiley, 1983.

5. Dean, Douglas, and John Mihalasky. *Executive ESP.* Englewood Cliffs, N.J.: Prentice-Hall, 1974. From 1962 to 1972 Dean, Mihalasky, and associates conducted extensive experiments through their Psi Communications Project in the Newark College of Engineering at the University of Pittsburgh. They used scientific approaches to obtain reliable information about the effects of ESP on executive decision-making.

6. Durden-Smith, Jo. *Sex and the Brain.* New York: Arbor House, 1983.

7. Hickman, Craig R., and Michael A. Silva. *Creative Excellence.* New York: Penguin, 1984.

8. Nierenberger, Gerard I. *The Art of Creative Thinking.* New York: Simon and Schuster, 1989. The author gives step-by-step methods for increasing your creativity and mental abilities. He includes suggestions for using greater creativity in thinking, writing, researching, negotiating, composing, inventing, problem-solving, and decision-making.

9. Rowan, Roy. *The Intuitive Manager.* New York: Berkley Books, 1986. This *Fortune Magazine* writer gives suggestions for harnessing your powers of instinct, recognizing the subconscious elements of success, unlocking your intuitive abilities, and mastering the process of major decision-making.

10. Von Oech, Roger. *A Whack on the Side of the Head.* New York: Warner Books, 1983. This book discusses ten mental locks to creativity.

11. Von Oech, Roger. *A Kick in the Seat of the Pants.* New York: Harper & Row, 1986. The author discusses ways to activate your creative thinking by adopting the mind-set of an explorer getting off the beaten path, an artist looking at things in new ways, a judge questioning assumptions and making decisions, and a warrior determined to reach objectives once decisions are made.

Chapter Twelve

Planning and Organizing for Results: Productivity Through Performance Planning

"A woman is known for the company she organizes."

Pamela M. Suber

The two keys to effective managerial planning are (1) focusing more on end results than on activities and (2) including your team members in the planning process, rather than doing it yourself and then telling them. To use the first key, you should understand the difference between efficiency and effectiveness. Peter Drucker has defined it this way:

- *Efficiency = Doing things right*
- *Effectiveness = Doing the right things*

Think about it. How many people have you known who focused on increasing their speed and accuracy in completing detail work, yet failed to move ahead in their careers? The promotable woman looks at the total picture and sets her objectives and priorities to ensure she is doing the right things — those things that will move her toward her top objectives.

In this chapter you will have the opportunity to

1. Learn the basic components of planning systems

2. Develop clearly stated job objectives and performance plans

3. Design appropriate standards and controls for achieving objectives

4. Understand how participative performance planning systems operate

5. Learn the bases for organizing work — organizational structure, departmental structure, and individual job design

6. Understand tactics for using your planning and organizing skills to best advantage

The Best-Laid Plans

Erika smiles as Brian, her assistant, walks through the door. "Say, Brian, you did a great job of handling that Resort/Holiday Fashion Preview. There was no sign of Murphy's Law in action."

"Thanks to your coaching," Brian responds. "But I guess there's no rest for the weary — what's this I hear about a new line of sportswear?"

"Oh, the new Viva line. I think it will be a real winner, and headquarters is planning to spend plenty to promote it. Now we've got to decide how we're going to promote it at the regional level. We need to develop some departmental goals for this line, set quotas for each of the sales people, come up with job assignments for the other personnel in the department, and work out the details for advertising, merchandising, and generally promoting the line."

"Wow. And when do we need all this — yesterday?"

Erika laughs. "Almost. I'm calling a staff meeting two weeks from today; so you and I should meet every morning till we get our plans in good shape."

Two weeks later, Erika and Brian are rehashing the staff meeting held earlier in the day.

"Do you think they really understood our goals for the Viva line, Brian?"

"Well, they must have. Only two or three people had questions — and those were on minor items."

"We did cover everything, didn't we?" Erika looks over her notes. "Explanation of the new line and its target market, departmental goals, quotas, job assignments. Somehow I thought there would be more discussion. I just feel the others aren't as enthusiastic as we are."

A month later, Erika and Brian are going over sales reports for the Viva line.

"Brian, I'm a little disappointed in these figures. I thought we'd be getting bigger orders than this by now — and more of them."

"Maybe the sales reps need a little motivating."

"Well, I've been praising those people who seem to be paying special attention to the Viva line. And I've called in several who aren't and stressed its importance. I don't know. Part of it may be that we didn't get as much budget money for the promotion as we requested. And I have to fight for any support from Advertising and from Administrative Services. How can I support my sales people properly if I can't get the support I need myself?"

At the end of the quarter, a couple of the top sales people are discussing the salary/commission situation:

"You know, Kerr *talks* a lot about rewarding performance, but when it comes to recommending people for raises, she pays a lot more attention to who gets their paperwork in on time," says Frank Andreini.

"Yeah," responds Ken Cypert, "and a lot depends on who she likes to have lunch with. Like Joe — I just found out he was recommended for a bigger raise than I was. I think I did a better job pushing the new line than he did!"

Frank shook his head. "These women are hard to figure out. I'm never sure exactly what she's looking for or how well I'm doing."

"Yeah," agreed Ken. "I'm getting pretty fed up. I think I'll start looking around."

Word of dissatisfaction filters back to Erika. She's not surprised; she's been sensing it for some time. She picks up the phone.

"Jan, I'm in trouble. I need help, and you're the best person at managing sales that I know. When can we get together?"

1. What planning strategies do you think Erika has overlooked?

2. How has her method of planning affected the motivation of her people?

3. Is she using good decision-making strategies in formulating her plans? Explain your response.

4. If you were Jan, what suggestions would you make to Erika now?

THE PLANNING PROCESS — AN OVERVIEW

All the planning skills in the world will do you no good unless you have a positive attitude toward planning so that you actually use your skills at the right time. Therefore, we'll first analyze attitudes toward planning, including why managers don't plan when they should and the payoffs for planning before taking action. Next, we'll look at the planning process as a system that involves the whole organization. You'll see how an ideal system of organizational planning might work. Then we'll discuss in more detail some key aspects of planning, and you'll have a chance to improve your planning skills by applying planning techniques to actual situations. First, to stimulate your thinking further about payoffs for planning, complete Exercise 12-1.

Why Plan?

Powerful leaders have powerful strategic visions of where the organization can go, as dis-

cussed in Chapter 2. Such visions are the basis for planning and are most likely to materialize as part of the process of regular, ongoing planning. They rarely appear out of nowhere in the midst of a planning vacuum. The missions, objectives, and strategies of excellent companies are based on powerful visions that are specific and have a time frame. President Kennedy had a clear vision of an American astronaut on the moon by the end of the 1960s. European leaders had a vision of joining their countries into a single market by the end of 1992. In this sense, planning is the essence of effective leadership.

In another sense, effective planning is the essence of good management. It is impossible to manage without planning. If you don't plan properly, then you are managed by the circumstances that surround you, instead of managing your time and energy to achieve your objectives and make the full contribution you're capable of making. Since it's so vital to good management, why do you suppose planning is so often neglected by managers?

To Make Things Happen Some managers are frightened by "thinking big." Setting up a year's objectives and action plans overwhelms them. Some managers don't like the risks involved in committing themselves to challenging objectives. They're more comfortable with day-to-day or week-to-week activities. What they call "objectives" may be merely intentions or hopes to complete certain activities. Such

EXERCISE 12-1: ANALYZING ATTITUDES TOWARD PLANNING

1. Why don't managers take time to plan when they should? List as many reasons as you can.

2. Why should managers take time to plan? When should planning be done? List as many reasons and instances as you can.

managers will never be leaders who make things happen.

As many leaders say, "There are three kinds of people: (1) people who make things happen, (2) people who watch what is happening, and (3) people who ask, 'What happened?'" Of course, you want to be a manager who makes things happen, not a passive observer. When you plan effectively, you make those things happen that you want to happen. You get the results you intend to get.

Planning is more important than ever in these times of rapid change. New technology, products, and services are increasingly available. Other products, services, and ways of providing them are becoming obsolete. Companies are reorganizing, eliminating some old jobs and creating new ones. All aspects of modern business are touched by rapid change.

You can make plans to anticipate these changes and take advantage of the opportunities they offer. Such plans can give direction to your own activities and to your workers' activities. By planning to anticipate and create change, you avoid becoming a passive victim of its effects. Instead, you *make things happen*.

To Become Promotable   Managers who don't take adequate time to plan don't fully understand that it can put them in control of their destiny. When managers focus on activities — the "doing" of their jobs — they have little chance of creating constructive changes that will make them visible to top management. Such changes require effective planning, which in turn is based on well-conceived, clearly stated objectives. Other managers say they rarely have time to sit down and plan. They haven't learned that adequate time spent planning complex projects or tasks saves time in actually doing the job. Planning efforts pay off, also, in better results. In a nutshell, the ability and tendency to plan well are key factors in being pegged for promotion.

To Provide an Effective Framework for Decision-Making   You won't always have as much time as you'd like to work out a decision. If you have clearly stated job objectives, however, you can make good decisions even under pressure. You brainstorm possible courses of action. Then you select the alternative that seems most likely to move you toward your objectives.

To Eliminate Unpleasant Surprises   Don't wait until crises occur to think about how you will handle them. As soon as you acquire new responsibilities, start analyzing the types of problems that could crop up, ways of preventing them, and your objectives for handling each of them. Then formulate plans you can put into action readily should the need arise. That way you won't be caught by surprise and perhaps make a poor crisis decision. The larger the organization, the less its top management likes surprises.

Managers who are caught by surprise can cause significant financial loss or embarrassment for the company and can find themselves quickly relieved of their responsibilities. Regardless of the size of your organization, you'll get more predictable results if you anticipate all eventualities. Then plan either to make them happen, prevent them, or cope with them. See the discussion on crisis management later in this chapter.

To Give Direction to Motivational Drive   To get something you want, you must have both motivational drive and direction. When you select goals that have value and meaning to you and to your company, goals that are worth the effort, then you tie your goals to your drive to achieve. You give the necessary direction to that drive by taking time now to decide on future actions. Some people think of planning as "coming up with a lot of stuff I've got to do, stuff that I'll feel guilty about if I don't get it done." High achievers think of it as essential to getting what they want. If you can sell your people on this idea, you'll gain a group of eager planners.

You can use the type of planning we'll discuss here to increase your own productivity and that of your work team, even though your organization has no integrated planning system. The truth is that most organizations still engage in formal planning only at the top and inform middle managers of what they want from them. Then middle managers direct others in ways they hope will produce the expected results. Workers seldom see the big picture and frequently are unclear about why they are performing certain tasks. Formal planning, like anything else, can be overdone, but the problem in most organizations tends to be inadequate planning.

Suppose you're fortunate enough to find an organization that uses planning on a system-wide basis. In other words, everyone in the firm is involved in planning, and all plans are integrated so that they work together and support each other in achieving the organization's objectives. We'll look first at how such a planning process might be set up (see Figure 12-1). Then we'll look at the role supervisors and middle managers play in the planning process, ways of improving your planning skills, and how to help your workers become skilled planners. Since virtually every step of the planning process involves decision-making, you should first develop problem-solving/decision-making skills, which were covered in Chapter 11.

How an Organizational Planning Process Works

A system of organizational planning, as shown in Figure 12-1, normally begins with top management's selecting a mission and setting organizational objectives based on forecasts of business opportunities and the company's capabilities. Top management then develops strategies and policies to guide others in carrying out

their plans to support the objectives. In participative companies middle managers and/or team leaders help formulate these organizational plans. Middle managers may in turn call in team leaders to set departmental objectives and develop tactics, rules, and procedures to guide them in carrying out their plans to support those objectives. Next, team leaders include their work teams in setting unit objectives that support the department objectives. Each team leader then meets with each member of the team to set individual worker objectives that support the work unit's objectives. Leaders and team members also jointly develop the action steps, standards, and controls that will guide workers in the day-to-day activities necessary to attain individual and work-unit objectives.

Defining the Mission Initial organizational planning begins even before a company starts operating, of course, and begins with top management's vision of the customer or client needs the company intends to meet—its reason for existence. This vision should include how the company differs from other, similar companies in the type of customer, products or services the company provides, and/or the way it provides them. To be successful, a company should see itself as being at least slightly unique in some way: it should fill a market niche or need. This reason for being is often referred to as the company's mission—and defining it, along with making forecasts, is the first step in the planning process shown in Figure 12-1.

Successful companies not only manage to select an appropriate mission, they regularly reassess it as client needs, technology, and markets change—and they reformulate it when it begins to become obsolete. Lighthouse Design's mission was "providing women's clothing for the mass market in the top-of-the-moderate price range in misses sizes." This mission was effective for over twenty years, but

FIGURE 12-1: An Organizational Planning Process

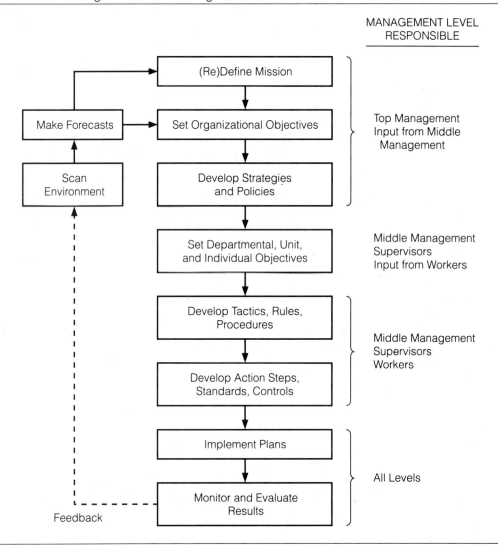

recently they forecast changing demands and responded to them. Now they've expanded their mission to: ". . . in misses, petite, and large sizes."

Scanning the External Environment Global competition of the 1990s underlines the leadership skills of scanning a fast-paced environment and intuiting how developments can affect the organization. These developments might include new customers and trends on the horizon, new ways of competing, new technology for getting things done, changing values and interests, and changing laws, government regulations, and court decisions. Leaders must determine what's going out and what's coming in, what's hot and what's not. They must intuit how and where the company can fill a need, make some money, or reap some benefit out of all this. They must also predict how these changes could leave the organization in the dust, taking a loss.

Making Forecasts Top management is also responsible for developing effective forecasts about how much the company can expect to sell during the coming year(s); how much it can produce; what its needs for financing, supplies, and workers will be; and other factors necessary for effective planning. The middle managers whose departments deal directly with these aspects of company operations are of course called on to help develop forecasts. The more accurate the forecasts, the more effective the company's objectives are likely to be. Challenging yet attainable objectives must be based on realistic forecasts.

Formulating Objectives, Strategies, and Policies Next, top management sets long-range (about five years) and short-range (usually one year) objectives for the entire organization, again with the input of the middle managers whose departments will carry out the resulting plans. Do you remember what you learned about stating effective personal goals in Chapter 3? We used the term "goal" there because it has a clear personal meaning for most people. In this chapter we'll use the term "objective" to discuss all types of organizational goals, from systemwide to individual worker goals. "Objectives" and "goals," as used in this book, have exactly the same meaning — that is, an end result we intend to achieve at some point in the future. Since most business organizations use the term "objectives" to refer to targeted business results, we'll use that term in this chapter.

After top management has developed forecasts, defined or redefined the organization's mission, and set long-range and short-range objectives, it develops strategies for attaining the objectives and policies to guide managers in carrying out plans. Strategies are long-range, broad decisions about the company's style or approach into achieving

objectives. One Lighthouse Design strategy, for example, is "to work closely with retail store buyers in developing new fashion lines."

The activities required to achieve organizational objectives will be carried out at lower levels and are often expressed as objectives at those levels. An organizational objective of "to increase sales by 15 percent" will be supported by a number of Sales Department objectives. "To increase market share to 30 percent in the Western Region" might be one. What the Sales Department might view as activities for increasing the market share ("obtain $10,000 in orders from the Village Life clothing chain") would become an objective for a particular salesperson. That salesperson's activities in turn might be expressed as "call on every Village Life buyer at least once a month."

The planning process shown in Figure 12-1 can apply to nonprofit organizations as well as profit-making firms. Profit-making firms are primarily concerned with providing particular goods or services within specific cost and profit constraints. Their objectives reflect this by focusing to some extent on profitability and productivity. On the other hand, nonprofits are concerned mainly with cost constraints; the budget and funding are of prime importance. Their objectives revolve around providing a specific service within specific budget limits and reflect a higher relative stress on social responsibility.

Deciding on Tactics, Rules, Procedures Middle management is usually responsible for developing tactics, rules, and procedures for carrying out the activities that will lead to the attainment of the objectives. Supervisors and workers participate in this ongoing process to the extent that their work is affected (in companies that practice participative management). Middle managers are usually in the best position to identify effective tactics. For example, a tactic Erika Kerr used to carry out the organizational strategy of "working closely with retail buyers in developing new fashion lines" was "to invite key buyers to preview the colors and base fabrics to be used in new lines."

Setting Up Action Steps, Standards, Controls
On the other hand, supervisors are often in the best position to develop or evaluate rules and procedures that affect their workers. And workers can often develop or improve on action steps, standards, and controls for carrying out their jobs. However, supervisors are usually responsible for approving and monitoring these aspects of the planning process.

Monitoring, Evaluating Once plans are made, everyone in the company has individual objectives as well as guidelines for ways of achieving them. When objectives and standards are clear, specific, and measurable, and when the information necessary to monitor actual performance is readily available, everyone in the company has the tools to practice self-control and self-evaluation of their own performance. With effective worker self-monitoring, the supervisor's role can truly become one of resource person and coach. Performance problems might signal the need for joint problem-solving rather than reprimands. Actual performance provides feedback on how well plans were carried out and input for making new forecasts and setting new objectives.

DEVELOPING PLANNING SKILLS

Now that you have an understanding of how an organizational planning process works, let's focus on your role as supervisor or manager and the planning skills you need to work with your boss and your people on departmental, work-unit, and individual worker objectives. The key aspects of your role in the planning process, as shown in Figure 12-2, are helping people identify the contributions they can make; setting clearly stated, effective objectives; developing challenging, attainable standards for

measuring performance; and establishing controls for monitoring performance.

Identifying Contributions People Can Make

The contributions a work unit or a department is able to make toward organizational objectives depends of course on what the individuals in that group can and will do. Chapter 10 gives suggestions for identifying the types of tasks that tie in to different kinds of needs that motivate people to perform, such as achievement, affiliation, and power. Chapter 13 gives further suggestions for assigning tasks.

The most powerful position you can take, however, in matching people to tasks, is to let

FIGURE 12-2: Departmental Planning Process

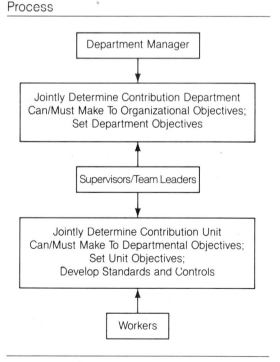

them take the lead while you serve as resource person. So instead of initially suggesting contributions your people can make, ask them to do their own thinking about contributions. Not only will you get a more accurate picture of what they're able and willing to do, they're likely to see themselves as capable of making greater contributions than you could require of them. In turn, they're likely to set up more challenging objectives and standards for themselves than you could impose—and to attain them.

If you ask your people to identify any obstacles they see to making each contribution, you're likely to gain much valuable information about what your people are thinking, department problems that need solving, and ways

of training and developing your people. Exercise 12-2 provides a structure for identifying possible contributions and obstacles to making them and for analyzing obstacles and attitudes. This exercise works well for managers too; so try it now for yourself.

Setting Clearly Stated, Specific Objectives
Clearly stated, specific objectives are the basis of all good plans, yet an amazing number of workers, and even managers, don't know what their boss expects of them, much less what her or his objectives are or how to formulate them effectively. How much do you know about the objectives of the firms you've worked for? Complete Exercise 12-3 before we talk about techniques for writing objectives. Later you

EXERCISE 12-2: IDENTIFYING YOUR CONTRIBUTIONS TO THE COMPANY

Step A. Think about what you see as the greatest contributions that you, in your present position, can make to the company. List them. Then ask yourself what obstacles are keeping you—or will keep you—from making those contributions. List them beside each contribution.

Step B. Look at the obstacles you listed and answer a few questions about them. How many of them are *really* external obstacles?

1. Do any of the obstacles originate within *you* rather than with external circumstances? How?

2. Would changing your viewpoint or behavior remove any of the obstacles? How?

3. Are any of the obstacles caused by a lack of clearly stated objectives?

4. Think about your attitude toward your job when you believe you're making a contribution. Describe your thoughts and feelings.

5. Think about your attitude toward your job when you believe you're "just working." Describe your thoughts and feelings.

6. Think about your productivity and effectiveness when you believe you're making a contribution rather than just working. Describe the differences.

EXERCISE 12-3: OBJECTIVES THAT AFFECT YOU

Note: If you are not working now, use the last job you had for this exercise.

1. What is one organizational objective that your company as a whole now has?

2. What is one objective for your department or unit?

3. What is one personal, job-related objective that you have?

4. If you were unable to answer any of the above questions, is it because no objectives exist? If they exist, how can you find out about them?

---

may want to rewrite these objectives, stating them more clearly.

A format for stating objectives clearly and specifically is shown in Exhibit 12-1. The most effective objectives always include an action verb and a single key result that expresses just what you intend to accomplish, as well as a deadline date. Where possible, your single key result (for example, "increase sales") should include a standard that is measurable (for example, "by 10 percent," or "to $500,000"). Where possible, your objective should also include a measurable cost (for example, "at no increase in salary expense," or "using no more than 300 additional work hours"). After all, it's fairly easy to attain some objectives if you spend enough money on extra help, equipment, or advertising. However, if your boss expected you to do it with no increase in those budget items, you may be in trouble.

The best way to determine if an objective is specific enough is to ask yourself, "On the deadline date, will it be clear to me and my boss whether I have achieved this objective? Is there room for argument? Will we agree on how close I've come or how far I've exceeded it?" A clearly stated, specific objective leaves no room for argument as to whether it has been achieved.

Using the model for stating objectives shown in Exhibit 12-1 and the examples of clearly stated, specific objectives shown in Exhibit 12-2, rewrite any poorly stated objectives shown in Exercise 12-4.

Planning with Your Boss   In the planning process described in this chapter, you as a work-unit supervisor or department manager (and your peers in your department) will be expected to meet with your boss in formulating the objectives for his or her department or division (see Figures 12-1 and 12-2). You'll need to help forecast opportunities, problems, and capabilities that involve your work area. Once the objectives have been set for your department or division, then it's your turn to meet with your people (as shown in Figure 12-2) to get their input on what the contributions and resulting objectives for your own department or work unit should be.

Planning with Your Work Team   Of course, it's quicker — and perhaps easier in the short run — to merely set the objectives for your unit on your own. After all, it's your responsibility, and in many companies your peers will be doing just that. On the other hand, there's a great deal of long-range power to be gained from getting your people involved in setting

EXHIBIT 12-1: Format for Stating Objectives in Clear, Specific Terms

> To: . . . (Action or Accomplishment Verb)
> (Single Key Result)
> By: . . . (Target Date)
> At: . . . (Cost)

EXHIBIT 12-2: Examples of Objectives at Various Organizational Levels

	Organizational Level	Departmental Level	Work-Unit Level	Individual Level
1.	To increase total sales by 10% by June 1, 19xx, at no more than 2% increased overhead cost	To increase sales of SuAnne Sportswear by 10% by June 1, 19xx, with 2% increase in promotional costs.	To increase sales of SuAnne Sportswear in Nevada by 10% by June 1, 19xx, with a 2% increase in promotional costs	To increase my total sales to all outlets by 10% by June 1, 19xx
2.	To reduce customer complaints by 25% during 19xx at no increased cost	To increase quality standards for SuAnne Sportswear during 19xx at no increased cost	To increase quality control inspections from 25% of pieces produced to 100% during 19xx by changing procedures for self-monitoring	To decrease defective merchandise that leaves my work station to zero during 19xx
3.	To reduce operating costs by 8% during 19xx	To save the company $120,000 in computer costs during 19xx by installing a new input system	Install computer input system and have it operating by June 1	Write programs for accounting input to new computer system and have them debugged by May 1

the objectives for the work unit or department you manage. When people have a real, meaningful share in creating a plan, they are almost certain to become committed to making that plan work. So in the long run, you'll save time and get better results by taking time in the beginning to include your people in the planning.

In fact, the objective-setting session should include some development of action steps, standards, and controls that will make the plan work. A problem-solving team approach usu-ally leads to good results. In fact, if your work group is large — over twenty or thirty people — you may want to ask work teams of five to seven each to work out proposals for plans that the entire group can then discuss and decide on.

Planning with Each Team Member   Once you've settled on the specific objectives for your work unit or department, it's time to meet with each of your people and to determine

EXERCISE 12-4: MAKING OBJECTIVES CLEAR AND SPECIFIC

Do you think the following statements are clearly stated objectives? If so, write "o.k." beside the statement. If not, rewrite it, adding any assumed information you need. Remember to include measurable standards where possible.

1. Capture as much of the petite-size clothing market as we can.

2. Achieve maximum profit.

3. Increase the level of training for supervisors.

4. Improve the quality of our sweater imports.

5. Develop additional sources of supply.

6. Reduce the number of employee grievances.

7. Establish a research and development department.

8. Carry out assigned responsibilities within approved budget.

9. Conduct a market research survey.

10. Install a new computer system.

---

jointly what their contributions toward these objectives will be. Of course you should discuss individual contributions at the very beginning of your work relationship with each person. It's also a good idea to review and update understandings about these contributions and obstacles to making them. This review can provide the basis for setting the individual's objectives for the coming year.

After you've settled on three to five major objectives, let the worker take the lead in formulating the action steps needed to attain each objective. Although each objective will include some measurable standards, they may not be sufficient to cover all the action steps leading to the objective. So you'll need to reach an agreement about any standards needed for the action steps. For example, an objective of the shipping clerk at Lighthouse is "To ship all orders for SuAnne products so that customers receive them within the time specified on the order at no increase in shipping budget." One action step is "Package merchandise for shipping." What performance standards might be included here? "So that no merchandise is damaged because of inadequate packaging"? "Within an average of fifteen minutes per order"? The key is to look for the level of performance — how much and how well — the worker will be aiming for.

Next, the two of you must decide how the worker, and you, will know if these standards are being maintained. What sort of record-keeping or feedback from others must be set up? But that comes under the heading of controls, which we'll discuss in the next section.

A word to the wise on setting individual objectives: *Keep them simple and few in number.*

EXHIBIT 12-3: Types of Controls and Their Purpose

Purpose of Control	Form of Control
To standardize quality of product or service	Employee training, inspections, statistical quality control, employee incentive systems
To standardize performance	Production schedules, written procedures, inspections
To protect assets (from theft, waste)	Division of responsibility, dual authorization, auditing procedures, recordkeeping requirements
To limit individual power	Job descriptions, accounting requirements, policy directives, rules

People can remember three to five simple objectives easily, and you want those objectives to be up front in their awareness every day. Then anytime they need to make a quick decision, such as what to do next, they can choose the alternative that will best move them toward one of their objectives. It's a good idea to rank the objectives in order of priority, for the same reason.

Later in this chapter we'll discuss individual performance plans, which are simply a comprehensive set of objectives and action steps developed or updated by each employee and approved by his or her manager each year. They include standards for quantity and quality of performance.

Developing Effective Controls

Controls are simply ways of determining how well plans are being carried out and when corrective or preventive action needs to be taken. Exhibit 12-3 shows some types of controls management uses for various purposes.

Standards provide the basis for controlling or monitoring progress toward objectives. Measurable standards can be expensive to measure and control objectively, especially quality standards. It makes sense therefore to weigh the costs of setting up control measures for standards against the payoffs the firm can

expect from their use. In the tactic for conveying a company image mentioned earlier, for example, management must decide whether the cost of a client survey can be justified in terms of a probable short- or long-range sales increase. Or would it make more sense for the management team to use their subjective judgment in evaluating the effectiveness of the tactic?

Preventive Controls   These are measures taken to minimize deviations from plans before they have a chance to occur. They in turn minimize the need for corrective action. Some examples include training and coaching individuals in performing their job responsibilities, providing job-related information, and setting up procedures and rules, such as those governing the handling of cash.

Corrective Controls   These are measures taken to correct a significant deviation after it occurs. Since errors or deviations will occur occasionally, even with the best preventive controls, checkpoints must be established to identify these deviations. In the manufacture of equipment, for example, the manager and workers must decide which parts can and should be tested before assembly proceeds. In the textbook publishing business, the editor and author must decide at what stages of book development the materials will be sent to reviewers for evaluation.

The corrective control process often includes the following elements:

Define the subsystem. Is the control process established to monitor an individual's performance? A department's? The entire organization's? Or is it designed to monitor specific inputs (such as raw materials), production processes (such as assembly of certain parts or the actual performance of certain services), or outputs, (such as inventory of finished goods on hand or service jobs completed)? The category you select is referred to here as the subsystem.

Identify characteristics to be measured. What are the most vital elements of the subsystem that account for most of the major variations in performance? How can they be measured most effectively and economically? Erika determined that an up-to-date, accurate record of items sold by salespersons would help her know where efforts needed to be increased as early as possible. She arranged for salespersons to carry portable computers with them when they call on buyers. Not only can they immediately enter the items ordered, they can access the headquarters computer via a telephone modem and tell buyers what items are on hand for immediate delivery. At the end of each day, they report the total items sold.

Set standards. What measures will you use for determining if the activities undertaken by the subsystem are acceptable — that is, if the quantity and quality of the subsystem's output are adequate to support organizational objectives? With input from all salespersons, Erika and her salespeople set quantity standards as part of departmental sales objectives. The one they set for this year, "To increase sales by 10 percent over last year," reflects a quantity standard of "10 percent increase." The quality standard is expressed in another objective, "To reduce customer service complaints by 15 percent." This approach assumes that customer complaints are a valid measure of the quality of service provided by salespersons.

Collect information. How will you get information on how well each of the selected characteristics of the action plan is being handled? From oral or written reports? Mechanical or computerized readouts? From the people who perform the activities? Inspectors? Auditors? Customers? Will feedback on performance be automatic — that is, built into the process? If not, how will it be activated or initiated? At what points in the process (checkpoints)?

Compare. Determine what differences exist between what is being done (performance) and what should be done (standards). If there are no significant deviations, then no further action needs to be taken except to continue collecting information.

Diagnose deviations and implement corrections. Determine the types, amounts, and causes of any deviations from standards. Decide on the best course of action for eliminating these deviations and determining how the new action plan will be monitored.

When establishing controls, try for the following: Let the work team take the lead, to get as many ideas as possible and to get worker commitment. Establish as many preventive (versus corrective) controls as feasible. Set up checkpoints as early in the process as feasible. (Generally speaking, the sooner errors or deviations are caught, the easier it is to correct them.) Look for controls that can be built into the system, that give feedback automatically, that let the individual performer know almost immediately when a deviation occurs. Where appropriate, adopt controls suggested by the individuals or groups they're designed to monitor. You're more likely to get their co-operation in making the control work.

Built-in controls and worker participation in establishing controls foster self-control. And assuming that people are committed to achieving their job objectives, the more they can exercise self-control, the more productive they tend to be.

ORGANIZING FOR PRODUCTIVITY

An integral part of planning for results is determining how to divide the total work of the organization into divisions, departments, and work units. Top management wants to design the best structure for helping people work together to fulfill the firm's mission, carry out its strategies, and achieve its objectives. An organization's structure is the arrangement and interrelationships of its various parts and job positions. The structure defines the formal division of work activities and shows how all functions or activities are linked together. It also indicates the organization's formal hierarchy and authority structure and shows reporting relationships.

First we'll discuss some elements common to all organizations that affect their structure. Then we'll look at some key factors top management must consider when they organize and some types of organizational structure (ways of dividing into departments) you should be familiar with. Finally, we'll talk about ways of organizing the work within a department and a work unit, right down to designing individual job positions.

Structuring Organizational Activities

The structuring of activities has traditionally begun at the top when management initially decides on an organizational plan and period-ically reevaluates and modifies it. To help you understand how this process works, let's look at some common elements that affect structure, some key factors in determining structure, and some ways of structuring activities into departments or divisions.

Elements of Organizational Structure   Management normally must take into consideration at least five common elements of organizational structure when deciding how to organize its activities: (1) the degree of job specialization, (2) the degree of standardization of job procedures, (3) the size of the work unit, (4) the type and extent of coordination of activities, and (5) the degree of centralization of decision-making.

The first three elements—specialization, standardization, and size of the work unit—pertain mainly to individual job positions or to work teams, so we'll discuss them in the next section. The fourth element, coordination of activities, refers to ways management ensures that all departments and units work together to achieve organizational objectives. The fifth element, centralization and decentralization of decision-making, refers to ways of delegating decision-making power. The more decentralized decision-making is, the more autonomy managers and workers at all levels are likely to have in planning, implementing, and controlling their own performance.

Key Factors in Determining Organizational Structure   The five elements just discussed are experimented with and finally established in the process of designing an organizational structure. Five key factors that determine *how* they are decided on and set up are the following:

The strategy for achieving the organization's mission and long-range objectives is important, especially in determining the lines of authority and channels of communication between various managers and subunits. Strategy also affects how information flows along those lines and what mechanisms are used for planning and decision-making. For example, some companies have adopted a strategy of staying in close touch with customers in order to anticipate their wants and satisfy their needs. To implement this strategy, they may decide to divide activities according to type of customer to be served.

The outputs of the organization are the source of its revenues and, in a sense, its reason for being. Outputs may be products, services, information, or programs—anything that customers or clients will pay for. Some experts say that outputs should be the major building blocks of organizational design, rather than positions, technology, or other types of structure.

The technology used to create the products or services the organization offers especially affects the degree of standardization and specialization of work activities. Technology also affects the size of work units, the level at which decisions are made, and how units are coordinated. The rapidly changing technology of the computer-manufacturing industry, for example, creates a need for flexible structures that provide for experimentation and team problem-solving. Industries based on a more established technology may have evolved to a fairly high degree of specialization and standardization that is very efficient.

The people involved in the organization's activities affect every aspect of organizational structure. The attitudes, beliefs, and abilities of managers, workers, customers, suppliers, and others—and their need to work with each other in specific ways—must be taken into account. When the work of the organization involves large, long-term projects that require the expertise of people from various functional areas, for example, a matrix or project type of organization may work best. Any structural form that is highly decentralized and depends on worker participation in planning and decision-making must be staffed with people who believe such a system can work and who are willing to accept responsibility.

In the past most companies have viewed such factors as capital assets, products, competitive position, or unique technology as the foundation for success. Today organizations that focus on their human resources as the foundation for success are emerging as the leaders in their respective fields [9, pp. 263–64].

The size of the overall organization and its major divisions, if any, affects the need for specialization and standardization. Generally, the larger the organization, the higher the degree of specialization and standardization needed to maintain adequate control and coordination of activities. For this and other reasons, facilities with fewer than 100 employees are often perceived by workers as "better places to work," and levels of motivation and productivity appear to be higher [3].

Types of Organizational Departmentation
Organizations are usually divided into departments according to (1) the functions workers are to perform, (2) the products or services produced, (3) the location of the markets that are serviced, (4) the type of customer buying the products or services, or, most frequently, (5) some combination of these categories (see Figure 12-3). We'll pay special attention to the combination known as a matrix structure, shown in Figure 12-4.

Functional departmentation is by far the most common and basic type of division of organizational activities. All persons engaged in

FIGURE 12-3: Organizational Structure; Product Division Combined with Other Forms

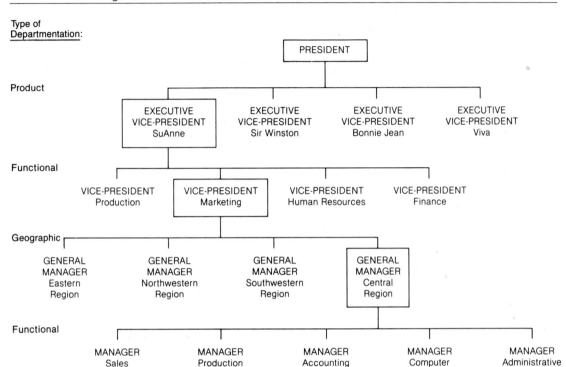

one type of activity — such as sales, manufacturing, finance, personnel, and so on — are grouped into a department. Functional departmentation fosters a higher degree of specialization. For example, when everyone involved in sales belongs to one department, specialized sales skills may become increasingly sophisticated. If the firm becomes quite large, however, it may become difficult to coordinate sales of many products to large and diverse markets.

Product or market departmentation is usually used, therefore, when an organization becomes so large that basic functional de-

partmentation is unwieldy. In small- to medium-sized companies the top managers are usually functional managers in charge of all sales or some other function for the entire company. In larger companies top managers may be in charge of a product line, all operations in a geographic location, or all operations for a particular customer category rather than heading up one functional area. Each of these divisions may have its own sales, manufacturing, accounting, and other functional departments. Each division may also be accountable for its own profits, operating almost as a separate business but with some direction from home

FIGURE 12-4: Matrix Organization

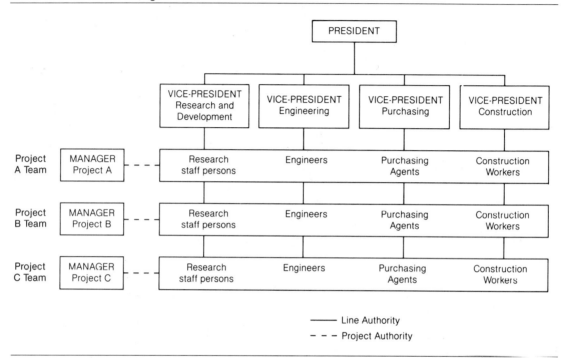

office top management. Let's take a look at product or market divisions and some combinations.

Product departmentation is often used by large manufacturers, such as General Motors (Chevrolet Division, Cadillac Division, and so forth). It may also be used by large construction companies and other firms that engage in large, long-term projects; a department may be formed for each project. Lighthouse Designs has a SuAnne Division responsible for women's fashion wear in misses sizes, a Sir Winston Division responsible for men's sportswear, a Bonnie Jean Division responsible for women's fashion wear in large sizes, and a Viva Division for petite-size clothing. The partial organization chart shown in Figure 12-3 shows this division by product with further division of work activities by function and location.

Geographical divisions are formed when activities must be performed close to (1) major markets, such as bank customers or product buyers in foreign countries, (2) major sources of raw materials, such as oil to be refined or coal to be mined, or (3) specialized labor markets, such as computer specialists in the Silicon Valley area near San Francisco. When location is of prime importance, then each region may be headed by an executive vice-president with functional vice-presidents serving under her or him. In the example shown in Figure 12-3, the type of product is most important to the company, so regional division occurs farther down the hierarchy.

Customer divisions may be formed when the operations involving various categories of customers are distinctly different. For example, a meat-packing plant may have different divisions for handling products going

FIGURE 12-5: Model of a Fluid,
Open Organization

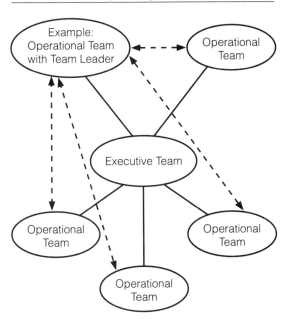

——— Direct Accountability

- - - Interaction Among Teams; Advisory

to grocery stores, to restaurants, and to institutions.

Combinations of these types of work division are used more often than a pure form. Normally there is a functional division at the top, with a vice-president overseeing sales of all kinds, for example. Under that vice-president there may be a further division by product, customer, and/or geography. A combination that has received much attention because it violates a strict chain of command is the matrix structure.

Matrix structure is a composite of a basic functional structure with an overlay of project or product teams, each with its own project managers. This structure is frequently used by companies that contract for large

projects (such as power plant or airport construction) that may last for months or years. Teams made up of various types of designers, engineers, skilled workers, and staff people are needed to complete the project. Each team member has a home base within a functional department (such as plant design or electrical engineering) but spends most of his or her time working with a project team. As soon as work on one project is completed, team members are normally assigned to a newly organized project team.

This dual structure, shown in Figure 12-4, complicates the chain of command because project team members report to two managers, the head of their functional (home-base) department and the project team manager. When an employee reports to two bosses, the authority and control of each boss can be weakened. The potential problems this situation might create must be weighed against the major advantage of bringing together specialized skills from various departments to focus on the problems of a particular project. Since these persons become a team, working together as a group, coordination problems are minimized. Also, each project is assigned only the number of people it needs, which minimizes duplication of effort and therefore costs.

Fluid, open structures are becoming more common in the 1990s, as mentioned in Chapter 2. Firms that operate within fast-paced, highly competitive, fluid, open marketplaces must organize themselves to respond quickly to their changing environment. As customer demands change, as the competition changes, as new opportunities open up and then quickly fade, new work teams or operating units must spring up to meet these needs, then reorganize quickly to meet new needs. Note the model of a fluid, open organization shown in Figure 12-5; remember, it is a simplified example of just one form a fluid organization might take. All operational teams communicate and interact with one another, so in a more complete model you would see an intricate web of interconnecting broken lines symbolizing this pattern of multiple, informal communication networks.

Structuring Work-Unit and Individual Job Activities

Now let's talk about the design of your work unit (if you're in a small facility, it may be referred to as a department). Your structure of course will be based on your unit objectives and the tactics you'll use in attaining them. How much freedom you have to set these objectives and tactics and to organize your unit accordingly will depend on the philosophy of the firm's top management. The more you can involve your workers in dividing up the activities necessary to attaining objectives, the better.

During the organizing process, keep in mind the elements, key factors, and ways of departmenting we just discussed. Which concepts can help you determine the best way of organizing your unit's activities? Two elements of special significance at this level are degree of specialization and standardization. The degree of specialization addresses the question, How routine or complex shall various jobs be? The degree of standardization looks at the question, How much autonomy shall workers have in doing their jobs?

Degree of Specialization   Both during and after the objective-setting process, you and your people should jointly determine what work must be done within the work unit to achieve its objectives. Next you must determine how that work will be divided into tasks that individual or work teams will perform. Will each person get a large chunk of a task or project—a chunk that includes a variety of activities? Or will each person specialize in a small part of each project—doing that part over and over in project after project?

The answers to these kinds of questions can greatly affect the level of motivation and productivity in your unit. The more routine, or repetitive and specialized, the job is, the easier it is to master and the more likely workers are to become bored once they become expert at it. On the other hand, the more complex the job and the more varied the functions included in it, the more difficult it is to learn and the longer workers take to become productive. However, the challenge and variety are likely to motivate workers if they are able eventually to master the job.

Degree of Standardization   How much guidance and control will you exercise over the tasks you delegate? Will you design jobs that are highly standardized and controlled, thus providing the worker with guidance in tried and proven procedures? At the other extreme, job design can provide the worker with maximum autonomy in deciding how to achieve job objectives. Such a design may result in false starts and dead-end approaches but will enhance the motivation of most capable workers. The degree of standardization in most jobs falls somewhere between these two examples. Your decision will depend on the type of work to be done, the technology involved, the demands of the situation, the needs and abilities of your workers, and the attitude of top management toward worker participation and autonomy.

Job Designs That Motivate   Of course, you'll want to design jobs for the greatest employee motivation and productivity. You know from our discussion on motivation in Chapter 10 that workers are most likely to be productive on a long-term basis when (1) the work is meaningful to them, (2) they feel responsible for the outcome of their work, and (3) they get timely feedback on the actual results of their work activities. You also know that when job design calls for (1) a variety of skills and activities, (2) chunks of projects that are large enough for the worker to identify as his or hers, and (3) results that are viewed as significant, workers tend to view the job as meaningful.

Work teams can be one solution to the problem of degree of specialization and standardization. Team members can gradually train each other in their respective specialties, for example, and then decide on how to rotate jobs to enhance skill variety. The work team can be responsible for a larger chunk of the work and therefore experience the feelings of pride, or disappointment and renewed determination, that go along with task identity and significance.

Once teams experience a sense of responsibility for what they produce, members usually begin to monitor each other, and peer pressure effectively replaces some of the external control that was previously necessary. Your role may become that of facilitator of group-planning, problem-solving, and decision-making, and the teams may become relatively self-managed and therefore relatively autonomous. Such a design works best when teams operate democratically.

On the other hand, if your organization and its workers are committed to a traditional type of work structure, you will need to determine which jobs carry more authority and responsibility than others. Then you must establish a hierarchy for coordinating the activities of your unit. Delegation and building work teams are discussed in more detail in Chapter 13.

A PARTICIPATIVE PERFORMANCE PLANNING SYSTEM

A Participative Performance Planning System is one approach to planning that uses the type of planning process and the kinds of planning and organizing skills we've discussed so far. The performance plans developed by every person, managers and workers alike, are de-signed to support organizational objectives and strategies, as well as departmental, unit, and work-team objectives and tactics, as indicated in Figure 12-6. One major purpose of this system is to encourage people to think in terms of objectives and priorities instead of duties and tasks. Another major purpose is to provide the basis for self-appraisal and self-control of performance.

The development of individual performance plans includes the following steps, as shown in Figure 12-7: (1) Each employee meets with his or her team leader for a one-on-one initial Planning Conference at which the employee presents an initial draft of a performance plan. The draft is jointly refined, and a Performance Plan is agreed on that includes ongoing and periodic objectives and the action steps needed to attain them. (2) Regular, spontaneous conferences and coaching augment self-evaluation of the individual's achievement of objectives throughout the year. (3) One year later the employee and team leader hold a one-on-one Yearly Planning Conference to formally discuss achievement of the past year's objectives and to plan the coming year's objectives. (4) At this conference they verbally describe the past year's performance and document it, along with the coming year's plan, in a Yearly Performance Planning Report.

The Performance Plan

It is all too common to encounter employees who focus on activities, duties, and tasks, some of which may be spelled out in a job description. Other employees are not even sure what their job description entails. It is relatively rare to encounter employees who are clear about their job objectives and priorities—who can reel them off on a moment's notice. Performance Plans are more comprehensive and results oriented than traditional job descriptions. A job description usually consists of a list

FIGURE 12-6: A Participative Performance Planning System

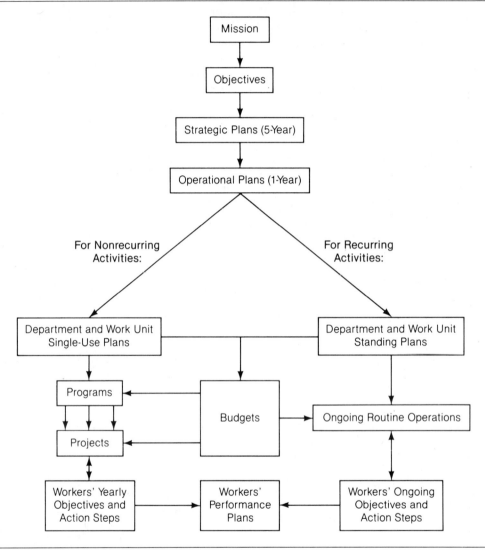

of functional responsibilities and tasks with perhaps a statement of the level of education and experience required, as shown in Exhibit 12-4.

On the other hand, Performance Plans are based on the outputs needed from each person. Team leaders and members base output goals on the organization's needs and the members' abilities. The description of performance goals often becomes the job description. Rewards, such as salary increases, commissions, and bonuses, are based on the types of outputs produced, on their quantity and quality. Performance Plans not only describe the tasks (ac-

FIGURE 12-7: A Participative Performance Planning Process

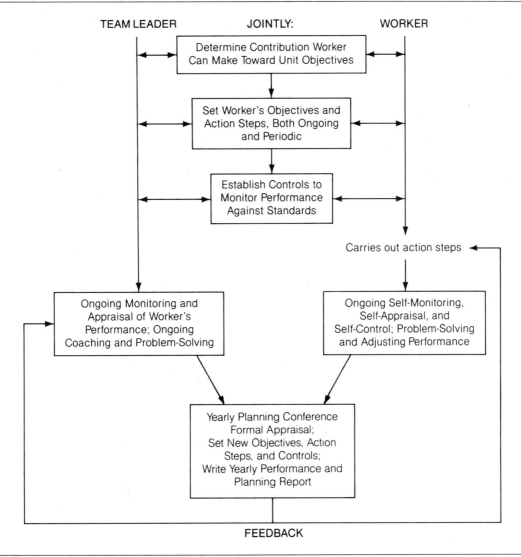

tion steps) the job entails, they relate the tasks to the achievement of objectives. In addition to these ongoing objectives, new organizational objectives are agreed on periodically (usually each year), and the team member integrates these periodic objectives into his or her Performance Plan, as shown in Exhibit 12-5.

Ongoing (Standing) Plans When individuals sit down to prepare their Performance Plans, they start with their existing job descriptions, if available. If not, they must start from scratch in identifying performance areas (or functional areas) they are responsible for on an ongoing basis. These responsibilities support

EXHIBIT 12-4: Job Description

Job Title: Buyer 1

Functional Area: Manufacturing

Subfunctional: Purchasing

Primary Responsibility:

Assist in obtaining materials, components, equipment, and services.
Check requisitions, obtain quotations, and examine bids.
Coordinate purchasing activities with Manufacturing and Engineering Departments, maintaining inventory at planned levels.
As required, monitor the cost, schedule, and scope aspects of assigned subcontracts.

Job Level:

Entry level: Learn to use professional concepts and company's internal policies and procedures to solve routine problems.

Education/Experience:

Two years of college or equivalent. No prior experience necessary. Good writing and verbal communication ability preferred.

---

the organization's standing plans. The next step is to formulate a key objective for each performance area.

Individuals at the managerial or professional staff level may find it helpful first to list two major performance categories: professional and technical. The professional category includes the ongoing managerial functions present in every team leader's job, such as planning, organizing, leading, and controlling. The individual should formulate a key ongoing objective in each major functional area for which he or she is responsible. Technical subcategories will vary according to the particular position. For example, an Advertising Manager's technical functions might include "identify target markets for XYZ product; create advertising materials that will appeal to target markets; identify optimal media sources for advertising materials."

The next step is to develop a miniplan for each major objective. That miniplan must include what the individual will do to achieve the objective, deadline dates for key actions, and standards that state the level of achievement desired — the quantity and quality of output from these activities. It might also include tac-

tics for achieving the objective. One tactic might be to delegate certain action steps to team members or to an ad agency; another might be to use only certain types of advertising media.

These plans make up the basic, ongoing Performance Plan for achieving recurring job objectives. The individual and his or her team leader formally update it each year. It should tie in with the manager's performance plan and support the work-unit objectives.

Single-Use Plans (Special Projects, One-Time Objectives) Individuals are also assigned periodic, nonrecurring responsibilities that contribute to the programs and resulting projects that are developed to meet nonrecurring organizational or departmental objectives. The other part of your Performance Plan will consist of specific objectives for meeting these responsibilities, along with key action steps for achieving each objective. For example, the objective "to develop an advertising campaign for ABC product" might call for the following action steps: (1) Select an ad agency using departmental screening steps; (2) develop standards for acceptance of advertising materials from

EXHIBIT 12-5: Partial Performance Plan

Name: Jean Casey
Position: Buyer
Department: Purchasing

Performance Areas:

1. Production buyer
2. Responsible for past-due purchase orders
3. Maintain purchase price variance
4. Responsible for returning defective merchandise or overshipments of merchandise to vendor
5. Interface with Accounts Payable
6. Responsible for revision changes with vendor
7. Responsible for all change orders received from Production Planning Department

Performance Area 1:   Production Buyer

Ongoing Objectives:

To purchase product materials in a cost-effective and timely manner in order to meet production work schedule determined by corporate requirements.

Action Steps:

1. After receipt of Traveling Requisition (TR) from Production Planning Department, contact vendor(s) (at least three) for pricing and delivery, after checking Approved Source List (APSL). Quotes may be verbal or written as required.
2. Select vendor, based on best price/delivery quotes and/or level of service offered.
3. Issue Purchase Order (PO) to vendor with TR data.
4. Complete TR card with vendor data.
5. Deliver TR card to Purchasing Clerk for computer entry.
6. TR is returned with confirmation PO for signature and quotation summary if dollar amount exceeds $1,000.
7. Review weekly PO status report for accuracy.
8. Attend SuAnne production meetings when necessary.
9. Interface with designers and manufacturing engineers for verification of APSL or to establish an alternative material.
10. Consult with Production Planner as required.

Yearly Objective:

To decrease cost of materials purchased by 3 percent, without decreasing quality, during fiscal year 19xx.

Action Steps:

1. Contact other Lighthouse Designs buyers for vendor information.
2. Contact buyers at other manufacturing companies for vendor information.
3. When time permits, contact more than three vendors for quotes.

Note: Although detailed objectives and action steps for only the first performance area of this plan are shown here, detailed plans are developed for all performance areas.

the agency, based on policy guidelines; (3) interpret marketing information from company sources and communicate it to the agency so they can develop appropriate advertising materials as evaluated by Executive Committee.

The formal written Performance Plan that is confirmed by an individual's boss may contain only major objectives and action steps, along with any standards that can be built in. But informal planning doesn't stop there; the written plan is merely the broad base for more detailed advance planning, for daily planning, and for monitoring of performance and results. Each broad action step may need a detailed plan of its own, with appropriate standards. These detailed action plans may be formalized into procedures for recurring objectives. Control plans should also be included in the Performance Plan, where appropriate. They should state when, where, and how performance will be checked against standards.

Ongoing Self-Evaluation and Monitoring

When the Performance Plan system is used effectively, it eliminates the individual's dependence on formal performance appraisals, which are generally ineffective and are usually dreaded by both employees and their team leaders or managers. Instead of waiting for a formal performance appraisal to find out how the boss thinks they are doing, individuals are guided by the Performance Plan in practicing self-evaluation on a continuous basis. This continual self-evaluation is essential to the success of the Performance Plan system. The plan must become a guide for making decisions, managing time, and allocating resources.

Also essential to the success of the system is the use the individuals' team leaders make of the Performance Plan. They must use it consistently to monitor the individuals' performance and to provide a fair and understandable basis

for giving needed feedback, coaching, information, and other resources. Obviously, there need be no surprises when it's time for the Yearly Planning Conference, since both the individual and the manager know specifically how performance has measured up to plans throughout the year.

Yearly Planning Conference

At the end of the year individuals meet with their team leaders or managers for a Yearly Planning Conference, which replaces the traditional performance evaluation with a more positive process. Here the focus is on the broad view of the employee's role and contributions in interacting with all elements of company operations. It is a joint endeavor in which employee and manager look at past experience, present status, and future needs and plans. Actual performance for the past year is surveyed in light of the Performance Plan. Achievements, areas of needed development, and career direction are discussed and identified.

Individuals and their team leaders agree on the level of the individual's achievement for the past year as specified and agreed on during their planning conference the previous year. They must describe the achievement level, both quantitatively and qualitatively, where appropriate, for each performance objective. Such verbal descriptions tend to be individual and appropriate to each employee's unique job situation, and therefore they are more effective than filling in checklist appraisal forms.

Leaders tend to inspire a higher level of employee motivation and accountability when they encourage employees to take the lead in evaluating their own performance, in pinpointing accountability for results, and in generating objectives for the coming year. When handled effectively, the conference eliminates the negative connotations for the employee of being evaluated. However, it still requires that the employee be responsible for his or her own performance.

The Yearly Planning Conference is much more future oriented than the traditional performance appraisal session. The conference provides a chance to step back and get an overview of the past year's performance. Employee and leader discuss important experiences in trying to meet last year's objectives and attempt to learn from those experiences. They identify what functional areas, action steps, and skill areas need to be expanded. For example, employees might attempt to identify what performance areas or portions of performance areas they enjoy the most and what future job position would allow them to use the skills involved in that performance area.

The Yearly Performance and Planning Report

The documentation process begins with the individual and his or her leader's determining if each objective was achieved. Then they verbally describe the level of achievement — that is, how close, over or under, the employee came to meeting the target. If the objective was not achieved, they note any action steps that were taken or overlooked. If similar objectives will be set in the future, they note any action steps that will be changed, added, or omitted. They also evaluate the performance of the action steps leading to each objective in order to gain a more detailed, specific picture of employee performance. This evaluation can help pinpoint strong areas and problem areas.

The form provided for documenting the Yearly Performance Planning Report does not provide performance categories with boxes that can be easily checked off. When such appraisal forms are used, leaders tend to stereotype employees as generally excellent, average, or poor. The forms are so quick and easy that

leaders often don't carefully analyze the employee's performance in each category. On the other hand, when people must verbally describe an achievement level for each objective and its action steps, they tend to become more engaged in the process, and a higher level of involvement and communication results.

As a result of this yearly conference and report process, the employee and the manager agree on Performance Plan Development Areas. These are the areas for training, coaching, growth, and development. They represent not only areas that need strengthening to achieve objectives in present performance areas, but areas that need to be developed for future career expansion and movement. These areas are included in the report.

Finally, the employee offers his or her ideas on what objectives and action steps should be included in the Performance Plan for the coming year. These ideas are discussed, the leader offers his or her ideas, and the two agree on a plan the employee is willing to make a commitment to achieving. The new objectives become part of the Yearly Performance and Planning Report as well as a part of the Performance Plan for the coming year. Thus the cycle is completed and the stage is set for goal-directed action and ongoing self-evaluation for the future.

Why the System Works

The Participative Performance Planning System works because the individuals themselves formulate the contributions they intend to make toward organizational objectives. They develop a clear picture of the expectations they, and their boss, have for their performance. They therefore know exactly how they are going to be measured. And when they are actually measured according to the stated objectives and agreed-on action steps, they are better able to perform at a level of productivity that gives them the satisfaction of achievement and also meets management's expectations.

THE POLITICAL SIDE OF PLANNING AND ORGANIZING

All management functions have their political aspects. We've talked about the more formal aspects of planning and organizing. Now let's discuss some of the political aspects — namely, how actual priorities and power lines may differ from formal plans and organization charts, how to handle crises, how to use a planning system to get what you want, and what to do when your boss resists formal planning.

Reading Between the Lines: What Formal Plans and Organizational Charts Don't Tell You

The larger the organization, the more deviation you may discover between formal, published objectives, policies, and so forth, and what your boss considers most important. The more complex the company, the greater the power gap may be between lines of authority shown on the formal organization chart and the actual informal power people can muster.

A major company objective and supporting policies may be to improve product or service quality. However, your boss's top priority may be to increase profits. He or she may prefer to sacrifice a little on quality if the resulting increase in profit is large enough. Don't assume therefore that formal organizational plans tell the whole story. Discuss them with your boss and other key decision-makers to determine where they really stand.

In a similar vein, the formal organizational chart may indicate that a certain person has only a staff relationship to your department and therefore has no line authority over you.

Find out what authority such people actually wield. It's not rare for a strong person who has the support of someone in top management to turn a staff job into a powerful position that carries the equivalent of line authority. Also, a certain group, either formal or informal, may have the ear of key decision-makers and therefore exercise informal power and influence that far exceed their formal authority as shown on the organization chart.

The point is, don't be naïve enough to assume that the formal planning system tells the whole story or that the organization chart gives the full picture of power and authority relationships. Try to determine where your boss and other key people really stand. Chapters 1 and 8 discuss some of these political aspects of power and authority. As pointed out in Chapter 8, you'll need to become aware of alliances, support networks, and cliques, as well as enmities, skirmishes, and vendettas in order to deal knowledgeably and effectively with people. Such savvy can help you tie into the right support networks and gain the cooperation of others. It can help you recognize and overcome barriers created by conflict between two managers. And it can help you steer clear of battles that don't directly concern you.

Planning for the Unexpected: Crisis Management

Savvy business leaders have always planned ahead for responding to natural disasters and accidents. The increased incidence of certain unfortunate events in the 1980s and 1990s demands that leaders also plan ahead for responding to terrorist threats and acts. Crisis situations — such as sabotage, hostage-taking, random or mass murder, arson, and building pollution — can affect the organization's image, reputation, products, or services. Intensifying the problem is the fact that about half of all terrorist threats worldwide during the 1980s were directed toward U.S. business. And businesses take on additional risks when they move into emerging markets, especially in underdeveloped countries with unstable governments.

Any crisis may grab immediate worldwide attention, forcing a company's leaders to make a quick response. Satellite news networks are making Marshall McLuhan's global village a reality. People throughout the global village watch newsworthy occurrences unfold almost (or literally) at the moment they happen. If an organization's leaders come across as stonewalling the global village, or lying to it, their company's image will be permanently tarnished. Whether a crisis arises from a terrorist act, a political coup, a dangerous product, or an environmental hazard, managers must communicate the message that the company is proactive in responding to the crisis and is open in its communication with the public.

In responding to a crisis, you may find that law enforcers' needs for conducting their investigation are in conflict with your firm's needs for maintaining its open, proactive image and even ensuring its survival. Before disaster strikes, the firm's leaders should form a crisis management team to develop policies that will help the organization cooperate with law enforcers, act in the public interest, deal with the media, cope with community groups, handle its own sales and marketing process, and protect its image and survival. Crisis management expert Dr. Deborah Lowe offers these guidelines [5]:

- Respond to the media as quickly as possible, within twenty-four to forty-eight hours, to show concern for the public well-being.

- Set up procedures for effective and quick threat assessment so you can report facts to the media.

- Do not speculate without facts.

- Learn some appropriate responses to typical media questions. If you don't know the an-

swer, try "I can't tell you that, but I can tell you about the process and the steps we are taking to investigate and handle the situation." Talk about what you *do* know and never say "no comment."

- Top management should select and cross-train company leaders and company spokespersons to understand and respond effectively to the media. Managers at outlying facilities need a local crisis management team. Keep the number of spokespersons to a minimum.

- Characterize the organization as a victim responding effectively to an unforeseeable misfortune, to prevent any undertone of a "villain" image.

By following an effective crisis management plan, you and your firm can reassure the public that (1) the organization is alert, aware, and on top of the situation; (2) it is doing everything in its power to mitigate disastrous effects; (3) it will protect its customers and the general public in every way possible; and (4) effective measures will be taken to prevent or effectively cope with similar crises in the future.

Using Your Plans — Beyond Formal Objectives

By now you're probably convinced that developing objectives for your work unit, yourself, and your people can lead to higher levels of achievement. You can also use your plans politically to increase your personal and leadership effectiveness.

With Your Boss   If your boss is also involved in formal planning, you're in a good position to deal with him or her in terms of priorities and objectives. For example, what if your boss keeps piling too much work on you or your department without giving you additional resources for getting the work done? Instead of playing the passive martyr, you can suggest that you'll handle work necessary to attain top-priority objectives and put other work on the back burner. Or you can suggest that if you try to complete all the work, top-priority work will probably be neglected. Or you can ask your boss to specify priorities for completing various items.

When you want additional resources, such as more workers, equipment, or supplies, show how they will help meet work-unit and department objectives. Do the same when you're defending budget requests.

When asking for a raise or promotion, refer to your record of achieving objectives. Chapter 14 discusses this in more detail.

With Your Peers What if one of your peers makes unreasonable demands or requests for service from your department? An acceptable way of refusing may be to explain that if you comply with such a request, you will have to neglect high-priority work that is necessary to meet departmental objectives.

Sometimes peers simply don't understand what your people are trying to do. When you have a performance plan on file for everyone, you can easily communicate the objectives and activities involved in every position.

With Your Work Team You'll probably get the most mileage out of a planning system within your own work unit. After all, workers can make unreasonable requests and demands too. And it helps when you evaluate requests, make decisions, and explain them in terms of how they tie in with department objectives.

The planning process helps you nail down each worker's willingness and ability to perform. It can help you pinpoint areas that need changing or reorganizing, such as dividing work loads, shifting responsibilities or activities, or reorganizing work flow. It can help separate important from unimportant activities so they can be managed on a priority basis. This

in turn helps eliminate energy drains and time-wasters.

From the time a worker comes on board until he or she moves out of the department, the planning process can pay off in greater effectiveness. Performance plans can be tools for orientation, career development, coaching and counseling, evaluation, and salary and promotion decisions.

A new worker can use the performance plan of the worker who previously held the position to gain a comprehensive, detailed, goal-oriented picture of job responsibilities and tasks.

By studying others' performance plans, you and your workers can pinpoint jobs in a career path leading to achievement of their career goals.

A well-developed performance plan helps you evaluate performance objectively because it provides specific, agreed-on areas of responsibility, objectives, tasks, and standards. It enables you to identify areas of needed development as well as areas of strength that can be expanded and enhanced. Therefore, you can do a better job of coaching workers to higher performance and counseling them in self-development.

Perhaps the major use you can make of the planning process is to motivate workers. A good planning process provides a higher level of autonomy, attainable challenges, guidelines for success, and the satisfaction of experiencing and being recognized for achieving specific results.

Performance plans also provide a fair basis for granting merit increases based on specific performance and results. In fact, they must be tied in with the reward the company gives if they are to continue to have meaning for workers. It's also crucial to base personnel decisions on how well workers meet performance objectives. Reward those who perform well with the promotions, transfer those who need development in other areas, and terminate those who repeatedly fail to perform adequately.

Every team leader dreads firing a worker. A good planning process provides the basis for making such a decision and explaining it to the worker. When you explain it in terms of the necessity for meeting specific objectives and standards, you separate the decision from the personalities involved. You can take a counseling approach in guiding the worker toward needed development or other occupations better suited to his or her abilities and interests.

When There's No Formal Planning in Your Firm

Although adopting a formal planning system will not automatically eliminate organizational problems, numerous research studies indicate that it will result in a higher level of organizational achievement. In spite of these facts, you may find yourself in a firm where little or no formal planning exists, especially below the top-management level. Management consultant Paul Warner confirms the observations of many planning consultants when he discusses how the bright, well-educated young woman with planning skills and ideas can threaten an older male manager: "Most men at middle management level in small to medium-sized organizations, where most of the jobs are, don't engage in formal planning and have no training in it. Most of the training that does take place occurs in university business schools."

Such managers may feel threatened by a woman with a business degree who comes to him with planning ideas and suggestions. The team member he previously viewed as average he now sees as someone able to "work smarter" than he works. The fact that the subordinate is a woman may intensify his discomfort. Of course, female bosses may also feel threatened in such circumstances. If you have such a boss, and you push the planning issue, she or he may develop an antiplanning bias. On the other hand, you needn't abandon your planning expertise. Just adopt an informal, non-threatening planning approach that is sensitive to your boss's preferences.

Start with Your Own Job Needs   Instead of pushing for a large-scale planning system, settle for getting some commitment from your boss on what your own job objectives should be and the basis she or he will use for evaluating your performance. First, carefully work out the plan *you* would like to establish — do this privately, even at home. And leave any formal written versions of it there. Then find a quiet time at the office to have a relaxed discussion with your boss.

Avoid the Vocabulary of Formal Planning   Carefully select the words you use to discuss matters pertaining to your privately developed performance plan. Instead of talking about strategic planning, objectives, tactics, action steps, and standards, ask your boss's opinion about what you should be accomplishing. You can say you have given some thought to this and you want to touch bases to be sure you're on the right track. You might ask what you need to work on in order to receive a good evaluation, a promotion, a raise, or whatever payoff seems appropriate for your situation.

Keep It Informal   Chances are your boss will not be able to come up with many specific objectives you should be working toward, much less standards, tactics, or key action steps. This can be to your advantage if you play your cards right because it means you can probably get agreement on the plan you've developed. But remember, you've left your written plan at home. You now discuss just the meat of the plan with your boss. "I thought one area I could work toward would be decreasing shipping errors, even reducing them to no more than 1 percent of all orders by the end of the year. What do you think?" Go through your key objectives in this manner, getting your boss's ideas and reaching a mutual understanding on each.

Document by Informal Memo Only Written planning documents tend to be viewed as much more formal, and therefore threatening, than oral discussion. However, it's to your advantage to follow up this meeting with an informal memo, using such terminology as "confirming our discussion about job direction." You might mention that you want to be sure you're clear about his or her thoughts on the subject. If appropriate, you might flesh out the discussion by saying, "In the meantime, I've had some additional thoughts . . ." Add more items to your plan, and conclude, "I'll assume this follows the thrust of our talk and meets with your approval unless I hear otherwise."

Carefully file away your copy of this memo. Of course, you'll be using your more complete, formal performance plan between now and evaluation time. Just before your formal evaluation, review the memo to refresh your memory as to just what your boss agreed to. If his evaluation is not based on those items and seems unfair to you, you now have a leg to stand on. Remind him tactfully of your agreements; if necessary, you can later produce a copy of them to refresh his memory.

Use Similar Tactics for Your Team Members You can use these same nonthreatening tactics in working with your people to improve their productivity. You can establish the entire planning process, merely changing the vocabulary to terms your boss and other key managers are comfortable with and documenting with informal memos. If your firm has a formal performance appraisal program, adapt the process to it.

SUMMARY

The two keys to effective managerial planning are (1) focusing more on end results than on activities and (2) including your team members in the planning process rather than doing it yourself and then telling them. When you focus on end results, you are more likely to be effective — to do the right things, the things that will bring about those results. This is much more important than being efficient — focusing on activities and doing them right — which can cause you to do relatively unimportant things at the expense of crucial items.

You must learn to plan effectively if you want to make things happen rather than be a passive bystander. Good planning (1) makes you more promotable, (2) provides you with a basis for making effective decisions, (3) can eliminate unpleasant surprises caused by lack of forecasting, and (4) gives direction to motivational drive — yours and your workers'.

The organizational planning process begins at the top-management level and includes defining the organization's mission, making forecasts, and setting organizational objectives. The next phase involves formulating strategies and policies that help achieve objectives. Middle management then develops departmental objectives, along with tactics, rules, and procedures for implementing them. Supervisors and workers set up work-unit and individual objectives, along with action steps for reaching them. They also devise standards and controls to help monitor and evaluate performance.

Important steps in the planning process include identifying the contributions each person can make and developing clearly stated individual objectives that support company objectives. Performance standards provide the basis for controls. These controls should serve to alert the right people to deviations from standards and allow corrections to be made before problems develop.

An integral part of planning for results is determining how to divide the total work of the organization into divisions, departments, and work units. Top management wants to design the best structure for helping people work together to fulfill the firm's mission, carry out its strategies, and achieve its objectives. An organization's structure is the arrangement and interrelationships of its various parts and job positions. The structure defines the formal division of work activities and shows how all functions or activities are linked together. It also indicates the organization's formal hierarchy and authority structure and shows reporting relationships.

The structuring of activities begins at the top when management initially decides on an organizational plan and periodically reevaluates and modifies it. Some key factors to consider when determining organizational structure are (1) the strategy for achieving the organization's mission and long-range objectives, (2) the outputs of the organization, (3) the technology used to create the products or services the organization offers, (4) the people involved in the organization's activities, and (5) the size of the overall organization and its major divisions.

Organizations are usually divided into departments according to (1) the functions workers are to perform, (2) the products or services produced, (3) the location of the markets that are serviced, (4) the type of customer buying the products or services, or, most frequently, (5) some combination of these categories.

When organizing the work in your unit and the individual job activities of your workers, pay special attention to the degree of specialization and standardization that will produce the best results. Look for job designs that motivate, such as self-managed work teams that provide a variety of activities and needed skills along with a measure of autonomy.

A Participative Performance Planning System encourages people to think in terms of objectives and priorities instead of duties and tasks. It provides the basis for self-control and self-appraisal of performance. The Performance Plan includes: (1) an initial planning conference at which workers and team leaders agree to ongoing and periodic objectives and action steps for the coming year; (2) regular, spontaneous conferences and coaching throughout the year; (3) a Yearly Planning Conference at the end of the year to discuss formally the achievement of the past year's objectives and to develop the coming year's objectives; and (4) the documentation of the Yearly Planning Conference, called the Yearly Performance Planning Report.

In addition to gaining knowledge and skills in planning and organizing, you will be wise to gain an understanding of the political aspects. Your boss's actual priorities and objectives may differ from his or her formal ones. Formal organization charts never show all the lines of informal influence and power.

You can use your plans politically to increase your effectiveness with your boss, your peers, and your work team. For example, you can base either agreement to or refusal of requests on how they affect objectives.

Use political public relations savvy by forming an effective crisis management team and policies before disaster strikes. The policies should guide the firm in cooperating with law enforcement, acting in the public interest, dealing with the media, coping with community groups, handling its own sales and marketing process, and protecting its image and survival.

Political savvy with workers includes using Performance Plans to help orient, develop, evaluate, motivate, coach, and counsel them. To be meaningful, however, Performance Plans must be tied in with the rewards of salary increase and promotion.

Your planning and organizing skills may threaten bosses who don't have such skills. You can still use them, beginning with setting objectives for your own performance. Be sensitive, however, to your boss's resistance to formal planning by using informal language and documentation. Use the same non-threatening approach when you establish a planning process with your work team — keep it informal.

Additional Exercises

EXERCISE 12-5: DEVELOPING OBJECTIVES AND CONTROLS WITH YOUR ASSISTANT

You have accepted the position of National Convention Chairperson for your professional association. This of course means you are responsible for the entire convention that will be held in your city six months from now. You want your assistant to assume responsibility for all routine correspondence in connection with the convention. You ask him to develop a set of attainable yet challenging objectives, standards, and controls for this area of responsibility. In the meantime, develop your own set so that you will be ready to discuss these items with him and make needed suggestions.

EXERCISE 12-6: DEVELOPING YOUR PERFORMANCE PLAN

If you are now working, develop a Performance Plan for your current job. If you are not working, develop a Performance Plan for any job you previously held, either part-time or full-time. On a sheet of paper write the following labels and then fill in the details:

Performance Areas
Performance Area 1 — Key Ongoing Objective
Action Steps
Performance Area 1 — Periodic Objective
Action Steps

Note: Using additional sheets of paper, repeat this process for each performance area.

EXERCISE 12-7: DEL ORO — DESIGNING AN ORGANIZATIONAL STRUCTURE

You are the manager of a Del Oro Boutique that sells apparel and gifts imported from Mexico. The boutique is part of Del Oro Enterprises, owned by Vickie Drew and her cousin Maria Sanchez. Seven years ago they started with a small Mexican restaurant in the Phoenix area. The business has grown to include eight restaurants with adjoining boutiques and Mexican delicatessens, scattered across a sixty-mile radius.

Almost from the beginning the restaurants displayed a few gift items Maria bought on her frequent trips to Mexico to visit her father's relatives. They sold so well that separate boutiques were set up at each restaurant location. Because of the many requests Del Oro received to cater parties in private homes and to provide take-out food, the cousins eventually opened a separate but adjacent Mexican Deli. This operation was so successful that delicatessens are now included at each of the eight restaurant locations.

Recently sales of Mexican beer and Margarita ingredients have been so great that the cousins are considering adding bottle shops at some of the locations. If they are successful, they would add bottle shops at all locations.

So far Vickie has been overseeing all aspects of the restaurant operations, Maria is mainly responsible for the boutique operations, and they have been sharing responsibility for the deli/catering operations. At each of the eight locations they have three managers who are responsible for the restaurant, boutique, and deli operations, respectively. Today they are holding a special meeting with these twenty-four local managers to begin plans for reorganizing the company.

V: We've experienced fantastic growth in the last few years, so we must have been doing something right. But Maria and I feel it's time for a reevaluation of our organizational structure.

M: Yes. For one thing, Vickie and I feel things have gotten a little beyond our control. It's difficult for us to keep up with our diverse operations.

V: And we may be missing real growth opportunities. We think this bottle shop idea may be very profitable, but frankly Maria and I don't feel like taking on more complexity when we can hardly manage what we have now.

M: That's right. Vickie and I have been working sixty to seventy hours a week with very few breaks for the past seven years. Basically, our headquarters staff consists of several highly paid assistants and secretaries who have learned various aspects of the business. Their titles don't begin to reflect their duties and responsibilities. It's time we promoted some people and perhaps hired some specialists for certain areas. We need some help in managing this operation, but we haven't decided just how to go about it. We're open to suggestions.

Your assignment:

Step 1. Draw a rough sketch of the Del Oro Enterprises organizational structure as it now exists. Indicate type of departmentation.

Step 2. Determine at least two ways the company could be reorganized. Draw rough sketches of the resulting organizational structure for each.

Step 3. Discuss the advantages and disadvantages of each type of organizational structure you devised in Step 2. Which would you recommend?

EXERCISE 12-8: THE BARRON CASE

You haven't had a chance to really chat with your friend and colleague Lauren Barron for the past few weeks. (Lauren supervises administrative services in your office.) Today she stops by your office. After a few minutes of catching up, Lauren starts talking about her job.

"I just came from another meeting with the boss. He says we'll all need to do more advance planning. I'm already so busy, I don't have time to think! This new computer system is about to get me down. I just can't keep up with everything anymore.

"You know, I've spent years learning all about this company—how to find out what needs doing and how to go about getting it done. You and I have talked about the fact that whenever someone wants to know how something is done in this division, they usually come to me. You know those procedures I set up a couple of months ago for word processing? I just got the bugs worked out and now they want me to change it.

"They just keep piling up things for me to do. I don't know how I can keep up with it all. I'm still worn out from this remodeling we just finished. It seemed as if I was running in four or five directions at once — answering one request and complaint after another, telling one person why she gets an L-shaped work space and another why his is square. I'm just trying to get along. But it seems no matter how hard I try, some people are upset.

"I've always liked this company, and I want to keep my job, but it's getting me down. Maybe I'm in over my head, now that everything is changing so fast."

You've never heard Lauren talk this way before; in fact, she has rarely complained at all in the past. What do you think are the major sources of Lauren's problems? What should she stop doing? Start doing?

REFERENCES

1. Bickel, Joyce. Director of Imports and Sweater Division, Koret of North America, San Francisco.

2. Drucker, Peter. *Management.* New York: Harper & Row, 1974. A classic — required reading in nearly all business schools. If you can read only one basic management book, read this one.

3. Hackman, J. Richard. *Improving Life at Work.* Santa Monica, Calif.: Goodyear, 1988.

4. Hellriegel, Don, and John W. Slocum, Jr. *Management.* 5th ed. Reading, Mass.: Addison-Wesley, 1990.

5. Lowe, Deborah. "Terrorism Against Business: Executive Crisis Communications Choices." *San Francisco State University School of Business Journal,* Vol. III, No. 2 (1991), pp. 47–54.

6. Newman, William H. *Constructive Control: Design and Use of Control Systems.* Englewood Cliffs, N.J.: Prentice-Hall, 1984. An extensive examination of control systems with models, diagrams, examples, and explanations.

7. Peters, Thomas J., and Robert H. Waterman. *In Search of Excellence.* New York: Harper & Row, 1982.

8. Schneider-Jenkins, Carol. Human Resources Manager, Oximetrix, Inc., Mountain View, Calif.

9. Stoner, James A. F. *Management.* 3rd ed. Englewood Cliffs, N.J.: Prentice-Hall, 1987.

10. Warner, Paul H. Executive Director, Management Resource Group, Consultants in Strategic Planning, Product Development, and Marketing, Oakland, Calif.

Chapter Thirteen

Team Development: Empowering, Delegating, Coaching, Interviewing

*"People support what they help create and
decisions are best made at the levels where
they will be carried out."*

Fran Rees

Team development allows you to bring together personal and leadership skills in the day-to-day functioning of your work team. Most leaders say it is the most challenging, demanding, and satisfying work they do. In this chapter you can learn more about

1. Understanding what work teams are and how to develop them

2. Empowering, challenging, and supporting workers and work teams

3. Facilitating team meetings that achieve team objectives

4. Leading Hot Teams, Continuous Improvement, and Total Quality Management

5. Leading demographically diverse teams

6. Delegating tasks to enhance team and worker empowerment, development, and training

7. Analyzing performance problems and coaching workers to top performance

8. Evaluating performance fairly and coherently

9. Interviewing and selecting new team members

10. Orienting new team players

11. Using fair processes when team members must be transferred or dismissed

 The Magic of Involvement

"You must have had a good day," Scott smiles at Erika as she breezes through the front door.

"Oh, Scott, I think this job is really beginning to click! And it all seems so easy, now that I know what to do."

"Sure. I knew you would do it. And to what do you attribute your sudden success?"

"I've finally learned how to get people involved. Now I know how to include them in the planning, the problem-solving, and the decision-making and still maintain their respect—you know, still project the right image of power and authority. It's like I use that sense of power to challenge them to learn and grow and achieve, but they also know I respect them and support them. Oh, I'm high on this feeling of success!" Erika twirls around the room.

"Say, it sure makes things nice around here, too," Scott grins, catching her in his arms. "What do you say we celebrate with a night on the town?"

Erika is tuned in to the feelings of her staff. Just that day Frank Andreini, one of her salespersons, ran into Hal Roach, a former Lighthouse salesman, whose Sales Manager is George Rodriguez.

F: Hi, Hal. How are things at Nob Hill?

H: Oh, so-so. How about you? I hear you have a new boss at Lighthouse.

F: That's right. Erika Kerr. Yeah, things are going real well. We have a whole new system of doing things—more like a team. At first I didn't know how I was going to like it, but it's working out okay. I never made so much money. The customers like what we're doing. And the best part is, the company lets me in on what's going on—in fact, they adopted a couple of my ideas already. Actually, all the sales people work together to decide what to do and how to do it.

H: That's a switch. I remember we were in the dark most of the time at Alexis, and I feel that way at Nob Hill too.

F: It really makes a difference when you're included in the decisions before they're made—and when you know you'll have a chance to speak your piece and to make a difference. You know, we've been talking about career goals in our department, and I think I might enjoy being a Sales Manager with this kind of system.

H: What? An old rebel like you? You've always sworn you could never put up with bureaucratic red tape and the other hassles of managing.

F: I know, but I think I would be good at this type of team leadership. The sales people work together on the hassles, and I know I'm a pretty good coach. I've been coaching some of the new sales reps—I've made just about all the mistakes, so I can tell them what *not* to do, if nothing else.

H: Maybe it isn't always a bummer to get a woman boss—you sound like a different person now. I've heard pretty awful things about Alexis since they hired Jane Osgood as Sales Manager.

F: Oh? What's the deal?

H: Mainly, a heavy maternal presence. She hovers—and picks, picks over little details. It's hard to know what she wants, but she'll pull the rug out from under anyone who blows an assignment. So the guys have to keep running to her to be sure they're doing things right. It gets pretty tense.

---

1. What effective leadership attitudes and actions do you see revealed in this story?

2. Why do you think they are effective?

3. What ineffective attitudes and actions do you see?

4. Why are they ineffective?

UNDERSTANDING WORK TEAMS AND TEAM DEVELOPMENT

Before we explore ways of developing a work team, you need to understand some terminology used by businesspersons and management consultants. A work group is not necessarily a work team, and team building is not the same as team development.

EXHIBIT 13-1: Traditional Work Groups and Work Teams

	Traditional Work Group	**Self-Directed Work Team**
Roles	Fixed	Interchangeable
Tasks	Rigid	Flexible
Skills	Specialized	Multiskilled
Control	Individual	Group
Status	Different	Equal
Leadership	Outside the group	Within the group
Work Effort	Divided	Cohesive

What Is a Work Team?

A work team, as the term is used here, is not just a group of people working together; that is really a work group [10]. A *work group* is usually led by one person; the work of each member is performed through additive, integrative, or interactive processes; and the group is the primary unit of performance in the organization. In a **work team,** however, members cooperate in performing all aspects of their tasks. They share in the traditional management functions: planning, organizing the team, setting performance goals, assessing the team's performance, developing their own strategies to manage change, and getting their own resources. A comparison of traditional work groups and self-directed work teams is shown in Exhibit 13-1.

When work teams do what work groups do, they accomplish more. Sharing information is easier, issues are aired openly, and conflicts are resolved quickly and with positive results. The best work teams are extremely persistent and have a higher level of consistency, intensity, and restless dissatisfaction than work groups.

Team Building or Team Development?

Most managers probably use the term "team building" for all team-improvement activities. Author Dennis Kinlaw makes an important distinction between team building and team development, similar to the difference between employee training and employee development [10].

Team building and team development focus on different issues. *Team building* focuses on a team's deficits that block performance, whereas **team development** focuses on a team's positive opportunities for continuous improvement. The two processes are compared in Exhibit 13-2.

HOW TO DEVELOP A TEAM

Leading-edge organizations aim for teams that become as self-directed as feasible. Teams and the people within them have important needs that must be met for the team to stay alive and productive. Facilitative leaders view teamwork as an ongoing negotiation among diverse individuals working together toward common goals. Facilitation skills help leaders blend different views into a consensus so the team can achieve its goals. In this section we'll discuss the basics of empowering a team and relating to its members, the meaning of Running Hot, how Hot Teams work together, why teamwork is essential for TQM, facilitating team meetings, valuing diverse members, and resolving conflict.

EXHIBIT 13-2: Team Development and Team Building

	Team Building	Team Development
Duration of Process	Short-term "fix-it" program	Long-term way of life; setting up systems for the long haul
Intensity of Process	Intense, usually a few hours to a few days because of time limits for fixing problems	Diffused and ongoing, a part of the day-to-day processes of work
Primary Goal	To improve relationships among team members	To create and improve the team's systems to ensure they support sustained superior performance and continuous development
Purpose	To fix breakdowns in such functions as:	To transform firm to meet global competition by transforming all key aspects of the organization:
	Communication: People won't give helpful information to other members; management doesn't welcome suggestions or freely share company plans and actions; many hidden agendas exist; team fears expressing disagreement or hostility	*Organizational culture*
		Strategies that get at a company's values
	Decision-making: Management does not consult people	*Systems,* including
		▪ human resource development plan
	Intrapreneurship: People are afraid to take risks; they play it safe	▪ appraisal and reward systems that enhance long-term team development
	Conflict resolution: No workable process exists for resolving conflict; people refuse to cooperate with each other, spend a lot of energy to avoid each other, go out of their way to create obstacles for each other, and enjoy each other's failure	▪ organizational structure ▪ policies ▪ practices
		Definitions of leadership, management, and work teams
	Mutual respect: Members are suspicious of each other's motives, often assuming teammates are incompetent or indifferent	*Roles and functions* (namely, supervisors encourage team development)
	Teamwork: People perceive themselves or their group in a win/lose type of competition; they pursue their own goals at the expense of team goals	
	Accountability: People blame others for their own mistakes, excuse or rationalize their mistakes, spend a lot of energy defending their own security or power base, don't take responsibility for the team's goals or decisions	

Empowering a Team

Seven major steps in team development are encouraging enlightened self-interest instead of dependency and manipulation, empowering the team to direct itself, creating a shared vision and focusing on common goals, establish-ing informal day-to-day processes, providing challenge and support, nurturing positive team feelings, and leading in ways that enhance self-direction.

Encouraging Enlightened Self-Interest

Workers in traditional bureaucratic organizations typically adopt an attitude of narrow self-interest based on a sense of dependency on bosses; this attitude leads to negative politics and manipulation. In developing a team, help members link their personal goals to the team's and organization's goals, to see how putting the team first can lead to achievement of a broader range of personal goals in the long run. Show workers how the following process will empower them:

- Setting goals and activities that have meaning to you and are needed by the team. Focusing on activities that have meaning, depth, and substance for the team.

- Contributing to the team and its purpose, with an awareness of your unique contribution and the team's unique value. Being willing to give all you can give and to share as much valuable information as you can. Seeing other teams in the organization as customers to be served. Focusing on contribution and service allows people to let go of struggles for control and territory.

- Speaking up and speaking honestly. Putting into words what you see happening, telling people what is really going on within the team and what you see going on outside the team, making only those promises you can keep, admitting your mistakes. Giving feedback honestly and with respect, even if it is not pleasant. Criticizing people to their face, not behind their backs.

- Supporting team members.

- Continually learning and gaining mastery. Learning as much as you can about your job. Welcoming new challenges and opportunities to learn new jobs and gain new skills. Performing well simply for its own sake, because it helps you be your best.

- The rewards for enlightened self-interest are autonomy and enthusiasm. As a team member, you pursue mastery, meaning, contribution, integrity, and service because your

team is in charge. You do not perform just to please a boss. The team operates as a group of entrepreneurs, setting their own goals and focusing on them as if the team were a small business.

Enlightened self-interest is a long-run strategy that requires team members to take a broader view and to envision future achievements. And organizational leaders must maintain integrity, deliver on promises, and support the team in order to maintain their trust.

Empowering the Team to Direct Itself The more the team is able to direct itself, the more committed and powerful it will become. Teams can be empowered to perform the following management functions:

- Set goals and determine how they will be achieved

- Solve problems they are capable of solving

- Make decisions that they must carry out

- Identify who will make what types of day-to-day decisions

- Redesign jobs and procedures so team members interact to do the work

Some leadership strategies that help empower teams include (1) seeking their input, (2) working toward consensus, (3) supporting their decisions, (4) promoting self-evaluation, and (5) giving genuine praise.

Seek members' input. Ask for their ideas, opinions, and reactions. Don't judge them personally for the type of input they give (although you may not necessarily agree with the input itself). Never punish them, in any way, for what they say — either in the short run or in the long run. Listen actively, ask questions, paraphrase what was said, thank them, and resist having the last word.

Work toward consensus. The team should reach for general agreement on key issues because team power will be lost if people are divided. Use conflict resolution techniques. Encourage direct expressions of thoughts, feelings, and concerns. Discourage and confront passive behavior, which is often an extreme form of withholding or an indirect strategy used to achieve a personal goal such as getting others to feel guilty or sorry for them. Usually, such people have been getting their way since childhood using passive strategies. They are not as vulnerable as they seem.

Promote self-evaluation. Give people the freedom to choose their own path to results. Encourage the team to structure work so that people do a whole job instead of a piece of it. Alternatively, encourage cross-training and task rotation so members are more likely to stay challenged, interested, and enthusiastic. Provide regular feedback, as quickly as possible. The most valuable feedback and evaluation are performed by the members themselves. Be sure everyone's performance is evaluated fairly. Give the team regular opportunities to evaluate team performance. Give guidance in how to measure performance—both how well the team is achieving its goals and how well it's doing as a team. Are relationships being built? How is team spirit? Are people cooperating? Are they working out differences? How are ground rules working?

Give genuine praise. The most powerful praise is specific and timely—normally just after performance. Give praise regularly but keep it meaningful. Keep it separate from problems, so it stands out as positive feedback.

Creating a Shared Vision and Focusing on Common Goals Just as individuals gain autonomy from bureaucratic dependency when they learn to create visions of greatness and make them reality, teams follow the same process. Everyone can and does have a vision, often at the subconscious level because of dependency on bosses or pessimism about having any influence anyway. To make a vision reality, the team must continually develop clear, specific goals. Otherwise, members be-

come apathetic or begin to focus on their own goals. The team must decide on strategies for (1) making the best use of each member's assets, (2) focusing on TQM, (3) aiming for continuous improvement, and (4) establishing communication processes that support team achievement.

Creating a vision. One way to start this process is to ask each member to pick an important project he or she cares about and is frustrated with. Then have them ask themselves why they care so much about it. They should keep asking why until they get to the root of the concern. Next, ask them to imagine the team three years in the future. What does their ideal way of working with customers look like? How do team members treat each other? Start a dialogue on these topics. Remind members that they are not likely to treat customers any better than they treat one another. If they are cautious, judgmental, and competitive with one another, they probably behave that way with customers. If they use fear and punishment to control a member, that member is likely to take out frustration on customers. The team's vision should reflect its members' deepest values about how people treat each other.

Describe to members the signposts that let them know they are reaching a vision they can commit to: The vision has depth; that is, it is personal and from the heart. It has clarity; that is, it is specific, not vague. They feel a sense of responsibility for it; that is, they begin to talk about the team as theirs to transform in any way.

Making the best use of team members' assets includes using their knowledge, skill, experience, and motivation by challenging, stretching, training, coaching, and supporting them. The more skills a person has a chance to use, the more skills he or she tends to develop. Look for opportunities to extend people's skills to other jobs within the team and within the larger organization. Look for opportunities to expand the depth of a job area—from giving information about something, to developing new ideas about it, to solving problems and making decisions concerning it. Team members need special skills in solving work problems and interpersonal problems and in making team meetings work. Exercises 13-1, 13-2, and 13-3 are designed to help you commit your skills and influence to team purposes and to contribute to your team.

Focusing on Total Quality Management means producing excellent services or products, even against all odds, overcoming all barriers. Encourage members to get results, to go beyond their expectations, to be flexible and innovative. Reward them for such efforts.

Targeting continuous improvement means always reaching a little higher and challenging the limits of quality. It means incrementally reducing error rates, improving customer satisfaction, increasing output, and so on. (This subject is discussed later in the chapter.)

Helping the Team Establish Day-to-Day Processes   Self-directed teams need to continually develop processes for helping their members respond well and adapt well — to change, to each other, to problems, to challenges, to the unexpected — often in new and different ways. They need processes to enhance their ability to identify opportunities that change may offer, processes for thriving on adversity, and dreaming up innovative ways around problems. These processes must ensure that members are able to influence and improve every aspect of the team's work, helping it to stay on

EXERCISE 13-1: USING YOUR SKILLS AND INFLUENCE AS A TEAM MEMBER

You may use this exercise independently if you now have a job or have recently had a job. If you are a team member or leader, you may want your entire team to do the exercise.

Step 1. Brainstorm as a team, or list individually, how you use your skills and influence in the following situations:

- Applying your mental abilities to the way you do your job, the way the team (or your work unit) operates, the way the organization is run

- Doing the work of the team, producing its output

- Giving information and answers that help you move toward goals — job goals, team goals, organizational goals

- Improving the individual, team, and organizational results

- Making decisions about your job, the team's work, the organization's work

- Solving problems that affect your job, the team, the organization

Step 2: Brainstorm as a team, or list individually, the additional ways your skills and influence might be used. How would you like to expand their use? How do other team members think they might expand their use?

EXERCISE 13-2: BREAKING THROUGH LIMITATIONS

Respond to the following questions with statements or drawings. Do not try to analyze your responses or give the "right" answers. You will probably find meaning in all responses that randomly come to mind if you think them over later.

About Your Caution:

1. What organizational signals, dangers, or ambiguities drive you toward caution?

About Your Feelings:

2. How are you feeling about your job, your unit, the organization?

3. What things happened in the past two months that made you proud?

4. What things happened in the past two months that you are sorry about?

About Your Wants:

5. What would you want for your unit if it were your own business?

6. What fears do you have about achieving this vision?

7. What frustrations would you encounter in trying to carry it out?

8. What price would you have to pay to achieve it?

9. What rewards would you experience from achieving it?

EXERCISE 13-3: CREATING A VISION OF GREATNESS

In response to the following questions, write statements and draw pictures. Be spontaneous; do not evaluate or edit. Whatever pops into your mind is valid. Anything your mind can conceive is attainable in some sense.

You are in a time capsule, visiting your unit five years from now. You are hovering above the scene like a spaceship.

1. What do you see happening?

2. How are people working with customers and users?

3. How are people working with each other?

4. You are watching a typical meeting. What is happening? How do people act?

5. You are reviewing the budget. What does it look like?

6. What kinds of projects are people working on?

7. How are people spending their time?

8. What does your product look like as it comes out the door?

9. What does your service include? How is it delivered?

---

a positive improvement slope. The team process focuses on members' appreciation of each other's contributions and the team's achievements. The team can celebrate in many ways — from pats on the back to special parties. Even the most routine processes can have a great impact on team spirit. Routine processes include those that foster team participation, decision-making, communication, and conflict resolution.

Participation processes must be developed. All team members must actively contribute to achieve synergy and team spirit. If even one member starts slacking off, hiding out, and otherwise not participating, his or her attitude will infect the others. To promote participation, the team might focus on questions such as, How do we want support to be expressed within the group? How do we want to handle internal competition? For example, what if we evaluated performance according to how much members contributed to other members' success? What balance between teamwork and individual work do we want?

Team decision processes must be adopted. Decision power is a cornerstone of effective team development. When team members develop ideas, solve problems, make decisions, and carry them out, the very process is developing ways to get along together. The team should focus on the things it has the power to influ-

ence. Once it decides on *content* matters — the tasks to be done — the team should have the power to implement those decisions. The group must also be able to decide *process* issues — how decisions will be made, whether majority vote or consensus will be the major mode, how minority rights will be protected, how the work will be structured and distributed, and the general ground rules of working together. Unresolved conflict about process can sabotage team productivity.

Communication processes are crucial. Frequent communication is essential to team success. The best teams tend to contact each other and customers more, talk more, interact more, and meet more often. Members must feel free to express themselves, especially to the leader. Informal channels must be open to pass on information, bring up new ideas, and make suggestions. The team must have the time and the means to communicate with each other, discuss issues, and share information. This means that team meetings are extremely important.

Processes for conflict resolution must be effective. Even the best teams will experience some conflict. Therefore, before it erupts, the team should decide how conflict and disagreements will be managed. Then, when a disagreement occurs, the team can focus on the *content* and not become bogged down in arguments over a process that may favor one side or another. The key to managing conflict is to get it out in the open before it festers and builds. Encourage members to express their concerns and feelings and come to some agreement. Even if full consensus cannot be reached, members are most likely to implement decisions when they feel the conflict resolution process was fair and equitable. Some guidelines are discussed later in this chapter.

Providing Challenge and Support Individuals and teams function most productively and enthusiastically when they feel challenged to achieve and supported in pursuing that challenge.

Challenging team members to improve their performance and to take on more challenging tasks can include

- Encouraging them to develop a vision of greatness, accept more difficult and challenging tasks, clarify performance goals and standards, identify performance problems, devise strategies to improve performance, and develop greater commitment to continuous improvement

- Helping them visualize a clear picture of end results

- Showing them the latitude they have to try out their ideas in doing tasks

- Helping them develop target dates and deadlines

- Encouraging them to seek out and accept chances to learn something new, to stretch their capabilities; finding ways to enable this process

- Encouraging a sense of friendly competition with themselves as well as with other members and teams

- Getting the team and its members to make a commitment to perform

- Pointing out or opening up opportunities to gain recognition or praise

Supporting the team and its members provides a model of behavior for all team members to follow. It signals the importance of team autonomy and promotes trust. Here are some specific supportive actions:

- Show a positive attitude, offer assistance when needed, run interference, explain to higher management what the team is doing, give encouragement

- Find out what people need and want in order to do their jobs

- Provide the necessary tools to meet the challenges — authority, information, supplies, staff support, facilities

- Give training and coaching; serve as mentor

- Recognize team and individual achievements, ideas, innovations, projects; fight for rewards for achievement

- Back up the team and members in well-meaning decisions and actions

- Take a constructive, problem-solving approach to mistakes and view them as part of the learning process; "This will give you a chance to follow through on the valuable know-how you picked up last month"

- Avoid dwelling on past histories, blaming, defending, getting bogged down in details — discourage these behaviors

- Communicate support — they can do the job, you'll be there for them, and you're rooting for them

Nurturing Positive Team Feelings The feelings most typical of top-performing teams are self-esteem, belonging, commitment, support, pride, trust, and mutual respect.

Self-esteem is the basis for all other positive feelings. Each member must be heard, acknowledged, and valued. Members must be able to be themselves and must feel that all members are treated fairly and equitably. Self-esteem grows when members see they have influence and can contribute to the team's successes.

Belongingness is a powerful asset to develop. Each member feels he or she belongs to a desirable group in which individuals are accepted for who they are, are respected for their uniqueness, and are rewarded for performance.

Commitment to the team's goals and its successes grows out of the feelings of belonging and self-esteem and is based on being part of the decision-making process.

Support for team members and for the team as a whole grows out of self-esteem, belongingness, and commitment. An important element of team spirit is the sense of "all for one and one for all" that impels members to root for each other and help out when they can.

Pride in the team's output, in its overcoming of obstacles, and in its camaraderie evolves as the other feelings develop and as the team works together in fruitful, positive ways.

Trust in one another and in the team develops from positive experiences. Members must discuss the types of behavior and attitudes that build or break trust. For example, when commitments are not met, confidentialities are betrayed, or dishonesty occurs, trust can be difficult to rebuild.

Mutual respect is essential. A team is a collection of diverse individuals, each with a unique character and potential for contributing to team success. The best team leaders capitalize on differences and do not try to force conformity.

Leading in Ways that Enhance Self-Direction
Team leaders must have enough respect and influence to get cooperation from members, to build relationships with groups and people outside the team, to lead in coordinating the work of the team, to communicate effectively, and to get everyone involved. A facilitative leadership style is essential for self-directed teams to survive and thrive. This style was in-

troduced in Chapter 9. Some other aspects of this style are discussed here.

Being a team player, while also being leader, is accomplished by focusing on team performance more than on individual performances and on getting results through each person's commitment to the team's performance rather than through control.

Focusing on both team development (processes) and team performance is achieved by giving special attention to structuring the team so everyone is clear about goals and values even more than about specific job responsibilities. Help the team track and evaluate its own progress in achieving goals *and* in developing as a team.

Creating shared visions of excellence. In Chapter 8 we discussed the importance of scanning the environment and visioning the future. Encourage everyone on the team to participate in such actions and to discuss them in team meetings. Shared visions are the basis for deciding on shared goals, values, and standards.

Filling the roles of initiator, role model, and coach is begun by initiating the actions and processes needed to build a work unit into an excellent team. Involve the team members at the very beginning, then become a member of the team as the team starts developing itself. Model the behavior you want team members to develop, by being a good team member—performing your own tasks and interacting with people in a team-oriented way. Coach members in the following ways:

- *Counseling* and assisting team members to clarify issues, develop strategies, and resolve problems. The process of counseling may include helping a person explore alternatives, accurately describe a problem and its root cause, gain technical or organizational insight, air strong feelings, understand some required change, or resolve some confusion or misunderstanding.

- *Mentoring* and helping team members understand company politics, the values and biases of key managers, and career opportunities within the firm. The process may include helping a person gain political savvy, understand the way the organization works, learn how to build a support system or network, better manage his or her career, develop greater commitment to team goals and values, and develop sensitivity to the values and biases of others.

- *Tutoring* and helping team members learn new skills. This process can include helping team members improve their technical competence and understanding, become an expert in an area, learn more rapidly, and develop greater commitment to continuous learning.

Leading Innovative Intrapreneurial Teams

In the past employees who were entrepreneurs at heart had no choice but to leave the company and form their own enterprises if they wanted to work their entrepreneurial magic. Today, these entrepreneurs can join one of the leading-edge companies that encourage such ventures and become **intrapreneurs** running their **intraprises** within the company [14]. How do you know if you are an intrapreneur, or how do you spot one? See Exercise 13-4.

Intrapreneurial Phases Intrapreneurial **phases** include the Solo, Network, Bootleg, and Formal Team phases. In the beginning the intrapreneur works alone, building the vision until the basic idea is clear. During the Network Phase, the intrapreneur gets feedback and casual help. She shares the vision with a few close friends and trusted customers. She gets their reactions and learns more about the concept's strengths and weaknesses. Remember that when you tell people you've heard great things about their expertise and invite them to lunch so you can bounce your idea off them, they tend to rise to the occasion and even become allies. During the Bootleg Phase, an informal team

forms around the idea. The intrapreneur works with and tests people who may end up as formal team members. A hungry bootleg team, borrowing time wherever it can find it, is usually very productive in simplifying ideas. The people who stay are drawn to the intrapreneur's vision and leadership style. They are also people who can get things done.

When company management gives its blessing to the project, the Formal Team Phase has begun. Each team member adds to the vision and helps execute it. Members have been selected so the team is functionally complete, acts autonomously, and normally stays together from the development of the project through its commercialization and beyond. Team members provide the breadth of talent necessary to address all the issues and tasks of a complex start-up and to establish the management depth needed for expansion.

Successful intrapreneurial leaders communicate the vision of the end results they want, setting the direction for the team. They attract motivated, capable people who add to the vision. They give members the freedom to figure out ways of doing their part. They respect team members and trust them to do their part. They listen to all comers, but reserve the right to make any final decisions they view as crucial to success.

Corporate Cultures That Foster Intrapreneurs How do you know if an organization provides enough freedom for intrapreneurs to blossom? Try applying the following questions; look for "yes" answers [14].

1. Does the firm encourage the self-appointed intrapreneur?

2. Does the firm provide ways for intrapreneurs and their teams to stay with their intraprises instead of handing them off to other parts of the firm?

3. Are people in the firm permitted to do the job in their own way, or are they constantly

EXERCISE 13-4: ARE YOU AN INTRAPRENEUR?

For each of the following questions, record the number that best represents your response:

5 = Yes, definitely; 4 = Yes, somewhat or most of the time; 3 = Don't know, neutral; 2 = No, probably not or not usually; 1 = No, definitely not.

1. Do you often get excited about your work?
2. Do you work at least as hard at making things work better as at maintaining the status quo?
3. Do you ever get in trouble for exceeding your authority at work?
4. Do you think about new business ideas when you are away from work — at odd times?
5. Can you visualize concrete steps for action when you think about ways to make a new idea happen?
6. Can you keep an idea a secret until you've had time to develop and test it?
7. Have you had the persistence to keep working on a project even though it looked as if it might fail?
8. Are you somewhat controversial, with your share of fans and critics?
9. Do you have a network of supporters at work you can count on for help?
10. Do you get annoyed easily by others' incompetent attempts to carry out portions of your pet ideas?
11. Do you have a perfectionist streak that causes you to want to do all the work on a pet project yourself?
12. Can you overcome perfectionism and share responsibility for your ideas with a team?
13. Would you take a lower salary in exchange for the freedom to try out your business idea, if the rewards for success were adequate?

Adapted from *Intrapreneurship* by Gifford Pinchot III (New York: Harper & Row, 1985).

stopping to explain their actions and ask for permission? Some companies push decisions up through a multilevel approval process so the doers and the deciders never even meet.

4. Does the firm provide any quick, informal ways to get the resources needed to try out new ideas? Intrapreneurs need discretionary resources to explore and develop new ideas. Some firms give employees the free-

dom to use a percentage of their time on projects of their own choosing and set aside funds to explore new ideas when they occur.

5. Has the firm developed ways to manage many small, experimental products and businesses? Most corporate cultures favor a few well-studied, well-planned attempts to hit a home run. Others realize that no firm bats 1,000, so they bet on trying more often with less tedious, precise, and expensive preparation for each try.

6. Are the firm's systems set up to encourage risk-taking and to tolerate mistakes? Innovation cannot be achieved without risk and mistakes. Even successful innovation generally begins with some blunders and false starts.

7. Can the firm decide to try something and stick with the experiment long enough to see if it will work, even when that may take years and several false starts? Innovation takes time, even decades sometimes, but the rhythm of corporations is annual planning.

8. Are people in the firm more concerned with new ideas or with defending their territory? Because new ideas almost always cross the boundaries of existing patterns of firms, a jealous tendency to territoriality blocks innovation.

9. How easy is it to form functionally complete, autonomous teams in the firm's environment? Small teams with full responsibility for developing an intraprise solve many of the basic problems of innovation. But some firms resist their formation.

10. Do intrapreneurs face internal monopolies, or are they free to use the resources of other divisions and outside vendors if they choose? If the intrapreneur is not free to

select from among many options for producing the product and getting it to the customer, a good idea may die an unnecessary death.

Running-Hot Intrapreneurial Teams

Running-Hot firms are developing intrapreneurial **Hot Teams.** They are more entrepreneurial and less democratic than some of the Self-Directed Teams in slower-paced organizations. Global competition is redefining the way businesses earn their right to exist in the marketplace. Competition can be met only if employees persistently cut down on slack; namely, excess scrap and inventory, wasted time and effort, needless delays and bottlenecks. Continuous improvement, continuous learning, and Total Quality Management are the essence of world-class operations. To meet these demands, a new team intrapreneurship is emerging. R. B. Reich, Harvard economist, has said, "We must begin to celebrate collective intrapreneurship, endeavors in which the whole of the effort is greater than the sum of individual contributions" [20, p. 5]. The traditional "we/they" approach to managing is giving way to a synergy between leaders and teams of employees.

Reich sees intrapreneurship as people following up on opportunities for creating new wealth — typically a lengthy, ongoing process. Alex Stewart defines a **Running-Hot firm** [20, p. 31] as an entrepreneurial firm that seizes an opportunity to serve a tough market for a service or product, on which their business must then depend. The firm is *pulled* by opportunities to create new wealth more than *pushed* by the resources it already has in place for doing business. The Hot firm then embraces its customers' demands, the pressures created by such demands, and how the demands define the firm's mission. It sets about fulfilling this mission through focus — a focus on action, on the one product or service, and on the particular operational requirements. One person, or a handful of people, with excellent industry skills, the human crafts for nurturing a team, and the vision of a clearly focused mission set the team action in play.

Tasks are carried out by small teams, developed in an informal internal labor market, and led by one or two people with specific skills. Members tend to think individually as employees, but act collectively as entrepreneurs. They play above their apparent levels of competence; that is, above their heads. With little experience of conventional approaches, the members and teams work out procedures themselves. They manage by inventiveness and faith in their teammates. With their new collective skills, and incrementally added, inexpensive equipment, they find themselves creating careers, and wealth.

Running-Hot teams stretch past their previous abilities, in learning how to solve customers' problems. They come up with procedures that manage to get the customer's total job done. Methods are learned incrementally and in practice. People on the floor are not second-guessed by intervening specialists, so Running Hot becomes the members' own game. The difficult mission, which at first was set from above, becomes redefined by teams as their own. They assume a pride of ownership as they create a system that works, that grows, and that wins.

Control is based on the detailed operational skills of a few coaches at the top. Their personal authority is clearly recognized and skill-based. The Running-Hot structure has been compared to a hospital emergency ward, which has clear, centralized authority at the top, with equals below doing what needs to be done. Although Hot teams are empowered in their everyday work, they are rarely involved in making strategic decisions. This is done by the leaders, who are skilled in seizing opportunities, understanding the particular business, building Hot teams, and sustaining the Running.

Hot teams are specific, evolving human systems and thus are difficult to imitate. Components of the Running-Hot model include tough competition, entrepreneurial cultures, customer focus, team-based organizational designs, and profit-sharing. Here are some guidelines:

- Keep each establishment small, no more than 100 people.

- Use measurements and appraisals that are operational (that is, relevant to customers) as well as financial.

- Ensure that everyone stays close to the customers.

- Give members a sense of security; honor promises of long-term reward. The high levels of competition make team members feel vulnerable.

- Give special rewards for those who Run Hot (that is, for continuous learning and high performance) and for those who can set up a new Hot establishment.

- Recruit members with broadly, not specifically, suitable backgrounds and the ability to work well within groups. Promote them through career paths that start at the bottom and include lateral transfers, from job to job.

- Delegate responsibility for the procedures needed to cope with pressures. Minimize staff specialists, and seldom overrule your line members.

- Prod members to understand matters they probably wouldn't learn if left to themselves; share information.

- Encourage planning, especially setting clear goals and prioritizing goals and activities.

Leading Continuous Improvement

Continuous improvement incorporates forward feed from customers about their changing needs so the team can plan ways of responding. The model, shown in Figure 13-1, also uses forward feed to and from suppliers to help provide for the team's changing needs. The goal is to produce a flow of incremental improvements with a focus on quicker, more competitive responses to changing customer requirements.

The model works for any team that produces goods or services for a customer, whether that customer is within the company or outside the company. Customer forward feed is advance information about customers' anticipated changing needs, requirements, desires, and preferences that helps the team plan changes to its work processes and outputs. Feedback is information about user satisfaction with inputs and outputs.

Teams can use the model to identify a wide variety of improvement opportunities and to anticipate how improvements in one part of the system may impact other parts of the system. They can brainstorm opportunities for improving its output, looking also at its inputs and processes as they affect output. Then they can prioritize the order in which they will work on each improvement. Suppliers provide the team with the forms, requests, materials, raw materials, products, or services that the team uses to perform its work. The team processes, or takes actions, using the input, to produce its output, the product or service for the customer. Supplier forward feed is advance information that (1) alerts teams to a changing supply picture and (2) helps suppliers anticipate the team's changing needs.

Leading TQM

Total Quality Management focuses on teamwork within teams and throughout the organization for the purpose of providing a total quality experience for the customer. The goal is total quality in both the basic product or service that a customer buys and in all the support services. These services may range from initially attracting the customer through communicating, shipping, billing, extending credit, to following up, servicing, and fulfilling warranties.

Management experts say the companies that are surviving and thriving in the 1990s have developed a culture that focuses on TQM; that is, a strategic approach to producing the best product and service possible through constant

FIGURE 13-1: Model for Continuous Team Improvement

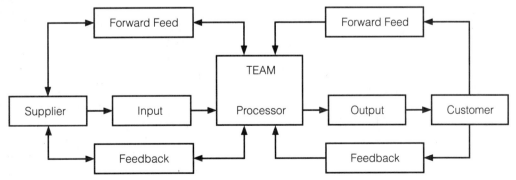

innovation [12, 13]. A commitment to TQM is a recognition that concentrating on the service side of the business — not just on the production side — is essential for success. Many companies can produce zero-defect products, but the company's quality will still be lacking if other functions and departments don't deliver. If the product isn't delivered on time, if the billing is not right, if credit arrangements are botched, if the sales representative doesn't follow up — any one of these failures means less-than-top quality. Not only do such problems irritate customers, they may cost the company money in the short run and lose customers in the long run.

Leaders must somehow build room for responding to the accelerating change that's occurring; they must build in time for the renewal and innovation that change demands. They must deal with the competitive advantage of quality and of speed; getting products to customers faster, increasing market share while reducing inventory costs. Getting products to market before your competitors is more important than ever, say consultants at McKinsey & Company. A high-tech product that comes to market six months late, but within budget, will earn on average 33 percent less profit (than if it had come out on time) over the next five years. On the other hand, if that high-tech product comes out on time, even if it's 50 percent over budget, expected profits are likely to be reduced by only 4 percent as a result of the budget overrun [13].

Leaders are beginning to understand that to continue to do business with customers will require a dedication to getting things right — the first time, every time. TQM is an organizationwide commitment to getting things right.

The greater the top leaders' commitment to TQM, the faster it becomes the dominant culture. Key goals of a TQM system include

- Team development and participation

- Meeting customer requirements

- Preventing errors

- Taking preventive action

- Achieving continuous improvement

- Setting a competitive pace

The types of actions leaders must engage in and inspire are

- Choosing and recording cost-of-quality (COQ) indicators (what less-than-top quality is costing the company in terms of fixing problems, lost customers, and so on)

- Agreeing on tangible milestones to assess progress

- Ensuring that all TQM objectives are achievable, measurable, and compatible with company objectives

- Leading agreement on how objectives will be met and by whom

FACILITATING TEAM MEETINGS: A POWERFUL FORUM

Team meetings are the major vehicle by which the team carries out its management functions of planning, organizing, goal-setting, problem-solving, and decision-making. They are also a major forum for communicating, bonding, building team spirit, and similar team-development functions. The most important thing to remember about team meetings is, *They are extremely important; never take them for granted.*

As team leader, your role at meetings is more that of facilitator than a traditional chair or leader. In Chapter 7 you learned some guidelines for meetings in general. Now we'll consider some specific suggestions for making team meetings work. We'll look at the skills you'll need, the key factors to keep in mind, and the techniques and activities you can use to accomplish meeting objectives.

Facilitation Skills

Women are socialized to develop many skills that team facilitators must have. The following essential skills are based on effective communication skills:

- *Interpersonal skills* include helping each other develop information, communicating respect, and developing positive relations with other members.

- *Task achievement skills* include (1) resourcing—giving information, proposing alternatives, suggesting procedures; (2) clarifying—interpreting ideas, clarifying confusion in discussions, finding common ground; (3) decision testing—checking for agreement, testing to see if the team is ready to make a decision; and (4) summarizing—pulling together related ideas at the right moment.

- *Group process skills* include (1) reminding—about team norms, past agreements, and decisions; (2) monitoring participation—making sure everyone gets a chance to speak, keeping communication channels open between members, helping everyone participate; (3) tracking meeting progress—helping the team keep track of where it is as it follows an agenda or problem-solving plan; and (4) monitoring meeting progress—making the team conscious of breakdowns in the communication process, such as when people start interrupting and stop listening.

The key factors in structuring a work-team meeting are determining roles, norms, goals/agenda, meeting process and methods, and meeting evaluation [10].

Roles: Will there be a leader? Will some members' votes count more than others? Are some people nonvoting members? Are some considered experts?

Norms: Norms are written and unwritten rules. The most important rules concern how the team will make its decisions. Complete consensus? General consensus? Majority vote? Another major norm concerns how people will interact. Open, give-and-take? Direct confrontation? How will conflict be resolved? Will everyone have a fair share of time to speak? How will fairness be ensured? What role will the leader play? Facilitator? Participant? Leader? Who will record the team's ideas and decisions?

Goals, agendas, and processes: They are more effective when the leader works toward

1. Clear objectives, agreement on objectives (the content of the meeting)

2. A defined process, agreement on process (the methods used to get the work of the meeting done)

3. Active participation by all members—encouraging, welcoming, accepting and considering expression of different viewpoints and innovative ideas and approaches

4. Closure on objectives—resolving something, providing adequate time for analyzing and solving difficult issues

5. Members leave the meeting committed to follow through on the decisions that are made—achieving reasonable consensus

Meeting process and methods: These may vary, depending on the purpose and objectives of the meeting. Help members explore and understand the various processes and methods that might work. Guide them to agreement on which ones to use for each type of meeting. For example, a rational process for meetings that focus on problem-solving and decision-making is to (1) define the problem, (2) develop a strategy for analyzing the problem, (3) collect and analyze information, (4) generate alternative solutions, (5) evaluate and select a solution, and (6) plan action steps and systems for accountability and evaluation. Within this overall process are many methods the team can use, such as small-group assignments, brainstorming, and nominal-group technique. Other specific processes and methods are discussed in the next section.

Meeting evaluation: The team can explore ways of regularly evaluating its meeting performance. Some typical evaluation questions are, Did we achieve the purpose of the meeting? Did we accomplish the meeting's goals? Did the processes and methods expedite goal achievement? Did the processes and methods enhance team development? Did they enhance team synergy, cohesiveness, innovativeness, trust?

Activities and Techniques for Facilitating Meeting Objectives

To determine the activities that will work best for your team meetings, ask yourself the following key questions [15]. See also Exhibit 13-3.

1. *How can I get everyone to participate as early in the meeting as possible? What activity will get the group off to a good start?*
   Whatever is done in the first five minutes of a meeting establishes the norm for it. Providing an inclusive activity signals that the norm state is one of equal influence by all. Devise an introductory activity that will re-

EXHIBIT 13-3: Facilitating Team Meetings: Key Leader Actions

Facilitative Skills	Participative Actions
Maintain a climate conducive to participating, listening, understanding, learning, creating.	Ask open-ended questions.
Provide structure and guidance to increase the likelihood that goals will be accomplished.	Phrase requests to encourage more responses — "tell us . . .," "describe . . .," "explain . . ."
Keep the team focused on its goals.	Acknowledge and positively respond to contributions made by members.
Encourage dialogue and interaction among members.	Ask for more specifics or examples.
Suggest and direct processes that empower and mobilize the team to get work done.	Redirect questions or comments to other members of the team — "what do others think about that?"
Encourage the team to evaluate its own progress or development.	Encourage nonvocal members to participate — "Jane, we haven't heard from you yet."
Utilize differences among team members for the common good of the team.	Ask for and encourage different points of view — avoid groupthink.
Remain neutral on content and be active in suggesting and directing the process.	Paraphrase for clarity and understanding.
Protect members and their ideas from being attacked or ignored.	Avoid stating your opinion or interjecting your own ideas while facilitating.
Make sure all members have a chance to speak their piece.	Refer to contributions people have made — "that's similar to what John said earlier" — to help reach consensus, to encourage participation.
Use facilitation skills to tap the team's reservoir of knowledge, experience, creativity.	Start a "speakers' list" when several people want to speak at once.
Sort, organize, and summarize team inputs or get the team to do so.	
Help the team move to healthy consensus, define steps, and reach timely closure.	

Adapted from *How to Lead Work Teams* by Fran Rees (San Diego: Pfeiffer and Company, 1991).

quire everyone's input, such as a quick poll of members' expectations, or opinions, or concerns, about the first objective. Ask them to use one-liners.

2. *How can I focus the group on the purpose of the meeting?*

   - *Post the meeting objectives* in a noticeable place. Refer to them. When the team strays too far for too long, remind them.

   - *Sidetrack stray issues.* Decide ahead of time how you will handle them. You can (1) appoint someone to record stray ideas on a notepad and later consider them as agenda items for future meetings, or (2) record stray ideas on a flipchart, and at the end of the meeting, ask the team how it wants to handle them.

   - *Balance open participation with structure.* Teams need enough time for participation and enough structure to keep them on track and on schedule. They may need to stray off the topic a bit and be creative. Little sidetrips can be productive but should not dominate.

3. *What group processes will best accomplish the meeting objectives?*

   - *Keep presentations short* and use them only when necessary. Allow ample time for questions and answers.

   - *Keep roles in mind.* Team members should do 80 to 90 percent of the talking. You should listen, record, and suggest processes.

   - *Work in pairs, small groups, or subgroups.* Subgroups of five or seven work well. Whenever possible, let people form their own subgroups. Keep the large group intact for some of the work. Bring the subgroups back together frequently for discussion, review, and final decisions. Ask subgroups to share ideas or report findings. You want to maintain the larger

team's identity and cohesiveness. Use subgroups when you need as many ideas or as much information as possible, when members need a jump-start in verbalizing and interacting, or to break up large tasks into manageable chunks.

   - *Start a speakers' list* when several people want to speak at once. When members can't speak their piece, they may become frustrated, angry, bored, or disgusted. Some may start interrupting or yelling; others may give up and withdraw. Keeping a speakers' list can avert these common problems. Members signal that they want to speak on the current issue by raising their hands. You or an assistant add their names to the list, and call on them when their turn comes up.

   - *Record ideas and decisions* where all can see and refer to them.

   - *Begin and end the meeting* with team members interacting as one cohesive group.

   - *Summarize.* Stop and summarize to refocus the team on its objective, or ask a team member to summarize. Then move on quickly to the next question or activity.

   - *Bridge.* Show the big picture and how the detailed activities fit together to form the whole. Summarize the previous work and then explain to the team what is going to happen next and how it relates to the previous work and to the meeting objectives.

   - *Mirror.* Reflect back to the team what you see them doing. Report what you see going on in the process or content of the meeting and ask the team to respond to that. Mirroring is used to help the team monitor itself. "We agreed we would get each members' input before generating solutions, but I'm hearing solutions. How will this affect our process and outcome?"

   - *Move out of dead ends.* If the team gets bogged down in specifics, ask them to move on to generalities (the big picture — what we are really trying to achieve here). When it gets sidetracked on an issue that doesn't relate directly to the objective, ask the team to come back to the objective.

- *Clear up confusion.* If the team gets mired in confusion, acknowledge it. Mirror to the team what you are hearing. Try to sort out what the team is confused about. List confusing points. Look for a pattern. Suggest a process that will help the team move on or ask for suggestions.

4. *How can I read the team's thoughts and moods?* Because participative meetings are *not* highly controlled, they usually do not "run smoothly." Learn to recognize problems and adjust. Pay attention to what is going on for individuals as well as for the team as a whole. People signal their feelings through such nonverbal clues as:

- Level of enthusiasm and energy
- Inattention (doing something else)
- Boredom or discomfort (yawning, looking away, reading)
- Anger, disdain, exasperation (glaring, frowning, rolling the eyes)
- Agreement or satisfaction (nodding and smiling)
- Degree of participation
- Focus of the discussion; what is *not* being discussed
- Balance between facts and feelings
- General clarity or confusion
- How leadership is being used — shared, monopolized
- How individuals are helping or hindering the team's progress

If there is a fairly high energy level and most members seem interested and involved, the meeting is probably going well. Some healthy disagreement usually means people are being open and feel secure enough to express themselves.

When you sense something is wrong but don't know what it is, ask the team, "What is happening right now?" "What do we need to do now to regain our energy?" "There is a lot of energy on this topic, but we are losing our productivity. Let's discuss one point at a time." Ask yourself if the team is balancing discussion of facts with expression of feelings. If the focus has been on facts, ask for a reading on feelings, or vice versa. Are some members dominating? Ask for the input of quiet members.

5. *How do I deal with difficult members?* Difficult situations can arise when members behave in a disruptive manner. Typical disruptive behaviors include being overly talkative, rambling, being unable to articulate ideas coherently, refusing to talk, being obstinate, holding side conversations, doing something else, arriving late, and leaving early.

Some general rules: (a) handle the problem before it gets out of hand; (b) avoid embarrassing anyone; (c) protect members' self-esteem; and (d) take control in a firm, positive, constructive way. If the difficult situation is significantly affecting the team's productivity and enjoyment, you need to intervene. When you can handle the situation in front of the group, do so. If not, take a break and meet with the difficult member privately. If the problem continues, you may need to ask the team to discuss this type of problem in general and arrive at a team solution.

- *The Talker.* Cut across this person's talk with a summarizing statement and a direct question to someone else. "That's an interesting point; now let's hear from Juanita."
- *The Rambler.* When this person stops for breath, say thank you, and refocus at-

tention by restating any relevant points, remind the group of its objective, and move on.

- *The Struggler.* Listen carefully, then restate the person's ideas. Or ask, "do you mean . . ."
- *The Nontalker.* Try to determine whether the cause is boredom, indifference, timidity, feelings of superiority or insecurity, or cultural differences. Ask direct questions that you are sure the person can answer. Ask for the person's agreement or opinion on views expressed by others.
- *The Stubborn Mule.* Get the others to help this person see their point of view. Then ask, "Would you consider the other members' view for now?"
- *The Side-Talkers.* Ask them if there is something they would like to share with the rest of the group. Or state, "Jay and Sonia, I'd like to have only one meeting at a time." Move toward them until they stop talking.
- *The Preoccupied.* Pull this person into the discussion by asking for facts or an opinion. Repeat often enough that he or she must stay involved in order to respond.
- *The Latecomer.* In private, find out why the person is habitually late. Point out why this behavior is disruptive, and ask the person to help you figure out a solution.
- *The Early Leaver.* At the beginning of the meeting, check to see if everyone can stay until the end. Then be sure that your meetings keep to the scheduled time, are not too unstructured or boring, and involve everyone.

6. *How can I achieve closure and move to necessary steps the team will take?*
Consensus is not achieved by voting, imposing a win/lose outcome, dictating the conclusion, or abdicating or giving in. To reach consensus, group members share ideas, discuss and evaluate, debate, organize and prioritize ideas, and struggle to reach the best conclusions together. A good test for consensus is to ask, "Can you support this decision?" If everyone can say yes, the team has reached 100 percent consensus.

The process requires good group problem-solving and decision-making skills and is often time-consuming and draining. It's worth the time and energy when the team must make an important decision that requires a high degree of support and commitment from all members in order to be implemented. In the case of decisions about what the team will do, members should clearly understand what the team's decision is, feel they can support that decision, and identify the action steps and responsibilities needed to carry out that decision (who will need to do what).

VALUING DIVERSE TEAM MEMBERS

We've discussed why our U.S. business culture is predominantly a white male culture and why that culture is changing to include women and minorities. The Labor Department study *Workforce 2000* [24] indicates that by the year 2000, women will represent 47 percent of the work force, racial minorities will comprise 45 percent, workers over 50 will make up 50 percent, the Hispanic population will triple, and 4 to 7 million immigrants will join the work force.

Approaches to Diversity

Valuing Diversity is an approach that maximizes the contributions of people from every segment of the employee population; this in turn helps the organization reach its objectives. When we value diversity among people, we value all the things that make them unique or different. Everyone is encouraged

FIGURE 13-2: Primary and Secondary Dimensions of Diversity

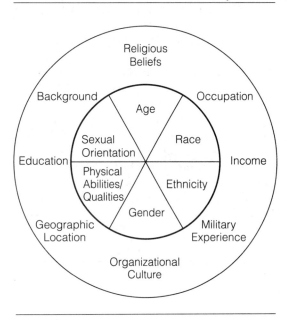

As a result, rapport can develop between and among members and team spirit is enhanced.

This approach contrasts with the *Melting Pot Approach,* which at its best is based on the Golden Rule. The problem with "doing unto others as you would have them do unto you" in this case is that the basis is still "your values," meaning white male values. Diverse others who want to move up in such organizations are expected to learn the rules of the game and change their styles to white male styles. White males are encouraged to be open to the idea that some of these newcomers might be able to fit in.

Valuing Diversity also contrasts with the *Affirmative Action Approach,* in which organizations accommodate members of disadvantaged groups with special advantages to compensate for the barriers they must face. White males are encouraged to be sensitive to the unique concerns of the disadvantaged group. Valuing Diversity does not attempt to replace AA, but to go beyond it to form more powerful beliefs and attitudes.

to be conscious of and responsive to a wide range of deviations from the white male standard — deviations based on race, gender, class, native language, national origin, physical ability, sexual preference, professional experience, and even work style. Primary and secondary dimensions of diversity are shown in Figure 13-2.

When work teams and entire organizations adopt the *Valuing Diversities Approach,* pluralism at its best emerges — a unity that encompasses wide diversity. A synergy develops in which teams can achieve more than the mere sum of individual contributions could provide. One member stimulates another with the expression of different beliefs, attitudes, thoughts, and feelings, which in turn trigger new ways of seeing problems and opportunities. People are encouraged to honor multiple viewpoints and to incorporate this approach into their daily and weekly activities to meet team goals.

Results of Valuing Diversity

When diverse teams are allowed to do what comes naturally, the results are often miscommunication, a lack of cohesion, and stress. Some arenas in which cultural values differ and create misunderstandings include use of time; work styles; presentation styles; level and expression of individualism; expression of masculinity/femininity; attitudes toward achievement, power, and risk-taking; and tolerance for uncertainty. Misunderstandings based on different values can lead to "cultural collisions." Further, when diverse others fear they will be excluded, they tend to cluster with one another, sometimes speaking their own language, thus excluding members of the dominant group.

When leaders focus on managing diversity, the outcomes include increased creativity, enhanced understanding among team members, and increased productivity. When members are encouraged and rewarded to honor diverse viewpoints and styles, they open themselves to a wider range of perspectives, so they emerge with more and better ideas for capitalizing on opportunities and solving problems. When there is less **groupthink,** teams can better define the problems and opportunities they face. They come up with more alternatives and are more likely to arrive at better solutions and decisions.

Team members move from miscommunication to understanding. When they are encouraged to take responsibility for understanding diverse viewpoints, they are likely to see more clearly other ideas, the unique meanings that events and concepts may hold for others, and what lies behind their arguments. Teams move from a lack of consensus and concerted action, because ideas and people are not validated, to greater cohesion. Teams become more effective and productive. Much of the conflict, disagreement, and counterproductive behavior that typically creates stress within teams that don't value diversity is replaced by the satisfaction, even excitement, of belonging to a creative, achieving work team.

Leading a Valuing-Diversity Approach

Here are some ideas for encouraging this approach in your team. Ensure that all team members are sensitized to the uniqueness and differences of other members or potential members. Ensure that they have the skills necessary for functioning on a diverse team. Do not make or tolerate inappropriate jokes or comments that belittle others because of their differences. Initiate training sessions, bring in diversity consultants, show training films, and lead team discussions, experiences, and role plays. (A listing of Valuing-Diversity materials is given in the reference section at the end of this chapter [25].)

Be aware of your own preconceptions and stereotypes. Then get to know each person as an individual and don't operate on myths or assumptions. Challenge your own and others' conclusions or assessments that seem to be based on assumptions. Communicate openly and honestly about differences, but be sensitive to the reactions and experiences of others.

When "cultural collisions" occur, be willing to listen, evaluate, negotiate, and accommodate. Actively listen to what the other has to say and to how she or he says it. Avoid expressing anger, shock, or amusement; focus on evaluating the cause of the problem. Is it a violation of expectations? An intrusion from an external source? Lack of role clarification? Negotiate by first granting that the other person has a right to his or her opinion. Explain your own viewpoint. Offer options, and allow the person to choose any option that causes no harm to any party. Accommodate the other by explaining the organizational values and assumptions that apply. Then explain, and demonstrate if necessary, the actions that will be taken.

When you introduce diverse others to the team, stress their qualifications and track records. Make it clear that they are well qualified. Assign the new person a buddy or mentor who can give them valuable information about the corporate culture and the work of the team. Serve as a mentor yourself, giving them insight about norms and roles within the team and other aspects of team life.

Expect the same high performance of diverse others that you do of all team members, but be willing to give them wide latitude on the *way* they achieve goals. Clearly establish performance expectations and measurements and provide timely, accurate, and balanced feedback. Address any performance problems early. Maintain high expectations and be willing to serve as a resource person and to give support.

Share the organizational and team vision with diverse newcomers. Enlist their ideas for focusing the vision, expressing it, sharing it, making it real, and for bringing multicultural perspectives into the corporate culture. Develop new slogans, stories, one-liners, and soundbites about diverse others. Include them and their escapades among the organizational heroes and myths. Enhance the corporate language bank. Celebrate events that honor diversity. On a practical level, develop job aids that accommodate cultural differences. Create incentives for valuing diversity. Institute creative rewards and forms of recognition.

RESOLVING CONFLICT WITHIN THE TEAM

As team leader you are expected to see that any conflict between and among team members is resolved. A constructive approach involves these steps:

1. Seeing conflict as an opportunity to look at all sides of an issue and to get at the heart of problems

2. Identifying types of competition among team members and guiding it into constructive channels

3. Openly airing the views of the people involved in the conflict in a group meeting

4. Isolating the real cause of the conflict: determining whether it is faulty communication, resentment of another's behavior, conflicting goals, conflicting choice of solutions, or some other root cause

5. Determining the resolution strategy of each party to the conflict: Is it competitive, collaborative, sharing, avoidant, or accommodative?

6. Reaching a resolution that is best for the organization and for all parties, one that provides control for the possibility of creating a

related and more intense conflict in the future

We will discuss each step in detail.

Seeing Conflict as Opportunity

Perhaps the most common way of viewing conflict is to see it as undesirable, something that should be avoided. From another perspective, however, conflict may add force, energy, and more intense interest in the idea or situation in question. When conflict is handled constructively, opposing opinions and ideas are discussed openly. This airing of ideas can lead to creative, innovative approaches.

If you view conflict as a natural and healthy aspect of group effort, your team members are more likely to be open about their opinions and ideas. Conflicts among your people will surface, and it will be possible to discuss problem situations at a stage when candid discussion is most helpful in defining the source of problems and in developing alternate solutions. In other words, people can air their differences at an optimal point in the problem-solving process — before the creative, brainstorming phase.

Also, if people can discuss their differences as soon as they surface, negative emotions they feel in connection with the conflict are more likely to be dissipated. When people keep their differences bottled up, along with accompanying negative emotions arising from squelched opinions, their resentments tend to fester and grow. When people harbor such resentments, they tend to block the process of cooperating to arrive at a problem solution and carry it out. As a manager, therefore, your key to avoiding *ongoing* conflict lies in accepting *initial* conflict among workers and airing it as openly as possible.

As leader of your group, you have the greatest influence on how conflict is handled. If you are watchful for signs of differences of opinion and see that they are considered and respected, you will teach your people by your actions that conflict can be constructive.

Constructively Handling Competition Among Members

To handle competition among your teammates in a constructive way, you should first identify the kind of competition that is involved. Let's look at three major categories: (1) friendly competition, (2) constructive group action, and (3) destructive politics.

Friendly competition occurs when participants, knowing that others are being considered for promotion to the jobs they want, intensify their efforts. They may develop personal, innovative approaches to their jobs as well as additional skills and traits needed for the promotion. They may set more challenging objectives and higher standards for themselves. When a competitor is promoted, the others are generally able to work cooperatively with their former rival. Most leaders *encourage friendly competition: It creates challenge and interest.*

Sometimes employees need to unite in *constructive group action* if they are to promote their individual interests and also meet organizational objectives. Group members may also need to team up with their peers to prevent action by another that would prevent them from adequately meeting their own job objectives. For example, one unit or department may be so successful in getting the lion's share of the budget that the other units or departments are shortchanged. They may have to unite to get their fair share. Most leaders *encourage this type of political action: It helps build the group into a top-producing team.*

Total concentration on the process of promotion rather than on the job at hand is a warning sign of *destructive politics;* for example,

attempts to block a qualified peer's promotion, teaming up with peers to stop a front runner, automatically siding with friends against enemies, and logrolling (you scratch my back, I'll scratch yours, even if the company suffers in the process).

As a leader, *let people know that you will not tolerate this destructive kind of company politics.* If you know someone is involved in that kind of behavior, nip it in the bud. You want word to get around: "That sort of thing just won't work. It's more likely to result in being demoted or fired than in promotion."

Reward cooperation among competitors. Look for instances where members bring in competitors on projects and where they cooperate with competitors in meeting objectives and in developing constructive, innovative approaches to implementing objectives. Make sure these people are recognized and rewarded for working as a team.

Airing Opposing Views

Here are some suggestions to keep in mind as you lead the group in a discussion of differences of opinion.

1. Provide a supportive atmosphere for airing differences and reaching solutions.

2. Provide incentives for resolving the conflict. Each side must understand that more is to be gained by resolving the conflict than by continuing it.

3. Establish ground rules. Make sure that each side has equal time to present its views. Take steps to see that the most powerful or aggressive people don't dominate the situation unfairly.

4. Make sure that the parties to the conflict are ready to sit down and try to resolve it. Until they are, everyone will be wasting time.

5. Establish an atmosphere that supports openness. Allow for expression of feelings without attack. Accept the feelings that are expressed. Encourage open communication. Be noncritical and nonevaluative.

6. Listen, clarify, summarize, and give feedback. Encourage and support team members. Try to find mutual feeling and common ground. Look for opportunities to reduce tensions. Your goal should be to strengthen the personal relationships between the parties or at least to avoid their deterioration.

Isolating the Cause of the Problem

Once conflicting opinions and ideas have been adequately discussed, your function is to guide the parties to a satisfactory resolution of the conflict. To do so, you must first be aware of the sources or causes of the conflict. Look at four main areas: faulty communication, resentment of another's past behavior, conflicting goals, and conflicting choice of solution.

Conflicts resulting from *faulty communication* are often more imagined than real. First look for signs of faulty perception, misunderstanding, or oversensitivity. The best way to reduce imagined conflicts is to encourage frequent discussion of problems.

Constructive discussion of a problem may be jeopardized because you or one of your team members is harboring *resentment of another member's past behavior*. See whether such resentment can be brought out in the open. Try to get the person who resents the behavior to state the objection and describe the behavior specifically. Frequently the first objections brought up do not get at the heart of the problem. Conflicts based on unvoiced resentment need to be explored in an atmosphere in which feelings are respected so that true feelings can come to the surface.

Problems that arise because of *conflicting goals* are often the most difficult to resolve. Try to get each party to the conflict to pinpoint the specific goals she or he wants to see as an outcome of the situation. Then see whether they can agree on some common goal, such as increased productivity or even the survival of the company.

Sometimes everyone agrees on the major goal to be achieved in a situation, but two or more factions espouse a *conflicting choice of solutions* to best achieve that goal. When this happens, be sure everyone thoroughly discusses and understands the conflicting approaches. If conflict persists, search for alternate courses of action that incorporate the best aspects of the conflicting solutions.

Determining the Resolution Strategy of Each Party

It is important to know how each party to the conflict is trying to resolve the problem. An awareness of strategies for conflict resolution can help you make sure that individuals' concerns or feelings are not squelched, ignored, or avoided. It can also help you equalize power in the situation. Here are five basic strategies for resolving conflict.

1. *Competitive.* A win/lose approach in which one party attempts to dominate the other(s) and to win sympathy for his or her concerns at the expense of the other(s)

2. *Collaborative.* A cooperative approach in which all parties try to integrate their concerns so that all are fully satisfied

3. *Sharing.* A give-and-take approach that seeks to find a solution somewhere in-between the desires of all parties, giving each party moderate but incomplete satisfaction

4. *Avoidant.* A head-in-the-sand approach characterized by an indifference to the concerns

of other parties and to the conflict itself; behaviors include withdrawal, isolation, evasion, flight, and/or apathy

5. *Accommodative.* A nonassertive approach characterized by appeasement; one party tries to make peace by giving in to the other's concerns without taking care of his or her own concerns

Reaching a Resolution

Determine what each party sees as a possible solution and whether there *can* be a solution that will satisfy all parties. Explore possible alternatives that the parties have not considered. The solution that is adopted should (1) be best for the organization, (2) be best for *all* parties, and (3) provide control of the possibility of creating a related and more intense conflict in the future. Your role is to guide your people in selecting the solution that best meets these criteria and negotiate differences in reaching a solution that all can live with. See Chapter 11 for a detailed discussion of the entire problem-solving process.

DELEGATING EFFECTIVELY

When we think of day-to-day supervision, we usually think first of delegating tasks. In the broadest sense, delegation involves training and developing your workers and your team, directing and following up assignments, analyzing performance problems, coaching to overcome problems, and evaluating performance.

Before we discuss techniques for effective delegation, examine your ideas on the subject by completing Exercise 13-5.

Deciding When to Delegate

Whether you are doing the delegating yourself or are training team members to delegate, you need to understand typical barriers to delegation and how to decide when to delegate. First, let's review some reasons why leaders don't delegate as much as they should.

Why Leaders Don't Delegate You've given your ideas on this question in Exercise 13-5. Compare your responses with the summary of barriers to delegation—in the delegator, the delegatee, and the situation—listed in Exhibit 13-4.

Now we'll discuss some of these barriers in detail, along with attitudes and actions that can help you overcome them.

> *It's easier to do it myself, and I know it will be done right if I do it.* This is a short-range view, of course. Sure, it may take extra time and effort to train people to take over certain tasks. However, once they are properly trained, your time is freed up for more productive tasks. Also, with proper training and controls some people may eventually do an even better job than you are doing.

EXERCISE 13-5: EXAMINING YOUR APPROACH TO DELEGATION

1. Why don't leaders delegate when they should? List five or more reasons.

2. When should leaders delegate? List five or more reasons.

EXHIBIT 13-4: Barriers to Effective Delegation

Barriers in the Delegator

Preference for operating rather than planning when both need doing (delegating requires planning)	Lack of confidence in workers
	Perfectionism, leading to overcontrol
Demand that everyone "know all the details"	Lack of organizational skill in balancing the workload
The "I can do it better myself" fallacy	
Lack of experience in the job or in delegating	Failure to delegate authority commensurate with responsibility
Insecurity	
Fear of being disliked by workers	Uncertainty over tasks and inability to explain them
Refusal to allow mistakes	Disinclination to develop workers
	Failure to establish effective controls and to follow up

Barriers in the Delegatee

Lack of experience	Disorganization
Lack of competence	Overload of work
Avoidance of responsibility	Immersion in trivia
Overdependence on the leader	Lack of commitment to team goals

Barriers in the Situation

One-man-show policy	Urgency, leaving no time to explain (crisis management)
No toleration of mistakes	
Involvement of critical decisions	Confusion in responsibilities and authority
	Understaffing

Adapted from R. Alec MacKenzie, *The Time Trap* (New York: McGraw-Hill, 1982), p. 133.

I don't have enough confidence in the person. You may doubt that a worker can handle the task properly, and this may be a valid reason for not delegating at times. Take a look at whether you've properly evaluated the person's potential. Perhaps you need to weed out some of your marginal people and replace them with people you can have more confidence in.

I'm afraid of what my boss will think. This fear can come from being unclear about what your boss expects. If you are going to advance in your job, you must train and develop your own people. You must use some of your time to grow and develop by taking on new challenges. Discuss this with your boss. If your boss is unwilling or unable to see the value of your delegating to team members, consider looking for a different position under a more enlightened boss.

I like to get personal credit for these tasks. Sometimes we don't realize that the higher we go in an organization, the less we actually *do* on a project and the more we *get done* through our team. That means our value, and therefore the source of our personal credit, lies in our team's achievements. By delegating to members and giving them personal or team credit for the achievements, we demonstrate our leadership ability.

I thought I had plenty of time to do it myself. Sometimes we simply bite off more than we can chew. One way to avoid this trap is to always ask first, "How much of this can I delegate?" instead of, "How much of this can I do myself?" Delegate as much as possible.

I'm afraid the worker will feel I'm imposing on him or her. This reason tends to come from women managers, almost never from men. Remember, your *job* is to assign tasks; you must become comfortable in that role.

Think of assignments as opportunities for the worker to contribute, not as impositions.

When Leaders Should Delegate You're on your way to recognizing barriers that prevent you from delegating. Next, look at some typical situations in which you'd be wise to delegate.

Delegate to empower the work team. The essence of self-directed work teams is group power to make decisions about goals, tasks, and roles. If the team can decide who will do what by when and with whom—in order to achieve team goals—you are likely to see high team performance and cooperation. So bring delegation decisions to team meetings as often as feasible.

Delegate when doing so will help develop and motivate the worker. We discussed this in detail in the previous section. In the long run, this is the key to deciding when and what to delegate.

Delegate when you can do more productive work. This includes any time a higher-level task can be worked on (for example, one that requires longer-range planning, greater risks, a larger impact on departmental objectives, and so forth). It also includes any time there are assignments or projects to be done that will help you learn and grow.

Delegate when doing so won't show undue favoritism. It's easy to give all the most challenging tasks to star performers. It's also tempting to always send a star to represent you in meetings with higher-level bosses be-

cause you know they'll make you look good. Pass around some of the plum assignments, where appropriate, so you gain a reputation for being fair and for giving everyone a chance to shine.

Delegate when you are continually under too much time pressure. When you regularly find yourself struggling to meet even your top-priority objectives and the others get no attention at all, it's definitely time to look for areas where you can delegate. Work out a plan for easing your burden by training members to take over appropriate tasks.

Delegate when you are willing to take the time and effort to turn over the job skillfully. It's better to do a job yourself and do it right than to dump it on people, expecting them to sink or swim. This approach usually leads to anxiety and resentment on the worker's part and to your having to salvage poor-to-disastrous results before the job is completed.

When Leaders Should Do It Themselves Some management experts believe that a team leader should not be doing the actual work of the unit or department more than 20 percent of the time. When *is* it appropriate to be doing the actual work? Here are some suggestions.

1. To instruct new people

2. To test or check out equipment

3. To try out a new method

4. When available people are overloaded due to a temporary, abnormal situation and it is impractical to recruit additional workers (If this is a frequent occurrence, you may not be foreseeing and avoiding problems adequately.)

5. When operating difficulties occur and corrective measures are beyond the ability of the workers (If this occurs frequently, you may not be training workers properly.)

Turning Over Tasks

Once you have decided that a task should be delegated, the next step is to turn over the job as skillfully as possible. Here are some suggestions.

Practice Delegation To become skilled at delegating and comfortable with it, you must practice. Delegating becomes easier as you go along. Don't get directly involved with the work you delegate. Instead, spend your time and effort trying to see that it gets done effectively by others. Set a goal that delegated work will be done entirely by others and will be done well.

Match the Job to the Worker As thoughtfully and carefully as possible, select both the job and the worker who will do it. Consider short-range, long-range, practical, and psychological factors in deciding on the best match.

Prepare Yourself and the Worker Think through the key aspects of the task. Visualize yourself doing it and make notes of key tasks. Take time to do it right. Meet with the worker in private; try to avoid having interruptions during the session. Put the worker at ease. Where possible, recall past successes she or he has experienced in similar situations. Review the task thoroughly and, where necessary, give appropriate training. Prepare the worker by first giving a general overview of the task. Find out what the worker knows about it already.

Explain the Assignment Start with why the task must be done. The more routine or repetitive the job is, the more essential it is for the worker to understand its importance. You must convey that you believe the task is important. Explain how completion of the task will help meet objectives — the worker's, the team's, the department's, the organization's. In other words, help the worker understand how completion of the task fits into the big picture, the overall scheme of things. If you think of the task as mere drudgery or dirty work, your atti-

tude will come across to the worker and will have a powerful demotivating effect.

Focus on the Goal for the Task Give the worker as clear a picture as possible of the end result you expect. Set target dates or times for completion of each phase of the project. Give the worker as much leeway as possible to reach the end result. In other words, if there are several ways or methods of achieving the goal, let the worker determine the best way, where possible.

Review the Assignment Thoroughly If appropriate, go over the task step by step, explaining it by telling, showing, illustrating. Keep explanations as simple and logical as possible. Use visual illustrations or examples where appropriate. Stress each key point. Don't give workers more than they can master at one time. When complex tasks are involved, consider holding several training sessions.

Check for Understanding Where appropriate, have workers perform a sample of the task. Have them explain key points to you as they understand them so you can identify and correct misinterpretations. Ask for questions, but don't depend on "Do you have any questions?" to verify that they understand how to do the job. Ask the worker to repeat back what you have said, to walk through the job, or to perform part or all of it. Ask "smoke-out" questions: "Suppose you don't get all the statements by the fifteenth, what will you do?" "What's the next step?" "What do you have to do before sending the invoices to the Accounting Department?" Determine what training, if any, the worker needs to succeed in this assignment.

Discuss Standards of Performance Get workers involved in setting standards for tasks. Where appropriate, reassure them that standards will be relaxed until they have had time to learn the job and gain skill at it. Transmit confidence that with experience they will perform well. Then discuss the quantity and quality of work they should eventually achieve.

Remember that standards should be challenging but realistic in light of the individual's ability.

Provide Necessary Support   Be sure you delegate both the authority the worker will need to accomplish a task and the responsibility for getting the job done and maintaining minimum standards. Define the limits of responsibility and authority. Give as much decision-making authority as is feasible.

For example, suppose you make a worker responsible for getting a report done on time, and she needs information from one or more persons in the company to complete it. Let those people know that she is responsible for the report and that you have given her the authority to set deadlines for getting the necessary information.

Remember to see that the worker gets all the information she will need to do the job. Provide for the proper flow of information.

Encourage Independence   Give workers time to try out new tasks without peering over their shoulders. But let them know you are available to help. Check at appropriate times to see how they are doing.

Follow Up, Give Feedback, and Maintain Contact   Remember that you are responsible for the results of the task even though you've delegated it. Set up a system of periodic reports or checkpoints so you can review progress.

Consider keeping a delegation file. Include in it all information about the tasks and projects you have delegated to someone else, including objectives, standards, and deadline dates. Also put deadline dates for completion of key parts of each delegated assignment on your calendar, or in your tickler file. This procedure will help ensure that you follow up on workers' progress at appropriate times to maintain adequate contact.

There are many ways to keep in touch with what's going on. One that's often overlooked is "management by walking around." This involves moving around among your people as often as necessary. Wander around and directly observe what's going on. Casually ask questions. If this is done in a friendly, offhand way, it won't be interpreted as peering over the shoulder—and in fact is not. Occasionally ask, "What are you working on today?" as you pass by someone's desk, especially if the work looks interesting or different. When you pass someone in the hall, occasionally ask about a project or assignment to see how well informed a worker is about what's going on. You don't have to play detective all the time, but remember it's your business to know what's going on. Also, your presence and your interest alone signal that members and their work are important.

Evaluate and Give Feedback   Build in self-evaluation and self-control. In addition, discuss progress at appropriate checkpoints. Then immediately after the assignment has been completed, give a clear picture of your evaluation of the performance. Objectives and standards set earlier will be the basis for the evaluation. Give ample praise and recognition for good performance. If the performance was poor, ask the worker first for a self-evaluation. If there is a weak area the worker isn't aware of, you can say something like, "I think you could have done better on that. What did you learn from it?" More on this later.

Keeping the Ball in the Right Court

Sometimes workers will try to throw a large portion of a delegated task back on you by (1) asking you to solve problems that arise, (2) asking you to make tough decisions, or (3) expecting you to put the finishing touches on the project or to check for their errors. If you allow them to get away with this, you're teaching them that it's okay to stay dependent on you and dump problems back in your lap. You are also partially defeating the purpose of freeing up your own time and developing team members.

The first step to solving this problem is to identify *why* the worker is dumping problems back on you. Is it to avoid taking risks? Is the worker afraid of being criticized for making a mistake? Does the worker lack confidence? Does the worker lack necessary information or resources? Or are *you* the main source of the problem?

Pay special attention to the last possibility. Do you need to be needed? Do you want to feel indispensable? Your attitude comes across to your people. Examine it. Do you find it impossible to say "no" when the worker runs to you for help? Use your judgment, say "no" assertively when appropriate; otherwise, you'll be inviting the ball back into your court.

To keep the ball in their court, insist that workers come up with at least one possible solution to a problem before discussing it with you. If a problem is really thorny, give the worker just enough help so that she or he begins to see possibilities for a solution.

If possible, tell workers to make the decisions involved. Unless the decision turns out to be a poor one that would be really costly, support it. Discuss how to improve the decision next time around.

At the very least, insist that workers make a firm recommendation when they bring you a problem: "Come back when you can tell me which course of action *you* think would be best."

Remember that people must have the freedom to make *some* mistakes in order to become confident and independent. If they are constantly running to you for solutions to problems and for decisions, you're not doing the job of training and developing properly. On the other hand, when they successfully work through problems (with minimal coaching), they experience more satisfaction and enjoyment.

Another approach to delegation that's designed to keep the ball in the worker's court is called "managing by exception."

Managing by Exception

Once a team member knows the job you've delegated, you may want to try management by exception (or reporting by exception). You and the team, or the team member, agree on the limits of his or her authority. Everything outside those limits is considered an exception—significantly different or of greater magnitude or importance than usual: "If you have never had anything like it before, check with me." "If it involves more than X dollars, let me see it."

The same applies for reporting progress toward meeting objectives. The team agrees on minimum progress that members must achieve at certain points and members report to you immediately when they begin to fall behind in quantity, quality, or timing. In some cases the team may need to set upper limits to be sure that necessary adjustments are made to handle any extra load on the system: "We'll let you (leader) know if sales go above X units."

One of the advantages of management by exception is that everything is handled at as low a level as possible, with a minimum drain on the time and attention of higher authority at every level. Another is that the leader spends time on the things that need special attention rather than on the routine or on what went right.

A potential disadvantage of managing by exception is succumbing to the temptation of requiring members to report routine transactions on your pet project or in an area that was formerly your specialty. Although you may find it difficult to let go of the details in those situations, doing so is essential to your progress.

The *major* disadvantage of managing by exception is the tendency to focus on the negative. You can offset this by giving credit and recognition when people meet objectives.

When no exceptions are reported, you know people are on top of things—or are they? After all, exceptions are, at least to some extent, admissions of failure. Therefore people may shade exceptions in their favor. You can overcome this tendency by actively monitoring their progress. First, figure out which elements of a person's job may vary and which elements are most likely to have a decisive effect on whether a worker meets the objectives. Then determine beforehand what could become reportable exceptions and stay on top of them. Use your tickler file or calendar notations to remind yourself when to make inquiries or to schedule periodic reviews so that projects don't get lost in the shuffle.

Evaluating and Coaching for Top Performance

Once you've effectively handed over an assignment, the next step is to lead the follow up and evaluation of the worker's performance. If evaluation is to result in improved performance, you and the worker must identify areas of strength and weakness. Then the two of you must analyze any problems to determine their cause. Only then can you take specific action to improve performance.

One approach to analyzing performance problems is to first determine which of three basic categories they fall in:

1. *Environmental circumstances.* The worker has the skills and the desire to perform the tasks satisfactorily, but some barrier affecting the work situation prevents him or her from doing so.
2. *Skill deficiency.* The worker is unable to meet acceptable standards for performing the task because he or she lacks the necessary skills.
3. *Attitude deficiency.* The worker *could* perform the task satisfactorily but doesn't.

Exercise 13-6, on the following page, lists a number of typical performance problems. How would you categorize them?

Actually there are no right or wrong answers. The aim of the exercise is to help you experience the difficulty of dealing effectively with performance problems without first analyzing them thoroughly. First, determine whether the performance problem is best analyzed by the entire team, all team members who perform similar jobs, or solely by you and the worker. Then follow this step-by-step analytical sequence.

Describe and Evaluate the Discrepancy First, describe as specifically as possible the performance discrepancy. For example, item 1 in Exercise 13-6 is "arrives at work late." A specific description would be "Has arrived at work late as follows: October 1, 15 minutes late; October 6, 20 minutes late; October 9, 30 minutes late."

Then determine whether the discrepancy is important. In the example just given, the lateness would be very important if the worker is responsible for serving customers or handling callers. There might be situations, however, where the behavior would be unimportant, such as when a technical or professional person is working in relative isolation and is meeting objectives satisfactorily.

Categorize the Source of the Discrepancy If there is a problem, determine its probable source. First, ask if it might be the result of environmental circumstances. If not, look next at the possibility that the worker is lacking in some skill. If neither of these categories appears to be the source of the problem, it may be the worker's attitude.

The simplest deficiencies to correct are often environmental ones, so look for them first. If the problem appears to result from an *environmental deficiency*, meet with the worker to attempt to discover the obstacles to performance. Your first step is to determine whether the worker understands the objectives and standards. Find out if the worker knows what is expected; is clear about timing, deadlines, and

EXERCISE 13-6: ANALYZING PERFORMANCE PROBLEMS

Categorize each problem by determining whether its source is most likely a skill, attitude, or environmental deficiency. Place the number 1 under the category that represents the most likely source. If you think that more than one category may be the source, rank the deficiency by placing 1, 2, and possibly 3 in the appropriate spaces.

Performance Problem	Skill Deficiency	Attitude Deficiency	Environmental Deficiency
1. Arrives at work late	_____	_____	_____
2. Has a sloppy appearance	_____	_____	_____
3. Works slowly and creates bottlenecks	_____	_____	_____
4. Makes too many mistakes in paperwork	_____	_____	_____
5. Doesn't follow necessary procedures	_____	_____	_____
6. Gives fellow workers incorrect information	_____	_____	_____
7. Leaves work early	_____	_____	_____
8. Takes sick leave too frequently	_____	_____	_____
9. Leaves out important steps of task	_____	_____	_____
10. Is rude to customers	_____	_____	_____
11. Misses deadline dates	_____	_____	_____
12. Sends letters to wrong addresses	_____	_____	_____

workflow; has conflicting demands on his or her time.

The second step is to determine whether the worker has the resources necessary to perform adequately. Does the worker have the authority necessary to complete the task? Has he or she been given a reasonable length of time to complete the task and the tools, staff support, and other resources needed to perform adequately?

The third step is to determine whether there are bottlenecks or other barriers to performance. Are there bottlenecks that can be eliminated? Can the flow of work or paper to the worker be improved? Does company policy or the attitudes of others need to be changed? ("That can't be done." "We have always done it this way.")

Physical factors may be creating barriers to performance. You may need to change lighting or colors, modify the work position, reduce noise, provide more privacy, or take other steps to increase the worker's comfort. Are interruptions creating problems? If so, focus on reducing phone calls, visitors, "crises," and other demands that are more immediate but less important than the tasks in question.

If the problem is not an environmental one, chances are it's caused by a *skill deficiency*. There are three steps you can take. The first is to meet with the worker to try to determine these things:

1. Could the worker do the task satisfactorily if he or she really had to (if it were a matter

of survival)? Under normal circumstances, are the worker's present skills adequate for the desired performance?

2. Was the worker able to perform the task satisfactorily in the past? If not, consider providing formal training. If so, has the worker forgotten how to perform the task satisfactorily?

3. How often is the skill used? If the worker rarely performs the task, consider providing opportunities for practice.

4. Does the worker find out how well he or she is doing? Does the worker routinely get feedback about performance? If not, consider devising standards and control systems so that the worker gets feedback as frequently and automatically as is feasible.

The second step is to determine whether the team can solve the problem by changing the job, providing written instructions or checklists, showing the worker how to perform, or providing informal on-the-job training.

The third step is to determine whether the worker has the aptitude to gain the necessary skills. Could the worker learn the job with a reasonable amount of formal training? Does he or she have the physical and mental potential to perform adequately, or is the worker over-qualified for the job?

After you've eliminated the possibility of environmental or skill deficiency, you're left with the probability that the source of the performance problem lies in the worker's attitude. Inspiring others to change their attitudes is a challenging task! All you can do is give it your best shot — and, remember, it's up to the worker to make the grade or not.

If the problem appears to reflect an *attitude deficiency*, meet with the worker to attempt to discover the source of the unproductive attitude. First, determine whether the results of performing well are perceived as rewarding or as punishing by the worker. Find out what the

worker sees as the consequences of performing well. Does he or she think there are certain penalties for performing well — for example, that standards will probably be increased and more work will be required? Does the worker feel his or her world would become a little less pleasant or interesting if he or she performed better, or does the worker anticipate rewards for performing well?

Next, determine what payoffs the worker gets for *not* performing well. Find out specifically what the worker gets out of doing it his or her way instead of your way. Look for payoffs the worker gets from his or her present performance — for example, group belonging, prestige, status, revenge, attention, help, sympathy, pity, more time and energy for personal or favored activities.

Does the worker need more attention? Perhaps he or she gets more attention for poor performance than for satisfactory performance. Perhaps you are inadvertently rewarding poor performance with attention and ignoring good performance.

Finally, determine whether the worker perceives good performance as important. Find out how important satisfactory performance is to the worker. Does he or she anticipate a favorable outcome for performing well and an undesirable outcome for performing poorly? Does the worker receive any personal satisfaction from good performance, and is he or she able to take pride in good performance as an individual and as a team member? Are any of the worker's needs satisfied through good performance?

Determine the Optimal Solution   After analyzing the deficiency, select the best solution to the performance problem and see that it is carried out. Determine which solutions are most appropriate and feasible and which solutions are obviously too costly.

First, figure out the cost (including time and energy) of carrying out each solution and the resources needed. Next, figure the added value to the company of successfully carrying out each solution. Then decide whether each solution is worth carrying out. Compare to see which solution will probably give the best results with the least effort and which the team is best equipped to try. Keep in mind the intangible factors, too, such as which solution will be the most interesting to those involved and the most supportive of team goals.

Making Coherent Formal Evaluations

One of the most meaningful empowerment signals you can give your team is their inclusion in the formal evaluation and reward process. Fully self-directed teams develop their own processes for evaluating performance and giving rewards, within corporate policy. Your role is to facilitate team consensus on these processes and to administer the procedures the team agrees to. Keep in mind the following suggestions.

First, remember that evaluations must not be limited to a formal procedure. They should be ongoing and as immediate as possible.

Second, never focus on trivia in the formal evaluation discussion. Focus on important matters. Be sure to evaluate the person's performance, not the person. Be as specific as possible about what achievements were satisfactory or unsatisfactory.

Third, the team may want each member to know how he or she ranks within the team. For example, a statement such as "Your performance on XYZ projects ranks third out of the fifteen team members working on these projects" tells a worker that he or she is doing well and is valued. It also lets the worker know that there is some room for improvement. On the other hand, "Your achievement of work objectives for the quarter ranks tenth among the twelve team members" may serve as a spur to those who never before realized how much room they have for improvement. And it can do so without creating a problem of personal jealousies through comparison by names.

Fourth, the team should develop a process for allocating the merit raise budget. It may be up to you to negotiate with your boss for the largest budget possible for your team, but the fully self-directed team will feel more responsible and committed if they decide how to divvy up the rewards. The team may want to use the ranking technique to identify top, average, and marginal performers. For example, some teams use a ratio of 2:1:0; the top performers get twice as much as those who made some progress (average performers) and the marginals get no raises. Next, the team must decide whether the amount to be divided up among each group will be based on a percentage of each person's salary or whether the same lump-sum raise will be given to everyone in a particular performance group.

Finally, everyone should keep in mind that the goal is to reward the achievement of specific objectives that you, the team, and each worker have agreed on — and to do it in as fair and reasonable a way as possible. Giving merit increases to those who don't deserve them waters down the impact of what the top performers get and encourages marginal workers to disbelieve what you and the team *say* about the importance of performance.

SELECTING TEAM MEMBERS

Periodically the team will be selecting and training new workers. Be sure to take full advantage of this opportunity to add persons who fit in. Your goal is to build an effective work team. You may inherit some people who are difficult to work with and perhaps even more difficult to move into different departments. It is worth taking special precautions to assure that each new team member is the best one available for the job and the team.

The process of selecting workers differs from company to company, depending on company size, policy, and job requirements. You and your team may have complete responsibility for selecting new workers — from announcing job openings to making the final decision about who is hired. On the other hand, if your company is one of those rare ones in which the Human Resources Department handles the entire selection process, you may have virtually no say about who is hired. In most cases, however, you will at least interview applicants for jobs in your unit or department and have some input into the hiring decision.

Your main goal in leading the interview process is to determine which applicants are likely to be successful or unsuccessful in the job position. Once you have differentiated between probable successful and unsuccessful candidates, your goal is to determine which of the successful ones is best suited to the position. To achieve these goals, you and your members must (1) distinguish between personal biases, prejudices, or stereotypes and valid intuitive judgment of each applicant's suitability for the job; (2) devise a form and procedures for recording your evaluations of the candidates' qualifications; (3) determine relevant questions to ask; and (4) establish an atmosphere that brings out essential information about each candidate's skills, knowledge, experience, and social/motivational aptitude for the particular position. (See Exercise 13-9 for practice at interviewing.)

Identifying Personal Biases

Only you can determine whether your positive or negative feelings about a job applicant reflect an inappropriate bias or a valid intuitive judgment. An inappropriate bias can cause you to select a person who is unsuited for the job or to reject a person who is well suited.

For example, you may take an immediate liking to an applicant who reminds you of a good friend or relative. You may subsequently assume that the applicant has the same admirable personal characteristics of your friend. However, the applicant may in fact have quite differ-

ent characteristics that you failed to discover because of your false conclusion.

On the other hand, you may immediately take a negative attitude toward a candidate who reminds you of, say, your brother-in-law, whom you believe is lazy, inconsiderate, and generally obnoxious. Unless you are aware of your bias and make a special effort to dig deeper and try to determine just what this applicant is really like, you may pass over the best candidate for the job.

Exercise 13-7 is designed to help you become aware of some of your biases and to pinpoint some areas where you will want to be especially cautious about jumping to false conclusions. In this exercise you have a chance to identify general categories in which you are biased, such as "same sex." Under that category, you will list specific types of people of the same sex that you have a positive bias toward — for example, "liberated women." Then you will list factors you have especially noticed and admired about this type of person — for example, "assertive, independent, direct in their dealings." You will also list specific types of people you have a negative bias toward — for example, "catty women." And you will mention negative factors about these people, such as "concerned with trivialities; tend to be sneaky."

Providing Necessary Structure

In addition to being aware of your personal biases, you must establish an atmosphere conducive to open communication. Then you must ask questions that will help you uncover the factors that are essential to making the best decision about whom to hire. Most of the experts who have researched the field of interviewing agree that the structured interview usually gives the best results. As a matter of fact, most interviews could be improved by more advance planning and structure. This includes formulating a set of questions to cover all bases with every applicant. Good questions

EXERCISE 13-7: IDENTIFYING PERSONAL BIASES

On a separate sheet of paper, make three columns and label them as shown below. In the first column list specific types of people toward whom you have positive or negative biases. For example, opposite "same sex," you might put "bright women" or "catty women." In the middle column, list *positive* factors (traits, actions, attitudes) that you especially notice and *like*. In the last column, list *negative* factors that you especially notice and *dislike*.

General Type	Specific Type	Positive Factors	Negative Factors
Same Sex	Catty Women (example)		
Opposite Sex			
Ethnic or Racial Minorities (list)			
Age			
Physical Ability or Appearance			
Education			
Socioeconomic Background			
Sexual Preference or Lifestyle			
Religion			
Other (list)			

will help you predict a good fit in the social/ motivational aspects of the job as well as in the skill/knowledge aspects.

Prepare for the interview thoroughly so you can make it as effective and relaxed as possible. Here are some suggestions.

1. Examine the job requirements and the application form.

2. Map out the areas that need to be covered by the interview.

3. Review, select, or develop a rating form that you will use for the candidates for this job. (A discussion of rating forms follows.)

4. Plan and organize questions that will help you get the essential information in each area without violating EEO guidelines on discrimination. (A discussion of effective questions follows.)

5. Try to interview each applicant in the same setting so that the only element that's altered is the applicant being interviewed. In this way your comparisons will have greater validity.

6. Pick a setting that's pleasant and quiet. Take steps to prevent interruptions during the interview.

FIGURE 13-3: Finding a Good Applicant/Job Position Fit

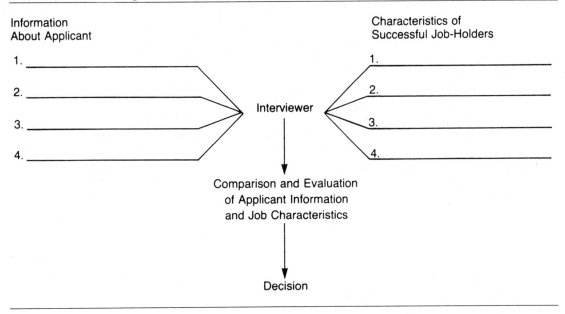

7. Before each candidate arrives, review his or her completed application form. Look for gaps in education and employment. Decide which items on the form need to be discussed so you can better understand the applicant's qualifications. From the application form determine what things about the candidate need to be confirmed or explained in the interview. Add these individualized questions to your list of questions designed for all candidates for this job position.

8. Keep the questions and the rating form handy for reference during the interview.

Select or Develop a Rating Form   A rating form will help you record and evaluate whether each candidate has the characteristics of a person likely to be successful in the particular position. Figure 13-3 depicts the process of selecting the best job candidate. The first step is to determine the characteristics necessary for success in the job. The next step is to discover each applicant's relevant characteristics. Then compare the two sets of characteristics to determine how well they fit and to decide whether the applicant merits further consideration. After this initial screening, compare the relative suitability of the top candidates and make a final decision about who will receive the job offer.

Only the team can formulate what it thinks are the essential characteristics for success in the position you have available. It is a good idea to consider more than the skill, experience, and education required for success. Look also at how well the person will fit in with the team members. Ask, "Will the applicant probably be happy and motivated to perform well in this work situation?" In other words, consider the social and motivational factors in job success as well as the technical factors.

Exhibit 13-5 is a model for a rating form that covers technical, social, and motivational predictors of job success.

EXHIBIT 13-5: Outline for an Applicant-Rating Form

1. *Knowledge, skills, and abilities (list)*

2. *Work experience* (extent to which applicant's work history indicates an ability to learn and understand the job requirements)

   Experience in performing tasks

   Experience in team work

   Past failures due to lack of ability

   Knowledge of equipment, tools, and work procedures

   Past job assignments

   Assignment to task forces or special projects

   Achievement in special projects, task forces

3. *Training*

   Adequate education for job position

   Relevant on-the-job training

   Relevant vocational or trade school training

   Participation in seminars, workshops, continuing education classes, etc.

   Self-study (programmed instruction, correspondence courses, etc.)

4. *Ability to understand and respond to questions*

   Listening skills

   Clear, concise answers

   On-target, relevant responses

5. *Ability to communicate ideas*

   Ability to organize and present ideas coherently

   Ability to communicate feelings, as well as logical thoughts and ideas, appropriately

6. *Manner and appearance* (how others react to applicant)

   Overall appearance

   Tactfulness

   Self-confidence

   Sensitivity to others' needs

   Appropriateness of dress

   Health and physical condition adequate for job duties

7. *Congeniality* (prediction of ability to get along with others and work as a member of a team)

   Previous problems with supervisors, peers, or workers

   Preference for working with others

   Tendency to be a "loner" in social activities

   Involvement in community, social, religious, or athletic activities

   Excessive reaction to criticism

   Openness and candidness in communication

8. *Goal congruence* (prediction of extent to which applicant's goals and aspirations are consistent with available opportunities)

   Level of ability and qualifications are consistent with available opportunity here

   Level of ambition is consistent with available opportunity in the company

9. *Job satisfaction* (prediction of the extent to which applicant will be involved in the job and will gain personal satisfaction from it)

   Past participation in job-related activities (societies, associations, etc.)

   Degree of success and satisfaction in school and work situations

Participation in company-sponsored opportunities to develop job-related skills

Personal interest in goals, hobbies, avocations that fit in with job activities

10. *Reward structure* (prediction of the extent to which rewards available in this position will be perceived as motivational rewards by the applicant)

Will soon expect higher pay than will be available

The job itself will be rewarding

Needs more recognition and praise than job offers

11. *Initiative and productivity* (prediction of applicant's ability to use good judgment in doing the job, taking initiative when appropriate, and getting help when needed)

Ability to think and act independently to meet work standards

Ability to exercise leadership when appropriate

Willingness to take responsibility for work delays and interruptions as well as for producing results

Capacity for persistence, thoroughness, "professionalism"

Past record for meeting deadlines and achieving objectives and standards

12. *Poise and stability* (prediction of applicant's ability to perform well under pressure and to respond effectively to emergencies)

History of reactions in emergencies (impulsive or composed)

Indications of the quality of applicant's work in emergencies or under pressure (suffers or remains high)

Ability to adjust to changes in work procedures

Ability to adjust to changes in work environment, such as work interruptions or schedule changes

13. *Dependability* (prediction of applicant's work habits and attendance record)

Past attendance record (absenteeism, lateness, regularity, promptness)

Previous reprimands or commendations for work performance

Safety record (instance of involvement in accidents, work interruptions, accident prevention, etc.)

Other indications of work habits

Factual Reasons for Hiring:

Factual Reasons for Rejecting:

Plan and Organize Questions The questions you pose to a candidate should ferret out the necessary facts without violating **Equal Employment Opportunity (EEO) laws** concerning discrimination against women, minorities, and other covered groups. Avoiding illegal questions while giving applicants an opportunity to express their ideas and feelings candidly requires special thought.

Any question that focuses on an applicant's sex, race, ethnic origin, religion, physical condition, or age is off limits *unless* it's a **Bona Fide**

Occupational Question (BFOQ). BFOQ, a term used in connection with EEO laws, refers to interview questions that are necessary to determine an applicant's *bona fide,* or relevant and essential, qualifications for the job. All qualifications set up for the job must be (1) objective, stated in terms of basic and observable facts, (2) uniform in application to all candidates, (3) consistent in their effect on all candidates, and (4) essential to the successful performance of the job. An effective interview question is helpful in gathering job-related information, is tactful, and is in compliance with Equal Employment Opportunity guidelines. Here are some examples.

1. *Work Experience*

   "One of the things I am particularly interested in is your work experience. Will you please describe your current position?"

   "What do you feel have been some of your particularly strong points in accomplishing your work? Why?"

   "What are some of the things about your present job that you have found difficult to do? Why?"

   "Have you worked on team projects? Tell me about those experiences."

   "How much supervision do you have? Do you feel that's the most appropriate amount for you?"

   "What do you feel are the major problems that you have encountered and how have you solved them?"

2. *Feelings and Attitudes About Past Jobs*

   "Do you consider your progress in your present position representative of your ability? Why or why not?"

   "How do you feel about the progress that you have made with your present employer?"

   "In what ways do you feel that your present job has developed you to assume greater responsibilities?"

   "How you feel about the responsibilities that you have assumed in former positions?"

   "What part of your job do you enjoy the most? The least? Why?"

   "Do you feel that your salary is adequate for the work you now perform? If not, why?"

   "What are your reasons for wanting to leave your present job?"

3. *Attitude Toward the Job Being Offered*

   "What are some of the things in a job that are most important to you?"

   "How do you feel this company can provide what's important for you?"

   "What do you feel should be the qualifications for this job?"

   "What do you feel you'd like best about this job?"

   "What do you expect would be the typical problems in this job?"

   "What reservations do you have about this job?"

   "What do you think is likely to make the difference between success and failure in this position?"

4. *Relationships with Others*

   "Describe the perfect boss for you. How does your boss differ?"

   "What kinds of people upset you the most?"

   "What are some of the problems you've encountered while working with other people?"

   "What would you like to do to strengthen your dealings with others? How?"

   "How do you feel your supervisor has increased your capabilities, or not developed them?"

   "How do you feel your previous or current supervisor would describe you?"

5. *Self-Esteem*

   "What are some of the things in a job that motivate you?"

"What has been your biggest disappointment? Why? How did you handle it?"

"What kinds of situations make you feel tense or nervous?"

"What obstacles have you had to overcome?"

"What's the hardest thing you've ever done?"

"What do you feel is your greatest strength?"

"What do you feel you could most improve on?"

"What are you doing to improve those things which you feel need improvement?"

6. *Career Goals*

"What is your long-range career goal?"

"How do you plan to reach this goal?"

"How do you feel this company can help you reach your career goals?"

"What do you want from your next job that you are not getting from your current job?"

"What kind of position do you want to have in five years?"

Conducting the Interview

You'll want to do a thorough job of both preparing for and conducting the job interview because it's your best chance to get and give essential information and to make a personal impact on potential team members. Determine the role team members will play in the interview process. A group interview could be followed up with an individual interview. Keep in mind that top applicants will be interviewing you and the company too. Therefore it is important to put your best foot forward in order to attract the best people to your team. Here are some pointers.

Opening the Interview   Begin the interview with a few minutes of light conversation, putting the applicant at ease as much as possible. Start establishing an atmosphere of trust and open communication. Next, ask the applicant how she or he learned of the job. This can help you establish a relationship between the applicant and the company. Mention early in the interview how much time you can spend. Mention again when you have only five or ten minutes left to talk so that important questions and information can be exchanged.

Exchanging Relevant Information   Move into important topics as soon as some rapport is established. Describe the essential responsibilities and requirements of the job. Clarify any job requirements the applicant is not clear about.

Use appropriate questions and techniques to get the information you need. Try to use the same sequence of questions with all applicants to help in making valid comparisons. Begin with broad general questions to give the applicant an opportunity to show what she or he thinks is most important for you to know. Probe incomplete answers and problem areas while maintaining an atmosphere of trust. Make follow-up comments and summaries of the discussion where appropriate.

Avoid questions that can be answered "yes" or "no" when you want complete information. Use open phrasing that encourages the applicant to give a complete idea or thought: "What did you like best (or least) about school?" rather than "Did you like school?" However, if you are having trouble getting an answer from an applicant who rambles and digresses, you may want to ask some closed questions, such as "Can you operate the XYZ machine without further training?" Other types of questions to be avoided are those that

Prompt a specific kind of reply (leading questions): "Working as part of a team is very satisfying, isn't it?"

May be argumentative: "Wouldn't you have more flexibility if you were willing to transfer?"

Have no bearing on the applicant's qualifications for the job

Tend to be viewed as discriminatory (such as some questions regarding children, arrests, religion, military discharge, credit rating, and age)

Have been answered adequately on the application form

Avoid interjecting your own opinion or attitude in your questions or comments without good reason. For example, do not make remarks such as these: "It's difficult to work with that type of person." "I wouldn't put up with that either." When an applicant makes a statement that is too general to be meaningful, ask for specifics to clarify what is meant. For example, the applicant says, "I'm good at planning and organizing." You respond, "Could you give me some examples of how you have used those abilities?"

Take notes during the interview so you will be able to recall important factual items clearly, as well as your feelings and general impressions about each candidate. If the applicant seems tense about note-taking, explain its purpose in a reassuring way. Note *how* a person answers questions as well as *what* is said. Does the applicant get to the point or wander and ramble? Answer concisely and clearly? Listen to questions closely? Second-guess what the question will be?

Throughout the interview, show concern for the applicant's feelings but maintain control of the interview. React appropriately to applicant's comments and questions as well as to nonverbal messages. Set a tone of warmth and trust by showing a positive interest in the applicant and by using encouragement and praise where appropriate.

Let the applicant do most of the talking while you focus on getting the information you need to make a decision. Give the applicant adequate time to formulate thoughts into logical replies. Don't feel you have to keep the air filled with words. In fact one technique for getting more information is simply to pause for a few seconds. The applicant will usually volunteer an additional response.

Closing and Documenting the Interview
Your main goal when closing is to leave the applicant feeling that she or he has been treated fairly, courteously, and with consideration. Whether the applicant is eventually hired or not, it's important that she or he leave with positive feelings about the company. A major factor in treating applicants fairly is to be as candid as possible about the status of their applications.

When the applicant *will not be hired,* use this procedure: If you have already determined that the applicant is not adequately qualified for the job, give him or her the decision and the reasons for it. Use only job-related reasons for not hiring applicants. This helps avoid feelings of discrimination. Where appropriate, offer suggestions for gaining the knowledge or experience needed to become qualified for such a job.

Be as tactful as possible in informing applicants that they will not be hired. Take special care to be encouraging and supportive so that the applicant will retain a positive image of the company.

When the applicant *may be hired,* use this procedure: Tell the applicant that he or she is qualified. Reveal the approximate number of other applicants you are considering and express this in terms of any one applicant's probability of being hired: "We're interviewing ten or so people. Therefore, there is roughly one chance in ten that any one of you will be hired." By giving this kind of information, you help the applicant formulate reasonable expectations. A subsequent refusal is less likely to be incorrectly interpreted as a case of discrimination. Tell qualified applicants how you will notify them of the final decision and approximately when they may expect to hear from you.

Studies show that vital information given toward the end of an interview is often not heard or remembered accurately. Therefore, be sure you present a clear plan of action to the applicant when closing the interview. A clear, concise summary of this plan should be repeated to be sure there is no misunderstanding.

Proper documentation of the interview process can save you and your company the ordeal of a discrimination suit. By taking notes and using a rating form correctly, you can explain to anyone why a particular applicant was hired or not.

Don't allow any interruptions until you have completed the rating form. Research indicates that even one phone call between the end of an interview and the documentation of it reduces your ability to remember all the essential information you gained during the interview.

Exhibit 13-5 mentions *factual reasons* for hiring or rejecting an applicant. The term "factual" as used here refers to specific actions or statements made by the applicant rather than vague, general statements or your personal feelings and opinions about the person. For example, "sloppy appearance" is an opinion, not a fact. "Applicant was wearing soiled, wrinkled, patched jeans and a tee shirt. He was wearing sandals with no socks." These are facts that are specific. They can readily be verified by others who met the applicant.

"Applicant is not highly motivated" is an opinion, not a fact. "Applicant stated that she had difficulty sitting at a desk for long periods. She stated that her family thought that she should work in a bank." These are specific, factual statements.

"Applicant lacks the necessary skills" is a vague statement. "Applicant's Verbal Skills exam score is 60, which is 20 points below minimum job standards." This is a specific reason for rejection.

Selecting the Best Candidate   Once you have completed interviewing all the applicants, you're ready to carefully analyze the information you obtained about them. If you have taken adequate notes and have completed your rating form properly, you'll have a good picture of each applicant and his or her qualifications and characteristics.

A word to the wise: Don't hire men or women who are openly hostile or reticent about working for a woman manager. There's no need to burden yourself unnecessarily with the tough and thankless job of trying to win them over.

ORIENTING NEW TEAM MEMBERS

Once you have a new team member, you'll want to retain his or her positive image of the company, and you'll also want to help the new worker get off to a good start. Perhaps the most common mistake leaders make in orienting new workers is throwing too much information at them at one time. Another common mistake is devoting too little time to preparing for and orienting the worker. Too often the new worker gets a half-day orientation—much of it conducted on the spur of the moment or almost as an afterthought. On the other hand, supervisors sometimes depend on canned, superficial presentations by the Human Resources Department for nearly all of the orientation process.

An effective orientation not only gives new workers basic information about the company and the job, it also enhances their motivation to achieve and their future productivity on the job. First, decide which workers you will ask to help with the orientation; select people you think will relate well to the new employee, people with positive, enthusiastic attitudes toward the work, the team, and the company. Ask their help in determining what information and training should be included in the orientation and how long the orientation period needs to be. Then prepare a brief written outline showing information that will be presented on each day of the orientation period. Plan short daily sessions designed to give the new employee a little information or instruction each day for about two weeks. The worker can spend the remainder of each day applying any instruction to job tasks. The exact pattern and length of time for orientation will of course depend on each specific situation.

Now we've come full circle. After the new worker has had time to become an accepted team member, master the job, and establish a fairly stable level of performance, the next step is to delegate appropriate new assignments.

REMOVING TEAM MEMBERS

Perhaps the most challenging task of a team leader is removing a team member from the team. This becomes necessary when the organization must cut back, or when members are unable or unwilling to perform the tasks that must be done and are unable to share team values and goals to such a degree that they create disruption and negatively affect team spirit and performance. In other words, some people simply do not fit the requirements of the job and are unwilling or unable to develop the needed skills or motivation. Releasing members with sensitivity is important for your relationship with the remaining team members and for the organization's reputation within the community. Potential applicants will be influenced by the stories they hear. A major goal is to foster a feeling of goodwill that the member will retain long after he or she leaves the team.

First, put yourself in the person's place and imagine what it would feel like to be released. Have the courage to meet face-to-face with the person and to support him or her in any way

possible. Consider any alternatives, such as transfer, job-sharing or part-time status. Think through the process you will use.

Layoffs

When layoffs must occur, a crucial rule of thumb is to lay off the right number of people from the start. When people are picked off like flies, morale takes a nose dive. So work with other leaders before making a clean sweep. Study the situation. Understand your resources, and be conservative about how much money you'll have to work with. The worst thing you can do is make cuts, tell the remaining people that they are your team — and then make more cuts. It totally undermines your credibility. Further do's and don'ts are given in Exhibit 13-6.

Dismissals

When you must release a team member because of a poor fit, your chore is easier if he comes to his own conclusion that the job is a poor fit for him and decides to leave on his own. Start a dialogue to get the individual to talk about what he wants from his career, his job, his work situation — and then to conclude that he can't get that in his current work situation.

If the member is primarily interested in the paycheck, and has little self-awareness or career vision, this approach will probably be fruitless. Focus on the reasons for the dismissal, on the person's performance, not on his personality. Do all you can to help him maintain a high level of self-esteem by viewing the dismissal as a learning experience and an opportunity to move into a more appropriate job fit. Be as supportive as possible, but make it very clear that the job is over. Offer whatever you can in the way of company or personal assistance in helping him through the transition to a new job situation.

EXHIBIT 13-6: Guidelines for Removing Team Members

Do's	Don'ts
Give as much warning about mass layoffs as possible.	Don't be ambiguous when releasing someone. The person should clearly understand that the job is over.
Provide written explanation of severance benefits.	
Provide outplacement services.	Don't get into a debate.
Be sure you deliver the message before the employee hears it from some other source.	Don't make personal comments; keep the conversation professional.
Express appreciation for what the employee has contributed.	Don't rush the employee off-site unless security is really an issue.
Be as supportive as possible.	Avoid releasing people on or around important holidays such as Christmas or vacation.

SUMMARY

A work team is a special type of work group in which members cooperate in all aspects of their tasks. Self-directed work teams share in carrying out the traditional management functions, with the leader functioning as a member and as a facilitator of team achievement. Team development is broader and more long term than team building with a primary goal of creating and improving all the team's systems.

Seven major steps in team development are encouraging enlightened self-interest, empowering the team to direct itself, providing challenge and support, creating a shared vision and focusing on common goals, establishing informal day-to-day processes, nurturing positive team feelings, and leading in ways that encourage self-direction.

Leading-edge companies now encourage intrapreneurs to develop informal, then formal innovative teams to carry their ideas to fruition. The key intrapreneurial phases are Solo, Network, Bootleg, and Formal. Running-Hot firms are developing intrapreneurial Hot Teams that are more entrepreneurial and less democratic than some of the Self-Directed Teams in slower-paced organizations. Hot firms seize rapidly evolving opportunities to serve a tough market for a service or product. They are usually small ad hoc teams, put together from within the company, and led by one or two people with specific skills. Members learn as they go, working out procedures themselves. Their purpose is to meet specific market opportunities and resulting company needs. As those needs change, teams disband and members are incorporated into new Hot Teams.

Continuous improvement incorporates forward feed from customers about their changing needs so the team can plan ways of responding. The model also uses forward feed that helps suppliers provide for the team's changing needs. The goal is to produce a flow of incremental improvements with a focus on quicker, more competitive responses to changing customer requirements. Total Quality Management focuses on teamwork within teams and throughout the organization for the purpose of providing a total quality experience for the customer. The goal is total quality in both the basic product or service that a customer buys and in all the support services. These services may range from initially attracting the customer through communicating, shipping, billing, extending credit, to following up, servicing, and fulfilling warranties.

Team meetings are the major vehicle by which the team carries out its management functions. Meetings are also a major forum for building team cohesiveness. The key factors in structuring a work team meeting are determining roles, norms, goals/agenda, process and methods, and evaluation. The meeting facilitator must get full participation as early in the meeting as possible, focus the team on the purpose of the meeting, use group processes that will accomplish the meeting objectives, read the team's moods, deal effectively with difficult members, and achieve closure and follow-up so the members leave feeling committed to decisions taken.

Valuing Diversity is an approach that maximizes the contributions of people from every segment of the employee population, which in turn helps the organization reach its objectives. It contrasts with the Melting Pot and AA approaches. Valuing Diversity does not replace Affirmative Action but goes beyond it to form more powerful beliefs and attitudes. The outcomes include increased creativity, enhanced understanding among team members, and increased productivity. Unmanaged diversity can result in miscommunication, lack of cohesiveness, and stress.

Resolving conflict within the team involves six key steps: seeing it as an opportunity to root out problems before they fester, identifying types of competition and guiding it constructively, openly airing the views of the people involved in a group meeting, isolating the real cause of the conflict, determining the resolution strategy of each party, and reaching a resolution that is best for all parties.

A key to effective day-to-day team leadership is knowing when and how to delegate. To develop a top-performing team, match tasks to be delegated to workers with the potential to successfully complete the tasks and benefit from the assignments. By delegating as many tasks as possible, you free up your own time for doing more productive tasks and acquiring new leadership skills. By delegating authority and responsibility, you empower the team and provide training and development opportunities, thereby increasing members' level of interest, challenge, and motivation. You can adopt various strategies for overcoming barriers to effective delegation within you, the workers, or the environment. Once you delegate a task, don't let the worker dump it back on you. Insist that she or he come up with at least tentative solutions, recommendations, or decisions before you step in to help.

Consider using the management-by-exception technique. You become involved only in the exceptions to the routine — decisions outside the limits of workers' authority, or their failure to make minimum progress in terms of quantity, quality, or timing of performance. Avoid potential problems with this technique by establishing an effective follow-up system.

To evaluate a worker's performance of delegated tasks, carefully analyze any performance problems before attempting to deal with them. First describe as specifically as possible the performance discrepancy and determine whether it's important. If it is, try to categorize it as a skill, attitude, or environmental deficiency. Then meet with the worker to further investigate and determine the source of the problem. Finally, select the best solution to the performance problem and see that it is carried out.

The team can develop evaluation and reward processes that you administer. When you make formal evaluations, stick with the really important matters. You may help the worker understand the situation if you explain how his or her performance ranks within the department. Be consistent in your actions and explain your line of reasoning to all concerned. Reward the accomplishment of specific objectives.

When selecting new team players, the job interview is a key tool. First determine which applicants are likely to be successful or unsuccessful in the job. Then determine which of the successful candidates is best suited to the job. To prepare properly for the interview, formulate a predetermined set of questions to ask so you'll cover all bases with every applicant. Good questions will help you predict a good fit in the social/motivational aspects and the skill/ knowledge aspects of the job. They'll also help you comply with the EEO guidelines. Close the interview so the applicant leaves feeling that she or he has been treated fairly. Immediately document what happened so you can refer back to key points. Record factual reasons for hiring or rejecting the person, not vague or general comments or your personal feelings about the applicant.

Once you have a new team member, plan an effective orientation that provides basic information about the company, the team, and the job and also enhances motivation. Spread the orientation over several days to give the new member time to absorb all the information.

Removing team members who don't fit is a more challenging task than laying off members because of budget problems. Focus on performance, not personality. Ask the member to discuss job and career aspirations, how well the current situation fits, and encourage the member to arrive at the conclusion of a poor fit. Provide all the support that you can with the goal of maintaining goodwill.

Additional Exercises

EXERCISE 13-8: DELEGATION

Jill has taken a deep look at herself and her department and has decided she must delegate more to her employees for the following reasons: (1) She has been working fifty hours a week instead of forty. (2) The pressure of getting everything done has put her on edge with some of the staff. (3) She has not been sleeping well because of worry. Last night she spent three hours formulating the following list of responsibilities she might delegate to her five employees. What goals should Jill keep in mind when she ranks these tasks in order of priority for delegating? Rank the tasks in order of priority for delegating.

Priority
Ranking:

_____ A. A weekly report that takes fifty minutes to prepare. This report could easily be delegated to Rose, but it would reveal certain departmental figures that have always been kept away from the employees. There is nothing secret about the data, but Jill feels she might lose some control if everybody knows what goes on.

_____ B. A weekly fun job that Jill has always enjoyed doing. Frances would love to do the job (she would probably do it better than Jill), but Jill wants to keep it because it keeps her closer to her employees and facilitates communication. The job usually takes about one hour.

_____ C. A very routine weekly stock or supply room count that takes an hour and a half. Jill has delegated this job before, but she always winds up taking it back because the grumbling from the employee disturbs her more than doing the job herself. Besides, sometimes the count is wrong and she winds up doing the job herself anyway.

_____ D. A short (fifteen-minute) telephone call every day at 4:00 P.M. to get some data to the computer center. Jill has refused to delegate this because if it is not done accurately, she will be reprimanded by her boss. Calvin would be able to do the job and not be overloaded.

_____ E. A daily (ten-minute) delivery job of a special report to higher management. Jill has kept this to do herself because it gives her a chance to have a cup of coffee and she can play a little politics with the executives.

_____ F. A special routine meeting each month, which many supervisors already delegate. George could learn a lot from this assignment. Jill has kept it to herself because she is afraid that something will happen at the meeting that she won't know about. The meetings last from one to two hours.

EXERCISE 13-9: INTERVIEWING: QUESTIONING TECHNIQUES

This activity will help you become more skillful in conducting interviews through using open-ended questions, responding to free information, and paraphrasing. (See Exhibit 13-7 and the accompanying discussion on phrasing questions.)

Interview your partner for a job in your office. Concentrate first on using open-ended questions, then on responding to free information, and finally on integrating paraphrasing into the interview. Switch roles.

Exhibit 13-7 presents some examples of closed and open-ended questioning and some possible responses. Note that closed questions can be answered by a simple yes or no, but open-ended questions call for a more detailed reply. Although some individuals *may* respond more fully to closed questions than shown here, nonassertive people frequently won't. Open-ended questions offer more encouragement to talk extensively.

EXHIBIT 13-7: Closed and Open-Ended Questions

Closed Questioning	Open-Ended Questioning
Q: Were you a salesman at Apex?	Q: *What* did you do at Apex?
A: Yes.	A: I was a salesman for the first two years and a sales supervisor for the last six months.
Q: Did you like being a sales supervisor?	Q: *How* did you feel about being a sales supervisor?
A: No.	A: It was frustrating because I really liked to sell and I'm not comfortable supervising others.
Q: And you supervised the Central City Territory?	Q: *Tell me* about the Central City Territory.
A: Yes.	A: Well, it includes twenty-one major accounts and . . .

Another way to encourage conversation is to occasionally respond to the *free information* the other person gives to your open-ended questioning and give your own opinions, disclosures, or information:

Q: How were your commissions paid at Apex?

A: We received two percent of gross sales each quarter.

Q: Our commissions are comparable, and they are paid each month. Most salespersons really appreciate getting that check every month.

If you don't have anything to say in response to your partner's free information, yet you'd like for him or her to continue talking on the topic, try *paraphrasing:*

Q: How is the Sales Department structured at Apex?

A: There are four hundred or so salespersons reporting to thirty or so sales supervisors. Supervisors are expected to make a few calls with each sales person every month.

Q: It sounds as if the supervisors have their hands full.

REFERENCES

1. Adler, Nancy J. *International Dimensions of Organizational Behavior.* Boston: PWS-Kent, 1991.

2. Asplund, Giselle. *Women Managers: Changing Organizational Cultures.* New York: Wiley, 1988.

3. Belasco, James A. *Teaching the Elephant to Dance.* New York: Crown Publishers, 1990. Empowering change in your organization is the theme in this book, along with moving from the status quo to innovative ways of meeting global competition. Visions make the difference, people are the key, and the corporate culture is the tool.

4. Bennis, Warren. *Why Leaders Can't Lead.* San Francisco: Jossey-Bass Publishers, 1989. Bennis says that the unconscious conspiracy continues, the consensus reality that keeps current myths about leadership in place. He gives suggestions for confounding the conspiracy.

5. Block, Peter. *The Empowered Manager.* San Francisco: Jossey-Bass Publishers, 1987. Power in the organization is seen as stemming from the ability to empower others by creating a vision of greatness, building support for it, empowering others to implement it. The author brings in positive political skills and leadership strategies.

6. Bolman, Lee G. *Reframing Organizations: Artistry Choice, and Leadership.* San Francisco: Jossey-Bass Publishers, 1991. Become a more versatile and masterful leader by using reframing (i.e., deliberately looking at situations from a variety of vantage points). Four major frames are structure, human resource, political, and symbolic.

7. Byham, William C. *Zapp! The Lightning of Empowerment.* Pittsburgh: Development Dimensions International Press, 1989. The theme is how to improve productivity, quality and employee satisfaction.

8. Gershon, David. *Empowerment: The Art of Creating Your Life as You Want It.* New York: Dell Publishing, 1989.

9. Hackman, J. Richard. *Groups That Work (And Those That Don't).* San Francisco: Jossey-Bass Publishers, 1990. This book focuses on creating conditions for effective teamwork.

10. Kinlaw, Dennis C. *Developing Superior Work Teams.* Lexington, Mass.: Lexington Books, 1991. The author describes how to build quality and the competitive edge into the organizational structure by developing productive self-managing teams.

11. Kotter, John P. *Power and Influence.* New York: The Free Press, 1985. The author discusses going beyond formal authority to use personal power and influence in leadership roles.

12. Kouzes, James M., and Barry Z. Posner. *The Leadership Challenge.* San Diego: University Associates, 1988. How to accomplish extraordinary things in organizations through new ways of leading.

13. Naisbett, John, and Patricia Aburdene. *Megatrends 2000: Ten New Directions for the 1990's.* New York: William Morrow and Company, Inc., 1990.

14. Pinchot, Gifford. *Intrapreneuring.* New York: Harper & Row, 1985. Pinchot tells why you don't have to leave the corporation to become an entrepreneur.

15. Rees, Fran. *How to Lead Work Teams: Facilitation Skills.* San Diego: Pfeiffer and Company, 1991. An excellent how-to for leading self-directed work teams.

16. Rowan, Roy. *The Intuitive Manager.* New York: Berkley Books, 1986.

17. Schein, Edgar H. *Organizational Culture and Leadership: A Dynamic View.* San Francisco: Jossey-Bass Publishers, 1985. Learn how leaders can create, manage, and if necessary modify an organizational culture.

18. Senge, P. *The Fifth Discipline: Mastering the Five Practices of the Learning Organization.* New York: Doubleday, 1990.

19. Simons, George. *Working Together.* Los Altos, Calif.: Crisp Publications, 1989. The author discusses how to become more effective in a multicultural organization and to work successfully with people different from you.

20. Stewart, Alex. *Team Entrepreneurship.* Newbury Park, Calif.: Sage Publications, 1989. Stewart describes Running Hot, Hot Teams, and how they function to create World Class Operations in the global markets of the 1990s.

21. Stringer, Robert A. *Strategy Traps.* Lexington, Mass.: D. C. Heath, 1986. The author tells how to manage corporate culture and develop and implement strategic planning.

22. Thomas, Kenneth. "Conflict and Conflict Management." In Marvin D. Dunette (Ed.), *Handbook of Industrial and Organizational Psychology.* Chicago: Rand McNally, 1981.

23. Torres, Crescencio, and Jerry Spiegel. *Self-Directed Work Teams: A Primer.* San Diego: Pfeiffer and Company, 1990. The authors explain how to structure and lead teams in ways that enable organizations to compete in the rapidly expanding global market, meet the challenges of deregulation, and keep abreast of rapid technological change.

24. U.S. Department of Labor. *Workforce 2000.* Washington, D.C.: Government Printing Office, 1985.

25. Valuing Diversity materials:

    Copeland-Griggs, 302 23rd Avenue, San Francisco, 94121. Copeland has a series of seven training films on valuing diversity; they present in-house and public seminars on the topic.

    Films for the Humanities & Sciences, P.O. Box 2053, Princeton, N.J. 08543-2053. This organization has a series of ten films called *The Mosaic Workplace,* which deal with diversity issues.

    Working Together: How to Become More Effective in a Multicultural Organization by George Simons. Los Altos, Calif.: Crisp Publications, Inc. 1989. This small book consists mainly of self-analysis activities for use by individuals. Such activities can serve as preparation for group discussions of diversity issues.

    A Workshop for Managing Diversity in the Workplace by S. Kanu Kogod. San Diego: Pfeiffer and Company, 1991. This notebook contains structure experiences, lecturettes, and handouts for conducting a workshop on diversity.

26. Vogt, Judith F., and Kenneth L. Murrell. *Empowerment in Organizations.* San Diego: University Associations, Inc. 1990. Learn how to spark exceptional performance through empowering workers.

Chapter Fourteen

Moving Up the Ladder: Promotions and Career Paths

*"Being good at something is only half the battle.
The other half is mastering the art of self-
presentation, positioning, and connecting."*

Adele Scheele

The culmination of developing and managing yourself and of developing and practicing effective leadership skills is getting the promotions that move you on up the ladder to your ultimate career goal. Whether that ultimate goal is head of the Human Resources Department of a relatively small company or Chief Executive Officer of a large multinational corporation, you must know how to negotiate promotions and raises in order to get there. Although you will base your requests on specific achievements and results, you must develop negotiating skills and techniques in order to make the most of your accomplishments.

In this chapter you will have an opportunity to learn how to

1. Base your requests on standards and accomplishments

2. Set job standards you can meet

3. Estimate the value of your work in terms of the company's profits

4. Get around promotion blocks

5. Size up your competition

6. Study your boss's position in the promotion game

7. Get rid of your false fears

8. Overcome barriers in your boss's mind

9. Stand up for your ideas without antagonizing your boss

10. Time your request for a raise or promotion

11. Adapt your visibility during the raise-getting period

12. Turn negatives into positives for promotion purposes

13. Handle special problems during promotion negotiations

14. Create demand for your services

15. Close the promotion negotiation proceedings

16. Position yourself for your next promotion

17. Deal with unfair discrimination

18. Identify four major career phases

19. Evaluate typical career detours and paths

Sweet Success

"For she's a jolly good fellow, for she's a jolly good fellow . . . " Erika's eyes are misty as she looks around at the staff of the branch, their glasses raised in a toast to her, their voices joined in song at this, her farewell party.

John Brockfield holds up his hand. "I just want to say that I've never seen a better Sales Manager than Erika. You've touched all our lives, and we'll always remember you — even when you're ensconced in that big Sales V.P. office in Dallas, with all the big guns."

Erika laughs. "And I'll never forget a one of you — I'll always remember all I've learned from you and all we've done together."

Next day, as Erika is packing the items she plans to take to Dallas with her, Kate Blakeley enters her office.

"Erika, before you get away, you've got to give me one more lesson — on getting promotions. I heard you had some stiff competition for this new Sales V.P. position they created at headquarters — like Fred Rosen, who's already a Sales Account Executive at headquarters, and Margo Malquist, who's made a name for herself at the New Orleans branch. Tell me, how did you pull it off?"

Erika searches Kate's face. "All right, Kate, but this is just between the two of us. Well, first I sized up my competition and figured that Margo was my closest competitor. The advantage she had over me was her computer knowledge. So my next step was to do some 'horse trading' with Vince Dietz."

"Oh, the head of our Computer Department," responds Kate. "But — horse trading?"

"Sure. Vince wanted to know more about the sales end of the business, so I swapped my knowledge about that for his knowledge of our computer setup and how to use it. In the meantime, I worked on my ILM file."

"What, pray tell, is an ILM file?"

Erika grins. "I love me. Jan coined the term, I guess, and told me about it. It's just a way to remind yourself vividly that you should be your own best friend. One way of doing that is to document your achievements — goals you've reached, deadlines you've met, increases in sales volume you've effected, decreases in expenses. You see, the President is a financial type; he understands people who talk in terms of the dollar value of their contributions and how resources should be allocated. I felt that Jan probably favored me for the promotion, but she had to sell her recommendation to the Executive Committee — mainly the President. So I needed to provide her with a strong case on my behalf."

"So, did she recommend you to the Committee?" prompts Kate.

"Yes, and they approved the promotion, but I had to go before them to discuss the terms and conditions of the appointment — meaning mainly the salary I would get. I was nervous, but I did my homework. You know, like my contribution to company profits, how I'd maintained an adequate profit margin, how my department's efforts affect cash flow. The Committee did raise some questions and objections, but I kept returning to my main points. I figured I might as well go for the best raise possible. So I laid the groundwork for computing my value to the company in dollars and cents, tracing my work in the Sales Department down to that magic 'bottom line.'"

Erika continues, "My main point was that I had achieved every one of the goals John Brockfield and I agreed on for my department each year. We increased the number of customer accounts by 15 percent, which gave the company the opportunity to expand its market in the region. In addition, my people increased our sales volume by 20 percent. And in spite of the extra expenses such increases always incur, I held the expense increase down to 5 percent. Finally, I provided the Committee with a table showing item by item how these and other achievements of my department had contributed to the net worth and the profit of the company."

"But how did you know how much to ask for?" Kate asks.

"To begin with, I let them make an offer first, just to be sure I didn't ask for too little. When they asked what amount I thought was fair, I said I'd like to hear what the Committee thought about that. They mentioned a 15 percent increase over my present salary. I had laid the groundwork for showing how I had made contributions beyond those of any previous Sales Manager—contributions worth well over 50 percent of my present salary. I said I felt it was only fair for them to split the difference and give me a 25 percent raise."

"And they bought it?" asks Kate.

"Yes. They all got a kick out of my line of reasoning. They said I was just the person to sell the Board on the new projects we'll be lining up. Believe me, I assured them that I'd make them look good and that they were making a good investment."

Kate sighs. "What a lovely success story. I hope I can tell one like it myself some day."

Kate hugs her friend. "You're just an inspiration, Erika, because you're managing to have it all—a good career, a good marriage, and real personal growth. And you deserve it all."

Where Did They Go Astray?

You have just seen how a successful campaign for a promotion can work. For every success story, however, there are probably a dozen stories of frustration, rejection, or disappointment. Let's look at a couple of them.

Too Little Margo Malquist knows that she deserves a promotion. She has improved productivity and lowered expenses significantly during the past year. She discusses her performance and her hopes with her colleague Lee Chin.

"Lee, I know Ms. Arguello's pleased with the job I've been doing. Nearly every time I see her, she comments about the great results I'm getting and how much improvement she sees in my department. I sure hope she recommends me for this promotion. I need a good raise too."

"Have you asked her about it, Margo?"

"No, I don't want to appear too greedy or pushy. Ms. Arguello tells me how much she appreciates my devotion and loyalty to the company. We have such a good relationship; I don't want to take a chance on upsetting it. I think she'll take care of me at promotion time and she'll probably recommend an even bigger raise if I let her decide on the amount."

"But what if she doesn't?"

"Well, at least our rapport will not be damaged. If I don't put her in a position of having to turn me down, then we won't have any negative feelings to have to work through."

As we know, Malquist doesn't get the promotion. She feels disappointed and finds it a little difficult to maintain her previous level of enthusiasm. She holds on to her hopes, however, that someday she will get the promotion she deserves.

Actually, Arguello decides that the new job assignment would be too tough and demanding for Margo. Handling some of the characters she would have to deal with in the new position requires more savvy and drive than she seems to have.

Too Much Back at headquarters, Fred Rosen, Sales Account Executive, decides to go all out for the promotion. He makes it a point to fully support Arguello's every idea, suggestion, and action. She can always depend on Rosen to agree with her.

Fred also wants Jan to see that he is a person who knows how to dress and how to live. He wears his best Italian-made shoes to the office. When he takes Jan to lunch he drives his new foreign sports car. And he invites her and several colleagues to dinner at his swank apartment with an impressive view of the city.

He makes sure Jan knows that he's aware of the pressing problems of the organization and that he needs Jan's advice and guidance. He looks for problems he can bring to her to solve.

To impress Jan with his diligence and dedication, Fred begins to show up much earlier and to stay much later at the office than usual. The amount of paperwork coming out of his office nearly doubles, with copies of almost everything going to Jan to be sure that she's aware of his activities.

Fred discusses the details of his campaign with his colleagues to get their reaction and to encourage them to share techniques with him. He begins to feel sure he'll get the promotion. In fact, he's so sure that he's already planning how he'll spend the raise that goes with it. He mentions a few of his plans to colleagues.

When it's announced that Erika Kerr is getting the new position, Fred is upset and resentful. He can't understand why he failed after putting so much time and energy into his campaign.

----

1. As you read this story, what actions and attitudes did you think were most effective in preparing for and getting a promotion? Why?

2. What actions and attitudes were most ineffective? Why?

ONGOING STRATEGIES FOR PROMOTABILITY

In most companies, upward mobility and power go hand in hand. In Chapter 1 we discussed Rosabeth Kanter's finding about the difficulty of managers in dead-end, low-power positions. Most managers consider it crucial to keep moving up. More than three years in a job is probably a danger sign of being "stuck." After completing Chapters 2 and 3, you should have some tools for developing an effective career path within your company. When you feel

it is time to be promoted or to receive a raise, you'll need to apply your assertiveness skills and plan a promotion campaign.

Overcoming Archaic Attitudes

Winning the right promotion and the raises and privileges that go with it is the proof of the pudding. These are the rewards that really count, the outward proof of your success as a leader and as an astute organization person. The further up you attempt to go, the more likely you are to encounter barriers based on stereotyped ideas about the roles women are suited for, what women *really* want, what women need (such as less money than men), and so forth. To overcome these barriers, you will need to use all the experience and knowledge you have gained about the hierarchy, influence and power, organizational politics, the mentor relationship, and leadership skills.

Perhaps the barriers you face are more internal than external. Take a good look at your own attitude toward taking the initiative to wage an assertive promotion campaign. Since women have traditionally been spectators rather than participants in the money game of business, they can be handicapped in successfully negotiating higher positions and salaries.

Have you, like most women, been taught that if you work hard and wait, you will be rewarded, that it's bad taste to make monetary demands? This defensive attitude places more value on approval than on money. It also overlooks the viewpoint of business executives who understand that they work for a proportionate share of the company's money — a share that reflects the value of their contributions.

Furthermore, anyone who is "worth his or her salt" is expected to ask for substantial raises. Waiting for a promotion or raise is low-echelon thinking. If you never ask, you're not likely to get what you're worth. Moreover, if you don't place a high value on your worth, no one else will. Regular merit increases are almost always mere tokens of appreciation, as small as the company can get away with and still keep satisfactory employees quiet.

As discussed in Chapter 1, women frequently view risk in a negative way. Examine your attitude toward the risks involved in pushing for a promotion or a significant raise. What are the possible payoffs? What are the possible negative results? Are you hanging back because the status quo is comfortable and that higher-level job is a little scary? What do you really have to lose? Will it be the end of the world if you don't succeed?

Once you've decided to go for the next promotion, give it all you've got. Be persistent and assertive.

Clarifying Your Career Goals

Before you start selecting specific strategies for waging your promotion campaign, first be sure the promotion you have in mind will lead to jobs that will further your career. Carefully consider any promotion offer that is not a part of your plan. It may be best to turn down a promotion that will not help you acquire the experience you need for your long-term goal. To determine whether a promotion is right for you, ask yourself questions such as these:

- "Will the new position lead directly to a higher position?"

- "Will I gain experience in the job that will make me more valuable to the company?"

- "Will this job give me an opportunity to make more or bigger decisions?"

- "Is this job a good temporary step — even if it's not in the direct line of my career goal? (For example, you could learn about many phases of company activities by working for a short time as an assistant to a senior executive. Be careful, however, that the new position isn't a dead end — and that you stay in it no longer than a couple of years.)

Once you're sure what your next position should be, you can focus your energy on ways of lining it up.

Expanding Your Present Job

Suppose you find yourself with a company you like and want to stay with. However, your upward mobility is temporarily blocked by older people above you, people waiting to retire, and lack of company growth. What can you do? Two likely approaches are to (1) enlarge your job or (2) get some small jobs attached to your position — jobs that show on the organization chart and that you can take on while you're holding down your main job. Here are some specific tactics.

- Volunteer for jobs no one is doing anything about. Look for things you can tackle. If the boss asks you to look into a project or problem, even very informally, accept the assignment happily and begin to formalize the request through the reports you write and by your attitude.

- Make yourself visible as someone who is interested in company progress and problems and ferrets out opportunities.

- Send your boss some progress reports with copies to others who might be interested.

- Talk to appropriate department heads and other executives.

- See whether you can get some colleagues to work with you on the project. Their reasons for working on it may be similar to yours. Now you have a task force.

- Try to get your new responsibilities or positions formalized on the organization chart. Whether you are able to do so or not, you can provide your boss with justification for giving you a raise outside the salary range for your position.

Executives who get what they want expend about half their time performing their work and the other half calling attention to it in an assertive, nonbragging manner. The decision-makers in your company must value your presence before they'll promote you, and they can't value what is not visible.

Creating Demand for Your Services

Without neglecting or jeopardizing your job, never miss an opportunity to make contacts with other companies, departments, or executives who might be interested in hiring you. There are several advantages to doing this.

- Your confidence and self-esteem are enhanced when you get job offers without soliciting them.

- Word may get around to your boss without your saying anything. As a result, you will appear more valuable to him or her while incurring no risk to yourself.

- During the promotion or raise negotiation period, you may be able to use other offers to reinforce your case. Be careful not to threaten or bluff, however, unless you're ready to carry it out.

- If you're turned down, you can always come back with the news that you have a firm offer that's better than your present salary.

Basing Your Requests on Standards and Accomplishments

Your boss will certainly be unwilling to lose you if he or she is clear about what you have contributed in the past and can contribute in the future. Rather than thinking in terms of how much additional money you need, therefore, focus on how much you're worth in the current job market and on what you can produce.

Setting Job Objectives and Standards You Can Meet   When the boss criticizes your performance and performance standards have previously been set, get your boss's comments on how the job could be done better, no matter how vague they may be. Get his or her agreement on what good performance would consist of. Get yourself in a position to suggest objectives and standards yourself. When you do, don't make them too easy but be sure that they are attainable (see Chapters 7 and 12).

To prevent unfair or unexpected criticism of your performance, develop a plan, including times when you will report your results to the boss. Set deadlines for accomplishment of each goal. Then make an appointment for a discussion with the boss in a relaxed atmosphere (preferably in your office so you'll have a "home court" advantage). During the meeting, get the boss to talk about what she or he thinks is important in your job. Get clarification on how your role fits into the overall scheme of the business. This information will help you pinpoint attributes you possess that are important to the company and know what points to stress later when you ask for a promotion.

When the boss gives you a lead in an area you handle well, follow it. Agree with the idea that this is truly a vital function and you'll do your best to achieve more than has ever been accomplished before. Reach an agreement on objectives and standards you know you can meet. Try to phrase them in words that will either give a great deal of credit to your boss or will help him or her report your achievements in glowing terms when justifying your promotion at some future time.

If you have some weak areas that the boss mentions or that you're sure will inevitably surface in carrying out your responsibilities, invite the boss's recommendations. If he or she has no good ones, take the opportunity to discuss the awesome difficulty of achieving in this area. Then work toward establishing a standard that involves motions without necessarily involving accomplishment—for example, paperwork and meetings. Turn the negative into a positive by at least appearing to be working on it and improving.

Once you have a set of goals and standards that you like, document them. Send your boss a follow-up memo confirming the conversation. Such records will serve you well when you prepare your case for getting a promotion or raise.

Learning How Your Work Affects the Bottom Line Compute the value of your achievements, your productivity. To do this, learn the arithmetic of your business and how it affects you. Find out how to understand financial statements and talk about them. You'll become identifiable as a profit-minded person and will probably learn more than your associates—and perhaps more than your boss—about the financial end of the business. Team up with someone who works with the finances of the company and exchange information. You can learn about the profits, losses, expenses, and costs of the business and teach your friend about your end of the business.

If you work in a staff position rather than as a line manager, your department will probably be viewed as an expense rather than as a profit source. Don't let that intimidate you. The services of your department must be contributing to the overall profit of the company or they would soon be eliminated. Your services at least indirectly affect profits. What would happen if these services were not provided by your department? Would the company pay freelance people to provide them or farm them out to another firm that specializes in such services? How much would that cost? What advantages does your company enjoy by securing these services through your department instead? The answers to these questions can help you figure the dollar value of your contributions.

Perhaps your services have resulted in a decrease in company expenses as well as an increase in profits. Have you reorganized the workflow, restructured job descriptions, developed new procedures, or formulated better controls that resulted in a saving of time, money, or both? Time saved represents money saved. Convert the time you've saved the company into the hourly wages of the workers, who can now use that time to accomplish other tasks and therefore to achieve a higher level of productivity.

If you're a manager in a government or non-profit organization, your department is contributing a valuable service to the public; otherwise it wouldn't be in existence for long. With a little thought and ingenuity, you can place a value on your services. What would they cost if they were provided by a profit-making organization? How much do they add to the lives of the people who receive them? What would happen if these services weren't provided at all? What resulting costs would society have to pay? Analyze also the increases in productivity and reductions in expenses you've been responsible for and translate them into dollars.

If you're a secretary or an assistant to a manager, your value is tied in with your boss's contributions. What does your boss do to increase profits and decrease expenses? What value can you place on his or her overall contribution to the organization each year? How do you help the boss in making that contribution? What percentage do you contribute to the boss's value to the company? Twenty-five percent? Fifty percent? Are there any projects or procedures you have pursued on your own for increasing departmental productivity or decreasing expenses? Figure dollar values and add them all together to arrive at a figure representing your achievements.

Whether you are a manager or a worker; in a profit-making, government, or nonprofit organization; in a line or staff position, you can make some effort to determine your value to the firm. You *must* do it if you want to prepare the most effective case possible for getting a promotion or raise. Follow the suggestions we've just discussed to complete Exercise 14-1.

EXERCISE 14-1: ESTIMATING YOUR VALUE TO THE ORGANIZATION

Analyze your activities and your achievements in terms of how much they contribute to company profits and how much they've helped the company save on costs and expenses. Evaluate time saved in terms of salary expense for each hour saved. If you can't determine exact amounts, make the closest estimate you can.

Step 1. *Evaluate activities that increased profits.*

A. List your key activities that directly increased profits and estimate their dollar value to the organization.
B. List activities that indirectly increased profits via:
   Services you provided and the cost to the firm if your services had to be contracted with freelancers or other firms.
   Increased productivity of other persons resulting from services you provide — in dollar value, based on salaries per hour.
C. Estimate the total dollar value from these activities.

Step 2. *Evaluate activities that helped decrease expenses.*

A. List your key activities that *directly* decreased expenses and estimate dollars saved.
B. List your key activities that *indirectly* decreased expenses and estimate dollars saved.
C. Estimate total dollars saved by these activities.

Step 3. *Estimate your market value to other similar organizations.*

A. Investigate three companies and determine the salary range for jobs similar to yours.
B. Estimate your probable starting salary at each firm.
C. Arrive at a salary range you could expect if you went to work for another firm.

Step 4. *Consider other factors.*

A. How has inflation affected your spending power since your last raise? Estimate the percentage reduction and dollar decrease.
B. What new skills and knowledge have you gained since your last raise? Estimate their dollar value to the firm.
C. What is the average salary increase for similar positions in your field (or similar positions in general) during the past year, according to the *Wall Street Journal* or other sources? Translate the percentage increase into a dollar amount based on your current salary.

Setting Your Asking Price Now you should have some basis for determining the size of your next raise. In figuring an exact asking price, keep in mind that you should always ask for more than you expect to get and you should phrase the increase in thousands of dollars per year. Here are some other factors to consider in setting your asking price:

What you have contributed or can contribute to the firm

How the rate of inflation has affected the buying power of your salary dollars since your last raise

What the *men* who perform similar functions in the company are making

The top figure your boss is probably willing to give you

The bottom figure you are willing to take

What competing firms are willing to pay you

The difference between the bottom figure you are willing to take (a $5,000 raise, for example) and the top figure your boss is willing to give ($3,000, for example) is the area of negotiation. Your goal is to negotiate for as close to your figure as possible. If you asked for $1,000 more than you expected to receive and are able to convince your boss that you deserve $4,000, you will each have made a $1,000 concession and you'll still end up with the raise you expected. Identify perks, benefits, and other rewards you would be willing to accept in lieu of cash. Be sure to consider all tax implications.

Building on Your Reputation for Assertiveness

You establish a reputation as a promotable woman beginning with the job interview and continuing through every phase of establishing yourself in the company. Keep in mind that you want your boss to respect you without feeling threatened by you. Therefore you don't want to be a "yes person," but you won't want to antagonize either. In other words, assertiveness with your boss throughout the year pays off at promotion time.

Occasionally disagree or express strong reservations about some idea or position of your boss. Don't make your disagreement too visible or too personal, however. Express it in a way that doesn't cast doubts on the boss's intelligence or reasoning power. If the boss strongly backs his or her position, come around to agreeing. You want to be known as a person who is not afraid to speak up but one who is also willing to listen to reason. If it later turns out that you were partially or completely right on the point, don't bring it up. Don't let any "I told you so" messages come through, however subtle. You also want to be known as a person who may disagree but then forgets her disagreement and pitches in to get the job done.

PREPARING TO ASK FOR A PROMOTION AND RAISE

In addition to ongoing strategies for moving into your next job position, you can adopt some specific strategies as you approach the time to discuss your promotion request. These include sizing up your competition, studying the boss's position, anticipating and overcoming barriers in your boss's mind, and getting rid of your false fears.

Sizing Up Your Competition

You need to understand the circumstances that will affect your chances of getting a promotion. Therefore it is important to size up the people who will be competing with you for the position you want. Exercise 14-2 provides some questions to consider. Of course you will *not* use this information to attack your competi-

EXERCISE 14-2: EVALUATING YOUR COMPETITION

Focusing on the person in your classification who seems to be your strongest rival, answer the following questions.

1. How long has Rival A been here?

2. How good is Rival A?

3. What is management's perception of how good Rival A is? (The answer to this one is often quite different from how well your competitor actually produces.)

4. What are Rival A's strong points?

5. What are Rival A's weak points?

6. How do I compare to Rival A, point by point?

7. What is management's perception of my strengths?

8. What is management's perception of my weaknesses?

9. How much is Rival A probably making?

10. What kind of raise is Rival A likely to ask for?

11. Does Rival A seem to be successful in getting promotions and raises?

Adapted from John J. Tarrant, *How to Negotiate a Raise* (New York: Simon and Schuster, 1984), pp. 81–82.

tors; in fact, you won't even mention rivals in most cases. When you're having your interview with your boss about your promotion, your competition is a strong *unmentioned* presence. Therefore stress at least one area in which you are unique or unquestionably stronger even though you don't make comparisons or even mention your competition. This gives your boss some ideas for justifying his or her selection of you. If you must discuss areas where your competition is stronger than you, associate yourself with your competitor. Talk about how you work together in these areas and the similarities you share.

In getting raises, strangely enough, your biggest problem may be the competitor that is an "old reliable" who never asks for a big raise. This person may have been around longer than you and on the whole may even do a better job than you. The boss is aware of "old reliable's" quiet worth and may mentally compare you with him or her. Since the boss may hesitate to give you a larger increase than "old reliable," your own chances of getting a good raise may be greatly increased if you can convince your complacent colleague to ask for more.

How you go about this will depend on the situation. Use the same rationale you use to determine your own worth to the company and the amount of increase you should get to convince your colleague of his or her worth and why he or she should receive a larger increase.

Studying Your Boss's Position

Perhaps the most important suggestion for successfully getting the raise or promotion you want is to put yourself in your boss's shoes. To do this, try to study his or her position — upward, downward, and laterally — in the raise-getting process within the company.

Your boss has many concerns besides your promotion. Before planning your approach to getting a promotion or raise, study the situation from your boss's viewpoint. Your boss is your adversary, even if you're the best of friends, if he or she is the one who has the most influence over the size of your raise. If you can determine the answers to the questions posed in Exercise 14-3, you'll go a long way toward understanding your boss's viewpoint.

How do you get good answers to all these questions? Sometimes the best way is through informal channels: getting to know as many people as possible who have access to the information you want, chatting with them occasionally about what's going on in the company, chatting with your boss about his or her plans. Listen, observe, ask questions. By all means, get all the *official* information you can through the Human Resources Department, company manuals, annual reports to stockholders, minutes of meetings, accessible files and records, and so forth. But don't depend on easily available data to give you the whole picture.

EXERCISE 14-3: STUDYING YOUR BOSS'S POSITION

Study the official position of your boss and of the company. Then ask yourself these questions.

1. What is the pattern of raises given to me and to others in similar jobs?

2. To what extent is compensation a part of a fixed budget process?

3. What degree of freedom does the boss have in deciding on raises?

4. What's the current condition of business within the company and industry?

5. What are the company's plans for the immediate future?

6. What's the boss's overall pattern of conduct toward me?

7. To what degree does she or he praise or criticize parts of my performance?

8. What is the boss's position in the firm and ambitions for growth?

9. To what extent does she or he take me for granted?

10. How much knowledge does the boss have of exactly what I do and how valuable that work is?

Adapted from John J. Tarrant, *How to Negotiate a Raise* (New York: Simon and Schuster, 1984), p. 13.

Overcoming Barriers in Your Boss's Mind

Remember that bosses *do* think about how the employee will use the raise. Plant the seed of need in the boss's mind, but be sure the picture he or she gets about how you'll spend the raise will not trigger resentful, envious, or disapproving feelings. Male bosses frequently believe women don't *need* as much money as men because they don't have the same financial obligations. Watch for that barrier so you can change his or her picture. Get across the idea that money represents the company's recognition of your achievements, not just buying power, and that therefore raises and promotions keep you motivated to perform better.

Getting Rid of False Fears

Get rid of any fear or apprehension you have about asking for an increase. Let's look at two major reasons we don't like to ask for a raise or promotion: (1) fear of being turned down and (2) fear of losing rapport with the boss.

These are false fears. Actually, the employee who doesn't take initiative on raises and promotions may give the impression of being too satisfied and too "nice" to handle a more difficult job assignment. If necessary, review the techniques for asserting yourself in Chapter 6 and select and complete appropriate exercises at the end of that chapter. Also, use the relaxation and visualization techniques described in Chapter 5.

MAKING YOUR REQUEST

In addition to adequate preparation, you must consider strategies for actually making your promotion request. You must decide exactly when to make it and you must be aware of your image in the boss's mind as part of your timing. Once you go into the meeting, you should be prepared for any response the boss makes and be ready to turn negatives into positives. Know what you plan to do if the boss balks or says "no."

Timing Your Request

If you've estimated your boss's position adequately, you'll know when budget requests are made and adjust your timing accordingly. Regardless of this, don't overlook the importance of asking for a promotion or raise shortly after you've done an outstanding job, made your boss look especially good, greatly outshined all your competitors, or otherwise pulled off a coup. Strike while the iron is hot. Even if the boss can't come through immediately, you may be able to extract a promise for a promotion or raise later.

Don't let your request for a raise or promotion be handled in a casual, spur-of-the-moment, or offhand manner. If your boss attempts to handle it that way, tell him or her you think this is not a good time to discuss the subject and ask for an appointment. If all else fails, ask for an appointment to discuss another work-related topic and bring it up then.

When should you reveal how much you're asking for? Should you announce the amount in advance of the interview or toward the end of the interview? Exercise 14-4 can provide guidelines for making that decision.

Fine-Tuning Your Image

Once your boss knows you're asking for a raise or promotion, he or she will be looking at you in a different light for a while. Give some thought to how you look during this period. Here are some do's and don'ts.

Don't make waves, although it's all right to talk to your boss about making waves that will

EXERCISE 14-4: DECIDING WHEN TO REVEAL THE AMOUNT YOU'RE REQUESTING

Rate each factor as it applies to your job situation by placing the appropriate number next to the item.

0 = Not a factor
1 = Somewhat a factor
2 = Definitely a factor
3 = Weighs heavily as a factor

Conditions Conducive to Telling How Much You Want in Advance

1. You have a strong case, one that is likely to be strengthened by developments between the time you tip your hand and the actual negotiation.

2. Your boss needs time to get used to the idea, and he or she is not likely to use the time to figure out ways to combat you.

3. Your boss must make preliminary judgments about how much of a gross figure he or she must set aside for raises.

4. Other conditions.

Factors Indicating You Should Wait to Reveal the Amount You Want

1. Little or nothing is going to happen in the interim to make you more deserving.

2. The boss is known as a haggler or bargainer who will begin to carve away at your request as soon as he or she knows what it is.

3. The boss has the leeway to make the decision and is apt to make it fast. (You want him or her to make it *after* you've presented a strong case.)

4. You are thinking of taking a strong stand, boldly striking for a very large amount, and you plan to win agreement through persuasion.

5. Your boss has to sell your raise to others and needs full knowledge and coaching in the supporting arguments you can provide. (You don't want him or her to start selling until you've provided that support.)

6. News of your request is likely to get around and stimulate others to jack up their own demands.

7. Other factors.

support him or her if you think a show of assertiveness will be helpful. However, don't get involved with your own in-fighting now.

Don't bring major problems or sticky questions to your boss if you can avoid it. If you have a good solution to the problem, fine. Otherwise, try to postpone it until after you get your raise.

Don't try to make a good impression by drastically changing your work habits or behavior. You probably won't fool anyone, and it may well go against you.

Don't talk about the progress of your raise or promotion with anyone. The only time you should talk about that is after you've received a tentative turndown or when you're being stalled. Then you might want to rally support.

Don't be away from the work scene if you can help it. Even if you're doing important work elsewhere, long absences sometimes unjustly trigger the suspicion that you're goofing off.

Do be a problem-solver. In fact, you can even emphasize your image as a problem-solver if you postpone solving small, nagging problems until the campaign period. Make sure you get credit — not by boasting but by making modest references to all the help other people gave you, including the boss.

When it comes to big problems, you may not have a solution. However, there may be something you can do toward solving them, such as reporting ways in which similar problems have been handled in other companies, by describing the difficulty in a way that gives clues to what must be done, or at least by showing you're determined to overcome barriers to getting the problem solved.

Do maintain a confident — but not complacent — attitude. Be positive in your communications.

Do make the boss look good while you are making yourself look good. You can avoid being a "yes person" and at the same time make your boss look good. For example, ask searching questions about his or her plans or proposals at meetings only when you are fairly sure he or she will be able to back them up with facts and figures and therefore win points with the others.

Do make life easier for your boss and give reassurance that he or she can depend on you to take care of responsibilities in a way that makes the boss look good with minimal hassle. Try to contribute to your boss's peace of mind. At the same time, you should appear to be working effortlessly.

In summary, fine-tune your image so the boss pictures you as a calm, efficient, supportive, positive leader with a forward-looking focus on preventing and solving problems and achieving goals that contribute to company profits.

Turning Negatives into Positives

Some of the most valuable strategies you can learn involve ways of turning negatives into positives, especially in the promotion/raise interview.

What should you do if you think your boss will fight your request for a promotion or raise by criticizing an area where you've been weak? What can you do to offset this attack? First, prepare yourself by finding some evidence — no matter how small — of progress in your weak area. At least try to come up with something that can be considered hopeful. Don't reveal it to the boss until you're in the interview; you don't want to give him or her extra time to pick it apart.

If the boss brings up the weak area, don't deny that it is a problem. Instead, encourage the boss to focus on this problem. Try to get him or her to verbalize it as the main or only obstacle to granting your request. Don't give your boss any solutions or progress reports until he or she has done this. The boss who thinks he or she is making a strong case you can't refute is more likely to concentrate on the weak area to the exclusion of any others.

Next, get the boss to express support for your work in other areas. Your boss will be more comfortable supporting you if he or she thinks your request can reasonably be denied because of your poor showing in the weak areas you've been discussing. If possible, get the boss to state that he or she would take a supportive position toward your request when and if you show improvement in the weak area.

Now produce evidence of improvement or reason for hope. This can be some minor result, some form of solution, a plan of action, or anything that shows promise. State clearly how you intend to take advantage of this improvement and what your plan of action is. Remind the boss that you can do your best work once your request has been granted and your mind is free to concentrate fully on the job.

Mention the job objectives and standards the two of you agreed on at the last interview of this type. Stress how well you have met most of them. Go over your strengths and your weakness, stressing that your evidence indicates that this weakness is in the process of becoming a strength. Keep stressing your strong points and achievements during the interview.

If the boss argues that your evidence is weak, counter with the fact that his or her objections were based on *complete* lack of results in the weak area. Appeal to his or her sense of fairness in giving you credit. Ask the boss whether he or she *really* demands perfect performance in every area before giving promotions or raises. Mention how monetary recognition of your achievements provides a strong stimulus to your becoming more effective and productive. Ask for advice and support in making improvements. Stress the boss's value to you

as a leader and guide in achieving these improvements.

Be patient and firm in maintaining your position that the boss was prepared to accept a slight show of progress and that you have given him or her that as well as a strong showing in other areas.

What if you've botched an assignment? How can you redeem yourself? As soon as you know how extensive the problem is, have a frank discussion about it with your boss. Get it over with right away — as far in advance of promotion or raise discussions as possible. Give him or her all the facts; get across the feeling that you are really leveling.

Don't give excuses or alibis, even though justified. Take responsibility for the problem. Express your concern and dismay and don't try to minimize the problem. If anything, let the boss reassure you and put things in perspective. Let him or her make you feel better, but stress that you have learned a lesson.

In the weeks that follow, don't go overboard in compensating for your error. However, when you're able to call the boss's attention to a real achievement, even though minor, indicate that you were able to learn from your previous error. When the promotion or raise negotiation period arises and you present your supporting evidence, be frank about the fact that you botched an assignment. Indirectly remind the boss that he or she said it wasn't so bad and that you have learned from your mistake.

Coping with the Boss Who Balks

It is possible to overcome all the barriers mentioned so far and still be faced with a boss who won't say "yes." Here are some strategies for handling the balky boss.

The Boss Who Says Money Is in Short Supply Prepare yourself for a disagreement. Collect facts that support your claim that the operation has been functioning properly and at a profit. Collect company statements and comments of executives that refute a "no money" argument. Find out the percentage of increase the top executives received last year, including stock options and other "perks."

The Hostile Boss If your boss gets angry when you ask for a promotion or raise, remain cool. Try to get as much information as you can about whether his or her upset is directed at you or is a general one. If the boss is displeased with your work, try to find out whether the displeasure is aimed at one particular area of your performance or several. Once you've discovered the major problem, you can then select the tactics you want to use.

The Boss Who Says "Trust Me" or Delays Making a Decision If your boss won't make a commitment, use one of these responses: (1) Appeal to his or her self-image as a decision-maker, someone who quickly and easily makes on-the-spot decisions. (2) Tactfully hint at the possible unfortunate results of delaying or giving a negative answer. (3) Reassure the boss that he or she will not regret a decision in your favor. Indicate that you will be appreciative and do everything in your power to merit an affirmative answer. When you've done everything you can do, stop talking. Use one more powerful tool—silence, no matter how long it gets.

Closing the Raise or Promotion Negotiation Proceedings

When you feel it's time to bring negotiations to a close, take the initiative and move on. Base your statements on the assumption that all questions are answered and that the promotion or raise will be granted. Summarize the main arguments for the promotion and ask for it.

If your boss balks, smoke out the main objection. Focus on *it* as the main obstacle to granting your request, answer the objection, and then restate your request. Imply the negative results that may result from delay or from a "no," and reassure the boss that he or she will be making the right move by saying "yes." If necessary, make one concession and then wait for the boss's answer.

If you get the promotion or raise, thank the boss, and reassure him or her that the decision is a sound one. Write a brief memo summing up any agreements and repeating your thanks.

POSITIONING FOR THE NEXT RAISE

As soon as the promotion or raise interview is over, regardless of its outcome, it's time for you to start positioning yourself for your next promotion.

If You Get the Promotion or Raise

First, do anything you can to help the boss resolve any ambiguous feelings about granting your request. Don't give the least reason to suspect you're gloating about getting a "yes" answer. Show how seriously you take your job, how much you appreciate the granting of the request, and stay busy.

Don't go all out to show an artificially high level of performance immediately after the increase. When you can't keep it up, the boss will later become disappointed. Don't hang around the boss asking numerous questions about your job. This may merely create more problems for the boss. Just do your job and be reasonably natural.

Reassure your boss of your good intentions by outlining the big plans you've made, the big problems you're going to solve, and the big goals you will begin to accomplish (long-term items are even better than short-term ones). Above all, give your boss reassurance that he or she made the right decision. Start positioning yourself for your next raise.

If You Don't Get the Promotion or Raise

If the boss says "no" and sticks with it, handle the turndown gracefully but show your concern. Ask for specific reasons for the denial. Pin down exactly what you must do to ensure getting it the next time around. Focus on your career goals rather than on blaming or complaining. If you do in fact achieve the objectives stated by your boss as criteria for promotion, you'll be in a stronger position next time. You can use the fact that you were previously turned down as a "playing chip," subtly implying "You owe me one."

If you've created a demand for your services with other firms, now may be the time to pin them down on the terms of an offer. Then you can tell your boss that you're seriously thinking of taking the offer, even though you'd prefer to stay with the company if they can match the offer.

You can say you realize that your job, as it's presently described, isn't worth the salary you expect. Then ask for promotion to one that is, or ask if there's any way of broadening your present duties or changing the title so both you and the company will be getting fair value. This strategy can open the door for renegotiation, and your boss can change the original decision without losing face.

Should You Always Accept a Promotion?

Suppose you don't get the promotion you asked for, but your boss offers you another position or assignment instead? How do you decide whether this move is in your best interests? Here are some questions to consider before saying "yes."

- *Will you have adequate authority?* Find out what the job or position requires. Whose cooperation must you have? What resources will

it take? What kind of latitude will you have as the project moves in different directions?

- *Will you have to move in on someone's territory?* Must part of the assignment be carried out in someone else's domain? Figure out what others have to lose or gain because of your work on this new assignment? How much resistance are you likely to meet from others. Ask to meet such people before you accept the assignment.

- *How much moral support can you count on?* Who can you count on to help you? How supportive will your immediate boss be? Your boss's boss? If inadequate support may be a problem, try to determine why.

- *Is there a hidden agenda?* This is the toughest question to answer. Your boss may not know of a hidden agenda coming from or through higher management levels. Or your boss may have his or her own agenda, or may not want to level with you until you are committed to the job.

- *Is the money there?* Analyze the position carefully and try to determine the budget you'll need to accomplish your objectives. What are management's budgetary priorities? Identify the route in your company that makes funds available and determine whether and how soon you can get the money you'll need.

- *How about productive capacity?* If producing a product is involved, examine your overhead, equipment, and space. Is something lurking there to drag you down? Determine how much space and equipment you'll need and be sure you can get it.

- *Will you have enough time?* An unrealistic deadline or ongoing schedule can complicate or even doom your project(s). Ask how much time you'll have for projects, and assess whether it is realistic. Find out who set the schedule and why it is set up that way. Ask whether the staff will be willing to work overtime if necessary.

- *Will you have qualified people?* Does the staff have the skills necessary to do what you'll delegate to them? Ask to meet them. If they come up lacking, make sure you have the budget and the authority to hire people with the necessary skills.

- *How's the team spirit?* Have there been attitude problems? Difficult people? Are they likely to be suspicious of you? Will they be taking cuts that are likely to make them dissatisfied or angry? Are they committed to old habits that need changing? Are they receptive to new ideas?

- *Is technology up-to-date?* If you're to be responsible for a product, does it reflect state-of-the-art technology. Examine the technology used in products, production facilities, research and development, and administration. Is the technology in each current? Is it so new, it's risky?

- *What's the turnover history of the job?* How long have others stayed in this position? Why did they leave? Excessive turnover can signal a problem. In large companies the normal term in a job is two or three years. If possible, talk with your predecessors about their experiences in the job.

If You Are Being Discriminated Against

If you think you haven't been promoted as fast as you should have been, or you think you haven't been given as much responsibility as a male counterpart would have been given, ask yourself whether your employer is unfairly discriminating against you because you are a woman. If you think the answer is "yes," here are some steps to consider.

1. Talk the problem over with your immediate boss, even if you are sure it won't do any good. Remember, your boss may resent your stand and seek revenge. On the other hand, he or she may respect your assertiveness and bend over backward to prevent accusations of discrimination. Either way, it's best to decide whether you are prepared to take the matter further before you talk it over with your boss. If you do confront your boss, keep in mind these suggestions:

   Talk about unfairness rather than discrimination so the boss won't overreact to what appears to be a threat of legal action.

   Give specific examples of unfairness.

   Talk about the facts of the situation without blaming or accusing.

   Take an effective, problem-solving approach, not an emotional one or one that reflects "just a gripe."

   Be clear about your exact purpose—what you want from this meeting. Prepare before you go in. Make a list of your specific complaints and of specific results that show what you've been producing. Practice what you're going to say.

2. If you are not satisfied with what your boss says or does, then go to his or her boss or to the Human Resources Department.

3. If you have done everything you know to do within the company without getting satisfactory results, and if you want to stay with the company, contact the nearest Department of Labor, Wage and Hour Division; Equal Employment Opportunity Commission office; State Fair Employment agency; and/or a lawyer experienced in handling discrimination cases. It's usually best to select a female lawyer who will have a special interest in the case and a rapport with your situation. Taking legal action should be a last resort since these cases take several years to resolve.

HANDLING TEAM MEMBERS' REQUESTS FOR PROMOTIONS

You now have some strategies for getting your boss to grant your request for a promotion or a raise. Now switch to the other side of the desk and ask yourself what you need to keep in mind when your team members come in with their own requests for promotions or raises. Perhaps the first point to remember is that since you are familiar with most of the strategies, you can more easily prepare yourself to respond appropriately to them.

Base your decision on how well the member has achieved the objectives the two of you agreed on earlier. If the objective-setting process is to have any meaning and impact, it must be as the basis for these kinds of personnel decisions. Be sure the members understand this basis for your decision. Whether your answer is "yes," "no," or somewhere in between, communicate specific reasons that are clearly tied in with the person's performance.

Remember that Rosabeth Kanter found that people will do almost anything for a boss who has power and is willing to fight for them. So where appropriate let members know you are willing to go to bat for them in getting their requests approved. However, guard against making promises you're not sure you can fulfill.

If you must deny all or part of the request, be firm but encouraging. Where appropriate, offer helpful suggestions for bringing performance up to par, gaining needed knowledge and experience, and so forth. Ask yourself about the basic needs of this particular member of the team (see Chapter 10). Social? Belonging? Status? Recognition? Self-Development? Other? Will the promotion or raise really fulfill these needs best? What else can you offer this person? Consider other rewards, such as more authority, status, or time off. Benefits or perks that are not taxable for the employee might be as satisfactory as twice the amount of straight salary increase.

How does your decision fit in with company and team needs and plans? See Chapter 13 for suggestions on evaluating workers' achievements and giving merit raises.

Effectively handling requests for promotions and raises is an important skill to develop. The major goals involved are making the best use of available job positions and salary funds while keeping workers' morale and productivity high, effectively training and developing workers, and providing for company and team needs and goals.

WOMEN'S CAREER PATHS: FOUR PHASES, POSSIBLE DETOURS

Chances are you, like many others, will go through four basic phases of career development: (1) gaining formal education and training and waging a job campaign, (2) paying your dues and mastering the basics needed to reach your ultimate job goal, (3) operating at a level where you can use position power and personal style in your job, and (4) exercising more freedom to choose a new career direction. As a woman, you are more likely than your male peers to take some career detours. For example, you may hit the glass ceiling during Phase 2 or 3 and decide to jump over to Phase 4 and take a new career direction. Or you may have children during any of these phases and either put your career on hold or focus less energy on it for a while.

Phases 1 and 2: Getting a Job and Paying Your Dues

The previous chapters of this book address many aspects of Phase 1. Part of your preparation for a business career is learning about the business culture, special preparation that women need to succeed in that culture, and basic leadership and business-related skills that apply to most organizations. Another important part of your preparation is learning to develop an effective job campaign to get the job that is best for you. This book also addresses many aspects of Phase 2, such as making the transition into a leadership role, applying your education and skills in developing effective work teams, and moving up the organizational ladder.

Phase 3: Using Position Power and Personal Style

Once you master the basics and pay your dues, you will soon find yourself promoted to a position of formal organizational power. If you have also been unlocking your personal power, you will be able to truly influence the course of the organization and its people in a constructive way. While you were paying your dues, others undoubtedly tutored and mentored you. Now it's your turn to offer support to those coming up the ladder behind you. This need not be an onerous, time-consuming task if you think of yourself as being there to influence in the moment that opportunities arise. If you make inspiring and supporting others part of your personal purpose, supportive actions become second nature, something done naturally in the course of each day. It may take just a moment to inspire, a few words here and there. Now you can use your personal power, position power, and personal style to fully empower yourself and others. Just remember to stay alert and keep expanding your horizons.

Staying Alert   You can never afford to become smug and complacent or to rest on your laurels for long. The cofounder of Apple Computer was forced out of his own company by the man he hired to run day-to-day operations. You must keep on your toes — even if your organization does not demand it. A typical cycle of high achievers seems to be stretching out to meet a new challenge and then falling back into a comfort zone for a while. The first part of the cycle fosters enthusiasm; the second part helps prevent stress buildup. Getting stuck for too long in the first phase results in overstress; in the second, apathy.

Even though your position is relatively secure now, it pays to keep your antennae up. To retain your organizational power, stay alert to your responsibilities, tuned in to the political climate, focused on excellence, and committed to further empowering yourself and others. If you keep moving toward projects and activities that are meaningful and worthwhile to you, you will naturally increase your competence, achievements, and power throughout your career.

Expanding Your Horizons   Now that you've paid your dues, it's time to expand your support network, your personal growth activities, and other facets of your life. Is it lonely at the top? The higher you go, the smaller your in-house peer group becomes. To avoid isolation, many executives and professionals become more active in business and professional associations, forming alliances outside the company. Well-rounded executives also build relationships with people they meet as they pursue hobbies and leisure activities.

If you became somewhat one-dimensional, a workaholic, while you were learning the basics, now is the time to expand. Most workaholics are lonely without their work, and their sense of self-worth depends on an endless string of career achievements. Their career is their life. If you tend toward this profile, the antidote is to increase your awareness of the various layers and facets of your personality and to spend more time on personal development outside the demands of your job. You can focus more on becoming a well-rounded, independent person. When you view your career as a vehicle for expressing yourself rather than as "your life," you're getting there. Most people who have taken sabbaticals claim that personal-development time feeds back into career excellence and expansion.

Phase 4: Exercising Freedom of Choice

When you have gained some level of mastery and excellence within a powerful organizational position, your career choices expand. They expand even further when you achieve some measure of financial independence. Now you have a high level of knowledge, expertise, position power, and personal power — as well as experience in using these assets to achieve results. You are entering the period of your life when you can experience the greatest freedom, have the greatest influence, and make the greatest contribution. Let's look at five major directions you might take at this career stage:

- Expanding your contribution to the organization

- Finding another organization that needs your talents or another career that will enhance personal growth

- Becoming a consultant to other organizations

- Teaching in your area of specialization

- Creating your own business organization

Only you can decide which direction is best for you, and many factors will affect your decision. For one thing, you may be blocked from reaching your ultimate career goal within your organization. Many women and minorities at midmanagement levels have recently found themselves up against a glass ceiling of subtle, invisible discrimination that blocks advancement to the most powerful positions. In response, they may leave the organization to follow one of the paths just mentioned. A second factor is your need for further personal development. Perhaps you simply cannot develop to your full potential or make your ulti-

mate contribution within your current organization. A third important factor is your need for a satisfying family life. A career change may be the only solution to carving out enough time for the close family relationships you crave.

The most important factor is following what you perceive to be your destiny. Putting this process into words and describing how to discover and follow your destiny is extremely difficult, but we'll make a stab at it. See if the following suggestions ring any bells for you.

Listen to your inner self. The most satisfying career guidance comes from tuning into messages from your heart, your feelings, your intuition, your higher self. Many sections of this book discuss ways of doing this. Distinguish between ego-driven feelings and deeper feelings coming from your inner self, between goodwill-based and fear-based feelings, between intuition and false hopes/false alarms. If the feelings and messages involve your contribution to a greater purpose beyond your ego needs, you're probably on the right track.

Alternative 1: Expand Your Contribution to Your Organization   You may be able to make your greatest contribution within your current organization. You already have a great deal of power, support, and influence there. It may be the place where you influence and touch people in ways that are most meaningful to you. Or perhaps your destiny is to improve, expand, redirect, or otherwise change the organization. You're probably in an excellent position to do this, using the power base you've built over the years. Do the other factors fit well? How about the meaningfulness of your contribution? Your needs for personal growth or family time? If everything fits, staying with the organization may be the best path for you. But first, listen to your heart.

Alternative 2: Find Another Organization or Career   Perhaps your career advancement or personal growth is blocked in your present organization. Perhaps you've already learned the major things to be learned from this career vantage point. Maybe your major contributions have already been made. If so, it's probably time to move on.

Consider changing careers as well as organizations. Does the idea appeal to you? First, consider branching off into a career that relates to yours, where you already have most of the skills you'll need. Such a move means you won't lose time, money, and momentum going back almost to ground zero and starting over. Next, look at any hobbies or avocations that you care passionately about; could one of these be expanded into a career? Finally, do a relaxed visualization process and picture yourself having the type of career you most want now. See yourself doing the things you most want to do, with the people you most want to interact with, in the places you most want to be. This dream may be completely different from your current career, avocation, or hobby, but if it's where your heart wants to take you, pay attention to it.

Which possibility best fills your needs for personal growth? Which best fits into your particular needs for free time? If you decide to pursue a new career, analyze how you can transfer current skills, experience, and interests. Perhaps your new career will be some combination of careers, such as consulting, teaching, lecturing, and writing.

Alternative 3: Become a Consultant   During their fourth career phase, some people serve as consultants to other organizations. Consultants are people who thrive on moving into new situations and solving challenging problems. If this describes you, think about joining or organizing a consulting firm. As a consultant, you can bring to client firms the knowledge of the business or profession you've mastered. You deal with such challenges as identifying and solving problems, capitalizing on or creating opportunities, managing change, and planning the future of the firm. What you miss is the day-to-day implementation and administration of plans, the ongoing teamwork, and the security and comfort of an established position.

It's a good idea to learn the ropes of the consulting game by working with a consulting firm before starting your own. Do your homework—a number of books are available on this topic, and you can meet other consultants by joining the right professional organizations. Many consultants lead a feast-or-famine existence, so it's a good idea to have some bread-and-butter income from another source. Teaching courses in your specialty may provide that stability. Other parts of the package might include making professional speeches (lecturing) and writing.

Alternative 4: Become a Teacher   You may want to use teaching as the vehicle for passing on to others the benefit of your experience and knowledge. Think about teaching either part-time or full-time at a college or university. You may prefer teaching seminars to business or professional people through seminar organizations, business and professional organizations, and Human Resources Departments of firms that provide their own seminars. Teaching gives you maximum personal interaction with people, which can be most gratifying. It is also very demanding, so you must be committed and be good in order to succeed. It is not enough to know about a specialty. You must also be skilled at communicating what you know and at involving people in the learning process.

Alternative 5: Create Your Own Business   Women created their own businesses during the 1980s at twice the rate men did. Many of them are doing so because they've hit the glass ceiling. Pride of ownership is extremely motivating to most people. It turns them on to know that the profits they make will belong to them and that if the business succeeds, their career is a success. Running your own business can be exciting and fun, but it also means you are totally responsible for results. The losses are all yours as well. You may want to start a smaller version of the business organization you've been working for. Or your business might fill a smaller niche in the industry, one you're qualified to run. If you're convinced you need help in making this move, consider incorporating with one or two colleagues. For example, a powerful combination for a wholesale operation might be a sales expert, a purchasing expert, and a finance/administrative expert. If you feel you need maximum autonomy to meet your needs and make your contribution, starting your own business may be the path for you.

Now that you have more freedom of choice, you can also choose to add phases to the life of your career. For example, you might follow several of the paths just described, one after another, or even two or three at a time. Whatever your mind can conceive, you can achieve.

Typical Career Detours Women Are Taking

The road to your ultimate target job in an organization may not always be direct and straight-up. Besides the glass ceiling phenomenon, women of the 1990s are encountering such obstacles as the following:

- *Thinning of midmanagement ranks.* In an era of global competition, the lean, mean business machine tends to win out, so many companies have eliminated most mid-management jobs. They now rely more on self-directed work teams and leader/facilitators who are skilled at coordinating with other work teams and with top management. This strategy serves multiple purposes: Employees tend to be more motivated and communication lines are richer.

- *Baby-boomer competition.* All those babies born in the 1950s and early 1960s are moving into middle age during the 1990s. Many now have the experience and expertise to move up the organizational ladder. In some areas this causes a competitive crunch, meaning otherwise qualified people will not get promoted as quickly.

- *Recessions.* A prolonged business recession in the early 1990s has meant that many organizations have reduced their operations or gone out of business.

- *Child-care, elder-care responsibilities.* Most women who broke through the leadership ranks in the 1970s either remained childless or had their children during their 20s. Child-care issues were not as problematic to these women, who were in their 30s or older. In the 1980s and 1990s the typical pattern for the Promotable Woman was to complete a college degree, become established in a career, then have one or two children. She's finding child care a major problem and may be facing elder-care problems with aging parents.

To overcome these obstacles, some women are taking the following types of detours from the usual upward career path:

- *Mommy tracks.* Some women see any type of Mommy Track as too risky, believing that regardless of what company policy says, their career is likely to remain sidetracked. Other women are willing to take the risk. For some, it means doing much of their work in a home office with a fax, a computer, or other equipment in place. For others, it means working fewer hours or days per week, perhaps sharing a job with another Mommy-Tracker.

- *Rent-an-exec.* Some business and professional women handle career detours by contracting their services on a temporary basis. A new type of temporary agency matches people who have executive, professional, or technical expertise with firms that are in a transition stage and want to "rent-an-exec." This arrangement provides great flexibility for women who want to keep their hand in without a long-term commitment.

- *Midcareer training.* Some women take a mid-career break that coincides either with a sabbatical for child-care purposes or a career plateau. Many firms are willing to finance or supplement a master's program, mid-career training program, or other appropriate training.

- *Lateral moves.* More managers and professionals than ever are accepting lateral transfers into completely different functional areas of the organization and into new geographic areas. In general, the higher you want to go, the more breadth of knowledge and experience you need. The days of CEOs who came straight up through marketing, production, or finance are numbered. With organizations moving rapidly out of one market niche and into another, leaders must have broad-based business savvy that is transferable from one type of business to another. Leaders who have completed assignments in all functional areas and in various regions of the United States and the world are better prepared to understand the global ramifications of marketplace events.

SUMMARY

You will need to use all the knowledge you've gained from this book and all your experience to get the promotions you want and the salary you're worth. First, you may need to overcome some archaic attitudes about women and salaries—both others' and your own. Before you go for a particular job move, clarify your career goals and be sure the new job will contribute to your plan.

Get around promotion blocks by enlarging your job or by getting small jobs attached to it—jobs that show on the organizational chart and that you can take on while holding down your main job. Gain all the visibility you can.

To strengthen your hand, create a demand for your services from other departments and other companies. Of course, you don't want to jeopardize your job in the process.

Base your requests on your standards and accomplishments. Think and talk in those terms, beginning with the job interview and carrying through with every discussion of performance or rewards. Set realistic job standards and objectives that you're reasonably sure you can meet. Learn how your contribution affects company profits. The more you can quantify your achievements, the more likely you are to be compensated for them.

Size up your competition so you can stress areas in which you're unique or unquestionably stronger when you meet with your boss. Don't knock your competitors. Instead, if one of their strengths must be discussed, talk about similarities you share and how you work well together in those areas.

Prepare well for the promotion interview by studying your boss's position so you'll understand his or her viewpoint and be able to anticipate arguments, responses, and ploys. Get rid of false fears of being turned down or losing rapport with the boss. Your assertiveness will be respected. Overcome barriers in your boss's mind about your need for the raise.

Time your request for best results. Don't allow the request to be handled in a casual or offhand manner. Study the conditions surrounding your situation and determine whether it's best to tell your boss in advance how much salary increase you want or to wait until the meeting. Adapt your visibility during the performance evaluation period. The boss is most likely to base the evaluation on your most recent behavior. Make it good, but don't overdo it.

Turn negatives in your performance into positives by focusing on progress, strong areas, plans for improvement, and evidence that objectives and standards have been met.

Close the promotion interview by summarizing your main arguments and requesting the promotion. If the boss has objections, determine the major one and focus on it by answering it and repeating the promotion request. If necessary, make one concession and wait for the boss's response.

Position yourself for the next promotion or raise by going about your business in a natural way and following through with the plans and agreements you made in the promotion interview. If you got the promotion or raise, make the boss glad he or she recommended it. If you didn't, find out exactly what you need to do to get it next time. If you deliver, you're in a stronger position for having requested and been turned down before.

If you don't get the position you want but are offered an alternative position or assignment, ask some key questions to determine whether the career move is right for you. You should at least have a fighting chance at success.

If you're being discriminated against, talk the problem over first with your boss. Remain objective and factual by discussing unfairness rather than discrimination and by giving specific examples. If you're not satisfied with your boss's response, go to his or her boss or to the Human Resources Department. If you still get poor results, contact the nearest EEOC office and/or a lawyer.

Handle your team members' requests for promotions and raises constructively by basing your decision on how well he or she has achieved the objectives and met the standards you agreed on earlier. Guard against making promises you can't fulfill; then fight for rewards your people deserve. If you must deny part or all of a request, be firm and specific but encouraging.

Careers tend to fall into four basic phases for most people: preparing for and getting a career-level job, paying your dues and mastering the basics, reaching your ultimate target job and using position power and personal style on the job, and exercising more freedom to choose a new career direction. Some alternative directions at the fourth phase include expanding your contribution to your organization, finding another organization or career, becoming a consultant or teacher, and creating your own business.

Many women take career detours during the second or third phase. Some factors in this decision include the thinning of midmanagement ranks, baby-boomer competition, economic recessions, and child-care and elder-care concern. Some typical solutions are Mommy Tracks, rent-an-exec agencies, midcareer training, and lateral moves.

REFERENCES

1. Administrative Management Society. *AMS Guide to Management Compensation.* Maryland Road, Willow Grove, Penn. 19090.

2. Bloomfield, Horace R. *Negative Factors in the Employment of Women as Corporate Executives.* Institute of Economists & Financiers, 1989. Includes the arguments against promotion of women that you need to counter.

3. *Directory of Women Business Owners: Megamarketplace East-West.* Washington, D.C.: Government Printing Office, 1987.

4. *Entrepreneurial Woman*, Vol. 1, No. 7 (September 1991). This monthly magazine provides valuable information to women who run their own businesses.

5. Fisher, Roger, and William Ury. *Getting to Yes: Negotiating Agreement Without Giving In.* New York: Penguin Books, 1983. The authors provide practical suggestions based on their experiences directing the Harvard Negotiation Project.

6. Hickman, Craig R., and Michael A. Silva. *Creative Excellence.* New York: Penguin, 1984.

7. Ilich, John, and Barbara S. Jones. *Successful Negotiating Skills for Women.* Grand Rapids, Mich.: Bengal Press, 1990.

8. Jaffe, Dennis T., and Cynthia D. Scott. *Take This Job and Love It.* New York: Simon and Schuster, 1988. The authors offer strategies for changing your work without changing your job. Strategies include shifting to creative involvement and intra-preneurship, becoming a change master, and harnessing your inner resources to create personal power and caring connections.

9. Kozmetsky, Ronya. *Women in Business: Succeeding As a Manager, Professional, or Entrepreneur.* Austin: Texas Monthly Press, 1989.

10. LaSota, Marcia. *Women & Business Ownership: A Bibliography.* New York: Media Marketing Group, 1987.

11. Lawnes, Millicent. *The Purple Rose Within: A Woman's Basic Guide for Developing a Business Plan.* Nashville, Tenn.: A Business of Your Own, 1989.

12. Morall, Patricia A. *The Directory of Women Entrepreneurs: A National Sourcebook.* Wind River, Ga.: Author, 1990.

13. Nierenberg, Gerard I. *Women and the Art of Negotiating.* New York: Simon and Schuster, 1985.

14. Rossman, Marlene L. *The International Business Woman of the 90s.* New York: Praeger, 1990. This book is a guide to success in the international marketplace. It contains information about various countries, local customs, and how to use your own natural abilities.

15. Tarrant, John J. *How to Negotiate a Raise.* New York: Simon and Schuster, 1984.

16. Ury, William. *Getting Past No: Negotiation with Difficult People.* New York: Bantam, 1991.

17. Vipperman, Carol. *Professional Selling: A Woman's Guide: Surviving & Thriving.* (Self-Counsel Business Service) ISC Press, 1990.

18. Who's Who in Entrepreneurial Women Staff Editors. *Who's Who in Entrepreneurial Women.* Lauderhill, Fla.: General Research of America, Inc., 1990.

19. Wilkens, Joanne. *Her Own Business.* New York: McGraw-Hill, 1987. Success secrets of entrepreneurial women are revealed. Everything from success stories to preparing a business plan to market research to women's networks.

20. *Women Entrepreneurs: Selling to the Government.* Washington, D.C.: Government Printing Office, 1987.

21. Women's World Banking Staff. *The Women's World Banking Atlas of Global Trade.* New York: Women's World, 1989–90.

22. Wright, John W. *The American Almanac of Jobs and Salaries.* New York: Avon Books, 1988. See listing in Chapter 3 References.

23. Zuckerman, Laurie B. *On Your Own: A Woman's Guide to Building a Business.* Dover, N.H.: Upstart Publishing, 1990.

Women's Networks

Use this appendix to develop your networking skills and to develop a power base. First, review the five keys to attaining networking power. Second, use the list of national headquarters of women's networks as a resource.

FIVE KEYS TO NETWORKING POWER

Networking must be more than socializing and small talk—if you want to gain mutual power through the process. Five keys to networking power include planning ahead, creating impact, being direct, picking up on opportunities, and taking the next step.

Plan Ahead   Before you go to an event, ask yourself two questions: What do I have to give? What do I want to get? On your "get" list put problems you want to solve and opportunities you want to discover—things you want to learn about, understand, connect with, or find. On your "give" list put ideas, referrals, expertise, enthusiasm—opportunities and solutions you want to share.

Planning also includes selecting people to include in your ever-expanding support network. Before and after each event, identify at least two or three people to target for each category. Most supporters will also be supportees sooner or later, of course.

Create Impact   Introduce yourself with a memorable one-liner and follow up with supporting information—during the event, or later. Create a one-liner that captures the essence of what you have to offer. Some examples are: "I create events that people remember," "I position people as niche experts," "I bring the woman's angle to commercial banking."

Be Direct   Don't be afraid to talk about what you really want. For example, when you realize you want to collaborate with someone, say "I have an idea. Are you interested?"

Pick Up on Opportunities   When someone asks, "What's new?" or "How are you?" the small-talk answer is some variation of "Not much" or "Just fine." Instead, be ready to answer with something from your "get" or "give" list. "I'm looking for an experienced journalist to coauthor an article on networking. Do you know anyone?" or "I'm fine, and I'll be even better when I find a computer consultant. Do you know of a good one?"

Take the Next Step   End conversations in a way that opens up future possibilities. This may be as simple as telling the person what was valuable or what you enjoyed about meeting her. "I especially enjoyed hearing about your new project." It may include making plans for the next step in your relationship. "I'll call you next Wednesday to get that information."

NATIONAL HEADQUARTERS

Every large city in the United States has numerous organizations devoted to promoting equal opportunity, career education, mutual support, and upward mobility for women. One way to find an organization that may fit your needs is to scan the following list, select one or more groups that seem to fit, and contact the national headquarters office shown. *Ask if there is a local group or chapter of the organization in your area.*

You can also check your local telephone directory, ask your librarian if there are local directories of organizations, and watch the newspaper for clues to the activities of local women's groups. Women's magazines, such as *Executive Female*, *Savvy*, and *Ms*, include information about women's networks and associations.

NATIONAL HEADQUARTERS OF WOMEN'S ORGANIZATIONS

American Agri-women
2006 Broadway
Box 726
Mt. Vernon, IL 62864
Phone: (618) 242-4311
          (618) 787-4501 (eve.)

American Association for
 Affirmative Action
11 E. Hubbard St., Ste. 200
Chicago, IL 60611
Phone: (312) 329-2512

American Business Women's
 Assn.
National Headquarters
9100 Ward Pky.
Box 8728
Kansas City, MO 64114
Phone: (816) 361-6621

American Economic Assn.
Committee on the Status of
 Women in the Economics
 Profession
Federal Aviation Agency
Washington, D.C.

American Society of Inventors
Box 58426
Philadelphia, PA 19104-8466
Phone: (215) 546-6601

Business and Professional
 Women
2012 Massachusetts Ave., NW
Washington, D.C. 20036
Phone: (202) 293-1200
          (202) 861-0298 (fax)

Center for Women Policy Studies
2000 P. St., NE, #508
Washington, D.C. 20037
Phone: (202) 872-1770

Committee on the Status of
Women in Linguistics
1325 18th St., NW, Ste. 211
Washington, D.C. 20036
Phone: (202) 835-1714

Committee on Women's
Employment and Related Social
Issues
National Research Council
2101 Constitution Ave.,
Rm. HA 178
Washington, D.C. 20418
Phone: (202) 334-3590

Congressional Caucus for
Women's Issues
2471 Rayburn House Office Bldg.
Washington, D.C. 20515
Phone: (202) 225-6740

Coordinating Committee on
Women in the Historical
Profession
527 Clinton
Oak Park, IL 60304
Phone: (312) 386-1829

Delegation for Friendship
Among Women
2219 Caroline Ln.
South St. Paul, MN 55075
Phone: (612) 455-5620

Displaced Homemakers Network
1411 K St., N.W., Ste. 930
Washington, D.C. 20005
Phone: (202) 628-6767

Eleanor Association
1550 N. Dearborn Pkwy.
Chicago, IL 60610

Equity Policy Center
2000 P St., N.W., #508
Washington, D.C. 20036

Federally Employed Women
1400 I St., NW, Ste. 425
Washington, D.C. 20005

Federation of Organizations for
Professional Women
2001 S St., NW, Ste. 540
Washington, D.C. 20009
Phone: (202) 328-1415

Feminists Concerned for Better
Feminist Leadership
Box 1348, Madison Square
Station
New York, NY 10159
Phone: (212) 796-1467

Fund for the Feminist Majority
1600 Wilson Blvd., Ste. 704
Arlington, VA 22209
Phone: (703) 522-2214

General Commission of the
Status and Role of Women
1200 Davis St.
Evanston, IL 60201
Phone: (312) 869-7330

Institute of Women Today
1307 S. Wabash Ave.
Chicago, IL 60605
Phone: (312) 341-9159

International Black Women's
Congress
1081 Bergen St.
Newark, NJ 07112
Phone: (201) 926-0570

International Center for Research
on Women
1717 Massachusetts Ave., NW,
Suite 501
Washington, D.C. 20036
Phone: (202) 797-0007

International Institute for
Women's Political Leadership
1101 14th St., NW, Ste. 200
Washington, D.C. 20005
Phone: (202) 842-1523

International Women's Tribune
Centre
777 U.N. Plaza, 3rd Fl.
New York, NY 10017
Phone: (212) 687-8633

International Women's Writing
Guild
Box 810, Grace Station
New York, NY 10028
Phone: (212) 737-7536

Justice for Women
100 Witherspoon St.
Louisville, KY 40202
Phone: (502) 569-5385

Know, Inc.
Box 86031
Pittsburgh, PA 15221
Phone: (412) 241-4844

Leads Club (to increase business)
Box 279
Carlsbad, CA 92008
Phone: (800) 783-3761
        (619) 434-3761
        (619) 729-7797 (fax)

Legal Advocates for Women
320 Clement
San Francisco, CA 94118

Mexican American Women's
National Association
1201 16th St., NW, Ste. 230
Washington, D.C. 20036
Phone: (202) 822-7888

Mormons for ERA
5540 N. 32nd St.
Arlington, VA 22207
Phone: (703) 536-2398

MS. Foundation for Women
141 Fifth Ave. Ste. 6-S
New York, NY 10010
Phone: (212) 353-8580

National Abortion Rights League
1101 14th Street, NW, 5th Fl.
Washington, D.C. 20005
Phone: (202) 408-4600

National Association of
Commissions for Women
YWCA Bldg., M-10
624 Ninth St., NW
Washington, D.C. 20001
Phone: (202) 628-5030

National Association of Cuban-
American Women of the U.S.A.
2119 S. Webster
Ft. Wayne, IN 46802
Phone: (219) 745-5421

National Association of
Insurance Women
1847 E. 15th St.
Box 4410
Tulsa, OK 74159-4410

National Association of Negro
Business & Professional
Women's Clubs
1806 New Hampshire Ave., NW
Washington, D.C. 20009
Phone: (202) 483-4206

National Association of Women
in Construction
327 South Adams
Fort Worth, TX 76104
Phone: (800) 552-3506

National Black Women's Political
Leadership Caucus
3005 Bladensburg Rd., NE,
No. 217
Washington, D.C. 20018
Phone: (202) 529-2806

National Coalition of 100 Black
Women
50 Rockefeller Plaza
Concourse Level, Rm. 46
New York, NY 10020
Phone: (212) 974-6140

National Commission for
Women's Equality
C/o American Jewish Cong.
15 E. 84th St.
New York, NY 10028
Phone: (212) 879-4500

National Commission on
Working Women
1325 G St., NW
Washington, D.C. 20005
Phone: (202) 737-5764

National Committee on Pay
Equity
1201 16th St., NW, Rm. 422
Washington, D.C. 20036
Phone: (202) 822-7304

National Conference of Puerto
Rican Women
Five Thomas Circle
Washington, D.C. 20005
Phone: (202) 387-4716

National Congress of
Neighborhood Women
249 Manhattan Ave.
Brooklyn, NY 11211
Phone: (718) 388-6666

National Council for Research on
Women
Sara Delano Roosevelt Memorial
House
47-49 E. 65th St.
New York, NY 10021
Phone: (212) 570-5001

National Council of Career
Women
3222 N St., NW, #32
Georgetown Ct.
Washington, D.C. 20007
Phone: (202) 333-8578

National Council of Negro
Women
1211 Connecticut Ave., NW,
Ste. 702
Washington, D.C. 20036
Phone: (202) 659-0006

National Council of Women of
the United States
777 United Nations Plaza
New York, NY 10017
Phone: (212) 697-1278

National Federation of Business
and Professional Women's
Clubs, Inc. of the U.S.A.
2012 Massachusetts Ave., NW
Washington, D.C. 20036
Phone: (202) 293-1100

National Hook-Up of Black
Women
5117 S. University Ave.
Chicago, IL 60615
Phone: (312) 643-5866

National Identification Program
for Advancement of Women in
Higher Education
Administration
C/o American Council on
Education
Office of Women in Higher
Education
One Dupont Circle, NW, Rm. 829
Washington, D.C. 20036
Phone: (202) 939-9390
       (202) 833-4760 (fax)

National Institute for Women
of Color
1301 20th St., NW, Ste. 702
Washington, D.C. 20036
Phone: (202) 296-2661

National Network of Hispanic
Women
12021 Wilshire Blvd., Ste. 353
Los Angeles, CA 90025
Phone: (213) 225-9895

National Organization for
Women
1000 16th St., NW, Ste. 700
Washington, D.C. 20036
Phone: (202) 331-0066

National Savings and Loan
League
1101 15th St., NW
Washington, D.C. 20005

National Society of Hispanic
MBAs
Box 862651
Terminal Annex Station
Los Angeles, CA 90086-2651

National Woman's Party
Sewall-Belmont House
144 Constitution Ave., NE
Washington, D.C. 20002
Phone: (202) 546-1210

National Women's Conference
Committee
Box 65605
Washington, D.C. 20035-5605
Phone: (202) 842-2790

National Women's Employment
and Education
650 S. Spring St.
Los Angeles, CA 90014
Phone: (213) 221-9124

National Women's Law Center
1616 P St., NW
Washington, D.C. 20036
Phone: (202) 328-5160

National Women's Political
Caucus
1275 K St., NW, Ste. 750
Washington, D.C. 20005
Phone: (202) 898-1100

National Women's Studies
Association
University of Maryland
College Park, MD 20742

New Ways to Work
149 Ninth St.
San Francisco, CA 94103
Phone: (415) 552-1000

New York Exchange for Woman's
Work
660 Madison Ave.
New York, NY 10021
Phone: (212) 753-2330

9 to 5 National Association of
Working Women
614 Superior Ave., NW, Rm. 852
Cleveland, OH 44113
Phone: (216) 566-9308

9 to 5 Working Women Education
Fund
614 Superior Ave., NW
Cleveland, OH 44113
Phone: (216) 566-1699

NOW Legal Defense and
Education Fund
99 Hudson St., 12th Fl.
New York, NY 10013
Phone: (212) 925-6635

OEF International
1815 H St., NW, 11th Fl.
Washington, D.C. 20006
Phone: (202) 466-3430

Organization of Chinese
American Women
1439 Rhode Island Ave., NW
Washington, D.C. 20005
Phone: (202) 328-3185

Organization of Pan Asian
American Women
Box 39218
Washington, D.C. 20016
Phone: (202) 659-9370

Professional & Technical
Consultants Assn.
1330 S. Bascom Ave., Ste. D
San Jose, CA 95128
Phone: (408) 287-8703

Radical Women
523A Valencia St.
San Francisco, CA 94110
Phone: (415) 864-1278

Radio Free Women
1213 N. Leithgow St.
Philadelphia, PA 19122
Phone: (215) 763-4760

Sagaris, Inc.
10 Second St., NE, No. 100
Minneapolis, MN 55413
Phone: (612) 379-2640

Smaller Business Assn. of New
England, Inc.
69 Hickory Dr.
Waltham, MA 02254-9117
Phone: (617) 890-9070

Task Force on Equality of Women
in Judaism
838 Fifth Ave.
New York, NY 10021
Phone: (212) 249-0100

The Woman Activist
2310 Barbour Rd.
Falls Church, VA 22043-2940
Phone: (703) 573-8716

The Woman Activist Fund
2310 Barbour Rd.
Falls Church, VA 22043-2940
Phone: (703) 573-8716

Third World Women's Project
Inst. for Policy Studies
1601 Connecticut Ave., NW
Washington, D.C. 20009
Phone: (202) 234-9382

United Nations Development
Fund for Women
304 E. 45th St., 6th Fl.
New York, NY 10017
Phone: (212) 906-6400

Venture Clubs of America
1616 Walnut St.
Philadelphia, PA 19103
Phone: (215) 732-0512

Wider Opportunities for Women
1325 G St., N.W. Lower Level
Washington, D.C. 20005
Phone: (202) 638-3143

Women Achieving Greater
Economic Status
Box 585766
Orlando, FL 32858
Phone: (407) 295-1941

Women and Foundations/
Corporate Philanthropy
141 Fifth Ave., Fl. 7-S
New York, NY 10010
Phone: (212) 460-9253

Women Employed Institute
22 W. Monroe, Ste. 1400
Chicago, IL 60603
Phone: (312) 782-3902

Women for Racial and Economic
Equality
198 Broadway, Rm. 606
New York, NY 10038
Phone: (212) 385-1103

Women in Sales Assn., Inc.
Eight Madison Ave.
Box M
Valhall, NY 10595
Phone: (914) 946-3802
(914) 946-3633 (fax)

Women Involved in Farm
  Economics
Box 191
Hingham, MT 59528

Women of the World
  (entrepreneurs)
13 Lake Dr.
Darien, CT 06820
Phone: (203) 359-9080

Women's Action Alliance
141 Fifth Ave., 8th Fl.
New York, NY 10010
Phone: (212) 532-8330

Women's Business Development
  Center
230 N. Michigan Ave., #1800
Chicago, IL 60601
Phone: (312) 853-3477

Women's Campaign Fund
1601 Connecticut Ave., NW,
  Ste. 800
Washington, D.C. 20009
Phone: (202) 234-3700

Women's Council of Realtors
430 N. Michigan Ave.
Chicago, IL 60611
Phone: (312) 329-8483

Women's Economic Rights
  Project
C/o NOW Legal Defense and
  Education Fund
99 Hudson St., 12th Fl.
New York, NY 10013
Phone: (212) 925-6635

Women's Information Exchange
Box 68
Jenner, CA 95450
Phone: (707) 632-5763

Women's Institute for Freedom of
  the Press
3306 Ross Place, NW
Washington, D.C. 20008
Phone: (202) 966-7783

Women's International Network
187 Grant St.
Lexington, MA 02173
Phone: (617) 862-9431

Women's International Resource
  Exchange
475 Riverside Dr., Rm. 570
New York, NY 10115
Phone: (212) 870-2783

Women's Law Fund
57 E. Washington St.
Chagrin Falls, OH 44022
Phone: (216) 687-3947

Women's Law Project
125 S. Ninth St., Ste. 401
Philadelphia, PA 19107
Phone: (215) 928-9801

Women's Legal Defense Fund
2000 P St., NW, #400
Washington, D.C. 20036
Phone: (202) 887-0364

Women's Media Project
1333 H St. NW, 11th Fl.
Washington, D.C. 20005
Phone: (202) 682-0940

Women's Research and Education
  Institute
1700 18th St., NW, Ste. 400
Washington, D.C. 20009
Phone: (202) 328-7070

Women's Rights Committee
C/o Human Rights Dept.
555 New Jersey Ave., NW
Washington, D.C. 20001
Phone: (202) 879-4400

Women's Rights Project
C/o American Civil Liberties
  Union
132 W. 43rd St.
New York, NY 10036
Phone: (212) 944-9800

Women's Student Association
C/o Hebrew Union College
Jewish Institute of Religion
One W. Fourth St.
New York, NY 10012
Phone: (212) 674-5300

Women U.S.A. Fund
1133 Broadway, Ste. 924
New York, NY 10010
Phone: (212) 691-7316

Magazines for Career Women

Business Week   P.O. Box 597, Hightstown, NJ 08520-9956.
A good weekly summary of news, important to all businesspersons.

Executive Female   421 Fourth Street, Annapolis, MD 21403
A bimonthly publication of the National Association for Female Executives (NAFE). This magazine offers a fairly sophisticated level of helpful articles for women managers. Each issue usually centers around a particular theme, such as functional skills, working relationships, or financial savvy. You must join NAFE to receive the magazine. Some advantages of membership include (1) access to a list of NAFE network directors as well as the opportunity to become a network director yourself, (2) a career placement service called MATCHPOINT, (3) career aids such as aptitude testing, résumé guidance, and a credit handbook, (4) personal benefits such as a group hospitalization option and hotel and car rental discounts.

Harvard Business Review   Soldier Field, Boston, MA 02163
An excellent journal for all executives. Rosabeth Moss Kanter became the editor in 1989.

Intercambios, P.O. Box 390543, Mountain View, CA 94039
A publication of the National Network of Hispanic Women, this magazine was launched in 1981. It focuses on success strategies and recent developments of interest to women.

Ms   370 Lexington Ave., New York, NY 10017
A monthly publication that includes articles on the sources and impact of sex-role stereotyping, discrimination, networking, sources of supportiveness for women, and other items of interest to women. It's an excellent source of current information on women's rights and the women's movement.

New Woman   314 Royal Poinciana Way, Palm Beach, FL 33480
A bimonthly publication that bridges the gap between *Good Housekeeping* and *Ms.* This magazine is for women who are just beginning to look seriously at alternate lifestyles and career choices. Some articles on self-development of interest to the aspiring woman manager are included.

Savvy   111 Eighth, Ave., Suite 1517, New York NY 10001
A sophisticated monthly publication that combines some aspects of *Ms.* and *Executive Female*. This is an excellent, well-rounded magazine for the woman manager.

Women's Health   Rodale Press, Emmaus, PA 18049.
This monthly newsletter takes a preventive, assertive approach to health care. It features news you won't find in newspapers or most women's magazines.

Working Mother   McCall Publishing Company, 230 Park Avenue, New York, NY 10169
A bimonthly magazine that includes articles of interest to all working women as well as information and advice specifically geared to the working mother.

Working Woman   P.O. Box 10132, Des Moines, IA 50340
An excellent monthly magazine for women who are thinking about upward mobility and for new women supervisors and managers. Basic articles of interest to working women at all levels are included.

Answers to Selected Exercises

Chapter 2 Case Incident: Career Decisions (pp. 28–29)

1. Actions and attitudes that tend to enhance a person's promotability include taking initiative in making career moves; taking responsibility for your own career; learning how to wage an effective job campaign; generating several job offers, thereby enhancing your negotiating power; viewing job interviews as exciting experiences and as a means to sharpen interviewing skills; being willing to risk rejection in applying for a better job; viewing the job campaign as a game and not tying the outcome to your sense of self-worth; communicating to your boss about your career goals.

2. Specific actions and attitudes that tend to sabotage career goals include failing to take the actions listed in Item 1; expecting your boss to take responsibility for your career progress, notice your accomplishments, and promote you; letting fear of failure or a negative view of risk-taking dominate your life; giv-

ing in to apathy and being willing to stay in the comfortable rut of the same old job.

3 and 4. Words associated with the word "risk" and how most successful businesspeople view risk are as follows: Most females tend to associate the concept of loss with the idea of risk and therefore think of risk as something negative, unwelcome, and to be avoided. Males are more likely to view risk in a balanced way: balancing the probability of success with the possibility and consequences of failure. They are as likely to view risk as an opportunity to gain or achieve something as to lose. Most successful businesspeople have an entrepreneurial view of risk. Entrepreneurs are by definition risk-takers. They risk the capital they invest in return for the probability of making a profit on the investment, and they constantly look for profit opportunities.

Exercise 2-1: Assessing Viewpoints That Affect Promotability (pp. 30–31)

Scoring Instructions: Place a check mark in the space to the left of the answer that corresponds to your responses for each of the ten items. For example, if your response to Item 1 was "a," place a check beside "1a"

below. When you have checked off all the items, add the number of check marks you have in each column and write the total for each category on the bottom line.

Category A (Viewpoints typical of the promotable woman)	Category B (Viewpoints typical of the marginally promotable woman)	Category C (Viewpoints typical of the nonpromotable woman)
_____ 1c	_____ 1a	_____ 1b
_____ 2b	_____ 2a	_____ 2c
_____ 3b	_____ 3c	_____ 3a
_____ 4a or c	_____ 4b	_____ 4d
_____ 5b	_____ 5a	_____ 5c
_____ 6b	_____ 6a or c	_____
_____ 7a	_____ 7c	_____ 7b
_____ 8a	_____ 8b	_____ 8c
_____ 9b	_____ 9a	_____ 9c
_____ 10b*	_____ 10a	_____ 10c
_____ Total	_____ Total	_____ Total

Scoring Interpretation: You can make a general evaluation of your current level of promotability by merely noting the category in which you have the highest score. The more detailed explanation that follows in Chapter 8 can help you further diagnose your areas of strength and weakness.

---

*You should include in your plans how many people you'll need to handle the increased workload.

Exercise 2-3: Pinpointing Your Attitude (p. 47)

This exercise is designed to pinpoint any conflict you may harbor about career success. Do any of the statements in your story reflect negative consequences? Negative consequences might include any form of social or family difficulty or rejection; some decrease in eligibility or desirability as a date or marriage partner; becoming isolated, lonely, or unhappy in some way as a result of succeeding. Expecting negative consequences leads to the arousal of some degree of fear of success, which in turn leads to self-sabotage unconsciously designed to avoid the negative consequences.

Chapter 3 Case Incident: Life Directions (pp. 54–55)

---

1. Erika's resistance to goal-setting is typical. Most people tend to resist inner reflection, in-depth thinking about life plans and career plans that are based on their aptitudes, talents, interests, and skills—and the resulting periodic goal-setting and risk assessment.
5. Florence Chadwick's goal was to swim from Catalina Island to Long Beach. When she took the time to develop a clear image or vision of that goal, she achieved it. Increase the probability of achieving all your goals by developing a clear picture of that goal. Picture yourself having it. (See Chapter 5 for more on the visualization process.)

Chapter 4 Case Incident: Freewheeling or Frantic? (pp. 106–108)

1. Effective time-management attitudes and actions include clearing your desk at the end of each day except for the materials needed to start tomorrow's first activity; setting aside quiet time to work on important projects; delegating such tasks as sorting mail, handling routine correspondence, fielding visitors and telephone calls; managing appointments; calling meetings only for specific purposes; coordinating with assistants.

2. Jan's assistant is clear about her job goals and duties. Workers understand the reasons for Jan's routines and procedures and respect them. Jan is in control and can take time to meet with workers when they need her. Jan is considered a role model of effective time management. Jan is able to guide and coach others to use effective time-management practices.

3. Kate is too busy to deal effectively with people. She isn't delegating enough. She shouldn't initiate telephone calls when she's expecting a visitor momentarily. When Frank comes in, she should end the call and ask her assistant to hold her calls till he leaves. She should give Frank her full attention and make a recommendation on the spot. She should send out a meeting agenda with a stated purpose and goals. The meeting should end with a summary of how well the purpose and goals were met and what follow-up actions are needed.

4. Frank feels ignored and frustrated; he doesn't like having his time wasted. Phil is frustrated and demotivated; his talents are not being fully utilized. Workers are unclear about the purpose of the meetings; they dislike boring, unproductive meetings.

Chapter 5 Case Incident: Getting Stress Under Control (pp. 135–137)

1. Erika is not taking full responsibility for her actions. She is playing the victim and blaming others for "picking on her." She is not asserting herself effectively. She is letting others pull her emotional strings, then acting out her hurt and anger in unprofessional ways. Erika also has some poor eating habits. She is using ineffective coping behavior to deal with stress, such as using caffeine, nicotine, and alcohol. She is not using effective time-management techniques; she's working too many hours and allowing too little time for personal life, exercise routines, relaxation, and rest.

2. Poor nutrition, lack of exercise, substance abuse, and overwork all contribute to stress buildup. Erika is like a pressure cooker ready to blow up. She is becoming a prime candidate for illness.

Chapter 6 Case Incident: Recognizing Assertiveness Gaps (pp. 165–166)

1. Erika remained calm and cool with Tom, taking a problem-solving approach and asking probing questions. To get at the root of the problem, she welcomed criticism as constructive feedback but didn't let it intimidate her or divert her from taking action to reach her goals. In her interaction with Perry, however, Erika allowed criticism to block her. She went into a nonassertive mode; she did not persist in getting at the root of the conflict.

3. One plan is to ask for a brainstorming session with Sue and Wayne to find a way to overcome the problems that concern Perry.

4. See the sections on "To Assert or Not Assert?" and "Payoffs."

5. See the section on "Payoffs."

Exercise 6-2: Identifying Assertive, Aggressive, and Nonassertive Behavior (pp. 167–169)

1. As   2. N   3. Ag   4. As   5. Ag   6. As   7. N   8. As   9. Ag   10. N   11. As   12. As   13. N   14. As   15. N   16. As   17. As   18. As   19. Ag   20. Ag

Exercise 6-3: Giving Feedback Messages (pp. 180–181)

If possible, get someone to read your response and to define or summarize it by selecting one verb that best represents its tone. Some possibilities include: "assume, evaluate, praise, blame, solve, lecture, psych, sympathize, accuse, warn, scold, order, imply, question, hint, kid." If you can't get someone to read your response, evaluate it yourself *after* you read the following discussion.

Underline any judgmental or evaluative words you can find in your response. Do any of your statements imply that Lois's behavior is bad or wrong in and of itself? Consider the fact that her behavior might seem good to some apartment mates, who would be happy that Lois likes to really relax and let her hair down once in a while. Such behavior could conceivably put such a partner at ease so that she would feel free to behave in a similar manner herself.

Here is an example of a feedback message that objectively describes Lois's behavior: "Lois, I want to talk with you. I notice that your coat, shoes, and briefcase are lying in the entry hall, that some of your clothes and the newspaper are lying around the living room, that there are peanuts and an empty beer can on the floor, and that the TV is playing loudly. This is the third or fourth time this has occurred. When it happens, I feel . . . (angry/frustrated/unhappy/glad to see you relaxed but worried about the furniture/that guests might drop in/etc.)"

Do you see that objectively describing behavior is merely repeating the specific actions as you observe them? Words such as "mess, lazy, sloppy, inconsiderate" are judgmental and should be avoided. A matter-of-fact tone should be used with no hint of hostility or resentment.

The feedback message should also include the effects Lois's behavior has on her roommate. For example, "I am beginning to hesitate to invite people over." At some point in the conversation the message should also include the specific behavior the sender would prefer. In most cases, including this one, the most effective approach is to get the receiver's ideas about behavior change first. However, if the receiver does not propose a change that is satisfactory to the sender, the sender should assert herself clearly by making tactful queries or suggestions. For example, "When you relax in this way, could you confine your activities and possessions to your bedroom?"

This feedback message may not "work" in the sense that you and Lois are able to reach a mutual agreement on lifestyles and housekeeping habits. In fact, you may decide now or later that you should not share an apartment because of these differences. However, if you have given effective feedback messages, both you and Lois will be clear about exactly why the living arrangement didn't work out. This way, Lois will not worry and wonder about what went wrong. She's not likely to think you dislike her as a person or even that you have negative emotions in connection with other aspects of her behavior. Therefore, unfounded resentments and hurt feelings are likely to be avoided. Although Lois may not like your honesty at the time, she's likely to respect it and to respect you. Your chances of an amicable living arrangement—or an amicable parting—and goodwill in the future are enhanced through effective feedback.

Chapter 7 Case Incident: A Focus on the Message (pp. 210–211)

1. The strong points included effective note cards for a spontaneous but well-organized presentation, effective visual aids, and good rehearsal techniques for clarity and self-confidence. Her weak points were overconcern about remembering all the details of the speech and an inability to manage nervous energy and to transform it into enthusiasm.

2. Yes, these techniques apply to many situations: Getting adequate information and preparing to communicate; focusing on the message and on getting it across to others; achieving deep relaxation followed by a focus on desired results.

Exercise 7-2: Preparing Action Agenda Items (p. 231)

1. The meeting objectives are (a) to set sales targets, (b) to approve a marketing plan for the new XYZ product, (c) to develop a layoff policy, and (d) to set the next meeting date.
2. The results-oriented questions are (a) What will be our sales target for 19xx? OR How can we increase sales by 10%? (b) Shall we develop the new XYZ product? OR How can we best market the new XYZ product? (c) How can we improve our layoff policy? OR What shall our layoff policy be? (d) When should we meet again?

Exercise 7-4: Choosing the Best Graph (pp. 250–251)

1. Broken-line. 2. Bar. 3. Pie. 4. Broken-line with projection in dots or similar differentiation. Text or footnote should give basis for projection and statistical technique used. 5. Bar, each bar with three differentiated segments. 6. Bar, if for comparison. 7. Broken-line. 8. Pie.

Exercise 7-5: Constructing and Interpreting a Graph (pp. 251–252)

1. True.
2. You can't tell. You can only make projections, using statistical treatment.
3. You can't tell—*something* does.
4. You can't say, since you have no costs or expenses shown.
5. True.
6. June and July, but not October.

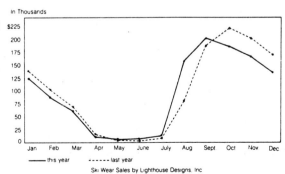

Chapter 8 Case Incident: Preparing for the Big Move (pp. 257–259)

1. Important aspects of making a successful transition include: shifting your focus from doing the work to leading and coaching others in the performance of the work; from pleasing your boss in every detail to leading your team in achieving its objectives; from depending on your boss's credibility and competence to handle organizational politics to becoming adept at handling difficulties, asserting yourself, and projecting a powerful image; from "trying hard to please" and being a pal to establishing appropriate distances in work relationships.

Exercise 8-1: Self-Assessment: Making the Transition to Leader (pp. 255–257)

Scoring Instructions: Transfer the numbers you placed in the blanks in Exercise 2-1 to the corresponding blanks shown here. Add the numbers in each column to get your total score in each category.

Category 1 (Savvy leader)	Category 2 (Aggressive/loner)	Category 3 (Submissive detail person)
_____ 1b	_____ 1c	_____ 1a
_____ 2a	_____ 2b	_____ 2c
_____ 3c	_____ 3a	_____ 3b
_____ 4b	_____ 4c	_____ 4a
_____ 5c	_____ 5b	_____ 5a
_____ 6a	_____ 6c	_____ 6b
_____ 7b	_____ 7c	_____ 7a
_____ 8c	_____ 8b	_____ 8a
_____ 9b	_____ 9a	_____ 9c
_____ 10a	_____ 10b	_____ 10c

Scoring Interpretation: You can make a general evaluation of your readiness to make a successful transition by simply noting the categories in which you scored the highest and the lowest. The categories may be interpreted as follows:

Category 1, Savvy leader — Your identification with these responses indicates that you're already tuned into ways of projecting a competent, professional image. You can probably avoid the typical problems that face the new career woman.

Category 2, Aggressive/loner — Your identification with these responses may indicate a tendency to "go it alone" and to sometimes overreact to others' stereotypes of women in the business world. Actions perceived as overaggressive may leave you wide open to being labeled a hostile feminist or a grouch. Loner actions may create barriers to developing a support network. See Chapter 6 for suggestions on changing your aggressiveness to assertiveness.

Category 3, Submissive detail person — Your identification with these responses may indicate that you strongly identify with typical female behavior patterns. While these patterns can contribute to success in secretarial/clerical roles, they are nonproductive in a leadership role. Focus on seeing the "big picture," on taking a power stance, and on upward mobility for you and your workers. See Chapter 6 for developing your assertiveness.

Chapter 9 Case Incident: Different Strokes (pp. 296–297)

See the Chapter 10 case incident in this answer key.

Exercise 9-1: How Do You View Workers? (p. 299)

Answers to odd-numbered
questions (1, 3, 5, 7, 9):

Total of + scores _____
Total of − scores _____
Difference _____ (Y) score

Answers to even numbered
questions (2, 4, 6, 8, 10):

Total of + scores _____
Total of − scores _____
Difference _____ (X) score

Interpretation:
A Y-Score or an X-Score of 7 to 10 indicates you are strongly oriented toward that theory. A Y-Score or an X-Score of 4 to 7 indicates you are moderately oriented toward that theory. A Y-Score or an X-Score of 3 to 0 or any minus amount indicates little or no orientation toward that theory.

Exercise 9-2: How Do You Lead? (p. 303)

The higher your *A* score, the more you tend toward a traditional, directive leadership style. The higher your *B* score, the more you tend toward a facilitative team-leader style. The following categories are rough estimates of your tendency toward one style or the other:

52−65 = Extremely characteristic of you
39−51 = Very characteristic of you
25−38 = Not very to somewhat characteristic of you
13−24 = Slightly to not very characteristic of you

Exercise 9-3: Identifying Behavior Characteristics of Defensive and Supportive Climates (p. 325)

	"A" Response	*"B" Response*
1.	Control	Cooperation
2.	Superiority	Equality
3.	Description	Evaluation
4.	Indifferent	Concerned
5.	Know-it-all	Open to ideas
6.	Manipulative	Spontaneous

The purpose of this exercise is to reinforce concepts and to stimulate thinking, not to determine "right answers." The answers shown here are merely intended to suggest the categories of behavior involved in each of the situations.

Chapter 10 Case Incident: Firefighting Strategies (pp. 329–331)

1. Erika let the clerks know exactly what she expected of them and what they were to do. Her detailed directions helped them achieve their goals. They were motivated to achieve the goals she set for them and believed that if they tried, they could succeed.
2. The salesmen were demotivated because they felt demoted when they were given less responsibility and autonomy.
3. The clerks don't know what is expected of them. They should have clear, specific objectives, as discussed in Chapter 12. Lin needs a more structured style. She needs to understand the expectancy theory of motivation and apply the path-goal approach (both are discussed in this chapter).
4. Since Lin reports to her, Erika is responsible for coaching Lin on this aspect of leadership. She

should serve as a role model by working with Lin to set clear performance objectives. Then she should ask Lin how she plans to work with her own people in setting such objectives. She can go on to an in-depth discussion of motivational strategies in connection with goal-setting and rewards.

Exercise 10-1: Identifying Motivational Priorities (p. 332)

Your self-assessment will depend on how you interpret each factor, of course. Most of the managers who have worked through Exercise 10-1 have interpreted these factors as follows:

Factor	Suggested Level — Maslow's Hierarchy	Category
Adequate salary	Physiological or security	A
Responsibilities assigned	Self-actualization	B
Relationship with fellow employees	Social	B
The work itself	Self-actualization	B
Opportunity for advancement	Ego or self-actualization	B
Working conditions	Safety	A
On-the-job achievement	Self-actualization	B
Kind of supervision received	Social	A
Recognition	Ego	B
Company policy	Security	A
Opportunities for personal growth	Self-actualization	B

Exercise 10-4: Matching Needs to Jobs (pp. 348–349)

The responses can vary depending on the particular job situation and the unique combination of needs perceived by each person. The responses shown are to stimulate your thinking.

1. *EDP program librarian:* Ach. The job is highly task oriented with little interaction with other people.
2. *EDP systems analyst:* Ach/Aff. The job calls for task-oriented technical skills as well as good human relations skills. Need to listen, question, identify others' needs, and communicate effectively.
3. *Personnel interviewer:* Aff. Extensive interaction with people. High level of human relations skills required.
4. *Word-processing operator:* Ach. Highly task-oriented job with almost immediate feedback and measurable results.

5. *Word-processing supervisor:* Aff/Ach. Although a task-oriented background is required, at this level human relations skills are more important. Much interaction with people; ability to keep workers and users satisfied is important.
6. *Labor relations specialist:* P/Aff. To the extent the union is demanding and hostile, ability to project and exercise power is crucial, especially in negotiations. High level of human relations skills is also required to anticipate others' behavior, to communicate effectively, and to smooth over ruffled feelings.
7. *Personnel benefits administrator:* Ach. Highly task-oriented job. Little interaction with people.
8. *Purchasing analyst:* Ach. Highly task oriented; little interaction.

9. *Buyer:* Aff/P. Much interaction with vendors; some interaction with production people. Good human relations skills, ability to communicate well are important. To extent management allows autonomy in bargaining with vendors and deciding on bids, power needs may be met.

10. *Account Executive:* Ach. Since results are so important and visible, and since they depend so greatly on the individual's effort and abilities, this job is first and foremost achievement oriented. Since it requires a high level of interaction and human relations skills, it may also satisfy affiliation needs. However, the successful account executive is comfortable with risk-taking and uncertainty. Because success can lead to rapid advancement, the job can also meet power needs.

Exercise 10-5: The Leslie Case (pp. 349–350)

The clerks are exhibiting strong affiliation needs at the expense of achievement or power needs. Here are various steps Lin can take to handle the situation and to enhance the motivation of the clerks.

1. Discuss goals and standards; implement the concepts of performance planning.
2. Attempt to find a way to achieve goal congruence and to channel the affiliation needs of the clerks so that the goals of the unit are also met.
3. Consider organizing the clerks formally into a project team with specific goals.
4. Consider separating the clerks on the job, putting them into jobs that allow maximum contact with others and giving them adequate responsibility to keep them challenged. Consider transferring them to other departments in carrying out this action.

5. Determine if achievement needs lie hidden behind the obvious affiliation needs. If so, try to find out what rewards are most motivating: recognition? training for more responsible tasks or positions?
6. If affiliation is actually the predominant motive, what types of rewards will be more satisfying than socializing on the job? Praise? Giving challenging tasks that require interaction with interesting people?
7. Determine if the clerks are viewing their jobs as mere drudgery. If so, how can Lin make the jobs appear more important and essential to them.
8. Determine if Lin can delegate some of her tasks to the clerks, tasks that will be rewarding to them.
9. Watch for opportunities to reward the clerks when they are obviously concentrating on work and performing tasks effectively.

Chapter 11 Case Incident: Breaking Murphy's Law (p. 353)

1. The effective actions and attitudes included willingness to admit mistakes, honesty; focusing on opportunities; willingness to take calculated risks; estimating the likelihood of problems occurring in order to plan ways of preventing and managing them.
2. These actions may inspire, model effective behavior, and motivate others.

3. The ineffective actions and attitudes include the fear of taking risks and focusing on probable loss, and solving problems for team members instead of training them to problem-solve.
4. These actions may encourage self-limiting beliefs of team members; lower self-confidence; make team members feel and act more dependent; and limit their personal growth and development.

Exercise 11-1: Discovering Your Approach to Decision-Making (p. 371)

Phillip Marvin found that the typical successful entrepreneur and top-level executive exhibits the decision-
making profile shown here:

	Nearly Always	Frequently	Frequently	Nearly Always	
1. Solve problems.					1. Capitalize on opportunities.
2. Generally dissatisfied with things as they are.					2. Satisfied with things as they are.
3. Don't care what others think.					3. Want to know what others think.
4. Get things going.					4. Avoid making waves.
5. Want to continue doing what I'm doing.					5. Want to shift to more rewarding activities.
6. Keep learning within my area of expertise.					6. Still in the process of searching for my best area of expertise; quickly bored.
7. Tend to do things in well-tested ways.					7. Tend to develop new ways of doing things.
8. Get ready for tomorrow's job while doing today's job.					8. Concentrate on today's job.
9. Do it myself.					9. Seek available counsel and advice.
10. Do what I'm told to do.					10. Make continuing reappraisals of the value of what I'm doing.
11. Adhere to rules.					11. Will break rules; rules are only guidelines.
12. Avoid risk as a matter of principle.					12. Accept "calculated" risk when it may optimize achievement.

Exercise 11-2: The Manning Case (p. 380)

1. Some of the sources of Manning's problems are:
   (a) Lack of a preventive attitude toward problems.
   (b) Failure to use Murphy's Law to prevent unpleasant surprises. (c) Failure to consult the people who are involved in carrying out the decisions. (d) Failure to brief people in groups, face-to-face, where possible. (e) Lack of participation of others in the decision-making process; for example, in deciding how details of the campaign will be carried out. (f) Lack of adequate controls to ensure that any deviations from the plan will be discovered in time to prevent failure.
2. By using the techniques mentioned above, Mary could have handled the situation more effectively.
3. Mary is in real trouble because she has blown her first real chance to show her managerial effectiveness. What's worse, the results will be visible to the top decision-makers in the company.
4. The best approach Mary can take now is to admit her problems and seek help. The first step would be to think through her problems and figure out how some can be remedied and how to prevent any of them from occurring again. Then she should go to Jan Arguello and discuss the whole matter, sharing her insights and asking Jan for her advice. If Mary shows that she has learned a great deal from this experience and is determined to perform better in the future, she may be able to redeem herself eventually.

Exercise 11-3: Making Decisions Under Pressure (p. 381)

The key to handling this situation effectively is the decision you make regarding Item E. Any time all production is halted in your department, your company is losing money rapidly. If the average salary of your workers is $20 an hour including benefits and you have ten workers, the company loses $200 worth of productivity for each hour your work unit is idle or unproductive. Since you're the only one who can fix the equipment (a situation that should be remedied in the future, by the way), you must handle this item at once if you are to get everyone else back to work as soon as possible.

Meanwhile, how are you going to salvage some productivity from your idle workers? Are you going to run around frantically trying to handle all the listed items by yourself while they sit around watching you? If you didn't decide to delegate as many of the other items as possible, you need to work on your attitude toward delegation! Pay special attention to this section in Chapter 13.

Here are suggested priorities and sequence of handling the items:

Importance	Sequence	Item
8	11	A
2	2	B
6	9	C
4	1	D
1	8	E
6	4	F
5	5	G
6	7	H
7	6	I
3	3	J

Suggestions for handling items in sequence are shown below.

Item D. If a worker is nearby, have her or him answer the phone and take the message. If not, answer it, ask them to hold, then get someone to take the message.

Item B. Send someone to your boss to explain the situation and to set up a later appointment.

Item J. Send someone to get a sandwich or other fast food that you can eat when you finish repairing the equipment.

Item F. Send someone to find out what the young man wants and to get his name and number so you can call him next week.

Item G. Have someone call the Los Angeles operator and talk with the party to determine whether or not it is an emergency.

Item I. Send someone to the lounge to relay your permission to Ann; let her go home.

Item H. Send someone to tell Jim of your situation and to get a message from him as to the nature of his call and/or how long it can wait.

Item E. After you have delegated the above items, which should take no more than five minutes, repair the equipment.

After the equipment is repaired, review the messages returned to you by the workers you sent on errands. Decide which need handling first and whether any can be further delegated.

Item C. You could have delegated the opening of the company mail earlier. (If you have a secretary, she should routinely open all company mail anyway.) Since anyone with an urgent time target would not handle a request by mail, you can assume the mail can wait. However, you may want to check it by midafternoon in case you want a reply to go out in the Friday afternoon mail.

Item A. Your talk to Scott can wait till next week. Think about it over the weekend.

Chapter 12 Case Incident: The Best-Laid Plans (p. 384)

1. Overlooked planning strategies included getting people involved in the planning and decision-making process; that is, deciding how to promote the new line, developing departmental goals for the line, deciding on quotas and job assignments, working out details for advertising, merchandising, and promotion. There is no mention of working out specific job objectives or performance plans for team members.

2. Her planning method has affected motivation in the following ways: lack of enthusiasm and motivation because people don't "own" the action plans,

they feel left out, alienated; limited understanding of plans; less-than-optimal performance; difficulty getting support from other departments without communicating how requests tie in with departmental objectives that in turn support the firm's objectives; no clear link between performance and rewards.

3. No, she has failed to get people involved in making the decisions relating to the plans.

4. See number 1 and the specifics given in the chapter.

Exercise 12-4: Making Objectives Clear and Specific (p. 394)

1. This statement needs to be more specific and measurable. A possible rewrite: Increase our share of the petite-size clothing market from 10 percent to 25 percent by January 19xx with no more than a 2 percent increase in our department budget.

2. A possible rewrite: Increase our net profit to 12 percent of sales for fiscal year 19xx.

3. A possible rewrite: Provide at least 100 contact hours of appropriate classroom training for each

supervisor during fiscal year 19xx within a budget of $250,000.

4. A possible rewrite: Set quality control standards for sweater imports to meet or exceed those of Competitors X and Y, while maintaining a profit margin of 13 percent.

5. A possible rewrite: Develop twelve additional sources of supply by January 1, 19xx, at a cost of no more than 100 working hours.

6. A possible rewrite: Reduce the number of employee grievances to no more than ten per quarter, by quarter ending April 1, 19xx, at a cost not to exceed $20,000.
7. A possible rewrite: Establish a research and development department with a staff of twelve and a first-year operating budget of $1,200,000 by September 1, 19xx, at a developmental cost of $565,000.
8. Ideally, an objective does not represent an "assigned responsibility." It is a measurable goal to be achieved by a certain date. "Carrying out assigned responsibilities" carries the connotation of "just working" to most people. The estimated resources to be used in achieving the objectives are agreed on by worker and boss during the objective-setting process. Securing the necessary resources is part of the action or implementation process. Therefore, "within approved budget" is inappropriate language for stating clear objectives.
9. A possible rewrite: Conduct a market research survey to determine the major emerging styles desired by businesswomen; results to be reported by March 1, 19xx; budget allowance, $20,000.
10. A possible rewrite: Install XYZ system by October 15, 19xx, at a cost not to exceed $150,000.

Exercise 12-5: Developing Objectives and Controls with Your Assistant (p. 416)

There are many possible responses to this exercise. Here is one:

1. Key objective: To initiate and respond to all routine correspondence in connection with the XYZ convention to be held on April 8, 19xx.
2. Additional standards: (1) All letters and memos will be effective; that is, they will get the desired results. (2) All letters and memos will be grammatically correct. (3) All correspondence will be typographically correct (no uncorrected errors). (4) The normal length of time for completing an average letter (one-half to one page long) will be fifteen minutes.
3. Controls: During the first few weeks of this project, you will sign all correspondence before it is sent. You should check each letter thoroughly before signing it, using standards (1) through (3) as the basis for approval. Later, you will only spot-check routine correspondence. During the entire project, your assistant will practice self-evaluation, using all agreed-on standards. Standard (4) is difficult to control when the assistant has a variety of duties and may be frequently interrupted. However, it can serve as a guideline.

Exercise 12-7: Del Oro Enterprises — Designing an Organizational Structure (pp. 417–418)

The Current Organizational Chart and the Possible New Chart A show departmentation by product or service: (1) in-house food service, (2) take-out or off-premises food service, (3) boutique products, and (4) alcoholic beverage products.

In Chart A, Drew and Sanchez capitalize on their individual strengths — Drew's in food services and Sanchez's in the buying/selling game of retail operations. Each has two vice-presidents reporting directly to her, which will help take some pressure off their jobs and yet provide top-management coverage of all areas. A disadvantage of this structure is that all four top managers must oversee all functional areas within their product areas. They may lack needed expertise in some functional areas, and there will probably be some overlap and duplication of functions.

Chart B shows departmentation by functional area. The operations area (equivalent to production in a manufacturing operation) is divided into two functional areas: Food Service Operations, covering restaurant and deli operations, and Retail Operations, covering boutique and bottle shop operations. These two types of operations are significantly different and call for different types of experience and expertise. Functional expertise can be brought to other areas too, such as marketing. The Vice-President of Marketing can handle promotion and advertising for all operations, possibly resulting in significant savings and better results. The major disadvantage is that the vice-presidents will be reporting to two bosses, and the lines of authority for Drew and Sanchez are not as clear-cut as in Chart A.

Current Organizational Chart:

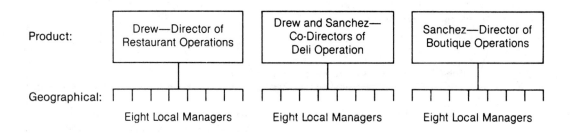

Possible New Chart A—Using Product Departmentation:

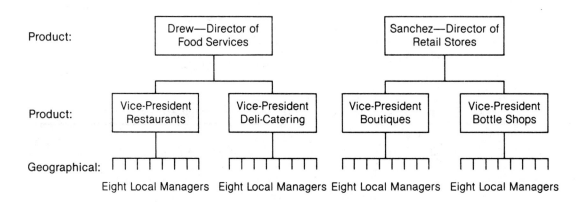

Possible New Chart B—Using Functional Departmentation:

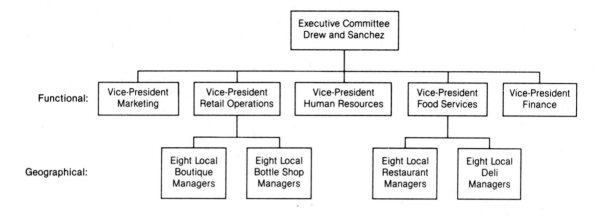

Exercise 12-8: The Barron Case (pp. 418–419)

Lauren Barron should stop trying so hard to do everything herself, to be all things to all people, and to please everyone. She should start planning by formulating some realistic goals and action plans, deciding what she can delegate and what additional resources she needs, discussing potential plans with her boss, and getting some agreement from the boss. She must revise her goals and plans regularly to keep up with rapid change.

Chapter 13 Case Incident: The Magic of Involvement (pp. 420–421)

1. Effective leadership actions and attitudes included getting people involved, using power to challenge and support, projecting an image of power and authority, and showing respect for team members.
2. These actions were effective because people feel included, a sense of ownership, motivated, and inspired to grow.
3. Ineffective attitudes and actions included keeping team members in the dark; hovering, carping on details; not communicating clear goals and expectations; punishing members who don't meet expectations.
4. They were ineffective because members tend to become either confused, dependent, demotivated, passive or angry, tense.

Exercise 13-4. Are You an Intrapreneur? (p. 432)

40 to 65 = You are an intrapreneur; at least you have the traits to be one.
25 to 39 = You have some potential for intrapreneuring.
13 to 24 = If you want to become an intrapreneur, you must examine your current attitudes and actions and be willing to change.

Exercise 13-8: Delegation (pp. 469–470)

Jill's rationale for priority ranking should be as follows: (1) The amount of time that Jill will free up for herself. (2) The extent to which workers' jobs will be enriched, their skills expanded, and their motivation increased without overburdening them. (3) The extent to which Jill will be focusing on higher-level functions rather than on routine details.

If Jill delegates all the tasks listed except E, she can reduce her workweek by an average of five hours, to forty-five hours per week. Perhaps she can shave off another five hours by streamlining some of her procedures for her remaining tasks. She can also help her workers streamline their tasks. As workers gain skill in performing current and new tasks more efficiently, Jill can delegate even more of her activities to them.

Priority Ranking	Job No.	Delegatee	No. Hours Involved (Per Week)	Comments
1	D	Calvin	1¼	Enrich Calvin's job. Train him properly and maintain close control until she is confident he will maintain accuracy.
2	C	Rotate	1½	Rotate the job each week to a different worker. Develop detailed written procedures for doing the task and include it in each worker's job description and performance plan. Maintain close control; require worker to redo task if count is wrong.
3	A	Rose	¾	If there is nothing secret about the data, Jill should let go and delegate the task. Job enrichment for Rose and free time for Jill should receive higher priority. Jill could stress the importance of the job and its confidentiality to Rose.
4	F	George	½ (Two per month)	If the other supervisors don't attend, it's unlikely Jill will miss much of importance. She can instruct George about the types of information he should note and report back to her.
5	B	Frances	1	Enrich Frances's job and develop her skills. Jill should find other, less time-consuming ways to interact with workers. If this proves too difficult, she may decide to keep this job for herself. If not, delegating it should rank third in priority because of the relatively large amount of time that can be saved.
6	E	None	1¼	It has been estimated by many experts that about 75 percent of managerial failures are due to office politics rather than to incompetence. Maintaining constructive political contacts is a crucial part of Jill's job. She should delegate this task only on extremely busy days; then rotate it.

Chapter 14 Case Incident: Sweet Success (pp. 475–477)

1. Erika's effective actions and attitudes included sizing up the competition, trading favors with her peers, documenting her own achievements, giving her backers plenty of information to make a strong case, understanding the decision-makers' viewpoints, estimating the dollar value of her contributions to the firm, stressing her own achievement of goals, and mapping out a negotiation plan for the promotion/raise meeting.

2. Margo's ineffective actions and attitudes included hoping for recognition and rewards instead of planning for them and communicating goals to decision-makers, avoiding risk, focusing on negative loss rather than positive gain, and projecting an image of low ambition or naivete. Fred's ineffectiveness included a lack of sincerity and openness, being a "yes-person," trying to impress the boss, displaying a relatively lavish lifestyle, bringing problems to the boss without proposed solutions, trying too hard to impress the boss regarding activities, productivity, "counting chickens before they hatch" and blabbing plans prematurely, and focusing on anger and resentment over being passed over instead of finding out why.

Key Terms

Achievement need A socially acquired need to continually set and achieve personal goals. It implies a willingness to solve problems, take calculated risks, and seek feedback on performance.

Active listening An approach to interacting constructively with another person through listening with a specific purpose in mind, such as indentifying the speaker's key thoughts, habit patterns, or desire for change; reflecting back main ideas; checking out the speaker's feelings.

Affiliation need A socially acquired need to be with others, to be liked and approved by them, and to relate to them in a mutually supportive, positive way.

Affirmative action guidelines Specific policies and procedures for achieving the goals of an affirmative action program within a prescribed time period. Guidelines may cover practices in employment, upgrading, demotion, transfer, recruitment, layoff, termination, salary, benefits, and training of employees.

Affirmative action program A set of specific results-oriented actions, commitments, and procedures designed to systematically achieve an equitable redistribution of both sexes in all racial groups within a work force.

Affirmative action target dates Deadline dates built into a company's affirmative action program for achieving various goals.

Aggressiveness Standing up for personal rights and expressing thoughts, feelings, and beliefs in ways that violate the rights of another person. Such expressions are usually inappropriate, domineering, manipulative, humiliating, degrading, belittling, or dishonest in some way.

Analytical messages Messages that can be broken down into parts so that each part can be examined to see how it relates to a particular situation or problem.

Assertiveness Standing up for personal rights and acting in ways that express thoughts, feelings, and beliefs in direct, honest, and appropriate ways that don't violate another person's rights.

Bar graph A graph consisting of bars that represent events that occurred at the same time or during the same period of time. Effective for making comparisons.

Body time Personal patterns of body functions that include preferred hours of waking, sleeping, and working; fluctuations in energy level; degree of sociability; and amount of charisma.

Bona Fide Occupational Questions (BFOQ) A term used in connection with EEO laws. BFOQs are interview questions that are necessary to determine an applicant's bona fide, or relevant and essential, qualifications for a job.

Broken-line graph A graph consisting of one or more lines that show progress such as trends and fluctuations over a period of time.

Business cycle A period during which there is a pattern of fluctuation in consumer demand for a product or service. Typically, demand increases until it reaches a high point, remains there for a time, begins to decrease until a low point is reached, and remains there for a time until the next cycle begins.

Cafeteria approach Allowing employees to choose from an array of possible benefits to tailor a "benefit package" (within a set budget) that fits their particular needs.

Chain of command An organizational structure in which each person is responsible to one immediate boss, who in turn is responsible to his or her immediate boss. If a worker goes to a vice-president for an assignment instead of to his or her supervisor, he or she would be violating the chain of command.

Communication process The steps involved in getting an idea from the mind of a sender to the mind of a receiver.

Company operations The day-to-day business activities and transactions necessary to achieve company goals.

Comparable pay for comparable worth Pay scales based on analyses of all types of jobs, male- and female-dominated, in which levels of education, experience, responsibility, difficulty, and hardship are the determining factors, rather than tradition or supply-and-demand.

Conformity pressures The attempts of members of a group to influence the behavior of others to conform to the group's ideas. Tactics such as a show of approval, disapproval, acceptance, or nonacceptance may be used.

Confrontive assertion Confronting a broken agreement by describing what the other person agreed to, what he or she actually did, and what the speaker wants done.

Content level (of messages) The verbal content of the message that focuses on the topic being discussed.

Contract option Giving a person who has violated your rights the chance to change his or her behavior before you take action to enforce your rights. A statement of the action you will take if the behavior is not changed.

Control checkpoint A step in a work process at which the work is checked to see how well standards are being met.

Control system The entire set of procedures established to provide feedback on the performance of a particular work process.

Controls Methods or procedures established to keep both management and workers informed about how well objectives and standards are being met.

Cost reduction Procedures for eliminating part or all of a particular cost or expense by finding new and better ways of doing things and by discovering what things can be eliminated entirely.

Criteria Specifications of the quality a good solution should have. Criteria help distinguish between good and bad alternatives. They are the standards a solution must meet.

Criteria matrix The matrix is a table in which the alternative actions, solutions, or selections are listed vertically as line headings. Major criteria that have been decided upon for measuring each alternative are listed horizontally as column headings. The criteria matrix allows you to organize and display the alternatives and criteria and to record your evaluation of how well each alternative meets each of the criteria.

Crunching numbers Using mathematical, statistical, or financial skills to solve business problems.

Dead-end jobs Positions that are not considered by top management to be on a career path leading to middle and upper management. People holding dead-end jobs are rarely if ever considered for promotion to "growth" positions. They are usually overlooked entirely by management in its planning for managerial training and development.

Dead-time A period of time when one is doing nothing that directly leads to the accomplishment of a high-level objective. Examples are time spent sleeping, eating, commuting, and waiting in line.

Decode To translate or interpret a message; to fit it into one's background of experience.

Dovetailing The coordinating of objectives at various hierarchical levels of an organization.

Economic pressures The need for persons or families to increase their income due to decreased purchasing power. The situation may result because of persons receiving relatively lower wages, facing higher costs of living, or both.

Encode To put a thought or feeling into some form for possible communication to another person.

Entrepreneurial Concerned with the process of searching for and finding promising business opportunities and taking calculated risks by investing money, time, and effort in business ventures with the expectation of making a profit.

Equal Employment Opportunity (EEO) laws Federal legislation designed to provide equal opportunity to be hired, retained, trained, and promoted for all persons regardless of sex, race, ethnic origin, religion, physical condition, or age.

Expectancy theory A motivational approach based on the assumption that people will not act to satisfy a need unless they believe they have the capability to perform satisfactorily so that their performance will actually lead to a reward that will satisfy the need.

Fast track A series of jobs leading to middle and top management in less time than usual. A career path chosen for "fair-haired boys" (and girls) by top-level decision-makers.

Fear of success Usually an unconscious fear of achieving career success based on an underlying belief that such success conflicts with other desirable female roles.

Feedback Information concerning a specific activity or performance.

Feedback assertion Information the speaker gives about how another person's specific behavior is violating the speaker's rights and affecting his or her life, the feelings the speaker has about the behavior, and what behavior the speaker would prefer.

Fiedlar's contingency theory A situational management philosophy that focuses on (1) leader/follower relations, (2) the leader's position power, and (3) the degree of structure in the workers' tasks as the three keys to determining the level of the manager's influence. A Theory Y approach works best in situations where a manager has moderate influence, a Theory X approach in situations of low or high influence.

Financial management system A coordinated arrangement of unit and departmental goals and budgets that results in a company-wide profit goal, budget, and management control system.

First-line supervisor A person who directly supervises the workers in an organization and who is usually skilled at doing the work itself. Her or his area of decision-making is usually limited to minor day-to-day operations within the work unit.

Fixed assets Assets such as buildings and equipment that are retained over a period of years.

Fixed costs Costs that remain the same regardless of the level of business activity, such as buildings, equipment, property insurance, and certain taxes.

Flexible operating budget An operating budget that is changed as the level of business activity changes. Variable costs are increased or decreased accordingly.

Flextime A system of scheduling in which the worker achieves some of his or her highly valued goals in the process of achieving specific organizational goals.

Glass ceiling An invisible barrier to promotion into higher level positions in certain organizations that may be experienced by women, ethnic minorities, and other "diverse" groups.

Goal congruence A work situation in which the worker achieves some of his or her highly valued goals in the process of achieving specific organizational goals.

Groupthink A state that occurs when members of a group appear to think as one and any deviation by one member results in severe negative sanctions by the others.

Hidden agenda A person's goals for a meeting that he or she does not spontaneously reveal to the group, often a political maneuver.

Holistic An overall systems approach, as opposed to an approach that deals with only isolated parts or subsystems of something.

Holistic health An approach to health care that recognizes the importance of every aspect of psychological and physical well-being and the effects of their interactions. This approach focuses mainly on the responsibility of each person for becoming aware of body signals and for preventing illness through optimal nutrition, exercise, mental attitude, and environmental control. Treatment of illness focuses on a patient/doctor partnership in which all relevant aspects of the patient's life situation are considered.

Hot teams Customer-focused teams that thrive in the midst of tough competition, within entrepreneurial cultures and team-based, profit-sharing structures.

Housekeeping Activities involved in keeping a work station in a neat, safe, and well-functioning condition.

Human Resources Department This department is often called "Personnel." Its responsibilities include screening applications for employment, maintaining current employee records, and conducting employee orientation and training meetings.

I-message A statement that expresses the speaker's honest feelings and experiences without evaluating, judging, or interpreting the motives of others.

Input Incoming information.

Intrapreneurial Behaving in an entrepreneurial way — scanning for profit opportunity, developing innovative ideas for capitalizing on profit opportunities, and taking risks — but as an employee of a corporation rather than as an owner.

Intraprises Intrapreneurial activities or projects within a corporation.

Job description A list of the typical functions, duties, skills, and tasks included in a particular position on an ongoing and continuous basis.

Job-sharing A setup where one job position is shared by two people — each working half of each day, week, or month (or other agreed-upon division).

Letting go Releasing tension; releasing a tension-producing need to have a goal, while retaining the relaxed intention to achieve it.

Line jobs Positions in the organizational hierarchy that are directly in the flow of authority and responsibility from top manager to worker. Career paths to top management are usually through line jobs.

Management By Objectives (MBO) A results-oriented approach to managing that emphasizes forecasting and planning for future events. The focus is on participation by workers at all levels and on improvement of both individual and organizational effectiveness. The process includes formulating clear objectives, developing action plans to achieve them, systematic measuring of performance, and taking corrective actions necessary to achieve the planned results.

Management functions Kinds of actions and areas of responsibility within a manager's job position, such as planning, organizing, and directing. Functional areas within a firm include sales, production, and personnel.

Managerial supervisor A person with a broader area of responsibility than the first-line supervisor. He or she may be responsible for two or more units, coordinating and directing their work, with the unit supervisors reporting to him or her. The managerial supervisor usually has some influence on departmental decisions.

Maslow's hierarchy of needs A motivational theory developed by psychologist Abraham Maslow that identifies five ascending categories of innate needs. The average person is motivated to act in ways that satisfy his or her most pressing unfulfilled need. Only when that need is adequately satisfied is a person motivated by a higher-level need.

Matrix organization A temporary organization of project teams that operates concurrently with the ongoing permanent organizational structure. Team members are pulled from various departments to work on projects and return to their departments upon the completion of each project.

Medium (of communication) The form a message takes, such as face-to-face meeting, letter, report, telegram, telephone call, or radio or television broadcast.

Mentor A person with experience and power within an organization who adopts a younger, less experienced protégé and helps him or her up the organizational ladder.

Middle manager A person who is responsible for a department, branch, or sometimes a division and who has a broader area of decision-making, coordinating and cooperating with other middle managers and top management in achieving organization goals. Middle managers usually have some influence on top-level policy-making and company direction.

Mind chatter The internal dialogue people carry on in their minds most of the time.

Murphy's law "If anything can go wrong, it will."

New hires Recently hired employees of an organization.

Nonassertiveness Letting oneself be victimized by failing to act in ways that express honest feelings, thoughts, and beliefs, or expressing them in such an apologetic or unsure way that others can easily disregard them. Allowing one's rights to be violated without adequate challenge.

Nonprofit organization Any organization—governmental, charitable, or other publicly or privately funded group—that exists to provide a service rather than to earn a profit for owners.

Objectives Targets or goals to be achieved within a specific time frame.

Open-door policy A manager's stated practice of being regularly available to listen to subordinates' ideas and problems. The policy implies an openness to accepting and trying out workers' suggestions.

Operational decisions Those decisions that directly concern the day-to-day business activities of the company.

Operational employees The line employees who actually make the products or perform the services that bring in company revenue.

Opportunity value The value of opportunities that are given up when a particular course of action is decided upon. Because limited resources must be committed to carry out the chosen plan, they are not available to take advantage of other opportunities that may arise. The value of the chosen plan should therefore be greater than the anticipated value of the other opportunities that may be sacrificed.

Organizational hierarchy The various levels of authority and responsibility within a company beginning with the worker level and going up through the supervisory, middle, and top management levels to the board of directors, which represents the stockholders, who own the company.

Output Outgoing information.

Parent messages Instructions about how to behave that small children pick up from parent figures and internalize so that the messages become a subconscious part of the child's, and later the adult's, value system.

Parkinson's law "Work expands to fill the time available for its completion."

Path-goal approach A motivational approach to management that focuses on showing workers how meeting their job objectives will satisfy their personal needs and help them get some of the rewards they want most.

Pay equity *See* **Comparable worth.**

Personnel assessment center A private or company-sponsored service for analyzing and evaluating a person's education, experience, performance, and aptitude in order to recommend the types of jobs the applicant is likely to handle well.

Pie graph A circular graph the shape of a pie with the "slices" representing parts of the whole. Effective for showing how the proportion of each of the items in a group relates to the whole amount.

Position power The power that is inherent in a particular job position regardless of the job-holder's personal traits and abilities.

Power base The political power gained through a combination of such factors as (1) support network, (2) job position, (3) visibility, (4) ability to fill a pressing company need, and (5) personal expertise, credibility, savvy, and charisma.

Power need A socially acquired need to gain and use power and authority over others.

Production cycle The process of converting cash into finished goods and back into cash again. It's often called the working capital cycle by accountants.

Production department The department responsible for manufacturing the products the company is set up to make.

Production schedules Detailed plans of the number and types of items a company will produce. These schedules are adjusted from week to week as customer demand changes.

Profit center A unit, department, branch, or division of a company that is directly responsible for generating a portion of company profits. Its revenues and expenses are figured or estimated separately so that a specific profit figure is arrived at.

Quality control circle A group of workers who hold regular problem-solving meetings. The group may analyze quality control problems, determining why standards are not being met and suggesting methods for improvement.

Quiet hour An hour set aside each day for uninterrupted concentration on work projects. No phone calls or visitors are received, and there is no unnecessary talking or moving about.

Relationship level (of messages) Predominantly nonverbal aspects of a message that focus on the way one person values or accepts the other person.

Resource person Someone who is available to others to provide information, expertise, advice, and instruction.

Resources Anything of value that is used in achieving company goals, such as cash; employees' labor, skill, and expertise; plant facilities; and equipment.

Role conflict A state of being in which a person believes that if she succeeds in one role she desires, such as manager, her success in another desired role, such as housewife, will be undermined. The resulting conflict often occurs at an unconscious level and leads to self-sabotage in one or both of the roles.

Running hot When teams stretch past their previous abilities, in learning how to solve customers' problems, in coming up with procedures to get the customer's total job done.

Sales forecast A prediction made by the Sales Department of sales volume for the coming year or years.

Self-actualization An ideal state in which a person achieves his or her full potential. Self-actualizing needs, the highest in Maslow's hierarchy, are needs for continuous growth and development in the pursuit of becoming all that one is potentially capable of becoming.

Self-concept The picture a person has of herself or himself, including strengths, weaknesses, looks, personality.

Socialization messages Parent-like messages that focus on "socially acceptable" behavior a child should adopt.

Socially acquired needs Needs that are socially acquired from interaction with people in a particular cultural environment, as differentiated from innate or biological needs.

Staff jobs Positions in the organizational hierarchy that are essentially advisory in nature. Staff departments specialize in a particular area of service or expertise and usually report to a line manager in an advisory capacity.

Standards Measures of acceptable work performance. A standard defines the cutoff point between acceptable and unacceptable performance of an activity engaged in to achieve a job objective.

Stereotype A belief about a certain group of people and their predictable characteristics that causes the holder to prejudge individual members of that group and to interpret their actions and motives according to predetermined expectations.

Stress Significant disruptions in an individual's environment, originating from within the person in such forms as fears and hurts or from the external environment in such forms as family conflicts or job promotions.

Stressor A source of stress; any situation or event that causes stress for an individual.

"Stuck" position A job position that the company decision-makers do not view as preparatory for promotion to other positions that in turn lead to top management.

Supervisor A lower-level manager who is directly responsible for getting workers to carry out the action plans of the organization. *See* **First-line supervisor** and **Managerial supervisor**.

Support system (or Support network) An assortment of people at various levels and positions in various departments within the company as well as outside the company who are carefully selected and developed by a manager for their ability and willingness to stand behind her or him. Ideally, supporters are selected from various areas so that the network is structured to enhance the manager's political power.

Synthesizing (messages) Putting together the parts of a message to understand the relationships between the parts. Putting together many messages to build a mental model of a situation, an organization, or a particular environment.

Team building A process for improving team performance that focuses on a team's deficits that block performance.

Team development A process for improving team performance that focuses on a team's positive opportunities for continuous improvement.

Territory A sphere of dominance, control, or power. Examples are a specific geographical space, a group of people, or an area of decision-making authority.

Theory X A management philosophy based on the assumption that people are basically lazy and unambitious, work mainly for security purposes, and therefore must be controlled and coerced to work toward organizational objectives.

Theory Y A management philosophy based on the assumption that workers will exercise self-direction in achieving the organization's goals if they believe their efforts will result in rewards they value. It assumes the average worker has the ingenuity to contribute to management decisions.

Theory Z An American adaptation of key aspects of Japanese management style, which is characterized by mutual trust between employees and management, informal relationships, employee involvement in decision-making, nonspecialized careers, a slow evaluation process for employees, long-term employment, flexibility, and adaptability.

"To Do" list A manager's daily plan of activities, noted in order of priority according to importance in achieving specific goals.

Top manager A high-level manager who is concerned with the overall mission and objectives of the company, its future direction, and the formulation of broad policies for implementing the objectives.

Total Quality Management (TQM) A focus on teamwork within teams and throughout the organization for the purpose of providing a total quality experience for the customer — in both the basic product or service that a customer buys and in all the support services.

Transactional analysis (TA) A comprehensive approach to awareness of the subtleties and meanings that underlie people's behavior, interactions, motivations, and games. TA offers a model or framework for understanding oneself and others and for changing nonproductive behavior.

Transmit (a message) To deliver or broadcast a message from a person sending the message to a person receiving the message.

Valuing Diversity Valuing all the things that make people, or specific groups of people, unique or different, while appreciating and accepting those differences. An approach to working with others that maximizes the contributions of people from every segment of the employee population, which in turn can help the organization to reach its objectives.

Work group A group of workers usually led by one person. The work of each group member is performed through processes that are additive, integrative, or interactive. The group is the primary unit of performance in the organization.

Work team A work group in which members cooperate in all aspects of doing their tasks. They all share in the traditional management functions of planning, organizing, setting performance goals, assessing the team's performance, developing strategies to manage change, and getting resources.

You-message Statements that focus on another person's actions or motives and are frequently judgmental.

Index